Rail Guide

2019

Main Line Systems

Colin J. Marsden

Crécy Publishing Ltd

First published 2010
Reprinted 2010,
Revised editions 2011, 2012, 2013, 2014, 2015, 2016, 2017, 2018
This Tenth Edition published 2019 by Crécy Publishing

ISBN 978 1 9108 09556

Printed in Bulgaria by Multiprint

Crécy Publishing Ltd
1a Ringway Trading Estate
Shadowmoss Road
Manchester
M22 5LH
Tel +44 (0) 161 499 0024

www.crecy.co.uk

Front cover top: *Eversholt Rail owned, Great Western Railway-operated, Class 802 IET No. 802001 passes Starcross 16 June 2018 with a staff training run from Exeter St Davids to Par.* **CJM**

Front cover bottom: *CrossRail 'Elizabeth Line' Class 345 No. 345017 approaches Acton Main Line on 26 June 2018 with the 09.47 Hayes & Harlington to London Paddington.* **CJM**

Back cover top: *Plasser & Theurer 09-03x Duomatic Tamper and Liner No. DR73120 is seen at Swindon, coupled at the far end, to Plasser & Theurer USP 5000 Ballast Regulator No. DR77909.* **CJM**

Back cover bottom: *Irish Rail Class 201 No. 216 painted in Belmond Pullman 'Grand Hibernian' dark blue livery is recorded at Portarlington on 5 July 2018.* **CJM**

Acknowledgement – The Author would like to record his thanks to the many railway staff who have provided
invaluable information for the production of this book. Also to the many photographers, especially
Antony Christie, Nathan Williamson and John Binch, for providing many of the images. I would also like to express
my thanks to Keith Ewins, Antony Christie and Russell Watkins for reading the updated manuscript. **CJM**

Welcome to the 2019 edition of the *ABC Rail Guide*. Over the past year we have seen considerable change on the railway, especially in terms of rolling stock. The huge benefits of new trains are starting to be seen, more new train orders have been placed and changes to operational franchises made.

During 2018, InterCity Express Trains continued to be introduced on the Great Western network, with around half of the HST fleet removed from service. Class 802s have been introduced. It is planned that GWR will convert to full IET working in spring 2019. The HSTs will not totally disappear, eleven 2+4 sliding door 'Castle' sets are to operate between Cardiff-Bristol-Taunton-Paignton-Plymouth and Penzance.

On the East Coast, the IET introduction was delayed from 2018 until spring 2019 due to technical issues. Once introduced, the HST and Class 91 and Mk4 stock will be withdrawn.

Many of the displaced HSTs from GWR are being refurbished for use in Scotland on the new 'Inter7City' services, these short sets are refurbished and fitted with sliding doors. This introduction has allowed a number of DMUs to be cascaded. Delivery has been slow, with production issues at Wabtec, Doncaster.

Class 385 EMUs have been introduced in Scotland, allowing modernisation of the Edinburgh-Glasgow corridor. Stock cascades has seen withdrawal of Class 314s.

A massive change in terms of rolling stock is taking place on Greater Anglia, with total fleet replacement, using multiple units. For the first time true bi-mode trains have been introduced, able to operate from the 25kV overhead or from on-board diesel engines. Elsewhere on Greater Anglia 12-car EMU sets are being introduced on InterCity and Stansted Airport services.

On the Northern franchise, Class 195 DMU and 331 EMU sets are on delivery, these will see the Class 14x 'Pacer' sets withdrawn.

On TransPennine Express, Class 802 IETs, Class 395 EMUs and Mk5 passenger stock, powered by Class 68s are being introduced.

The Class 345 sets, which should have commenced operation through the core section of CrossRail (Elizabeth Line) in late 2018 have been deferred for one year, however Class 345s are in use on the eastern and western ends of the route, allowing some Class 315 sets to be sent for scrap.

In late 2018, the first of the end door fitted 'Desiro City' Class 717 sets entered service on the GTR Great Northern route, seeing Class 313 sets withdrawn.

The Vivarail 'D' Stock conversion project has progressed with firm orders placed, the first production trains are now working for West Midlands.

The new Transport for Wales franchise was launched in autumn 2018 and with it came announcement of major new stock orders, to be fulfilled by both CAF and Stadler, including a fleet of TramTrains. In terms of Tram Train technology, the long awaited introduction of the extension of the Sheffield Super Tram project came to fruition in October 2018 with the launch of a service between Sheffield Cathedral and Rotherham Parkgate using Class 399 stock.

During the course of 2018 the ill-fated East Coast franchise was returned to Government control, this saw the rebranding of the route as LNER.

New stock for the Caledonian Sleeper operation has been delivered for type test approval, a planned introduction in late 2018 was deferred to early 2019.

On the freight side, business has generally been slow. The DB-C fleet still has huge spare capacity for the number of trains operated and further locos could be exported. GBRf have continued to expand in terms of traction, with a deal to take on 10 former DB Class 66s finalised and the take over of 10 previously Colas-operated Class 60s.

The rebuilding and refurbishment of the more modern displaced trains is now big business for the owners. In many cases, new trains have displaced stock with a good life expectancy. Porterbrook Leasing has masterminded the rebuild of Class 319 stock into bi-mode units by installing a diesel raft under the driving cars. Orders are currently being fulfilled for Northern and Transport for Wales. Great Western have gone one stage further, by ordering a fleet of tri-mode 'Flex' sets able to operate from electric, diesel or battery technology.

Various projects have been announced to adapt stock to bi-mode operation, including installing diesel rafts below Class 350/2s due off lease in 2019-2020. Alternative fuel technology is also being investigated with the development of hydrogen fuel cell systems.

Due to the amount of data we include in the *ABC Rail Guide*, from this edition we will be producing two books, one covering Main Line systems, and a companion volume *ABC Light Rail and Heritage Lines*, this will provide expanded coverage of the Light Rail, and now includes some of the minor systems, as well as an enlarged section covering the preserved traction. *ABC Light Rail and Heritage Lines*, gives a complete list of all preserved railways, together with a full numeric list of preserved steam and diesel locos and multiple units. Also, for the first time, *ABC Light Rail and Heritage Lines* provides full numeric listing of all London Underground stock.

The Editor and Publishers of *ABC Rail Guide* hope you continue to enjoy observing and recording the UK Rail scene, as ever, if any reader has any additional information, we welcome this to be sent to the editorial address, together with a picture if possible.

Always, when on or about the railways, please keep your eyes about you and report anything suspicious, enthusiasts act as extra eyes for the rail industry and never be afraid to mention anything unusual to staff. However, stay safe and do not trespass on railway property, always keep to the public areas.

Colin J. Marsden
Editor
February 2019

Rail Guide information is correct to 1 February 2019

Train Operators, The Rail Operations Group, and Network Rail welcome rail enthusiasts and photographers, but in today's safety-led railway and with the continued concerns about possible transport terrorism, guidelines are very important and we encourage all to follow these published guidelines as much as possible. They are available to view and download from the National Rail and ROG websites, but are reproduced in full below to assist you with this information. ■

The Official Railway Enthusiasts Guidelines

■ Network Rail welcomes rail enthusiasts to our stations.

■ The following guidelines are designed to help you to have a safe and enjoyable experience. Please keep them with you when you are at Network Rail-managed stations.

■ You may also wish to take a copy of the Railway by-laws which are available from the Office of Public Sector Information website.

Before you enter the platform

■ When you arrive at a station, please let the staff at the Network Rail Reception Desk know that you are on the station. This will help keep station staff informed so that they can go about their duties without concern as to your reasons for being there.

■ You may require a platform ticket to allow access to platforms.

While you are on the platform

■ You need to act safely and sensibly at all times.
- Stay clear of the platform edge and stay behind the yellow lines where they are provided.
- Be aware of your surroundings.

Please DO NOT:
- Trespass on to the tracks or any other part of the railway that is not available to passengers.
- Use flash photography because it can distract train drivers and train despatch staff and so is potentially very dangerous.
- Climb on any structure or interfere with platform equipment.
- Obstruct any signalling equipment or signs which are vital to the safe running of the railway.
- Wear anything which is similar in colour to safety clothing, such as high-visibility jackets, as this could cause confusion to drivers and other railway employees.
- Gather together in groups at busy areas of the platform (e.g. customer information points, departure screens, waiting areas, seating etc.) or where this may interfere with the duties of station staff.

■ If possible, please try to avoid peak hours which are Monday – Friday 6:00am (06.00) – 10:30am (10.30) and 3:30pm (15.30) – 7:30pm (19.30).

Extra eyes and ears

■ If you see anything suspicious or notice any unusual behaviour or activities, please tell a member of staff immediately.

■ For emergencies and serious incidents, either call:
The British Transport Police on 0800 40 50 40. Or text a message to61016
The Police on 999, or 101

■ Your presence at a station can be very helpful to us as extra 'eyes and ears' and can have a positive security benefit.

Photography

■ You can take photographs at stations provided you do not sell them. However, you are not allowed to take photographs of security-related equipment, such as CCTV cameras.

■ Flash photography on platforms is not allowed at any time. It can distract train drivers and train despatch staff and so is potentially very dangerous.

■ Tripod legs must be kept away from platform edges and behind the yellow lines. On busy stations, you may not be allowed to use a tripod because it could be a dangerous obstruction to passengers.

Railway by-laws

For safety and ease of travel on the railway system (which includes passengers, staff, property and equipment), the by-laws must be observed by everyone. A copy of the by-laws can be obtained at stations or downloaded from the Office of Public Sector Information website.

General

Train operators must put the safety of their passengers and staff first. You may very occasionally be asked by station staff to move to another part of the station or to leave the station altogether. Station staff should be happy to explain why this is necessary. If you are travelling by train, they may ask you to remain in the normal waiting areas with other passengers. If this occurs, please follow their instructions with goodwill as staff have many things to consider, including the safety and security of all passengers, and are authorised to use judgement in this regard.

Below: *Some of the latest trains to enter service are the CAF built Class 195 DMU and 331 EMU stock for the Northern franchise, replacing the majority of older stock, currently on the operators books. Four-car Class 331 EMU No. 331102 is illustrated at Crewe on 2 November 2018 while undergoing test running.* **CJM**

Contents

New Train Orders

Class	Builder	Operator	Owner	Type	Number of sets	Status
195	CAF	Northern Rail	Eversholt	DMU	55	On Delivery
196	CAF	West Midlands	Corelink Rail	DMU	26	Design
19x	CAF	Transport for Wales	Transport for Wales	DMU	77	Design
1xx	Stadler	Transport for Wales	Transport for Wales	DMU	11	Design
230	Vivarail	West Midlands		BMU	3	In Service
230	Vivarail	Transport for Wales		BMU	5	Conversion
331	CAF	Northern Rail	Eversholt	EMU	43	On Delivery
345	Bombardier	Crossrail / TfL	Transport for London	EMU	70	In Service
385	Hitachi	ScotRail	Caledonian Leasing	EMU	70	On Delivery
387	Bombardier	Great Western	Porterbrook	EMU	45	In Service
397	CAF	TransPennine	Eversholt	EMU	12	On Delivery
700	Bombardier	GTR	Cross London Trains	EMU	115	In Service
701	Bombardier	SWR	Rock Rail	EMU	90	Construction
707	Siemens	SWT	Angel Trains	EMU	30	In Service
710	Bombardier	London Overground	London Rail Leasing	EMU	45	In Service
711	Bombardier	c2c	Porterbrook	EMU	6	Design
717	Siemens	GTR	Rock Rail	EMU	25	In Service
720	Bombardier	Greater Anglia	Angel Trains	EMU	111	Construction
730	Bombardier	West Midlands	Corelink Rail	EMU	81	Design
745	Stadler	Greater Anglia	Rock Rail	EMU	20	On Delivery
755	Stadler	Greater Anglia	Rock Rail	BMU	38	On Delivery
75x	Stadler	Transport for Wales	Transport for Wales	BMU	24	Design
769	Wabtec*	Great Western	Porterbrook	BMU	19	Conversion
769	Wabtec*	Northern Rail	Porterbrook	BMU	8	Conversion
769	Wabtec*	Transport for Wales	Porterbrook	BMU	9	Conversion
777	Stadler	MerseyRail	Mersey Travel	EMU	52	Construction
7xx	Stadler	Transport for Wales	Transport for Wales	EMU	36	Design
800	Hitachi	Great Western	Agility Trains	BMU	57	In Service / On Delivery
800	Hitachi	LNER	Agility Trains	BMU	23	On Delivery
801	Hitachi	LNER	Agility Trains	EMU	42	On Delivery
802	Hitachi	TransPennine	Angel Trains	BMU	19	On Delivery
802	Hitachi	Hull Trains	Angel Trains	BMU	5	On De;ivery
802	Hitachi	Great Western	Eversholt	BMU	36	In Service / On Delivery

* Rebuild by Porterbrook / Wabtec of Class 319

Below: *The 30 Siemens 'Desiro City' Class 707 five-car sets, owned by Angel Trains and at present leased to South Western Railway are scheduled to come off lease when SWR Class 701 stock is commissioned in 2020-2021. This brand new stock will then be available to re-lease to a new operator. Set No. 707008 is seen at Clapham Junction yard in March 2018.* **CJM**

c2c - Essex/East Thameside

Address: ✉ 2nd Floor, Cutlers Court, 115 Houndsditch, London, EC3A 7BR
⌨ contact@c2crail.co.uk
✆ 03457 444422
ⓘ www.c2c-online.co.uk

Managing Director: Julian Drury
Franchise Dates: 26 May 1996 - 8 November 2029
Principal Routes: London Fenchurch Street - Shoeburyness
Barking - Pitsea via Purfleet
Ockendon branch
London Liverpool Street - Barking (limited service)
Depots: East Ham (EM), Shoeburyness*
* Stabling point
Parent Company: Trenitalia

Note: Under the terms of the c2c East Thameside franchise, a fleet of six 10-car Bombardier 'Aventra' units were ordered in late 2017 for delivery from 2020-2021. These sets will be funded by Porterbrook. When delivered, the existing Class 387 sets will be taken off lease.

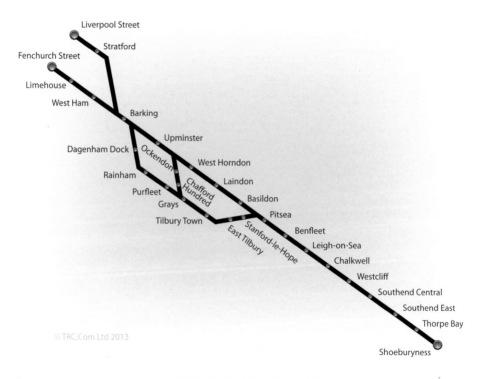

Class 357/0
Electrostar

Vehicle Length: (Driving) 68ft 1in (20.75m) Width: 9ft 2½in (2.80m)
(Inter) 65ft 11½in (20.10m) Horsepower: 2,011hp (1,500kW)
Height: 12ft 4½in (3.78m) Seats (total/car): 282S, 71S/78S/62S/71S

Number	Formation DMSO(A)+MSO+PTSO+DMSO(B)	Depot	Livery	Owner	Op'r	Name
357001	67651+74151+74051+67751	EM	C2C	PTR	c2c	Barry Flaxman
357002	67652+74152+74052+67752	EM	C2C	PTR	c2c	Arthur Lewis Stride 1841-1922
357003	67653+74153+74053+67753	EM	C2C	PTR	c2c	Southend City on Sea
357004	67654+74154+74054+67754	EM	C2C	PTR	c2c	Tony Amos
357005	67655+74155+74055+67755	EM	C2C	PTR	c2c	Southend : 2017 Alternative City of Culture
357006	67656+74156+74056+67756	EM	C2C	PTR	c2c	Diamond Jubilee 1952 - 2012
357007	67657+74157+74057+67757	EM	C2C	PTR	c2c	Sir Andrew Foster
357008	67658+74158+74058+67758	EM	C2C	PTR	c2c	
357009	67659+74159+74059+67759	EM	C2C	PTR	c2c	
357010	67660+74160+74060+67760	EM	C2C	PTR	c2c	
357011	67661+74161+74061+67761	EM	C2C	PTR	c2c	John Lowing
357012	67662+74162+74062+67762	EM	C2C	PTR	c2c	
357013	67663+74163+74063+67763	EM	C2C	PTR	c2c	
357014	67664+74164+74064+67764	EM	C2C	PTR	c2c	
357015	67665+74165+74065+67765	EM	C2C	PTR	c2c	
357016	67666+74166+74066+67766	EM	C2C	PTR	c2c	
357017	67667+74167+74067+67767	EM	C2C	PTR	c2c	
357018	67668+74168+74068+67768	EM	C2C	PTR	c2c	Remembering the Fallen 88 1914-1918
357019	67669+74169+74069+67769	EM	C2C	PTR	c2c	
357020	67670+74170+74070+67770	EM	C2C	PTR	c2c	
357021	67671+74171+74071+67771	EM	C2C	PTR	c2c	
357022	67672+74172+74072+67772	EM	C2C	PTR	c2c	
357023	67673+74173+74073+67773	EM	C2C	PTR	c2c	
357024	67674+74174+74074+67774	EM	C2C	PTR	c2c	
357025	67675+74175+74075+67775	EM	C2C	PTR	c2c	
357026	67676+74176+74076+67776	EM	C2C	PTR	c2c	
357027	67677+74177+74077+67777	EM	C2C	PTR	c2c	
357028	67678+74178+74078+67778	EM	C2C	PTR	c2c	London, Tilbury & Southend Railway 1854-2004
357029	67679+74179+74079+67779	EM	C2C	PTR	c2c	Thomas Whitelegg 1840-1922
357030	67680+74180+74080+67780	EM	C2C	PTR	c2c	Robert Harben Whitelegg 1871-1957
357031	67681+74181+74081+67781	EM	C2C	PTR	c2c	
357032	67682+74182+74082+67782	EM	C2C	PTR	c2c	
357033	67683+74183+74083+67783	EM	C2C	PTR	c2c	
357034	67684+74184+74084+67784	EM	C2C	PTR	c2c	

Below: *Used exclusively on the c2c network are the fleet of 46 four-car Class 357/0 'Electrostar' non-gangway sets. Based at East Ham, this fleet and the like design Class 357/2 and 357/3s form the backbone of London Tilbury and Southend line services. Set No. 357027 is seen at Pitsea with a coast bound service.* **CJM**

c2c

357035	67685+74185+74085+67785	EM	C2C	PTR	c2c
357036	67686+74186+74086+67786	EM	C2C	PTR	c2c
357037	67687+74187+74087+67787	EM	C2C	PTR	c2c
357038	67688+74188+74088+67788	EM	C2C	PTR	c2c
357039	67689+74189+74089+67789	EM	C2C	PTR	c2c
357040	67690+74190+74090+67790	EM	C2C	PTR	c2c
357041	67691+74191+74091+67791	EM	C2C	PTR	c2c
357042	67692+74192+74092+67792	EM	C2C	PTR	c2c
357043	67693+74193+74093+67793	EM	C2C	PTR	c2c
357044	67694+74194+74094+67794	EM	C2C	PTR	c2c
357045	67695+74195+74095+67795	EM	C2C	PTR	c2c
357046	67696+74196+74096+67796	EM	C2C	PTR	c2c

Class 357/2 & 357/3
Electrostar

Vehicle Length: (Driving) 68ft 1in (20.75m) Width: 9ft 2½in (2.80m)
(Inter) 65ft 11½in (20.10m) Horsepower: 2,011hp (1,500kW)
Height: 12ft 4½in (3.78m) Seats (total/car): 282S, 71S/78S/62S/71S
Class 357/3 sets are fitted with revised interiors using 2+2 low-density layout with total seating for 223S passengers

Number	Formation DMSO(A)+MSO+PTSO+DMSO(B)	Depot	Livery	Owner	Operator	Name
357201	68601+74701+74601+68701	EM	C2C	ANG	c2c	*Ken Bird*
357202	68602+74702+74602+68702	EM	C2C	ANG	c2c	*Kenny Mitchell*
357203	68603+74703+74603+68703	EM	C2C	ANG	c2c	*Henry Pumfrett*
357204	68604+74704+74604+68704	EM	C2C	ANG	c2c	*Derek Flowers*
357205	68605+74705+74605+68705	EM	C2C	ANG	c2c	*John D'Silva*
357206	68606+74706+74606+68706	EM	C2C	ANG	c2c	*Martin Aungier*
357207	68607+74707+74607+68707	EM	C2C	ANG	c2c	*John Page*
357208	68608+74708+74608+68708	EM	C2C	ANG	c2c	*Dave Davis*
357209	68609+74709+74609+68709	EM	C2C	ANG	c2c	*James Snelling*
357210	68610+74710+74610+68710	EM	C2C	ANG	c2c	
357211	68611+74711+74611+68711	EM	C2C	ANG	c2c	
357312 (357212)	68612+74712+74612+68712	EM	C2C	ANG	c2c	
357313 (357213)	68613+74713+74613+68713	EM	C2C	ANG	c2c	
357314 (357214)	68614+74714+74614+68714	EM	C2C	ANG	c2c	*Upminster IECC*
357315 (357215)	68615+74715+74615+68715	EM	C2C	ANG	c2c	
357316 (357216)	68616+74716+74616+68716	EM	C2C	ANG	c2c	
357317 (357217)	68617+74717+74617+68717	EM	C2C	ANG	c2c	*Allan Burnell*
357318 (357218)	68618+74718+74618+68718	EM	C2C	ANG	c2c	
357319 (357219)	68619+74719+74619+68719	EM	C2C	ANG	c2c	
357320 (357220)	68620+74720+74620+68720	EM	C2C	ANG	c2c	
357321 (357221)	68621+74721+74621+68721	EM	C2C	ANG	c2c	
357322 (357222)	68622+74722+74622+68722	EM	C2C	ANG	c2c	
357323 (357223)	68623+74723+74623+68723	EM	C2C	ANG	c2c	
357324 (357224)	68624+74724+74624+68724	EM	C2C	ANG	c2c	
357325 (357225)	68625+74725+74625+68725	EM	C2C	ANG	c2c	
357326 (357226)	68626+74726+74626+68726	EM	C2C	ANG	c2c	
357327 (357227)	68627+74727+74627+68727	EM	C2C	ANG	c2c	*Southend United*
357328 (357228)	68628+74728+74628+68728	EM	C2C	ANG	c2c	

Left: *Originally a second batch of like-design Class 357/2 sets were introduced on the c2c network, funded by Angel Trains. Today 11 sets remain classified as Class 357/2. These have a higher seating capacity of 282 and use a 2+3 internal layout. Set No. 357205 is viewed at Pitsea. All sets are painted in standard c2c white livery, with dark blue contrasting passenger doors.* **CJM**

Right: *A fleet of 17 Class 357/2 sets were modified several years ago as 'Metro' sets, with less seating, using the 2+2 low-density layout and more standing room, especially in the door positions. Roof hanging 'straps' were also provided for passengers to hold. These sets, branded 'Metro' on the doors and bodyside, are scheduled to operate on the busy local routes, but in reality can be found throughout the network. 'Metro' set No. 357317 is recorded passing Limehouse, forming an empty stock duty to the main c2c depot at East Ham.* **CJM**

Class 387
Electrostar

Vehicle Length: (Driving) 66ft 9in (20.3m) Width: 9ft 2in (2.79m)
(Inter) 65ft 6in (19.96m) Horsepower: 2,012hp (1,500kW)
Height: 12ft 4in (3.75m) Seats (total/car): 223S. 56S/62S/45S/60S

Number	Formation DMSO(A)+MSO+TSO+DMSO(B)	Depot	Livery	Owner	Operator
387301	421301+422301+423301+424301	EM	C2C	PTR	c2c
387302	421302+422302+423302+424302	EM	C2C	PTR	c2c
387303	421303+422303+423303+424303	EM	C2C	PTR	c2c
387304	421304+422304+423304+424304	EM	C2C	PTR	c2c
387305	421305+422305+423305+424305	EM	C2C	PTR	c2c
387306	421306+422306+423306+424306	EM	C2C	PTR	c2c

Below: *To cope with high passenger demand until new purpose-built stock is delivered, six Class 387/3 'Electrostar' sets entered traffic in 2016. The sets are based on the GTR Class 387/1 stock and will be returned to Porterbrook when new c2c Class 711 Bombardier 'Aventra' sets enter service around 2020-2021. Set No. 387306 is seen at Upminster with a Fenchurch Street to Shoeburyness duty.* **Antony Christie**

Chiltern Railways

Address: ✉ 2nd floor, Western House, Rickfords Hill, Aylesbury, Buckinghamshire, HP20 2RX
🖳 Via website (www.chilternrailways.co.uk)
℡ 08456 005165   ⓘ www.chilternrailways.co.uk

Managing Director: Dave Penney
Franchise Dates: 21 July 1996 - 21 December 2021
Principal Routes: London Marylebone - Birmingham Snow Hill
London Marylebone - Aylesbury
London Marylebone - Stratford-upon-Avon
Depots: Aylesbury (AL), Wembley*   * Stabling point
Parent Company: Deutsche Bahn AG (DB Regio)

Passenger Train Operating Companies - Chiltern Railways

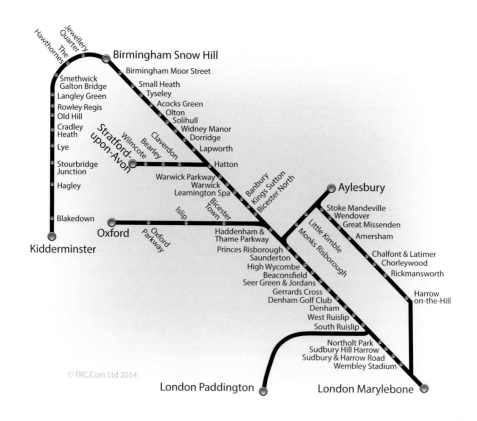

© TRC.Com Ltd 2014

Class 165/0 (2-car)
Networker Turbo

Vehicle Length: (Driving) 75ft 2½in (22.91m), (Inter) 74ft 6½in (22.72m)
Height: 12ft 5¼in (3.79m)   Engine: 1 x Perkins 2006 TWH of 350hp per vehicle
Width: 9ft 2½in (2.81m)   Horsepower: 700hp (522kW)
Seats (total/car): 183S, 89S/94S

Number	Formation DMSL+DMS	Depot	Livery	Owner	Operator
165001	58801+58834	AL	CRW	ANG	CRW
165002	58802+58835	AL	CRR	ANG	CRW
165003	58803+58836	AL	CRW	ANG	CRW
165004	58804+58837	AL	CRW	ANG	CRW
165005	58805+58838	AL	CRR	ANG	CRW
165006	58806+58839	AL	CRR	ANG	CRW
165007	58807+58840	AL	CRW	ANG	CRW
165008	58808+58841	AL	CRW	ANG	CRW
165009	58809+58842	AL	CRR	ANG	CRW
165010	58810+58843	AL	CRW	ANG	CRW
165011	58811+58844	AL	CRW	ANG	CRW
165012	58812+58845	AL	CRW	ANG	CRW
165013	58813+58846	AL	CRW	ANG	CRW
165014	58814+58847	AL	CRW	ANG	CRW
165015	58815+58848	AL	CRW	ANG	CRW
165016	58816+58849	AL	CRW	ANG	CRW
165017	58817+58850	AL	CRW	ANG	CRW
165018	58818+58851	AL	CRW	ANG	CRW
165019	58819+58852	AL	CRW	ANG	CRW
165020	58820+58853	AL	CRW	ANG	CRW
165021	58821+58854	AL	CRW	ANG	CRW
165022	58822+58855	AL	CRW	ANG	CRW
165023	58873+58867	AL	CRR	ANG	CRW
165024	58874+58868	AL	CRW	ANG	CRW
165025	58875+58869	AL	CRW	ANG	CRW
165026	58876+58870	AL	CRW	ANG	CRW
165027	58877+58871	AL	CRR	ANG	CRW
165028	58878+58872	AL	CRW	ANG	CRW

Right: *The Class 165 'Networker Turbo' fleet is still the main passenger stock for Chiltern suburban operations. A fleet of 28 two-car sets are based at Aylesbury. These have been upgraded from their original design and now sport air conditioning, and thus have no opening passenger windows. Set No. 165003 is seen at Marylebone.*
Antony Christie

Class 165/0 (3-car)
Networker Turbo

Vehicle Length: (driving) 75ft 2½in (22.91m), (Inter) 74ft 6½in (22.72m)
Height: 12ft 5¼in (3.79m)   Engine: 1 x Perkins 2006 TWH of 350hp per vehicle
Width: 9ft 2½in (2.81m)   Horsepower: 1,050hp (783kW)
Seats (total/car): 289S, 89S/106S/94S

Number	Formation DMSL+MS+DMS	Depot	Livery	Owner	Operator
165029	58823+55404+58856	AL	CRW	ANG	CRW
165030	58824+55405+58857	AL	CRW	ANG	CRW
165031	58825+55406+58858	AL	CRW	ANG	CRW
165032	58826+55407+58859	AL	CRW	ANG	CRW
165033	58827+55408+58860	AL	CRW	ANG	CRW
165034	58828+55409+58861	AL	CRW	ANG	CRW
165035	58829+55410+58862	AL	CRR	ANG	CRW
165036	58830+55411+58863	AL	CRW	ANG	CRW
165037	58831+55412+58864	AL	CRR	ANG	CRW
165038	58832+55413+58865	AL	CRW	ANG	CRW
165039	58833+55414+58866	AL	CRW	ANG	CRW

Right: *In 2018 a start was made at repainting the Class 165 Chiltern fleet into a slightly revised livery, adding a blue cant rail band, removing the red sole bar band and applying a 'by Arriva' slogan on the bodyside below the Chiltern name. Showing the revised livery is three-car set No. 165035 departing from London Marylebone.*
Antony Christie

Passenger Train Operating Companies - Chiltern Railways

Chiltern Railways

Class 168/0
Turbostar

Vehicle Length: 77ft 6in (23.62m)		*Engine: 1 x MTU 6R 183TD13H pf 422hp per vehicle*			
Height: 12ft 4½in (3.77m)		*Horsepower: 1,688hp (1,259kW)*			
Width: 8ft 10in (2.69m)		*Seats (total/car): 278S, 60S/73S/77S/68S*			

Number	Formation DMSL(A)+MSL+MS+DMSL(B)	Depot	Livery	Owner	Operator
168001	58151+58651+58451+58251	AL	CRG	PTR	CRW
168002	58152+58652+58452+58252	AL	CRG	PTR	CRW
168003	58153+58653+58453+58253	AL	CRG	PTR	CRW
168004	58154+58654+58454+58254	AL	CRG	PTR	CRW
168005	58155+58655+58455+58255	AL	CRG	PTR	CRW

Left: *The very first batch of Adtranz 'Turbostar' stock was built for Chiltern, when the Class 168/0s were introduced in 1997. Sporting a very different front end to the standard 'Turbostar' style, the five original Class 168/0s operate in a core pool with the Aylesbury-based '168s' and can be found on any main line duty. Set No. 168004 painted in Chiltern main line livery passes South Ruislip.* **CJM**

Class 168/1
Turbostar

Vehicle Length: 77ft 6in (23.62m)		*Engine: 1 x MTU 6R 183TD13H of 422hp per vehicle*		
Height: 12ft 4½in (3.77m)		*Horsepower: 3/4-car 1,266hp (944kW)/1,688hp (1,259kW)*		
Width: 8ft 10in (2.69m)		*Seats (total/car): 3-car - 208S, 59S/73S/76S, 4-car - 284S, 59S/73S/76S/76S*		

Number	Formation DMSL(A)+MS+MS+DMSL(B)	Depot	Livery	Owner	Operator	Notes
168106	58156+58756§+58456+58256	AL	CRG	PTR	CRW	§ is a MSL vehicle
168107	58157+58457+58757§+58257	AL	CRG	PTR	CRW	§ is a MSL vehicle
168108	58158+58458+58258	AL	CRG	PTR	CRW	
168109	58159+58459+58259	AL	CRG	PTR	CRW	
168110	58160+58460+58260	AL	CRG	PTR	CRW	
168111	58161+58461+58261	AL	CRG	EVL	CRW	58461 was originally 58661
168112	58162+58462+58262	AL	CRG	EVL	CRW	58462 was originally 58662
168113	58163+58463+58263	AL	CRG	EVL	CRW	58463 was originally 58663

Below: *The first follow-on order for Class 168s were built with the standard 'Turbostar' front end design and classified as 168/1. A total of 26 vehicles were constructed, formed into two 4-car and six 3-car units, numbered in the range 106-113. These sets have a deep front valance and three-section marker/head lights. Set No. 168111 is shown.* **CJM**

Class 168/2
Turbostar

Vehicle Length: 77ft 6in (23.62m)
Height: 12ft 4½in (3.77m)
Width: 8ft 10in (2.69m)
Engine: 1 x MTU 6R 183TD13H of 422hp per vehicle
Horsepower: 3/4-car 1,266hp (944kW)/1,688hp (1,259kW)
Seats (total/car): 3-car - 204S, 59S/76S/69S, 4-car - 277S, 59S/73S/76S/69S

Number	Formation DMSL(A)+MS+MS+DMSL(B)	Depot	Livery	Owner	Operator
168214	58164+58464+58264	AL	CRG	PTR	CRW
168215	58165+58465+58365+58265	AL	CRG	PTR	CRW
168216	58166+58466+58366+58266	AL	CRG	PTR	CRW
168217	58167+58467+58367+58267	AL	CRG	PTR	CRW
168218	58168+58468+58268	AL	CRG	PTR	CRW
168219	58169+58469+58269	AL	CRG	PTR	CRW

Right: *A fleet of 21 vehicles of Class 168/2 were introduced by Chiltern between 2003-2006 and formed into three 4-car and three 3-car sets. These units, which share work with the other '168' main line sets have a shallow front valance and revised light clusters. Four-car set No. 168215 is shown passing South Ruislip.* **CJM**

Class 168/3
Turbostar

Vehicle Length: 77ft 6in (23.62m)
Height: 12ft 4½in (3.77m)
Width: 8ft 10in (2.69m)
Engine: 1 x MTU 6R 183TD13H of 422hp per vehicle
Horsepower: 844hp (629kW)
Seats (total/car): 8F/108S 8F-43S/65S

Number	Formation DMCL+DMS	Depot	Livery	Owner	Operator
168321	50301+79301	AL	CRG	PTR	CRW
168322	50302+79302	AL	CRG	PTR	CRW
168323	50303+79303	AL	CRG	PTR	CRW
168324	50304+79304	AL	CRG	PTR	CRW
168325	50305+79305	AL	CRG	PTR	CRW
168326	50306+79306	AL	CRG	PTR	CRW
168327	50307+79307	AL	CRG	PTR	CRW
168328	50308+79308	AL	CRG	PTR	CRW
168329	50399+79399	AL	CRG	PTR	CRW

Previously numbered 170301 - 170309 and operated by South West Trains and First TransPennine

Below: *Nine additional Class 168 two-car sets entered service with Chiltern in 2015-16 when nine former SWT/TPE Class 170s were adapted for use, refurbished and fitted with trip cocks. Painted in Chiltern main line livery, set No. 168325 is illustrated in one of the bays at Oxford.* **Nathan Williamson**

Chiltern Railways

Class 172/1

Vehicle Length: 73ft 4in (22.37m)
Height: 12ft 4½in (3.77m)
Width: 8ft 8in (2.69m)

Engine: MTU 6H1800 of 360kW
Horsepower: 965hp (720kW)
Seats (total/car): 121S, 53S/68S

Number	Formation DMS+DMS	Depot	Livery	Owner	Operator		Number	Formation	Depot	Livery	Owner	Operator
172101	59111+59211	AL	CRW	ANG	CRW		172103	59113+59213	AL	CRW	ANG	CRW
172102	59112+59212	AL	CRW	ANG	CRW		172104	59114+59214	AL	CRW	ANG	CRW

Left: *To provide extra trains for the Chiltern network, Angel Train supplied four new Class 172/1 sets in 2009-10. Painted in the earlier Chiltern blue/white colours, the four sets are not fitted with trip cock equipment which restricts their area of operation. Set No. 172101 is seen at Marylebone.* **Antony Christie**

Class 68 'UK Light'

Vehicle Length: 67ft 3in (20.5m)
Height: 12ft 6½in (3.82m)
Speed: 100mph (161km/h)

Engine: Caterpillar C175-16
Horsepower: 3,750hp (2,800kW)
Electrical Equipment: ABB

Above: *Chiltern Railways operates its core long distance services between London Marylebone and the West Midlands with a fleet of loco-hauled Mk3s. Traction is provided by a fleet of six Class 68s hired from Direct Rail Services, with locos Nos. 68010-015 painted in Chiltern two-tone grey livery. Complete with Chiltern Railways branding, No. 68015 is shown.* **CJM**

Number	Depot	Pool	Livery	Owner	Operator		Number	Depot	Pool	Livery	Owner	Operator
68010	CR	XHVE	CRG	BEA	DRS/CRW		68013	CR	XHVE	CRG	BEA	DRS/CRW
68011	CR	XHVE	CRG	BEA	DRS/CRW		68014	CR	XHVE	CRG	BEA	DRS/CRW
68012	CR	XHVE	CRG	BEA	DRS/CRW		68015	CR	XHVE	CRG	BEA	DRS/CRW

Name applied - **68010** *Oxford Flyer*

Mk3 Hauled Stock (Passenger)

Vehicle Length: 75ft 0in (22.86m)
Height: 12ft 9in (3.88m)   Width: 8ft 11in (2.71m)
Bogie Type: BT10

AJ1F - GFW *Seating 30F (Catering out of use)*

Number		Depot	Livery	Owner
10271	(10236/10018)	AL	CRG	DBR
10272	(10208/40517)	AL	CRG	DBR
10273	(10230/10021)	AL	CRG	DBR
10274	(10255/11010)	AL	CRG	DBR

AC2G - TSO/TSOL* *Seating 72S*

Number		Depot	Livery	Owner
11029		AL	CRG	DBR
11031		AL	CRG	DBR
12017		AL	CRG	DBR
12036		AL	CRG	DBR
12043		AL	CRG	DBR
12094		AL	CRG	DBR
12119		AL	CRG	DBR
12602	(12072)	AL	CRG	DBR
12603*	(12053)	AL	CRG	DBR
12604	(12131)	AL	CRG	DBR
12605*	(11040)	AL	CRG	DBR
12606	(12048)	AL	CRG	DBR
12607*	(12038)	AL	CRG	DBR
12608	(12069)	AL	CRG	DBR
12609*	(12014)	AL	CRG	DBR
12610	(12117)	AL	CRG	DBR
12613*	(12173/11042)	AL	CRG	DBR
12614	(12145)	AL	CRG	DBR
12615*	(12059)	AL	CRG	DBR
12616	(12127)	AL	CRG	DBR
12617*	(12174/11050)	AL	CRG	DBR
12618	(12169)	AL	CRG	DBR
12619*	(12175/11052)	AL	CRG	DBR
12620	(12124)	AL	CRG	DBR
12621	(11046)	AL	CRG	DBR
12623	(11019)	AL	CRG	DBR
12625	(11030)	AL	CRG	DBR
12627	(11054)	AL	CRG	DBR

Above: *The modified Mk3s operated by Chiltern have sliding plug doors. TSO No. 12614 is shown. All are painted in CR 'mainline' colours.* **CJM**

Mk3 Hauled Stock (NPCCS)

Vehicle Length: 75ft 0in (22.86m)
Height: 12ft 9in (3.88m)
Width: 8ft 11in (2.71m)
Bogie Type: BT7

NZAG - DVT

Number	Depot	Livery	Owner		Number	Depot	Livery	Owner
82301 (82117)	AL	CRG	DBR		82304 (82130)	AL	CRG	DBR
82302 (82151)	AL	CRG	DBR		82305 (82134)	AL	CRG	DBR
82303 (82135)	AL	CRG	DBR		82309 (82104)	AL	CRG	DBR

Class 960 – Service Units

Length: 64ft 6in (19.66m)
Height: 12ft 8½in (3.87m)
Width: 9ft 3in (2.81m)
Engine: 2 x Leyland 150hp
Horsepower: 300hp (224kW)
Seats (total/car): None

Number	Formation	Depot	Livery	Owner	Operator	Notes
960014	977873	AL	BLG	CRW	CRW	Ex-Class 121 55022, Route Learning/Sandite

Class 01.5 (0-6-0)

Number		Depot	Pool	Livery	Owner	Operator	Name
01509	(433) RH468043	AL	MBDL	BLU	CRW	CRW	*Lesley*

CrossCountry Trains

Address: ✉ Cannon House, 18 The Priory, Queensway, Birmingham, B4 6BS
🖂 info@crosscountrytrains.co.uk
✆ 0870 0100084
ⓘ www.crosscountrytrains.co.uk

Managing Director: Andy Cooper
Franchise Dates: 11 November 2007 - December 2024
Principal Routes: Penzance / Paignton -
Manchester / Edinburgh / Aberdeen
Bournemouth - Manchester /
Edinburgh / Aberdeen
Birmingham - Stansted
Nottingham - Cardiff
Depots: Central Rivers (CZ),
Tyseley (TS),
Laira (LA)
Parent Company: Deutsche Bahn AG
(DB Regio) / Arriva

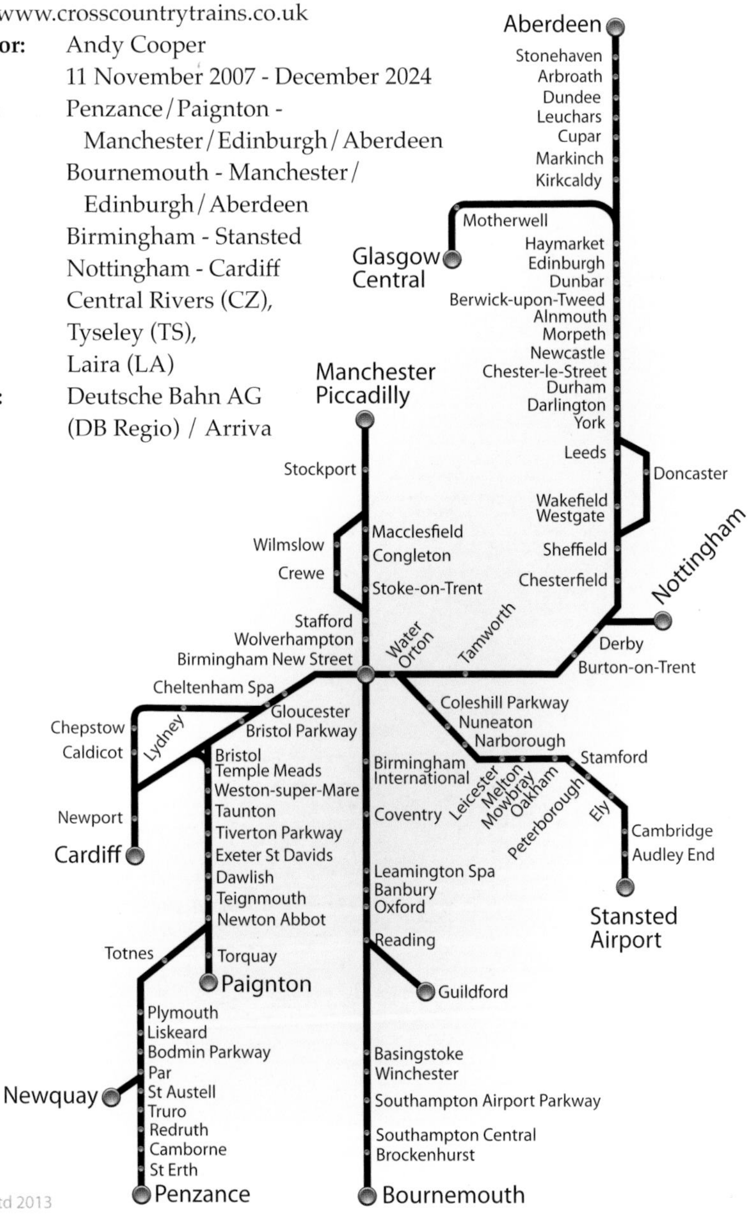

Aberdeen
Stonehaven
Arbroath
Dundee
Leuchars
Cupar
Markinch
Kirkcaldy
Motherwell
Glasgow Central
Haymarket
Edinburgh
Dunbar
Berwick-upon-Tweed
Alnmouth
Morpeth
Newcastle
Chester-le-Street
Durham
Darlington
York
Manchester Piccadilly
Leeds
Doncaster
Stockport
Wakefield Westgate
Wilmslow
Macclesfield
Congleton
Sheffield
Nottingham
Crewe
Stoke-on-Trent
Chesterfield
Stafford
Wolverhampton
Birmingham New Street
Water Orton
Tamworth
Derby
Burton-on-Trent
Cheltenham Spa
Chepstow
Gloucester
Bristol Parkway
Coleshill Parkway
Nuneaton
Narborough
Caldicot
Lydney
Bristol Temple Meads
Weston-super-Mare
Birmingham International
Leicester
Melton Mowbray
Oakham
Stamford
Newport
Taunton
Tiverton Parkway
Coventry
Peterborough
Ely
Cambridge
Cardiff
Exeter St Davids
Dawlish
Teignmouth
Newton Abbot
Audley End
Leamington Spa
Banbury
Oxford
Stansted Airport
Totnes
Torquay
Reading
Plymouth
Paignton
Guildford
Liskeard
Bodmin Parkway
Par
St Austell
Basingstoke
Winchester
Newquay
Truro
Redruth
Camborne
St Erth
Southampton Airport Parkway
Southampton Central
Brockenhurst
Penzance
Bournemouth

© TRC.Com Ltd 2013

Class 43 – HST

Vehicle Length: 58ft 5in (18.80m)			Engine: MTU 16V4000 R41R		
Height: 12ft 10in (3.90m)			Horsepower: 2,250hp (1,680kW)		
Width: 8ft 11in (2.73m)			Electrical Equipment: Brush		

Number	Depot	Pool	Livery	Owner	Operator
43207 (43007)	LA	EHPC	AXC	ANG	AXC
43285 (43085)	LA	EHPC	AXC	PTR	AXC
43301 (43101)	LA	EHPC	AXC	PTR	AXC
43303 (43103)	LA	EHPC	AXC	PTR	AXC
43304 (43104)	LA	EHPC	AXC	ANG	AXC
43321 (43121)	LA	EHPC	AXC	PTR	AXC
43357 (43157)	LA	EHPC	AXC	PTR	AXC
43366 (43166)	LA	EHPC	AXC	ANG	AXC
43378 (43178)	LA	EHPC	AXC	ANG	AXC
43384 (43184)	LA	EHPC	AXC	ANG	AXC

Right: *With Edinburgh Craigentinny depot now operated by Hitachi for Class 800/801 maintenance, the CrossCountry HST fleet is now based at Laira depot, Plymouth. A fleet of 10 Class 43s are on the roster, all are refurbished with MTU power units and usually supply traction for a maximum of four HST consists in service daily. No. 43285 is shown at Bristol Parkway. All power cars have been modified to operate with sliding door HST stock.* **CJM**

HST passenger fleet

Vehicle Length: 75ft 0in (22.86m)			Bogie Type: BT10		
Height: 12ft 9in (3.88m)					
Width: 8ft 11in (2.71m)					

GH1G - TF   *Seating 40F*

Number		Depot	Livery	Owner	
41026		LA	AXC	ANG	
41035		LA	AXC	ANG	
41193	(11060)	LA	AXC	PTR	
41194	(11016)	LA	AXC	PTR	
41195¤	(11020) §	LA	AXC	PTR	¤ = TFD

GH2G - TS   *Seating 82S*

Number	Depot	Livery	Owner
42036§	LA	AXC	ANG
42037	LA	AXC	ANG
42038	LA	AXC	ANG
42051	LA	AXC	ANG
42052	LA	AXC	ANG
42053	LA	AXC	ANG
42097	LA	AXC	ANG
42234	LA	AXC	PTR
42290	LA	AXC	PTR
42342 (44082)	LA	AXC	ANG
42366 (12007)	LA	AXC	PTR
42367 (12025)	LA	AXC	PTR
42368 (12028)	LA	AXC	PTR
42369 (12050)	LA	AXC	PTR
42370 (12086)§	LA	AXC	PTR
42371 (12052)	LA	AXC	PTR
42372 (12055)	LA	AXC	PTR
42373 (12071)	LA	AXC	PTR

Number	Depot	Livery	Owner	
42374 (12075)	LA	AXC	PTR	
42375 (12113)	LA	AXC	PTR	
42376 (12085) §	LA	AXC	PTR	
42377 (12102) §	LA	AXC	PTR	
42378 (12123)§	LA	AXC	PTR	
42379* (41036)	LA	AXC	ANG	*=TSD
42380* (41025)	LA	AXC	ANG	*=TSD

GJ2G - TGS   *Seating 67S*

Number	Depot	Livery	Owner
44012	LA	AXC	ANG
44017	LA	AXC	ANG
44021	LA	AXC	ANG
44052 §	LA	AXC	PTR
44072	LA	AXC	PTR

GH3G - TCC   *Seating 30F/10S*

Number	Depot	Livery	Owner
45001 (12004)	LA	AXC	PTR
45002 (12106)	LA	AXC	PTR
45003 (12076) §	LA	AXC	PTR
45004 (12077)	LA	AXC	PTR
45005 (12080)	LA	AXC	PTR

§ fitted with power operated sliding doors

CrossCountry Trains

Above: *A fleet of 40 HST Mk3 vehicles are based at Laira and are usually formed into four passenger rakes. In 2018-19 an ongoing project was underway to fit sliding doors to this fleet. Sliding door fitted TCC No. 45003 is illustrated from its first class end.* **CJM**

Class 170/1
Turbostar

Vehicle Length: 77ft 6in (23.62m)
Height: 12ft 4½in (3.77m)
Width: 8ft 10in (2.69m)

Engine: 1 x MTU 6R 183TD13H of 422hp per vehicle
Horsepower: 1,266hp (944kW)
Seats (total/car): 9F/191S 52S/80S/9F-59S

Number	Formation DMS+MS+DMCL	Depot	Livery	Owner	Operator
170101	50101+55101+79101	TS	AXC	PTR	AXC
170102	50102+55102+79102	TS	AXC	PTR	AXC
170103	50103+55103+79103	TS	AXC	PTR	AXC
170104	50104+55104+79104	TS	AXC	PTR	AXC
170105	50105+55105+79105	TS	AXC	PTR	AXC
170106	50106+55106+79106	TS	AXC	PTR	AXC
170107	50107+55107+79107	TS	AXC	PTR	AXC
170108	50108+55108+79108	TS	AXC	PTR	AXC
170109	50109+55109+79109	TS	AXC	PTR	AXC
170110	50110+55110+79110	TS	AXC	PTR	AXC

Left: *The Cross-Country east-west services are operated by a fleet of Class 170, formed as either two or three-car sets based at Tyseley in the West Midlands. The fleet is formed of members from several different sub-classes. All have been refurbished to a common high-quality standard offering 2+2 low-density seating. All sets are painted in XC silver and deep maroon livery. First class accommodation has been retained and provided in one driving car of each set. A pair of two-car Class 170/1s, led by No. 170114 is seen near Severn Tunnel Junction with a Cardiff to Nottingham service.* **CJM**

Vehicle Length: 77ft 6in (23.62m)
Height: 12ft 4½in (3.77m)
Width: 8ft 10in (2.69m)

Engine: 1 x MTU 6R 183TD13H of 422hp per vehicle
Horsepower: 844hp (629kW)
Seats (total/car): 9F-111S 59S/9F-52S

Number	Formation DMS+DMCL	Depot	Livery	Owner	Operator
170111*	50111+79111	TS	AXC	PTR	AXC
170112	50112+79112	TS	AXC	PTR	AXC
170113	50113+79113	TS	AXC	PTR	AXC
170114	50114+79114	TS	AXC	PTR	AXC
170115	50115+79115	TS	AXC	PTR	AXC
170116	50116+79116	TS	AXC	PTR	AXC
170117	50117+79117	TS	AXC	PTR	AXC

* Fitted with passenger counters

Passenger Train Operating Companies - CrossCountry Trains

Above: *The three-car Class 170s operated by CrossCountry seat 9 first and 191 standard class passengers. On busy services, two two-car or a two and three-car set can operate together. Viewed from its DMCL end, set No. 170104 hurries through Longbridge with a Nottingham to Cardiff service.* **CJM**

Class 170/3
Turbostar

	Vehicle Length: 77ft 6in (23.62m)			Engine: 1 x MTU 6R 183TD13H of 422hp per vehicle	
	Height: 12ft 4½in (3.77m)			Horsepower: 1,266hp (944kW)	
	Width: 8ft 10in (2.69m)			Seats (total/car): 9F-191S 59S/80S/9F-52S	

Number	Formation	Depot	Livery	Owner	Operator
	DMSL+MS+DMCL				
170397	50397+56397+79397	TS	AXC	PTR	AXC
170398	50398+56398+79398	TS	AXC	PTR	AXC

Class 170/5
Turbostar

Vehicle Length: 77ft 6in (23.62m)	Engine: 1 x MTU 6R 183TD13H of 422hp per vehicle
Height: 12ft 4½in (3.77m)	Horsepower: 844hp (629kW)
Width: 8ft 10in (2.69m)	Seats (total/car): 9F-111S 59S/9F-52S

Number	Formation	Depot	Livery	Owner	Operator		Number	Formation	Depot	Livery	Owner	Operator
	DMSL+DMCL						170520	50520+79520	TS	AXC	PTR	AXC
							170521	50521+79521	TS	AXC	PTR	AXC
170518	50518+79518	TS	AXC	PTR	AXC		170522	50522+79522	TS	AXC	PTR	AXC
170519	50519+79519	TS	AXC	PTR	AXC		170523	50523+79523	TS	AXC	PTR	AXC

Class 170/6
Turbostar

	Vehicle Length: 77ft 6in (23.62m)			Engine: 1 x MTU 6R 183TD13H of 422hp per vehicle	
	Height: 12ft 4½in (3.77m)			Horsepower: 1,266hp (944kW)	
	Width: 8ft 10in (2.69m)			Seats (total/car): 9F-191S 59S/80S/9F-52S	

Number	Formation	Depot	Livery	Owner	Operator
	DMSL+MS+DMCL				
170636	50636+56636+79636	TS	AXC	PTR	AXC
170637	50637+56637+79637	TS	AXC	PTR	AXC
170638	50638+56638+79638	TS	AXC	PTR	AXC
170639	50639+56639+79639	TS	AXC	PTR	AXC

Right: *When the split of assets was done at privatisation in the mid-1990s, CrossCountry was allocated six two-car Class 170/5 and four three-car Class 170/6s. Together with members of 170/1 and 170/3 a number of different interiors were found. Soon a global refurbishment was undertaken bringing all sets to the same standard, allowing the different sub-classes to operate in a common pool. Three-car Class 170/6 set No. 170637 is shown on a Cardiff to Nottingham service at Longbridge.* **CJM**

CrossCountry Trains

Class 220
Voyager

Vehicle Length: 77ft 6in (23.62m)		Engine: 1 x Cummins of 750hp per vehicle
Height: 12ft 4in (3.75m)		Horsepower: 3,000hp (2,237kW)
Width: 8ft 11in (2.73m)		Seats (total/car): 26F/174S 42S/66S/66S/26F

Number	Formation DMS+MS+MS+DMF	Depot	Livery	Owner	Operator
220001	60301+60701+60201+60401	CZ	AXC	BEA	AXC
220002	60302+60702+60202+60402	CZ	AXC	BEA	AXC
220003	60303+60703+60203+60403	CZ	AXC	BEA	AXC
220004	60304+60704+60204+60404	CZ	AXC	BEA	AXC
220005	60305+60705+60205+60405	CZ	AXC	BEA	AXC
220006	60306+60706+60206+60406	CZ	AXC	BEA	AXC
220007	60307+60707+60207+60407	CZ	AXC	BEA	AXC
220008	60308+60708+60208+60408	CZ	AXC	BEA	AXC
220009	60309+60709+60209+60409	CZ	AXC	BEA	AXC
220010	60310+60710+60210+60410	CZ	AXC	BEA	AXC
220011	60311+60711+60211+60411	CZ	AXC	BEA	AXC
220012	60312+60712+60212+60412	CZ	AXC	BEA	AXC
220013	60313+60713+60213+60413	CZ	AXC	BEA	AXC
220014	60314+60714+60214+60414	CZ	AXC	BEA	AXC
220015	60315+60715+60215+60415	CZ	AXC	BEA	AXC
220016	60316+60716+60216+60416	CZ	AXC	BEA	AXC
220017	60317+60717+60217+60417	CZ	AXC	BEA	AXC
220018	60318+60718+60218+60418	CZ	AXC	BEA	AXC
220019	60319+60719+60219+60419	CZ	AXC	BEA	AXC
220020	60320+60720+60220+60420	CZ	AXC	BEA	AXC
220021	60321+60721+60221+60421	CZ	AXC	BEA	AXC
220022	60322+60722+60222+60422	CZ	AXC	BEA	AXC
220023	60323+60723+60223+60423	CZ	AXC	BEA	AXC
220024	60324+60724+60224+60424	CZ	AXC	BEA	AXC
220025	60325+60725+60225+60425	CZ	AXC	BEA	AXC
220026	60326+60726+60226+60426	CZ	AXC	BEA	AXC
220027	60327+60727+60227+60427	CZ	AXC	BEA	AXC
220028	60328+60728+60228+60428	CZ	AXC	BEA	AXC
220029	60329+60729+60229+60429	CZ	AXC	BEA	AXC
220030	60330+60730+60230+60430	CZ	AXC	BEA	AXC
220031	60331+60731+60231+60431	CZ	AXC	BEA	AXC
220032	60332+60732+60232+60432	CZ	AXC	BEA	AXC
220033	60333+60733+60233+60433	CZ	AXC	BEA	AXC
220034	60334+60734+60234+60434	CZ	AXC	BEA	AXC

Below: *The main CrossCountry fleet, used on the majority of long distance services are Class 220 'Voyager' and Class 221 'Super Voyager' sets. These are based at the Bombardier-operated Central Rivers depot near Burton. The 34 sets have been refurbished from their original days but are now tired and in need of attention. Set No. 220021 passes Eastleigh on 30 November 2017 with the 07.27 Manchester Piccadilly to Bournemouth service.* **CJM**

Class 221
Super Voyager

Vehicle Length: 77ft 6in (23.62m)	Engine: 1 x Cummins of 750hp per vehicle
Height: 12ft 4in (3.75m)	Horsepower: 3,750hp (2,796kW)
Width: 8ft 11in (2.73m)	Seats (total/car): 26F/236S 42S/66S/66S/62S/26F

Originally fitted with tilt system to allow higher speeds over curves. Equipment now isolated.

Number	Formation DMS+MS+MS+MS+DMF	Depot	Livery	Owner	Operator	
221119	60369+60769+60969+60869+60469	CZ	AXC	BEA	AXC	
221120	60370+60770+60970+60870+60470	CZ	AXC	BEA	AXC	
221121	60371+60771+60971+60871+60471	CZ	AXC	BEA	AXC	
221122	60372+60772+60972+60872+60472	CZ	AXC	BEA	AXC	
221123	60373+60773+60973+60873+60473	CZ	AXC	BEA	AXC	
221124	60374+60774+60974+60874+60474	CZ	AXC	BEA	AXC	
221125	60375+60775+60975+60875+60475	CZ	AXC	BEA	AXC	
221126	60376+60776+60976+60876+60476	CZ	AXC	BEA	AXC	
221127	60377+60777+60977+60877+60477	CZ	AXC	BEA	AXC	
221128	60378+60778+60978+60878+60478	CZ	AXC	BEA	AXC	
221129	60379+60779+60979+60879+60479	CZ	AXC	BEA	AXC	
221130	60380+60780+60980+60880+60480	CZ	AXC	BEA	AXC	
221131	60381+60781+60981+60881+60481	CZ	AXC	BEA	AXC	
221132	60382+60782+60982+60882+60482	CZ	AXC	BEA	AXC	
221133	60383+60783+60983+60883+60483	CZ	AXC	BEA	AXC	
221134	60384+60784+60984+60884+60484	CZ	AXC	BEA	AXC	
221135	60385+60785+60985+60885+60485	CZ	AXC	BEA	AXC	
221136	60386+60786+-+60886+60486	CZ	AXC	BEA	AXC	(four-car set)
221137	60387+60787+60987+60887+60487	CZ	AXC	BEA	AXC	
221138	60388+60788+60988+60888+60488	CZ	AXC	BEA	AXC	
221139	60389+60789+60989+60889+60489	CZ	AXC	BEA	AXC	
221140	60390+60790+-+60890+60490	CZ	AXC	BEA	AXC	(four-car set)
221141	60391+60791+60991+-+60491	CZ	AXC	BEA	AXC	(four-car set)
221144	60394+60794+60990+-+60494	CZ	AXC	BEA	AXC	(four-car set)

Below: In 2018-2019, CrossCountry operates a fleet of 24 Class 221 'Super Voyager' sets, these are formed as 20 five-car and four four-car units. Originally these were tilting sets, which could takes curves at a higher speed while retaining passenger comfort, however the expensive system has now been isolated. On all 'Voyager' stock, one driving car is set aside for first class occupancy with 26 seats, from the outside, this vehicle is identifiable by a yellow cant-rail band and a yellow cover to the coupling box. Five-car set No. 221132 passes Powderham on 19 April 2018 forming train 1S41, the 07.25 Plymouth to Edinburgh Waverley. **CJM**

Elizabeth Line (CrossRail)

Address: ✉ 6th Floor, St Mary Axe, London, EC3A 8NH
          ✍ helpdesk@crossrail.co.uk
          ✆ 03432 2211234
          ① http://www.crossrail.co.uk

Managing Director: Steve Murphy
Principal Routes: Present - Liverpool Street - Shenfield
                          Paddington - Hayes and Harlington
                          Future - Reading to Shenfield/Abbey Wood, Heathrow spur
Depots: Ilford (IL), Old Oak Common (OC)
Parent Company: MTR Corporation (Crossrail) Limited
                        Transport for London

Through services due to commence from late 2019.

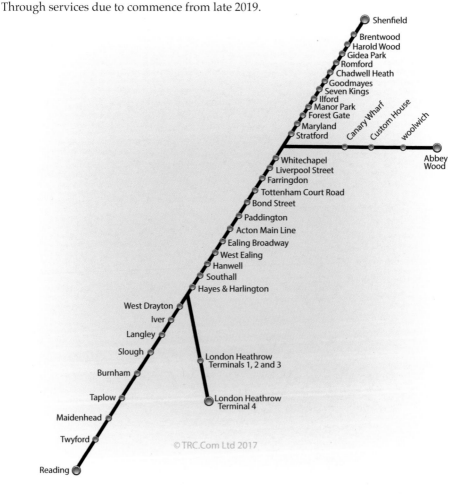

Class 315

	Vehicle Length: (Driving) 64ft 11½in (19.80m)	Width: 9ft 3in (2.82m)
	(Inter) 65ft 4½in (19.92m)	Horsepower: 880hp (656kW)
	Height: 11ft 6½in (3.58m)	Seats (total/car): 318S, 74S/86S/84S/74S

Number	Formation DMSO(A)+TSO+PTSO+DMSO(B)	Depot	Livery	Owner	Operator	Name
315818	64495+71298+71406+64496	IL	CRO	EVL	CRO	
315819	64497+71299+71407+64498	IL	CRO	EVL	CRO	
315820	64499+71300+71408+64500	IL	CRO	EVL	CRO	
315821	64501+71301+71409+64502	IL	CRO	EVL	CRO	
315822	64503+71302+71410+64504	IL	CRO	EVL	CRO	
315823	64505+71303+71411+64506	IL	CRO	EVL	CRO	
315824	64507+71304+71412+64508	IL	CRO	EVL	CRO	
315825	64509+71305+71413+64510	IL	CRO	EVL	CRO	
315826	64511+71306+71414+64512	IL	CRO	EVL	CRO	
315827	64513+71307+71415+64514	IL	CRO	EVL	CRO	
315829	64517+71309+71417+64518	IL	CRO	EVL	CRO	*London Borough of Havering Celebrating 40 Years*
315830	64519+71310+71418+64520	IL	CRO	EVL	CRO	
315831	64521+71311+71419+64522	IL	CRO	EVL	CRO	
315833	64525+71313+71421+64526	IL	CRO	EVL	CRO	
315834	64527+71314+71422+64528	IL	CRO	EVL	CRO	
315836	64531+71316+71424+64532	IL	CRO	EVL	CRO	
315837	64533+71317+71425+64534	IL	CRO	EVL	CRO	
315838	64535+71318+71426+64536	IL	CRO	EVL	CRO	
315839	64537+71319+71427+64538	IL	CRO	EVL	CRO	
315842	64543+71322+71430+64544	IL	CRO	EVL	CRO	
315843	64545+71323+71431+64546	IL	CRO	EVL	CRO	
315844	64547+71324+71432+64548	IL	CRO	EVL	CRO	
315847	64553+71327+71435+64554	IL	CRO	EVL	CRO	
315848	64540+71328+71436+64556	IL	CRO	EVL	CRO	
315849	64557+71329+71437+64558	IL	CRO	EVL	CRO	
315851	64561+71331+71439+64562	IL	CRO	EVL	CRO	
315852	64563+71332+71440+64564	IL	CRO	EVL	CRO	
315853	64565+71333+71441+64566	IL	CRO	EVL	CRO	
315854	64567+71334+71442+64568	IL	CRO	EVL	CRO	
315856	64571+71336+71444+64572	IL	CRO	EVL	CRO	
315857	64573+71337+71445+64574	IL	CRO	EVL	CRO	
315858	64575+71338+71446+64576	-	CRO	EVL	-	
315859	64577+71339+71447+64578	IL	CRO	EVL	CRO	

Below: *The 1972-design Class 315 sets are now being reduced in numbers following introduction of new Class 345 stock on the Crossrail route. When the full 'Elizabeth Line' is open from 2020-2021, the '315s' will finally be withdrawn. At present the sets are maintained at Ilford and are painted in Transport for London white with a blue base band and blue passenger doors. Set No. 315823 is seen passing Stratford, East London. Some sets were sent for scrap in late 2018.* **CJM**

CrossRail

Class 345
Aventra

Train Length: (Driving) - 7-car - 524ft (159.74m)	Width: - 9ft 2in (2.78m)
- 9-car - 673ft (205m)	Max Speed: 90mph (145km/h)
Weight: - 7-car - 252.7t	Seats (total/car): 9-car - 406S (7-car - 314S)
9-car - 327.1t	46S/46S/46S/46S/38S/46S/46S/46S/46S

Sets 345002-017/022 have been delivered as seven-car units to allow operation on Shenfield- Liverpool Street and Hayes & Harlington to Paddington services until platform extension and software work is complete. The full Elizabeth Line/ CrossRail service is due to commence running at the end of 2019.

Number	Formation	Depot	Livery	Owner	Operator
	DMSO(A)+PMSO(A)+MSO+MSO+TSO+MSO+MSO+PMSO+DMSO(B)				
345001	340101+340201+340301+*340401*+340501+*340601*+340701+340801+340901	IL	CRO	TFL	CRO
345002	340102+340202+340302+*340402*+340502+*340602*+340702+340802+340902	IL	CRO	TFL	CRO
345003	340103+340203+340303+*340403*+340503+*340603*+340703+340803+340903	IL	CRO	TFL	CRO
345004	340104+340204+340304+*340404*+340504+*340604*+340704+340804+340904	IL	CRO	TFL	CRO
345005	340105+340205+340305+*340405*+340505+*340605*+340705+340805+340905	IL	CRO	TFL	CRO
345006	340106+340206+340306+*340406*+340506+*340606*+340706+340806+340906	IL	CRO	TFL	CRO
345007	340107+340207+340307+*340407*+340507+*340607*+340707+340807+340907	IL	CRO	TFL	CRO
345008	340108+340208+340308+*340408*+340508+340608+340708+340808+340908	IL	CRO	TFL	CRO
345009	340109+340209+340309+*340409*+340509+*340609*+340709+340809+340909	IL	CRO	TFL	CRO
345010	340110+340210+340310+*340410*+340510+*340610*+340710+340810+340910	IL	CRO	TFL	CRO
345011	340111+340211+340311+*340411*+340511+*340611*+340711+340811+340911	IL	CRO	TFL	CRO
345012	340112+340212+340312+*340412*+340512+*340612*+340712+340812+340912	IL	CRO	TFL	CRO
345013	340113+340213+340313+*340413*+340513+*340613*+340713+340813+340913	IL	CRO	TFL	CRO
345014	340114+340214+340314+*340414*+340514+*340614*+340714+340814+340914	IL	CRO	TFL	CRO
345015	340115+340215+340315+*340415*+340515+*340615*+340715+340815+340915	IL	CRO	TFL	CRO
345016	340116+340216+340316+340416+340516+340616+340716+340816+340916	OC	CRO	TFL	CRO
345017	340117+340217+340317+340417+340517+340617+340717+340817+340917	OC	CRO	TFL	CRO
345018	340118+340218+340318+340418+340518+340618+340718+340818+340918	OC	CRO	TFL	CRO
345019	340119+340219+340319+340419+340519+340619+340719+340819+340919	OC	CRO	TFL	CRO
345020	340120+340220+340320+340420+340520+340620+340720+340820+340920	OC	CRO	TFL	.CRO
345021	340121+340221+340321+340421+340521+340621+340721+340821+340921	OC	CRO	TFL	CRO
345022	340122+340222+340322+340422+340522+340622+340722+340822+340922	OC	CRO	TFL	CRO
345023	340123+340223+340323+340423+340523+340623+340723+340823+340923	OC	CRO	TFL	CRO
345024	340124+340224+340324+340424+340524+340624+340724+340824+340924	OC	CRO	TFL	CRO
345025	340125+340225+340325+340425+340525+340625+340725+340825+340925	OC	CRO	TFL	CRO
345026	340126+340226+340326+340426+340526+340626+340726+340826+340926	OC	CRO	TFL	CRO
345027	340127+340227+340327+340427+340527+340627+340727+340827+340927	OC	CRO	TFL	CRO
345028	340128+340228+340328+340428+340528+340628+340728+340828+340928	OC	CRO	TFL	CRO
345029	340129+340229+340329+340429+340529+340629+340729+340829+340929	OC	CRO	TFL	CRO
345030	340130+340230+340330+340430+340530+340630+340730+340830+340930	OC	CRO	TFL	CRO
345031	340131+340231+340331+340431+340531+340631+340731+340831+340931	OC	CRO	TFL	CRO
345032	340132+340232+340332+340432+340532+340632+340732+340832+340932	OC	CRO	TFL	CRO
345033	340133+340233+340333+340433+340533+340633+340733+340833+340933	OC	CRO	TFL	CRO
345034	340134+340234+340334+340434+340534+340634+340734+340834+340934	OC	CRO	TFL	CRO
345035	340135+340235+340335+340435+340535+340635+340735+340835+340935	OC	CRO	TFL	CRO
345036	340136+340236+340336+340436+340536+340636+340736+340836+340936	OC	CRO	TFL	CRO
345037	340137+340237+340337+340437+340537+340637+340737+340837+340937	OC	CRO	TFL	CRO
345038	340138+340238+340338+340438+340538+340638+340738+340838+340938	OC	CRO	TFL	CRO
345039	340139+340239+340339+340439+340539+340639+340739+340839+340939	OC	CRO	TFL	CRO
345040	340140+340240+340340+340440+340540+340640+340740+340840+340940	OC	CRO	TFL	CRO
345041	340141+340241+340341+340441+340541+340641+340741+340841+340941	OC	CRO	TFL	CRO
345042	340142+340242+340342+340442+340542+340642+340742+340842+340942	OC	CRO	TFL	CRO
345043	340143+340243+340343+340443+340543+340643+340743+340843+340943	OC	CRO	TFL	CRO
345044	340144+340244+340344+340444+340544+340644+340744+340844+340944	OC	CRO	TFL	CRO
345045	340145+340245+340345+340445+340545+340645+340745+340845+340945	OC	CRO	TFL	CRO
345046	340146+340246+340346+340446+340546+340646+340746+340846+340946	OC	CRO	TFL	CRO
345047	340147+340247+340347+340447+340547+340647+340747+340847+340947	OC	CRO	TFL	CRO
345048	340148+340248+340348+340448+340548+340648+340748+340848+340948	OC	CRO	TFL	CRO
345049	340149+340249+340349+340449+340549+340649+340749+340849+340949	OC	CRO	TFL	CRO
345050	340150+340250+340350+340450+340550+340650+340750+340850+340950	OC	CRO	TFL	CRO
345051	340151+340251+340351+340451+340551+340651+340751+340851+340951	OC	CRO	TFL	CRO
345052	340152+340252+340352+340452+340552+340652+340752+340852+340952	OC	CRO	TFL	CRO
345053	340153+340253+340353+340453+340553+340653+340753+340853+340953	OC	CRO	TFL	CRO
345054	340154+340254+340354+340454+340554+340654+340754+340854+340954	OC	CRO	TFL	CRO

345055	340155+340255+340355+340455+340555+340655+340755+340855+340955	OC	CRO	TFL	CRO
345056	340156+340256+340356+340456+340556+340656+340756+340856+340956	OC	CRO	TFL	CRO
345057	340157+340257+340357+340457+340557+340657+340757+340857+340957	OC	CRO	TFL	CRO
345058	340158+340258+340358+340458+340558+340658+340758+340858+340958	OC	CRO	TFL	CRO
345059	340159+340259+340359+340459+340559+340659+340759+340859+340959	OC	CRO	TFL	CRO
345060	340160+340260+340360+340460+340560+340660+340760+340860+340960	OC	CRO	TFL	CRO
345061	340161+340261+340361+340461+340561+340661+340761+340861+340961	OC	CRO	TFL	CRO
345062	340162+340262+340362+340462+340562+340662+340762+340862+340962	OC	CRO	TFL	CRO
345063	340163+340263+340363+340463+340563+340663+340763+340863+340963	OC	CRO	TFL	CRO
345064	340164+340264+340364+340464+340564+340664+340764+340864+340964	OC	CRO	TFL	CRO
345065	340165+340265+340365+340465+340565+340665+340765+340865+340965	OC	CRO	TFL	CRO
345066	340166+340266+340366+340466+340566+340666+340766+340866+340966	OC	CRO	TFL	CRO
345067	340167+340267+340367+340467+340567+340667+340767+340867+340967	OC	CRO	TFL	CRO
345068	340168+340268+340368+340468+340568+340668+340768+340868+340968	OC	CRO	TFL	CRO
345069	340169+340269+340369+340469+340569+340669+340769+340869+340969	OC	CRO	TFL	CRO
345070	340170+340270+340370+340470+340570+340670+340770+340870+340970	OC	CRO	TFL	CRO

Above: *The 70 Class 345 'Aventra' sets are currently on delivery to CrossRail. A total of 17 sets have been delivered as seven-car units to allow operation on Liverpool Street-Shenfield and Paddington-Hayes services in advance of the full east-west service commencing from late 2019. Full length sets are currently being stored at Old Oak Common and Ilford. Reduced length set No. 345007 with promotional bodyside branding is seen on a Liverpool Street-Shenfield working in summer 2018.* **CJM**

Below: *Full length nine-car set No. 345046 was used to promote the CrossRail project at the 2018 Rail Live event at Long Marston. The Class 345s were the first units delivered to take advantage of the no yellow front end rule.* **CJM**

East Midlands Trains

Address: ✉ 1 Prospect Place, Millennium Way, Pride Park, Derby, DE24 8HG
✆ getintouch@eastmidlandstrains.co.uk
✆ 08457 125678
ⓘ www.eastmidlandstrains.co.uk

Managing Director: Jake Kelly
Franchise Dates: 11 November 2007 - March 2019 (Extended by agreement)
Principal Routes: St Pancras - Sheffield/York/Leeds/Nottingham
Norwich/Skegness/Cleethorpes - Nottingham/Crewe/
Liverpool and Matlock
Depots: Derby (DY), Nottingham (NM), Neville Hill (NL)
Parent Company: Stagecoach Group

Class 08

Vehicle Length: 29ft 3in (8.91m)			Engine: English Electric 6K			
Height: 12ft 8⅝in (3.87m)			Horsepower: 400hp (298kW)			
Width: 8ft 6in (2.59m)			Electrical Equipment: English Electric			

Number	Depot	Pool	Livery	Owner	Operator	Name
08405	NL	EMSL	RSS	RSS	EMT	
08525	NL	EMSL	EMT	EMT	EMT	Duncan Bedford
08690	NL	EMSL	EMT	EMT	EMT	David Thirkill
08899	DY	EMSL	MAR	EMT	EMT	Midland Counties Railway 175 1839-2014
08908	DY	EMSL	EMT	EMT	EMT	
08950	NL	EMSL	EMT	EMT	EMT	David Lightfoot

Class 43/0 – HST

Vehicle Length: 58ft 5in (18.80m) — Engine: Paxman VP185
Height: 12ft 10in (3.90m) — Horsepower: 2,100hp (1,565kW)
Width: 8ft 11in (2.73m) — Electrical Equipment: Brush

Number	Depot	Pool	Livery	Owner	Operator
43043	NL	EMPC	SCE	PTR	EMT
43044	NL	EMPC	SCE	PTR	EMT
43045	NL	EMPC	SCE	PTR	EMT
43046	NL	EMPC	SCE	PTR	EMT
43047	NL	EMPC	SCE	PTR	EMT
43048	NL	EMPC	SCE	PTR	EMT
43049	NL	EMPC	SCE	PTR	EMT
43050	NL	EMPC	SCE	PTR	EMT
43052	NL	EMPC	SCE	PTR	EMT
43054	NL	EMPC	SCE	PTR	EMT
43055	NL	EMPC	SCE	PTR	EMT
43058	NL	EMPC	SCE	PTR	EMT
43059	NL	EMPC	SCE	PTR	EMT
43060	NL	EMPC	SCE	PTR	EMT
43061	NL	EMPC	SCE	PTR	EMT
43064	NL	EMPC	SCE	PTR	EMT
43066	NL	EMPC	SCE	PTR	EMT
43073	NL	EMPC	SCE	PTR	EMT
43075	NL	EMPC	SCE	PTR	EMT
43076	NL	EMPC	SCE	PTR	EMT
43081	NL	EMPC	SCE	PTR	EMT
43082	NL	EMPC	SCE	PTR	EMT
43083	NL	EMPC	SCE	PTR	EMT
43089	NL	EMPC	SCE	PTR	EMT

Names applied
43045 EMT Customer Service Week #TrainWatch
43048 T. C. B. Miller MBE
43049 Neville Hill
43055 The Sheffield Star 125 Years
43076 In Support of Help for Heroes
43082 Railway Children Fighting for Street Children

Class 43/4 – HST

Vehicle Length: 58ft 5in (18.80m) — Engine: MTU 16V4000 R41R
Height: 12ft 10in (3.90m) — Horsepower: 2,250hp (1,680kW)
Width: 8ft 11in (2.73m) — Electrical Equipment: Brush

Number	Depot	Pool	Livery	Owner	Operator
43423 (43123)	NL	EMPC	SCF	ANG	EMT
43465 (43065)	NL	EMPC	SCF	ANG	EMT
43467 (43067)	NL	EMPC	SCF	ANG	EMT
43468 (43068)	NL	EMPC	SCF	ANG	EMT
43480 (43080)	NL	EMPC	SCF	ANG	EMT
43484 (43084)	NL	EMPC	SCF	ANG	EMT

Below: *A fleet of 30 Class 43s are on the books of East Midlands Trains, 24 Class 43/0 and six 43/4s. The Class 43/0s carry standard EMT livery, as shown on No. 43060 at East Midlands Parkway. The 43/4s carry a revised livery.* **Nathan Williamson**

Names applied
43423 'Valenta' 1972 - 2010
43467 Nottinghamshire Fire and Rescue service / British Transport Police Nottingham
43480 West Hampstead PSB

East Midlands Trains

Class 153

Vehicle Length: 76ft 5in (23.29m)	Engine: 1 x NT855R5 of 285hp
Height: 12ft 3⅛in (3.75m)	Horsepower: 285hp (213kW)
Width: 8ft 10in (2.70m)	Seats (total/car): 66S

Number	Formation DMSL	Depot	Livery	Owner	Operator	Number	Formation DMSL	Depot	Livery	Owner	Operator
						153357	57357	NM	EMT	ANG	EMT
						153368	52368	NM	EMT	ANG	EMT
153302	52302	NM	EMT	ANG	EMT	153372	52372	NM	EMT	ANG	EMT
153308	52308	NM	EMT	ANG	EMT	153374	57374	NM	EMT	ANG	EMT
153310	52310	NM	EMT	PTR	EMT	153376	57376	NM	EMT	PTR	EMT
153311	52311	NM	EMT	PTR	EMT	153379	57379	NM	EMT	PTR	EMT
153313	52313	NM	EMT	PTR	EMT	153381	57381	NM	EMT	PTR	EMT
153318	52318	NM	EMT	ANG	EMT	153382	52382	NM	EMT	ANG	EMT
153319	52319	NM	EMT	ANG	EMT	153383	57383	NM	EMT	PTR	EMT
153321	52321	NM	EMT	PTR	EMT	153384	57384	NM	EMT	PTR	EMT
153326	52326	NM	EMT	PTR	EMT	153385	57385	NM	EMT	PTR	EMT
153355	57355	NM	EMT	ANG	EMT						

Name applied
153376 *X-24 Expeditious*
153383 *Ecclesbourne Valley Railway 150 years*

Left: *EMT operate a fleet of 21 single car Class 153s for rural line operations. Owned by either Porterbrook or Angel Trains, the Nottingham fleet carry Stagecoach/EMT long-distance blue livery. No. 153374 is shown from its small cab end at Doncaster.* **CJM**

Class 156

Vehicle Length: 75ft 6in (23.03m)	Engine: 1 x Cummins NT855R5 of 285hp
Height: 12ft 6in (3.81m)	Horsepower: 570hp (425kW)
Width: 8ft 11in (2.73m)	Seats (total/car): 148S, 72S/76S

Number	Formation DMSL+DMS	Depot	Livery	Owner	Operator	Number	Formation	Depot	Livery	Owner	Operator
						156411	52411+57411	NM	EMT	PTR	EMT
						156413	52413+57413	NM	EMT	PTR	EMT
156401	52401+57401	NM	EMT	PTR	EMT	156414	52414+57414	NM	EMT	PTR	EMT
156403	52403+57403	NM	EMT	PTR	EMT	156415	52415+57415	NM	EMT	PTR	EMT
156404	52404+57404	NM	EMT	PTR	EMT	156470	52470+57470	NM	EMT	PTR	EMT
156405	52405+57405	NM	EMT	PTR	EMT	156473	52473+57473	NM	EMT	PTR	EMT
156406	52406+57406	NM	EMT	PTR	EMT	156497	52497+57497	NM	EMT	PTR	EMT
156408	52408+57408	NM	EMT	PTR	EMT	156498	52498+57498	NM	EMT	PTR	EMT
156410	52410+57410	NM	EMT	PTR	EMT						

Below: *Medium and longer distance East Midlands services are in the hands of two-car Class 156s, based at Nottingham Eastcroft. Sets are painted in blue livery, off-set by orange, red and yellow ends. Set No. 156401 is shown, carrying a 'non-multi' sign in the non driving cab window, indicating the set must not couple to another.* **John Binch**

Passenger Train Operating Companies - East Midlands Trains

Class 158

Vehicle Length: 76ft 1¾in (23.21m)
Height: 12ft 6in (3.81m)
Width: 9ft 3¼in (2.82m)

Engine: 158770-813, 889 - 1 x Cummins
NT855R5 of 350hp
Horsepower: 700hp (522kW)
Engine: 158846-862 - 1 x Perkins 2006TWH of 350hp
Horsepower: 700hp (522kW)
Engine: 158863-866 - 1 x Cummins NT855R5 of 400hp
Horsepower: 800hp (597kW)
Seats (total/car): 146S - 74S, 72S

Number	Formation	Depot	Livery	Owner	Operator
	DMSL+DMSL				
158770	52770+57770	NM	SCE	PTR	EMT
158773	52773+57773	NM	SCE	PTR	EMT
158774	52774+57774	NM	SCE	PTR	EMT
158777	52777+57777	NM	SCE	PTR	EMT
158780	52780+57780	NM	SCE	ANG	EMT
158783	52783+57783	NM	SCE	ANG	EMT
158785	52785+57785	NM	SCE	ANG	EMT
158788	52788+57788	NM	SCE	ANG	EMT
158799	52799+57799	NM	SCE	PTR	EMT
158806	52806+57806	NM	SCE	PTR	EMT
158810	52810+57810	NM	SCE	PTR	EMT
158812	52812+57812	NM	SCE	PTR	EMT
158813	52813+57813	NM	SCE	PTR	EMT
158846	52846+57846	NM	SCE	ANG	EMT
158847	52847+57847	NM	SCE	ANG	EMT
158852	52852+57852	NM	SCE	ANG	EMT
158854	52854+57854	NM	SCE	ANG	EMT
158856	52856+57856	NM	SCE	ANG	EMT
158857	52857+57857	NM	SCE	ANG	EMT
158858	52858+57858	NM	SCE	ANG	EMT
158862	52862+57862	NM	SCE	ANG	EMT
158863	52863+57863	NM	SCE	ANG	EMT
158864	52864+57864	NM	SCE	ANG	EMT
158865	52865+57865	NM	SCE	ANG	EMT
158866	52866+57866	NM	SCE	ANG	EMT
158889	52808+57808	NM	SCE	PTR	EMT§

Names applied
158773 *Eastcroft Depot*
158847 *Lincoln Castle Explorer*
158854 *The Station Volunteer*
§ On loan from SWR

Right: *Long distance local services operated by East Midlands Trains are in the hands of 25 two-car Class 158s, painted in stagecoach white livery and based at Nottingham Eastcroft. Set No. 158889, on long term loan from South Western Railway, is recorded at Longport. The '2' painted on the front, indicated the 52xxx vehicle.*
Cliff Beeton

Class 222

Vehicle Length: 77ft 6in (23.62m)
Height: 12ft 4in (3.75m)
Width: 8ft 11in (2.73m)
Engine: 1 x Cummins OSK9R of 750hp per vehicle

Horsepower: 5,250hp (3,914kW)
Seats (total/car): 106F/236S
38S/68S/68S/62S/42F/42F/22F

Number	Formation	Depot	Livery	Owner	Op'r	Name
	DMS+MS+MS+MSRMB+MF+MF+DMRFO					
222001	60161+60551+60561+60621+60341+60445+60241	DY	SCE	EVL	EMT	*The Entrepreneur Express*
222002	60162+60544+60562+60622+60342+60346+60242	DY	SCE	EVL	EMT	*The Cutlers' Company*
222003	60163+60553+60563+60623+60343+60446+60243	DY	SCE	EVL	EMT	*Tornado*
222004	60164+60554+60564+60624+60344+60345+60244	DY	SCE	EVL	EMT	*Childrens Hospital Sheffield*
222005	60165+60555+60565+60625+60443+60347+60245	DY	SCE	EVL	EMT	
222006	60166+60556+60566+60626+60441+60447+60246	DY	SCE	EVL	EMT	*The Carbon Cutter*

Vehicle Length: 77ft 6in (23.62m)
Height: 12ft 4in (3.75m)
Width: 8ft 11in (2.73m)
Engine: 1 x Cummins OSK9R of 750hp per vehicle

Horsepower: 3,750hp (2,796kW)
Seats (total/car): 50F/190S
38S/68S/62S/28F-22S/22F

Number	Formation	Depot	Livery	Owner	Operator	Name
	DMS+MS+MSRMB+MC+DMRFO					
222007	60167+60567+60627+60442+60247	DY	SCE	EVL	EMT	
222008	60168+60545+60628+60918+60248	DY	SCE	EVL	EMT	*Derby Etches Park*
222009	60169+60557+60629+60919+60249	DY	SCE	EVL	EMT	
222010	60170+60546+60630+60920+60250	DY	SCE	EVL	EMT	
222011	60171+60531+60631+60921+60251	DY	SCE	EVL	EMT	*Sheffield City Battalion 1914 - 1918*
222012	60172+60532+60632+60922+60252	DY	SCE	EVL	EMT	

East Midlands Trains

222013	60173+60536+60633+60923+60253	DY	SCE	EVL	EMT	
222014	60174+60534+60634+60924+60254	DY	SCE	EVL	EMT	
222015	60175+60535+60635+60925+60255	DY	SCE	EVL	EMT	
222016	60176+60533+60636+60926+60256	DY	SCE	EVL	EMT	*175 Years of Derby's Railways 1839-2014*
222017	60177+60537+60637+60927+60257	DY	SCE	EVL	EMT	*Lions Clubs International Centenary 1917-2017*
222018	60178+60444+60638+60928+60258	DY	SCE	EVL	EMT	
222019	60179+60547+60639+60929+60259	DY	SCE	EVL	EMT	
222020	60180+60543+60640+60930+60260	DY	SCE	EVL	EMT	
222021	60181+60552+60641+60931+60261	DY	SCE	EVL	EMT	
222022	60182+60542+60642+60932+60262	DY	SCE	EVL	EMT	*Invest in Nottingham*
222023	60183+60541+60643+60933+60263	DY	SCE	EVL	EMT	

Left: East Midlands main line core services between London and Sheffield, Derby and Nottingham are operated by a fleet of six 7-car and 17 5-car Class 222 units, working alongside a fleet of HSTs. The Class 222 sets are painted in long distance Stagecoach white livery. Set No. 222001, a seven car set, is seen at Sheffield station. All the Class 222s are based at Derby Etches Park. **CJM**

Class 222/1

Vehicle Length: 77ft 6in (23.62m)	Horsepower: 3,000hp (2,237kW)
Height: 12ft 4in (3.75m)	Seats (total/car): 33F/148S
Width: 8ft 11in (2.73m)	22F/11F-46S/62S/40S
Engine: 1 x Cummins QSK9R of 750hp per vehicle	

Number	Formation DMF+MC+MSRMB+DMS	Depot	Livery	Owner	Operator
222101	60271+60571+60681+60191	DY	SCE	EVL	EMT
222102	60272+60572+60682+60192	DY	SCE	EVL	EMT
222103	60273+60573+60683+60193	DY	SCE	EVL	EMT
222104	60274+60574+60684+60194	DY	SCE	EVL	EMT

Left: The East Midlands Trains Class 222 fleet is supplemented by four Class 222/1 four-car sets. These were originally operated by Hull Trains and after replacement by Class 180s were absorbed into the East Midlands fleet. The sets have now been overhauled and refurbished in line with the Class 222/0 units. No. 222102 is shown at East Midlands Parkway. **Nathan Williamson**

HST Passenger Fleet

Vehicle Length: 75ft 0in (22.86m)	Width: 8ft 11in (2.71m)
Height: 12ft 9in (3.88m)	Bogie Type: BT10

GN1G - TRFB *Seating 23F*

Number	Depot	Livery	Owner
40204	DY	SCE	ANG
40205	DY	SCE	ANG
40221	DY	SCE	ANG

GK1G - TRFB *Seating 17F*

Number	Depot	Livery	Owner
40700	NL	SCE	PTR
40728	NL	SCE	PTR

40730	NL	SCE	PTR
40741	NL	SCE	PTR
40746	NL	SCE	PTR
40749	NL	SCE	PTR
40753	NL	SCE	PTR
40754	NL	SCE	PTR
40756	NL	SCE	PTR
40805	NL	SPL	ANG

GH1G - TF *Seating 46F*

Number	Depot	Livery	Owner
41041	NL	SCE	PTR
41046	NL	SCE	PTR
41057	NL	SCE	PTR
41061	NL	SCE	PTR
41063	NL	SCE	PTR
41064	NL	SCE	PTR
41067	NL	SCE	PTR
41069	NL	SCE	PTR
41070	NL	SCE	PTR
41071	NL	SCE	PTR
41072	NL	SCE	PTR
41075	NL	SCE	PTR
41076	NL	SCE	PTR
41077	NL	SCE	PTR
41079	NL	SCE	PTR
41084	NL	SCE	PTR
41111	NL	SCE	PTR
41113	NL	SCE	PTR
41117	NL	SCE	PTR
41156	NL	SCE	PTR

GH1G - TF *Seating 48F*

Number		Depot	Livery	Owner
41204	(11023)	DY	SCE	ANG
41205	(11036)	DY	SCE	ANG
41206	(11055)	DY	SCE	ANG
41207	(42403/12033)	DY	SCE	ANG
41208	(42406/12112)	DY	SCE	ANG
41209	(42409/12088)	DY	SCE	ANG

GH2G - TS *Seating 74S*

Number	Depot	Livery	Owner
42100	NL	SCE	PTR
42111	NL	SCE	PTR
42113	NL	SCE	PTR
42119	NL	SCE	PTR
42120	NL	SCE	PTR
42121	NL	SCE	PTR
42124	NL	SCE	PTR
42131	NL	SCE	PTR
42132	NL	SCE	PTR
42133	NL	SCE	PTR
42135	NL	SCE	PTR
42136	NL	SCE	PTR
42137	NL	SCE	PTR

42139	NL	SCE	PTR
42140	NL	SCE	PTR
42141	NL	SCE	PTR
42148	NL	SCE	PTR
42149	NL	SCE	PTR
42151	NL	SCE	PTR
42152	NL	SCE	PTR
42153	NL	SCE	PTR
42155	NL	SCE	PTR
42156	NL	SCE	PTR
42157	NL	SCE	PTR
42164	NL	SCE	PTR
42165	NL	SCE	PTR
42220	NL	SCE	PTR
42230	NL	SCE	PTR
42327	NL	SCE	PTR
42328	NL	SCE	PTR
42329	NL	SCE	PTR
42331	NL	SCE	PTR
42337	NL	SCE	PTR
42339	NL	SCE	PTR
42341	NL	SCE	PTR
42384¤	NL	SCE	PTR

¤ **Modified from 41078**

GH2G - TS *Seating 64S*
TSD Seating 60S

Number		Depot	Livery	Owner
42401	(12149)	DY	SCE	ANG
42402	(12155)	DY	SCE	ANG
42404	(12152)	DY	SCE	ANG
42405	(12136)	DY	SCE	ANG
42407	(12044)	DY	SCE	ANG
42408	(12121)	DY	SCE	ANG

Number		Depot	Livery	Owner
42584	(41201/11045)	DY	SCE	ANG
42585	(41202/11017)	DY	SCE	ANG
42586	(41203/11038)	DY	SCE	ANG

GJ2G - TGS *Seating 63S*

Number	Depot	Livery	Owner
44041	NL	SCE	PTR
44044	NL	SCE	PTR
44046	NL	SCE	PTR
44047	NL	SCE	PTR
44048	NL	SCE	PTR
44051	NL	SCE	PTR
44054	NL	SCE	PTR
44070	NL	SCE	PTR
44071	NL	SCE	PTR
44085	NL	SCE	PTR

Right: *A fleet of 94 Mk3 HST vehicles are allocated to East Midlands Trains, with a wide variety of vehicle types. With a row of red dots above the window indicating first class, FO No. 41067 is shown.* **Nathan Williamson**

Eurostar

Address: ✉ Eurostar, Times House, Bravingtons Walk, Regent Quarter,
London, N1 9AW
✍ new.comments@eurostar.com
✆ 08701 606 600
ⓘ www.eurostar.com

CEO: Mike Cooper

Principal Routes: St Pancras International - Brussels and Paris, also serving
Disneyland Paris, and a winter sport service to
Bourg St Maurice

Owned Stations: St Pancras International, Stratford International, Ebbsfleet

Depots: Temple Mills [UK] (TI), Forest [Belgium] (FF), Le Landy [France] (LY)

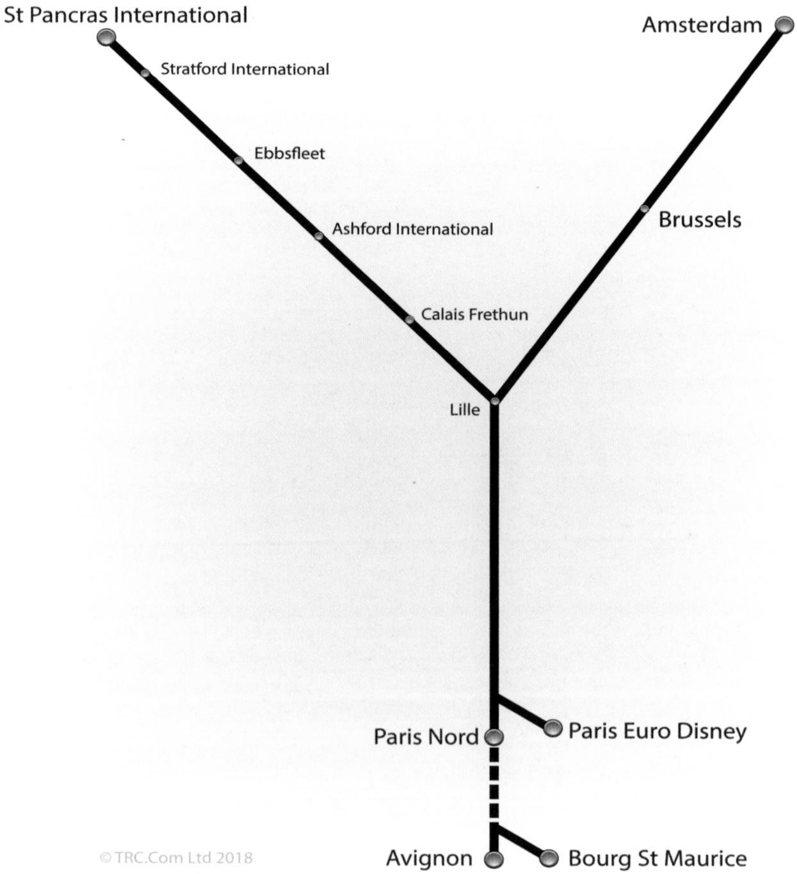

Passenger Train Operating Companies - Eurostar

St Pancras International

Stratford International

Ebbsfleet

Ashford International

Calais Frethun

Lille

Amsterdam

Brussels

Paris Nord

Paris Euro Disney

Avignon

Bourg St Maurice

© TRC.Com Ltd 2018

Class 373 (e300)

Vehicle Length: (DM) 72ft 8in (22.15m), (MS) 71ft 8in (21.84m)
(TS, RB, TF, TBF) 61ft 4in (18.70m)
Height: 12ft 4½in (3.77m)
■ *Modified for 1500V dc operation*
Width: 9ft 3in (2.81m)
Horsepower: 16,400hp (12,249kW)
Seats (total/car): 102F/272S, 0/48S/56S/56S/56S/56S/0/39F/39F/24F

Number	*Formation* DM+MSO+TSO+TSO+TSO+TSO+RB+TFO+TFO+TBFO	*Depot*	*Livery*	*Owner*	*Operator*	*Name*
UK sets (Class 373/0)						
373007	3730070+3730071+3730072+3730073+3730074+3730075+3730076+3730077+3730078+3730079	TI	EUB	EUS	EUS	*Waterloo Sunset*
373008	3730080+3730081+3730082+3730083+3730084+3730085+3730086+3730087+3730088+3730089	TI	EUB	EUS	EUS	*Waterloo Sunset*
373015	3730150+3730151+3730152+3730153+3730154+3730155+3730156+3730157+3730158+3730159	TI	EUB	EUS	EUS	
373016	3730160+3730161+3730162+3730163+3730164+3730165+3730166+3730167+3730168+3730169	TI	EUB	EUS	EUS	
373021§	3730210+3730211+3730212+3730213+3730214+3730215+3730216+3730217+3730218+3730219	TI	EUS	EUS	EUS	
373022§	3730220+3730221+3730222+3730223+3730224+3730225+3730226+3730227+3730228+3730229	TI	EUS	EUS	EUS	
French sets (Class 373/2)						
373205	3732050+3732051+3732052+3732053+3732054+3732055+3732056+3732057+3732058+3732059	LY	EUB	SNF	EUS	
373206	3732060+3732061+3732062+3732063+3732064+3732065+3732066+3732067+3732068+3732069	LY	EUB	SNF	EUS	
373209	3732090+3732091+3732092+3732093+3732094+3732095+3732096+3732097+3732098+3732099	LY	EUB	SNF	EUS	
373210	3732100+3732101+3732102+3732103+3732104+3732105+3732106+3732107+3732108+3732109	LY	EUB	SNF	EUS	
373211	3732030+3732031+3732032+3732033+3732034+3732035+3732036+3732037+3732038+3732039	LY	EUB	SNF	EUS	
373212	3732040+3732041+3732042+3732043+3732044+3732045+3732046+3732047+3732048+3732049	LY	EUB	SNF	EUS	
373213●	3732130+3732131+3732132+3732133+3732134+3732135+3732136+3732137+3732138+3732139	LY	IZY	SNF	EUS	
373214§	3732140+3732141+3732142+3732143+3732144+3732145+3732146+3732147+3732148+3732149	LY	EUS	SNF	EUS	
373215§	3732150+3732151+3732152+3732153+3732154+3732155+3732156+3732157+3732158+3732159	LY	EUB	SNF	EUS	
373216§	3732160+3732161+3732162+3732163+3732164+3732165+3732166+3732167+3732168+3732169	LY	EUB	SNF	EUS	
373217	3732170+3732171+3732172+3732173+3732174+3732175+3732176+3732177+3732178+3732179	LY	EUS	SNF	EUS	
373218	3732180+3732181+3732182+3732183+3732184+3732185+3732186+3732187+3732188+3732189	LY	EUS	SNF	EUS	
373219	3732190+3732191+3732192+3732193+3732194+3732195+3732196+3732197+3732198+3732199	LY	EUB	SNF	EUS	
373220	3732200+3732201+3732202+3732203+3732204+3732205+3732206+3732207+3732208+3732209	LY	EUB	SNF	EUS	
373221	3732210+3732211+3732212+3732213+3732214+3732215+3732216+3732217+3732218+3732219	LY	EUB	SNF	EUS	
373222	3732220+3732221+3732222+3732223+3732224+3732225+3732226+3732227+3732228+3732229	LY	EUB	SNF	EUS	
373223§	3732230+3732231+3732232+3732233+3732234+3732235+3732236+3732237+3732238+3732239	LY	EUS	SNF	EUS	
373224●	3732240+3732241+3732242+3732243+3732244+3732245+3732246+3732247+3732248+3732249	LY	ISY	SNF	EUS	
373229	3732290+3732291+3732292+3732293+3732294+3732295+3732296+3732297+3732298+3732299	LY	EUS	SNF	EUS	*The Da Vinci Code*
373230	3732300+3732301+3732302+3732303+3732304+3732305+3732306+3732307+3732308+3732309	LY	EUS	SNF	EUS	*The Da Vinci Code*

§ Scheduled for early withdrawal.
● For use by Thalys on Paris to Brussells route for low cost Izy services

Eurostar

Spare DM

Number		Depot	Livery	Owner	Operator
3999	(Spare vehicle used as required to cover for maintenance.)	TI	EUB	EUS	EUS

Above: *A significant number of the original Class 373 Eurostar sets have now been withdrawn, replaced by Class 374 e320 stock. Only around eight (16 half sets) will eventually remain in service. Painted in the latest livery, set No. 373008/007 are seen heading south towards the Channel Tunnel at Lenham.* **CJM**

Below: *Spare Eurostar power car No. 373999 is usually kept at Temple Mills depot when not in use. The vehicle is able to take the place of any Class 373 driving car if required. No. 3999 is seen emerging from North Downs Tunnel.* **CJM**

Class 374 (e320)

Vehicle Length: Car 1 - 26.075m, Car 2-8 - 24.775m.
Height: Details awaited
Horsepower: 25kV ac operation - 21,000hp (16,000kW) 3,000V dc, 1,500V dc tba
Seats (total/car): 107F/336S. 40F/36F/31F/76S/76S/76S/76S/32S (half train)
Electrical Equipment: Siemens

Train length (8-car) 199.46m
Width: Details awaited

Set No.	DMFO	TBFO	MFO	TSO	TSO	MSO	TSO	MSORB
374001	93 70 3740 011	+93 70 3740 012	+93 70 3740 013	+93 70 3740 014	+93 70 3740 015	+93 70 3740 016	+93 70 3740 017	+93 70 3740 018
374002	93 70 3740 021	+93 70 3740 022	+93 70 3740 023	+93 70 3740 024	+93 70 3740 025	+93 70 3740 026	+93 70 3740 027	+93 70 3740 028
374003	93 70 3740 031	+93 70 3740 032	+93 70 3740 033	+93 70 3740 034	+93 70 3740 035	+93 70 3740 036	+93 70 3740 037	+93 70 3740 038
374004	93 70 3740 041	+93 70 3740 042	+93 70 3740 043	+93 70 3740 044	+93 70 3740 045	+93 70 3740 046	+93 70 3740 047	+93 70 3740 048
374005	93 70 3740 051	+93 70 3740 052	+93 70 3740 053	+93 70 3740 054	+93 70 3740 055	+93 70 3740 056	+93 70 3740 057	+93 70 3740 058
374006	93 70 3740 061	+93 70 3740 062	+93 70 3740 063	+93 70 3740 064	+93 70 3740 065	+93 70 3740 066	+93 70 3740 067	+93 70 3740 068
374007	93 70 3740 071	+93 70 3740 072	+93 70 3740 073	+93 70 3740 074	+93 70 3740 075	+93 70 3740 076	+93 70 3740 077	+93 70 3740 078
374008	93 70 3740 081	+93 70 3740 082	+93 70 3740 083	+93 70 3740 084	+93 70 3740 085	+93 70 3740 086	+93 70 3740 087	+93 70 3740 088
374009	93 70 3740 091	+93 70 3740 092	+93 70 3740 093	+93 70 3740 094	+93 70 3740 095	+93 70 3740 096	+93 70 3740 097	+93 70 3740 098
374010	93 70 3740 101	+93 70 3740 102	+93 70 3740 103	+93 70 3740 104	+93 70 3740 105	+93 70 3740 106	+93 70 3740 107	+93 70 3740 101
374011	93 70 3740 111	+93 70 3740 112	+93 70 3740 113	+93 70 3740 114	+93 70 3740 115	+93 70 3740 116	+93 70 3740 117	+93 70 3740 118
374012	93 70 3740 121	+93 70 3740 122	+93 70 3740 123	+93 70 3740 124	+93 70 3740 125	+93 70 3740 126	+93 70 3740 127	+93 70 3740 128
374013	93 70 3740 131	+93 70 3740 132	+93 70 3740 133	+93 70 3740 134	+93 70 3740 135	+93 70 3740 136	+93 70 3740 137	+93 70 3740 138
374014	93 70 3740 141	+93 70 3740 142	+93 70 3740 143	+93 70 3740 144	+93 70 3740 145	+93 70 3740 146	+93 70 3740 147	+93 70 3740 148
374015	93 70 3740 151	+93 70 3740 152	+93 70 3740 153	+93 70 3740 154	+93 70 3740 155	+93 70 3740 156	+93 70 3740 157	+93 70 3740 158
374016	93 70 3740 161	+93 70 3740 162	+93 70 3740 163	+93 70 3740 164	+93 70 3740 165	+93 70 3740 166	+93 70 3740 167	+93 70 3740 168
374017	93 70 3740 171	+93 70 3740 172	+93 70 3740 173	+93 70 3740 174	+93 70 3740 175	+93 70 3740 176	+93 70 3740 177	+93 70 3740 178
374018	93 70 3740 181	+93 70 3740 182	+93 70 3740 183	+93 70 3740 184	+93 70 3740 185	+93 70 3740 186	+93 70 3740 187	+93 70 3740 188
374019	93 70 3740 191	+93 70 3740 192	+93 70 3740 193	+93 70 3740 194	+93 70 3740 195	+93 70 3740 196	+93 70 3740 197	+93 70 3740 198
374020	93 70 3740 201	+93 70 3740 202	+93 70 3740 203	+93 70 3740 204	+93 70 3740 205	+93 70 3740 206	+93 70 3740 207	+93 70 3740 208
374021	93 70 3740 211	+93 70 3740 212	+93 70 3740 213	+93 70 3740 214	+93 70 3740 215	+93 70 3740 216	+93 70 3740 217	+93 70 3740 218
374022	93 70 3740 221	+93 70 3740 222	+93 70 3740 223	+93 70 3740 224	+93 70 3740 225	+93 70 3740 226	+93 70 3740 227	+93 70 3740 228
374023	93 70 3740 231	+93 70 3740 232	+93 70 3740 233	+93 70 3740 234	+93 70 3740 235	+93 70 3740 236	+93 70 3740 237	+93 70 3740 238
374024	93 70 3740 241	+93 70 3740 242	+93 70 3740 243	+93 70 3740 244	+93 70 3740 245	+93 70 3740 246	+93 70 3740 247	+93 70 3740 248
374025	93 70 3740 251	+93 70 3740 252	+93 70 3740 253	+93 70 3740 254	+93 70 3740 255	+93 70 3740 256	+93 70 3740 257	+93 70 3740 258
374026	93 70 3740 261	+93 70 3740 262	+93 70 3740 263	+93 70 3740 264	+93 70 3740 265	+93 70 3740 266	+93 70 3740 267	+93 70 3740 268
374027	93 70 3740 271	+93 70 3740 272	+93 70 3740 273	+93 70 3740 274	+93 70 3740 275	+93 70 3740 276	+93 70 3740 277	+93 70 3740 278
374028	93 70 3740 281	+93 70 3740 282	+93 70 3740 283	+93 70 3740 284	+93 70 3740 285	+93 70 3740 286	+93 70 3740 287	+93 70 3740 288
374029	93 70 3740 291	+93 70 3740 292	+93 70 3740 293	+93 70 3740 294	+93 70 3740 295	+93 70 3740 296	+93 70 3740 297	+93 70 3740 298
374030	93 70 3740 301	+93 70 3740 302	+93 70 3740 303	+93 70 3740 304	+93 70 3740 305	+93 70 3740 306	+93 70 3740 307	+93 70 3740 308
374031	93 70 3740 311	+93 70 3740 312	+93 70 3740 313	+93 70 3740 314	+93 70 3740 315	+93 70 3740 316	+93 70 3740 317	+93 70 3740 318
374032	93 70 3740 321	+93 70 3740 322	+93 70 3740 323	+93 70 3740 324	+93 70 3740 325	+93 70 3740 326	+93 70 3740 327	+93 70 3740 328
374033	93 70 3740 331	+93 70 3740 332	+93 70 3740 333	+93 70 3740 334	+93 70 3740 335	+93 70 3740 336	+93 70 3740 337	+93 70 3740 338
374034	93 70 3740 341	+93 70 3740 342	+93 70 3740 343	+93 70 3740 344	+93 70 3740 345	+93 70 3740 346	+93 70 3740 347	+93 70 3740 348

Above: *The 34 Siemens 'Velaro' half sets forming 17 20-car Eurostar e320 sets now form the core of Eurostar services from London St Pancras International to Mainland Europe. The impressive sets are only authorised to operate over HS1 in the UK and are unable to operate over Network Rail classic lines. Led by set No. 374020 with No. 374019 on the rear, train 9I33, the 12.52 Brussels Midi to St Pancras is seen near Harrietsham on 25 April 2018.* **CJM**

Class 08

Vehicle Length: 29ft 3in (8.91m)		Engine: English Electric 6K	
Height: 12ft 8⅝in (3.87m)		Horsepower: 400hp (298kW)	
Width: 8ft 6in (2.59m)		Electrical Equipment: English Electric	

Number	Depot	Pool	Livery	Owner	Operator
08948	TI	GPSS	TTG	EUS	EUS

First Great Western Railway

Address:	✉ Milford House, 1 Milford Street, Swindon, SN1 1HL
	✍ gwrfeedback@gwr.com
	✆ 08457 000125 ⓘ www.gwr.com
Managing Director:	Mark Hopwood
Franchise Dates:	1 April 2006 - Extension to April 2019
Principal Routes:	Paddington - Penzance/Paignton, Bristol, Swansea
	Thames Valley local lines, to Worcester, Hereford and Gloucester
	Local lines in Bristol, Exeter, Plymouth and Cornwall
	Bristol - Weymouth, Portsmouth/Brighton/Great Malvern
Depots:	Exeter (EX) Laira (LA), St Philip's Marsh (PM), Penzance (PZ),
	Reading (RG), North Pole (NP) Stoke Gifford (ST)
Parent Company:	First Group PLC

Class 08

Vehicle Length: 29ft 3in (8.91m)	Engine: English Electric 6K
Height: 12ft 8⅝in (3.87m)	Horsepower: 400hp (298kW)
Width: 8ft 6in (2.59m)	Electrical Equipment: English Electric

Number	Depot	Pool	Livery	Owner	Operator
08410	LA	EFSH	GRN	FGP	GWR
08483	LA	EFSH	BLK	FGP	GWR
08641	LA	EFSH	BLU	FGP	GWR
08644	PZ	EFSH	BLU	FGP	GWR
08645	LE	EFSH	GRY	FGP	GWR
08663	PM	EFSH	BLU	FGP	GWR
08795	LE	EFSH	BLK	FGP	GWR
08822	LE	EFSH	ICS	FGP	GWR

Number	Depot	Pool	Livery	Owner	Operator
08836	RG	EFSH	GWG	FGP	GWR

Names applied

08641	*Pride of Laira*
08644	*Laira Diesel Depot 50 years 1962-2012*
08645	*Mike Baggott*
08663	*St Silas*
08822	*Dave Mills*

Below: *At present the main Great Western depots of Reading, Bristol St Philips Marsh, Plymouth Laira and Penzance, have a daily need for shunting stock, especially the make up of HST and loco hauled sets. Following full introduction of Class 800 and 802 stock this will diminish. Currently nine Class 08s are funded by Great Western for this work. Painted in 1970s BR Rail Blue with yellow ends No. 08641 Pride of Laira is seen shunting HST stock at Laira depot.* **Antony Christie**

Great Western Railway

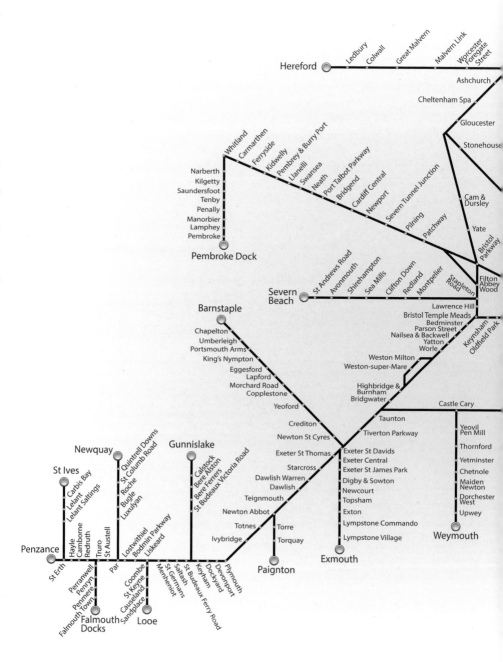

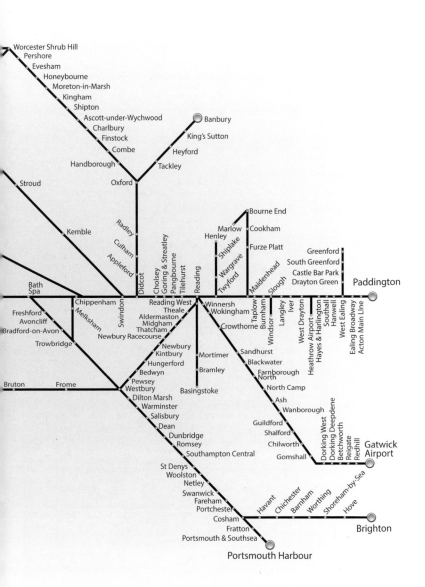

Class 43 – HST

Vehicle Length: 58ft 5in (18.80m)
Height: 12ft 10in (3.90m)
Width: 8ft 11in (2.73m)
Engine: MTU 16V4000 R41R
Horsepower: 2,250hp (1,680kW)
Electrical Equipment: Brush

Number	Depot	Pool	Livery	Owner	Operator
43002	LA	EFPC	SPL±	ANG	GWR
43004	LA	EFPC	GWG	ANG	GWR
43005	LA	EFPC	GWG	ANG	GWR
43009	LA	EFPC	FGB	ANG	GWR
43010	LA	EFPC	FGB	ANG	GWR
43016	LA	EFPC	GWG	ANG	GWR
43017	LA	EFPC	FGB	ANG	GWR
43018	LA	EFPC	FGB	ANG	GWR
43020	LA	EFPC	FGB	ANG	GWR
43022	LA	EFPC	FGB	ANG	GWR
43023	LA	EFPC	FGB	ANG	GWR
43024	LA	EFPC	FGB	ANG	GWR
43025	LA	EFPC	FGB	ANG	GWR
43027	LA	EFPC	FGA¶	ANG	GWR
43029	LA	EFPC	FGB	ANG	GWR
43040	LA	EFPC	GWG	ANG	GWR
43041	LA	EFPC	GWG	ANG	GWR
43042	LA	EFPC	GWG	ANG	GWR
43053	LA	EFPC	FGB	PTR	GWR
43056	LA	EFPC	FGB	PTR	GWR
43063	LA	EFPC	FGB	PTR	GWR
43069	LA	EFPC	FGB	PTR	GWR
43070	LA	EFPC	FGB	PTR	GWR
43071	LA	EFPC	FGB	PTR	GWR
43078	LA	EFPC	FGB	PTR	GWR
43079	LA	EFPC	FGB	PTR	GWR
43086	LA	EFPC	FGB	PTR	GWR
43087	LA	EFPC	FGB	PTR	GWR
43088	LA	EFPC	FGB	PTR	GWR
43091	LA	EFPC	FGB	PTR	GWR
43092	LA	EFPC	GWG	PTR	GWR
43093	LA	EFPC	SPL■	PTR	GWR
43094	LA	EFPC	FGB	PTR	GWR
43097	LA	EFPC	FGB	PTR	GWR
43098	LA	EFPC	GWG	PTR	GWR
43122	LA	EFPC	FGB	FGP	GWR
43153	LA	EFPC	GWG	FGP	GWR
43154	LA	EFPC	GWG	FGP	GWR
43155	LA	EFPC	FGB	FGP	GWR
43156	LA	EFPC	FGB	PTR	GWR
43158	LA	EFPC	FGB	FGP	GWR
43159	LA	EFPC	FGB	PTR	GWR
43160	LA	EFPC	FGB	PTR	GWR
43161	LA	EFPC	FGB	PTR	GWR
43162	LA	EFPC	FGB	ANG	GWR
43165	LA	EFPC	FGB	ANG	GWR
43170	LA	EFPC	GWG	ANG	GWR
43171	LA	EFPC	FGB	ANG	GWR
43172	LA	EFPC	SPL	ANG	GWR
43174	LA	EFPC	FGB	ANG	GWR
43180	LA	EFPC	FGB	PTR	GWR
43185	LA	EFPC	ICS	ANG	GWR
43186	LA	EFPC	GWG	ANG	GWR
43187	LA	EFPC	GWG	ANG	GWR
43188	LA	EFPC	GWG	ANG	GWR
43189	LA	EFPC	GWG	ANG	GWR
43190	LA	EFPC	FGB	ANG	GWR
43191	LA	EFPC	FGB	ANG	GWR
43192	LA	EFPC	FGB	ANG	GWR
43193	LA	EFPC	FGB	PTR	GWR
43194	LA	EFPC	GWG	FGP	GWR
43195(S)	LA	-	FGB	PTR	-
43196	LA	EFPC	FGB	PTR	GWR
43197	LA	EFPC	FGB	PTR	GWR
43198	LA	EFPC	GWG	FGP	GWR

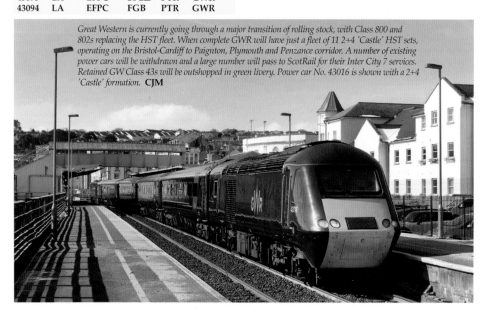

Great Western is currently going through a major transition of rolling stock, with Class 800 and 802s replacing the HST fleet. When complete GWR will have just a fleet of 11 2+4 'Castle' HST sets, operating on the Bristol-Cardiff to Paignton, Plymouth and Penzance corridor. A number of existing power cars will be withdrawn and a large number will pass to ScotRail for their Inter City 7 services. Retained GW Class 43s will be outshopped in green livery. Power car No. 43016 is shown with a 2+4 'Castle' formation. **CJM**

Passenger Train Operating Companies - Great Western Railway

SPL± - Heritage yellow/blue   FGA¶ - 90 Glorious Years branding SPL■ - GW green with OC Legends branding

Names applied

43002	*Sir Kenneth Grange*
43004	*First for the Future / First ar gyfer y dyfodol*
43017	*Hannahs discoverhannahs.org*
43020	*MTU Power Passion Partnership*
43022	*The Duke of Edinburgh's Award Diamond Anniversary 1956-2016*
43023	*Sqn Ldr Harold Starr One of the Few*
43024	*Great Western Society 1961-2011 Didcot Railway Centre*
43025	*The Institution of Railway Operators*
43041	*Meningitis Trust Support for Life*
43053	*University of Worcester*
43056	*The Royal British Legion*
43070	*The Corps of Royal Electrical and Mechanical Engineers*
43087	*11 Explosive Ordnance Disposal Regiment Royal Logistic Corps*
43093	*Old Oak Common HST Depot 1976-2018*
43097	*Environment Agency*
43155	*The Red Arrows 50 Seasons of Excellence*
43156	*Dartington International Summer School*
43160	*Sir Moir Lockhead OBE*
43165	*Prince Michael of Kent*
43172	*Harry Patch The last survivor of the trenches*
43185	*Great Western*
43198	*Oxfordshire 2007*

To indicate the planned movement of GW power cars in 2019-2020, colour coding is used. **Black** indicates cars which will remain on Great Western, and Red shows those going off-lease and stored.

Right: *By the time this edition of* Rail Guide *is published, the majority of FGW blue liveried Class 43s should have gone. This illustration shows the FGW livery style. Power car No. 43154 is owned by First Group and is scheduled to remain in operation with GWR. No. 43154 is seen at the London end of a train at Plymouth, adjacent to a CrossCountry Class 43.* **CJM**

Class 57/6

Vehicle Length: 63ft 6in (19.38m)	Engine: EMD 645-12E3
Height: 12ft 10¹⁄sin (3.91m)	Horsepower: 2,500hp (1,860kW)
Width: 9ft 2in (2.79m)	Electrical Equipment: Brush

Number	Depot	Pool	Livery	Owner	Operator	Name
57602 (47337)	PZ	EFOO	GWG	PTR	GWR	*Restormel Castle*
57603 (47349)	PZ	EFOO	GWG	PTR	GWR	*Tintagel Castle*
57604 (47209)	PZ	EFOO	GWR	PTR	GWR	*Pendennis Castle*
57605 (47206)	PZ	EFOO	GWG	PTR	GWR	*Totnes Castle*

Right: *Four Class 57/6 locos are based at Penzance and are responsible for powering the Great Western 'Night Riviera' sleeper services linking London Paddington with Penzance. Three of the fleet are painted in GW green and one, No. 57604 displays a Great Western Railway historic livery. The locos occasionally power GW empty HST moves. In the London area the Class 57/6s receive maintenance with the sleeper stock at Reading depot. No. 57603 is shown at Newton Abbot with an empty stock move, it is rare to find these locos operating during daylight hours.* **Antony Christie**

Passenger Train Operating Companies - Great Western Railway

HST Passenger Fleet

Vehicle Length: 75ft 0in (22.86m) *Width: 8ft 11in (2.71m)*
Height: 12ft 9in (3.88m) *Bogie Type: BT10*

GN2G - TSRMB *Seating 70S*

Number		Dep	Livery	O'nr
40101 (42170)	(S)	PZ	FGW	PTR
40102 (42223)	(S)	LE	FGW	PTR
40103 (42316)		LA	GWG	PTR
40104 (42254)	(S)	LE	FGW	PTR
40107 (42334)	(S)	LE	FGW	PTR
40109 (42262)	(S)	LE	FGW	PTR
40111 (42248)		LA	FGW	PTR
40112 (42336)	(S)	LE	FGW	PTR
40113 (42309)	(S)	PZ	GWG	PTR
40114 (42086)	(S)	LE	FGW	PTR
40115 (42320)		LA	FGW	PTR
40116 (42147)	(S)	PZ	GWG	PTR
40117 (42249)	(S)	LE	GWG	PTR
40118 (42338)		LA	FGW	PTR
40119 (42090)	(S)	LE	FGW	PTR

GN1G - TRFB *Seating 23F*

Number	Depot	Livery	Owner
40207*	LA	FGW	ANG
40231	LA	FGW	ANG

GK1G - TRFB *Seating 17F*

Number	Depot	Livery	Owner
40703	LA	FGW	ANG
40707	LA	FGW	ANG
40710	LA	FGW	ANG
40713	LA	FGW	ANG
40715	LA	GWG	ANG
40716	LA	FGW	ANG
40718	LA	FGW	ANG
40721	LA	FGW	ANG
40722	LA	FGW	ANG
40727	LA	FGW	ANG

40733	LA	FGW	ANG
40734	LA	FGW	ANG
40739	LA	FGW	ANG
40743	LA	GWG	ANG
40752	LA	GWG	ANG
40755	LA	GWG	ANG
40757	LA	FGW	ANG

GL1G - TRFB *Seating 17F*

Number	Depot	Livery	Owner
40801	LA	GWG	PTR
40803	LA	GWG	PTR
40807(S)	LE	FGW	PTR
40808	LA	FGW	PTR
40809	LA	FGW	PTR
40810(S)	LE	FGW	PTR
40811(S)	LE	FGW	PTR

* Currently in Scotland

GN1G - TRB *Seating 23F*

Number	Depot	Livery	Owner
40900(S)	LE	FGW	FGP
40901(S)	LE	GWG	FGP
40902(S)	LE	FGW	FGP
40903(S)	LE	GWG	FGP
40904(S)	LE	GWG	FGP

GH1G - TF *Seating 48F*

Number	Depot	Livery	Owner
41008	LA	FGW	ANG
41018	LA	FGW	ANG
41028	LA	FGW	ANG
41030	LA	FGW	ANG
41032	LA	FGW	ANG
41034	LA	FGW	ANG

41056	LA	FGW	ANG
41059	LA	GWG	FGP
41089	LA	FGW	ANG
41102	LA	FGW	ANG
41106	LA	FGW	ANG
41110	LA	FGW	ANG
41122	LA	FGW	ANG
41132	LA	FGW	ANG
41138	LA	FGW	ANG
41144	LA	FGW	ANG
41146	LA	GWG	ANG
41149	LA	GWG	PTR
41160	LA	GWG	FGP
41161	LA	GWG	PTR
41162	LA	GWG	FGP
41166	LA	GWG	FGP
41167	LA	FGW	FGP
41182	LA	GWG	PTR
41183	LA	GWG	PTR
41186	LA	FGW	PTR
41187	LA	FGW	PTR
41189	LA	GWG	PTR

GH2G - TS *Seating 68-84S*

Number	Depot	Livery	Owner
42003	LA	FGW	ANG
42004	LA	FGW	ANG
42005	LA	GWG	ANG
42008	LA	FGW	ANG
42015	LA	GWG	ANG
42016	LA	GWG	ANG
42019	LA	FGW	ANG
42021	LA	FGW	ANG
42023	LA	FGW	ANG
42024	LA	FGW	ANG

Below: *Once all new trains are introduced and the HST fleet reduced, Great Western will just have a fleet of 48 vehicles, modified with sliding doors for 'Castle' operations. Painted in GW green livery, TSRMB No. 40108 is seen from its catering end at Totnes. This vehicle was rebuilt from TS No. 42314 and is likely to be withdrawn following the fleet changes.* **Nathan Williamson**

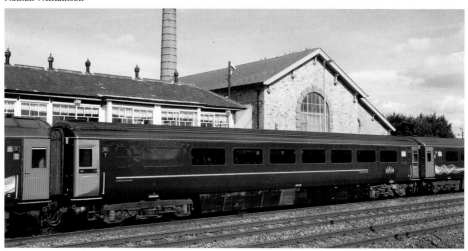

42025	LA	FGW	ANG		42201	LA	FGW	ANG		42381 (41058) LA FGW PTR
42026	LA	FGW	ANG		42202	LA	FGW	ANG		42383 (12172) LA GWG PTR
42027	LA	FGW	ANG		42203	LA	FGW	ANG		42501 (40744) LA FGW ANG
42039	LA	FGW	ANG		42204	LA	FGW	ANG		42503 (40712) LA FGW ANG
42040	LA	FGW	ANG		42207	LA	FGW	ANG		42504 (40714) LA FGW ANG
42041	LA	FGW	ANG		42211	LA	FGW	ANG		42505 (40228) LA FGW ANG
42042	LA	FGW	ANG		42212	LA	FGW	ANG		42506 (40724) LA FGW ANG
42044	LA	FGW	ANG		42213	LA	FGW	ANG		42509 (40736) LA GWG ANG
42046	LA	FGW	ANG		42214	LA	FGW	ANG		42510 (40717) LA FGW ANG
42047	LA	FGW	ANG		42217	LA	FGW	PTR		42512 (40208) LA GWG ANG
42048	LA	FGW	ANG		42218	LA	FGW	FGP		42514 (40726) LA FGW ANG
42049	LA	FGW	ANG		42222	LA	FGW	ANG		42515 (40747) LA FGW ANG
42050	LA	FGW	ANG		42222	LA	FGW	FGP		42516 (40723) LA FGW ANG
42055	LA	FGW	ANG		42231	LA	FGW	FGP		42517 (40745) LA FGW ANG
42062	LA	FGW	ANG		42233	LA	FGW	PTR		42518 (40403) LA FGW ANG
42066	LA	FGW	ANG		42236	LA	FGW	ANG		42519 (40416) LA FGW ANG
42067	LA	FGW	ANG		42247	LA	FGW	PTR		42520 (40434) LA FGW ANG
42068	LA	FGW	ANG		42251	LA	FGW	ANG		42552 (41007) LA FGW ANG
42071	LA	FGW	ANG		42258	LA	FGW	FGP		42554 (41011) LA GWG ANG
42073	LA	FGW	ANG		42260	LA	FGW	ANG		42556 (41017) LA FGW ANG
42074	LA	FGW	ANG		42264	LA	FGW	ANG		42560 (41027) LA FGW ANG
42079	LA	FGW	ANG		42266	LA	FGW	FGP		42561 (41031) LA GWG ANG
42080	LA	FGW	ANG		42283	LA	FGW	ANG		42563 (41045) LA FGW FGP
42081	LA	FGW	ANG		42284	LA	FGW	ANG		42565 (41085) LA FGW FGP
42083	LA	FGW	ANG		42285	LA	FGW	ANG		42566 (41086) LA FGW FGP
42085	LA	FGW	FGP		42294	LA	FGW	PTR		42568 (41101) LA FGW ANG
42087	LA	GWG	ANG		42295	LA	FGW	ANG		42569 (41105) LA FGW ANG
42089	LA	FGW	ANG		42296	LA	FGW	ANG		42570 (41114) LA FGW FGP
42092	LA	FGW	PTR		42299	LA	GWG	ANG		42571 (41121) LA FGW ANG
42094	LA	FGW	FGP		42300	LA	GWG	ANG		42575 (41131) LA FGW ANG
42095	LA	FGW	FGP		42301	LA	GWG	ANG		42578 (41143) LA FGW ANG
42098	LA	FGW	ANG		42302	LA	FGW	PTR		42579 (41145) LA GWG ANG
42101	LA	FGW	FGP		42303	LA	FGW	PTR		42580 (41155) LA FGW PTR
42103	LA	FGW	PTR		42304	LA	FGW	FGP		42581 (41157) LA GWG ANG
42105	LA	FGW	PTR		42305	LA	GWG	PTR		42582 (41163) LA FGW FGP
42108	LA	FGW	PTR		42310	LA	FGW	PTR		42583 (42385) LA GWG PTR
42126	LA	FGW	ANG		42317	LA	FGW	FGP		
42138	LA	FGW	ANG		42332	LA	FGW	ANG		**GJ2G - TGS** *Seating 67-71S*
42143	LA	FGW	ANG		42343	LA	FGW	ANG		*Number Depot Livery Owner*
42145	LA	FGW	ANG		42345	LA	FGW	ANG		44002	LA	FGW	ANG
42166	LA	FGW	PTR		42346	LA	FGW	ANG		44003	LA	FGW	ANG
42167	LA	FGW	FGP		42347	LA	GWG	ANG		44005	LA	GWG	ANG
42169	LA	FGW	PTR		42348	LA	FGW	ANG		44008	LA	FGW	ANG
42173	LA	FGW	PTR		42349	LA	FGW	ANG		44013	LA	FGW	ANG
42174	LA	FGW	FGP		42353	LA	FGW	PTR		44014	LA	FGW	ANG
42175	LA	FGW	FGP		42356	LA	GWG	ANG		44016	LA	FGW	ANG
42176	LA	GWG	PTR		42361	LA	GWG	ANG		44022	LA	FGW	ANG
42178	LA	FGW	PTR		42362	LA	FGW	ANG		44026	LA	FGW	ANG
42195	LA	FGW	PTR		42364	LA	GWG	PTR		44034	LA	FGW	ANG
42196	LA	FGW	ANG		42365	LA	FGW	FGP		44036	LA	FGW	ANG

Right: *Included to show the soon to go First Great Western 'Dynamic Lines' livery, a Trailer First (TF) is illustrated. These vehicle with low-density 2+1 seating accommodated 48. In recent years just one TF vehicle was formed in each set, formed between a power car and the refreshment vehicle. However, as the fleet numbers have reduced, several TFs have been seen in traffic declassified to Trailer Standards.*
CJM

Great Western Railway

Number	Depot	Livery	Owner
44039	LA	FGW	ANG
44040	LA	GWG	ANG
44042	LA	FGW	PTR
44043	LA	FGW	ANG
44059	LA	FGW	ANG
44060	LA	FGW	PTR
44064	LA	FGW	ANG
44067	LA	FGW	ANG
44068	LA	FGW	PTR
44069	LA	FGW	PTR
44074	LA	FGW	PTR
44076	LA	FGW	PTR

Number	Depot	Livery	Owner
44078	LA	FGW	PTR
44081	LA	FGW	PTR
44083	LA	FGW	FGP
44090	LA	FGW	FGP
44091	LA	FGW	PTR
44093	LA	FGW	ANG
44097	LA	FGW	FGP
44100	LA	FGW	PTR

GH3A - TC *Seating 24F/39S*

Number	Depot	Livery	Owner
46002 (41029)	LA	FGW	ANG

Number	Depot	Livery	Owner
46003 (41033)	LA	FGW	ANG
46004 (41055)	LA	FGW	ANG
46005 (41065)	LA	FGW	ANG
46006 (41081) §		FGW	PTR
46007 (41096) §		FGW	PTR
46009 (41119) §		FGW	PTR
46013 (41148) §		FGW	PTR
46015 (41179)	LA	FGW	ANG
46017 (41184) §		FGW	PTR

§ **Stored at Long Rock, Penzance**

Castle Stock

TS- *Seating 84S*

Number	Depot	Livery	Owner
48101 (42168)	LA	GWG	FGP
48102 (42177)	LA	GWG	FGP
48103 (42218)	LA	GWG	FGP
48104 (42365)	LA	GWG	FGP
48105 (42266)	LA	GWG	FGP
48106 (42258)	LA	GWG	PTR
48107 (42101)	LA	GWG	FGP
48108 (42317)	LA	GWG	FGP
48109 (42315)	LA	GWG	FGP
48110 (42285)	LA	GWG	FGP
48111 (42093)	LA	GWG	FGP
48112 (42224)	LA	GWG	FGP
48113 (42221)	LA	GWG	FGP
48114 (42174)	LA	GWG	FGP
48115 (42085)	LA	GWG	FGP
48116 (42044)	LA	GWG	ANG
48117 (42008)	LA	GWG	ANG

Number	Depot	Livery	Owner
48118 (42042)	LA	GWG	ANG
48119 (42204)	LA	GWG	ANG
48120 (42201)	LA	GWG	ANG
48121 (42027)	LA	GWG	ANG
48122 (42214)	LA	GWG	ANG
48123 (42211)	LA	GWG	ANG
48124 (42212)	LA	GWG	ANG
48125 (42203)	LA	GWG	ANG
48126 (42138)	LA	GWG	ANG
48127 (42349)	LA	GWG	ANG
48128 (42273)	LA	GWG	ANG
48129 (42271)	LA	GWG	ANG
48130 (42074)	LA	GWG	ANG
48131 (42102)	LA	GWG	FGP
48132 (42202)	LA	GWG	ANG
48133 (42003)	LA	GWG	ANG
48134 (42264)	LA	GWG	ANG
48135 (42251)	LA	GWG	ANG

TGS- *Seating 71S*

Number	Depot	Livery	Owner
49101 (44055)	LA	GWG	FGP
49102 (44083)	LA	GWG	FGP
49103 (44090)	LA	GWG	FGP
49104 (44101)	LA	GWG	FGP
49105 (44097)	LA	GWG	FGP
49106 (44014)	LA	GWG	ANG
49107 (44064)	LA	GWG	ANG
49108 (44067)	LA	GWG	ANG
49109 (44003)	LA	GWG	ANG
49110 (44033)	LA	GWG	ANG
49111 (44036)	LA	GWG	ANG
49112 (44079)	LA	GWG	FGP
49113 (44034)	LA	GWG	ANG

Numbers in light type are the *proposed* renumbering order

Below: *A fleet of 48 'Castle' HST vehicles are currently under conversion at Wabtec, Doncaster and fitted with Vapor pocket sliding doors. The 'Castle' sets operate in four-car formations of three TS and one TGS vehicle. All vehicles are fitted with retention toilets. The modified vehicles are allocated to Laira depot and operate with modified Class 43 power cars. TS No. 48111 is illustrated.* **CJM**

Class 143
Pacer

Vehicle Length: 51ft 0½in (15.55m)						*Engine: 1 x Cummins LTA10-R per vehicle*					
Height: 12ft 2¼in (3.73m)						*Horsepower: 460hp (343kW)*					
Width: 8ft 10½in (2.70m)						*Seats (total/car): 92S, 48S/44S*					

Number	Formation DMS+DMSL	Depot	Livery	Owner	Operator		Number	Formation	Depot	Livery	Owner	Operator
							143617	55644+55683	EX	GWG	PTR	FGW
							143618	55659+55684	EX	GWG	PTR	FGW
143603	55658+55689	EX	GWG	PTR	FGW		143619	55660+55685	EX	GWG	PTR	FGW
143611	55652+55677	EX	GWG	PTR	FGW		143620	55661+55686	EX	GWG	PTR	FGW
143612	55653+55678	EX	GWG	PTR	FGW		143621	55662+55687	EX	GWG	PTR	FGW

Right: *The Rail Vehicle Accessibility Regulations (RVAR) which come into force in January 2020 will require the present fleet of Great Western Class 143s to be taken out of service. Currently eight sets are based at Exeter and operate on the Exeter to Exmouth, Paignton and Barnstaple routes, with some occasional running to Plymouth, Bristol or even Penzance. The sets are painted in GW green. Set No. 143619 is viewed from its DMSL vehicle.* **CJM**

Class 150/0
Sprinter

Vehicle Length: (Driving) 65ft 9¾in (20.05m), (Inter) 66ft 2½in (20.18m)						
Height: 12ft 4½in (3.77m)				*Engine: 1 x Cummins NT855R4 of 285hp per vehicle*		
Width: 9ft 3⅛in (2.82m)				*Horsepower: 855hp (638kW)*		
				Seats (total/car): 240S, 72S/92S/76S		

Number	Formation DMSL+MS+DMS	Depot	Livery	Owner	Op'r		Number	Formation	Depot	Livery	Owner	Op'r
150001	55200+55400+55300	PM	GWG	ANG	GWR		150002	55201+55401+55301	PM	GWG	ANG	GWR

Below: *The two original three-car Class 150/0 sets are on the books of Great Western, based at St Philips Marsh, Bristol and are usually deployed on longer distance services. Both sets are refurbished and carry green livery. Set No. 150002 is seen near Cheltenham, forming a Great Malvern to Weymouth service.* **CJM**

Great Western Railway

Class 150/2
Sprinter

Vehicle Length: 64ft 9¾in (19.74m)			Engine: 1 x NT855R5 of 285hp per vehicle	
Height: 12ft 4½in (3.77m)			Horsepower: 570hp (425kW)	
Width: 9ft 3⅛in (2.82m)			Seats (total/car): 116S, 60S/56S	
			Refurbished * 108S 50S/58S	

Number	Formation DMSL+DMS	Depot	Livery	Owner	Operator
150202	52202+57202	EX	GWG	ANG	GWR
150207	52207+57207	PM	GWG	ANG	GWR
150216	52216+57216	EX	GWG	ANG	GWR
150219*	52219+57219	EX	FGB	PTR	GWR
150221	52221+57221	EX	GWG	PTR	GWR
150232*	52232+57232	EX	GWG	PTR	GWR
150233*	52233+57233	EX	GWG	PTR	GWR
150234*	52234+57234	EX	GWG	PTR	GWR
150238*	52238+57238	EX	FGB	PTR	GWR
150239	52239+57239	EX	FGL	PTR	GWR
150243	52243+57243	EX	GWG	PTR	GWR
150244	52244+57244	EX	GWG	PTR	GWR
150246*	52246+57246	EX	GWG	PTR	GWR
150247*	52247+57247	EX	GWG	PTR	GWR
150248*	52248+57248	EX	GWG	PTR	GWR
150249	52249+57249	EX	GWG	PTR	GWR
150261	52261+57261	EX	GWG	PTR	GWR
150263*	52263+57263	EX	GWG	PTR	GWR
150265	52265+57265	EX	GWG	PTR	GWR
150266*	52266+57266	EX	GWG	PTR	GWR

Left and Below: *A fleet of 20 Class 150/2 gangway fitted 'Sprinter' sets are allocated to either Exeter or Bristol St Philips Marsh depots and today form the backbone of Devon and Cornwall services, as well as working to Gloucestershire, Wiltshire, Somerset and Dorset. On the left, Set No. 150216 is seen near Cheltenham. While below, set No. 150249 is seen near Powderham with its DMS vehicle on the left forming a Bristol to Penzance service. The majority of sets are painted in GW green livery, but one or two still retain FGW blue. Both:* **CJM**

Class 153

Vehicle Length: 76ft 5in (23.29m)			Engine: 1 x NT855R5 of 285hp		
Height: 12ft 3⅛in (3.75m)			Horsepower: 285hp (213kW)		
Width: 8ft 10in (2.70m)			Seats (total/car): 72S		

Number	Formation DMSL	Depot	Livery	Owner	Operator
153325	52325	EX	ADV	PTR	GWR
153329	52329	EX	FGB	ANG	GWR
153333	52333	EX	ADV	PTR	GWR
153361	57361	EX	FGB	ANG	GWR
153369	57369	EX	FGB	ANG	GWR

Right: *Until early 2019 and further stock transfers following introduction of new trains, Great Western Exeter depot operates five Class 153 single car units. These are usually operated in multiple or supplement two-car sets to increase capacity. However, one or two duties see vehicles operating on their own over the main line between Exeter and Plymouth. Two sets display promotional liveries and three plain FGW blue. No. 153361 is seen strengthening a Class 150/2 formation. When displaced from Great Western, these vehicles are scheduled to move to Transport for Wales as part of their 'Pacer' withdrawal programme.* **CJM**

Class 158/0 (2-car)

Vehicle Length: 76ft 1¾in (23.21m)			Engine: 1 x Cummins NTA855R of 350hp per vehicle		
Height: 12ft 6in (3.81m)			Horsepower: 700hp (522kW)		
Width: 9ft 3¾in (2.82m)			Seats (total/car): 134S, 66S/68S		

Number	Formation DMSL+DMSL	Depot	Livery	Owner	Operator		Number	Formation	Depot	Livery	Owner	Operator
158763	52763+57763	PM	FGL	PTR	GWR		158766	52766+57766	PM	GWG	PTR	GWR

Class 158/0 (3-car)

158798			
Vehicle Length: 76ft 1¾in (23.21m)		Engine: 1 x Cummins NTA855R of 350hp per vehicle	
Height: 12ft 6in (3.81m)		Horsepower: 1,050hp (783kW)	
Width: 9ft 3¼in (2.82m)		Seats (total/car): 200S, 66S/66S/68S	

158950 - 158961			
Vehicle Length: 76ft 1¾in (23.21m)		Engine: 1 x Cummins NTA855R of 350hp per vehicle	
Height: 12ft 6in (3.81m)		Horsepower: 1,050hp (783kW)	
Width: 9ft 3¼in (2.82m)		Seats (total/car): 204S, 66S/70S/68S	

Number	Formation DMSL+MSL+DMSL	Depot	Livery	Owner	Operator
158798	52798+58715+57798	PM	GWG	PTR	GWR

Number	Formation DMSL+DMSL+DMSL		Depot	Livery	Owner	Operator
158950	(158751/761)	57751+52761+57761	PM	GWG	PTR	GWR
158951	(158751/764)	52751+52764+57764	PM	GWG	PTR	GWR
158952	(158745/762)	57745+52762+57762	PM	GWG	PTR	GWR
158953	(158745/750)	52745+52750+57750	PM	GWG	PTR	GWR
158954	(158747/760)	57747+52760+57760	PM	GWG	PTR	GWR
158955	(158747/765)	52747+52765+57765	PM	FGL	PTR	GWR
158956	(158748/768)	57748+52768+57768	PM	GWG	PTR	GWR
158957	(158748/771)	52748+52771+57771	PM	GWG	PTR	GWR
158958	(158746/776)	57746+52776+57776	PM	GWG	PTR	GWR
158959	(158746/778)	52746+52778+57778	PM	GWG	PTR	GWR
158960	(158769/749)	57769+52769+57749	PM	FGL	PTR	GWR
158961	(158767/749)	57767+52767+52749	PM	GWG	PTR	GWR

Left: *Bristol St Philips Marsh depot has 13 three-car and two 2-car Class 158 sets which are used on longer distance services. These will eventually operate mainly in the West Country when replaced on the Cardiff-Bristol-Portsmouth route. Of the three-car sets, one is an 'as built' three car and the others are formed of spreading three driving cars. Sets are in the process of repainting into GW green livery. Set No. 158951 is seen at Millbrook with a Cardiff to Portsmouth service.* **CJM**

Class 165/1 (3-car)
Networker Turbo

Vehicle Length: (Driving) 75ft 2½in (22.91m), (Inter) 74ft 6½in (22.72m)
Height: 12ft 5¼in (3.79m)
Width: 9ft 5½in (2.81m)
Engine: 1 x Perkins 2006TWH of 350hp per car
Horsepower: 1,050hp (783kW)
Seats (total/car): 286S, 82S/106S/98S

Number	Formation DMSL+MS+DMS	Depot	Livery	Owner	Operator
165101	58953+55415+58916	RG	GWG	ANG	GWR
165102	58954+55416+58917	RG	GWG	ANG	GWR
165103	58955+55417+58918	RG	GWG	ANG	GWR
165104	58956+55418+58919	RG	GWG	ANG	GWR
165105	58957+55419+58920	RG	GWG	ANG	GWR
165106	58958+55420+58921	RG	GWG	ANG	GWR
165107	58959+55421+58922	RG	GWG	ANG	GWR
165108	58960+55422+58923	RG	GWG	ANG	GWR
165109	58961+55423+58924	RG	GWG	ANG	GWR
165110	58962+55424+58925	RG	GWG	ANG	GWR
165111	58963+55425+58926	RG	GWG	ANG	GWR
165112	58964+55426+58927	RG	GWG	ANG	GWR
165113	58965+55427+58928	RG	GWG	ANG	GWR
165114	58966+55428+58929	RG	GWG	ANG	GWR
165116	58968+55430+58931	RG	GWG	ANG	GWR
165117	58969+55431+58932	RG	GWG	ANG	GWR

Left: *The 'Networker Turbo' or 'Thames Turbo' fleet introduced by Network SouthEast are now spreading their wings following introduction of electric stock in the London area. Class 165s still operate the Thames Valley branches and between Didcot and Oxford as well as some services to Worcester. The 165s come in both two and three-car formation. Three-car set No. 165112 is captured at Honeybourne.* **CJM**

Class 165/1 (2-car)
Networker Turbo

Vehicle Length: 75ft 2½in (22.91m)
Height: 12ft 5¼in (3.79m)
Width: 9ft 5½in (2.81m)
Engine: 1 x Perkins 2006TWH of 350hp per car
Horsepower: 700hp (522kW)
Seats (total/car): 16F/170S, 16F-72S/98S

Number	Formation DMCL+DMS	Depot	Livery	Owner	Operator	Number	Formation	Depot	Livery	Owner	Operator
						165122	58883+58937	PM	GWG	ANG	GWR
						165123	58884+58938	RG	GWG	ANG	GWR
165118	58879+58933	PM	GWG	ANG	GWR	165124	58885+58939	RG	GWG	ANG	GWR
165119	58880+58934	PM	GWG	ANG	GWR	165125	58886+58940	RG	GWG	ANG	GWR
165120	58881+58935	PM	GWG	ANG	GWR	165126	58887+58941	RG	GWG	ANG	GWR
165121	58882+58936	RG	GWG	ANG	GWR	165127	58888+58942	RG	GWG	ANG	GWR

165128	58889+58943	RG	GWG ANG	GWR
165129	58890+58944	PM	GWG ANG	GWR
165130	58891+58945	RG	GWG ANG	GWR
165131	58892+58946	RG	GWG ANG	GWR
165132	58893+58947	PM	GWG ANG	GWR

165133	58894+58948	RG	GWG ANG	GWR
165134	58895+58949	PM	GWG ANG	GWR
165135	58896+58950	RG	GWG ANG	GWR
165136	58897+58951	RG	GWG ANG	GWR
165137	58898+58952	PM	GWG ANG	GWR

Class 166
Networker Turbo Express

Vehicle Length: (Driving) 75ft 2½in (22.91m), (Inter) 74ft 6½in (22.72m)
Height: 12ft 5¼in (3.79m) Engine: 1 x Perkins 2006TWH of 350hp per car
Width: 9ft 5½in (2.81m) Horsepower: 1,050hp (783kW)
Seats (total/car): 16F/258S, 90S/96S/16F-72S

Number	Formation DMSL+MS+DMCL	Depot	Livery	Owner	Operator	Name
166201	58101+58601+58122	RG	FGB	ANG	GWR	
166202	58102+58602+58123	PM	FGB	ANG	GWR	
166203	58103+58603+58124	PM	FGB	ANG	GWR	
166204	58104+58604+58125	PM	GWG	ANG	GWR	*Norman Topsom MBE*
166205	58105+58605+58126	PM	GWG	ANG	GWR	
166206	58106+58606+58127	PM	GWG	ANG	GWR	
166207	58107+58607+58128	RG	FGB	ANG	GWR	
166208	58108+58608+58129	PM	GWG	ANG	GWR	
166209	58109+58609+58130	RG	FGB	ANG	GWR	
166210	58110+58610+58131	PM	GWG	ANG	GWR	
166211	58111+58611+58132	PM	FGB	ANG	GWR	
166212	58112+58612+58133	PM	GWG	ANG	GWR	
166213	58113+58613+58134	RG	GWG	ANG	GWR	
166214	58114+58614+58135	PM	GWG	ANG	GWR	
166215	58115+58615+58136	PM	FGB	ANG	GWR	
166216	58116+58616+58137	PM	GWG	ANG	GWR	
166217	58117+58617+58138	PM	GWG	ANG	GWR	
166218	58118+58618+58139	PM	GWG	ANG	GWR	
166219	58119+58619+58140	PM	GWG	ANG	GWR	
166220	58120+58620+58141	PM	GWG	ANG	GWR	*Roger Walkins - The GWR Master Train Planner*
166221	58121+58621+58142	PM	FGB	ANG	GWR	*Reading Train Care Depot*

Above: *At the start of 2017 the Class 166s were largely allocated to Bristol St Philips Marsh for use on Worcester, Great Malvern, Weymouth, Westbury and Severn Beach services. Sets operating from Bristol have to have a ride height adjustment to operate within the safety gauge envelope. In GW green livery, set No. 166206 is seen at Bristol Temple Meads.* **CJM**

Great Western Railway

Class 387
Electrostar

Vehicle Length: (Driving) 66ft 9in (20.3m) Width: 9ft 2in (2.79m)
(Inter) 65ft 6in (19.96m) Horsepower: 2,012hp (1,500kW)
Height: 12ft 4in (3.75m) Seats (total/car): 223S. 56S/62S/45S/60S

Number	Formation	Depot	Livery	Owner	Operator
	DMSO(A)+MSO+TSO+DMSO(B)				
387130	421130+422130+423130+424130	RG	GWG	PTR	GWR
387131	421131+422131+423131+424131	RG	GWG	PTR	GWR
387132	421132+422132+423132+424132	RG	GWG	PTR	GWR
387133	421133+422133+423133+424133	RG	GWG	PTR	GWR
387134	421134+422134+423134+424134	RG	GWG	PTR	GWR
387135	421135+422135+423135+424135	RG	GWG	PTR	GWR
387136	421136+422136+423136+424136	RG	GWG	PTR	GWR
387137	421137+422137+423137+424137	RG	GWG	PTR	GWR
387138	421138+422138+423138+424138	RG	GWG	PTR	GWR
387139	421139+422139+423139+424139	RG	GWG	PTR	GWR
387140§	421140+422140+423140+424140	RG	GWG	PTR	GWR
387141	421141+422141+423141+424141	RG	GWG	PTR	GWR
387142	421142+422142+423142+424142	RG	GWG	PTR	GWR
387143	421143+422143+423143+424143	RG	GWG	PTR	GWR
387144	421144+422144+423144+424144	RG	GWG	PTR	GWR
387145	421145+422145+423145+424145	RG	GWG	PTR	GWR
387146	421146+422146+423146+424146	RG	GWG	PTR	GWR
387147	421147+422147+423147+424147	RG	GWG	PTR	GWR
387148	421148+422148+423148+424148	RG	GWG	PTR	GWR
387149	421149+422149+423149+424149	RG	GWG	PTR	GWR
387150	421150+422150+423150+424150	RG	GWG	PTR	GWR
387151	421151+422151+423151+424151	RG	GWG	PTR	GWR
387152	421152+422152+423152+424152	RG	GWG	PTR	GWR
387153	421153+422153+423153+424153	RG	GWG	PTR	GWR
387154	421154+422154+423154+424154	RG	GWG	PTR	GWR
387155	421155+422155+423155+424155	RG	GWG	PTR	GWR
387156	421156+422156+423156+424156	RG	GWG	PTR	GWR
387157	421157+422157+423157+424157	RG	GWG	PTR	GWR
387158	421158+422158+423158+424158	RG	GWG	PTR	GWR
387159	421159+422159+423159+424159	RG	GWG	PTR	GWR
387160	421160+422160+423160+424160	RG	GWG	PTR	GWR
387161	421161+422161+423161+424161	RG	GWG	PTR	GWR
387162	421162+422162+423162+424162	RG	GWG	PTR	GWR
387163	421163+422163+423163+424163	RG	GWG	PTR	GWR
387164	421164+422164+423164+424164	RG	GWG	PTR	GWR
387165	421165+422165+423165+424165	RG	GWG	PTR	GWR
387166	421166+422166+423166+424166	RG	GWG	PTR	GWR
387167	421167+422167+423167+424167	RG	GWG	PTR	GWR
387168	421168+422168+423168+424168	RG	GWG	PTR	GWR
387169	421169+422169+423169+424169	RG	GWG	PTR	GWR
387170	421170+422170+423170+424170	RG	GWG	PTR	GWR
387171	421171+422171+423171+424171	RG	GWG	PTR	GWR
387172	421172+422172+423172+424172	RG	GWG	PTR	GWR
387173	421173+422173+423173+424173	RG	GWG	PTR	GWR
387174	421174+422174+423174+424174	RG	GWG	PTR	GWR

§ Heathrow Express modified

Left: *The 45 four-car Class 387/1 'Electrostar' sets based at Reading now operate the majority of Thames Valley services between London Paddington and Didcot. Trains are formed of up to three sets giving 12-car formations on peak services. The sets are all painted in GW green livery, with each set seating 223 passengers. In 2019 a batch of sets will be modified to operate the Heathrow Express service, taking over from Class 332 stock. Set No. 387135 is seen at Didcot.* **CJM**

Mk3 Hauled Stock

Vehicle Length: 75ft 0in (22.86m)   Width: 8ft 11in (2.71m)
Height: 12ft 9in (3.88m)   Bogie Type: BT10

AJ1G - RFB *Seating 18F*

Number	Depot	Livery	Owner
10217	PZ	GWG	PTR
10219	PZ	GWG	PTR
10221	PZ	WHT	PTR
10225	PZ	GWG	PTR

AU4G - SLEP *Comps 12*

Number	Depot	Livery	Owner
10532	PZ	GWG	PTR
10534	PZ	GWG	PTR
10563	PZ	GWG	PTR
10584	PZ	GWG	PTR

10589	PZ	GWG	PTR
10590	PZ	GWG	PTR
10594	PZ	GWG	PTR
10596	ZN	GWG	PTR
10601	PZ	GWG	PTR
10612	PZ	GWG	PTR
10616	PZ	GWG	PTR

AC2G - TSO *Seating 45S*

Number	Depot	Livery	Owner
12100	PZ	GWG	PTR
12142	PZ	GWG	PTE
12161	PZ	FGW	PTR

AE1H - BSO *Seating 36U*

Number	Depot	Livery	Owner
17173	PZ	GWG	PTR
17174	PZ	GWG	PTR
17175	PZ	GWG	PTR

Right: *The recently enlarged Penzance depot is the base for 21 Mk3 loco-hauled passenger vehicles which are used on the Night Riviera service providing sleeping car and seating coaches between London and Penzance six nights each week. Catering vehicle No. 10225 is illustrated from its seating end. Operational vehicles are painted in GW green livery.* **CJM**

Service Stock

HST Barrier Vehicles

Number	Depot	Livery	Owner	Former Identity
6330	LA	FGB	ANG	BFK - 14084
6336	PM	FGB	ANG	BG - 81591/92185

6338	LA	FGB	ANG	BG - 81581/92180
6348	PZ	FGB	ANG	BG - 81233/92963

Below: *To enable GW stock to be hauled by a standard locomotive, four barrier vehicles are on the books, which have standard draw gear at one end and buck-eye couplers at the other. The four can be found at any of the main depots and are frequently operated by Rail Operations Group locomotives. Three barrier cars are shown, with on the left GW No. 6330.* **CJM**

Class 769

Porterbrook 'Flex'

In 2018, Great Western ordered a fleet of 19 Class 769 'Flex' units from Porterbrook. These four-car sets, rebuilt from Class 319s are being technically modified by Brush Traction and Loughborough and will then receive an internal refurbishment by Knorr-Bremse at Wolverton.

The 19 sets, to be based at Reading will be tri-mode, able to operate from 750V DC third rail, 25kV AC overhead as well as from an on-board diesel engine below each driving vehicle.

The sets due to be converted are Nos. 319422/423/425/427/428/430/432/435/436/437/438/439/440/443/445/447/449/452/459, these will be renumbered in the 7699xx series and are due to enter traffic in 2019.

Passenger Train Operating Companies - Great Western Railway

Class 800/0 Bi-Mode 'IET' stock

5-car sets

Vehicle Length: (Driving) 85ft 4in (26m)
Height: 11ft 8¾in (3.62m)
Engine: MTU 12V 1600R80L of 750hp (560kW) x 3

Width: 8ft 10in (2.7m)
Horsepower: Electric 3,636hp (2,712kW)
Seats (total/car): 36F/290S -
18F, 18F/58S, 88S, 88S, 56F

Number	Formation DTRBFO+MC+MS+MS+DTSO	Depot	Livery	Owner	Operator	Name
800001*	811001+812001+813001+814001+815001§	NP	GWG	AGT	GWR	
800002*	811002+812002+813002+814002+815002§	NP	GWG	AGT	GWR	
800003*	811003+812003+813003+814003+815003	NP	GWG	AGT	GWR	Queen Elizabeth II / Queen Victoria
800004*	811004+812004+813004+814004+815004	NP	GWG	AGT	GWR	Sir Daniel Gooch / Isambard Kingdom Brunel
800005	811005+812005+813005+814005+815005	NP	GWG	AGT	GWR	
800006	811006+812006+813006+814006+815006	NP	GWG	AGT	GWR	
800007	811007+812007+813007+814007+815007	NP	GWG	AGT	GWR	
800008	811008+812008+813008+814008+815008	NP	GWG	AGT	GWR	
800009	811009+812009+813009+814009+815009	NP	GWG	AGT	GWR	Sir Gareth Edwards / John Charles
800010	811010+812010+813010+814010+815010	NP	GWG	AGT	GWR	Michael Bond / Paddington Bear
800011	811011+812011+813011+814011+815011	NP	GWG	AGT	GWR	
800012	811012+812012+813012+814012+815012	NP	GWG	AGT	GWR	
800013	811013+812013+813013+814013+815013	NP	GWG	AGT	GWR	
800014	811014+812014+813014+814014+815014	NP	GWG	AGT	GWR	
800015	811015+812015+813015+814015+815015	NP	GWG	AGT	GWR	
800016	811016+812016+813016+814016+815016	NP	GWG	AGT	GWR	
800017	811017+812017+813017+814017+815017	NP	GWG	AGT	GWR	
800018	811018+812018+813018+814018+815018	NP	GWG	AGT	GWR	
800019	811019+812019+813019+814019+815019	NP	GWG	AGT	GWR	Jonny Johnson MBE DFM / Joy Lofthouse
800020	811020+812020+813020+814020+815020	NP	GWG	AGT	GWR	Bob Woodward / Elizabeth Ralph
800021	811021+812021+813021+814021+815021	NP	GWG	AGT	GWR	
800022	811022+812022+813022+814022+815022	NP	GWG	AGT	GWR	
800023	811023+812023+813023+814023+815023	NP	GWG	AGT	GWR	
800024	811024+812024+813024+814024+815024	NP	GWG	AGT	GWR	
800025	811025+812025+813025+814025+815025	NP	GWG	AGT	GWR	
800026	811026+812026+813026+814026+815026	NP	GWG	AGT	GWR	Don Cameron
800027	811027+812027+813027+814027+815027	NP	GWG	AGT	GWR	
800028	811028+812028+813028+814028+815028	NP	GWG	AGT	GWR	
800029	811029+812029+813029+814029+815029	NP	GWG	AGT	GWR	
800030	811030+812030+813030+814030+815030	NP	GWG	AGT	GWR	
800031	811031+812031+813031+814031+815031	NP	GWG	AGT	GWR	
800032	811032+812032+813032+814032+815032	NP	GWG	AGT	GWR	
800033	811033+812033+813033+814033+815033	NP	GWG	AGT	GWR	
800034	811034+812034+813034+814034+815034	NP	GWG	AGT	GWR	
800035	811035+812035+813035+814035+815035	NP	GWG	AGT	GWR	
800036	811036+812036+813036+814036+815036	NP	GWG	AGT	GWR	

Left: At the start of 2019, the majority of GW main line services were in the hands of Class 800 and 802 stock. The Class 800s are owned by Agility Trains and form part of the Government led modernisation of the GW and LNER routes. Five-car set No. 800024 is seen alongside a GW HST at Swindon in spring 2018. **CJM**

Passenger Train Operating Companies - Great Western Railway

Class 800/3 Bi-Mode 'IET' stock

9-car sets

Vehicle Length: (Driving) 85ft 4in (26m)
Height: 11ft 8¾in (3.62m)
Engine: MTU 12V 1600R80L of 750hp (560kW) x 5
Width: 8ft 10in (2.7m)
Horsepower: Electric 6,061hp (4,520kW)
Seats (total/car): 93F/534S - 56S, 88S, 88S, 88S, 88S, 88S,30F/38S, 48F, 15F

Number	*Formation* DTRBFO+MF+MC+TS+MS+TS+MS+MS+DTSO	*Depot*	*Livery*	*Owner*	*Operator*
800301	821001+822001+823001+824001+825001+826001+827001+828001+829001	NP	GWG	AGT	GWR
800302*	821002+822002+823002+824002+825002+826002+827002+828002+829002	NP	GWG	AGT	GWR
800303*	821003+822003+823003+824003+825003+826003+827003+828003+829003	NP	GWG	AGT	GWR
800304	821004+822004+823004+824004+825004+826004+827004+828004+829004	NP	GWG	AGT	GWR
800305	821005+822005+823005+824005+825005+826005+827005+828005+829005	NP	GWG	AGT	GWR
800306	821006+822006+823006+824006+825006+826006+827006+828006+829006	NP	GWG	AGT	GWR
800307	821007+822007+823007+824007+825007+826007+827007+828007+829007	NP	GWG	AGT	GWR
800308	821008+822008+823008+824008+825008+826008+827008+828008+829008	NP	GWG	AGT	GWR
800309	821009+822009+823009+824009+825009+826009+827009+828009+829009	NP	GWG	AGT	GWR
800310	821010+822010+823010+824010+825010+826010+827010+828003+829010	NP	GWG	AGT	GWR
800311	821011+822011+823011+824011+825011+826011+827011+828011+829011§	NP	GWG	AGT	GWR
800312	821012+822012+823012+824012+825012+826012+827012+828012+829012§	NP	GWG	AGT	GWR
800313	821013+822013+823013+824013+825013+826013+827013+828013+829013	NP	GWG	AGT	GWR
800314	821014+822014+823014+824014+825014+826014+827014+828014+829014	NP	GWG	AGT	GWR
800315	821015+822015+823015+824015+825015+826015+827015+828015+829015	NP	GWG	AGT	GWR
800316	821016+822016+823016+824016+825016+826016+827016+828016+829016	NP	GWG	AGT	GWR
800317	821017+822017+823017+824017+825017+826017+827017+828017+829017	NP	GWG	AGT	GWR
800318	821018+822018+823018+824018+825018+826018+827018+828018+829018	NP	GWG	AGT	GWR
800319	821019+822019+823019+824019+825019+826019+827019+828019+829019	NP	GWG	AGT	GWR
800320	821020+822020+823020+824020+825020+826020+827020+828020+829020	NP	GWG	AGT	GWR
800321	821021+822021+823021+824021+825021+826021+827021+828021+829021	NP	GWG	AGT	GWR

* Built in Japan, delivered to the UK
§ 829011 and 829012 previously 815001 and 815002 from sets No. 800001/002

Names Applied. *800306 Allan Leonard Lewis VC / Harold Day DSC*

Right: *By summer 2018, the longer nine-car bi-mode Class 800/3 sets were entering GW service, Viewed from the first class end, identifiable by three blanked out windows where the kitchen is located, set No. 800306 is seen departing from Swindon towards London.* **CJM**

Class 802 Bi-Mode 'IET' stock

'West of England' sets

5-car sets 802/0

Vehicle Length: (Driving) 85ft 4in (26m)
Height: 11ft 8¾in (3.62m)
Engine: MTU 12V 1600R80L of 940hp (700kW) x 3
Seats (total/car): 36F/290S -18F, 18F/58S, 88S, 88S, 56F
Width: 8ft 10in (2.7m)
Horsepower: Electric 3,636hp (2,712kW)
Diesel 2,820hp (2,100kW)

Number	*Formation* DTRBFO+MC+MS+MS+DTSO	*Depot*	*Livery*	*Owner*	*Operator*	*Name*
802001*	831001+832001+833001+834001+835001	NP	GWG	EVL	GWR	
802002*	832002+832002+833002+834002+835002	NP	GWG	EVL	GWR	
802003	833003+832003+833003+834003+835003	NP	GWG	EVL	GWR	
802004	834004+832004+833004+834004+835004	NP	GWG	EVL	GWR	
802005	835005+832005+833005+834005+835005	NP	GWG	EVL	GWR	
802006	836006+832006+833006+834006+835006	NP	GWG	EVL	GWR	
802007	837007+832007+833007+834007+835007	NP	GWG	EVL	GWR	
802008	838008+832008+833008+834008+835008	NP	GWG	EVL	GWR	
802009	839009+832009+833009+834009+835009	NP	GWG	EVL	GWR	
802010	840010+832010+833010+834010+835010	NP	GWG	EVL	GWR	

Great Western Railway

802011	841011+832011+833011+834011+835011	NP	GWG	EVL	GWR	*Sir Joshua Reynolds PRA / Capt. Robert Falcon Scott RN CVO*
802012	842012+832012+833012+834012+835012	NP	GWG	EVL	GWR	
802013	843013+832013+833013+834013+835013	NP	GWG	EVL	GWR	
802014	844014+832014+833014+834014+835014	NP	GWG	EVL	GWR	
802015	845015+832015+833015+834015+835015	NP	GWG	EVL	GWR	
802016	846016+832016+833016+834016+835016	NP	GWG	EVL	GWR	
802017	847017+832017+833017+834017+835017	NP	GWG	EVL	GWR	
802018	848018+832018+833018+834018+835018	NP	GWG	EVL	GWR	
802019	849019+832019+833019+834019+835019	NP	GWG	EVL	GWR	
802020	850020+832020+833020+834020+835020	NP	GWG	EVL	GWR	
802021	851021+832021+833021+834021+835021	NP	GWG	EVL	GWR	
802022	852022+832022+833022+834022+835022	NP	GWG	EVL	GWR	

9-car sets 802/1

Vehicle Length: (Driving) 85ft 4in (26m)
Height: 11ft 8¾in (3.62m)
Engine: MTU 12V 1600R80L of 940hp (750kW) x 5
Seats (total/car): 101F/526S, 15F, 56F, 30F/38S 88S, 88S, 88S, 88S, 88S, 48S
Width: 8ft 10in (2.7m)
Horsepower: Electric 6,061hp (4,520kW)
Diesel 4,700hp (3,500kW)

Number	Formation DTRBFO+MF+MC+TS+MS+TS+MS+MS+DTSO		Depot	Livery	Owner	Operator
802101*	831101+832101+833101+834101+835101+836101+837101+838101+839101	NP	GWG	EVL	GWR
802102	831102+832102+833102+834102+835102+836102+837102+838102+839102	NP	GWG	EVL	GWR
802103	831103+832103+833103+834103+835103+836103+837103+838103+839103	NP	GWG	EVL	GWR
802104	831104+832104+833104+834104+835104+836104+837104+838104+839104	NP	GWG	EVL	GWR
802105	831105+832105+833105+834105+835105+836105+837105+838105+839105	NP	GWG	EVL	GWR
802106	831106+832106+833106+834106+835106+836106+837106+838106+839106	NP	GWG	EVL	GWR
802107	831107+832107+833107+834107+835107+836107+837107+838107+839107	NP	GWG	EVL	GWR
802108	831108+832108+833108+834108+835108+836108+837108+838108+839108	NP	GWG	EVL	GWR
802109	831109+832109+833109+834109+835109+836109+837109+838109+839109	NP	GWG	EVL	GWR
802110	831110+832110+833110+834110+835110+836110+837110+838110+839110	NP	GWG	EVL	GWR
802111	831111+832111+833111+834111+835111+836111+837111+838111+839111	NP	GWG	EVL	GWR
802112	831112+832112+833112+834112+835112+836112+837112+838112+839112	NP	GWG	EVL	GWR
802113	831113+832113+833113+834113+835113+836113+837113+838113+839113	NP	GWG	EVL	GWR
802114	831114+832114+833114+834114+835114+836114+837114+838114+839114	NP	GWG	EVL	GWR

* Built in Japan, delivered to the UK

Left and Below: *From summer 2018, the five and nine-car Eversholt-owned Great Western operated Class 802s entered traffic on the West of England corridor. Internally the same as 800s, the sets have technical differences to cope with the West Country gradients. On the left is five-car set No. 802001 passing Powderham, while below, is the first of the nine-car sets No. 802101 departing west from Dawlish. Both:* **CJM**

First Hull Trains

Address: ✉ Europa House, 184 Ferensway, Kingston-upon-Hull, HU1 3UT
✆ customer.services@hulltrains.co.uk
✆ 0345 071 0222 ⓘ www.hulltrains.co.uk

Managing Director: Louise Cheeseman
Franchise Dates: Private Open Access Operator, agreement to December 2029
Principal Route: London King's Cross - Hull **Depots:** Crofton (XW)
Parent Company: First Group PLC

Hull — Brough — Howden — Selby — Doncaster — Retford — Grantham — Stevenage — London King's Cross

© TRC.Com Ltd 2013

Class 180
Adelante

Vehicle Length: (Driving) 75ft 7in (23.71m), (Inter) 75ft 5in (23.03m)
Height: 12ft 4in (3.75m) Engine: 1 x Cummins OSK19 of 750hp per vehicle
Width: 9ft 2in (2.80m) Horsepower: 3,750hp (2,796kW)
Seats (total/car): 42F/226S, 46S/42F/68S/56S/56S

Number	Formation DMSL(A)+MFL+MSF+MSLRB+DMSL(B)	Depot	Livery	Owner	Operator	
180109(S)	50909+54909+55909+56909+59909	XW	FHT	ANG	FHT	
180110	50910+54910+55910+56910+59910	XW	FHT	ANG	FHT	Sets to be fitted with
180111	50911+54911+55911+56911+59911	XW	FHT	ANG	FHT	Alstom Atlas 2000
180113	50913+54913+55909+56913+59913	XW	FHT	ANG	FHT	ETCS systems.

Right: *Open access operator First Hull Trains is undergoing a rolling stock transition in 2019, with the replacement of its four Class 180s, with a brand new fleet of five-car bi-mode Class 802s, built by Hitachi in Pistoia, Italy. Once introduced, the '180s' will be returned to owner Angel Trains for re-deployment. First Hull Trains set No. 180113 is seen departing from London King's Cross.*
Antony Christie

■ Due to a shortage of stock, Hull Trains hired Mk3 HST vehicles Nos. 40716/18, 41018, 41102, 42024/026/347/506, 44002/034 from First Great Western in spring 2019.

Class 802/3
AT300

Vehicle Length: (Driving) 85ft 4in (26m) Width: 8ft 10in (2.7m)
Height: 11ft 8¼in (3.62m) Horsepower: Electric 3,636hp (2,712kW)
Engine: MTU 12V 1600R80L of 940hp (700kW) x 3 Diesel 2,820hp (2,100kW)
Seats (total/car): Awaited

Number	Formation DTRBFO+MSO+MSO+MSO+PDTSO	Depot	Livery	Owner	Operator
802301	831301+832301+833301+834001+835001	-	FHT	ANG	On delivery/commissioning
802302	831302+832302+833302+834002+835002	-	FHT	ANG	On delivery/commissioning
802303	831303+832303+833303+834003+835003	-	FHT	ANG	On delivery/commissioning
802304	831304+832304+833304+834004+835004	-	FHT	ANG	On delivery/commissioning
802305	831305+832305+833305+834005+835005	-	FHT	ANG	On delivery/commissioning

First TransPennine Express

Address: ✉ Floor 7, Bridgewater House, 60 Whitworth Street, Manchester, M1 6LT
🖷 tpecustomer.relations@firstgroup.com   ℰ 0845 600 1671
ⓘ www.tpexpress.co.uk

Managing Director: Leo Goodwin
Franchise Dates: 1 February 2004 - 31 March 2023
Principal Routes: Newcastle, Middlesbrough, Scarborough, Hull, Cleethorpes to
Manchester, Liverpool, Barrow, Carlisle, Edinburgh and Glasgow
Depots: Ardwick (AK), York (YK), Crofton (XW), Manchester (MA)
Parent Company: First Group PLC

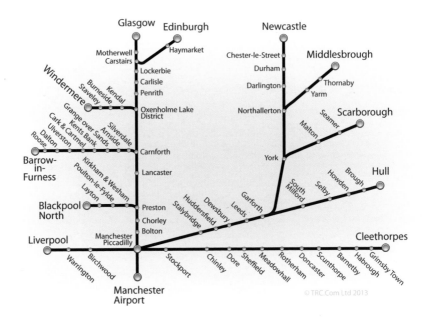

Class 68 'UK Light'

Vehicle Length: 67ft 3in (20.5m)					*Engine: Caterpillar C175-16*	
Height: 12ft 6½in (3.82m)					*Horsepower: 3,750hp (2,800kW)*	
Speed: 100mph (161km/h)					*Electrical Equipment: ABB*	

Number	Depot	Pool	Livery	Owner	Operator	Name (not yet fitted)
68019	CR	XHTP	FTN	BEA	DRS/TPE	*Brutus*
68020	CR	XHTP	FTN	BEA	DRS/TPE	*Reliance*
68021	CR	XHTP	FTN	BEA	DRS/TPE	*Tireless*
68022	CR	XHTP	FTN	BEA	DRS/TPE	*Resolution*
68023	CR	XHTP	FTN	BEA	DRS/TPE	*Achilles*
68024	CR	XHTP	FTN	BEA	DRS/TPE	*Centaur*
68025	CR	XHTP	FTN	BEA	DRS/TPE	*Superb*
68026	CR	XHTP	FTN	BEA	DRS/TPE	*(Nautilus)*
68027	CR	XHTP	FTN	BEA	DRS/TPE	*(Endeavour)*
68028	CR	XHTP	FTN	BEA	DRS/TPE	*Lord President*
68029	CR	XHVE	FTN	BEA	DRS/TPE	*(Destroyer)*
68030	CR	XHTP	FTN	BEA	DRS/TPE	*Black Douglas*
68031	CR	XHTP	FTN	BEA	DRS/TPE	*(Excelsior)*
68032	CR	XHVE	FTN	BEA	DRS/TPE	*(Patriot)*

Above: *The 14 DRS Class 68s leased to TransPennine to power Mk5 sets are finished in TPE colours and are devoid of a yellow warning end. No. 68019* Brutus *is seen passing Crewe in November 2018.* **CJM**

Class 185
Desiro

Vehicle Length: (Driving) 77ft 11in (23.76m), (Inter) 77ft 10½in (23.75m)	
Height: 12ft 4in (3.75m)	Engine: 1 x Cummins QSK19 of 750hp per vehicle
Width: 9ft 3in (2.81m)	Horsepower: 2,250hp (1,680kW)
	Seats (total/car): 15F/154S, 15F-18S/72S/64S

Number	Formation DMCL+MSL+DMS	Depot	Livery	Owner	Operator
185101	51101+53101+54101	AK	FTP	EVL	FTP
185102	51102+53102+54102	AK	FTN	EVL	FTP
185103	51103+53103+54103	AK	FTN	EVL	FTP
185104	51104+53104+54104	AK	FTN	EVL	FTP
185105	51105+53105+54105	AK	FTN	EVL	FTP
185106	51106+53106+54106	AK	FTN	EVL	FTP
185107	51107+53107+54107	AK	FTN	EVL	FTP
185108	51108+53108+54108	AK	FTN	EVL	FTP
185109	51109+53109+54109	AK	FTN	EVL	FTP
185110	51110+53110+54110	AK	FTN	EVL	FTP
185111	51111+53111+54111	AK	FTN	EVL	FTP
185112	51112+53112+54112	AK	FTP	EVL	FTP
185113	51113+53113+54113	AK	FTN	EVL	FTP
185114	51114+53114+54114	AK	FTN	EVL	FTP
185115	51115+53115+54115	AK	FTN	EVL	FTP
185116	51116+53116+54116	AK	FTP	EVL	FTP
185117	51117+53117+54117	AK	FTN	EVL	FTP
185118	51118+53118+54118	AK	FTN	EVL	FTP
185119	51119+53119+54119	AK	FTN	EVL	FTP
185120	51120+53120+54120	AK	FTP	EVL	FTP
185121	51121+53121+54121	AK	FTN	EVL	FTP
185122	51122+53122+54122	AK	FTP	EVL	FTP
185123	51123+53123+54123	AK	FTN	EVL	FTP
185124	51124+53124+54124	AK	FTN	EVL	FTP
185125	51125+53125+54125	AK	FTN	EVL	FTP
185126	51126+53126+54126	AK	FTN	EVL	FTP
185127	51127+53127+54127	AK	FTN	EVL	FTP
185128	51128+53128+54128	AK	FTN	EVL	FTP
185129	51129+53129+54129	AK	FTP	EVL	FTP
185130	51130+53130+54130	AK	FTN	EVL	FTP
185131	51131+53131+54131	AK	FTN	EVL	FTP
185132	51132+53132+54132	AK	FTN	EVL	FTP
185133	51133+53133+54133	AK	FTN	EVL	FTP
185134	51134+53134+54134	AK	FTN	EVL	FTP
185135	51135+53135+54135	AK	FTN	EVL	FTP
185136	51136+53136+54136	AK	FTP	EVL	FTP

First TransPennine Express

■ Following introduction of new stock, 22 Class 185s will be taken off lease.

Left: Another TOC undergoing major rolling stock change is TransPennine Express, currently introducing three new breads of train. This will see many of the existing Class 185s removed from service and returned to owner Eversholt Leasing. Class 185 No. 185124 with its first class DMCL coach leading, arrives at Doncaster. **CJM**

185137	51137+53137+54137	AK	FTP	EVL	FTP
185138	51138+53138+54138	AK	FTN	EVL	FTP
185139	51139+53139+54139	AK	FTN	EVL	FTP
185140	51140+53140+54140	AK	FTN	EVL	FTP
185141	51141+53141+54141	AK	FTN	EVL	FTP
185142	51142+53142+54142	AK	FTA	EVL	FTP
185143	51143+53143+54143	AK	FTN	EVL	FTP
185144	51144+53144+54144	AK	FTN	EVL	FTP
185145	51145+53145+54145	AK	FTN	EVL	FTP
185146	51146+53146+54146	AK	SPL	EVL	FTP
185147	51147+53147+54147	AK	FTN	EVL	FTP
185148	51148+53148+54148	AK	FTN	EVL	FTP
185149	51149+53149+54149	AK	FTN	EVL	FTP
185150	51150+53150+54150	AK	FTN	EVL	FTP
185151	51151+53151+54151	AK	FTP	EVL	FTP

Class 350/4
Desiro

Vehicle Length: 66ft 9in (20.4m)
Height: 12ft 1½in (3.78m)
Width: 9ft 2in (2.7m)

Horsepower: 1,341hp (1,000kW)
Seats (total/car): 19F/178S

Number	Formation	Depot	Livery	Owner	Operator
	DMSO(A)+TCO+PTSO+DMSO(B)				
350401	60691+60901+60941+60671	AK	FTN	ANG	FTP
350402	60692+60902+60942+60672	AK	FTN	ANG	FTP
350403	60693+60903+60943+60673	AK	FTN	ANG	FTP
350404	60694+60904+60944+60674	AK	FTN	ANG	FTP
350405	60695+60905+60945+60675	AK	FTN	ANG	FTP
350406	60696+60906+60946+60676	AK	FTN	ANG	FTP
350407	60697+60907+60947+60677	AK	FTN	ANG	FTP
350408	60698+60908+60948+60678	AK	FTN	ANG	FTP
350409	60699+60909+60949+60679	AK	FTN	ANG	FTP
350410	60700+60910+60950+60680	AK	FTN	ANG	FTP

Following introduction of new stock in 2019, these Class 350 sets will go off lease, they will be transferred to the new West Midlands (North Western) franchise.

Left: Until introduction of new CAF Class 397 'Civity' five-car sets, the TPE electric service from Manchester Airport to Scotland by way of the West Coast Main Line will be operated by a fleet of 10 Class 350/4 Siemens Desiro sets, based in Manchester. The sets carry full TransPennine livery and seat 19 first and 178 standard class passengers, which is frequently insufficient to meet demand. Set No. 350408 is seen arriving at Carlisle. **Nathan Williamson**

Class 397
'Civity' Nova 2

	Vehicle Length: awaited			Horsepower: awaited
	Height: awaited			Seats (total/car): 22F/264S
	Width: awaited			

Number	Formation	Depot	Livery	Owner	Operator
	DMF+PTS(A)+MS+PTS(B)+DMS				
397001	471001+472001+473001+474001+475001	MA	FTN	EVL	Under test
397002	471001+472002+473002+474002+475002	MA	FTN	EVL	Under test
397003	471003+472003+473003+474003+475003	MA	FTN	EVL	Under test
397004	471004+472004+473004+474004+475004	MA	FTN	EVL	(on delivery)
397005	471005+472005+473005+474005+475005	MA	FTN	EVL	(on delivery)
397006	471006+472006+473006+474006+475006	MA	FTN	EVL	(on delivery)
397007	471007+472007+473007+474007+475007	MA	FTN	EVL	(on delivery)
397008	471008+472008+473008+474008+475008	MA	FTN	EVL	(on delivery)
397009	471009+472009+473009+474009+475009	MA	FTN	EVL	(on delivery)
397010	471010+472010+473010+474010+475010	MA	FTN	EVL	(on delivery)
397011	471011+472011+473011+474011+475011	MA	FTN	EVL	(on delivery)
397012	471012+472012+473012+474012+475012	MA	FTN	EVL	(on delivery)

Class 802 Bi-Mode IET stock

5-car sets - Nova 1

	Vehicle Length: (Driving) 85ft 4in (26m)			Width: 8ft 10in (2.7m)
	Height: 12ft 4in (3.75m)			Horsepower: Electric 3,636hp (2,712kW)
	Engine: MTU 12V 1600R80L of 750hp (560kW) x 3			Seats (total/car): Awaited

Number	Formation	Depot	Livery	Owner	Operator
	DTRBFO+MSO+MSO+MSO+PDTSO				
802201*	831201+832201+833201+834201+835201	AK	FTN	ANG	Under test
802202*	831202+832202+833202+834202+835202	AK	WHT	ANG	Under test
802203	831203+832203+833203+834203+835203	AK	WHT	ANG	On order, delivery 2018-2019
802204	831204+832204+833204+834204+835204	AK	WHT	ANG	On order, delivery 2018-2019
802205	831205+832205+833205+834205+835205	AK	WHT	ANG	On order, delivery 2018-2019
802206	831206+832206+833206+834206+835206	AK	WHT	ANG	On order, delivery 2018-2019
802207	831207+832207+833207+834207+835207	AK	WHT	ANG	On order, delivery 2018-2019
802208	831208+832208+833208+834208+835208	AK	WHT	ANG	On order, delivery 2018-2019
802209	831209+832209+833209+834209+835209	AK	WHT	ANG	On order, delivery 2018-2019
802210	831210+832210+833210+834210+835210	AK	WHT	ANG	On order, delivery 2018-2019
802211	831211+832211+833211+834211+835211	AK	WHT	ANG	On order, delivery 2018-2019
802212	831212+832212+833212+834212+835212	AK	WHT	ANG	On order, delivery 2018-2019
802213	831213+832213+833213+834213+835213	AK	WHT	ANG	On order, delivery 2018-2019
802214	831214+832214+833214+834214+835214	AK	WHT	ANG	On order, delivery 2018-2019
802215	831215+832215+833215+834215+835215	AK	WHT	ANG	On order, delivery 2018-2019
802216	831216+832216+833216+834216+835216	AK	WHT	ANG	On order, delivery 2018-2019
802217	831217+832217+833217+834217+835217	AK	WHT	ANG	On order, delivery 2018-2019
802218	831218+832218+833218+834218+835218	AK	WHT	ANG	On order, delivery 2018-2019
802219	831219+832219+833219+834219+835219	AK	WHT	ANG	On order, delivery 2018-2019

* Built in Japan, remainder built in
Pistoia, Italy

Right: *Testing commenced in summer
2018 of the first of 19 five-car Class 802/2
sets for TPE, which will take over from
many of the Class 185s on Cross-Pennine
operations in 2019. In unbranded 'base'
colours, Hitachi set No. 802201 is seen
undergoing type test approval runs on
the East Coast Main Line. These bi-mode
sets will operate using their three diesel
engines for Pennine routes and overhead
power on the East and West Coast lines.*
Antony Christie

Passenger Train Operating Companies - First TransPennine Express

Passenger Train Operating Companies - First TransPennine Express

First TransPennine Express

Mk3 Hauled Stock

Vehicle Length: 75ft 0in (22.86m)	Width: 8ft 11in (2.71m)
Height: 12ft 9in (3.88m)	Bogie Type: BT10

Mk3 vehicles leased to First TransPennine for training.

AJ1G - RFB *Seating 18F*

Number	Depot	Livery	Owner
10212	AK	SIL	PTR

AD1G - FO *Seating 48F*

Number	Depot	Livery	Owner
11007	AK	SIL	PTR
11018	AK	SIL	PTR
11048	AK	SIL	PTR

AC2G - TS0 (*TSOD) *Seating 76/70*S*

Number	Depot	Livery	Owner
12011	AK	SIL	PTR
12078	AK	SIL	PTR
12122*	AK	SIL	PTR
12133	AK	SIL	PTR
12138	AK	SIL	PTR

Mk5a Hauled Stock
Nova 3

Vehicle Length: DTS/TF 22.37m,	Width: awaited
TS 22.2m	Bogie Type: CAF
Height: awaited	

Set Number	Formation DTS+T2(TS)+T3-1(TS)+T3-2(TS)+T1(TF)+Loco	Depot	Livery	Owner	Operator
001	12801+11703+11702+11701+11501	MA	FTN	BEA	FTP
002	12802+11706+11705+11704+11502	MA	FTN	BEA	FTP
003	12803+11709+11708+11707+11503	MA	FTN	BEA	FTP
004	12804+11712+11711+11710+11504	MA	FTN	BEA	FTP
005	12805+11715+11714+11713+11505	MA	FTN	BEA	FTP
006	12806+11718+11717+11716+11506	MA	FTN	BEA	FTP
007	12807+11721+11720+11719+11507	MA	FTN	BEA	FTP
008	12808+11724+11723+11722+11508	MA	FTN	BEA	FTP
009	12809+11727+11726+11725+11509	MA	FTN	BEA	FTP
010	12810+11730+11729+11728+11510	MA	FTN	BEA	FTP
011	12811+11733+11732+11731+11511	MA	FTN	BEA	FTP
012	12812+11736+11735+11734+11512	MA	FTN	BEA	FTP
013	12813+11739+11738+11737+11513	MA	FTN	BEA	FTP
Spare	12814	MA	FTN	BEA	FTP

Above & Left: *First TransPennine CAF-built Mk5 hauled stock and driving trailers commenced testing in autumn 2018 for a fleet introduction in 2019. The fixed formation five-car sets, powered by a hired-in DRS Class 68 carry the latest TPE multi-coloured livery. Sets are based at Manchester and will operate on all main Trans-Pennine routes. Above, Driving Trailer Standard No. 12801 arrives at Crewe, while the view left shows re-liveried DRS '68' No. 68020 Reliance. Both:* **Cliff Beeton**

Grand Central

Address: ✉ River House, 17 Museum Street, York, YO1 7DJ

✆ info@grandcentral.com

☎ 0845 603 4852

ⓘ www.grandcentral.co.uk

Managing Director: Richard McLean

Franchise Dates: Open Access Operator, to December 2026

Principal Routes: London King's Cross - Sunderland / Bradford

Depots: Heaton (HT)

Parent Company: Arriva PLC

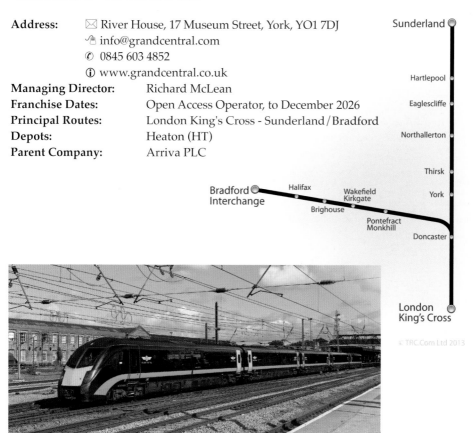

Sunderland
Hartlepool
Eaglescliffe
Northallerton
Thirsk
Bradford Interchange
Halifax
Wakefield Kirkgate
York
Brighouse
Pontefract Monkhill
Doncaster
London King's Cross

© TRC.Com Ltd 2013

Above: *Open access operator Grand Central, owned by Arriva Trains, currently operates a fleet of 10 Class 180 five-car Alstom sets on its routes from London King's Cross to Bradford and Sunderland. Over the last couple of years several former Great Western sets joined the fleet and now all units have been refurbished, carrying the regal-looking black and orange company livery. Set No. 180107 with its DMSL(B) leading, departs from Doncaster.* **CJM**

Class 180
Zephyr

Vehicle Length: (Driving) 75ft 7in (23.71m), (Inter) 75ft 5in (23.03m)			
Height: 12ft 4in (3.75m)		Engine: 1 x Cummins OSK19 of 750hp per vehicle	
Width: 9ft 2in (2.80m)		Horsepower: 3,750hp (2,796kW)	
		Seats (total/car): 42F/226S, 46S/42F/68S/56S/56S	

Number	Formation DMSL(A)+MFL+MSL+MSLRB+DMSL(B)	Depot	Livery	Owner	Operator	Name
180101	50901+54901+55901+56901+59901	HT	GTO	ANG	GTL	
180102	50902+54902+55902+56902+59902	HT	GTO	ANG	GTL	
180103	50903+54903+55903+56903+59903	HT	GTO	ANG	GTL	
180104	50904+54904+55904+56904+59904	HT	GTO	ANG	GTL	
180105	50905+54905+55905+56905+59905	HT	GTO	ANG	GTL	*The Yorkshire Artist Ashley Jackson*
180106	50906+54906+55906+56906+59906	HT	GTO	ANG	GTL	
180107	50907+54907+55907+56907+59907	HT	GTO	ANG	GTL	*Hart of the North*
180108	50908+54908+55908+56908+59908	HT	GTO	ANG	GTL	*William Shakespeare*
180112	50912+54912+55912+56912+59912	HT	GTO	ANG	GTL	*James Herriot Celebrating 100 Years 1916-2016*
180114	50914+54914+55914+56914+59914	HT	GTO	ANG	GTL	*Kirkgate Calling*

Greater Anglia

Address: ✉ 1 Ely Place, London, EC1N 6RY
✒ contactcentre@greateranglia.co.uk
✆ 0345 600 7245
ⓘ www.greateranglia.co.uk

Managing Director: Jamie Burles
Franchise Dates: 1 February 2012 - October 2025
Principal Routes: London Liverpool Street to Norwich, Cambridge, Enfield Town, Hertford East, Upminster, Southend Victoria, Southminster, Braintree, Sudbury, Clacton, Walton, Harwich Town, Felixstowe, Lowestoft, Great Yarmouth, Sheringham, Stansted Airport, Kings Lynn and Peterborough
Depots: Ilford (IL), Norwich (NC), Clacton (CC)
Parent Company: Abellio (60%), Mitsui (40%)

Class 90/0

Vehicle Length: 61ft 6in (18.74m)	Power Collection: 25kV ac overhead
Height: 13ft 0¼in (3.96m)	Horsepower: 7,860hp (5,860kW)
Width: 9ft 0in (2.74m)	Electrical Equipment: GEC

Number	Depot	Pool	Livery	Owner	Operator	Name
90001	NC	IANA	AWT	PTR	GAR	Crown Point
90002	NC	IANA	AWT	PTR	GAR	Eastern Daily Press 1870-2010 Serving Norfolk for 140 years
90003	NC	IANA	AWT	PTR	GAR	
90004	NC	IANA	AWT	PTR	GAR	City of Chelmsford
90005	NC	IANA	AWT	PTR	GAR	Vice-Admiral Lord Nelson
90006	NC	IANA	AWT	PTR	GAR	Roger Ford / Modern Railways Magazine
90007	NC	IANA	AWT	PTR	GAR	Sir John Betjeman
90008	NC	IANA	AWT	PTR	GAR	The East Anglian
90009	NC	IANA	AWT	PTR	GAR	
90010	NC	IANA	AWT	PTR	GAR	Bressingham Steam and Gardens
90011	NC	IANA	AWT	PTR	GAR	East Anglian Daily Times Suffolk & Proud
90012	NC	IANA	AWT	PTR	GAR	Royal Anglian Regiment
90013	NC	IANA	AWT	PTR	GAR	The Evening Star
90014	NC	IANA	AWT	PTR	GAR	Norfolk and Norwich Festival
90015	NC	IANA	AWT	PTR	GAR	Colchester Castle

Below: *A total train renewal policy is currently underway for Abellio Greater Anglia, with dozens of new main line and suburban trains currently on delivery. The present fleet of Class 90s will soon be replaced with new Class 745 multiple units. In GA white livery, No. 90009 leads a Mk3 rake into Ipswich, bound for London Liverpool Street.* **Nathan Williamson**

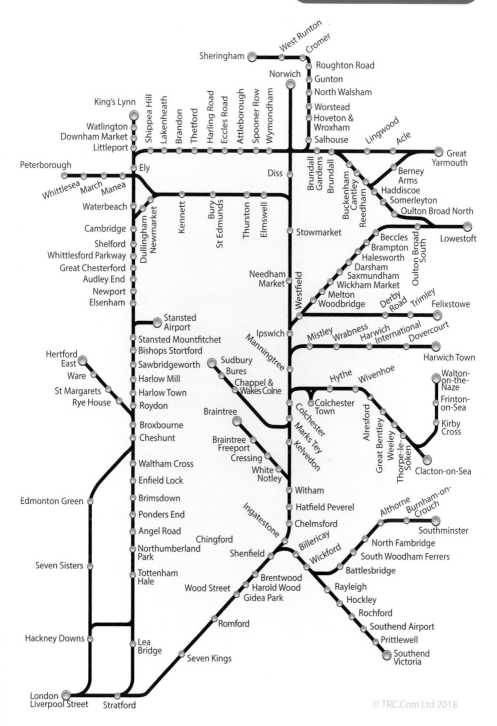

West Runton
Cromer
Sheringham
Roughton Road
Norwich
Gunton
North Walsham
Worstead
Hoveton &
Wroxham
Salhouse
Lingwood
Acle
Great
Yarmouth
King's Lynn
Shippea Hill
Lakenheath
Brandon
Thetford
Harling Road
Eccles Road
Attleborough
Spooner Row
Wymondham
Watlington
Downham Market
Littleport
Peterborough
Ely
Diss
Brundall
Gardens
Brundall
Berney
Arms
Haddiscoe
Somerleyton
Oulton Broad North
Whittlesea
March
Manea
Waterbeach
Kennett
Bury
St Edmunds
Thurston
Elmswell
Stowmarket
Buckenham
Cantley
Reedham
Cambridge
Shelford
Whittlesford Parkway
Great Chesterford
Audley End
Newport
Elsenham
Dullingham
Newmarket
Needham
Market
Westfield
Beccles
Brampton
Halesworth
Darsham
Saxmundham
Wickham Market
Melton
Woodbridge
Oulton Broad
South
Lowestoft
Derby
Road
Trimley
Felixstowe
Stansted
Airport
Ipswich
Mistley
Wrabness
Harwich
International
Dovercourt
Manningtree
Stansted Mountfitchet
Bishops Stortford
Harwich Town
Hertford
East
Ware
St Margarets
Rye House
Sawbridgeworth
Harlow Mill
Harlow Town
Roydon
Sudbury
Bures
Chappel &
Wakes Colne
Hythe
Wivenhoe
Walton-
on-the-
Naze
Frinton-
on-Sea
Kirby
Cross
Braintree
Colchester
Town
Alresford
Great Bentley
Weeley
Thorpe-le-
Soken
Broxbourne
Cheshunt
Colchester
Marks Tey
Kelvedon
Braintree
Freeport
Cressing
White
Notley
Clacton-on-Sea
Waltham Cross
Enfield Lock
Brimsdown
Ponders End
Angel Road
Witham
Hatfield Peverel
Althorne
Burnham-on-
Crouch
Edmonton Green
Chelmsford
Billericay
Wickford
Southminster
North Fambridge
South Woodham Ferrers
Ingatestone
Chingford
Shenfield
Battlesbridge
Northumberland
Park
Seven Sisters
Tottenham
Hale
Brentwood
Harold Wood
Gidea Park
Wood Street
Rayleigh
Hockley
Rochford
Southend Airport
Prittlewell
Romford
Hackney Downs
Lea
Bridge
Seven Kings
Southend
Victoria
London
Liverpool Street
Stratford

Greater Anglia

Mk3 Hauled Stock

Vehicle Length: 75ft 0in (22.86m)   Width: 8ft 11in (2.71m)
Height: 12ft 9in (3.88m)   Bogie Type: BT10

Passenger Train Operating Companies - Greater Anglia

AN2G - TSOB *Seating 52S*

10401 (12168)	NC	AWT	PTR
10402 (12010)	NC	AWT	PTR
10403 (12135)	NC	AWT	PTR
10404 (12068)	NC	AWT	PTR
10405 (12137)	NC	AWT	PTR
10406 (12020)	NC	AWT	PTR
10411 (10200)	NC	AWT	PTR
10412 (10203)	NC	AWT	PTR
10413 (10214)	NC	AWT	PTR
10414 (10216)	NC	AWT	PTR
10415 (10223)	NC	AWT	PTR
10416 (10228)	NC	AWT	PTR
10417 (10247)	NC	AWT	PTR

AD1G - FO, *FOD *Seating 48F/37F**

11066	NC	AWT	PTR
11067	NC	AWT	PTR
11068	NC	AWT	PTR
11069	NC	AWT	PTR
11070	NC	AWT	PTR
11072*	NC	AWT	PTR
11073*	NC	AWT	PTR
11075	NC	AWT	PTR
11076	NC	AWT	PTR
11077	NC	AWT	PTR
11078*	NC	AWT	PTR
11080	NC	AWT	PTR
11081	NC	AWT	PTR
11082	NC	AWT	PTR
11085*	NC	AWT	PTR
11087*	NC	AWT	PTR
11088*	NC	AWT	PTR
11090*	NC	AWT	PTR
11091*	NC	AWT	PTR
11092	NC	AWT	PTR
11093*	NC	AWT	PTR
11094*	NC	AWT	PTR
11095*	NC	AWT	PTR
11096*	NC	AWT	PTR
11098*	NC	AWT	PTR
11099*	NC	AWT	PTR
11100*	NC	AWT	PTR
11101*	NC	AWT	PTR

AC2G - TSO *Seating 80S*

12005	NC	AWT	PTR
12009	NC	AWT	PTR

12012	NC	AWT	PTR
12013	NC	AWT	PTR
12015	NC	AWT	PTR
12016	NC	AWT	PTR
12019	NC	AWT	PTR
12021	NC	AWT	PTR
12024	NC	AWT	PTR
12026	NC	AWT	PTR
12027	NC	AWT	PTR
12030	NC	AWT	PTR
12031	NC	AWT	PTR
12032	NC	AWT	PTR
12034	NC	AWT	PTR
12035	NC	AWT	PTR
12037	NC	AWT	PTR
12040	NC	AWT	PTR
12041	NC	AWT	PTR
12042	NC	AWT	PTR
12046	NC	AWT	PTR
12049	NC	AWT	PTR
12051	NC	AWT	PTR
12056	NC	AWT	PTR
12057	NC	AWT	PTR
12060	NC	AWT	PTR
12061	NC	AWT	PTR
12062	NC	AWT	PTR
12064	NC	AWT	PTR
12066	NC	AWT	PTR
12067	NC	AWT	PTR
12073	NC	AWT	PTR
12079	NC	AWT	PTR
12081	NC	AWT	PTR
12082	NC	AWT	PTR
12084	NC	AWT	PTR
12089	NC	AWT	PTR
12090	NC	AWT	PTR
12091	NC	AWT	PTR
12093	NC	AWT	PTR
12097	NC	AWT	PTR
12098	NC	AWT	PTR
12099	NC	AWT	PTR
12103	NC	AWT	PTR
12105	NC	AWT	PTR
12107	NC	AWT	PTR
12108	NC	AWT	PTR
12109	NC	AWT	PTR
12110	NC	AWT	PTR
12111	NC	AWT	PTR

12114	NC	AWT	PTR
12115	NC	AWT	PTR
12116	NC	AWT	PTR
12118	NC	AWT	PTR
12120	NC	AWT	PTR
12125	NC	AWT	PTR
12126	NC	AWT	PTR
12129	NC	AWT	PTR
12130	NC	AWT	PTR
12132	NC	AWT	PTR
12137	NC	AWT	PTR
12139	NC	AWT	PTR
12141	NC	AWT	PTR
12143	NC	AWT	PTR
12146	NC	AWT	PTR
12147	NC	AWT	PTR
12148	NC	AWT	PTR
12150	NC	AWT	PTR
12151	NC	AWT	PTR
12153	NC	AWT	PTR
12154	NC	AWT	PTR
12159	NC	AWT	PTR
12164	NC	AWT	PTR
12166	NC	AWT	PTR
12167	NC	AWT	PTR
12170	NC	AWT	PTR
12171	NC	AWT	PTR

NZAH - DVT

82102	NC	AWT	PTR
82103§	NC	AWT	PTR
82105	NC	AWT	PTR
82107	NC	AWT	PTR
82112	NC	AWT	PTR
82114	NC	AWT	PTR
82118	NC	AWT	PTR
82121	NC	AWT	PTR
82127	NC	AWT	PTR
82132	NC	AWT	PTR
82133	NC	AWT	PTR
82136	NC	AWT	PTR
82139	NC	AWT	PTR
82143	NC	AWT	PTR
82152	NC	AWT	PTR

§ Fitted with de-icing equipment

Left: *Currently, the London-Norwich service, which operates half hourly, is operated by Mk3 hauled stock formations, with Class 90s at the London end and DVTs at the country end. The Mk3s, all refurbished and carrying GA white livery, off-set with orange passenger doors are based at Norwich Crown Point depot. All Mk3s and Class 90s will go off-lease when new stock enters service. Much of which is unlikely to see further use. Mk3 TSO No. 12154 is shown.*
Antony Christie

Right: *Remote driving facilities on the Class 90/Mk3 formed Greater Anglia trains is provided by a fleet of Mk3 Driving Van Trailers (DVTs) which, some years ago, were displaced from the West Coast Main line. The DVTs are usually formed at the Norwich end of formations. All are painted in white/ black GA livery. DVT No. 82103 is shown.* **Nathan Williamson**

Class 153

Vehicle Length: 76ft 5in (23.29m)				Engine: 1 x NT855R5 of 285hp		
Height: 12ft 3½in (3.75m)				Horsepower: 285hp (213kW)		
Width: 8ft 10in (2.70m)				Seats (total/car): 72S		

Number	Formation DMSL	Depot	Livery	Owner	Operator	Name
153306	52306	NC	AWT	PTR	GAR	
153309	52309	NC	AWT	PTR	GAR	Gerard Fiennes
153314	52314	NC	AWT	PTR	GAR	
153322	52322	NC	AWT	PTR	GAR	Benjamin Britten
153335	52335	NC	AWT	PTR	GAR	Michael Palin

Right: *In 2019-2020 the existing fleet of five Class 153 'bubble' cars, based at Norwich Crown Point and deployed on rural routes, will be phased out of service as new Stadler 'Flirt' Class 755 sets enter traffic. These '153s' might see further use, possibly in Scotland, as luggage and cycle carriers. No. 153306 is seen at Great Yarmouth.* **Antony Christie**

Class 156

Vehicle Length: 75ft 6in (23.03m)				Engine: 1 x Cummins NT855R5 of 285hp per car		
Height: 12ft 6in (3.81m)				Horsepower: 570hp (425kW)		
Width: 8ft 11in (2.73m)				Seats (total/car): 136S, 62S/74S		

Number	Formation DMSL+DMS	Depot	Livery	Owner	Operator
156402	52402+57402	NC	AWT	PTR	GAR
156407	52407+57407	NC	AWT	PTR	GAR
156409	52409+57409	NC	AWT	PTR	GAR
156412	52412+57412	NC	AWT	PTR	GAR
156416	52416+57416	NC	AWT	PTR	GAR
156417	52417+57417	NC	AWT	PTR	GAR
156418	52418+57418	NC	AWT	PTR	GAR
156419	52419+57419	NC	AWT	PTR	GAR
156422	52422+57422	NC	AWT	PTR	GAR

Names applied
156416 *Saint Edmund*

156418 *ESTA 1965-2015*

Greater Anglia

Left: *For heavier used services radiating from Norwich, a fleet of nine two-car Class 156 'Super Sprinter' sets are based at Crown Point. Refurbished with disabled access toilets, these sets are likely to find new use when displaced from the Norwich area. With Wherry Line promotional branding, set No. 156409 stands at Norwich.*
Antony Christie

Class 170/2
Turbostar

Vehicle Length: 77ft 6in (23.62m)		Engine: 1 x MTU 6R 183TD13H of 422hp per vehicle
Height: 12ft 4½in (3.77m)		Horsepower: 1,266hp (944kW)
Width: 8ft 10in (2.69m)		Seats (total/car): 7F-173S 7F-39S/68S/66S

Number	Formation	Depot	Livery	Owner	Operator
	DMCL+MSL+DMSL				
170201	50201+56201+79201	NC	AWT	PTR	GAR
170202	50202+56202+79202	NC	AWT	PTR	GAR
170203	50203+56203+79203	NC	AWT	PTR	GAR
170204	50204+56204+79204	NC	AWT	PTR	GAR
170205	50205+56205+79205	NC	AWT	PTR	GAR
170206	50206+56206+79206	NC	AWT	PTR	GAR
170207	50207+56207+79207	NC	AWT	PTR	GAR
170208	50208+56208+79208	NC	AWT	PTR	GAR

Vehicle Length: 77ft 6in (23.62m)		Engine: 1 x MTU 6R 183TD13H of 422hp per vehicle
Height: 12ft 4½in (3.77m)		Horsepower: 844hp (629kW)
Width: 8ft 10in (2.69m)		Seats (total/car): 9F-110S 57S/9F-53S

Number	Formation	Depot	Livery	Owner	Operator		Number	Formation	Depot	Livery	Owner	Operator
	DMSL+DMCL						170271	50271+79271	NC	AWT	PTR	GAR
							170272	50272+79272	NC	AWT	PTR	GAR
170270	50270+79270	NC	AWT	PTR	GAR		170273	50273+79273	NC	AWT	PTR	GAR

Left: *The two breeds of Class 170 'Turbostar' allocated to GA at Norwich and used on some of the longer distance services, are scheduled to transfer to Transport for Wales when displaced by new Stadler 'Flirt' sets. The 170s have recently been refurbished and now sport GA white livery with orange passenger doors. Three-car set No. 170201 is seen at Lowestoft.*
Antony Christie

Class 317/3

Vehicle Length: (Driving) 65ft 0¾in (19.83m)	Width: 9ft 3in (2.82m)	
(Inter) 65ft 4¼in (19.92m)	Horsepower: 1,000hp (746kW)	
Height: 12ft 1½in (3.58m)	Seats (total/car): 22F/269S, 74S/79S/22F-46S/70S	

Number	Formation	Depot	Livery	Owner	Operator	Name
	DTSO+MSO+TCO+DTSO					
317337	77036+62671+71613+77084	IL	TLK	ANG	GAR	
317338	77037+62698+71614+77085	IL	TLK	ANG	GAR	
317339	77038+62699+71615+77086	IL	TLK	ANG	GAR	
317340	77039+62700+71616+77087	IL	TLK	ANG	GAR	
317341	77040+62701+71617+77088	IL	AWT	ANG	GAR	
317342	77041+62702+71618+77089	IL	TLK	ANG	GAR	
317343	77042+62703+71619+77090	IL	TLK	ANG	GAR	
317344	77029+62690+71620+77091	IL	AWT	ANG	GAR	
317345	77044+62705+71621+77092	IL	AWT	ANG	GAR	*Driver John Webb*

317346	77045+62706+71622+77093	IL	AWT	ANG	GAR	
317347	77046+62707+71623+77094	IL	AWT	ANG	GAR	
317348	77047+62708+71624+77095	IL	TLK	ANG	GAR	*Richard A. Jenner*

Right: *The Greater Anglia Class 317 stock is due to be replaced by brand new Bombardier-built Class 720 'Aventra' stock from 2019. The '317s' which started life as 'Bed-Pan' stock on the St Pancras to Bedford electrification are unlikely to find much further use, with a high number of quality electric sets due to come off lease in the near future. Class 317/3 No. 317341, a phase 1 set is seen at Harlow Town in unbranded white livery with sky blue passenger doors.* **CJM**

Class 317/5

Vehicle Length: (Driving) 65ft 0¾in (19.83m) Width: 9ft 3in (2.82m)
(Inter) 65ft 4¼in (19.92m) Horsepower: 1,000hp (746kW)
Height: 12ft 1½in (3.58m) Seats (total/car): 291S, 74S/79S/68S/70S

Number	Former Number	Formation DTSO(A)+MSO+TCO+DTSO(B)	Depot	Livery	Owner	Operator	Name
317501	(317301)	77024+62661+71577+77048	IL	AWT	ANG	GAR	
317502	(317302)	77001+62662+71578+77049	IL	AWT	ANG	GAR	
317503	(317303)	77002+62663+71579+77050	IL	AWT	ANG	GAR	
317504	(317304)	77003+62664+71580+77051	IL	AWT	ANG	GAR	
317505	(317305)	77004+62665+71581+77052	IL	AWT	ANG	GAR	
317506	(317306)	77005+62666+71582+77053	IL	AWT	ANG	GAR	
317507	(317307)	77006+62667+71583+77054	IL	AWT	ANG	GAR	*University of Cambridge 800 years 1209-2009*
317508	(317311)	77010+62697+71587+77058	IL	AWT	ANG	GAR	
317509	(317312)	77011+62672+71588+77059	IL	AWT	ANG	GAR	
317510	(317313)	77012+62673+71589+77060	IL	TLK	ANG	GAR	
317511	(317315)	77014+62675+71591+77062	IL	AWT	ANG	GAR	
317512	(317316)	77015+62676+71592+77063	IL	AWT	ANG	GAR	
317513	(317317)	77016+62677+71593+77064	IL	AWT	ANG	GAR	
317514	(317318)	77017+62678+71594+77065	IL	AWT	ANG	GAR	
317515	(317320)	77019+62680+71596+77067	IL	AWT	ANG	GAR	

Right: *Refurbished Class 317/5, upgraded from a Class 317/3, No. 317506 is seen on a West Anglia service from Liverpool Street passing Bethnal Green. These all standard class sets seat 291. The Greater Anglia '317s' are all based at Ilford depot. In autumn 2018, some sets were receiving universal toilets and a passenger information system, set No. 317506 was one of the first to be modified.* **CJM**

Class 317/6

Vehicle Length: (Driving) 65ft 0¾in (19.83m) Width: 9ft 3in (2.82m)
(Inter) 65ft 4¼in (19.92m) Horsepower: 1,000hp (746kW)
Height: 12ft 1½in (3.58m) Seats (total/car): 24F/244S, 64S/70S/62S/24F-48S

Number	Former Number	Formation DTSO+MSO+TSO+DTCO	Depot	Livery	Owner	Operator	Name
317649	(317349)	77200+62846+71734+77220	IL	AWT	ANG	GAR	
317650	(317350)	77201+62847+71735+77221	IL	AWT	ANG	GAR	

Greater Anglia

317651	(317351)	77202+62848+71736+77222	IL	AWT	ANG	GAR	
317652	(317352)	77203+62849+71739+77223	IL	AWT	ANG	GAR	
317653	(317353)	77204+62850+71738+77224	IL	AWT	ANG	GAR	
317654	(317354)	77205+62851+71737+77225	IL	NXU	ANG	GAR	*Richard Wells*
317655	(317355)	77206+62852+71740+77226	IL	AWT	ANG	GAR	
317656	(317356)	77207+62853+71742+77227	IL	AWT	ANG	GAR	
317657	(317357)	77208+62854+71741+77228	IL	NXU	ANG	GAR	
317658	(317358)	77209+62855+71743+77229	IL	AWT	ANG	GAR	
317659	(317359)	77210+62856+71744+77230	IL	AWT	ANG	GAR	
317660	(317360)	77211+62857+71745+77231	IL	AWT	ANG	GAR	
317661	(317361)	77212+62858+71746+77232	IL	AWT	ANG	GAR	
317662	(317362)	77213+62859+71747+77233	IL	AWT	ANG	GAR	
317663	(317363)	77214+62860+71748+77234	IL	AWT	ANG	GAR	
317664	(317364)	77215+62861+71749+77235	IL	AWT	ANG	GAR	
317665	(317365)	77216+62862+71750+77236	IL	AWT	ANG	GAR	
317666	(317366)	77217+62863+71752+77237	IL	NXU	ANG	GAR	
317667	(317367)	77218+62864+71751+77238	IL	AWT	ANG	GAR	
317668	(317368)	77219+62865+71753+77239	IL	AWT	ANG	GAR	
317669	(317369)	77280+62886+71762+77284	IL	NXU	ANG	GAR	
317670	(317370)	77281+62887+71763+77285	IL	AWT	ANG	GAR	
317671	(317371)	77282+62888+71764+77286	IL	AWT	ANG	GAR	
317672	(317372)	77283+62889+71765+77287	IL	AWT	ANG	GAR	

Left: *Phase 2 Class 317s were built with a rounded and more pleasing cab roof profile. This design is demonstrated by Class 317/6 set No. 317652 seen passing Bethnal Green. This set sports Greater Anglia white livery, off-set by dark blue passenger doors.* **CJM**

Class 317/8

Vehicle Length: (Driving) 65ft 0¾in (19.83m) Width: 9ft 3in (2.82m)
(Inter) 65ft 4¼in (19.92m) Horsepower: 1,000hp (746kW)
Height: 12ft 1½in (3.58m) Seats (total/car): 20F/265S, 74S/79S/20F-42S/70S

Number	Former Number	Formation DTSO(A)+MSO+TCO+DTSO(B)	Depot	Livery	Owner	Operator
317881	(317321)	77020+62681+71597+77068	IL	AWT	ANG	GAR
317882	(317324)	77023+62684+71600+77071	IL	NXU	ANG	GAR
317883	(317325)	77000+62685+71601+77072	IL	AWT	ANG	GAR
317884	(317326)	77025+62686+71602+77073	IL	AWT	ANG	GAR
317885	(317327)	77026+62687+71603+77074	IL	AWT	ANG	GAR
317886	(317328)	77027+62688+71604+77075	IL	AWT	ANG	GAR

Class 321/3

Vehicle Length: (Driving) 65ft 0¾in (19.83m) Width: 9ft 3in (2.82m)
(Inter) 65ft 4¼in (19.92m) Horsepower: 1,328hp (996kW)
Height: 12ft 4¾in (3.78m) Seats (total/car): 16F/292S, 16F-57S/82S/75S/78S

Number	Formation DTCO+MSO+TSO+DTSO	Depot	Livery	Owner	Operator	Name
321301	78049+62975+71880+77853	IL	GAZ	EVL	GAR	
321302	78050+62976+71881+77854	IL	GAZ	EVL	GAR	
321303	78051+62977+71882+77855	IL	GAZ	EVL	GAR	
321304	78052+62978+71883+77856	IL	GAZ	EVL	GAR	
321305	78053+62979+71884+77857	IL	GAZ	EVL	GAR	
321306	78054+62980+71885+77858	IL	GAZ	EVL	GAR	
321307	78055+62981+71886+77859	IL	GAZ	EVL	GAR	
321308	78056+62982+71887+77860	IL	GAZ	EVL	GAR	
321309	78057+62983+71888+77861	IL	GAZ	EVL	GAR	
321310	78058+62984+71889+77862	IL	GAZ	EVL	GAR	

Right: *Although the Class 321s will be phased out following the introduction of new stock, a major refurbishment project is currently being undertaken on the first 30 sets to convert them to ac traction and upgrade interiors with air conditioning and revised fittings including a disabled access toilet. The sets know as 'Renatus', display a revised Greater Anglia livery. Set No. 321309 is illustrated from its standard class driving car at Stratford.*
CJM

321311	78059+62985+71890+77863	IL	GAZ	EVL	GAR	
321312	78060+62986+71891+77864	IL	GAZ	EVL	GAR	
321313	78061+62987+71892+77865	IL	GAZ	EVL	GAR	
321314	78062+62988+71893+77866	IL	GAZ	EVL	GAR	
321315	78063+62989+71894+77867	IL	GAZ	EVL	GAR	
321316	78064+62990+71895+77868	IL	GAZ	EVL	GAR	
321317	78065+62991+71896+77869	IL	GAZ	EVL	GAR	
321318	78066+62992+71897+77870	IL	GAZ	EVL	GAR	
321319	78067+62993+71898+77871	IL	GAZ	EVL	GAR	
321320	78068+62994+71899+77872	IL	GAZ	EVL	GAR	
321321	78069+62995+71900+77873	IL	GAZ	EVL	GAR	*NSPCC Essex Full Stop*
321322	78070+62996+71901+77874	IL	GAZ	EVL	GAR	
321323	78071+62997+71902+77875	IL	GAZ	EVL	GAR	
321324	78072+62998+71903+77876	IL	GAZ	EVL	GAR	
321325	78073+62999+71904+77877	IL	GAZ	EVL	GAR	
321326	78074+63000+71905+77878	IL	GAZ	EVL	GAR	
321327	78075+63001+71906+77879	IL	GAZ	EVL	GAR	
321328	78076+63002+71907+77880	IL	GAZ	EVL	GAR	
321329	78077+63003+71908+77881	IL	GAZ	EVL	GAR	
321330	78078+63004+71909+77882	IL	GAR	EVL	GAR	
321331	78079+63005+71910+77883	IL	NXU	EVL	GAR	
321332	78080+63006+71911+77884	IL	NXU	EVL	GAR	
321333	78081+63007+71912+77885	IL	NXU	EVL	GAR	*Amsterdam*
321334	78082+63008+71913+77886	IL	NXU	EVL	GAR	
321335	78083+63009+71914+77887	IL	NXU	EVL	GAR	*Geoffrey Freeman Allen*
321336	78084+63010+71915+77888	IL	NXU	EVL	GAR	
321337	78085+63011+71916+77889	IL	NXU	EVL	GAR	
321338	78086+63012+71917+77890	IL	NXU	EVL	GAR	
321339	78087+63013+71918+77891	IL	NXU	EVL	GAR	
321340	78088+63014+71919+77892	IL	NXU	EVL	GAR	
321341	78089+63015+71920+77893	IL	NXU	EVL	GAR	
321342	78090+63016+71921+77894	IL	NXU	EVL	GAR	*R Barnes*
321343	78091+63017+71922+77895	IL	NXU	EVL	GAR	
321344	78092+63018+71923+77896	IL	NXU	EVL	GAR	
321345	78093+63019+71924+77897	IL	NXU	EVL	GAR	
321346	78094+63020+71925+77898	IL	NGU	EVL	GAR	
321347	78131+63105+71991+78280	IL	NXU	EVL	GAR	
321348	78132+63106+71992+78281	IL	NXU	EVL	GAR	
321349	78133+63107+71993+78282	IL	NGE	EVL	GAR	
321350	78134+63108+71994+78283	IL	NXU	EVL	GAR	*Gurkha*
321351	78135+63109+71995+78284	IL	NXU	EVL	GAR	*London Southend Airport*
321352	78136+63110+71996+78285	IL	NXU	EVL	GAR	
321353	78137+63111+71997+78286	IL	NXU	EVL	GAR	
321354	78138+63112+71998+78287	IL	NXU	EVL	GAR	
321355	78139+63113+71999+78288	IL	NXU	EVL	GAR	
321356	78140+63114+72000+78289	IL	NGU	EVL	GAR	
321357	78141+63115+72001+78290	IL	NGE	EVL	GAR	

Passenger Train Operating Companies - Greater Anglia

Greater Anglia

321358	78142+63116+72002+78291	IL	NXU	EVL	GAR	
321359	78143+63117+72003+78292	IL	AWT	EVL	GAR	
321360	78144+63118+72004+78293	IL	NXU	EVL	GAR	*Phoenix*
321361	78145+63119+72005+78294	IL	AWT	EVL	GAR	
321362	78146+63120+72006+78295	IL	AWT	EVL	GAR	
321363	78147+63121+72007+78296	IL	AWT	EVL	GAR	
321364	78148+63122+72008+78297	IL	AWT	EVL	GAR	
321365	78149+63123+72009+78298	IL	AWT	EVL	GAR	
321366	78150+63124+72010+78299	IL	AWT	EVL	GAR	

Class 321/4

Vehicle Length: (Driving) 65ft 0¾in (19.83m) Width: 9ft 3in (2.82m)
(Inter) 65ft 4¼in (19.92m) Horsepower: 1,328hp (996kW)
Height: 12ft 4¾in (3.78m) Seats (total/car): 16F/283S, 16F-52S/79S/74S/78S

Number	Formation	Depot	Livery	Owner	Operator	Name/Note
	DTCO+MSO+TSO+DTSO					
321403	78097+63065+71950+77945	IL	BLU	EVL	GAR	*(For ScotRail operation as 320/4)*
321405	78099+63067+71953+77947	IL	BLU	EVL	GAR	
321406	78100+63068+71954+77948	IL	BLU	EVL	GAR	
321407	78101+63069+71955+77949	IL	BLU	EVL	GAR	
321408	78102+63070+71956+77959	IL	BLU	EVL	GAR	
321409	78103+63071+71957+77960	IL	BLU	EVL	GAR	
321410	78104+63072+71958+77961	IL	BLU	EVL	GAR	
321419	78113+63081+71969+77963	IL	BLU	EVL	GAR	
321421	78115+63083+71969+77963	IL	NXU	EVL	GAR	
321422	78116+63084+71970+77964	IL	NXU	EVL	GAR	
321423	78117+63085+71971+77965	IL	NXU	EVL	GAR	
321424	78118+63086+71972+77966	IL	GAR	EVL	GAR	
321425	78119+63087+71973+77967	IL	AWT	EVL	GAR	
321426	78120+63088+71974+77968	IL	GAR	EVL	GAR	
321427	78121+63089+71975+77969	IL	GAR	EVL	GAR	
321428	78122+63090+71976+77970	IL	AWT	EVL	GAR	*The Essex Commuter*
321429	78123+62091+71977+77971	IL	GAR	EVL	GAR	
321430	78124+63092+71978+77972	IL	GAR	EVL	GAR	
321431	78151+63125+72011+78300	IL	GAR	EVL	GAR	
321432	78152+63126+72012+78301	IL	NXU	EVL	GAR	
321433	78153+63127+72013+78302	IL	NXU	EVL	GAR	
321434	78154+63128+72014+78303	IL	NXU	EVL	GAR	
321435	78155+63129+72015+78304	IL	NXU	EVL	GAR	
321436	78156+63130+72016+78305	IL	NXU	EVL	GAR	
321437	78157+63131+72017+78306	IL	NXU	EVL	GAR	
321438	78158+63132+72018+78307	IL	AWT	EVL	GAR	
321439	78159+63133+72019+78308	IL	AWT	EVL	GAR	
321440	78160+63134+72020+78309	IL	AWT	EVL	GAR	
321441	78161+63135+72021+78310	IL	AWT	EVL	GAR	
321442	78162+63136+72022+78311	IL	AWT	EVL	GAR	*Crouch Valley 1889-2014*
321443	78125+63099+71985+78274	IL	AWT	EVL	GAR	
321444	78126+63100+71986+78275	IL	AWT	EVL	GAR	*Essex Lifeboats*
321445	78127+63101+71987+78276	IL	AWT	EVL	GAR	
321446	78128+63102+71988+78277	IL	AWT	EVL	GAR	*George Mullings*
321447	78129+63103+71989+78278	IL	AWT	EVL	GAR	
321448§	78130+63104+71990+78279	IL	ADV	EVL	GAR	

§ Eversholt development train consisting of two vehicles with Metro interior and two with suburban, seating 246 passengers and allocated to Ilford for demonstration running on Abellio Greater Anglia services.

Class 360/1
Desiro

Vehicle Length: 66ft 9in (20.4m) Horsepower: 1,341hp (1,000kW)
Height: 12ft 1½in (3.7m) Seats (total/car): 16F/265S, 8F-59S/69S/78S/8F-59S
Width: 9ft 2in (2.79m)

Number	Formation	Depot	Livery	Owner	Operator
	DMCO(A)+PTSO+TSO+DMCO(B)				
360101	65551+72551+74551+68551	IL	FNA	ANG	GAR
360102	65552+72552+74552+68552	IL	FNA	ANG	GAR
360103	65553+72553+74553+68553	IL	FNA	ANG	GAR
360104	65554+72554+74554+68554	IL	FNA	ANG	GAR
360105	65555+72555+74555+68555	IL	FNA	ANG	GAR

360106	65556+72556+74556+68556	IL	FNA	ANG	GAR
360107	65557+72557+74557+68557	IL	FNA	ANG	GAR
360108	65558+72558+74558+68558	IL	FNA	ANG	GAR
360109	65559+72559+74559+68559	IL	FNA	ANG	GAR
360110	65560+72560+74560+68560	IL	FNA	ANG	GAR
360111	65561+72561+74561+68561	IL	FNA	ANG	GAR
360112	65562+72562+74562+68562	IL	FNA	ANG	GAR
360113	65563+72563+74563+68563	IL	FNA	ANG	GAR
360114	65564+72564+74564+68564	IL	FNA	ANG	GAR
360115	65565+72565+74565+68565	IL	FNA	ANG	GAR
360116	65566+72566+74566+68566	IL	FNA	ANG	GAR
360117	65567+72567+74567+68567	IL	FNA	ANG	GAR
360118	65568+72568+74568+68568	IL	FNA	ANG	GAR
360119	65569+72569+74569+68569	IL	FNA	ANG	GAR
360120	65570+72570+74570+68570	IL	FNA	ANG	GAR
360121	65571+72571+74571+68571	IL	FNA	ANG	GAR

Right: *Another fleet which will be returned to the lease owner after new stock has been introduced are the 21 Siemens 'Desiro' Class 360 four-car sets. These units are currently allocated to Ilford and operate longer distance outer-suburban services. Set No. 360113 is shown approaching Stratford.* **CJM**

Class 379
Electrostar

Vehicle Length: (Driving) 66ft 9in (20.40m)
(Inter) 65ft 6in (19.99m)
Height: 12ft 4in (3.77m)
Width: 9ft 2in (2.80m)
Horsepower: 2,010hp (1,500kW)
Seats (total/car): 20F/189S, 60S/62S/43S/20F-24S

Number	Formation	Depot	Livery	Owner	Operator	Name
	DMSO(A)+MSO+TSO+DMCO					
379001	61201+61701+61901+62101	IL	NXU	MAG	GAR	
379002	61202+61702+61902+62102	IL	NXU	MAG	GAR	
379003	61203+61703+61903+62103	IL	NXU	MAG	GAR	
379004	61204+61704+61904+62104	IL	NXU	MAG	GAR	
379005	61205+61705+61905+62105	IL	NXU	MAG	GAR	*Stansted Express*
379006	61206+61706+61906+62106	IL	NXU	MAG	GAR	
379007	61207+61707+61907+62107	IL	NXU	MAG	GAR	
379008	61208+61708+61908+62108	IL	NXU	MAG	GAR	
379009	61209+61709+61909+62109	IL	NXU	MAG	GAR	
379010	61210+61710+61910+62110	IL	NXU	MAG	GAR	
379011	61211+61711+61911+62111	IL	NXU	MAG	GAR	*Ely Cathedral*
379012	61212+61712+61912+62112	IL	NXU	MAG	GAR	*The West Anglian*
379013	61213+61713+61913+62113	IL	NXU	MAG	GAR	
379014	61214+61714+61914+62114	IL	NXU	MAG	GAR	
379015	61215+61715+61915+62115	IL	NXU	MAG	GAR	*City of Cambridge*
379016	61216+61716+61916+62116	IL	NXU	MAG	GAR	
379017	61217+61717+61917+62117	IL	NXU	MAG	GAR	
379018	61218+61718+61918+62118	IL	NXU	MAG	GAR	
379019	61219+61719+61919+62119	IL	NXU	MAG	GAR	
379020	61220+61720+61920+62120	IL	NXU	MAG	GAR	
379021	61221+61721+61921+62121	IL	NXU	MAG	GAR	
379022	61222+61722+61922+62122	IL	NXU	MAG	GAR	
379023	61223+61723+61923+62123	IL	NXU	MAG	GAR	
379024	61224+61724+61924+62124	IL	NXU	MAG	GAR	
379025	61225+61725+61925+62125	IL	NXU	MAG	GAR	*Go Discover*
379026	61226+61726+61926+62126	IL	NXU	MAG	GAR	

Greater Anglia

379027	61227+61727+61927+62127	IL	NXU	MAG	GAR
379028	61228+61728+61928+62128	IL	NXU	MAG	GAR
379029	61229+61729+61929+62129	IL	NXU	MAG	GAR
379030	61230+61730+61930+62130	IL	NXU	MAG	GAR

Left: Built as part of the Bombardier 'Electrostar' family in 2010-2011, the 30 Greater Anglia Class 379s used on the Liverpool Street to Stansted Airport route will soon be replaced with Class 744s. The future for these modern units is in doubt and they could face disposal if a new operator can not be found. With Greater Anglia/Stansted Airport branding, set No. 379021 is seen passing Bethnal Green en route to Stansted Airport. CJM

Class 720/1
Aventra

Vehicle Length: Driving: 24.47m
Int: 24.21m
Seats (total/car):

Horsepower:
Height:
Width:

10-car sets

Number Formation
DMSO+PMSOL+MSO+MSO+TSO+MSO+PMSOL+MSO+MSO+DTSOL
DT+M3L+M2+PM+EMLW I ET+M3+M2+PML+DM

Depot Livery Owner Op'r

720101	450101+451101+452101+453101+454101+455101+456101+457101+458101+459101	IL	GAR	ANG	GAR
720102	450102+451102+452102+453102+454102+455102+456102+457102+458102+459102	IL	GAR	ANG	GAR
720103	450103+451103+452103+453103+454103+455103+456103+457103+458103+459103	IL	GAR	ANG	GAR
720104	450104+451104+452104+453104+454104+455104+456104+457104+458104+459104	IL	GAR	ANG	GAR
720105	450105+451105+452105+453105+454105+455105+456105+457105+458105+459105	IL	GAR	ANG	GAR
720106	450106+451106+452106+453106+454106+455106+456106+457106+458106+459106	IL	GAR	ANG	GAR
720107	450107+451107+452107+453107+454107+455107+456107+457107+458107+459107	IL	GAR	ANG	GAR
720108	450108+451108+452108+453108+454108+455108+456108+457108+458108+459108	IL	GAR	ANG	GAR
720109	450109+451109+452109+453109+454109+455109+456109+457109+458109+459109	IL	GAR	ANG	GAR
720110	450110+451110+452110+453110+454110+455110+456110+457110+458110+459110	IL	GAR	ANG	GAR
720111	450111+451111+452111+453111+454111+455111+456111+457111+458111+459111	IL	GAR	ANG	GAR
720112	450112+451112+452112+453112+454112+455112+456112+457112+458112+459112	IL	GAR	ANG	GAR
720113	450113+451113+452113+453113+454113+455113+456113+457113+458113+459113	IL	GAR	ANG	GAR
720114	450114+451114+452114+453114+454114+455114+456114+457114+458114+459114	IL	GAR	ANG	GAR
720115	450115+451115+452115+453115+454115+455115+456115+457115+458115+459115	IL	GAR	ANG	GAR
720116	450116+451116+452116+453116+454116+455116+456116+457116+458116+459116	IL	GAR	ANG	GAR
720117	450117+451117+452117+453117+454117+455117+456117+457117+458117+459117	IL	GAR	ANG	GAR
720118	450118+451118+452118+453118+454118+455118+456118+457118+458118+459118	IL	GAR	ANG	GAR
720119	450119+451119+452119+453119+454119+455119+456119+457119+458119+459119	IL	GAR	ANG	GAR
720120	450120+451120+452120+453120+454120+455120+456120+457120+458120+459120	IL	GAR	ANG	GAR
720121	450121+451121+452121+453121+454121+455121+456121+457121+458121+459121	IL	GAR	ANG	GAR
720122	450122+451122+452122+453122+454122+455122+456122+457122+458122+459122	IL	GAR	ANG	GAR

Class 720/5
Aventra

Vehicle Length: Driving: 24.47m
Int: 24.21m
Seats (total/car):

Horsepower:
Height:
Width:

5-car sets

Number Formation
DMSO+PMSOL+MSO+MSO+DTSOL
DTLW+M3+M2+PML+DM

Depot Livery Owner Operator

720501	450501+451501+452501+453501+459501	IL	GAR	ANG	GAR
720502	450502+451502+452502+453502+459502	IL	GAR	ANG	GAR
720503	450503+451503+452503+453503+459503	IL	GAR	ANG	GAR
720504	450504+451504+452504+453504+459504	IL	GAR	ANG	GAR
720505	450505+451505+452505+453505+459505	IL	GAR	ANG	GAR
720506	450506+451506+452506+453506+459506	IL	GAR	ANG	GAR
720507	450507+451507+452507+453507+459507	IL	GAR	ANG	GAR

720508	450508+451508+452508+453508+459508	IL	GAR	ANG	GAR
720509	450509+451509+452509+453509+459509	IL	GAR	ANG	GAR
720510	450510+451510+452510+453510+459510	IL	GAR	ANG	GAR
720511	450511+451511+452511+453511+459511	IL	GAR	ANG	GAR
720512	450512+451512+452512+453512+459512	IL	GAR	ANG	GAR
720513	450513+451513+452513+453513+459513	IL	GAR	ANG	GAR
720514	450514+451514+452514+453514+459514	IL	GAR	ANG	GAR
720515	450515+451515+452515+453515+459515	IL	GAR	ANG	GAR
720516	450516+451516+452516+453516+459516	IL	GAR	ANG	GAR
720517	450517+451517+452517+453517+459517	IL	GAR	ANG	GAR
720518	450518+451518+452518+453518+459518	IL	GAR	ANG	GAR
720519	450519+451519+452519+453519+459519	IL	GAR	ANG	GAR
720520	450520+451520+452520+453520+459520	IL	GAR	ANG	GAR
720521	450521+451521+452521+453521+459521	IL	GAR	ANG	GAR
720522	450522+451522+452522+453522+459522	IL	GAR	ANG	GAR
720523	450523+451523+452523+453523+459523	IL	GAR	ANG	GAR
720524	450524+451524+452524+453524+459524	IL	GAR	ANG	GAR
720525	450525+451525+452525+453525+459525	IL	GAR	ANG	GAR
720526	450526+451526+452526+453526+459526	IL	GAR	ANG	GAR
720527	450527+451527+452527+453527+459527	IL	GAR	ANG	GAR
720528	450528+451528+452528+453528+459528	IL	GAR	ANG	GAR
720529	450529+451529+452529+453529+459529	IL	GAR	ANG	GAR
720530	450530+451530+452530+453530+459530	IL	GAR	ANG	GAR
720531	450531+451531+452531+453531+459531	IL	GAR	ANG	GAR
720532	450532+451532+452532+453532+459532	IL	GAR	ANG	GAR
720533	450533+451533+452533+453533+459533	IL	GAR	ANG	GAR
720534	450534+451534+452534+453534+459534	IL	GAR	ANG	GAR
720535	450535+451535+452535+453535+459535	IL	GAR	ANG	GAR
720536	450536+451536+452536+453536+459536	IL	GAR	ANG	GAR
720537	450537+451537+452537+453537+459537	IL	GAR	ANG	GAR
720538	450538+451538+452538+453538+459538	IL	GAR	ANG	GAR
720539	450539+451539+452539+453539+459539	IL	GAR	ANG	GAR
720540	450540+451540+452540+453540+459540	IL	GAR	ANG	GAR
720541	450541+451541+452541+453541+459541	IL	GAR	ANG	GAR
720542	450542+451542+452542+453542+459542	IL	GAR	ANG	GAR
720543	450543+451543+452543+453543+459543	IL	GAR	ANG	GAR
720544	450544+451544+452544+453544+459544	IL	GAR	ANG	GAR
720545	450545+451545+452545+453545+459545	IL	GAR	ANG	GAR
720546	450546+451546+452546+453546+459546	IL	GAR	ANG	GAR
720547	450547+451547+452547+453547+459547	IL	GAR	ANG	GAR
720548	450548+451548+452548+453548+459548	IL	GAR	ANG	GAR
720549	450549+451549+452549+453549+459549	IL	GAR	ANG	GAR
720550	450550+451550+452550+453550+459550	IL	GAR	ANG	GAR
720551	450551+451551+452551+453551+459551	IL	GAR	ANG	GAR
720552	450552+451552+452552+453552+459552	IL	GAR	ANG	GAR

Right: *During 2019, the large fleet of Bombardier 'Aventra' five and ten car sets will enter service on Greater Anglia, replacing many of the Class 317, 321, 360 and 379 sets. Built at the Derby Litchurch Lane factory, these sets commenced rolling off the production line in autumn 2018. The sets will be based at Ilford depot. One of the first complete vehicles is seen inside the Bombardier factory in Derby in September 2018.* **Antony Christie**

Greater Anglia

720553	450553+451553+452553+453553+459553	IL	GAR	ANG	GAR
720554	450554+451554+452554+453554+459554	IL	GAR	ANG	GAR
720555	450555+451555+452555+453555+459555	IL	GAR	ANG	GAR
720556	450556+451556+452556+453556+459556	IL	GAR	ANG	GAR
720557	450557+451557+452557+453557+459557	IL	GAR	ANG	GAR
720558	450558+451558+452558+453558+459558	IL	GAR	ANG	GAR
720559	450559+451559+452559+453559+459559	IL	GAR	ANG	GAR
720560	450560+451560+452560+453560+459560	IL	GAR	ANG	GAR
720561	450561+451561+452561+453561+459561	IL	GAR	ANG	GAR
720562	450562+451562+452562+453562+459562	IL	GAR	ANG	GAR
720563	450563+451563+452563+453563+459563	IL	GAR	ANG	GAR
720564	450564+451564+452564+453564+459564	IL	GAR	ANG	GAR
720565	450565+451565+452565+453565+459565	IL	GAR	ANG	GAR
720566	450566+451566+452566+453566+459566	IL	GAR	ANG	GAR
720567	450567+451567+452567+453567+459567	IL	GAR	ANG	GAR
720568	450568+451568+452568+453568+459568	IL	GAR	ANG	GAR
720569	450569+451569+452569+453569+459569	IL	GAR	ANG	GAR
720570	450570+451570+452570+453570+459570	IL	GAR	ANG	GAR
720571	450571+451571+452571+453571+459571	IL	GAR	ANG	GAR
720572	450572+451572+452572+453572+459572	IL	GAR	ANG	GAR
720573	450573+451573+452573+453573+459573	IL	GAR	ANG	GAR
720574	450574+451574+452574+453574+459574	IL	GAR	ANG	GAR
720575	450575+451575+452575+453575+459575	IL	GAR	ANG	GAR
720576	450576+451576+452576+453576+459576	IL	GAR	ANG	GAR
720577	450577+451577+452577+453577+459577	IL	GAR	ANG	GAR
720578	450578+451578+452578+453578+459578	IL	GAR	ANG	GAR
720579	450579+451579+452579+453579+459579	IL	GAR	ANG	GAR
720580	450580+451580+452580+453580+459580	IL	GAR	ANG	GAR
720581	450581+451581+452581+453581+459581	IL	GAR	ANG	GAR
720582	450582+451582+452582+453582+459582	IL	GAR	ANG	GAR
720583	450583+451583+452583+453583+459583	IL	GAR	ANG	GAR
720584	450584+451584+452584+453584+459584	IL	GAR	ANG	GAR
720585	450585+451585+452585+453585+459585	IL	GAR	ANG	GAR
720586	450586+451586+452586+453586+459586	IL	GAR	ANG	GAR
720587	450587+451587+452587+453587+459587	IL	GAR	ANG	GAR
720588	450588+451588+452588+453588+459588	IL	GAR	ANG	GAR
720589	450589+451589+452589+453589+459589	IL	GAR	ANG	GAR

Class 745
Flirt

Vehicle Length:	*Horsepower:*
Height:	*Seats (total/car):*
Width:	

Class 745/0 - InterCity main line sets

Number	Formation	Depot	Livery	Owner	Operator
	DMF+PTF+TS(A)+TS(B)+TS(C)+MS(A)+MS(B)+TS(D)+TS(E)+TS(F)+PTS+DMS				
745001	413001+426001+332001+343001+341001+301001+				
	302001+342001+344001+346001+322001+312001	NC	GAR	ROK	GAR
745002	413002+426002+332002+334002+341002+301002+				
	302002+342002+344002+346002+322002+312002	NC	GAR	ROK	GAR
745003	413003+426003+332003+343003+341003+301003+				
	302003+342003+344003+346003+322003+312003	NC	GAR	ROK	GAR
745004	413004+426004+332004+343004+341004+301004+				
	302004+342004+344004+346004+322004+312004	NC	GAR	ROK	GAR
745005	413005+426005+332005+343005+341005+301005+				
	302005+342005+344005+346005+322005+312005	NC	GAR	ROK	GAR
745006	413006+426006+332006+343006+341006+301006+				
	302006+342006+344006+346006+322006+312006	NC	GAR	ROK	GAR
745007	413007+426007+332007+343007+341007+301007+				
	302007+342007+344007+346007+322007+312007	NC	GAR	ROK	GAR
745008	413008+426008+332008+343008+341008+301008+				
	302008+342008+344008+346008+322008+312008	NC	GAR	ROK	GAR
745009	413009+426009+332009+343009+341009+301009+				
	302009+342009+344009+346009+322009+312009	NC	GAR	ROK	GAR
745010	413010+426010+332010+343010+341010+301010+				
	302010+342010+344010+346010+322010+312010	NC	GAR	ROK	GAR

Class 745/1 - Airport Express sets

Number	Formation DMS+PTS+TS(A)+TS(B)+TS(C)+MS(A)+MS(B)+TS(D)+TS(E)+TS(F)+PTS+SMS	Depot	Livery	Owner	Operator
745101	313001+326101+332101+343101+341101+301101+ 302101+342101+344101+346101+322101+312101	IL	GAR	ROK	GAR
745102	313002+326102+332102+343102+341102+301102+ 302102+342102+344102+346102+322102+312102	IL	GAR	ROK	GAR
745103	313003+326103+332103+343103+341103+301103+ 302103+342103+344103+346103+322103+312103	IL	GAR	ROK	GAR
745104	313004+326104+332104+343104+341104+301104+ 302104+342104+344104+346104+322104+312104	IL	GAR	ROK	GAR
745105	313005+326105+332105+343105+341105+301105+ 302105+342105+344105+346105+322105+312105	IL	GAR	ROK	GAR
745106	313006+326106+332106+343106+341106+301106+ 302106+342106+344106+346106+322106+312106	IL	GAR	ROK	GAR
745107	313007+326107+332107+343107+341107+301107+ 302107+342107+344107+346107+322107+312107	IL	GAR	ROK	GAR
745108	313008+326108+332108+343108+341108+301108+ 302108+342108+344108+346108+322108+312108	IL	GAR	ROK	GAR
745109	313009+326109+332109+343109+341109+301109+ 302109+342109+344109+346109+322109+312109	IL	GAR	ROK	GAR
745110	313010+326110+332110+343110+341110+301110+ 302110+342110+344110+346110+322110+312110	IL	GAR	ROK	GAR

Class 755/3
Flirt - Bi-Mode

Train Length: 65m   *Output Electric: 2,600kW, Diesel: 960kW*
TPP Length: 6.69m   *Seats (total/car): 136S 60S/-/32S/52S*
Width (pass): 2.72m, (PP) 2.82m

3-car sets

Number	Formation DMS(1)+ PP+PTSW+DMS(2)	Depot	Livery	Owner	Operator
755325	911325+971325+981325+912325	NC	GAR	ROK	GAR
755326	911326+971326+981326+912326	NC	GAR	ROK	GAR
755327	911327+971327+981327+912327	NC	GAR	ROK	GAR
755328	911328+971328+981328+912328	NC	GAR	ROK	GAR
755329	911329+971329+981329+912329	NC	GAR	ROK	GAR
755330	911330+971330+981330+912330	NC	GAR	ROK	GAR
755331	911331+971331+981331+912331	NC	GAR	ROK	GAR
755332	911332+971332+981332+912332	NC	GAR	ROK	GAR
755333	911333+971333+981333+912333	NC	GAR	ROK	GAR
755334	911334+971334+981334+912334	NC	GAR	ROK	GAR
755335	911335+971335+981335+912335	NC	GAR	ROK	GAR
755336	911336+971336+981336+912336	NC	GAR	ROK	GAR
755337	911337+971337+981337+912337	NC	GAR	ROK	GAR
755338	911338+971338+981338+912338	NC	GAR	ROK	GAR

Right: *The Class 755 interior is based on the 2+2 style, with a mix of airline and group seats. Each passenger coach has one pair of bi-parting sliding plug doors. The between coach gangway is of a wide, open style. Above seat luggage racks, arm rests, fixed tables or fold down tables, coat hooks and charging points are provided throughout. The floors are carpeted. The passenger walkway through the power pack car has a sliding door from the passenger saloons.* **CJM**

Passenger Train Operating Companies - Greater Anglia

Greater Anglia

Class 755/4
Flirt - Bi-Mode

Train Length: 80.7m	Output Electric: 2,600kW, Diesel: 1,920kW
TPP Length: 6.69m	Seats (total/car): 196S 60S/56S/-/32S/52S
Width (pass): 2.72m, (PP) 2.82m	

4-car sets

Number	Formation DMS(1)+PTS+PP+PTSW+DMS(2)	Depot	Livery	Owner	Operator
755401	911401+961401+971401+981401+912401	NC	GAR	ROK	GAR
755402	911402+961402+971402+981402+912402	NC	GAR	ROK	GAR
755403	911403+961403+971403+981403+912403	NC	GAR	ROK	GAR
755404	911404+961404+971404+981404+912404	NC	GAR	ROK	GAR
755405	911405+961405+971405+981405+912405	NC	GAR	ROK	GAR
755406	911406+961406+971406+981406+912406	NC	GAR	ROK	GAR
755407	911407+961407+971407+981407+912407	NC	GAR	ROK	GAR
755408	911408+961408+971408+981408+912408	NC	GAR	ROK	GAR
755409	911409+961409+971409+981409+912409	NC	GAR	ROK	GAR
755410	911410+961410+971410+981410+912410	NC	GAR	ROK	GAR
755411	911411+961411+971411+981411+912411	NC	GAR	ROK	GAR
755412	911412+961412+971412+981412+912412	NC	GAR	ROK	GAR
755413	911413+961413+971413+981413+912413	NC	GAR	ROK	GAR
755414	911414+961414+971414+981414+912414	NC	GAR	ROK	GAR
755415	911415+961415+971415+981415+912415	NC	GAR	ROK	GAR
755416	911416+961416+971416+981416+912416	NC	GAR	ROK	GAR
755417	911417+961417+971417+981417+912417	NC	GAR	ROK	GAR
755418	911418+961418+971418+981418+912418	NC	GAR	ROK	GAR
755419	911419+961419+971419+981419+912419	NC	GAR	ROK	GAR
755420	911420+961420+971420+981420+912420	NC	GAR	ROK	GAR
755421	911421+961421+971421+981421+912421	NC	GAR	ROK	GAR
755422	911422+961422+971422+981422+912422	NC	GAR	ROK	GAR
755423	911423+961423+971423+981423+912423	NC	GAR	ROK	GAR
755424	911424+961424+971424+981424+912424	NC	GAR	ROK	GAR

Left: *The new Class 755/3 and 755/4 Stadler 'Flirt' sets due to be introduced on Greater Anglia from 2019 are currently on test in Europe and the UK. Set No. 744405 is seen at the Innotrans Trade Fair in Germany in September 2018, where Stadler showcased the design.* **CJM**

Right: *For the first time in a UK modern train design, the Class 755s incorporate a Power Pack or 'PP' vehicle in the middle of the formation housing the main traction system, including the diesel/alternator packs (two on a three-car and four on a four-car set). Traction for the train is however performed by the outer bogie of each driving car. The articulated PP coach for set No. 755405 is shown.* **CJM**

Island Line

Address: ✉ Ryde St Johns Road Station, Ryde, Isle of Wight, PO33 2BA
✎ info@island-line.co.uk ℂ 01983 812591 ⓘ www.island-line.co.uk

General Manager: Andy Naylor
Franchise Dates: Part of SWR franchise until August 2023
Principal Route: Ryde Pier Head - Shanklin
Owned Stations: All
Depots: Ryde St Johns Road (RY)
Parent Company: First Group (70%), MTR (30%)

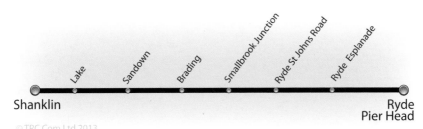

©TRC.Com Ltd 2013

Class 483

Vehicle Length: 52ft 4in (15.95m)	Horsepower: 670hp (500kW)
Height: 9ft 5½in (2.88m)	Seats (total/car): 82S, 40S/42S
Width: 8ft 8½in (2.65m)	

Number	Formation DMSO+DMSO	Depot	Livery	Owner	Operator
(483)002	122+222	RY	LUL	SWR	SWR §
(483)004	124+224	RY	LUL	SWR	SWR
(483)006	126+226	RY	LUL	SWR	SWR
(483)007	127+227	RY	LUL	SWR	SWR
(483)008	128+228	RY	LUL	SWR	SWR
(483)009	129+229	RY	LUL	SWR	SWR §

§ Stored out of service

Below: *Modernisation has still not been announced for the short, isolated, Isle of Wight line linking Ryde Pier Head with Shanklin. Currently a fleet of six two-car modified ex London Transport 1938 stock trains work the service, all are painted in mock LU red livery. Set No. 008 is seen heading towards Shanklin from Sandown. It has been put forward for investment, to purchase five, two-car Class 230 Vivarail sets, converted from ex-LUL 'D' stock.* **Antony Christie**

Govia Thameslink Railway

Address: Thameslink, Hertford House, 1 Cranwood Street, London, EC1V 9QS
✆ icustomer service@thameslinkrailway.com 📞 0345 0264700
ⓘ www.thameslinkrailway.com

Managing Director: Patrick Verwer.   **Chief Executive Officer:** Steve White

Franchise Dates: September 2014 - September 2021

Principal Routes: London Victoria / London Bridge to Brighton, 'Coastway' route, Uckfield / East Grinstead. Services to Surrey / Sussex, London King's Cross - King's Lynn, Peterborough / Cambridge, Moorgate - Hertford Loop / Letchworth, Bedford - Brighton / Sutton / Wimbledon

Depots: Bedford Cauldwell Walk (BF), Brighton (BI), Hornsey (HE), Selhurst (SU), Stewarts Lane (SL), Three Bridges (TB)

Parent Company: Govia

Passenger Train Operating Companies - Govia Thameslink Railway

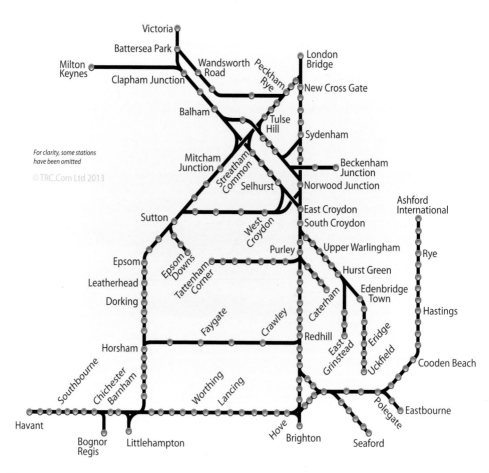

For clarity, some stations have been omitted

©TRC.Com Ltd 2013

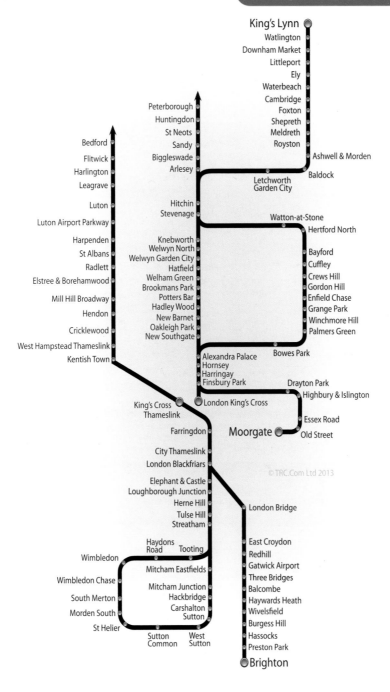

Passenger Train Operating Companies – Govia Thameslink Railway

Govia Thameslink Railway

Class 73/2

Vehicle Length: 53ft 8in (16.35m)
Height: 12ft 5⅜in (3.79m)
Width: 8ft 8in (2.64m)

Power: 750V dc third rail or English Electric 6K
Horsepower: E/D - 1,600hp (1,193kW) / 600hp (447kW)
Electrical Equipment: English Electric

Number	Depot	Pool	Livery	Owner	Operator	Name
73202 (73137)	SL	MBED	SOU	PTR	GTR	*Graham Stenning*

Class 171/2
Turbostar

Vehicle Length: 77ft 6in (23.62m)
Height: 12ft 4½in (3.77m)
Width: 8ft 10in (2.69m)

Engine: 1 x MTU 6R 183TD13H of 422hp per vehicle
Horsepower: 844hp (629kW)
Seats (total/car): 9F-107S 9F-43S/64S

Number	Former Number	Formation DMCL+DMSL	Depot	Livery	Owner	Operator
171201	(170421)	50421+79421	SU	SOU	EVL	GTR
171202	(170423)	50423+79423	SU	SOU	EVL	GTR

Class 171/4
Turbostar

Vehicle Length: 77ft 6in (23.62m)
Height: 12ft 4½in (3.77m)
Width: 8ft 10in (2.69m)

Engine: 1 x MTU 6R 183TD13H of 422hp per vehicle
Horsepower: 1,688hp (1,259kW)
Seats (total/car): 9F-259S 9F-43S/76S/76S/64S

Number	Former Number	Formation DMCL+MS+MS+DMSL	Depot	Livery	Owner	Operator
171401	(170422)	50422+56421+56422+79422	SU	SOU	EVL	GTR
171402	(170424)	50424+56423+56424+79424	SU	SOU	EVL	GTR

Class 171/7
Turbostar

Vehicle Length: 77ft 6in (23.62m)
Height: 12ft 4½in (3.77m)
Width: 8ft 10in (2.69m)

Engine: 1 x MTU 6R 183TD13H of 422hp per vehicle
Horsepower: 844hp (629kW)
Seats (total/car): 9F-107S 9F-43S/64S

Number	Formation DMCL+DMSL	Depot	Livery	Owner	Operator
171721	50721+79721	SU	SOU	PTR	GTR
171722	50722+79722	SU	SOU	PTR	GTR
171723	50723+79723	SU	SOU	PTR	GTR
171724	50724+79724	SU	SOU	PTR	GTR
171725	50725+79725	SU	SOU	PTR	GTR
171726	50726+79726	SU	SOU	PTR	GTR
171727	50727+79727	SU	SOU	PTR	GTR
171728	50728+79728	SU	SOU	PTR	GTR
171729	50729+79729	SU	SOU	PTR	GTR
171730	50392+79392	SU	SOU	PTR	GTR

171730 previously numbered 170392

Left: *The Southern operating arm of the Govia Thameslink franchise operates a fleet of Class 171 'Turbostar' sets on non electrified routes. The two and four-car sets are based at Selhurst and operate on duties from London Bridge. Further Class 170/4 sets are due to transfer from Scotland. Two-car set No. 171727 is viewed from its DMSL vehicle.* **CJM**

Class 171/8
Turbostar

Vehicle Length: 77ft 6in (23.62m)
Height: 12ft 4½in (3.77m)
Width: 8ft 10in (2.69m)

Engine: 1 x MTU 6R 183TD13H of 422hp per vehicle
Horsepower: 1,688hp (1,259kW)
Seats (total/car): 18F-241S 9F-43S/74S/74S/9F-50S

Number	Formation DMCL(A)+MS+MS+DMCL(B)	Depot	Livery	Owner	Operator
171801	50801+54801+56801+79801	SU	SOU	PTR	GTR
171802	50802+54802+56802+79802	SU	SOU	PTR	GTR
171803	50803+54803+56803+79803	SU	SOU	PTR	GTR
171804	50804+54804+56804+79804	SU	SOU	PTR	GTR
171805	50805+54805+56805+79805	SU	SOU	PTR	GTR
171806	50806+54806+56806+79806	SU	SOU	PTR	GTR

Above: *With its Driving Motor Composite Lavatory A (DMCL-A) nearest the camera, four car sets Nos. 171801 and 171806 pass Forest Hill, with a London Bridge to Uckfield service. The four-car Class 171s seat 18 first and 241 standard class passengers.* CJM

Class 313/0 & 313/1

Vehicle Length: (Driving) 64ft 11½in (20.75m)	Width: 9ft 3in (2.82m)
(Inter) 65ft 4¼in (19.92m)	Horsepower: 880hp (656kW)
Height: 11ft 9in (3.58m)	Seats (total/car): 231S, 74S/83S/74S

Number	Formation DMSO+PTSO+BDMSO	Depot	Livery	Owner	Operator	Name
313018	62546+71230+62160	HE	FCC	EVL	GTR	
313024	62552+71236+62616	HE	FCC	EVL	GTR	
313025	62553+71237+62617	HE	FCC	EVL	GTR	
313026	62554+71238+62618	HE	FCC	EVL	GTR	
313027	62555+71239+62619	HE	FCC	EVL	GTR	
313028	62556+71240+62620	HE	FCC	EVL	GTR	
313029	62557+71241+62621	HE	FCC	EVL	GTR	
313030	62558+71242+62622	HE	FCC	EVL	GTR	
313031	62559+71243+62623	HE	FCC	EVL	GTR	
313032	62560+71244+62643	HE	FCC	EVL	GTR	
313033	62561+71245+62625	HE	FCC	EVL	GTR	
313035	62563+71247+62627	HE	FCC	EVL	GTR	
313036	62564+71248+62628	HE	FCC	EVL	GTR	
313037	62565+71249+62629	HE	FCC	EVL	GTR	
313038	62566+71250+62630	HE	FCC	EVL	GTR	
313039	62567+71251+62631	HE	FCC	EVL	GTR	
313040	62568+71252+62632	HE	FCC	EVL	GTR	
313041	62569+71253+62633	HE	FCC	EVL	GTR	
313042	62570+71254+62634	HE	FCC	EVL	GTR	
313043	62571+71255+62635	HE	FCC	EVL	GTR	
313044	62572+71256+62636	HE	FCC	EVL	GTR	
313045	62573+71257+62637	HE	FCC	EVL	GTR	
313046	62574+71258+62638	HE	FCC	EVL	GTR	
313047	62575+71259+62639	HE	FCC	EVL	GTR	
313048	62576+71260+62640	HE	FCC	EVL	GTR	
313049	62577+71261+62641	HE	FCC	EVL	GTR	
313050	62578+71262+62649	HE	FCC	EVL	GTR	
313051	62579+71263+62624	HE	FCC	EVL	GTR	
313052	62580+71264+62644	HE	FCC	EVL	GTR	
313053	62581+71265+62645	HE	FCC	EVL	GTR	
313054	62582+71266+62646	HE	FCC	EVL	GTR	*Captain William Leefe Robinson VC*
313055	62583+71267+62647	HE	FCC	EVL	GTR	
313056	62584+71268+62648	HE	FCC	EVL	GTR	
313057	62585+71269+62642	HE	FCC	EVL	GTR	

Govia Thameslink Railway

313058	62586+71270+62650	HE	FCC	EVL	GTR	
313059	62587+71271+62651	HE	FCC	EVL	GTR	
313060	62588+71272+62652	HE	FCC	EVL	GTR	
313061	62589+71273+62653	HE	FCC	EVL	GTR	
313062	62590+71274+62654	HE	FCC	EVL	GTR	
313063	62591+71275+62655	HE	FCC	EVL	GTR	
313064	62592+71276+62656	HE	FCC	EVL	GTR	
313122	62550+71234+62614	HE	FCC	EVL	GTR	*Eric Roberts 1946-2012 'The Flying Nottsman'*
313123	62551+71235+62615	HE	FCC	EVL	GTR	
313134	62562+71246+62626	HE	FCC	EVL	GTR	*City of London*

Left: *Soon to be withdrawn and services taken over by new Class 717 'Desiro City' sets, the 1972-design Class 313s are currently allocated to Hornsey and operate on the Great Northern local services from Moorgate. Displaying Great Northern branded First Group 'Urban Lights' colours, set No. 313056 is seen between Drayton Park and Finsbury Park.*
Jamie Squibbs

Class 313/2

Vehicle Length: (Driving) 64ft 11½in (20.75m) Width: 9ft 3in (2.82m)
(Inter) 65ft 4½in (19.92m) Horsepower: 880hp (656kW)
Height: 11ft 9in (3.58m) Seats (total/car): 202S, 66S/70S/66S

Number	Formation DMSO+PTSO+BDMSO	Depot	Livery	Owner	Operator
313201 (313001/101)	62529+71213+62593	BI	BLG	BEA	GTR
313202 (313002/102)	62530+71214+62594	BI	SOU	BEA	GTR
313203 (313003/103)	62531+71215+62595	BI	SOU	BEA	GTR
313204 (313004/104)	62532+71216+62596	BI	SOU	BEA	GTR
313205 (313005/105)	62533+71217+62597	BI	SOU	BEA	GTR
313206 (313006/106)	62534+71218+62598	BI	SOU	BEA	GTR
313207 (313007/107)	62535+71219+62599	BI	SOU	BEA	GTR
313208 (313008/108)	62536+71220+62600	BI	SOU	BEA	GTR
313209 (313009/109)	62537+71221+62601	BI	SOU	BEA	GTR
313210 (313010/110)	62538+71222+62602	BI	SOU	BEA	GTR
313211 (313011/111)	62539+71223+62603	BI	SOU	BEA	GTR
313212 (313012/112)	62540+71224+62604	BI	SOU	BEA	GTR
313213 (313013/113)	62541+71225+62605	BI	SOU	BEA	GTR
313214 (313014/114)	62542+71226+62606	BI	SOU	BEA	GTR
313215 (313015/115)	62543+71227+62607	BI	SOU	BEA	GTR
313216 (313016/116)	62544+71228+62608	BI	SOU	BEA	GTR
313217 (313017/117)	62545+71229+61609	BI	SOU	BEA	GTR
313219 (313019/119)	62547+71231+61611	BI	SOU	BEA	GTR
313220 (313020/120)	62548+71232+61612	BI	SOU	BEA	GTR

Left: *Owned by Beacon Rail and operated by GTR Southern is a fleet of 19 Class 313/2s, allocated to Brighton for 'Coastway' services, radiating from Brighton. In 2017, set No. 313201 (the original 313001) was returned to traffic following overhaul painted near original BR blue and grey livery, now off-set by grey passenger doors. Displaying its 1970s livery, the set is seen at Ford.*
Antony Christie

Class 365
Networker Express

Vehicle Length: (Driving) 68ft 6½in (20.89m)	Width: 9ft 2½in (2.81m)		
(Inter) 65ft 9¼in (20.89m)	Horsepower: 1,684hp (1,256kW)		
Height: 12ft 4½in (3.77m)	Seats (total/car): 24F/239S, 12F-56S/59S/68S/12F-56S		

Number	Formation DMCO(A)+TSO+PTSO+DMCO(B)	Depot	Livery	Owner	Operator	Name
365502	65895+72243+72242+65936	HE	TLK	EVL	GTR	
365504	65897+72247+72246+65938	HE	TLK	EVL	GTR	
365506	65899+72251+72250+65940	HE	TLK	EVL	GTR	
365508	65901+72255+72254+65942	HE	TLK	EVL	GTR	
365510	65903+72259+72258+65944	HE	TLK	EVL	GTR	
365511	65904+72261+72260+65945	HE	TLK	EVL	-	
365512	65905+72263+72262+65946	HE	TLK	EVL	GTR	
365514	65907+72267+72266+65948	HE	TLK	EVL	GTR	
365516	65909+72271+72270+65950	HE	TLK	EVL	GTR	
365518	65911+72275+72274+65952	HE	TLK	EVL	GTR	
365520	65913+72279+72278+65954	HE	TLK	EVL	GTR	
365522	65915+72283+72282+65956	HE	TLK	EVL	GTR	
365524	65917+72287+72286+65958	HE	TLK	EVL	GTR	
365528	65921+72295+72294+65962	HE	TLK	EVL	GTR	
365530	65923+72299+72298+65964	HE	TLK	EVL	GTR	
365531	65924+72301+72300+65965	HE	TLK	EVL	-	
365532	65925+72303+72302+65966	HE	TLK	EVL	GTR	
365534	65927+72307+72306+65968	HE	TLK	EVL	GTR	
365536	65929+72311+72310+65970	HE	TLK	EVL	GTR	
365538	65931+72315+72314+65972	HE	TLK	EVL	GTR	
365539	65932+72317+72316+65973	HE	TLK	EVL	-	
365540	65933+72319+72318+65974	HE	TLK	EVL	GTR	
365541	65934+72321+72320+65975	HE	TLK	EVL	-	

Right: *Since the introduction of Class 385 and 700 sets on GTR Great Northern services, a large number of Class 365 'Networker Express' sets have been stored. Ten sets were transferred to Scottish Railways in 2018 to reduce problems with late delivery of Class 385 stock. It is expected that a large number of '365s' will be taken out of service and stored. Non operational set No. 365515 is illustrated passing Harringay.* **Nathan Williamson**

19 of the 40 sets are to be retained after the full fleets of Class 385 and 700s are in service, the remaining sets will be stored.

Class 377/1
Electrostar

Vehicle Length: (Driving) 66ft 9in (20.3m)	Width: 9ft 2in (2.79m)		
(Inter) 65ft 6in (19.96m)	Horsepower: 2,012hp (1,500kW)		
Height: 12ft 4in (3.75m)	Seats (total/car): 24F-210S or 244S 12F-48S(56S)/62S(70S)/52S(62S)/12F-48S(56S)		

Number	Formation DMCO(A)+MSO+TSO+DMCO(B)	Depot	Livery	Owner	Operator
377101	78501+77101+78901+78701	SU	SOU	PTR	GTR
377102	78502+77102+78902+78702	SU	SOU	PTR	GTR
377103	78503+77103+78903+78703	SU	SOU	PTR	GTR
377104	78504+77104+78904+78704	SU	SOU	PTR	GTR
377105	78505+77105+78905+78705	SU	SOU	PTR	GTR
377106	78506+77106+78906+78706	SU	SOU	PTR	GTR
377107	78507+77107+78907+78707	SU	SOU	PTR	GTR
377108	78508+77108+78908+78708	SU	SOU	PTR	GTR
377109	78509+77109+78909+78709	SU	SOU	PTR	GTR
377110	78510+77110+78910+78710	SU	SOU	PTR	GTR
377111	78511+77111+78911+78711	SU	SOU	PTR	GTR

Passenger Train Operating Companies - Govia Thameslink Railway

Govia Thameslink Railway

377112	78512+77112+78912+78712	SU	SOU	PTR	GTR
377113	78513+77113+78913+78713	SU	SOU	PTR	GTR
377114	78514+77114+78914+78714	SU	SOU	PTR	GTR
377115	78515+77115+78915+78715	SU	SOU	PTR	GTR
377116	78516+77116+78916+78716	SU	SOU	PTR	GTR
377117	78517+77117+78917+78717	SU	SOU	PTR	GTR
377118	78518+77118+78918+78718	SU	SOU	PTR	GTR
377119	78519+77119+78919+78719	SU	SOU	PTR	GTR
377120	78520+77120+78920+78720	SU	SOU	PTR	GTR
377121	78521+77121+78921+78721	SU	SOU	PTR	GTR
377122	78522+77122+78922+78722	SU	SOU	PTR	GTR
377123	78523+77123+78923+78723	SU	SOU	PTR	GTR
377124	78524+77124+78924+78724	SU	SOU	PTR	GTR
377125	78525+77125+78925+78725	SU	SOU	PTR	GTR
377126	78526+77126+78926+78726	SU	SOU	PTR	GTR
377127	78527+77127+78927+78727	SU	SOU	PTR	GTR
377128	78528+77128+78928+78728	SU	SOU	PTR	GTR
377129	78529+77129+78929+78729	SU	SOU	PTR	GTR
377130	78530+77130+78930+78730	SU	SOU	PTR	GTR
377131	78531+77131+78931+78731	SU	SOU	PTR	GTR
377132	78532+77132+78932+78732	SU	SOU	PTR	GTR
377133	78533+77133+78933+78733	SU	SOU	PTR	GTR
377134	78534+77134+78934+78734	SU	SOU	PTR	GTR
377135	78535+77135+78935+78735	SU	SOU	PTR	GTR
377136	78536+77136+78936+78736	SU	SOU	PTR	GTR
377137	78537+77137+78937+78737	SU	SOU	PTR	GTR
377138	78538+77138+78938+78738	SU	SOU	PTR	GTR
377139	78539+77139+78939+78739	SU	SOU	PTR	GTR
377140	78540+77140+78940+78740	SU	SOU	PTR	GTR
377141	78541+77141+78941+78741	SU	SOU	PTR	GTR
377142	78542+77142+78942+78742	SU	SOU	PTR	GTR
377143	78543+77143+78943+78743	SU	SOU	PTR	GTR
377144	78544+77144+78944+78744	SU	SOU	PTR	GTR
377145	78545+77145+78945+78745	SU	SOU	PTR	GTR
377146	78546+77146+78946+78746	SU	SOU	PTR	GTR
377147	78547+77147+78947+78747	SU	SOU	PTR	GTR
377148	78548+77148+78948+78748	SU	SOU	PTR	GTR
377149	78549+77149+78949+78749	SU	SOU	PTR	GTR
377150	78550+77150+78950+78750	SU	SOU	PTR	GTR
377151	78551+77151+78951+78751	SU	SOU	PTR	GTR
377152	78552+77152+78952+78752	SU	SOU	PTR	GTR
377153	78553+77153+78953+78753	SU	SOU	PTR	GTR
377154	78554+77154+78954+78754	SU	SOU	PTR	GTR
377155	78555+77155+78955+78755	SU	SOU	PTR	GTR
377156	78556+77156+78956+78756	SU	SOU	PTR	GTR
377157	78557+77157+78957+78757	SU	SOU	PTR	GTR
377158	78558+77158+78958+78758	SU	SOU	PTR	GTR

Left: *The core traction for GTR Southern, introduced to replace slam door stock is a sizeable fleet of Class 377s of various sub classes, allocated to Selhurst depot, with maintenance also carried out at Brighton. Class 377/1 No. 377131 is viewed from its DMSO(B). The TSO on these sets has a well for a pantograph but is not fitted for ac power collection.*
Antony Christie

377159	78559+77159+78959+78759	SU	SOU	PTR	GTR
377160	78560+77160+78960+78760	SU	SOU	PTR	GTR
377161	78561+77161+78961+78761	SU	SOU	PTR	GTR
377162	78562+77162+78962+78762	SU	SOU	PTR	GTR
377163	78563+77163+78963+78763	SU	SOU	PTR	GTR
377164	78564+77164+78964+78764	SU	SOU	PTR	GTR

Class 377/2
Electrostar

Vehicle Length: (Driving) 66ft 9in (20.3m)   *Width: 9ft 2in (2.79m)*
(Inter) 65ft 6in (19.96m)   *Horsepower: 2,012hp (1,500kW)*
Height: 12ft 4in (3.75m)   *Seats (total/car): 24F-222S, 12F-48S/69S/57S/12F-48S*

Number	Formation DMCO(A)+MSO+PTSO+DMCO(B)	Depot	Livery	Owner	Operator
377201	78571+77171+78971+78771	SU	SOU	PTR	GTR
377202	78572+77172+78972+78772	SU	SOU	PTR	GTR
377203	78573+77173+78973+78773	SU	SOU	PTR	GTR
377204	78574+77174+78974+78774	SU	SOU	PTR	GTR
377205	78575+77175+78975+78775	SU	SOU	PTR	GTR
377206	78576+77176+78976+78776	SU	SOU	PTR	GTR
377207	78577+77177+78977+78777	SU	SOU	PTR	GTR
377208	78578+77178+78978+78778	SU	SOU	PTR	GTR
377209	78579+77179+78979+78779	SU	SOU	PTR	GTR
377210	78580+77180+78980+78780	SU	SOU	PTR	GTR
377211	78581+77181+78981+78781	SU	SOU	PTR	GTR
377212	78582+77182+78982+78782	SU	SOU	PTR	GTR
377213	78583+77183+78983+78783	SU	SOU	PTR	GTR
377214	78584+77184+78984+78784	SU	SOU	PTR	GTR
377215	78585+77185+78985+78785	SU	SOU	PTR	GTR

Right: *Dual ac/dc power equipment is fitted to the 15 members of Class 377/2, thus enabling sets to operate from south to north London by way of the West London Line through Kensington Olympia. Today, while the ac/dc power equipment is retained, the units tend to operate GTR Southern domestic services. Set No. 377204 is shown at Hurst Green.* **Antony Christie**

Class 377/3
Electrostar

Vehicle Length: (Driving) 66ft 9in (20.3m)   *Width: 9ft 2in (2.79m)*
(Inter) 65ft 6in (19.96m)   *Horsepower: 2,012hp (1,500kW)*
Height: 12ft 4in (3.75m)   *Seats (total/car): 12F-163S, 60S/56S/12F-48S*

Number		Formation DMSO+TSO+DMCO	Depot	Livery	Owner	Operator
377301	(375311)	68201+74801+68401	SU	SOU	PTR	GTR
377302	(375312)	68202+74802+68402	SU	SOU	PTR	GTR
377303	(375313)	68203+74803+68403	SU	SOU	PTR	GTR
377304	(375314)	68204+74804+68404	SU	SOU	PTR	GTR
377305	(375315)	68205+74805+68405	SU	SOU	PTR	GTR
377306	(375316)	68206+74806+68406	SU	SOU	PTR	GTR
377307	(375317)	68207+74807+68407	SU	SOU	PTR	GTR
377308	(375318)	68208+74808+68408	SU	SOU	PTR	GTR
377309	(375319)	68209+74809+68409	SU	SOU	PTR	GTR
377310	(375320)	68210+74810+68410	SU	SOU	PTR	GTR
377311	(375321)	68211+74811+68411	SU	SOU	PTR	GTR

Govia Thameslink Railway

377312	(375322)	68212+74812+68412	SU	SOU	PTR	GTR
377313	(375323)	68213+74813+68413	SU	SOU	PTR	GTR
377314	(375324)	68214+74814+68414	SU	SOU	PTR	GTR
377315	(375325)	68215+74815+68415	SU	SOU	PTR	GTR
377316	(375326)	68216+74816+68416	SU	SOU	PTR	GTR
377317	(375327)	68217+74817+68417	SU	SOU	PTR	GTR
377318	(375328)	68218+74818+68418	SU	SOU	PTR	GTR
377319	(375329)	68219+74819+68419	SU	SOU	PTR	GTR
377320	(375330)	68220+74820+68420	SU	SOU	PTR	GTR
377321	(375331)	68221+74821+68421	SU	SOU	PTR	GTR
377322	(375332)	68222+74822+68422	SU	SOU	PTR	GTR
377323	(375333)	68223+74823+68423	SU	SOU	PTR	GTR
377324	(375334)	68224+74824+68424	SU	SOU	PTR	GTR
377325	(375335)	68225+74825+68425	SU	SOU	PTR	GTR
377326	(375336)	68226+74826+68426	SU	SOU	PTR	GTR
377327	(375337)	68227+74827+68427	SU	SOU	PTR	GTR
377328	(375338)	68228+74828+68428	SU	SOU	PTR	GTR

Left: *GTR Southern operates a fleet of 28 three-car Class 377s, classified as 377/3, these are devoid of the intermediate MSO vehicle. 377/3s tend to operate in twos or threes on services or strengthen four car sets to seven vehicles. Set No. 377319 is shown passing Forest Hill with its DTSO vehicle leading.* **CJM**

Class 377/4
Electrostar

Vehicle Length: (Driving) 66ft 9in (20.3m)
(Inter) 65ft 6in (19.96m)
Height: 12ft 4in (3.75m)
Width: 9ft 2in (2.79m)
Horsepower: 2,012hp (1,500kW)
Seats (total/car): 20F-221S, 10F-48S/69S/56S/10F-48S

Number	Formation	Depot	Livery	Owner	Operator
	DMCO(A)+MSO+TSO+DMCO(B)				
377401	73401+78801+78601+73801	SU	SOU	PTR	GTR
377402	73402+78802+78602+73802	SU	SOU	PTR	GTR
377403	73403+78803+78603+73803	SU	SOU	PTR	GTR
377404	73404+78804+78604+73804	SU	SOU	PTR	GTR
377405	73405+78805+78605+73805	SU	SOU	PTR	GTR
377406	73406+78806+78606+73806	SU	SOU	PTR	GTR
377407	73407+78807+78607+73807	SU	SOU	PTR	GTR
377408	73408+78808+78608+73808	SU	SOU	PTR	GTR
377409	73409+78809+78609+73809	SU	SOU	PTR	GTR
377410	73410+78810+78610+73810	SU	SOU	PTR	GTR
377411	73411+78811+78611+73811	SU	SOU	PTR	GTR
377412	73412+78812+78612+73812	SU	SOU	PTR	GTR
377413	73413+78813+78613+73813	SU	SOU	PTR	GTR
377414	73414+78814+78614+73814	SU	SOU	PTR	GTR
377415	73415+78815+78615+73815	SU	SOU	PTR	GTR
377416	73416+78816+78616+73816	SU	SOU	PTR	GTR
377417	73417+78817+78617+73817	SU	SOU	PTR	GTR
377418	73418+78818+78618+73818	SU	SOU	PTR	GTR
377419	73419+78819+78619+73819	SU	SOU	PTR	GTR
377420	73420+78820+78620+73820	SU	SOU	PTR	GTR
377421	73421+78821+78621+73821	SU	SOU	PTR	GTR
377422	73422+78822+78622+73822	SU	SOU	PTR	GTR
377423	73423+78823+78623+73823	SU	SOU	PTR	GTR
377424	73424+78824+78624+73824	SU	SOU	PTR	GTR
377425	73425+78825+78625+73825	SU	SOU	PTR	GTR

377426	73426+78826+78626+73826	SU	SOU	PTR	GTR
377427	73427+78827+78627+73827	SU	SOU	PTR	GTR
377428	73428+78828+78628+73828	SU	SOU	PTR	GTR
377429	73429+78829+78629+73829	SU	SOU	PTR	GTR
377430	73430+78830+78630+73830	SU	SOU	PTR	GTR
377431	73431+78831+78631+73831	SU	SOU	PTR	GTR
377432	73432+78832+78632+73832	SU	SOU	PTR	GTR
377433	73433+78833+78633+73833	SU	SOU	PTR	GTR
377434	73434+78834+78634+73834	SU	SOU	PTR	GTR
377435	73435+78835+78635+73835	SU	SOU	PTR	GTR
377436	73436+78836+78636+73836	SU	SOU	PTR	GTR
377437	73437+78837+78637+73837	SU	SOU	PTR	GTR
377438	73438+78838+78638+73838	SU	SOU	PTR	GTR
377439	73439+78839+78639+73839	SU	SOU	PTR	GTR
377440	73440+78840+78640+73840	SU	SOU	PTR	GTR
377441	73441+78841+78641+73841	SU	SOU	PTR	GTR
377342	73442+78642+73442	SU	SOU	PTR	GTR (Temp reduced to three car)
377443	73443+78843+78643+73843	SU	SOU	PTR	GTR
377444	73444+78844+78644+73844	SU	SOU	PTR	GTR
377445	73445+78845+78645+73845	SU	SOU	PTR	GTR
377446	73446+78846+78646+73846	SU	SOU	PTR	GTR
377447	73447+78847+78647+73847	SU	SOU	PTR	GTR
377448	73448+78848+78648+73848	SU	SOU	PTR	GTR
377449	73449+78849+78649+73849	SU	SOU	PTR	GTR
377450	73450+78850+78650+73850	SU	SOU	PTR	GTR
377451	73451+78851+78651+73851	SU	SOU	PTR	GTR
377452	73452+78852+78652+73852	SU	SOU	PTR	GTR
377453	73453+78853+78653+73853	SU	SOU	PTR	GTR
377454	73454+78854+78654+73854	SU	SOU	PTR	GTR
377455	73455+78855+78655+73855	SU	SOU	PTR	GTR
377456	73456+78856+78656+73856	SU	SOU	PTR	GTR
377457	73457+78857+78657+73857	SU	SOU	PTR	GTR
377458	73458+78858+78658+73858	SU	SOU	PTR	GTR
377459	73459+78859+78659+73859	SU	SOU	PTR	GTR
377460	73460+78860+78660+73860	SU	SOU	PTR	GTR
377461	73461+78861+78661+73861	SU	SOU	PTR	GTR
377462	73462+78862+78662+73862	SU	SOU	PTR	GTR
377463	73463+78863+78663+73863	SU	SOU	PTR	GTR
377464	73464+78864+78664+73864	SU	SOU	PTR	GTR
377465	73465+78865+78665+73865	SU	SOU	PTR	GTR
377466	73466+78866+78666+73866	SU	SOU	PTR	GTR
377467	73467+78867+78667+73867	SU	SOU	PTR	GTR
377468	73468+78868+78668+73868	SU	SOU	PTR	GTR
377469	73469+78869+78669+73869	SU	SOU	PTR	GTR
377470	73470+78870+78670+73870	SU	SOU	PTR	GTR
377471	73471+78871+78671+73871	SU	SOU	PTR	GTR
377472	73472+78872+78672+73872	SU	SOU	PTR	GTR
377473	73473+78873+78673+73873	SU	SOU	PTR	GTR
377474	73474+78874+78674+73874	SU	SOU	PTR	GTR
377475	73475+78875+78675+73875	SU	SOU	PTR	GTR

Right: *GTR-Southern operate a fleet of 75 four-car Class 377/4s, allocated to Selhurst and deployed on main line services. The sets seat 20 first and 221 standard class passengers. Set No. 377465 is shown passing Forest Hill, with a London Bridge to Epsom service.* **CJM**

Govia Thameslink Railway

Class 377/6
Electrostar

Vehicle Length: (Driving) 66ft 9in (20.3m) Width: 9ft 2in (2.79m)
(Inter) 65ft 6in (19.96m) Horsepower: 2,012hp (1,500kW)
Height: 12ft 4in (3.75m) Seats (total/car): 298S-60S/64S/46S/66S/62S

Number	Formation DMSO(A)+MSO+TSO+MSO+DMSO(B)	Depot	Livery	Owner	Operator
377601	70101+70201+70301+70401+70501	SU	SOU	PTR	GTR
377602	70102+70202+70302+70402+70502	SU	SOU	PTR	GTR
377603	70103+70203+70303+70403+70503	SU	SOU	PTR	GTR
377604	70104+70204+70304+70404+70504	SU	SOU	PTR	GTR
377605	70105+70205+70305+70405+70505	SU	SOU	PTR	GTR
377606	70106+70206+70306+70406+70506	SU	SOU	PTR	GTR
377607	70107+70207+70307+70407+70507	SU	SOU	PTR	GTR
377608	70108+70208+70308+70408+70508	SU	SOU	PTR	GTR
377609	70109+70209+70309+70409+70509	SU	SOU	PTR	GTR
377610	70110+70210+70310+70410+70510	SU	SOU	PTR	GTR
377611	70111+70211+70311+70411+70511	SU	SOU	PTR	GTR
377612	70112+70212+70312+70412+70512	SU	SOU	PTR	GTR
377613	70113+70213+70313+70413+70513	SU	SOU	PTR	GTR
377614	70114+70214+70314+70414+70514	SU	SOU	PTR	GTR
377615	70115+70215+70315+70415+70515	SU	SOU	PTR	GTR
377616	70116+70216+70316+70416+70516	SU	SOU	PTR	GTR
377617	70117+70217+70317+70417+70517	SU	SOU	PTR	GTR
377618	70118+70218+70318+70418+70518	SU	SOU	PTR	GTR
377619	70119+70219+70319+70419+70519	SU	SOU	PTR	GTR
377620	70120+70220+70320+70420+70520	SU	SOU	PTR	GTR
377621	70121+70221+70321+70421+70521	SU	SOU	PTR	GTR
377622	70122+70222+70322+70422+70522	SU	SOU	PTR	GTR
377623	70123+70223+70323+70423+70523	SU	SOU	PTR	GTR
377624	70124+70224+70324+70424+70524	SU	SOU	PTR	GTR
377625	70125+70225+70325+70425+70525	SU	SOU	PTR	GTR
377626	70126+70226+70326+70426+70526	SU	SOU	PTR	GTR

Above: *To meet passenger growth on GTR-Southern routes two fleets of longer five-car Class 377 'Electrostar' units have been introduced. This includes 26 Class 377/6s, allocated to Selhurst. These sets have 24 first class seats at the inner end of DMCO coach. These sets incorporate a track light housed in the front valance. Set No. 377619 is shown from its DMCO coach.* **CJM**

Class 377/7
Electrostar

Vehicle Length: (Driving) 66ft 9in (20.3m) Width: 9ft 2in (2.79m)
(Inter) 65ft 6in (19.96m) Horsepower: 2,012hp (1,500kW)
Height: 12ft 4in (3.75m) Seats (total/car): 298S-60S/64S/46S/66S/62S
Dual-voltage sets

Number	Formation DMSO(A)+MSO+TSO+MSO+DMSO(B)	Depot	Livery	Owner	Operator
377701	65201+70601+65601+70701+65401	SU	SOU	PTR	GTR

377702	65202+70602+65602+70702+65402	SU	SOU	PTR	GTR
377703	65203+70603+65603+70703+65403	SU	SOU	PTR	GTR
377704	65204+70604+65604+70704+65404	SU	SOU	PTR	GTR
377705	65205+70605+65605+70705+65405	SU	SOU	PTR	GTR
377706	65206+70606+65606+70706+65406	SU	SOU	PTR	GTR
377707	65207+70607+65607+70707+65407	SU	SOU	PTR	GTR
377708	65208+70608+65608+70708+65408	SU	SOU	PTR	GTR

Right: *Identical to the Class 377/6s are eight Class 377/7s, these sets however include dual voltage equipment, allowing operation from either the 25kV ac overhead or 750V dc third rail power supply. The sets can be used on south-north London services via Kensington Olympia/Willesden Junction. If not required for this route, sets are deployed on GTR-Southern domestic services. Set No. 377703 is illustrated passing Honor Oak Park.* **CJM**

Class 387/1
Electrostar

Vehicle Length: (Driving) 66ft 9in (20.3m) Width: 9ft 2in (2.79m)
(Inter) 65ft 6in (19.96m) Horsepower: 2,012hp (1,500kW)
Height: 12ft 4in (3.75m) Seats (total/car): 22F/201S, 22F/34S/62S/45S/60S

Number	Formation	Depot	Livery	Owner	Operator
	DMCO+MSO+TSO+DMSO				
387101	421101+422101+423101+424101	HE	TMK	PTR	GTR
387102	421102+422102+423102+424102	HE	TMK	PTR	GTR
387103	421103+422103+423103+424103	HE	TMK	PTR	GTR
387104	421104+422104+423104+424104	HE	TMK	PTR	GTR
387105	421105+422105+423105+424105	SL	TMK	PTR	GTR (working for GatEx)

Above: *A fleet of 29 Class 387/1 'Electrostar' units are based at Hornsey and operate on GTR Great Northern services. As these sets are deployed on longer distance services, first class accommodation (22 seats) are provided in one driving car. Set No. 387106 is seen at Hornsey.* **Antony Christie**

387106	421106+422106+423106+424106	HE	TMK	PTR	GTR
387107	421107+422107+423107+424107	HE	TMK	PTR	GTR
387108	421108+422108+423108+424108	HE	TMK	PTR	GTR
387109	421109+422109+423109+424109	HE	TMK	PTR	GTR
387110	421110+422110+423110+424110	HE	TMK	PTR	GTR
387111	421111+422111+423111+424111	HE	TMK	PTR	GTR
387112	421112+422112+423112+424112	HE	TMK	PTR	GTR
387113	421113+422113+423113+424113	HE	TMK	PTR	GTR
387114	421114+422114+423114+424114	HE	TMK	PTR	GTR
387115	421115+422115+423115+424115	HE	TMK	PTR	GTR
387116	421116+422116+423116+424116	HE	TMK	PTR	GTR
387117	421117+422117+423117+424117	HE	TMK	PTR	GTR
387118	421118+422118+423118+424118	HE	TMK	PTR	GTR
387119	421119+422119+423119+424119	HE	TMK	PTR	GTR
387120	421120+422120+423120+424120	HE	TMK	PTR	GTR
387121	421121+422121+423121+424121	HE	TMK	PTR	GTR
387122	421122+422122+423122+424122	HE	TMK	PTR	GTR
387123	421123+422123+423123+424123	HE	TMK	PTR	GTR
387124	421124+422124+423124+424124	HE	TMK	PTR	GTR
387125	421125+422125+423125+424125	HE	TMK	PTR	GTR
387126	421126+422126+423126+424126	HE	TMK	PTR	GTR
387127	421127+422127+423127+424127	HE	TMK	PTR	GTR
387128	421128+422128+423128+424128	HE	TMK	PTR	GTR
387129	421129+422129+423129+424129	HE	TMK	PTR	GTR

Class 387/2
Electrostar

Vehicle Length: (Driving) 66ft 9in (20.3m) Width: 9ft 2in (2.79m)
(Inter) 65ft 6in (19.96m) Horsepower: 2,012hp (1,500kW)
Height: 12ft 4in (3.75m) Seats (total/car): 201S/22F

Number	Formation	Depot	Livery	Owner	Operator
	DMCO+MSO+PTSO+DMSO				
387201	421201+422201+423201+424201	SL	GAT	PTR	GTR
387202	421202+422202+423202+424202	SL	GAT	PTR	GTR
387203	421203+422203+423203+424203	SL	GAT	PTR	GTR
387204	421204+422204+423204+424204	SL	GAT	PTR	GTR
387205	421205+422205+423205+424205	SL	GAT	PTR	GTR
387206	421206+422206+423206+424206	SL	GAT	PTR	GTR
387207	421207+422207+423207+424207	SL	GAT	PTR	GTR
387208	421208+422208+423208+424208	SL	GAT	PTR	GTR
387209	421209+422209+423209+424209	SL	GAT	PTR	GTR
387210	421210+422210+423210+424210	SL	GAT	PTR	GTR
387211	421211+422211+423211+424211	SL	GAT	PTR	GTR
387212	421212+422212+423212+424212	SL	GAT	PTR	GTR
387213	421213+422213+423213+424213	SL	GAT	PTR	GTR
387214	421214+422214+423214+424214	SL	GAT	PTR	GTR
387215	421215+422215+423215+424215	SL	GAT	PTR	GTR
387216	421216+422216+423216+424216	SL	GAT	PTR	GTR

Left: *As part of the modernisaion of the GTR-operated Gatwick Express route, a fleet of 27 four-car Class 387/2 sets are allocated to Stewarts Lane and operate the dedicated service. The interiors are much the same as the standard GTR sets. Externally the units carry the distinctive Gatwick Express red livery. Usually two or three sets operate in multiple to cope with high levels of passenger demand on this route. A three-set formation is seen arriving at London Victoria.* **Antony Christie**

387217	421217+422217+423217+424217	SL	GAT	PTR	GTR
387218	421218+422218+423218+424218	SL	GAT	PTR	GTR
387219	421219+422219+423219+424219	SL	GAT	PTR	GTR
387220	421220+422220+423220+424220	SL	GAT	PTR	GTR
387221	421221+422221+423221+424221	SL	GAT	PTR	GTR
387222	421222+422222+423222+424222	SL	GAT	PTR	GTR
387223	421223+422223+423223+424223	SL	GAT	PTR	GTR
387224	421224+422224+423224+424224	SL	GAT	PTR	GTR
387225	421225+422225+423225+424225	SL	GAT	PTR	GTR
387226	421226+422226+423226+424226	SL	GAT	PTR	GTR
387227	421227+422227+423227+424227	SL	GAT	PTR	GTR

Class 455/8

Vehicle Length: (Driving) 65ft 0½in (19.83m)
(Inter) 65ft 4½in (19.92m)
Height: 12ft 1½in (3.79m)
Width: 9ft 3¼in (2.82m)
Horsepower: 1,000hp (746kW)
Seats (total/car): 310S, 74S/78S/84S/74S

Number	Formation DTSO(A)+MSO+TSO+DTSO(B)	Depot	Livery	Owner	Operator
455801	77627+62709+71657+77580	SL	SOU	EVL	GTR
455802	77581+62710+71658+77582	SL	SOU	EVL	GTR
455803	77583+62711+71639+77584	SL	SOU	EVL	GTR
455804	77585+62712+71640+77586	SL	SOU	EVL	GTR
455805	77587+62713+71641+77588	SL	SOU	EVL	GTR
455806	77589+62714+71642+77590	SL	SOU	EVL	GTR
455807	77591+62715+71643+77592	SL	SOU	EVL	GTR
455808	77637+62716+71644+77594	SL	SOU	EVL	GTR
455809	77623+62717+71648+77602	SL	SOU	EVL	GTR
455810	77597+62718+71646+77598	SL	SOU	EVL	GTR
455811	77599+62719+71647+77600	SL	SOU	EVL	GTR
455812	77595+62720+71645+77626	SL	SOU	EVL	GTR
455813	77603+62721+71649+77604	SL	SOU	EVL	GTR
455814	77605+62722+71650+77606	SL	SOU	EVL	GTR
455815	77607+62723+71651+77608	SL	SOU	EVL	GTR
455816	77609+62724+71652+77633	SL	SOU	EVL	GTR
455817	77611+62725+71653+77612	SL	SOU	EVL	GTR
455818	77613+62726+71654+77632	SL	SOU	EVL	GTR
455819	77615+62727+71637+77616	SL	SOU	EVL	GTR
455820	77617+62728+71656+77618	SL	SOU	EVL	GTR
455821	77619+62729+71655+77620	SL	SOU	EVL	GTR
455822	77621+62730+71658+77622	SL	SOU	EVL	GTR
455823	77601+62731+71659+77596	SL	SOU	EVL	GTR
455824	77593+62732+71660+77624	SL	SOU	EVL	GTR
455825	77579+62733+71661+77628	SL	SOU	EVL	GTR
455826	77630+62734+71662+77629	SL	SOU	EVL	GTR
455827	77610+62735+71663+77614	SL	SOU	EVL	GTR
455828	77631+62736+71638+77604	SL	SOU	EVL	GTR
455829	77635+62737+71665+77636	SL	SOU	EVL	GTR
455830	77625+62743+71666+77638	SL	SOU	EVL	GTR
455831	77639+62739+71667+77640	SL	SOU	EVL	GTR
455832	77641+62740+71668+77642	SL	SOU	EVL	GTR
455833	77643+62741+71669+77644	SL	SOU	EVL	GTR
455834	77645+62742+71670+77646	SL	SOU	EVL	GTR
455835	77647+62738+71671+77648	SL	SOU	EVL	GTR
455836	77649+62744+71672+77650	SL	SOU	EVL	GTR
455837	77651+62745+71673+77652	SL	SOU	EVL	GTR
455838	77653+62746+71674+77654	SL	SOU	EVL	GTR
455839	77655+62747+71675+77656	SL	SOU	EVL	GTR
455840	77657+62748+71676+77658	SL	SOU	EVL	GTR
455841	77659+62749+71677+77660	SL	SOU	EVL	GTR
455842	77661+62750+71678+77662	SL	SOU	EVL	GTR
455843	77663+62751+71679+77664	SL	SOU	EVL	GTR
455844	77665+62752+71680+77666	SL	SOU	EVL	GTR
455845	77667+62753+71681+77668	SL	SOU	EVL	GTR
455846	77669+62754+71682+77670	SL	SOU	EVL	GTR

Above: *GTR-Southern suburban services are operated by a fleet of 46 four-car Class 455/8s based at Stewarts Lane. These 1980s built units now sport modified non-gangway front ends. Set No. 455844 is seen at Forest Hill.* **CJM**

Class 700
Desiro City

Vehicle Length: (Driving) 20m	Weight: 278tonne/410 tonne
(Inter) 20m	Power output: 3.3/5.0MW
Height: 3.79m	Seats (total/car): 8-car - 52F/375S, 18F,26S/54S/64S/56S/40S/64S/54S/28F, 16S
	12-car 52F/614S, 26F, 20S/54S/60S/56S/64S/56S/38S/64S/56S/60S/54S/26F, 20S

Number	Formation (RLU - Reduced Length Units) DMCO+PTSO+MSO+TSO+TSO+MSO+PTSO+DMCO	Depot	Livery	Owner	Operator
700001	401001+402001+403001+406001+407001+410001+411001+412001	TB	TMK	UKG	GTR
700002	401002+402002+403002+406002+407002+410002+411002+412002	TB	TMK	UKG	GTR
700003	401003+402003+403003+406003+407003+410003+411003+412003	TB	TMK	UKG	GTR
700004	401004+402004+403004+406004+407004+410004+411004+412004	TB	TMK	UKG	GTR
700005	401005+402005+403005+406005+407005+410005+411005+412005	TB	TMK	UKG	GTR
700006	401006+402006+403006+406006+407006+410006+411006+412006	TB	TMK	UKG	GTR
700007	401007+402007+403007+406007+407007+410007+411007+412007	TB	TMK	UKG	GTR
700008	401008+402008+403008+406008+407008+410008+411008+412008	TB	TMK	UKG	GTR
700009	401009+402009+403009+406009+407009+410009+411009+412009	TB	TMK	UKG	GTR
700010	401010+402010+403010+406010+407010+410010+411010+412010	TB	TMK	UKG	GTR
700011	401011+402011+403011+406011+407011+410011+411011+412011	TB	TMK	UKG	GTR
700012	401012+402012+403012+406012+407012+410012+411012+412012	TB	TMK	UKG	GTR
700013	401013+402013+403013+406013+407013+410013+411013+412013	TB	TMK	UKG	GTR
700014	401014+402014+403014+406014+407014+410014+411014+412014	TB	TMK	UKG	GTR
700015	401015+402015+403015+406015+407015+410015+411015+412015	TB	TMK	UKG	GTR
700016	401016+402016+403016+406016+407016+410016+411016+412016	TB	TMK	UKG	GTR
700017	401017+402017+403017+406017+407017+410017+411017+412016	TB	TMK	UKG	GTR
700018	401018+402018+403018+406018+407018+410018+411018+412018	TB	TMK	UKG	GTR
700019	401019+402019+403019+406019+407019+410019+411019+412019	TB	TMK	UKG	GTR
700020	401020+402020+403020+406020+407020+410020+411020+412020	TB	TMK	UKG	GTR
700021	401021+402021+403021+406021+407021+410021+411021+412021	TB	TMK	UKG	GTR
700022	401022+402022+403022+406022+407022+410022+411022+412022	TB	TMK	UKG	GTR
700023	401023+402023+403023+406023+407023+410023+411023+412023	TB	TMK	UKG	GTR
700024	401024+402024+403024+406024+407024+410024+411024+412024	TB	TMK	UKG	GTR
700025	401025+402025+403025+406025+407025+410025+411025+412025	TB	TMK	UKG	GTR
700026	401026+402026+403026+406026+407026+410026+411026+412026	TB	TMK	UKG	GTR
700027	401027+402027+403027+406027+407027+410027+411027+412027	TB	TMK	UKG	GTR
700028	401028+402028+403028+406028+407028+410028+411028+412028	TB	TMK	UKG	GTR
700029	401029+402029+403029+406029+407029+410029+411029+412029	TB	TMK	UKG	GTR
700030	410030+402030+403030+406030+407030+410030+411030+412030	TB	TMK	UKG	GTR
700031	401031+402031+403031+406031+407031+410031+411031+412031	TB	TMK	UKG	GTR
700032	401032+402032+403032+406032+407032+410032+411032+412032	TB	TMK	UKG	GTR
700033	401033+402033+403033+406033+407033+410033+411033+412033	TB	TMK	UKG	GTR
700034	401034+402034+403034+406034+407034+410034+411034+412034	TB	TMK	UKG	GTR
700035	401035+402035+403035+406035+407035+410035+411035+412035	TB	TMK	UKG	GTR
700036	401036+402036+403036+406036+407036+410036+411036+412036	TB	TMK	UKG	GTR
700037	401037+402037+403037+406037+407037+410037+411037+412037	TB	TMK	UKG	GTR
700038	401038+402038+403038+406038+407038+410038+411038+412038	TB	TMK	UKG	GTR
700039	401039+402039+403039+406039+407039+410039+411039+412039	TB	TMK	UKG	GTR
700040	401040+402040+403040+406040+407040+410040+411040+412040	TB	TMK	UKG	GTR
700041	401041+402041+403041+406041+407041+410041+411041+412041	TB	TMK	UKG	GTR

Number	Formation	Depot	Livery	Owner	Operator
700042	401042+402042+403042+406042+407042+410042+411042+412042	TB	TMK	UKG	GTR
700043	401043+402043+403043+406043+407043+410043+411043+412043	TB	TMK	UKG	GTR
700044	401044+402044+403044+406044+407044+410044+411044+412044	TB	TMK	UKG	GTR
700045	401045+402045+403045+406045+407045+410045+411045+412045	TB	TMK	UKG	GTR
700046	401046+402046+403046+406046+407046+410046+411046+412046	TB	TMK	UKG	GTR
700047	401047+402047+403047+406047+407047+410047+411047+412047	TB	TMK	UKG	GTR
700048	401048+402048+403048+406048+407048+410048+411048+412048	TB	TMK	UKG	GTR
700049	401049+402049+403049+406049+407049+410049+411049+412049	TB	TMK	UKG	GTR
700050	401050+402050+403050+406050+407050+410050+411050+412050	TB	TMK	UKG	GTR
700051	401051+402051+403051+406051+407051+410051+411051+412051	TB	TMK	UKG	GTR
700052	401052+402052+403052+406052+407052+410052+411052+412052	TB	TMK	UKG	GTR
700053	401053+402053+403053+406053+407053+410053+411053+412053	TB	TMK	UKG	GTR
700054	401054+402054+403054+406054+407054+410054+411054+412054	TB	TMK	UKG	GTR
700055	401055+402055+403055+406055+407055+410055+411055+412055	TB	TMK	UKG	GTR
700056	401056+402056+403056+406056+407056+410056+411056+412056	TB	TMK	UKG	GTR
700057	401057+402057+403057+406057+407057+410057+411057+412057	TB	TMK	UKG	GTR
700058	401058+402058+403058+406058+407058+410058+411058+412058	TB	TMK	UKG	GTR
700059	401059+402059+403059+406059+407059+410059+411059+412059	TB	TMK	UKG	GTR
700060	401060+402060+403060+406060+407060+410060+411060+412060	TB	TMK	UKG	GTR

Right: *The massive GTR-Thameslink operation linking north and south London by way of the Clerkenwell Tunnels via Farringdon and King's Cross now use a fleet of Class 700s, either formed as eight-car Reduced Length Units (RLU) or as 12-car Full Length Units (FLU). RLU set No. 700021 is shown at Blackfriars.* **CJM**

Number	Formation (FLU - Full Length Units) DMCO+PTSO+MSO+MSO+TSO+TSO+ TSO+TSO+MSO+MSO+PTSO+DMCO	Depot	Livery	Owner	Operator
700101	401101+402101+403101+404101+405101+406101+ 407101+408101+409101+410101+411101+412101	TB	TMK	UKG	GTR
700102	401102+402102+403102+404102+405102+406102+ 407102+408102+409102+410102+411102+412102	TB	TMK	UKG	GTR
700103	401103+402103+403103+404103+405103+406103+ 407103+408103+409103+410103+411103+412103	TB	TMK	UKG	GTR
700104	401104+402104+403104+404104+405104+406104+ 407104+408104+409104+410104+411104+412104	TB	TMK	UKG	GTR
700105	401105+402105+403105+404105+405105+406105+ 407105+408105+409105+410105+411105+412105	TB	TMK	UKG	GTR
700106	401106+402106+403106+404106+405106+406106+ 407106+408106+409106+410106+411106+412106	TB	TMK	UKG	GTR
700107	401107+402107+403107+404107+405107+406107+ 407107+408107+409107+410107+411107+412107	TB	TMK	UKG	GTR
700108	401108+402108+403108+404108+405108+406108+ 407108+408108+409108+410108+411108+412108	TB	TMK	UKG	GTR
700109	401109+402109+403109+404109+405109+406109+ 407109+408109+409109+410109+411109+412109	TB	TMK	UKG	GTR
700110	401110+402110+403110+404110+405110+406110+ 407110+408110+409110+410110+411110+412110	TB	TMK	UKG	GTR
700111	401111+402111+403111+404111+405111+406111+ 407111+408111+409111+410111+411111+412111	TB	TMK	UKG	GTR
700112	401112+402112+403112+404112+405112+406112+ 407112+408112+409112+410112+411112+412102	TB	TMK	UKG	GTR
700113	401113+402113+403113+404113+405113+406113+ 407113+408113+409113+410113+411113+412113	TB	TMK	UKG	GTR
700114	401114+402114+403114+404114+405114+406114+ 407114+408114+409114+410114+411114+412114	TB	TMK	UKG	GTR
700115	401115+402115+403115+404115+405115+406115+ 407115+408115+409115+410115+411105+412115	TB	TMK	UKG	GTR

Govia Thameslink Railway

Passenger Train Operating Companies - Govia Thameslink Railway

700116	401116+402116+403116+404116+405116+406116+ 407116+408116+409116+410116+411116+412116	TB	TMK	UKG	GTR
700117	401117+402117+403117+404117+405117+406117+ 407117+408117+409117+410117+411107+412117	TB	TMK	UKG	GTR
700118	401118+402118+403118+404118+405118+406118+ 407118+408118+409118+410118+411108+412118	TB	TMK	UKG	GTR
700119	401119+402119+403119+404119+405119+406119+ 407119+408119+409119+410119+411109+412119	TB	TMK	UKG	GTR
700120	401120+402120+403120+404120+405120+406120+ 407120+408120+409120+410120+411120+412120	TB	TMK	UKG	GTR
700121	401121+402121+403121+404121+405121+406121+ 407121+408121+409121+410121+411121+412121	TB	TMK	UKG	GTR
700122	401122+402122+403122+404122+405122+406122+ 407122+408122+409122+410122+411122+412122	TB	TMK	UKG	GTR
700123	401123+402123+403123+404123+405123+406123+ 407123+408123+409123+410123+411123+412123	TB	TMK	UKG	GTR
700124	401124+402124+403124+404124+405124+406124+ 407124+408124+409124+410124+411124+412124	TB	TMK	UKG	GTR
700125	401125+402125+403125+404125+405125+406125+ 407125+408125+409125+410125+411125+412125	TB	TMK	UKG	GTR
700126	401126+402126+403126+404126+405126+406126+ 407126+408126+409126+410126+411126+412126	TB	TMK	UKG	GTR
700127	401127+402127+403127+404127+405127+406127+ 407127+408127+409127+410127+411127+412127	TB	TMK	UKG	GTR
700128	401128+402128+403128+404128+405128+406128+ 407128+408128+409128+410128+411128+412128	TB	TMK	UKG	GTR
700129	401129+402129+403129+404129+405129+406129+ 407129+408129+409129+410129+411129+412129	TB	TMK	UKG	GTR
700130	401130+402130+403130+404130+405130+406130+ 407130+408130+409130+410130+411130+412130	TB	TMK	UKG	GTR
700131	401131+402131+403131+404131+405131+406131+ 407131+408131+409131+410131+411131+412131	TB	TMK	UKG	GTR
700132	401132+402132+403132+404132+405132+406132+ 407132+408132+409132+410132+411132+412132	TB	TMK	UKG	GTR
700133	401133+402133+403133+404133+405133+406133+ 407133+408133+409133+410133+411133+412133	TB	TMK	UKG	GTR
700134	401134+402134+403134+404134+405134+406134+ 407134+408134+409134+410134+411134+412134	TB	TMK	UKG	GTR
700135	401135+402135+403135+404135+405135+406135+ 407135+408135+409135+410135+411135+412135	TB	TMK	UKG	GTR
700136	401136+402136+403136+404136+405136+406136+ 407136+408136+409136+410136+411136+412136	TB	TMK	UKG	GTR
700137	401137+402137+403137+404137+405137+406137+ 407137+408137+409137+410137+411137+412137	TB	TMK	UKG	GTR
700138	401138+402138+403138+404138+405138+406138+ 407138+408138+409138+410138+411138+412138	TB	TMK	UKG	GTR
700139	401139+402139+403139+404139+405139+406139+ 407139+408139+409139+410139+411139+412139	TB	TMK	UKG	GTR
700140	401140+402140+403140+404140+405140+406140+ 407140+408140+409140+410140+411140+412140	TB	TMK	UKG	GTR
700141	401141+402141+403141+404141+405141+406141+ 407141+408141+409141+410141+411141+412141	TB	TMK	UKG	GTR
700142	401142+402142+403142+404142+405142+406142+ 407142+408142+409142+410142+411142+412142	TB	TMK	UKG	GTR
700143	401143+402143+403143+404143+405143+406143+ 407143+408143+409143+410143+411143+412143	TB	TMK	UKG	GTR
700144	401144+402144+403144+404144+405144+406144+ 407144+408144+409144+410144+411144+412144	TB	TMK	UKG	GTR
700145	401145+402145+403145+404145+405145+406145+ 407145+408145+409145+410145+411145+412145	TB	TMK	UKG	GTR
700146	401146+402146+403146+404146+405146+406146+ 407146+408146+409146+410146+411146+412146	TB	TMK	UKG	GTR
700147	401147+402147+403147+404147+405147+406147+ 407147+408147+409147+410147+411147+412147	TB	TMK	UKG	GTR
700148	401148+402148+403148+404148+405148+406148+ 407148+408148+409148+410148+411148+412148	TB	TMK	UKG	GTR

700149	401149+402149+403149+404149+405149+406149+ 407149+408149+409149+410149+411149+412149	TB	TMK	UKG	GTR
700150	401150+402150+403150+404150+405150+406150+ 407150+408150+409150+410150+411150+412150	TB	TMK	UKG	GTR
700151	401151+402151+403151+404151+405151+406151+ 407151+408151+409151+410151+411151+412151	TB	TMK	UKG	GTR
700152	401152+402152+403152+404152+405152+406152+ 407152+408152+409152+410152+411152+412152	TB	TMK	UKG	GTR
700153	401153+402153+403153+404153+405153+406153+ 407153+408153+409153+410153+411153+412153	TB	TMK	UKG	GTR
700154	401154+402154+403154+404154+405154+406154+ 407154+408154+409154+410154+411154+412154	TB	TMK	UKG	GTR
700155	401155+402155+403155+404155+405155+406155+ 407155+408155+409155+410155+411155+412155	TB	TMK	UKG	GTR

Class 717
Desiro City

Vehicle Length: (Driving) 20m / (Inter) 20m   Height: 3.79m   Weight: Power output: Seats (total/car):

717001	451001+452001+453001+454001+455001+456001	HE	TLK	RKR	GTR
717002	451002+452002+453002+454002+455002+456002	HE	TLK	RKR	GTR
717003	451003+452003+453003+454003+455003+456003	HE	TLK	RKR	GTR
717004	451004+452004+453004+454004+455004+456004	HE	TLK	RKR	GTR
717005	451005+452005+453005+454005+455005+456005	HE	TLK	RKR	GTR
717006	451006+452006+453006+454006+455006+456006	HE	TLK	RKR	GTR
717007	451007+452007+453007+454007+455007+456007	HE	TLK	RKR	GTR
717008	451008+452008+453008+454008+455008+456008	HE	TLK	RKR	GTR
717009	451009+452009+453009+454009+455009+456009	HE	TLK	RKR	GTR
717010	451010+452010+453010+454010+455010+456010	HE	TLK	RKR	GTR
717011	451011+452011+453011+454011+455011+456011	HE	TLK	RKR	GTR
717012	451012+452012+453012+454012+455012+456012	HE	TLK	RKR	GTR
717013	451013+452013+453013+454013+455013+456013	HE	TLK	RKR	GTR
717014	451014+452014+453014+454014+455014+456014	HE	TLK	RKR	GTR
717015	451015+452015+453015+454015+455015+456015	HE	TLK	RKR	GTR
717016	451016+452016+453016+454016+455016+456016	HE	TLK	RKR	GTR
717017	451017+452017+453017+454017+455017+456017	HE	TLK	RKR	GTR
717018	451018+452018+453018+454018+455018+456018	HE	TLK	RKR	GTR
717019	451019+452019+453019+454019+455019+456019	HE	TLK	RKR	GTR
717020	451020+452020+453020+454020+455020+456020	HE	TLK	RKR	GTR
717021	451021+452021+453021+454021+455021+456021	HE	TLK	RKR	GTR
717022	451022+452022+453022+454022+455022+456022	HE	TLK	RKR	GTR
717023	451023+452023+453023+454023+455023+456023	HE	TLK	RKR	GTR
717024	451024+452024+453024+454024+455024+456024	HE	TLK	RKR	GTR
717025	451025+452025+453025+454025+455025+456025	HE	TLK	RKR	GTR

Right: *During 2019, the Class 313 dual-voltage sets introduced for the Great Northern electrification in the 1970s will be phased out and replaced by a new fleet of six-car Siemens Desiro Class 717 sets. These are very similar to the Class 700s, except the front ends are fitted with an emergency egress door, which is hinged at the base and when opened deploys an escape ladder. The 25 sets to be based at Hornsey do not have yellow front end warning panels. Half of set No. 717017 is seen on display at Innotrans in Berlin in September 2018. The recess in the front door, in the light grey panel, is to allow opening with space to accommodate the coupling.*
CJM

Passenger Train Operating Companies - Govia Thameslink Railway

Heathrow Express /
Heathrow Connect

Address: ✉ 6th Floor, 50 Eastbourne Terrace, Paddington, London, W2 6LX

📧 queries@heathrowexpress.com or queries@heathrowconnect.com

📞 020 8750 6600

🌐 www.heathrowexpress.com or www.heathrowconnect.com

Managing Director: Keith Greenfield
Franchise Dates: Private Open Access Operator
Principal Routes: London Paddington - Heathrow Airport
Owned Stations: Heathrow Central, Heathrow Terminal 4, Heathrow Terminal 5
Depots: Old Oak Common HEX (OH)
Parent Company: Heathrow Express - Heathrow Airport Ltd
Heathrow Connect - Heathrow Airport Ltd / First Group

Heathrow Connect is operated by TfL

Heathrow Express

Heathrow Airport Terminal 5 — Heathrow Airport Terminals 1-3 — London Paddington

Heathrow Connect

Heathrow Airport Terminal 4 — Heathrow Airport Terminals 1-3 — Hayes — Southall — Hanwell — West Ealing — Ealing Broadway — London Paddington

Shuttle

Above: *Currently the Class 332s used on the Heathrow Express service carry Tata Communications livery, as shown on set No. 332003 at Paddington. These sets will be replaced by modified Great Western Class 387s in 2019-2020.* **CJM**

Class 332

	Vehicle Length: (Driving) 77ft 10¾in (23.74m)	Width: 9ft 1in (2.75m)
	(Inter) 75ft 11in (23.143m)	Horsepower: 1,876hp (1,400kW)
	Height: 12ft 1½in (3.70m)	Seats 4-car (total/car): 26F-148S, 26F/56S/44S/48S
		5-car (total/car): 26F-204S, 26F/56S/44S/56S/48S

Number	Formation	Depot	Livery	Owner	Operator
	DMFO+TSO+PTSO+(TSO)+DMSO				
332001	78400+72412+63400+ - +78401	OH	HEX	BAA	HEX
332002	78402+72409+63406+ - +78403	OH	HEX	BAA	HEX
332003	78404+72407+63402+ - +78405	OH	HEX	BAA	HEX
332004	78406+72405+63403+ - +78407	OH	HEX	BAA	HEX
332005	78408+72411+63404+72417+78409	OH	HEX	BAA	HEX
332006	78410+72410+63405+72415+78411	OH	HEX	BAA	HEX
332007	78412+72401+63401+72414+78413	OH	HEX	BAA	HEX

	Vehicle Length: (Driving) 77ft 10¾in (23.74m)	Width: 9ft 1in (2.75m)
	(Inter) 75ft 11in (23.143m)	Horsepower: 1,876hp (1,400kW)
	Height: 12ft 1½in (3.70m)	Seats 4-car (total/car): 14F-148S, 48S/56S/44S/14F
		5-car (total/car): 14F-204S, 48S/56S/44S/56S/14F

Number	Formation	Depot	Livery	Owner	Operator
	DMSO+TSO+PTSO+(TSO)+DMFLO				
332008	78414+72413+63407+72418+78415	OH	HEX	BAA	HEX
332009	78416+72400+63408+72416+78417	OH	HEX	BAA	HEX
332010	78418+72402+63409+ - +78419	OH	HEX	BAA	HEX
332011	78420+72403+63410+ - +78421	OH	HEX	BAA	HEX
332012	78422+72404+63411+ - +78423	OH	HEX	BAA	HEX
332013	78424+72408+63412+ - +78425	OH	HEX	BAA	HEX
332014	78426+72406+63413+ - +78427	OH	HEX	BAA	HEX

Class 360/2
Desiro

	Vehicle Length: 66ft 9in (20.4m)	Horsepower: 1,341hp (1,000kW)
	Height: 12ft 1½in (3.7m)	Seats (total/car): 340S, 63S/66S/74S/74S/63S
	Width: 9ft 2in (2.79m)	(360205 - 280S using 2+2 seats)

Number	Formation	Depot	Livery	Owner	Operator	
	DMSO(A)+PTSO+TSO+TSO+DMSO(B)					
360201	78431+63421+72431+72421+78441	OH	HEC	BAA	TfL	■ Class 360/2
360202	78432+63422+72432+72422+78442	OH	HEC	BAA	TfL	sets due off-
360203	78433+63423+72433+72423+78443	OH	HEC	BAA	TfL	lease following
360204	78434+63424+72434+72424+78444	OH	HEC	BAA	TfL	introduction of
360205	78435+63425+72435+72425+78445	OH	HEL	BAA	TfL	Class 345 stock.

Below: *In Spring 2018, the five Class 360/2 sets deployed on the stopping services between London Paddington and Heathrow Airport were transferred to Transport for London and given their branding. As soon as the Class 345 sets are fully commissioned, these will take over from the Class 360s on Airport-Paddington stopping services and the '360s' will be taken out of use. Set No. 360204 is seen passing Acton Main Line bound for Paddington.* **CJM**

Passenger Train Operating Companies - Heathrow Express / Heathrow Connect

London Overground

Address: ✉ 125 Finchley Road, London, NW3 6H
✆ overgroundinfo@tfl.gov.uk, ✆ 0845 601 4867, ⓘ www.tfl.gov.uk/overground

Managing Director: Steve Murphy

Principal Routes: Clapham Junction - Willesden, Richmond - Stratford, Gospel Oak - Barking, Euston - Watford, East London and Dalston - West Croydon, GE local services from Liverpool Street

Depots: Willesden (WN), New Cross Gate (NG), Ilford (IL),

Parent Company: Transport for London (TfL), operated by Arriva

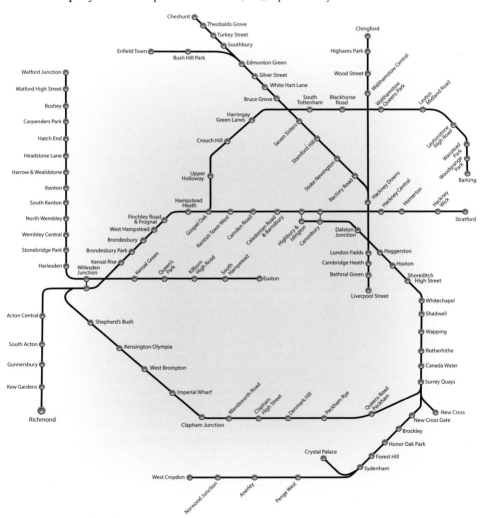

Class 09/0

Vehicle Length: 29ft 3in (8.91m)		Engine: English Electric 6K			
Height: 12ft 8⅜in (3.87m)		Horsepower: 400hp (298kW)			
Width: 8ft 6in (2.59m)		Electrical Equipment: English Electric			

Number	Depot	Pool	Livery	Owner	Operator
09007 (D3671)	WN	-	GRN	LOG	LOG

Class 315

Vehicle Length: (Driving) 64ft 11½in (19.80m)	Width: 9ft 3in (2.82m)	
(Inter) 65ft 4½in (19.92m)	Horsepower: 880hp (656kW)	
Height: 11ft 6½in (3.58m)	Seats (total/car): 318S, 74S/86S/84S/74S	

Right: *Soon to be replaced by Class 710 Bombardier 'Aventra' stock, 16 Class 315s allocated to Ilford currently operate on the Liverpool Street to Chingford, Cheshunt and Enfield Town lines. The sets are painted in London Overground white off-set with a blue and orange band with orange passenger doors. Set No. 315810 is seen at Bethnal Green.* **CJM**

Number	Formation	Depot	Livery	Owner	Operator	Name
	DMSO(A)+TSO+PTSO+DMSO(B)					
315801	64461+71281+71389+64462	IL	TFL	EVL	LOG	
315802	64463+71282+71390+64464	IL	TFL	EVL	LOG	
315803	64465+71283+71391+64466	IL	TFL	EVL	LOG	
315804	64467+71284+71392+64468	IL	TFL	EVL	LOG	
315805	64469+71285+71393+64470	IL	TFL	EVL	LOG	
315806	64471+71286+71394+64472	IL	TFL	EVL	LOG	
315807	64473+71287+71395+64474	IL	TFL	EVL	LOG	
315808	64475+71288+71396+64476	IL	TFL	EVL	LOG	
315809	64477+71289+71397+64478	IL	TFL	EVL	LOG	
315810	64479+71290+71398+64480	IL	TFL	EVL	LOG	
315811	64481+71291+71399+64482	IL	TFL	EVL	LOG	
315812	64483+71292+71400+64484	IL	TFL	EVL	LOG	
315814	64487+71294+71402+64488	IL	TFL	EVL	LOG	
315815	64489+71295+71403+64490	IL	TFL	EVL	LOG	
315816	64491+71296+71404+64492	IL	TFL	EVL	LOG	
315817	64493+71297+71405+64494	IL	TFL	EVL	LOG	*Transport for London*

Right: *Just one member of the Class 315 fleet carries a cast nameplate, No. 315817 which has the operators name Transport for London on the side.* **CJM**

Class 317/7

Vehicle Length: (Driving) 65ft 0¾in (19.83m)	Width: 9ft 3in (2.82m)	
(Inter) 65ft 4¼in (19.92m)	Horsepower: 1,000hp (746kW)	
Height: 12ft 1½in (3.58m)	Seats (total/car): 22F/172S, 52S/62S/42S/22F-16S	

Number	Former Number	Formation	Depot	Livery	Owner	Operator
		DTSO+MSO+TSO+DTCO				
317708	(317308)	77007+62668+71584+77055	IL	TFL	ANG	LOG
317709	(317309)	77008+62669+71585+77056	IL	TFL	ANG	LOG
317710	(317310)	77009+62670+71586+77057	IL	TFL	ANG	LOG
317714	(317314)	77013+62674+71590+77061	IL	TFL	ANG	LOG
317719	(317319)	77018+62679+71595+77066	IL	TFL	ANG	LOG
317723	(317323/393)	77022+62683+71599+77070	IL	TFL	ANG	LOG
317729	(317329)	77028+62689+71605+77076	IL	TFL	ANG	LOG
317732	(317332)	77031+62692+71608+77079	IL	TFL	ANG	LOG

Passenger Train Operating Companies - London Overground

Passenger Train Operating Companies - London Overground

London Overground

Left: *Two batches of Class 317 are on the books of London Overground. This includes the eight members of Class 317/7, which have a modified front end with a streamlined roof profile and revised light clusters. This modification was made by a previous operator for Stansted Airport services. Set No. 317709 is shown at Seven Sisters.* **Antony Christie**

Class 317/8

Vehicle Length: (Driving) 65ft 0¾in (19.83m)	Width: 9ft 3in (2.82m)
(Inter) 65ft 4¼in (19.92m)	Horsepower: 1,000hp (746kW)
Height: 12ft 1½in (3.58m)	Seats (total/car): 20F/265S, 74S/79S/20F-42S/70S

Left: *Six members of Class 317/8 are also operated, these are refurbished phase 1 sets with the warning horns at roof height. All 317s carry London Overground white, blue and orange livery, off-set by orange passenger doors. Set No. 317888 is seen at Seven Sisters.* **Antony Christie**

317887	(317330)	77043+62704+71606+77077	IL	TFL	ANG	LOG
317888	(317331)	77030+62691+71607+77078	IL	TFL	ANG	LOG
317889	(317333)	77032+62693+71609+77080	IL	TFL	ANG	LOG
317890	(317334)	77033+62694+71610+77081	IL	TFL	ANG	LOG
317891	(317335)	77034+62695+71611+77082	IL	TFL	ANG	LOG
317892	(317336)	77035+62696+71612+77083	IL	TFL	ANG	LOG	*Ilford Depot*

Class 378/1
Capitalstar

Vehicle Length: (Driving) 20.46m, (Inter) 20.14m	Width: 9ft 2in (2.80m)	
Height: 11ft 9in (3.58m)	Horsepower: 2,010hp (1,500kW)	
750V dc sets	Seats (total/car): 146S, 36S/40S/34S/36S	

Number	Formation DMSO+MSO+TSO+MSO+DMSO	Depot	Livery	Owner	Operator	Name
378135	38035+38235+38335+38435+38135	NG	LON	QWR	LOG	Daks Hamilton
378136	38036+38236+38336+38436+38136	NG	LON	QWR	LOG	
378137	38037+38237+38337+38437+38137	NG	LOG	QWR	LOG	
378138	38038+38238+38338+38438+38138	NG	LOG	QWR	LOG	
378139	38039+38239+38339+38439+38139	NG	LOG	QWR	LOG	
378140	38040+38240+38340+38440+38140	NG	LOG	QWR	LOG	
378141	38041+38241+38341+38441+38141	NG	LOG	QWR	LOG	
378142	38042+38242+38342+38442+38142	NG	LOG	QWR	LOG	
378143	38043+38243+38343+38443+38143	NG	LOG	QWR	LOG	
378144	38044+38244+38344+38444+38144	NG	LOG	QWR	LOG	
378145	38045+38245+38345+38445+38145	NG	LOG	QWR	LOG	
378146	38046+38246+38346+38446+38146	NG	LOG	QWR	LOG	
378147	38047+38247+38347+38447+38147	NG	LON	QWR	LOG	
378148	38048+38248+38348+38448+38148	NG	LOG	QWR	LOG	
378149	38049+38249+38349+38449+38149	NG	LOG	QWR	LOG	
378150	38050+38250+38350+38450+38150	NG	LON	QWR	LOG	
378151	38051+38251+38351+38451+38151	NG	LOG	QWR	LOG	

378152	38052+38252+38352+38452+38152	NG	LOG	QWR	LOG
378153	38053+38253+38353+38453+38153	NG	LOG	QWR	LOG
378154	38054+38254+38354+38454+38154	NG	LOG	QWR	LOG

Right: *A fleet of 57 Bombardier 'Capitalstar' five-car sets are in traffic allocated to New Cross Gate. These seat 146, with a huge amounts of standing room. Sets were originally built as three-car sets and augmented as passenger numbers grew. Most sets are painted in standard white and blue livery, but a start has been made on applying a new livery based on the Class 710. DC only set No. 378135 is shown in the new colours at Crystal Palace.* **Antony Christie**

Class 378/2
Capitalstar

Vehicle Length: (Driving) 20.46m, (Inter) 20.14m Width: 9ft 2in (2.80m)
Height: 11ft 9in (3.58m) Horsepower: 2,010hp (1,500kW)
Dual voltage - 750V dc third rail and 25kV ac overhead Seats (total/car): 146S, 36S/40S/34S/36S

Sets built as three-car units as Class 378/0, MSO added and reclassified as 378/2

Number	Formation	Depot	Livery	Owner	Operator	Name
	DMSO+MSO+PTSO+MSO+DMSO					
378201 (378001)	38001+38201+38301+38401+38101	NG	LOG	QWR	LOG	
378202 (378002)	38002+38202+38302+38402+38102	NG	LOG	QWR	LOG	
378203 (378003)	38003+38203+38303+38403+38103	NG	LOG	QWR	LOG	
378204 (378004)	38004+38204+38304+38404+38104	NG	LOG	QWR	LOG	*Professor Sir Peter Hall*
378205 (378005)	38005+38205+38305+38405+38105	NG	LOG	QWR	LOG	
378206 (378006)	38006+38206+38306+(38406)+38106	NG	LOG	QWR	LOG	(4-car set for Goblin)
378207 (378007)	38007+38207+38307+38407+38107	NG	LOG	QWR	LOG	
378208 (378008)	38008+38208+38308+38408+38108	NG	LOG	QWR	LOG	
378209 (378009)	38009+38209+38309+38409+38109	NG	LOG	QWR	LOG	
378210 (378010)	38010+38210+38310+38410+38110	NG	LOG	QWR	LOG	
378211 (378011)	38011+38211+38311+38411+38111	NG	LOG	QWR	LOG	
378212 (378012)	38012+38212+38312+38412+38112	NG	LOG	QWR	LOG	
378213 (378013)	38013+38213+38313+38413+38113	NG	LOG	QWR	LOG	
378214 (378014)	38014+38214+38314+38414+38114	NG	LOG	QWR	LOG	
378215 (378015)	38015+38215+38315+38415+38115	NG	LOG	QWR	LOG	
378216 (378016)	38016+38216+38316+38416+38116	NG	LOG	QWR	LOG	
378217 (378017)	38017+38217+38317+38417+38117	NG	LOG	QWR	LOG	
378218 (378018)	38018+38218+38318+38418+38118	NG	LOG	QWR	LOG	
378219 (378019)	38019+38219+38319+38419+38119	NG	LOG	QWR	LOG	
378220 (378020)	38020+38220+38320+38420+38120	NG	LOG	QWR	LOG	
378221 (378021)	38021+38221+38321+38421+38121	NG	LOG	QWR	LOG	
378222 (378022)	38022+38222+38322+38422+38122	NG	LOG	QWR	LOG	
378223 (378023)	38023+38223+38323+38423+38123	NG	LOG	QWR	LOG	
378224 (378024)	38024+38224+38324+38424+38124	NG	LOG	QWR	LOG	

Sets 378216-378220 fitted with de-icing equipment

Number	Formation	Depot	Livery	Owner	Operator	Name/Note
	DMSO+MSO+TSO+MSO+DMSO					
378225	38025+38225+38325+38425+38125	NG	LOG	QWR	LOG	
378226	38026+38226+38326+38426+38126	NG	LOG	QWR	LOG	
378227	38027+38227+38327+38427+38127	NG	LOG	QWR	LOG	
378228	38028+38228+38328+38428+38128	NG	LOG	QWR	LOG	
378229	38029+38229+38329+38429+38129	NG	LOG	QWR	LOG	
378230	38030+38230+38330+38430+38130	NG	LOG	QWR	LOG	
378231	38031+38231+38331+38431+38131	NG	LOG	QWR	LOG	
378232	38032+38232+38332+(38432)+38132	NG	LOG	QWR	LOG	(4-car set for Goblin) *Ian Brown CBE*
378233	38033+38233+38333+38433+38133	NG	LOG	QWR	LOG	
378234	38034+38234+38334+38434+38134	NG	LOG	QWR	LOG	
378255	38055+38255+38355+38455+38155	NG	LOG	QWR	LOG	
378256	38056+38256+38356+38456+38156	NG	LOG	QWR	LOG	
378257	38057+38257+38357+38457+38157	NG	LOG	QWR	LOG	

London Overground

Above: *Showing the original London Overground livery, dual-voltage set No. 378216 is illustrated at Camden Road operating from the 25kV ac overhead power supply.* **CJM**

Class 710
Aventra

Vehicle Length: (Driving)	Width:
Height:	Horsepower:
Dual voltage -	Seats (total/car):

Class 710/1
AC sets

Number	Formation DMSO(S)+MSO+PMSO+DMSO(B)	Depot	Livery	Owner	Operator
710101	431101+431201+431301+431501	IL	LON	SML	On delivery
710102	431102+431202+431302+431502	IL	LON	SML	On delivery
710103	431103+431203+431303+431503	IL	LON	SML	On delivery
710104	431104+431204+431304+431504	IL	LON	SML	On delivery
710105	431105+431205+431305+431505	IL	LON	SML	On delivery
710106	431106+431206+431306+431506	IL	LON	SML	On delivery
710107	431107+431207+431307+431507	IL	LON	SML	On delivery
710108	431108+431208+431308+431508	IL	LON	SML	On delivery
710109	431109+431209+431309+431509	IL	LON	SML	On delivery
710110	431110+431210+431310+431510	IL	LON	SML	On delivery
710111	431111+431211+431311+431511	IL	LON	SML	On delivery
710112	431112+431212+431312+431512	IL	LON	SML	On delivery
710113	431113+431213+431313+431513	IL	LON	SML	On delivery
710114	431114+431214+431314+431514	IL	LON	SML	On delivery
710115	431115+431215+431315+431515	IL	LON	SML	On delivery
710116	431116+431216+431316+431516	IL	LON	SML	On delivery
710117	431117+431217+431317+431517	IL	LON	SML	On delivery
710118	431118+431218+431318+431518	IL	LON	SML	On delivery
710119	431119+431219+431319+431519	IL	LON	SML	On delivery
710120	431120+431220+431320+431520	IL	LON	SML	On delivery
710121	431121+431221+431321+431521	IL	LON	SML	On delivery
710122	431122+431222+431322+431522	IL	LON	SML	On delivery
710123	431123+431223+431323+431523	IL	LON	SML	On delivery
710124	431124+431224+431324+431524	IL	LON	SML	On delivery
710125	431125+431225+431325+431525	IL	LON	SML	On delivery
710126	431126+431226+431326+431526	IL	LON	SML	On delivery
710127	431127+431227+431327+431527	IL	LON	SML	On delivery
710128	431128+431228+431328+431528	IL	LON	SML	On delivery
710129	431129+431229+431329+431529	IL	LON	SML	On delivery
710130	431130+431230+431330+431530	IL	LON	SML	On delivery
710131	431131+431231+431331+431531	IL	LON	SML	On delivery

Class 710/2
AC/DC four-car sets

Number	Formation DMSO(S)+MSO+PMSO+DMSO(B)	Depot	Livery	Owner	Operator
710256	432156+432256+432356+432556	WN	LON	SML	LOG
710257	432157+432257+432357+432557	WN	LON	SML	LOG
710258	432158+432258+432358+432558	WN	LON	SML	LOG
710259	432159+432259+432359+432559	WN	LON	SML	LOG
710260	432160+432260+432360+432560	WN	LON	SML	LOG
710261	432161+432261+432361+432561	WN	LON	SML	LOG
710262	432162+432262+432362+432562	WN	LON	SML	LOG
710263	432163+432263+432363+432563	WN	LON	SML	LOG
710264	432164+432264+432364+432564	WN	LON	SML	LOG
710265	432165+432265+432365+432565	WN	LON	SML	LOG
710266	432166+432266+432366+432566	WN	LON	SML	LOG
710267	432167+432267+432367+432567	WN	LON	SML	LOG
710268	432168+432268+432368+432568	WN	LON	SML	LOG
710269	432169+432269+432369+432569	WN	LON	SML	LOG
710270	432170+432270+432370+432570	WN	LON	SML	LOG
710271	432171+432271+432371+432571	WN	LON	SML	LOG
710272	432172+432272+432372+432572	WN	LON	SML	LOG
710273	432173+432273+432373+432573	WN	LON	SML	LOG

Class 710/3
AC/DC five-car sets

Number	Formation DMSO(S)+MSO+PMSO+MSO+DMSO(B)	Depot	Livery	Owner	Operator
710274	432174+432274+432374+432474+432574	WN	LON	SML	LOG
710275	432175+432275+432375+432475+432575	WN	LON	SML	LOG
710276	432176+432276+432376+432476+432576	WN	LON	SML	LOG
710277	432177+432277+432377+432477+432577	WN	LON	SML	LOG
710278	432178+432278+432378+432478+432578	WN	LON	SML	LOG
710279	432179+432279+432379+432479+432579	WN	LON	SML	LOG

Above and Right: *For modernisation of suburban lines in around London, Bombardier 'Aventra' sets were selected, classified as 710. In late 2018, early 2019, dual voltage ac/dc sets of Class 710/2, allocated to Willesden depot entered service on the Gospel Oak-Barking route and will soon be introduced on North London routes. Set No. 710261 is illustrated above, while Motor Standard 432258 from set 710258 is illustrated right, this vehicle is still to receive its final orange band bridging the white and blue at the base of the body.* **TfL / Antony Christie**

London North Eastern Railway

Passenger Train Operating Companies - LNER

Address: ✉ East Coast House, 25 Skeldergate, York, YO1 6DH
  ✆ customers@eastcoast.co.uk
  ✆ 08457 225225
  ⓘ www.eastcoast.co.uk

Managing Director: David Horne
Franchise Dates: 24 June 2018-UFN
Principal Routes: London King's Cross - Aberdeen/
  Inverness, Edinburgh, Glasgow
  Hull, Leeds, Bradford, Skipton
  and Harrogate
Depots: Bounds Green (BN),
  Craigentinny (EC),
  Doncaster (DR)

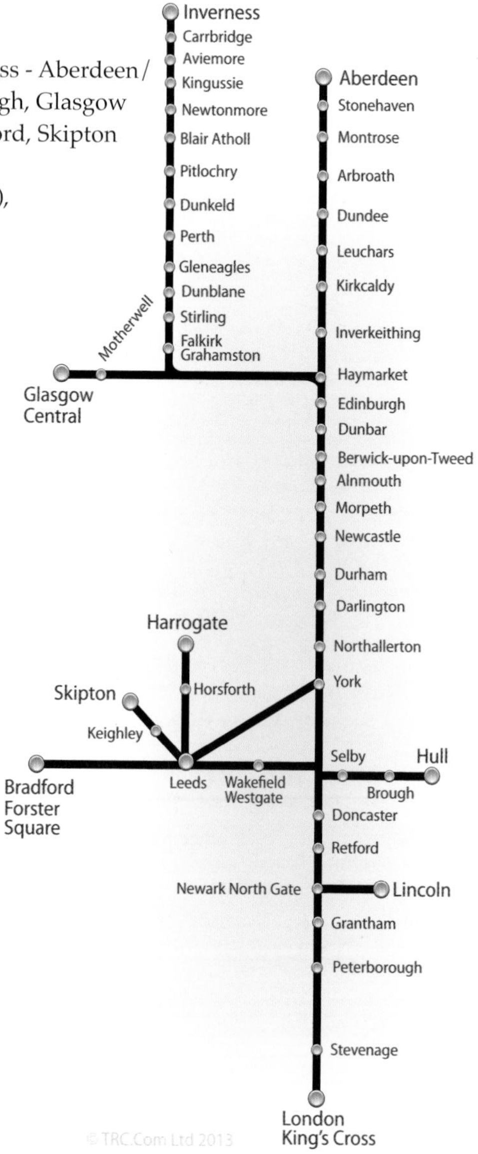

Inverness
Carrbridge
Aviemore
Kingussie
Newtonmore
Blair Atholl
Pitlochry
Dunkeld
Perth
Gleneagles
Dunblane
Stirling
Falkirk
Grahamston
Motherwell

Aberdeen
Stonehaven
Montrose
Arbroath
Dundee
Leuchars
Kirkcaldy
Inverkeithing
Haymarket

Glasgow
Central

Edinburgh
Dunbar
Berwick-upon-Tweed
Alnmouth
Morpeth
Newcastle
Durham
Darlington
Northallerton
York

Harrogate

Horsforth

Skipton

Keighley

Selby   Hull

Bradford   Leeds   Wakefield   Brough
Forster   Westgate
Square   Doncaster
Retford

Newark North Gate   Lincoln
Grantham
Peterborough

Stevenage

London
King's Cross

© TRC.Com Ltd 2013

Class 43 – HST

			Vehicle Length: 58ft 5in (18.80m)		Engine: MTU 16V4000 R41R	
			Height: 12ft 10in (3.90m)		Horsepower: 2,250hp (1,680kW)	
			Width: 8ft 11in (2.73m)		Electrical Equipment: Brush	

Number		Depot	Pool	Livery	Owner	Operator	Name
43206	(43006)	EC	IECP	LNR	ANG	LNE	Kingdom of Fife
43208	(43008)	EC	IECP	LNR	ANG	LNE	Lincolnshire Echo
43238	(43038)	EC	IECP	LNR	ANG	LNE	National Railway Museum 40 Years 1975-2015
43239	(43039)	EC	IECP	LNR	ANG	LNE	
43251	(43051)	EC	IECP	LNR	PTR	LNE	
43257	(43057)	EC	IECP	LNR	PTR	LNE	Bounds Green
43272	(43072)	EC	IECP	LNR	PTR	LNE	
43274	(43074)	EC	IECP	LNR	PTR	LNE	Spirit of Sunderland
43277	(43077)	EC	IECP	LNR	PTR	LNE	
43290	(43090)	EC	IECP	LNR	PTR	LNE	MTU Fascination of Power
43295	(43095)	EC	IECP	LNR	ANG	LNE	Perth is the Place - 2021 City of Culture bid
43296	(43096)	EC	IECP	LNR	PTR	LNE	
43299	(43099)	EC	IECP	LNR	PTR	LNE	
43300	(43100)	EC	IECP	LNR	PTR	LNE	Craigentinny
43302	(43102)	EC	IECP	LNR	PTR	LNE	World Speed Record - HST
43305	(43105)	EC	IECP	LNR	ANG	LNE	
43306	(43106)	EC	IECP	LNR	ANG	LNE	
43307	(43107)	EC	IECP	LNR	ANG	LNE	
43308	(43108)	EC	IECP	LNR	ANG	LNE	Highland Chieftain
43309	(43109)	EC	IECP	LNR	ANG	LNE	
43310	(43110)	EC	IECP	LNR	ANG	LNE	
43311	(43111)	EC	IECP	LNR	ANG	LNE	
43312	(43112)	EC	IECP	LNR	ANG	LNE	
43313	(43113)	EC	IECP	LNR	ANG	LNE	
43314	(43114)	EC	IECP	LNR	ANG	LNE	
43315	(43115)	EC	IECP	LNR	ANG	LNE	
43316	(43116)	EC	IECP	LNR	ANG	LNE	
43317	(43117)	EC	IECP	LNR	ANG	LNE	
43318	(43118)	EC	IECP	LNR	ANG	LNE	
43319	(43119)	EC	IECP	LNR	ANG	LNE	
43320	(43120)	EC	IECP	LNR	ANG	LNE	
43367	(43167)	EC	IECP	LNR	ANG	LNE	Deltic 50 1955 - 2005 v

Right: The LNER-operated East Coast Main Line is about to undergo massive change with the introduction of IEP Class 800 and 801 stock. The HST fleet will be phased out in 2019-2020. Displaying the former franchise operator Virgin Trains red livery, but with LNER branding, Class 43 No. 43310 stands at London King's Cross.
Antony Christie

Class 91

			Vehicle Length: 63ft 8in (19.40m)		Power Collection: 25kV ac overhead
			Height: 12ft 4in (3.75m)		Horsepower: 6,300hp (4,700kW)
			Width: 9ft 0in (2.74m)		Electrical Equipment: GEC

Number		Depot	Pool	Livery	Owner	Operator	Name
91101	(91001)	BN	IECA	SPL	EVL	LNE	Flying Scotsman
91102	(91002)	BN	IECA	LNR	EVL	LNE	City of York
91103	(91003)	BN	IECA	LNR	EVL	LNE	
91104	(91004)	BN	IECA	LNR	EVL	LNE	
91105	(91005)	BN	IECA	LNR	EVL	LNE	
91106	(91006)	BN	IECA	LNR	EVL	LNE	
91107	(91007)	BN	IECA	LNR	EVL	LNE	Skyfall

London North Eastern Railway

91108	(91008)	BN	IECA	LNR	EVL	LNE
91109	(91009)	BN	IECA	LNR	EVL	LNE	Sir Bobby Robson
91110	(91010)	BN	IECA	ADV	EVL	LNE	Battle of Britain Memorial Flight - Spitfire Hurricane Lancaster Dakota
91111	(91011)	BN	IECA	SPL	EVL	LNE	For the Fallen
91112	(91012)	BN	IECA	LNR	EVL	LNE
91113	(91013)	BN	IECA	LNR	EVL	LNE
91114	(91014)	BN	IECA	LNR	EVL	LNE	Durham Cathedral
91115	(91015)	BN	IECA	LNR	EVL	LNE	Blaydon Races
91116	(91016)	BN	IECA	LNR	EVL	LNE
91117	(91017)	BN	IECA	LNR	EVL	LNE	West Riding Limited
91118	(91018)	BN	IECA	LNR	EVL	LNE	The Fusiliers
91119	(91019)	BN	IECA	ICS	EVL	LNE	Bounds Green Intercity Depot 1977-2017
91120	(91020)	BN	IECA	LNR	EVL	LNE
91121	(91021)	BN	IECA	LNR	EVL	LNE
91122	(91022)	BN	IECA	LNR	EVL	LNE
91124	(91024)	BN	IECA	LNR	EVL	LNE
91125	(91025)	BN	IECA	LNR	EVL	LNE
91126	(91026)	BN	IECA	LNR	EVL	LNE	Darlington Hippodrome
91127	(91027)	BN	IECA	LNR	EVL	LNE
91128	(91028)	BN	IECA	LNR	EVL	LNE	InterCity 50
91129	(91029)	BN	IECA	LNR	EVL	LNE
91130	(91030)	BN	IECA	LNR	EVL	LNE	Lord Mayor of Newcastle
91131	(91031)	BN	IECA	LNR	EVL	LNE
91132	(91023)	BN	IECA	LNR	EVL	LNE	Time to Change

Left: *The Class 91s and Mk4 sets will be replaced by Hitachi Class 800 and 801 stock in 2019-2020. Showing Virgin Trains red livery but with present operator LNER branding, No. 91125 is shown at London King's Cross.* **Antony Christie**

■ With the full introduction of IET stock on LNER, six Class 91 and Mk4 sets will be retained, the remainder will go off-lease, it is speculated that some might find use with an open access operator between Blackpool and London and other Mk4s might find use in Wales or on the East Midlands network.

Mk3 HST Stock

Vehicle Length: 75ft 0in (22.86m)   Bogie Type: BT10
Height: 12ft 9in (3.88m)
Width: 8ft 11in (2.71m)

GK1G - TRFB *Seating 17F*

Number	Depot	Livery	Owner
40701	EC	LNR	PTR
40702	EC	LNR	PTR
40704	EC	LNR	ANG
40705	EC	LNR	ANG
40706	EC	LNR	ANG
40708	EC	LNR	PTR
40711	EC	LNR	ANG
40720	EC	LNR	ANG
40732	EC	LNR	PTR
40735	EC	LNR	ANG
40737	EC	LNR	ANG
40740	EC	LNR	ANG
40742	EC	LNR	ANG
40748	EC	LNR	ANG
40750	EC	LNR	ANG
40751	EC	LNR	PTR

GH1G - TF *Seating 48F*

Number	Depot	Livery	Owner
41039	EC	LNR	ANG
41040	EC	LNR	ANG
41043	EC	ECS	ANG
41044	EC	LNR	ANG
41058	EC	NXE	PTR
41062	EC	LNR	PTR
41066	EC	LNR	ANG
41067	EC	LNR	PTR
41083	EC	LNR	PTR
41087	EC	LNR	ANG
41088	EC	LNR	ANG
41090	EC	LNR	ANG
41091	EC	LNR	ANG
41092	EC	LNR	ANG
41095	EC	LNR	ANG

41097	EC	LNR	ANG
41098	EC	LNR	ANG
41099	EC	LNR	ANG
41100	EC	LNR	ANG
41112	EC	LNR	PTR
41115	EC	LNR	PTR
41118	EC	LNR	ANG
41120	EC	LNR	ANG
41150	EC	LNR	ANG
41151	EC	LNR	ANG
41152	EC	LNR	ANG
41154	EC	LNR	PTR
41159	EC	LNR	PTR
41164	EC	LNR	ANG
41165	EC	LNR	PTR
41170(41001)	EC	LNR	ANG
41185(42313)	EC	LNR	PTR
41190(42088)	EC	LNR	PTR

GH2G - TS (*TSD) *Seating 76/62*S*

Number	Depot	Livery	Owner
42057	EC	LNR	ANG
42058	EC	LNR	ANG
42059	EC	LNR	ANG
42063	EC	LNR	ANG
42064	EC	LNR	ANG
42065	EC	LNR	ANG
42091*	EC	LNR	ANG
42106	EC	LNR	ANG
42109	EC	LNR	PTR
42110	EC	LNR	PTR
42116*	EC	LNR	ANG
42117	EC	LNR	PTR
42122	EC	LNR	ANG
42123	EC	LNR	PTR
42125	EC	LNR	PTR
42127*	EC	LNR	ANG
42128*	EC	LNR	ANG
42130	EC	LNR	PTR
42134	EC	LNR	ANG
42146	EC	LNR	ANG
42147	EC	NXE	PTR
42150	EC	LNR	ANG
42154	EC	LNR	ANG
42158	EC	LNR	ANG
42159*	EC	LNR	PTR
42160	EC	LNR	PTR
42161*	EC	LNR	PTR
42163	EC	LNR	PTR
42171	EC	LNR	ANG
42172	EC	LNR	ANG
42179	EC	LNR	ANG
42180	EC	LNR	ANG
42181	EC	LNR	ANG
42182	EC	LNR	ANG
42186	EC	LNR	ANG
42188*	EC	LNR	ANG
42189*	EC	LNR	ANG
42190	EC	LNR	ANG
42191	EC	LNR	ANG
42192	EC	LNR	ANG
42193	EC	LNR	ANG
42194	EC	LNR	PTR
42198	EC	LNR	ANG
42199	EC	LNR	ANG
42205	EC	LNR	PTR
42210	EC	LNR	PTR
42215	EC	LNR	ANG
42219	EC	LNR	ANG
42225	EC	LNR	PTR
42226	EC	LNR	ANG
42227	EC	LNR	PTR
42228	EC	LNR	PTR
42229	EC	LNR	PTR
42235	EC	LNR	ANG
42237	EC	LNR	PTR
42238*	EC	LNR	ANG
42239*	EC	LNR	ANG
42240	EC	LNR	ANG
42241	EC	LNR	ANG
42242	EC	LNR	ANG
42243	EC	LNR	ANG
42244	EC	LNR	ANG
42286	EC	LNR	PTR
42306	EC	LNR	PTR
42307	EC	LNR	PTR
42322	EC	LNR	PTR
42323	EC	LNR	ANG
42326	EC	LNR	PTR
42330	EC	LNR	PTR
42335	EC	LNR	PTR
42340	EC	LNR	ANG
42352(41176)	EC	NXE	PTR
42354(41175)	EC	LNR	ANG
42355(41172)	EC	LNR	ANG
42357(41174)	EC	LNR	ANG
42363(41082)	EC	LNR	ANG

GJ2G - TGS *Seating 65S*

Number	Depot	Livery	Owner
44019	EC	LNR	ANG
44027	EC	LNR	PTR
44031	EC	LNR	ANG
44045	EC	LNR	ANG
44050	EC	LNR	PTR
44056	EC	LNR	ANG
44057	EC	LNR	PTR
44058	EC	LNR	ANG
44061	EC	LNR	ANG
44063	EC	LNR	ANG
44073	EC	LNR	PTR
44075	EC	LNR	PTR
44077	EC	LNR	ANG
44080	EC	LNR	ANG
44094	EC	LNR	ANG
44098	EC	LNR	ANG

Right: The entire Mk3 HST passenger fleet owned by Porterbrook and Angel Trains are expected to be taken off-lease following introduction of Class 800 and 802 stock on LNER services. These vehicles still retain slam doors and are unlikely to receive sliding/plug doors for operation after 2020. Many of these vehicles are likely to go for scrap. TRFB No. 40705 is seen from its seating end, when 17 first class seats are provided. The catering section of the vehicle is at the far end, seen from the kitchen side. **CJM**

Mk4 Stock

Vehicle Length: 75ft 5in (23m) Width: 8ft 11in (2.73m)
Height: 12ft 5in (3.79m) Bogie Type: BT41

AJ2J - RSB *Seating 30S*

Number	Depot	Livery	Owner
10300	BN	LNR	EVL
10301	BN	LNR	EVL
10302	BN	LNR	EVL
10303	BN	LNR	EVL
10304	BN	LNR	EVL
10305	BN	LNR	EVL
10306	BN	LNR	EVL
10307	BN	LNR	EVL
10308	BN	LNR	EVL
10309	BN	LNR	EVL
10310	BN	LNR	EVL
10311	BN	LNR	EVL
10312	BN	LNR	EVL
10313	BN	LNR	EVL
10315	BN	LNR	EVL
10317	BN	LNR	EVL
10318	BN	LNR	EVL
10319	BN	LNR	EVL
10320	BN	LNR	EVL
10321	BN	LNR	EVL
10323	BN	LNR	EVL
10324	BN	LNR	EVL
10325	BN	LNR	EVL
10326	BN	LNR	EVL
10328	BN	LNR	EVL
10329	BN	LNR	EVL
10330	BN	LNR	EVL
10331	BN	LNR	EVL
10332	BN	LNR	EVL
10333	BN	LNR	EVL

London North Eastern Railway

AD1J - FO *Seating 46F*

Number	Depot	Livery	Owner
11201	BN	LNR	EVL
11219	BN	LNR	EVL
11229	BN	LNR	EVL
11237	BN	LNR	EVL
11241	BN	LNR	EVL
11244	BN	LNR	EVL
11273	BN	LNR	EVL
11277(12408)	BN	LNR	EVL
11278(12479)	BN	LNR	EVL
11279(12521)	BN	LNR	EVL
11280(12523)	BN	LNR	EVL
11281(12418)	BN	LNR	EVL
11282(12524)	BN	LNR	EVL
11283(12435)	BN	LNR	EVL
11284(12487)	BN	LNR	EVL
11285(12537)	BN	LNR	EVL
11286(12482)	BN	LNR	EVL
11287(12527)	BN	LNR	EVL
11288(12517)	BN	LNR	EVL
11289(12528)	BN	LNR	EVL
11290(12530)	BN	LNR	EVL
11291(12535)	BN	LNR	EVL
11292(12451)	BN	LNR	EVL
11293(12536)	BN	LNR	EVL
11294(12529)	BN	LNR	EVL
11295(12475)	BN	LNR	EVL
11298(12416)	BN	LNR	EVL
11299(12532)	BN	LNR	EVL

AL1J - FOD *Seating 42F*

Number	Depot	Livery	Owner
11301(11215)	BN	LNR	EVL
11302(11203)	BN	LNR	EVL
11303(11211)	BN	LNR	EVL
11304(11257)	BN	LNR	EVL
11305(11261)	BN	LNR	EVL
11306(11276)	BN	LNR	EVL

11307(11217)	BN	LNR	EVL
11308(11263)	BN	LNR	EVL
11309(11262)	BN	LNR	EVL
11310(11272)	BN	LNR	EVL
11311(11221)	BN	LNR	EVL
11312(11225)	BN	LNR	EVL
11313(11210)	BN	LNR	EVL
11314(11207)	BN	LNR	EVL
11315(11238)	BN	LNR	EVL
11316(11227)	BN	LNR	EVL
11317(11223)	BN	LNR	EVL
11318(11251)	BN	LNR	EVL
11319(11247)	BN	LNR	EVL
11320(11255)	BN	LNR	EVL
11321(11245)	BN	LNR	EVL
11322(11228)	BN	LNR	EVL
11323(11235)	BN	LNR	EVL
11324(11253)	BN	LNR	EVL
11325(11231)	BN	LNR	EVL
11326(11206)	BN	ECG	EVL
11327(11236)	BN	LNR	EVL
11328(11274)	BN	LNR	EVL
11329(11243)	BN	LNR	EVL
11330(11249)	BN	LNR	EVL

AD1J - FO *Seating 46F (55F*)*

Number	Depot	Livery	Owner
11401(11214)	BN	LNR	EVL*
11402(11216)	BN	LNR	EVL
11403(11258)	BN	LNR	EVL
11404(11202)	BN	LNR	EVL
11405(11204)	BN	LNR	EVL
11406(11205)	BN	LNR	EVL
11407(11256)	BN	LNR	EVL
11408(11218)	BN	LNR	EVL
11409(11259)	BN	LNR	EVL
11410(11260)	BN	LNR	EVL
11411(11240)	BN	LNR	EVL
11412(11209)	BN	LNR	EVL

11413(11212)	BN	LNR	EVL
11414(11246)	BN	LNR	EVL
11415(11208)	BN	LNR	EVL
11416(11254)	BN	LNR	EVL
11417(11226)	BN	LNR	EVL
11418(11222)	BN	LNR	EVL
11419(11250)	BN	LNR	EVL
11420(11242)	BN	LNR	EVL
11421(11220)	BN	LNR	EVL
11422(11232)	BN	LNR	EVL
11423(11230)	BN	LNR	EVL
11424(11239)	BN	LNR	EVL
11425(11234)	BN	LNR	EVL
11426(11252)	BN	LNR	EVL
11427(11200)	BN	LNR	EVL
11428(11233)	BN	LNR	EVL
11429(11275)	BN	LNR	EVL
11430(11248)	BN	LNR	EVL
11998(10314)	BN	LNR	EVL
11999(10316)	BN	LNR	EVL

AI2J - TSOE *Seating 76S*

Number	Depot	Livery	Owner
12200	BN	LNR	EVL
12201	BN	LNR	EVL
12202	BN	LNR	EVL
12203	BN	LNR	EVL
12204	BN	LNR	EVL
12205	BN	LNR	EVL
12207	BN	LNR	EVL
12208	BN	LNR	EVL
12209	BN	LNR	EVL
12210	BN	LNR	EVL
12211	BN	LNR	EVL
12212	BN	LNR	EVL
12213	BN	LNR	EVL
12214	BN	LNR	EVL
12215	BN	LNR	EVL
12216	BN	LNR	EVL

Below: *Fitted with sliding plug doors, the Mk4 coaches meet 2020 regulations and most, are expected to find other use. Some vehicles are likely to replace Mk3s on the Transport for Wales Holyhead-Cardiff route, while others might well operate on East Midlands Trains to replace HST coaches or work for open access operators. First Open No. 11318 is seen at Doncaster.* **CJM**

12217	BN	LNR	EVL
12218	BN	LNR	EVL
12219	BN	LNR	EVL
12220	BN	LNR	EVL
12222	BN	LNR	EVL
12223	BN	LNR	EVL
12224	BN	LNR	EVL
12225	BN	LNR	EVL
12226	BN	LNR	EVL
12227	BN	LNR	EVL
12228	BN	LNR	EVL
12229	BN	LNR	EVL
12230	BN	LNR	EVL
12231	BN	LNR	EVL
12232	BN	LNR	EVL

AL2J - TSOD *Seating 68S*

Number	Depot	Livery	Owner
12300	BN	LNR	EVL
12301	BN	LNR	EVL
12302	BN	LNR	EVL
12303	BN	LNR	EVL
12304	BN	LNR	EVL
12305	BN	LNR	EVL
12307	BN	LNR	EVL
12308	BN	LNR	EVL
12309	BN	LNR	EVL
12310	BN	LNR	EVL
12311	BN	LNR	EVL
12312	BN	LNR	EVL
12313	BN	LNR	EVL
12315	BN	LNR	EVL
12316	BN	LNR	EVL
12317	BN	LNR	EVL
12318	BN	LNR	EVL
12319	BN	LNR	EVL
12320	BN	LNR	EVL
12321	BN	LNR	EVL
12322	BN	LNR	EVL
12323	BN	LNR	EVL
12324	BN	LNR	EVL
12325	BN	LNR	EVL
12326	BN	LNR	EVL
12327	BN	LNR	EVL
12328	BN	LNR	EVL
12329	BN	LNR	EVL
12330	BN	LNR	EVL
12331(12531)	BN	LNR	EVL

AC2J - TSO *Seating 76S*

Number	Depot	Livery	Owner
12400	BN	LNR	EVL
12401	BN	LNR	EVL
12402	BN	LNR	EVL
12403	BN	LNR	EVL
12404	BN	LNR	EVL
12405	BN	LNR	EVL
12406	BN	LNR	EVL

12407	BN	LNR	EVL
12409	BN	LNR	EVL
12410	BN	LNR	EVL
12411	BN	LNR	EVL
12414	BN	LNR	EVL
12415	BN	LNR	EVL
12417	BN	LNR	EVL
12419	BN	LNR	EVL
12420	BN	LNR	EVL
12421	BN	LNR	EVL
12422	BN	LNR	EVL
12423	BN	LNR	EVL
12424	BN	LNR	EVL
12425	BN	LNR	EVL
12426	BN	LNR	EVL
12427	BN	LNR	EVL
12428	BN	LNR	EVL
12429	BN	LNR	EVL
12430	BN	LNR	EVL
12431	BN	LNR	EVL
12432	BN	LNR	EVL
12433	BN	LNR	EVL
12434	BN	LNR	EVL
12436	BN	LNR	EVL
12437	BN	LNR	EVL
12438	BN	LNR	EVL
12439	BN	LNR	EVL
12440	BN	LNR	EVL
12441	BN	LNR	EVL
12442	BN	LNR	EVL
12443	BN	LNR	EVL
12444	BN	LNR	EVL
12445	BN	LNR	EVL
12446	BN	LNR	EVL
12447	BN	LNR	EVL
12448	BN	LNR	EVL
12449	BN	LNR	EVL
12450	BN	LNR	EVL
12452	BN	LNR	EVL
12453	BN	LNR	EVL
12454	BN	LNR	EVL
12455	BN	LNR	EVL
12456	BN	ECG	EVL
12457	BN	LNR	EVL
12458	BN	LNR	EVL
12459	BN	LNR	EVL
12460	BN	LNR	EVL
12461	BN	LNR	EVL
12462	BN	LNR	EVL
12463	BN	LNR	EVL
12464	BN	LNR	EVL
12465	BN	ECG	EVL
12466	BN	LNR	EVL
12467	BN	LNR	EVL
12468	BN	LNR	EVL
12469	BN	LNR	EVL
12470	BN	LNR	EVL
12471	BN	LNR	EVL
12472	BN	LNR	EVL

12473	BN	LNR	EVL
12474	BN	LNR	EVL
12476	BN	LNR	EVL
12477	BN	LNR	EVL
12478	BN	LNR	EVL
12480	BN	LNR	EVL
12481	BN	LNR	EVL
12483	BN	LNR	EVL
12484	BN	LNR	EVL
12485	BN	LNR	EVL
12486	BN	LNR	EVL
12488	BN	LNR	EVL
12489	BN	LNR	EVL
12513	BN	LNR	EVL
12514	BN	LNR	EVL
12515	BN	LNR	EVL
12518	BN	LNR	EVL
12519	BN	LNR	EVL
12520	BN	LNR	EVL
12522	BN	LNR	EVL
12526	BN	LNR	EVL
12533	BN	LNR	EVL
12534	BN	ECG	EVL
12538	BN	ECG	EVL

NZAJ - DVT

Number	Depot	Livery	Owner
82200	BN	LNR	EVL
82201	BN	LNR	EVL
82202	BN	LNR	EVL
82203	BN	LNR	EVL
82204	BN	LNR	EVL
82205	BN	LNR	EVL
82206	BN	ECG	EVL
82207	BN	LNR	EVL
82208	BN	LNR	EVL
82209	BN	LNR	EVL
82210	BN	LNR	EVL
82211	BN	LNR	EVL
82212	BN	LNR	EVL
82213	BN	LNR	EVL
82214	BN	LNR	EVL
82215	BN	LNR	EVL
82216	BN	LNR	EVL
82217	BN	LNR	EVL
82218	BN	LNR	EVL
82219	BN	LNR	EVL
82220	BN	LNR	EVL
82222	BN	LNR	EVL
82223	BN	LNR	EVL
82224	BN	LNR	EVL
82225	BN	LNR	EVL
82226	BN	LNR	EVL
82227	BN	LNR	EVL
82228	BN	LNR	EVL
82229	BN	LNR	EVL
82230	BN	LNR	EVL
82231	BN	LNR	EVL

Service Stock

HST and Mk4 Barrier Vehicles

Number	Depot	Livery	Owner	Former Identity					
6340	EC	BLU	ANG	BCK - 21251	6352	BN	HSB	HSB	SK - 19465
6344	EC	BLU	ANG	BG - 92080	6353	BN	HSB	HSB	SK - 19478
6346	EC	BLU	ANG	BSO - 9422	9393	EC	PTR	PTR	BG - 92196
					9394	EC	PTR	PTR	BG - 92906

Passenger Train Operating Companies - LNER

Class 800/1 Bi-Mode 'Azuma' IET stock
9-car sets

Vehicle Length: (Driving) 85ft 4in (26m)	Width: 8ft 10in (2.7m)
Height: 11ft 8¾in (3.62m)	Horsepower: Electric 6,061hp (4,520kW)
Engine: MTU 12V 1600R80L of 750hp (560kW) x 5	Seats (total/car): 93F/534S -
	56S, 88S, 88S, 88S, 88S, 88S,30F/38S, 48F, 15F

Number	Formation DTRBFO+MF+MC+TS+MS+TS+MS+MS+DTSO	Depot	Livery	Owner	Operator
800101 (T58)*	811101+812101+813101+814101+815101+816101+817101+818101+819101	DR	WHT	EVL	HIT
800102	811102+812102+813102+814102+815102+816102+817102+818102+819102	DR	WHT	EVL	LNE
800103*	811103+812103+813103+814103+815103+816103+817103+818103+819103	DR	LNE	EVL	LNE
800104	811104+812104+813104+814104+815104+816104+817104+818104+819104	DR	WHT	EVL	LNE
800105*	811105+812105+813105+814105+815105+816105+817105+818105+819105	DR	LNE	EVL	LNE
800106*	811106+812106+813106+814106+815106+816106+817106+818106+819106	DR	WHT	EVL	LNE
800107*	811107+812107+813107+814107+815107+816107+817107+818107+819107	DR	LNE	EVL	LNE
800108*	811108+812108+813108+814108+815108+816108+817108+818108+819108	DR	WHT	EVL	LNE
800109*	811109+812109+813109+814109+815109+816109+817109+818109+819109	DR	LNE	EVL	LNE
800110*	811110+812110+813110+814110+815110+816110+817110+818110+819110	DR	WHT	EVL	LNE
800111*	811111+812111+813111+814111+815111+816111+817111+818111+819111	DR	LNE	EVL	LNE
800112*	811112+812112+813112+814112+815112+816112+817112+818112+819112	DR	LNE	EVL	LNE
800113*	811113+812113+813113+814113+815113+816113+817113+818113+819113	DR	WHT	EVL	LNE

Class 800/2 Bi-Mode 'Azuma' IET stock
5-car sets

Vehicle Length: (Driving) 85ft 4in (26m)	Width: 8ft 10in (2.7m)
Height: 11ft 8¾in (3.62m)	Horsepower: Electric 3,636hp (2,712kW)
Engine: MTU 12V 1600R80L of 750hp (560kW) x 3	Seats (total/car): 45F/270S -
	56S, 88S,88S,30F/38S,15F

Number	Formation DTRBFO+MC+MS+MS+DTSO	Depot	Livery	Owner	Operator
800201*	811201+812201+813201+814201+815201	DR	WHT	EVL	HIT
800202	811202+812202+813202+814202+815202	DR	WHT	EVL	LNE
800203	811203+812203+813203+814203+815203	DR	WHT	EVL	LNE
800204	811204+812204+813204+814204+815204	DR	WHT	EVL	LNE
800205	811205+812205+813205+814205+815205	DR	WHT	EVL	LNE
800206	811206+812206+813206+814206+815206	DR	WHT	EVL	LNE
800207	811207+812207+813207+814207+815207	DR	WHT	EVL	LNE
800208	811208+812208+813208+814208+815208	DR	WHT	EVL	LNE
800209	811209+812209+813209+814209+815209	DR	WHT	EVL	LNE
800210	811210+812210+813210+814210+815210	DR	WHT	EVL	LNE

Class 801/1 Electric 'Azuma' IET stock
5-car sets

Vehicle Length: (Driving) 85ft 4in (26m)	Width: 8ft 10in (2.7m)
Height: 12ft 4in (3.75m)	Horsepower: 3,636hp (2,712kW)
Engine: MTU 12V 1600R80L of 750hp (560kW) x 1	Seats (total/car): 45F/270S -
	56S, 88S,88S,30F/38S,15F

Number	Formation DTRBFO+MC+MS+MS+DTSO	Depot	Livery	Owner	Operator
801101* (T71)	821101+822101+823101+824101+825101	DR	WHT	EVL	HIT
801102* (T72)	821102+822102+823102+824102+825102	DR	WHT	EVL	HIT
801103	821103+822103+823103+824103+825103	DR	AZU	EVL	LNE
801104	821104+822104+823104+824104+825104	DR	WHT	EVL	LNE
801105	821105+822105+823105+824105+825105	DR	WHT	EVL	LNE
801106	821106+822106+823106+824106+825106	DR	WHT	EVL	LNE
801107	821107+822107+823107+824107+825107	DR	WHT	EVL	LNE
801108	821108+822108+823108+824108+825108	DR	WHT	EVL	LNE
801109	821109+822109+823109+824109+825109	DR	WHT	EVL	LNE
801110	821110+822110+823110+824110+825110	DR	WHT	EVL	LNE
801111	821111+822111+823111+824111+825111	DR	WHT	EVL	LNE
801112	821112+822112+823112+824112+825112	DR	WHT	EVL	LNE

Class 801/2 Electric 'Azuma' IET stock

9-car sets
Vehicle Length: (Driving) 85ft 4in (26m)
Height: 11ft 8¾in (3.62m)
Engine: MTU 12V 1600R80L of 750hp (560kW) x 1

Width: 8ft 10in (2.7m)
Horsepower: 6,061hp (4,520kW)
Seats (total/car): 93F/534S -
56S, 88S, 88S, 88S, 88S, 88S,30F/38S, 48F, 15F

Number	Formation	Depot	Livery	Owner	Operator
	DTRBFO+MF+MC+TS+MS+TS+MS+MS+DTSO				
801201*	821201+822201+823201+824201+825201+826201+827201+828201+829201	DR	WHT	EVL	LNE
801202	821202+822202+823202+824202+825202+826202+827202+828202+829202	DR	WHT	EVL	LNE
801203	821203+822203+823203+824203+825203+826203+827203+828203+829203	DR	WHT	EVL	LNE
801204	821204+822204+823204+824204+825204+826204+827204+828204+829204	DR	WHT	EVL	LNE
801205	821205+822205+823205+824205+825205+826205+827205+828205+829205	DR	WHT	EVL	LNE
801206	821206+822206+823206+824206+825206+826206+827206+828206+829206	DR	WHT	EVL	LNE
801207	821207+822207+823207+824207+825207+826207+827207+828207+829207	DR	WHT	EVL	LNE
801208	821208+822208+823208+824208+825208+826208+827208+828208+829208	DR	WHT	EVL	LNE
801209	821209+822209+823209+824209+825209+826209+827209+828209+829209	DR	WHT	EVL	LNE
801210	821210+822210+823210+824210+825210+826210+827210+828210+829210	DR	WHT	EVL	LNE
801211	821211+822211+823211+824211+825211+826211+827211+828211+829211	DR	WHT	EVL	LNE
801212	821212+822212+823212+824212+825212+826212+827212+828212+829212	DR	WHT	EVL	LNE
801213	821213+822213+823213+824213+825213+826213+827213+828213+829213	DR	WHT	EVL	LNE
801214	821214+822214+823214+824214+825214+826214+827214+828214+829214	DR	WHT	EVL	LNE
801215	821215+822215+823215+824215+825215+826215+827215+828215+829215	DR	WHT	EVL	LNE
801216	821216+822216+823216+824216+825216+826216+827216+828216+829216	DR	WHT	EVL	LNE
801217	821217+822217+823217+824217+825217+826217+827217+828217+829217	DR	WHT	EVL	LNE
801218	821218+822218+823218+824218+825218+826218+827218+828218+829218	DR	WHT	EVL	LNE
801219	821219+822219+823219+824219+825219+826219+827219+828219+829219	DR	WHT	EVL	LNE
801220	821220+822220+823220+824220+825220+826220+827220+828220+829220	DR	WHT	EVL	LNE
801221	821221+822221+823221+824221+825221+826221+827221+828221+829221	DR	WHT	EVL	LNE
801222	821222+822222+823222+824222+825222+826222+827222+828222+829222	DR	WHT	EVL	LNE
801223	821223+822223+823223+824223+825223+826223+827223+828223+829223	DR	WHT	EVL	LNE
801224	821224+822224+823224+824224+825224+826224+827224+828224+829224	DR	WHT	EVL	LNE
801225	821225+822225+823225+824225+825225+826225+827225+828225+829225	DR	WHT	EVL	LNE
801226	821226+822226+823226+824226+825226+826226+827226+828226+829226	DR	WHT	EVL	LNE
801227	821227+822227+823227+824227+825227+826227+827227+828227+829227	DR	WHT	EVL	LNE
801228	821228+822228+823228+824228+825228+826228+827228+828228+829228	DR	WHT	EVL	LNE
801229	821229+822229+823229+824229+825229+826229+827229+828229+829229	DR	WHT	EVL	LNE
801230	821230+822230+823230+824230+825230+826230+827230+828230+829230	DR	WHT	EVL	LNE

* Built in Japan.

Below: *Class 800 bi-mode and 801 electric IETs will progressively enter traffic on LNER services in 2019. Based at Doncaster, the sets will take over all routes currently operated by HST sets and Class 91/Mk4 formations. Nine-car bi-mode set No. 800103 is seen in the full LNER 'Azuma' livery at London King's Cross.* **CJM**

Passenger Train Operating Companies - LNER

Merseyrail

Address: ✉ Rail House, Lord Nelson Street, Liverpool, L1 1JF
✍ comment@merseyrail.org
✆ 0151 702 2534
ⓘ www.merseyrail.org
Managing Director: Andy Heath
Franchise Dates: 20 July 2003 - 19 July 2028
Principal Routes: All non-main-line services
in Liverpool area
Depots: Birkenhead North (BD) maintenance undertaken by Stadler
Parent Company: Serco / Abellio

Passenger Train Operating Companies - Merseyrail

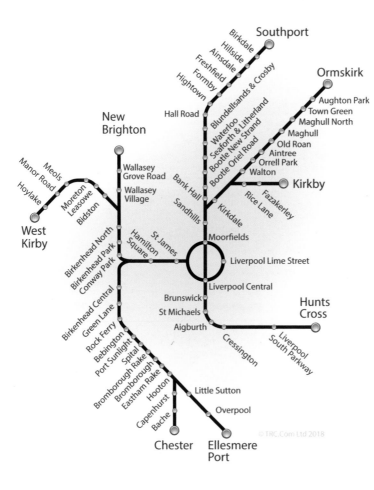

■ A new fleet of 52 Stadler four-coach (Class 777) articulated sets were ordered in December 2016 for delivery in 2019-2020.

A new depot is to be built at Kirkdale

Right: *Entering what is likely to be their final year of operation, the 1972-design Class 507s, share duties with Class 508s on the Merseyrail electric system. A total of 32 Class 507s are currently in traffic, allocated to Birkenhead. Set No. 507002 is seen carrying Liverpool Hope University promotional livery at Liverpool Central.*
Antony Christie

© TRC.Com Ltd 2018

Class 507

	Vehicle Length: (Driving) 64ft 11½in (19.80m)	Width: 9ft 3in (2.82m)
	(Inter) 65ft 4¼in (19.92m)	Horsepower: 880hp (656kW)
	Height: 11ft 6½in (3.58m)	Seats (total/car): 186S, 56S/74S/56S

Passenger Train Operating Companies - Merseyrail

Number	Formation DMSO+TSO+DMSO	Depot	Livery	Owner	Operator	Name
507001	64367+71342+64405	BD	MEY	ANG	MER	
507002	64368+71343+64406	BD	ADV	ANG	MER	
507003	64369+71344+64407	BD	MEY	ANG	MER	
507004	64388+71345+64408	BD	MEY	ANG	MER	Bob Paisley
507005	64371+71346+64409	BD	MEY	ANG	MER	
507006	64372+71347+64410	BD	MEY	ANG	MER	
507007	64373+71348+64411	BD	MEY	ANG	MER	
507008	64374+71349+64412	BD	MEY	ANG	MER	Harold Wilson
507009	64375+71350+64413	BD	MEY	ANG	MER	Dixie Dean
507010	64376+71351+64414	BD	MEY	ANG	MER	
507011	64377+71352+64415	BD	MEY	ANG	MER	
507012	64378+71353+64416	BD	MEY	ANG	MER	
507013	64379+71354+64417	BD	MEY	ANG	MER	
507014	64380+71355+64418	BD	MEY	ANG	MER	
507015	64381+71356+64419	BD	MEY	ANG	MER	
507016	64382+71357+64420	BD	MEY	ANG	MER	Merseyrail - celebrating the first ten years 2003-2013
507017	64383+71358+64421	BD	MEY	ANG	MER	
507018	64384+71359+64422	BD	MEY	ANG	MER	
507019	64385+71360+64423	BD	MEY	ANG	MER	
507020	64386+71361+64424	BD	MEY	ANG	MER	John Peel
507021	64387+71362+64425	BD	MEY	ANG	MER	Red Rum
507023	64389+71364+64427	BD	MEY	ANG	MER	Operating Inspector Stuart Mason
507024	64390+71365+64428	BD	MEY	ANG	MER	
507025	64391+71366+64429	BD	MEY	ANG	MER	
507026	64392+71367+64430	BD	MEY	ANG	MER	Councillor George Howard
507027	64393+71368+64431	BD	MEY	ANG	MER	
507028	64394+71369+64432	BD	MEY	ANG	MER	
507029	64395+71370+64433	BD	MEY	ANG	MER	
507030	64396+71371+64434	BD	MEY	ANG	MER	
507031	64397+71372+64435	BD	MEY	ANG	MER	
507032	64398+71373+64436	BD	MEY	ANG	MER	
507033	64399+71374+64437	BD	MEY	ANG	MER	

Class 508/1

Vehicle Length: (Driving) 64ft 11½in (19.80m)   Width: 9ft 3in (2.82m)
(Inter) 65ft 4¼in (19.92m)   Horsepower: 880hp (656kW)
Height: 11ft 6½in (3.58m)   Seats (total/car): 186S, 56S/74S/56S

Number	Formation DMSO+TSO+DMSO	Depot	Livery	Owner	Operator	Name
508103	64651+71485+64694	BD	MEY	ANG	MER	
508104	64652+71486+64964	BD	MEY	ANG	MER	
508108	64656+71490+64699	BD	MEY	ANG	MER	
508110	64658+71492+64701	BD	MEY	ANG	MER	
508111	64659+71493+64702	BD	SPL	ANG	MER	The Beatles
508112	64660+71494+64703	BD	MEY	ANG	MER	
508114	64662+71496+64705	BD	MEY	ANG	MER	
508115	64663+71497+64708	BD	MEY	ANG	MER	
508117	64665+71499+64908	BD	MEY	ANG	MER	
508120	64668+71502+64711	BD	MEY	ANG	MER	
508122	64670+71504+64713	BD	MEY	ANG	MER	
508123	64671+71505+64714	BD	MEY	ANG	MER	William Roscoe
508124	64672+71506+64715	BD	MEY	ANG	MER	
508125	64673+71507+64716	BD	MEY	ANG	MER	
508126	64674+71508+64717	BD	MEY	ANG	MER	
508127	64675+71509+64718	BD	MEY	ANG	MER	
508128	64676+71510+64719	BD	MEY	ANG	MER	
508130	64678+71512+64721	BD	MEY	ANG	MER	
508131	64679+71513+64722	BD	MEY	ANG	MER	
508134	64682+71516+64725	BD	MEY	ANG	MER	
508136	64684+71518+64727	BD	MEY	ANG	MER	
508137	64685+71519+64728	BD	MEY	ANG	MER	
508138	64686+71520+64729	BD	MEY	ANG	MER	
508139	64687+71521+64730	BD	MEY	ANG	MER	
508140	64688+71522+64731	BD	MEY	ANG	MER	
508141	64689+71523+64732	BD	MEY	ANG	MER	
508143	64691+71525+64734	BD	MEY	ANG	MER	

Passenger Train Operating Companies - Merseyrail

Above: Most Class 507s and 508s carry a dual yellow and silver livery, with a different colour on either side of the train. Showing the yellow livery, Class 508 No. 508126 departs from Hooton. The front ends of the 507s and 508s have been modified since delivery with revised light clusters. **Antony Christie**

Northern Rail

Address: ✉ Northern House, 9 Rougier Street, York, YO1 6HZ

✆ enquiries@northernrailway.co.ukg

✆ 0845 000125 ⓘ www.northernrailway.co.uk

Managing Director: David Brown

Franchise Dates: 12 December 2004 - March 2025

Principal Routes: Regional services in Merseyside, Greater Manchester, South/North Yorkshire, Lancashire, Cumbria and the North East

Depots: Newton Heath (NH), Heaton (HT), Longsight (LG), Neville Hill (NL), Allerton (AN)

Parent Company: Arriva Trains

Northern will withdraw Class 142 and 144 'Pacer' units by the end of 2019.

Class 142
Pacer

Vehicle Length: 51ft 0½in (15.55m)			*Engine: 1 x Cummins LTA10-R per vehicle*		
Height: 12ft 8in (3.86m)			*Horsepower: 460hp (343kW)*		
Width: 9ft 2¼in (2.80m)			*Seats (total/car): 106S, 56S/50S*		

Number	Formation DMS+DMSL	Depot	Livery	Owner	Operator
142001	55542+55592	NH	NOU	ANG	NOR
142003	55544+55594	NH	NOR	ANG	NOR
142004	55545+55595	NH	NOR	ANG	NOR
142005	55546+55596	NH	NOR	ANG	NOR
142007	55548+55598	NH	NOR	ANG	NOR
142009	55550+55600	NH	NOU	ANG	NOR
142011	55552+55602	NH	NOR	ANG	NOR
142012	55553+55603	NH	NOR	ANG	NOR
142013	55554+55604	NH	NOR	ANG	NOR
142014	55555+55605	NH	NOR	ANG	NOR
142015	55556+55606	HT	NOR	ANG	NOR
142016	55557+55607	HT	NOR	ANG	NOR
142017	55558+55608	HT	NOR	ANG	NOR
142018	55559+55609	HT	NOR	ANG	NOR
142019	55560+55610	HT	NOR	ANG	NOR
142020	55561+55611	HT	NOR	ANG	NOR
142021	55562+55612	HT	NOR	ANG	NOR
142022	55563+55613	HT	NOR	ANG	NOR
142023	55564+55614	NH	NOR	ANG	NOR
142024	55565+55615	HT	NOR	ANG	NOR
142025	55566+55616	HT	NOR	ANG	NOR
142026	55567+55617	HT	NOR	ANG	NOR
142027	55568+55618	NH	NOR	ANG	NOR
142028	55569+55619	NH	NOR	ANG	NOR
142029	55570+55620	NH	NOU	ANG	NOR
142030	55571+55621	NH	NOU	ANG	NOR
142031	55572+55622	NH	NOR	ANG	NOR
142032	55573+55623	NH	NOR	ANG	NOR
142033	55574+55624	NH	NOR	ANG	NOR
142034	55575+55625	HT	NOR	ANG	NOR
142035	55576+55626	NH	NOR	ANG	NOR
142036	55577+55627	NH	NOR	ANG	NOR
142037	55578+55628	NH	NOR	ANG	NOR
142038	55579+55629	NH	NOR	ANG	NOR
142039	55580+55630	NH	NOR	ANG	NOR
142040	55581+55631	NH	NOR	ANG	NOR
142041	55582+55632	NH	NOR	ANG	NOR
142042	55583+55633	NH	NOR	ANG	NOR
142043	55584+55634	NH	NOR	ANG	NOR
142044	55585+55635	NH	NOR	ANG	NOR
142045	55586+55636	NH	NOR	ANG	NOR
142046	55587+55637	NH	NOR	ANG	NOR
142047	55588+55638	NH	NOR	ANG	NOR
142048	55589+55639	NH	NOR	ANG	NOR
142049	55590+55640	NH	NOR	ANG	NOR
142050	55591+55641	HT	NOR	ANG	NOR
142051	55701+55747	NH	NOR	ANG	NOR
142052	55702+55748	NH	NOR	ANG	NOR
142053	55703+55749	NH	NOR	ANG	NOR
142054	55704+55750	NH	NOR	ANG	NOR
142055	55705+55751	NH	NOR	ANG	NOR
142056	55706+55752	NH	NOR	ANG	NOR
142057	55707+55753	NH	NOR	ANG	NOR
142058	55708+55754	NH	NOR	ANG	NOR
142060	55710+55756	NH	NOR	ANG	NOR
142061	55711+55757	NH	NOR	ANG	NOR
142062	55712+55758	NH	NOR	ANG	NOR
142063	55713+55759	HT	NOU	ANG	NOR
142064	55714+55760	NH	NOU	ANG	NOR
142065	55715+55761	HT	NOR	ANG	NOR
142066	55716+55762	HT	NOR	ANG	NOR
142067	55717+55763	NH	NOR	ANG	NOR
142068	55718+55764	NH	NOU	ANG	NOR
142070	55720+55766	HT	NOR	ANG	NOR
142071	55721+55767	HT	NOR	ANG	NOR
142078	55728+55768	HT	NOR	ANG	NOR
142079	55729+55769	HT	NOR	ANG	NOR
142084	55734+55780	HT	NOR	ANG	NOR
142086	55736+55782	HT	NOR	ANG	NOR
142087	55737+55783	HT	NOR	ANG	NOR
142088	55738+55784	HT	NOR	ANG	NOR
142089	55739+55785	HT	NOR	ANG	NOR
142090	55740+55786	HT	NOR	ANG	NOR
142091	55741+55787	HT	NOR	ANG	NOR
142092	55742+55788	HT	NOR	ANG	NOR
142093	55743+55789	HT	NOR	ANG	NOR
142094	55744+55790	HT	NOR	ANG	NOR
142095	55745+55791	HT	NOR	ANG	NOR
142096	55746+55792	HT	NOR	ANG	NOR

Passenger Train Operating Companies – Northern Rail

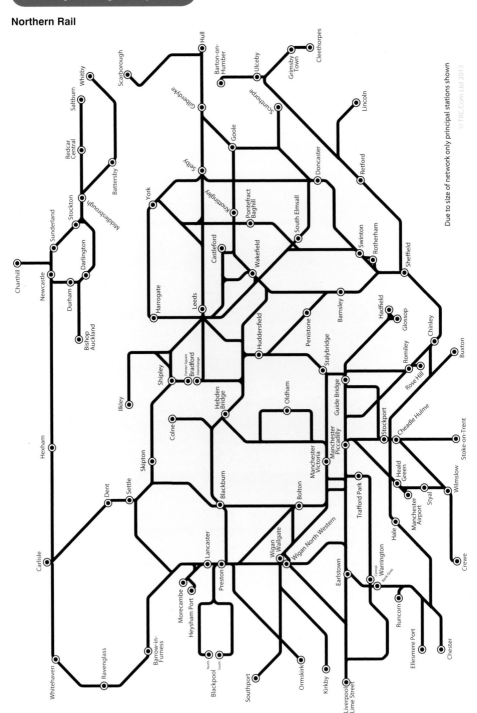

Due to size of network only principal stations shown

© TRC.Com Ltd 2013

Right: *To be withdrawn by the end of 2019, Northern currently still operates a large fleet of Class 142 and 144 'Pacer' sets. Painted in older Northern mauve and blue livery, set No. 142051 calls at Meadowhall with a Sheffield to Leeds stopping service.* **CJM**

Class 144
Pacer

Vehicle Length: 50ft 2in (15.25m)			Engine: 1 x Cummins LTA10-R per vehicle	
Height: 12ft 2½in (3.73m)			Horsepower: 460hp (343kW)	
Width: 8ft 10½in (2.70m)			Seats (total/car): 87S, 45S/42S	

Number	Formation DMS+DMSL	Depot	Livery	Owner	Operator
144001	55801+55824	NL	NOR	PTR	NOR
144002	55802+55825	NL	NOR	PTR	NOR
144003	55803+55826	NL	NOR	PTR	NOR
144004	55804+55827	NL	NOR	PTR	NOR
144005	55805+55828	NL	NOR	PTR	NOR
144006	55806+55829	NL	NOR	PTR	NOR
144007	55807+55830	NL	NOR	PTR	NOR
144008	55808+55831	NL	NOR	PTR	NOR
144009	55809+55832	NL	NOR	PTR	NOR
144010	55810+55833	NL	NOR	PTR	NOR
144011	55811+55834	NL	NOR	PTR	NOR
144012§	55812+55835	NL	NOA	PTR	NOR
144013	55813+55836	NL	NOR	PTR	NOR

§ Set 144012 modified as '144evolution' train with new-style interior, seating and toilet. DMS seats 43S and DMSL 35S.

Name applied
144001 *The Penistone Line Partnership*

Above: *A fleet of 13 two-car and 10 three-car Class 144 'Pacer' sets are in traffic at Leeds Neville Hill and operate alongside the '142' fleet on local services. One set No. 144012 was rebuilt by RVEL/Porterbrook as a demonstrator of what could be done with the 'Pacer' fleet of operators wanted to use them after 2020 to meet accessibility regulations. While making a major improvement, the project was not furthered, but the sets remains identifiable painted in a revised livery, as shown the set arrives at Doncaster.* **CJM**

Train Operating Companies

Northern Rail

						Engine: 1 x Cummins LTA10-R per vehicle

Vehicle Length: 50ft 2in (15.25m) Engine: 1 x Cummins LTA10-R per vehicle
Height: 12ft 2½in (3.73m) Horsepower: 690hp (515kW)
Width: 8ft 10½in (2.70m) Seats (total/car): 145S, 45S/58S/42S

Number	Formation DMS+MS+DMSL	Depot	Livery	Owner	Operator
144014	55814+55850+55837	NL	NOR	PTR	NOR
144015	55815+55851+55838	NL	NOR	PTR	NOR
144016	55816+55852+55839	NL	NOR	PTR	NOR
144017	55817+55853+55840	NL	NOR	PTR	NOR
144018	55818+55854+55841	NL	NOR	PTR	NOR
144019	55819+55855+55842	NL	NOR	PTR	NOR
144020	55820+55856+55843	NL	NOR	PTR	NOR
144021	55821+55857+55844	NL	NOR	PTR	NOR
144022	55822+55858+55845	NL	NOR	PTR	NOR
144023	55823+(55859)+55846	NL	NOR	PTR	NOR

Right: *The three-car Class 144s, were the only 'Pacer' stock built with an intermediate powered non-driving vehicle, and Northern tend to roster these for longer distance and more heavily used services. Set No. 144016 departs from Sheffield with a Huddersfield all stations service. On the three car sets, the intermediate vehicle is finished in all-over blue.*
CJM

Class 150/1
Sprinter

Vehicle Length: 64ft 9¾in (19.74m) Engine: 1 x NT855R5 of 285hp per vehicle
Height: 12ft 4½in (3.77m) Horsepower: 570hp (425kW)
Width: 9ft 3⅛in (2.82m) Seats (total/car): 124S, 59S/65S

Number	Formation DMSL+DMS	Depot	Livery	Owner	Operator
150101	52101+57101	NH	NNR	ANG	NOR
150102	52102+57102	NH	NNR	ANG	NOR
150103	52103+57103	NH	NOR	ANG	NOR
150104	52104+57104	NH	FGB	ANG	NOR
150106	52106+57106	NH	FGB	ANG	NOR
150108	52108+57108	NH	NNR	ANG	NOR
150110	52110+57110	NH	NOR	ANG	NOR
150111	52111+57111	NH	NOR	ANG	NOR
150112	52112+57112	NH	NNR	ANG	NOR
150113	52113+57113	NH	NOR	ANG	NOR
150114	52114+57114	NH	NOR	ANG	NOR
150115	52115+57115	NH	NOR	ANG	NOR
150116	52116+57116	NH	NNR	ANG	NOR
150117	52117+57117	NH	NOR	ANG	NOR
150118	52118+57118	NH	NOR	ANG	NOR
150119	52119+57119	NH	NOR	ANG	NOR
150120	52120+57120	NH	NNR	ANG	NOR
150121	52121+57121	NH	FGB	ANG	NOR
150122	52122+57122	NH	FGB	ANG	NOR
150123	52123+57123	NH	NNR	ANG	NOR
150124	52124+57124	NH	NNR	ANG	NOR
150125	52125+57125	NH	FGB	ANG	NOR
150126	52126+57126	NH	FGB	ANG	NOR
150127	52127+57127	NH	FGB	ANG	NOR
150128	52128+57128	NH	FGB	ANG	NOR
150129	52129+57129	NH	FGB	ANG	NOR
150130	52130+57130	NH	FGB	ANG	NOR
150131	52131+57131	NH	FGB	ANG	NOR
150132	52132+57132	NH	NNR	ANG	NOR
150133	52133+57133	NH	NNR	ANG	NOR
150134	52134+57134	NH	NNR	ANG	NOR
150135	52135+57135	NH	NOR	ANG	NOR
150136	52136+57136	NH	NNR	ANG	NOR
150137	52137+57137	NH	NNR	ANG	NOR
150138	52138+57138	NH	NNR	ANG	NOR
150139	52139+57139	NH	NOR	ANG	NOR
150140	52140+57140	NH	NNR	ANG	NOR
150141	52141+57141	NH	NNR	ANG	NOR
150142	52142+57142	NH	NNR	ANG	NOR
150143	52143+57143	NH	NNR	ANG	NOR
150144	52144+57144	NH	NNR	ANG	NOR
150145	52145+57145	NH	NNR	ANG	NOR
150146	52146+57146	NH	NNR	ANG	NOR
150147	52147+57147	NH	NNR	ANG	NOR
150148	52148+57148	NH	NOR	ANG	NOR
150149	52149+57149	NH	NNR	ANG	NOR
150150	52150+57150	NH	NOR	ANG	NOR

Right: *With the latest Northern franchise operated by Arriva, a slight livery change has been seen, with units repainted in a white and mauve livery, off-set by mauve passenger doors and stylized 'n' and Northern branding. Non-gangwayed Class 150/1 No. 150144 displays this latest livery at Leeds.* **CJM**

Class 150/2
Sprinter

	Vehicle Length: 64ft 9¾in (19.74m)	Engine: 1 x NT855R5 of 285hp per vehicle
	Height: 12ft 4½in (3.77m)	Horsepower: 570hp (425kW)
	Width: 9ft 3⅛in (2.82m)	Seats (total/car): 132S, 62S/70S

Number	Formation DMSL+DMS	Depot	Livery	Owner	Operator
150201	52201+57201	NH	NOR	ANG	NOR
150203	52203+57203	NH	NNR	ANG	NOR
150204	52204+57204	NH	NNR	ANG	NOR
150205	52205+57205	NH	NNR	ANG	NOR
150206	52206+57206	NH	NNR	ANG	NOR
150209	57212+57209	NH	GWR	ANG	NOR
150210	52210+57210	NH	NOR	ANG	NOR
150211	52211+57211	NH	NNR	ANG	NOR
150214	52214+57214	NH	NNR	ANG	NOR
150215	52215+57215	NH	NOR	ANG	NOR
150218	52218+57218	NH	NOR	ANG	NOR
150220	52220+57220	NH	NNR	ANG	NOR
150222	52222+57222	NH	NNR	ANG	NOR
150223	52223+57223	NH	NNR	ANG	NOR
150224	52224+57224	NH	NOR	ANG	NOR
150225	52225+57225	NH	NOR	ANG	NOR
150226	52226+57226	NH	NOR	ANG	NOR
150228	52228+57228	NH	NOR	PTR	NOR
150268	52268+57268	NH	NOR	PTR	NOR
150269	52269+57269	NH	NOR	PTR	NOR
150270	52270+57270	NH	NNR	PTR	NOR
150271	52271+57271	NH	NNR	PTR	NOR
150272	52272+57272	NH	NNR	PTR	NOR
150273	52273+57273	NH	NOR	PTR	NOR
150274	52274+57274	NH	NNR	PTR	NOR
150275	52275+57275	NH	NNR	PTR	NOR
150276	52276+57276	NH	NNR	PTR	NOR
150277	52277+57277	NH	NOR	PTR	NOR

Name applied
150214 *The Bentham Line - A Dementia-Friendly Railway*

Right: *A fleet of 28 two-car gangway fitted Class 150/2 sets are based at Newton Heath for Northern local services. In 2018-19 sets were passing through works for refurbishment and application of the latest Arriva Northern livery. Set No. 150203 is shown, displaying the latest colours.* **Antony Christie**

Class 153

	Vehicle Length: 76ft 5in (23.29m)	Engine: 1 x NT855R5 of 285hp
	Height: 12ft 3⅛in (3.75m)	Horsepower: 285hp (213kW)
	Width: 8ft 10in (2.70m)	Seats (total/car): 70S

Number	Formation DMSL	Depot	Livery	Owner	Operator
153301	52301	NL	NOR	ANG	NOR
153304	52304	NL	NOR	ANG	NOR
153305	52305	NL	SPL	ANG	NOR
153307	52307	NL	NOR	ANG	NOR
153315	52315	NL	NOR	ANG	NOR
153316	52316	NL	NOR	PTR	NOR
153317	52317	NL	NOR	ANG	NOR
153324	52324	NL	NOR	PTR	NOR
153328	52328	NL	NOR	ANG	NOR
153330	52330	NL	NOR	PTR	NOR
153331	52331	NL	NOR	ANG	NOR
153332	52332	NL	NOR	ANG	NOR
153351	57351	NL	NOR	ANG	NOR
153352	57352	NL	NOR	ANG	NOR

Northern Rail

Number	Formation	Depot	Livery	Owner	Operator	Number	Formation	Depot	Livery	Owner	Operator
153358	57358	NL	NOR	PTR	NOR	153370	57370	NL	GWG	ANG	NOR
153359	57359	NL	NOR	PTR	NOR	153373	57373	NL	GWG	ANG	NOR
153360	57360	NL	NOR	PTR	NOR	153378	57378	NL	NOR	ANG	NOR
153363	57363	NL	NOR	PTR	NOR	153380	57380	NL	GWG	ANG	NOR

Name applied
153316 *John 'Longitude' Harrison
Inventor of the Marine Chronometer*

Left: *Over the last year the compliment of Northern Class 153 'bubble' cars has increased by five vehicles, transferred in from Great Western. Based at Leeds Neville Hill, these cars tend to supplement two-car formations to increase capacity. Wearing older Northern livery, No. 153330 is seen at Leeds coupled to a Class 158.* **CJM**

Class 155
Super Sprinter

Vehicle Length: 76ft 5in (23.29m)
Height: 12ft 3½in (3.75m)
Width: 8ft 10in (2.70m)

Engine: 1 x NT855R5 of 285hp per vehicle
Horsepower: 570hp (425kW)
Seats (total/car): 156S, 76S/80S

Number	Formation DMSL+DMS	Depot	Livery	Owner	Operator	Number	Formation	Depot	Livery	Owner	Operator
155341	52341+57341	NL	NNR	PTR	NOR	155344	52344+57344	NL	NOR	PTR	NOR
155342	52342+57342	NL	NNR	PTR	NOR	155345	52345+57345	NL	NNR	PTR	NOR
155343	52343+57343	NL	NNR	PTR	NOR	155346	52346+57346	NL	NNR	PTR	NOR
						155347	52347+57347	NL	NNR	PTR	NOR

Left: *Leeds Neville Hill depot is the base for seven two-car Class 155 'Super Sprinter' sets. The larger proportion of these Leyland-built sets were later reformed into single car Class 153s. Painted in Northern 'pictogram' livery, No. 155344 is seen in one of the north facing bays at York.* **Mark V. Pike**

Class 156
Super Sprinter

Vehicle Length: 75ft 6in (23.03m)
Height: 12ft 6in (3.81m)
Width: 8ft 11in (2.73m)

Engine: 1 x Cummins NT855R5 of 285hp per car
Horsepower: 570hp (425kW)
Seats (total/car): 146S, 70/76S

Number	Formation DMSL+DMS	Depot	Livery	Owner	Operator	Number	Formation	Depot	Livery	Owner	Operator
156420	52420+57420	NH	NNR	PTR	NOR	156440	52440+57440	NH	NOR	PTR	NOR
156421	52421+57421	NH	NNR	PTR	NOR	156441	52441+57441	NH	§	PTR	NOR
156423	52423+57423	NH	NNR	PTR	NOR	156443	52443+57443	HT	NNR	ANG	NOR
156424	52424+57424	NH	NOR	PTR	NOR	156444	52444+57444	HT	NNR	ANG	NOR
156425	52425+57425	NH	NOR	PTR	NOR	156447	52447+57447	HT	SRB	ANG	NOR
156426	52426+57426	NH	NOR	PTR	NOR	156448	52448+57448	HT	NNR	ANG	NOR
156427	52427+57427	NH	NNR	PTR	NOR	156449	52449+57449	HT	SRB	ANG	NOR
156428	52428+57428	NH	NOR	PTR	NOR	156451	52451+57451	HT	NNR	ANG	NOR
156429	52429+57429	NH	NOR	PTR	NOR	156452	52452+57452	NH	NNR	PTR	NOR
156438	52438+57438	HT	NNR	ANG	NOR	156454	52454+57454	HT	NNR	ANG	NOR
						156455	52455+57455	NH	NOR	PTR	NOR
						156459	52459+57459	NH	NOR	PTR	NOR

156460	52460+57460	NH	NOR	PTR	NOR	156481	52481+57481	HT	NNR	ANG	NOR
156461	52461+57461	NH	NOR	PTR	NOR	156482	52482+57482	HT	NNR	ANG	NOR
156463	52463+57463	HT	NOR	ANG	NOR	156483	52483+57483	HT	NNR	ANG	NOR
156464	52464+57464	NH	SPL	PTR	NOR	156484	52484+57484	HT	NNR	ANG	NOR
156465	52465+57465	HT	SRB	ANG	NOR	156485	52485+57485	HT	SRB	ANG	NOR
156466	52466+57466	NH	NNR	PTR	NOR	156486	52486+57486	HT	NNR	ANG	NOR
156468	52468+57468	NH	NNR	ANG	NOR	156487	52487+57487	HT	NNR	ANG	NOR
156469	52469+57469	HT	NNR	ANG	NOR	156488	52488+57488	NH	NNR	ANG	NOR
156471	52471+57471	HT	NNR	ANG	NOR	156489	52489+57489	NH	NNR	ANG	NOR
156472	52472+57472	HT	NNR	ANG	NOR	156490	52490+57490	HT	NNR	ANG	NOR
156475	52475+57475	HT	NNR	ANG	NOR	156491	52491+57491	HT	NNR	ANG	NOR
156479	52479+57479	HT	NNR	ANG	NOR	156496	52496+57496	HT	SCR	ANG	NOR
156480	52480+57480	HT	SPL	ANG	NOR						

§ - Liverpool & Manchester Railway livery

Names applied
156440 *George Bradshaw*
156441 *William Huskisson MP*
156459 *Benny Rothman -*
    The Manchester Rambler

156460 *Driver John Axon GC*
156464 *Lancashire DalesRail*
156469 *The Royal Northumberland*
    Fusiliers (The Fighting Fifth)

156480 *RAF 100 Spirit of The*
    Royal Air Force

Right: *Northern operates a fleet of 47 Class 156 'Super Sprinter' sets, allocated to either Heaton (Newcastle) or Newton Heath (Manchester). These sets, many of which are now refurbished and in the latest white livery, are usually deployed on longer distance services. Painted in the white-based colours, set No. 156489 is seen at Leeds.* **CJM**

Class 158/0

Vehicle Length: 76ft 1¾in (23.21m)
Height: 12ft 6in (3.81m)
Width: 9ft 3¼in (2.82m)

Engine: 1 x Cummins NTA855R of 350hp per vehicle
Horsepower: 1,050hp (783kW)
Seats (total/car): 208S, 68S/66S/70S (Refurb-66S / 72S)

Number	Formation DMSL+MSL+DMSL	Depot	Livery	Owner	Op'r
158752	52752+58716+57752	NL	NNR	PTR	NOR
158753	52753+58710+57753	NL	NNR	PTR	NOR
158754	52754+58708+57754	NL	NNR	PTR	NOR
158755	52755+58702+57755	NL	NNR	PTR	NOR
158756	52756+58712+57756	NL	NNR	PTR	NOR
158757	52757+58706+57757	NL	NNR	PTR	NOR
158758	52758+58714+57758	NL	NNR	PTR	NOR
158759	52759+58713+57759	NL	NNR	PTR	NOR

Below: *Eight three-car Class 158/0s are on the books of Leeds Neville Hill depot, these have now all been refurbished and sport the Arriva Northern white livery. Blue ends are only applied to the outer ends of driving cars. Set No. 158755 is recorded arriving at Leeds City station.* **CJM**

Northern Rail

Class 158/0

Vehicle Length: 76ft 1¾in (23.21m)
Height: 12ft 6in (3.81m)
Width: 9ft 3¼in (2.82m)

Engine: 1 x Cummins NTA855R of 350hp per vehicle
Horsepower: 700hp (522kW)
Seats (total/car): 138S, 68S/70S (Refurb-66S / 72S)

Number	Formation DMSL+DMSL	Depot	Livery	Owner	Operator
158782	52782+57782	NL	SCR	ANG	NOR
158784	52784+57784	NL	NOR	ANG	NOR
158786	52786+57786	NL	SCR	ANG	NOR
158787	52787+57787	NL	NOR	ANG	NOR
158789	52789+57789	NL	SCR	ANG	NOR
158790	52790+57790	NL	NOR	ANG	NOR
158791	52791+57791	NL	NOR	ANG	NOR
158792	52792+57792	NL	NOR	ANG	NOR
158793	52793+57793	NL	NOR	ANG	NOR
158794	52794+57794	NL	NOR	ANG	NOR
158795	52795+57795	NL	NOR	ANG	NOR
158796	52796+57796	NL	NOR	ANG	NOR
158797	52797+57797	NL	NOR	ANG	NOR
158815	52815+57815	NL	NOR	ANG	NOR
158816	52816+57816	NL	NOR	ANG	NOR
158817	52817+57817	NL	NOR	ANG	NOR
158842	52842+57842	NL	NOR	ANG	NOR
158843	52843+57843	NL	NOR	ANG	NOR
158844	52844+57844	NL	NOR	ANG	NOR
158845	52845+57845	NL	NNR	ANG	NOR
158848	52848+57848	NL	NOR	ANG	NOR
158849	52849+57849	NL	NNR	ANG	NOR
158850	52850+57850	NL	NOR	ANG	NOR
158851	52851+57851	HT	NOR	ANG	NOR
158853	52853+57853	HT	NOR	ANG	NOR
158855	52855+57855	NL	NOR	ANG	NOR
158859	52859+57859	NL	NOR	ANG	NOR
158860	52860+57860	NL	NOR	ANG	NOR
158861	52861+57861	NL	NOR	ANG	NOR
158867	52867+57867	NL	SCR	ANG	NOR
158868	52868+57868	NL	SCR	ANG	NOR
158869	52869+57869	NL	SCR	ANG	NOR
158870	52870+57870	NL	SCR	ANG	NOR
158871	52871+57871	NL	SCR	ANG	NOR
158872	52872+57872	NL	NOR	ANG	NOR

Names applied
158784 Barbara Castle
158791 County of Nottinghamshire
158796 Fred Trueman - Cricketing Legend

158797 Jane Tomlinson
158860 Ian Dewhirst
158861 Magna Carta 800 - Lincoln 800
158910 William Wilberforce

Left: *Longer distance domestic Northern services are handled by a fleet of two-car Class 158s, with 35 sets on the roster at Neville Hill and Heaton in early 2019. Over the last year a number of extra sets have transferred south from ScotRail, following displacement by new stock. Set No. 158816 is seen in unbranded Northern mauve and blue with a turquoise roof at Doncaster.* **CJM**

Class 158/9

Vehicle Length: 76ft 1¾in (23.21m)
Height: 12ft 6in (3.81m)
Width: 9ft 3¼in (2.82m)

Engine: 1 x Cummins NTA855R of 350hp per vehicle
Horsepower: 700hp (522kW)
Seats (total/car): 142S, 70S/72S

Number	Formation DMSL+DMS	Depot	Livery	Owner	Operator
158901	52901+57901	NL	NOR	EVL	NOR
158902	52902+57902	NL	NOR	EVL	NOR
158903	52903+57903	NL	NOR	EVL	NOR
158904	52904+57904	NL	NOR	EVL	NOR
158905	52905+57905	NL	NOR	EVL	NOR
158906	52906+57906	NL	NOR	EVL	NOR
158907	52907+57907	NL	NOR	EVL	NOR
158908	52908+57908	NL	NOR	EVL	NOR
158909	52909+57909	NL	NOR	EVL	NOR
158910	52910+57910	NL	NOR	EVL	NOR

Left: *The 10 Class 158/9 sets were originally built with funding by West Yorkshire PTE and emerged in maroon and cream livery. Today, the sets are integrated with the normal '158' fleet allocated to Neville Hill depot. The sets carry Northern route pictogram livery. Set No. 158910 William Wilberforce is seen at Sheffield.* **CJM**

Class 170/4
Turbostar

Vehicle Length: 77ft 6in (23.62m)
Height: 12ft 4½in (3.77m)
Width: 8ft 10in (2.69m)

Engine: 1 x MTU 6R 183TD13H of 422hp per vehicle
Horsepower: 1,266hp (944kW)
Seats: 200S, 57S/76S/67S

Number		Depot	Livery	Own'r	Op'r
DMSL+MS+DMSL/DMCL§					
170453	50453+56453+79453	NL	BLU	PTR	NOR
170454	50454+56454+79454§	NL	BLU	PTR	NOR
170455	50455+56455+79455§	NL	BLU	PTR	NOR
170456	50456+56456+79456§	NL	BLU	PTR	NOR
170457	50457+56457+79457§	NL	BLU	PTR	NOR
170458	50458+56458+79458	NL	BLU	PTR	NOR
170459	50459+56459+79459	NL	BLU	PTR	NOR
170460	50460+56460+79460	NL	BLU	PTR	NOR
170461	50461+56461+79461	NL	BLU	PTR	NOR
170470	50470+56470+79470	NL	BLU	PTR	NOR
170471	50471+56471+79471	NL	BLU	PTR	NOR
170472	50472+56472+79472	NL	NNR	PTR	NOR
170473	50473+56473+79473	NL	NNR	PTR	NOR
170474	50474+56474+79474	NL	NNR	PTR	NOR
170475	50475+56475+79475	NL	NNR	PTR	NOR
170476	50476+56476+79476	NL	NNR	PTR	NOR
170477	50477+56477+79477	NL	BLU	PTR	NOR
170478	50478+56478+79478	NL	NNR	PTR	NOR

Right: *From mid 2018, following displacement in Scotland a batch of Class 170/4s have migrated to Northern, allocated to Leeds Neville Hill depot. These three-car high-quality sets are quickly being repainted into Northern white colours and used on longer distance services. Set No. 170476 is shown departing from Leeds.*
CJM

Class 195
Civity

Vehicle Length:
Height:
Width:

Engine:
Horsepower:
Seats:

Number	Formation	Depot	Livery	Owner	Op'r
	DMSL+DMS				
195001	101001+103001	NH	NNR	EVL	NOR
195002	101002+103002	NH	NNR	EVL	NOR
195003	101003+103003	NH	NNR	EVL	NOR
195004	101004+103004	NH	NNR	EVL	NOR
195005	101005+103005	NH	NNR	EVL	NOR
195006	101006+103006	NH	NNR	EVL	NOR
195007	101007+103007	NH	NNR	EVL	NOR
195008	101008+103008	NH	NNR	EVL	NOR
195009	101009+103009	NH	NNR	EVL	NOR
195010	101010+103010	NH	NNR	EVL	NOR
195011	101011+103011	NH	NNR	EVL	NOR
195012	101012+103012	NH	NNR	EVL	NOR
195013	101013+103013	NH	NNR	EVL	NOR
195014	101014+103014	NH	NNR	EVL	NOR
195015	101015+103015	NH	NNR	EVL	NOR
195016	101016+103016	NH	NNR	EVL	NOR
195017	101017+103017	NH	NNR	EVL	NOR
195018	101018+103018	NH	NNR	EVL	NOR
195019	101019+103019	NH	NNR	EVL	NOR
195020	101020+103020	NH	NNR	EVL	NOR
195021	101021+103021	NH	NNR	EVL	NOR
195022	101022+103022	NH	NNR	EVL	NOR
195023	101023+103023	NH	NNR	EVL	NOR
195024	101024+103024	NH	NNR	EVL	NOR
195025	101025+103025	NH	NNR	EVL	NOR

Number	Formation	Depot	Livery	Owner	Operator	Name
	DMSL+MS+DMS					
195101	101101+102101+103101	NH	NNR	EVL	NOR	
195102	101102+102102+103102	NH	NNR	EVL	NOR	
195103	101103+102103+103103	NH	NNR	EVL	NOR	
195104	101104+102104+103104	NH	NNR	EVL	NOR	
195105	101105+102105+103105	NH	NNR	EVL	NOR	
195106	101106+102106+103106	NH	NNR	EVL	NOR	
195107	101107+102107+103107	NH	NNR	EVL	NOR	
195108	101108+102108+103108	NH	NNR	EVL	NOR	*Northern Powerhouse*
195109	101109+102109+103109	NH	NNR	EVL	NOR	
195110	101110+102110+103110	NH	NNR	EVL	NOR	
195111	101111+102111+103111	NH	NNR	EVL	NOR	
195112	101112+102112+103112	NH	NNR	EVL	NOR	
195113	101113+102113+103113	NH	NNR	EVL	NOR	
195114	101114+102114+103114	NH	NNR	EVL	NOR	

Northern Rail

195115	101115+102115+103115	NH	NNR	EVL	NOR
195116	101116+102116+103116	NH	NNR	EVL	NOR
195117	101117+102117+103117	NH	NNR	EVL	NOR
195118	101118+102118+103118	NH	NNR	EVL	NOR
195119	101119+102119+103119	NH	NNR	EVL	NOR
195120	101120+102120+103120	NH	NNR	EVL	NOR
195121	101121+102121+103121	NH	NNR	EVL	NOR
195122	101122+102122+103122	NH	NNR	EVL	NOR
195123	101123+102123+103123	NH	NNR	EVL	NOR
195124	101124+102124+103124	NH	NNR	EVL	NOR
195125	101125+102125+103125	NH	NNR	EVL	NOR
195126	101126+102126+103126	NH	NNR	EVL	NOR
195127	101127+102127+103127	NH	NNR	EVL	NOR
195128	101128+102128+103128	NH	NNR	EVL	NOR
195129	101129+102129+103129	NH	NNR	EVL	NOR
195130	101130+102130+103130	NH	NNR	EVL	NOR
195131	101131+102131+103131	NH	NNR	EVL	NOR
195132	101132+102132+103132	NH	NNR	EVL	NOR
195133	101133+102133+103133	NH	NNR	EVL	NOR

Left: *In autumn 2018, the first of the CAF 'Civity' Class 195 sets was under test, first based at Allerton depot, but will soon move to new accommodation at Newton Heath. The sets sport standard Northern white and blue colours and sport full yellow warning ends. No. 195001 is seen passing Winwick Junction.* **Jamie Squibbs**

Class 319

Vehicle Length: (Driving) 65ft 0¾in (19.83m) Width: 9ft 3in (2.82m)
(Inter) 65ft 4¼in (19.92m) Horsepower: 1,326hp (990kW)
Height: 11ft 9in (3.58m) Seats (total/car): 300S, 70S/78S/74S/78S

Number	Formation	Depot	Livery	Owner	Operator	Name
	DTCO+MSO+TSO+DTSO					
319004	77297+62894+71775+77296	AN	NOE	PTR	NOR	
319218	77325+62908+71789+77324	AN	NOE	PTR	NOR	
319219	77327+62909+71790+77326	AN	NOE	PTR	NOR	
319361	77459+63043+71929+77458	AN	NNR	PTR	NOR	
319362	77461+63044+71930+77460	AN	NNR	PTR	NOR	*Northern Powerhouse*
319363	77463+63045+71931+77462	AN	NNR	PTR	NOR	
319364	77465+63046+71932+77464	AN	NNR	PTR	NOR	
319365	77467+63047+71933+77466	AN	NNR	PTR	NOR	
319366	77469+63048+71934+77468	AN	NNR	PTR	NOR	
319367	77471+63049+71935+77470	AN	NNR	PTR	NOR	
319368	77473+63050+71936+77472	AN	NNR	PTR	NOR	
319369	77475+63051+71937+77474	AN	NNR	PTR	NOR	
319370	77477+63052+71938+77476	AN	NNR	PTR	NOR	
319371	77479+63053+71939+77478	AN	NNR	PTR	NOR	
319372	77481+63054+71940+77480	AN	NNR	PTR	NOR	
319373	77483+63055+71941+77482	AN	NNR	PTR	NOR	
319374	77485+63056+71942+77484	AN	NNR	PTR	NOR	
319375	77487+63057+71943+77486	AN	NNR	PTR	NOR	
319376	77489+63058+71944+77488	AN	NNR	PTR	NOR	
319377	77491+63059+71945+77490	AN	NNR	PTR	NOR	
319378	77493+63060+71946+77492	AN	NNR	PTR	NOR	
319379	77495+63061+71947+77494	AN	NNR	PTR	NOR	
319380	77497+63062+71948+77496	AN	NNR	PTR	NOR	
319381	77973+63093+71979+77974	AN	NNR	PTR	NOR	
319382	77975+63094+71980+77976	AN	NNR	PTR	NOR	
319383	77977+63096+71981+77978	AN	NNR	PTR	NOR	

Passenger Train Operating Companies - Northern Rail

319385	77981+63097+71983+77982	AN	NNR	PTR	NOR
319386	77983+63098+71984+77984	AN	NNR	PTR	NOR
319446	77381+62936+71817+77380	AN	NNR	PTR	NOR

Right: *An increasing number of Class 319s are now operating for Northern, based at Allerton and deployed on Liverpool-Manchester-Crewe area routes. The four-car sets have been refurbished and the majority sport the latest Northern white livery. Some of these sets will be included in the Porterbrook 'Flex' project. Set No. 319381 is seen at Crewe.* **CJM**

Class 321/9

Vehicle Length: (Driving) 65ft 0¾in (19.83m) Width: 9ft 3in (2.82m)
(Inter) 65ft 4¼in (19.92m) Horsepower: 1,328hp (996kW)
Height: 12ft 4¾in (3.78m) Seats (total/car): 288S, 52/79S/78S/79S

Number	Formation	Depot	Livery	Owner	Operator
	DTSOL+MSO+TSO+DTSO				
321901	77990+63153+72128+77993	NL	NOE	EVL	NOR
321902	77991+63154+72129+77994	NL	NOE	EVL	NOR
321903	77992+63155+72130+77995	NL	NOE	EVL	NOR

Right: *The final three Class 321s to be built were funded by West Yorkshire PTE for use on the Doncaster-Leeds route to replace old secondhand former NSE stock. Based at Leeds Neville Hill, the sets are still deployed on the same route. Today, classified as 321/9, the sets sport Northern electric blue livery, off-set by grey passenger doors and carry Metro branding. Set No. 321903 is viewed at Leeds.* **CJM**

Class 322

Vehicle Length: (Driving) 65ft 0¾in (19.83m) Width: 9ft 3in (2.82m)
(Inter) 65ft 4¼in (19.92m) Horsepower: 1,328hp (996kW)
Height: 12ft 4¾in (3.78m) Seats (total/car): 291S, 74S/83S/76S/58S

Number	Formation	Depot	Livery	Owner	Operator
	DTSOL+MSO+TSO+DTSO				
322481	78163+63137+72023+77985	NL	NOR	EVL	NOR
322482	78164+63138+72024+77986	NL	NOR	EVL	NOR
322483	78165+63139+72025+77987	NL	NOR	EVL	NOR
322484	78166+63140+72026+77988	NL	NOR	EVL	NOR
322485	78167+63141+72027+77989	NL	NOR	EVL	NOR

Class 323

Vehicle Length: (Driving) 76ft 8¼in (23.37m) Width: 9ft 2¼in (2.80m)
(Inter) 76ft 10¾in (23.44m) Horsepower: 1,565hp (1,168kW)
Height: 12ft 4¾in (3.78m) Seats (total/car) 323223-225: 244S, 82S/80S/82S
323226-239: 284S, 98S/88S/98S

Number	Formation	Depot	Livery	Owner	Op'r	Number	Formation	Depot	Livery	Owner	Op'r
	DMSO(A)+PTSO+DMSO(B)					323231	64031+72231+65031	LG	NOR	PTR	NOR
323223	64023+72223+65023	LG	NOR	PTR	NOR	323232	64032+72232+65032	LG	NOR	PTR	NOR
323224	64024+72224+65024	LG	NOR	PTR	NOR	323233	64033+72233+65033	LG	NOR	PTR	NOR
323225	64025+72225+65025	LG	NOR	PTR	NOR	323234	64034+72234+65034	LG	NOR	PTR	NOR
323226	64026+72226+65026	LG	NOR	PTR	NOR	323235	64035+72235+65035	LG	NOR	PTR	NOR
323227	64027+72227+65027	LG	NOR	PTR	NOR	323236	64036+72236+65036	LG	NOR	PTR	NOR
323228	64028+72228+65028	LG	NOR	PTR	NOR	323237	64037+72237+65037	LG	NOR	PTR	NOR
323229	64029+72229+65029	LG	NOR	PTR	NOR	323238	64038+72238+65038	LG	NOR	PTR	NOR
323230	64030+72230+65030	LG	NOR	PTR	NOR	323239	64039+72239+65039	LG	NOR	PTR	NOR

Above: *Soon to be displaced by new Class 331 stock are the 17 Class 323s introduced in the early 1990s and currently operate local services in the Manchester area. The long term future for this class is unclear, at one time it was suggested they would move to the Birmingham area to operate with like sets allocated to Soho, but with new trains ordered for the West Midlands this is unlikely to happen. Set No. 323235 displays unbranded Northern livery.* **Cliff Beeton**

Class 331
Civity

Vehicle Length: (Driving) 77ft 10¾in (23.74m)
(Inter) 75ft 11in (23.14m)
Height: 12ft 1½in (3.79m)
Width: 9ft 0¼in (2.75m)
Horsepower: 1,475hp (1,100kW)
Seats (total/car): 3 Car - 203S, 51S/80S/72S
4 Car - 280S, 51S/80S/80S/72S

Number	Formation DMSL+PTS+DMS	Depot	Livery	Owner	Operator
331001	463001+464001+466001	AN	NNR	EVL	NOR
331002	463002+464002+466002	AN	NNR	EVL	NOR
331003	463003+464003+466003	AN	NNR	EVL	NOR
331004	463004+464004+466004	AN	NNR	EVL	NOR
331005	463005+464005+466005	AN	NNR	EVL	NOR
331006	463006+464006+466006	AN	NNR	EVL	NOR
331007	463007+464007+466007	AN	NNR	EVL	NOR
331008	463008+464008+466008	AN	NNR	EVL	NOR
331009	463009+464009+466009	AN	NNR	EVL	NOR
331010	463010+464010+466010	AN	NNR	EVL	NOR
331011	463011+464011+466011	AN	NNR	EVL	NOR
331012	463012+464012+466012	AN	NNR	EVL	NOR
331013	463013+464013+466013	AN	NNR	EVL	NOR
331014	463014+464014+466014	AN	NNR	EVL	NOR
331015	463015+464015+466015	AN	NNR	EVL	NOR
331016	463016+464016+466016	AN	NNR	EVL	NOR
331017	463017+464017+466017	AN	NNR	EVL	NOR
331018	463018+464018+466018	AN	NNR	EVL	NOR
331019	463019+464019+466019	AN	NNR	EVL	NOR
331020	463020+464020+466020	AN	NNR	EVL	NOR
331021	463021+464021+466021	AN	NNR	EVL	NOR
331022	463022+464022+466022	AN	NNR	EVL	NOR
331023	463023+464023+466023	AN	NNR	EVL	NOR
331024	463024+464024+466024	AN	NNR	EVL	NOR
331025	463025+464025+466025	AN	NNR	EVL	NOR
331026	463026+464026+466026	AN	NNR	EVL	NOR
331027	463027+464027+466027	AN	NNR	EVL	NOR
331028	463028+464028+466028	AN	NNR	EVL	NOR
331029	463029+464029+466029	AN	NNR	EVL	NOR
331030	463030+464030+466030	AN	NNR	EVL	NOR
331031	463031+464031+466031	AN	NNR	EVL	NOR

Number	Formation	Depot	Livery	Owner	Operator
	DMSL+PTS+TS+DMS				
331101	463101+464101+465101+466101	AN	NNR	EVL	NOR
331102	463102+464102+465102+466102	AN	NNR	EVL	NOR
331103	463103+464103+465103+466103	AN	NNR	EVL	NOR
331104	463104+464104+465104+466104	AN	NNR	EVL	NOR
331105	463105+464105+465105+466105	AN	NNR	EVL	NOR
331106	463106+464106+465106+466106	AN	NNR	EVL	NOR
331107	463107+464107+465107+466107	AN	NNR	EVL	NOR
331108	463108+464108+465108+466108	AN	NNR	EVL	NOR
331109	463109+464109+465109+466109	AN	NNR	EVL	NOR
331110	463110+464110+465110+466110	AN	NNR	EVL	NOR
331111	463111+464111+465111+466111	AN	NNR	EVL	NOR
331112	463112+464112+465112+466112	AN	NNR	EVL	NOR

Below: *The new state-of-the-art CAF 'Civity' three and four car EMUs sets commenced delivery to the UK in autumn 2018 with line testing and staff training commencing in October 2018. Allocated to Allerton depot close to Liverpool, the sets are scheduled to go into passenger service in early 2019. Set No. 331102. a four-car set is illustrated at Crewe.* **CJM**

Class 333

Vehicle Length: (Driving) 77ft 10³⁄₄in (23.74m)   Width: 9ft 0¹⁄₄in (2.75m)
(Inter) 75ft 11in (23.14m)   Horsepower: 1,877hp (1,400kW)
Height: 12ft 1¹⁄₂in (3.79m)   Seats (total/car): 353S, 90S/73S/100S/90S

Number	Formation	Depot	Livery	Owner	Op'r		Number	Formation	Depot	Livery	Owner	Op'r
	DMSO(A)+PTSO+TSO+DMSO(B)						333008	78465+74468+74484+78466	NL	NOM	ANG	NOR
							333009	78467+74469+74485+78468	NL	NOM	ANG	NOR
333001	78451+74461+74477+78452	NL	NNR	ANG	NOR		333010	78469+74470+74486+78470	NL	NOM	ANG	NOR
333002	78453+74462+74478+78454	NL	NOM	ANG	NOR		333011	78471+74471+74487+78472	NL	NOM	ANG	NOR
333003	78455+74463+74479+78456	NL	NOM	ANG	NOR		333012	78473+74472+74488+78474	NL	NOM	ANG	NOR
333004	78457+74464+74480+78458	NL	NOM	ANG	NOR		333013	78475+74473+74489+78476	NL	NNR	ANG	NOR
333005	78459+74465+74481+78460	NL	NOM	ANG	NOR		333014	78477+74474+74490+78478	NL	NOM	ANG	NOR
333006	78461+74466+74482+78462	NL	NOM	ANG	NOR		333015	78479+74475+74491+78480	NL	NOM	ANG	NOR
333007	78463+74467+74483+78464	NL	NOM	ANG	NOR		333016	78481+74476+74492+78482	NL	NOM	ANG	NOR

Names applied
333007 *Alderman J Arthur Godwin -*
  First Lord Mayor of Bradford 1907
333011 *Olicana Ilkley's Roman Fort*

Northern Rail

Above: *The Aire Valley electric network is dominated by Class 333s, built by CAF/Siemens in 2000. Allocated to Leeds Neville Hill the sets carry Northern electric red and blue livery, with light grey contrasting passenger doors. Set No. 333008 is shown departing from Leeds.* **CJM**

Class 399
CityLink

Train Length: 122ft 0¾in (37.2m)
Width: 8ft 8½in (2.65m)
Power supply: 750V dc overhead (equipped for 25kV ac operation)

Power equipment: 6 x 145kW VEM traction motors
Seats (total/car): 88S, 22S/44S/22S

Number	Formation DMOSW+MOS+DMOSW	Depot	Livery	Owner	Operator	Name
399201 (201)*	999001+999101+999201	§	SST	SST	SST	
399202 (202)*	999002+999102+999204	§	SST	SST	SST	*Theo The Childrens Hospital Charity*
399203 (203)*	999003+999103+999203	§	SST	SST	SST	
399204 (204)*(S)	999004+999104+999202	§	SST	SST	SST	
399205 (205)	999005+999105+999205	§	SST	SST	SST	
399206 (206)*	999006+999106+999206	§	SST	SST	SST	
399207 (207)	999007+999107+999207	§	SST	SST	SST	

* Authorised for TramTrain operation   § - Sheffield Nunnery   SST - Sheffield Super Tram

Left: *The three-section articulated TramTrain sets offers seating for 88, the same as on a conventional Sheffield Super Tram, but in a different layout. The sets are painted in Stagecoach style blue orange and red livery. Set No. 399205 calls at the Cathedral stop with a blue line service to Malin Bridge.* **CJM**

Above: *The fleet of seven Vossloh 'TramTrain' sets operating on the Sheffield Super Tram system also operate through services from Cathedral in Sheffield city centre to Rotherham Parkgate shopping centre. When not required for TramTrain operations, the sets augment the standard city centre fleet. Sets operating TramTrain services are required to have modified wheel profiles. Modified set No. 399201 passes through Rotherham Central Network Rail station. The low-level tram platforms are at the Sheffield end of the station. It looks very odd to see a low-level tram passing a standard height station.* **CJM**

Class 769
Flex

Vehicle Length: (Driving) 65ft 0¾in (19.83m)	Width: 9ft 3in (2.82m)
(Inter) 65ft 4¼in (19.92m)	Horsepower: electric 1,326hp (990kW)
Height: 11ft 9in (3.58m)	Horsepower: diesel 2x 523hp (390kW)
Engine: MAN D2876, LUE631	Seats (total/car): 300S, 70S/78S/74S/78S

Class 319 electric sets fitted with diesel engines in driving cars as dual power electro-diesel multiple units.

Number	Formation DMCO+MSO+TSO+DMSO	Depot	Livery	Owner	Operator
769424 (319424)	77337+62914+71795+77336	AN	NNR	PTR	*under conversion*
769431 (319431)	77351+62921+71802+77350	AN	NNR	PTR	**NOR**
769434 (319434)	77357+62924+71805+77356	AN	NNR	PTR	*under test*
769442 (319442)	77373+62932+71813+77372	AN	NNR	PTR	*under conversion*
769448 (319448)	77433+62962+71867+77432	AB	NNR	PTR	*under conversion*
769450 (319450)	77437+62964+71869+77436	AN	NNR	PTR	*under conversion*
769456 (319456)	77449+62970+71875+77448	AN	NNR	PTR	*under test*
769458 (319458)	77453+62972+71877+77452	AN	NNR	PTR	*under conversion*

Right: *A significant project, funded by Porterbrook will see a large number of redundant Class 319 dual-voltage EMUs converted to bi-mode sets under the 'Flex' name. The sets will be rebuilt with a diesel engine raft and alternator group under each driving trailer vehicle. Northern are committed to having a fleet of eight sets. Other main stream TOCs are also investing in the technology, especially Great Western. Demonstration 'Flex' set No. 769000 (319426) is illustrated painted in Northern colours.* **CJM**

Scotrail

Address: ✉ Atrium Court, 50 Waterloo Street, Glasgow, G2 6HQ

✉ customer.relations@scotrail.com, ✆ 0344 811 0141, ⓘ www.scotrail.com

Managing Director: Alex Haynes
Franchise Dates: 1 April 2015 - March 2030
Principal Routes: All Scottish services
Depots: Corkerhill (CK), Shields (GW), Haymarket (HA), Inverness (IS), Millerhill (ML)
Parent Company: Abellio

Class 43 – HST

Vehicle Length: 58ft 5in (18.80m)
Height: 12ft 10in (3.90m)
Width: 8ft 11in (2.73m)
Engine: MTU 16V4000 R41R
Horsepower: 2,250hp (1,680kW)
Electrical Equipment: Brush

Number	Depot	Pool	Livery	Owner	Operator
43003	HA	HPAC	SCI	ANG	ASR
43012	HA	HPAC	SCI	ANG	ASR
43015	HA	HPAC	BLU	ANG	ASR
43021	HA	HPAC	SCI	ANG	ASR
43026	HA	HPAC	SCI	ANG	ASR
43028	HA	HPAC	BLU	ANG	ASR
43030	HA	HPAC	BLU	ANG	ASR
43031	HA	HPAC	SCI	ANG	ASR
43032	HA	HPAC	SCI	ANG	ASR
43033	HA	HPAC	SCI	ANG	ASR
43034	HA	HPAC	BLU	ANG	ASR
43035	HA	HPAC	BLU	ANG	ASR
43036	HA	HPAC	SCI	ANG	ASR
43037	HA	HPAC	SCI	ANG	ASR
43124	HA	HPAC	BLU	ANG	ASR
43125	HA	HPAC	SCI	ANG	ASR
43126	HA	HPAC	SCI	ANG	ASR
43127	HA	HPAC	SCI	ANG	ASR
43128	HA	HPAC	SCI	ANG	ASR
43129	HA	HPAC	BLU	ANG	ASR
43130	HA	HPAC	SCI	ANG	ASR
43131	HA	HPAC	BLU	ANG	ASR
43132	HA	HPAC	SCI	ANG	ASR
43133	HA	HPAC	BLU	ANG	ASR
43134	HA	HPAC	SCI	ANG	ASR
43135	HA	HPAC	SCI	ANG	ASR
43136	HA	HPAC	BLU	ANG	ASR
43137	HA	HPAC	BLU	ANG	ASR
43138	HA	HPAC	BLU	ANG	ASR
43139	HA	HPAC	SCI	ANG	ASR
43140	HA	HPAC	SCI	ANG	ASR
43141	HA	HPAC	SCI	ANG	ASR
43142	HA	HPAC	SCI	ANG	ASR
43143	HA	HPAC	SCI	ANG	ASR
43144	HA	HPAC	BLU	ANG	ASR
43145	HA	HPAC	SCI	ANG	ASR
43146	HA	HPAC	SCI	ANG	ASR
43147	HA	HPAC	BLU	ANG	ASR
43148	HA	HPAC	SCI	ANG	ASR
43149	HA	HPAC	SCI	ANG	ASR
43150	HA	HPAC	SCI	ANG	ASR
43151	HA	HPAC	BLU	ANG	ASR
43152	HA	HPAC	SCI	ANG	ASR
43163	HA	HPAC	SCI	ANG	ASR
43164	HA	HPAC	SCI	ANG	ASR
43168	HA	HPAC	SCI	ANG	ASR
43169	HA	HPAC	SCI	ANG	ASR
43175	HA	HPAC	BLU	ANG	ASR
43176	HA	HPAC	SCI	ANG	ASR
43177	HA	HPAC	SCI	ANG	ASR
43179	HA	HPAC	SCI	ANG	ASR
43181	HA	HPAC	BLU	ANG	ASR
43182	HA	HPAC	BLU	ANG	ASR
43183	HA	HPAC	SCI	ANG	ASR

Names applied
43132 - Aberdeen Station 150th Anniversary

Left: *Made available by the introduction of Class 800 and 802 stock on Great Western, ScotRail have taken on a fleet of 26 2+3 and 2+4 HST sets to operate on the InterCity '7 City' network linking Glasgow, Edinburgh, Inverness, Aberdeen, Perth, Dundee and Stirling. The power cars have been modified by Brush at Loughborough and the trailers, rebuilt with sliding doors have been upgraded at Wabtec Doncaster. The trains now carry a striking Inter7City livery. Class 43 No. 43169 illustrates the new colours.* **CJM**

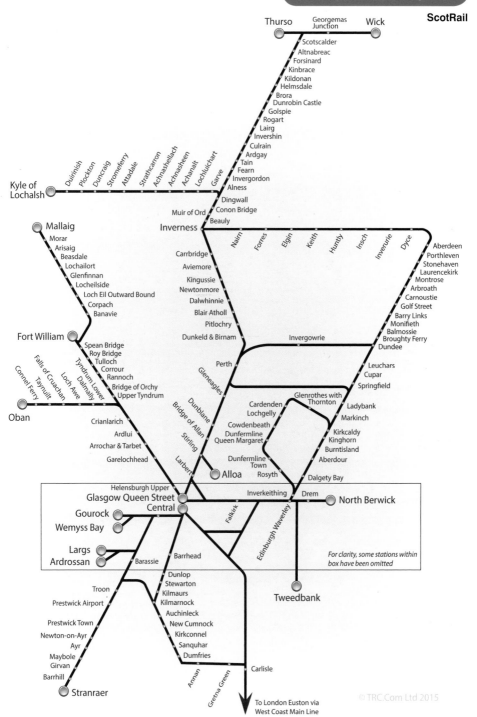

Thurso
Georgemas Junction
Wick

Scotscalder
Altnabreac
Forsinard
Kinbrace
Kildonan
Helmsdale
Brora
Dunrobin Castle
Golspie
Rogart
Lairg
Invershin
Culrain
Ardgay
Tain
Fearn
Invergordon
Alness

Duirinish
Plockton
Duncraig
Stromeferry
Attadale
Strathcarron
Achnashellach
Achnasheen
Achanalt
Lochluichart
Garve

Kyle of Lochalsh

Dingwall
Muir of Ord
Conon Bridge
Beauly

Mallaig
Morar
Arisaig
Beasdale
Lochailort
Glenfinnan
Locheilside
Loch Eil Outward Bound
Corpach
Banavie

Inverness

Nairn
Forres
Elgin
Keith
Huntly
Insch
Inverurie
Dyce

Aberdeen
Porthleven
Stonehaven
Laurencekirk
Montrose
Arbroath
Carnoustie
Golf Street
Barry Links
Monifieth
Balmossie
Broughty Ferry
Dundee

Carrbridge
Aviemore
Kingussie
Newtonmore
Dalwhinnie
Blair Atholl
Pitlochry
Dunkeld & Birnam

Invergowrie

Fort William

Spean Bridge
Roy Bridge
Tulloch
Corrour
Rannoch
Bridge of Orchy
Upper Tyndrum

Falls of Cruachan
Taynuilt
Connel Ferry
Loch Awe
Dalmally
Tyndrum Lower

Perth

Gleneagles

Leuchars
Cupar
Springfield

Oban

Crianlarich
Ardlui
Arrochar & Tarbet
Garelochhead

Dunblane
Bridge of Allan
Stirling
Larbert

Cardenden
Lochgelly
Cowdenbeath
Dunfermline Queen Margaret

Glenrothes with Thornton
Ladybank
Markinch
Kirkcaldy
Kinghorn
Burntisland
Aberdour

Dunfermline Town
Rosyth

Alloa

Dalgety Bay

Helensburgh Upper
Glasgow Queen Street
Central
Gourock
Wemyss Bay

Inverkeithing
Drem
North Berwick

Falkirk

Edinburgh Waverley

Largs
Ardrossan
Barassie
Barrhead

For clarity, some stations within box have been omitted

Troon
Prestwick Airport
Prestwick Town
Newton-on-Ayr
Ayr
Maybole
Girvan
Barrhill

Dunlop
Stewarton
Kilmaurs
Kilmarnock
Auchinleck
New Cumnock
Kirkconnel
Sanquhar
Dumfries

Tweedbank

Stranraer

Annan
Gretna Green
Carlisle

To London Euston via West Coast Main Line

© TRC.Com Ltd 2015

ScotRail

Passenger Train Operating Companies - ScotRail

Class 153

Vehicle Length: 76ft 5in (23.29m)
Height: 12ft 3⅛in (3.75m)
Width: 8ft 10in (2.70m)

Engine: 1 x NT855R5 of 285hp
Horsepower: 285hp (213kW)
Seats (total/car): TBA

In 2019-2020 ScotRail will be taking on five Class 153s to modify as cycle/baggage cars for Scottish scenic route services.

Number	Formation DML	Depot	Livery	Owner	Operator
153377	52377	-		ASR	ANG	ASR

Class 156
Super Sprinter

Vehicle Length: 75ft 6in (23.03m)
Height: 12ft 6in (3.81m)
Width: 8ft 11in (2.73m)

Engine: 1 x Cummins NT855R5 of 285hp per car
Horsepower: 570hp (425kW)
Seats (total/car): 142S, 70 or 72S

Number	Formation DMSL+DMS	Depot	Livery	Owner	Operator
156430	52430+57430	CK	SCR	ANG	ASR
156431	52431+57431	CK	SCR	ANG	ASR
156432	52432+57432	CK	SCR	ANG	ASR
156433	52433+57433	CK	SCR	ANG	ASR
156434	52434+57434	CK	SCR	ANG	ASR
156435	52435+57435	CK	SCR	ANG	ASR
156436	52436+57436	CK	SCR	ANG	ASR
156437	52437+57437	CK	SCR	ANG	ASR
156439	52439+57439	CK	SCR	ANG	ASR
156442	52442+57442	CK	SCR	ANG	ASR
156445	52445+57445	CK	SCR	ANG	ASR
156446	52446+57446	CK	SCR	ANG	ASR
156450	52450+57450	CK	SRB	ANG	ASR
156453	52453+57453	CK	SRB	ANG	ASR
156456	52456+57456	CK	SRB	ANG	ASR
156457	52457+57457	CK	SCR	ANG	ASR
156458	52458+57458	CK	SCR	ANG	ASR
156462	52462+57462	CK	SCR	ANG	ASR
156467	52467+57467	CK	SCR	ANG	ASR
156474	52474+57474	CK	SCR	ANG	ASR
156476	52476+57476	CK	SRB	ANG	ASR
156477	52477+57477	CK	SCR	ANG	ASR
156478§	52478+57478	CK	SCR	BRO	ASR
156492	52492+57492	CK	SCR	ANG	ASR
156493	52493+57493	CK	SCR	ANG	ASR
156494	52494+57494	CK	SCR	ANG	ASR
156495	52495+57495	CK	SCR	ANG	ASR
156499	52499+57499	CK	SRB	ANG	ASR
156500	52500+57500	CK	SCR	ANG	ASR
156501	52501+57501	CK	SCR	ANG	ASR
156502	52502+57502	CK	SCR	ANG	ASR
156503	52503+57503	CK	SCR	ANG	ASR
156504	52504+57504	CK	SCR	ANG	ASR
156505	52505+57505	CK	SCR	ANG	ASR
156506	52506+57506	CK	SCR	ANG	ASR
156507	52507+57507	CK	SCR	ANG	ASR
156508	52508+57508	CK	SCR	ANG	ASR
156509	52509+57509	CK	SCR	ANG	ASR
156510	52510+57510	CK	SCR	ANG	ASR
156511	52511+57511	CK	SCR	ANG	ASR
156512	52512+57512	CK	SCR	ANG	ASR
156513	52513+57513	CK	SCR	ANG	ASR
156514	52514+57514	CK	SCR	ANG	ASR

§ Owned by Brodie Engineering, prototype refurbished set.

Left: *The largest fleet of Class 156 'Super Sprinter' two-car sets are on the books of Abellio ScotRail, allocated to Corkerhill depot in Glasgow. The units operate longer-distance non-electrified routes and in the main most have been upgraded in recent years, with a number now carrying the latest Scottish Railways blue and white livery. Set No. 156505 is seen at Carlisle while operating a Glasgow & South Western service.*
Nathan Williamson

Class 158

Vehicle Length: 76ft 1¾in (23.21m)
Height: 12ft 6in (3.81m)
Width: 9ft 3¼in (2.82m)

Engine: 1 x Cummins NTA855R of 350hp per vehicle
Horsepower: 700hp (522kW)
Seats (total/car): 14F/116S, 14F-46S/70S, * 138S, 68S/70S

Number	Formation DMCL/DMSL *+DMS	Depot	Livery	Owner	Operator
158701	52701+57701	IS	SCR	PTR	ASR
158702	52702+57702	IS	SCR	PTR	ASR
158703	52703+57703	IS	SCR	PTR	ASR
158704	52704+57704	IS	SCR	PTR	ASR
158705	52705+57705	IS	SCR	PTR	ASR
158706	52706+57706	IS	SCR	PTR	ASR
158707	52707+57707	IS	SCR	PTR	ASR
158708	52708+57708	IS	SCR	PTR	ASR
158709	52709+57709	IS	SCR	PTR	ASR
158710	52710+57710	IS	SCR	PTR	ASR
158711	52711+57711	IS	SCR	PTR	ASR
158712	52712+57712	IS	SCR	PTR	ASR
158713	52713+57713	IS	SCR	PTR	ASR
158714	52714+57714	IS	SCR	PTR	ASR
158715	52715+57715	IS	SCR	PTR	ASR
158716	52716+57716	IS	SCR	PTR	ASR
158717	52717+57717	IS	SCR	PTR	ASR
158718	52718+57718	IS	SCR	PTR	ASR
158719	52719+57719	IS	SCR	PTR	ASR
158720	52720+57720	IS	SCR	PTR	ASR
158721	52721+57721	IS	SCR	PTR	ASR

158722	52722+57722	IS	SCR	PTR	ASR		158732	52732+57732	CK	SCR	PTR	ASR
158723	52723+57723	IS	SCR	PTR	ASR		158733	52733+57733	CK	SCR	PTR	ASR
158724	52724+57724	IS	SCR	PTR	ASR		158734	52734+57734	CK	SCR	PTR	ASR
158725	52725+57725	IS	SCR	PTR	ASR		158735	52735+57735	CK	SCR	PTR	ASR
158726	52726+57726	CK	SCR	PTR	ASR		158736	52736+57736	CK	SCR	PTR	ASR
158727	52727+57727	IS	SCR	PTR	ASR		158737	52737+57737	CK	SCR	PTR	ASR
158728	52728+57728	IS	SCR	PTR	ASR		158738	52738+57738	CK	SCR	PTR	ASR
158729	52729+57729	HA	SCR	PTR	ASR		158739	52739+57739	CK	SCR	PTR	ASR
158730	52730+57730	CK	SCR	PTR	ASR		158740	52740+57740	CK	SCR	PTR	ASR
158731	52731+57731	CK	SCR	PTR	ASR		158741	52741+57741	CK	SCR	PTR	ASR

Names applied
158715 Haymarket

Right: *Although the numbers are now reduced following cascade of some units to new operators following introduction of new stock in Scotland, ScotRail are still a major operator of Class 158s, with two-car sets based at both Inverness and Haymarket depots. A repaint policy is currently being undertaken to put all sets in Scottish Railways blue and white colours. Set No. 158715 is seen at North Queensferry.* **Antony Christie**

Class 170/3
Turbostar

Vehicle Length: 77ft 6in (23.62m)		Engine: 1 x MTU 6R 183TD13H of 422hp per vehicle
Height: 12ft 4½in (3.77m)		Horsepower: 1,266hp (944kW)
Width: 8ft 10in (2.69m)		Seats (total/car): 197S, 57S/76S/64S

Number	Formation	Depot	Livery	Owner	Operator
	DMSL+MS+DMSL				
170393	50393+56393+79393	HA	SCR	PTR	ASR
170394	50394+56394+79394	HA	SCR	PTR	ASR
170395	50395+56395+79395	HA	SCR	PTR	ASR
170396	50396+56396+79396	HA	SCR	PTR	ASR

Class 170/4
Turbostar

Vehicle Length: 77ft 6in (23.62m)		Engine: 1 x MTU 6R 183TD13H of 422hp per vehicle
Height: 12ft 4½in (3.77m)		Horsepower: 1,266hp (944kW)
Width: 8ft 10in (2.69m)		(170431/432 have 3 x 483hp engines giving 1,449hp)
		Seats (total/car): 18F/168S 9F-43S/76S/9F-49S

Number	Formation	Depot	Livery	Owner	Op'r		Number	Formation	Depot	Livery	Owner	Op'r
	DMCL+MS+DMCL						170415	50415+56415+79415	HA	SCR	PTR	ASR
							170416	50416+56416+79416	HA	SCB	EVL	ASR
170401	50401+56401+79401	HA	SCR	PTR	ASR		170417	50417+56417+79417	HA	SCB	EVL	ASR
170402	50402+56402+79402	HA	SCR	PTR	ASR		170418	50418+56418+79418	HA	SCB	EVL	ASR
170403	50403+56403+79403	HA	SCR	PTR	ASR		170419	50419+56419+79419	HA	SCB	EVL	ASR
170404	50404+56404+79404	HA	SCR	PTR	ASR		170420	50420+56420+79420	HA	SCB	EVL	ASR
170405	50405+56405+79405	HA	SCR	PTR	ASR		170425	50425+56425+79425	HA	SCR	PTR	ASR
170406	50406+56406+79406	HA	SCR	PTR	ASR		170426	50426+56426+79426	HA	SCR	PTR	ASR
170407	50407+56407+79407	HA	SCR	PTR	ASR		170427	50427+56427+79427	HA	SCR	PTR	ASR
170408	50408+56408+79408	HA	SCR	PTR	ASR		170428	50428+56428+79428	HA	SCR	PTR	ASR
170409	50409+56409+79409	HA	SCR	PTR	ASR		170429	50429+56429+79429	HA	SCR	PTR	ASR
170410	50410+56410+79410	HA	SCR	PTR	ASR		170430	50430+56430+79430	HA	SCR	PTR	ASR
170411	50411+56411+79411	HA	SCR	PTR	ASR		170431	50431+56431+79431	HA	SCR	PTR	ASR
170412	50412+56412+79412	HA	SCR	PTR	ASR		170432	50432+56432+79432	HA	SCR	PTR	ASR
170413	50413+56413+79413	HA	SCR	PTR	ASR		170433	50433+56433+79433	HA	SCR	PTR	ASR
170414	50414+56414+79414	HA	SCR	PTR	ASR		170434	50434+56434+79434	HA	SCR	PTR	ASR

Class 170/4
Turbostar

Vehicle Length: 77ft 6in (23.62m)		Engine: 1 x MTU 6R 183TD13H of 422hp per vehicle
Height: 12ft 4½in (3.77m)		Horsepower: 1,266hp (944kW)
Width: 8ft 10in (2.69m)		Seats: 170450-170457 (total/car) 9F/180S, 55S/76S/9F,49S

Number	Formation	Depot	Livery	Owner	Op'r
	DMSL+MS+DMCL				
170450	50450+56450+79450	HA	SCR	PTR	ASR
170451	50451+56451+79451	HA	SCR	PTR	ASR

170452	50452+56452+79452	HA	SCR	PTR	ASR

ScotRail

Left: *The majority of longer distance diesel services operated by ScotRail are formed of three car Class 170 'Turbostar' sets, based at Haymarket depot in Edinburgh. Sets sport Scottish Railways blue and white colour. Class 170/3 sets are standard class only, while 170/4 sets include first class seats. Set No. 170406 is seen at Glasgow Queen Street*
Antony Christie

Class 314

Vehicle Length: (Driving) 64ft 11¹⁄₂in (19.80m)
(Inter) 65ft 4¹⁄₄in (19.92m)
Height: 11ft 6¹⁄₂in (3.58m)
Width: 9ft 3in (2.82m)
Horsepower: 880hp (656kW)
Seats (total/car): 212S, 68S/76S/68S

Number	Formation DMSO(A)+PTSO+DMSO(B)	Depot	Livery	Owner	Operator
314201	64583+71450+64584	GW	SCC	ANG	ASR
314202	64585+71451+64586	GW	SCC	ANG	ASR
314203	64587+71452+64588*	GW	SCR	ANG	ASR
314204(S)	64589+71453+64590	GW	SCR	ANG	ASR
314205	64591+71454+64592	GW	SCR	ANG	ASR
314206	64593+71455+64594	GW	SCC	ANG	ASR
314207	64595+71456+64596	GW	SCC	ANG	ASR
314208	64597+71457+64598	GW	SCR	ANG	ASR
314209	64599+71458+64600	GW	SCC	ANG	ASR
314210	64601+71459+64602	GW	SCC	ANG	ASR
314211	64603+71460+64604	GW	SCR	ANG	ASR
314213(S)	64607+71462+64608	GW	SCC	ANG	ASR
314214	64609+71463+64610	GW	SCR	ANG	ASR
314215	64611+71464+64612	GW	SCC	ANG	ASR
314216	64613+71465+64614	GW	SCR	ANG	ASR

* 64588 was rebuilt from Class 507 car No. 64426 and seats 74S

Left: *A class set for early withdrawal is the 1972-design three-car Class 314s used on Glasgow local services. Based at Glasgow Shields Road depot, the fleet sport a mix of carmine and cream SPT colours and the latest Scottish Railways blue and white. Set No. 314204 (now stored) stands under the roof at Glasgow Central station.*
Antony Christie

Class 318

Vehicle Length: (Driving) 65ft 0³⁄₄in (19.83m)
(Inter) 65ft 4¹⁄₄in (19.92m)
Height: 12ft 1¹⁄₂in (3.70m)
Width: 9ft 3in (2.82m)
Horsepower: 1,328hp (996kW)
Seats (total/car): 216S, 66S/79S/71S

Number	Formation DTSO(A)+MSO+DTSO(B)	Depot	Livery	Owner	Operator
318250	77240+62866+77260	GW	SCR	EVL	ASR
318251	77241+62867+77261	GW	SCR	EVL	ASR
318252	77242+62868+77262	GW	SCR	EVL	ASR
318253	77243+62869+77263	GW	SCR	EVL	ASR

318254	77244+62870+77264	GW	SCR	EVL	ASR
318255	77245+62871+77265	GW	SCR	EVL	ASR
318256	77246+62872+77266	GW	SCR	EVL	ASR
318257	77247+62873+77267	GW	SCR	EVL	ASR
318258	77248+62874+77268	GW	SCR	EVL	ASR
318259	77249+62875+77269	GW	SCR	EVL	ASR
318260	77250+62876+77270	GW	SCR	EVL	ASR
318261	77251+62877+77271	GW	SCC	EVL	ASR
318262	77252+62878+77272	GW	SCR	EVL	ASR
318263	77253+62879+77273	GW	SCC	EVL	ASR
318264	77254+62880+77274	GW	SCR	EVL	ASR
318265	77255+62881+77275	GW	SCR	EVL	ASR
318266	77256+62882+77276	GW	SCR	EVL	ASR
318267	77257+62883+77277	GW	SCR	EVL	ASR
318268	77258+62884+77278	GW	SCR	EVL	ASR
318269	77259+62885+77279	GW	SCR	EVL	ASR
318270	77288+62890+77289	GW	SCR	EVL	ASR

Right: *A fleet of 21 Class 318 sets are operated by ScotRail, based at Glasgow Shields Road and used on Glasgow local lines. Originally these sets were built with a front gangway, but these were removed when cab improvements were made during refurbishment. The front end now offers much improved visibility. All sets sport Scottish Railways blue and white. Set No. 318257 is seen at Partick.*
Antony Christie

Class 320/3

Vehicle Length: (Driving) 65ft 0¾in (19.83m)
(Inter) 65ft 4¼in (19.92m)
Height: 12ft 4¾in (3.78m)
Width: 9ft 3in (2.82m)
Horsepower: 1,328hp (996kW)
Seats (total/car): 206S, 51S/78S/77S

Number	Formation DTSO(A)+MSO+DTSO(B)	Depot	Livery	Owner	Operator
320301	77899+63021+77921	GW	SCR	EVL	ASR
320302	77900+63022+77922	GW	SCR	EVL	ASR
320303	77901+63023+77923	GW	SCR	EVL	ASR
320304	77902+63024+77924	GW	SCR	EVL	ASR
320305	77903+63025+77925	GW	SCR	EVL	ASR
320306	77904+63026+77926	GW	SCR	EVL	ASR
320307	77905+63027+77927	GW	SCR	EVL	ASR
320308	77906+63028+77928	GW	SCR	EVL	ASR
320309	77907+63029+77929	GW	SCR	EVL	ASR
320310	77908+63030+77930	GW	SCR	EVL	ASR
320311	77909+63031+77931	GW	SCR	EVL	ASR
320312	77910+63032+77932	GW	SCR	EVL	ASR
320313	77911+63033+77933	GW	SCR	EVL	ASR
320314	77912+63034+77934	GW	SCR	EVL	ASR
320315	77913+63035+77935	GW	SCR	EVL	ASR
320316	77914+63036+77936	GW	SCR	EVL	ASR
320317	77915+63037+77937	GW	SCR	EVL	ASR
320318	77916+63038+77938	GW	SCR	EVL	ASR
320319	77917+63039+77939	GW	SCR	EVL	ASR
320320	77918+63040+77940	GW	SCR	EVL	ASR
320321	77919+63041+77941	GW	SCR	EVL	ASR
320322	77920+63042+77942	GW	SCR	EVL	ASR

Passenger Train Operating Companies - ScotRail

ScotRail

Class 320/4

	Vehicle Length: (Driving) 65ft 0¾in (19.83m)	Width: 9ft 3in (2.82m)
	(Inter) 65ft 4¼in (19.92m)	Horsepower: 1,328hp (996kW)
	Height: 12ft 4¾in (3.78m)	Seats (total/car): 28F/197S, 28F-40S/79S//78S

Number	Formation	Depot	Livery	Owner	Operator
	DTSO(A)+MSO+DTSO(B)				
320401 (321401)	78095+63063+77943	GW	SCR	EVL	ASR
320402 (321402)	78096+63064+77944	GW	SCR	EVL	ASR
320404 (321404)	78098+63066+77946	GW	SCR	EVL	ASR
320411 (321411)	78105+63073+77953	GW	SCR	EVL	ASR
320412 (321412)	78106+63074+77954	GW	SCR	EVL	ASR
320413 (321413)	78107+63075+77955	GW	SCR	EVL	ASR
320414 (321414)	78108+63076+77956	GW	SCR	EVL	ASR
320415 (321415)	78109+63077+77957	GW	SCR	EVL	ASR
320416 (321416)	78110+63078+77958	GW	SCR	EVL	ASR
320417 (321417)	78111+63079+77959	GW	SCR	EVL	ASR
320418 (321418)	78112+63080+77962	GW	SCR	EVL	ASR
320420 (321420)	78114+68032+77964	GW	SCR	EVL	ASR

Left: *Two batches of Class 320s operate for ScotRail. The 22 Class 320/3 sets were delivered new to Scotland in 1990, while in 2016-2019 a further batch of sets were introduced, when some displaced Class 321/4s were reduced to three-car formation by removal of the TSO and reclassified as 320/4 to supplement the fleet. One of the converted sets No. 320416 (modified from 321 No. 321416), is seen at Cambuslang.* **Antony Christie**

Class 334
Juniper

	Vehicle Length: (Driving) 69ft 0¾in (21.04m)	Width: 9ft 2¾in (2.80m)
	(Inter) 65ft 4½in (19.93m)	Horsepower: 1,448hp (1,080kW)
	Height: 12ft 3in (3.77m)	Seats (total/car): 178S, 64S/55S/59S

Number	Formation	Depot	Livery	Owner	Operator
	DMSO(A)+PTSO+DMSO(B)				
334001	64101+74301+65101	GW	SCR	EVL	ASR
334002	64102+74302+65102	GW	SCR	EVL	ASR
334003	64103+74303+65103	GW	SCR	EVL	ASR
334004	64104+74304+65104	GW	SCR	EVL	ASR
334005	64105+74305+65105	GW	SCR	EVL	ASR
334006	64106+74306+65106	GW	SCR	EVL	ASR
334007	64107+74307+65107	GW	SCR	EVL	ASR
334008	64108+74308+65108	GW	SCR	EVL	ASR
334009	64109+74309+65109	GW	SCR	EVL	ASR
334010	64110+74310+65110	GW	SCR	EVL	ASR
334011	64111+74311+65111	GW	SCR	EVL	ASR
334012	64112+74312+65112	GW	SCR	EVL	ASR
334013	64113+74313+65113	GW	SCR	EVL	ASR
334014	64114+74314+65114	GW	SCR	EVL	ASR
334015	64115+74315+65115	GW	SCR	EVL	ASR
334016	64116+74316+65116	GW	SCR	EVL	ASR
334017	64117+74317+65117	GW	SCR	EVL	ASR
334018	64118+74318+65118	GW	SCR	EVL	ASR
334019	64119+74319+65119	GW	SCR	EVL	ASR
334020	64120+74320+65120	GW	SCR	EVL	ASR
334021	64121+74321+65121	GW	SCR	EVL	ASR
334022	64122+74322+65122	GW	SCR	EVL	ASR
334023	64123+74323+65123	GW	SCR	EVL	ASR
334024	64124+74324+65124	GW	SCR	EVL	ASR
334025	64125+74325+65125	GW	SCR	EVL	ASR
334026	64126+74326+65126	GW	SCR	EVL	ASR
334027	64127+74327+65127	GW	SCR	EVL	ASR

334028	64128+74328+65128	GW	SCR	EVL	ASR
334029	64129+74329+65129	GW	SCR	EVL	ASR
334030	64130+74330+65130	GW	SCR	EVL	ASR
334031	64131+74331+65131	GW	SCR	EVL	ASR
334032	64132+74332+65132	GW	SCR	EVL	ASR
334033	64133+74333+65133	GW	SCR	EVL	ASR
334034	64134+74334+65134	GW	SCR	EVL	ASR
334035	64135+74335+65135	GW	SCR	EVL	ASR
334036	64136+74336+65136	GW	SCR	EVL	ASR
334037	64137+74337+65137	GW	SCR	EVL	ASR
334038	64138+74338+65138	GW	SCR	EVL	ASR
334039	64139+74339+65139	GW	SCR	EVL	ASR
334040	64140+74340+65140	GW	SCR	EVL	ASR

Right: *When seeking new trains in the late 1990s, ScotRail opted for a fleet of 40 Alstom 'Juniper' three-car sets. Based at Glasgow Shields Road depot, today the sets can be seen operating between Edinburgh and Glasgow and on suburban routes in the Glasgow area. All units sport Scottish Railways blue and white livery. Set No. 334040 is shown approaching Edinburgh Park.*
Antony Christie

Class 365
Networker Express

Vehicle Length: (Driving) 68ft 6½in (20.89m) *Width: 9ft 2½in (2.81m)*
(Inter) 65ft 9¼in (20.89m) *Horsepower: 1,684hp (1,256kW)*
Height: 12ft 4½in (3.77m) *Seats (total/car): 24F/239S, 12F-56S/59S/68S/12F-56S*

Number	Formation	Depot	Livery	Owner	Operator
	DMCO(A)+TSO+PTSO+DMCO(B)				
365509	65902+72257+72256+65943	GW	SCW	EVL	ASR
365513	65906+72265+72264+65947	GW	SCW	EVL	ASR
365517	65910+72273+72272+65951	GW	SCW	EVL	ASR
365519	65912+72277+72276+65953	GW	SCW	EVL	ASR
365521	65914+72281+72280+65955	GW	SCW	EVL	ASR
365523	65916+72285+72284+65957	GW	SCW	EVL	ASR
365525	65918+72289+72288+65959	GW	SCW	EVL	ASR
365529	65922+72297+72296+65963	GW	SCW	EVL	ASR
365533	65926+72305+72304+65967	GW	SCW	EVL	ASR
365537	65930+72313+72312+65971	GW	SCW	EVL	ASR

Right: *Due to very delayed delivery of new Class 385 stock from Hitachi to operate the newly electrified Edinburgh-Glasgow corridor, Scottish Railways took on 10 off-lease Class 365 'Networker Express' sets in 2018 to help out until the Class 385s could be commissioned. The Class 365s painted in GTR grey/white livery were given dark blue passenger doors and ScotRail bodyside branding. The sets will be taken off lease once the Class 385 fleet are commissioned. Set No. 365521 is shown at Edinburgh Park.*
Antony Christie

Left side (rotated): *Passenger Train Operating Companies - ScotRail*

Train Operating Companies

ScotRail

Class 380/0
Desiro

Vehicle Length: 77ft 3in (23.57m)			Horsepower: 1,341hp (1,000kW)			
Height: 12ft 1½in (3.7m)			Seats (total/car): 191S, 70S/57S/64S			
Width: 9ft 2in (2.7m)						

Number	Formation DMSO(A)+PTSO+DMSO(B)	Depot	Livery	Owner	Operator
380001	38501+38601+38701	GW	SCR	EVL	ASR
380002	38502+38602+38702	GW	SCR	EVL	ASR
380003	38503+38603+38703	GW	SCR	EVL	ASR
380004	38504+38604+38704	GW	SCR	EVL	ASR
380005	38505+38605+38705	GW	SCR	EVL	ASR
380006	38506+38606+38706	GW	SCR	EVL	ASR
380007	38507+38607+38707	GW	SCR	EVL	ASR
380008	38508+38608+38708	GW	SCR	EVL	ASR
380009	38509+38609+38709	GW	SCR	EVL	ASR
380010	38510+38610+38710	GW	SCR	EVL	ASR
380011	38511+38611+38711	GW	SCR	EVL	ASR
380012	38512+38612+38712	GW	SCR	EVL	ASR
380013	38513+38613+38713	GW	SCR	EVL	ASR
380014	38514+38614+38714	GW	SCR	EVL	ASR
380015	38515+38615+38715	GW	SCR	EVL	ASR
380016	38516+38616+38716	GW	SCR	EVL	ASR
380017	38517+38617+38717	GW	SCR	EVL	ASR
380018	38518+38618+38718	GW	SCR	EVL	ASR
380019	38519+38619+38719	GW	SCR	EVL	ASR
380020	38520+38620+38720	GW	SCR	EVL	ASR
380021	38521+38621+38721	GW	SCR	EVL	ASR
380022	38522+38622+38722	GW	SCR	EVL	ASR

Left: *During 2010-2011 two fleets of Class 380 Siemens 'Desiro' units were delivered to Scotland, three-car sets classified as 380/0 and four-car sets as Class 380/1. Sets are based at Glasgow Shields Road and can be found operating in both the Edinburgh and Glasgow area. Three-car set No. 380007 is shown at Drem with an Edinburgh to North Berwick service.* **Antony Christie**

Class 380/1
Desiro

Vehicle Length: 77ft 3in (23.57m)			Horsepower: 1,341hp (1,000kW)			
Height: 12ft 1½in (3.7m)			Seats (total/car): 265S, 70S/57S/74S/64S			
Width: 9ft 2in (2.7m)						

Number	Formation DMSO(A)+PTSO+MSO+DMSO(B)	Depot	Livery	Owner	Operator
380101	38551+38651+38851+38751	GW	SCR	EVL	ASR
380102	38552+38652+38852+38752	GW	SCR	EVL	ASR
380103	38553+38653+38853+38753	GW	SCR	EVL	ASR
380104	38554+38654+38854+38754	GW	SCR	EVL	ASR
380105	38555+38655+38855+38755	GW	SCR	EVL	ASR
380106	38556+38656+38856+38756	GW	SCR	EVL	ASR
380107	38557+38657+38857+38757	GW	SCR	EVL	ASR
380108	38558+38658+38858+38758	GW	SCR	EVL	ASR
380109	38559+38659+38859+38759	GW	SCR	EVL	ASR
380110	38560+38660+38860+38760	GW	SCR	EVL	ASR
380111	38561+38661+38861+38761	GW	SCR	EVL	ASR

380112	38562+38662+38862+38762	GW	SCR	EVL	ASR
380113	38563+38663+38863+38763	GW	SCR	EVL	ASR
380114	38564+38664+38864+38764	GW	SCR	EVL	ASR
380115	38565+38665+38865+38765	GW	SCR	EVL	ASR
380116	38566+38666+38866+38766	GW	SCR	EVL	ASR

Class 385/0
AT200

Vehicle Length: 77ft 3in (23.57m) Horsepower: 1,341hp (1,000kW)
Height: awaited 12ft 2in (3.7m) Seats (total/car): 190S , 48S/80S/62S
Width: 9ft 2in (2.74m)

Number	Formation DMSO(A)+PTSO+DMSO(B)	Depot	Livery	Owner	Operator
385001	441001+442001+444001	EC	SCR	SMB	ASR
385002	441002+442002+444002	EC	SCR	SMB	ASR
385003	441003+442003+444003	EC	SCR	SMB	ASR
385004	441004+442004+444004	EC	SCR	SMB	ASR
385005	441005+442005+444005	EC	SCR	SMB	ASR
385006	441006+442006+444006	EC	SCR	SMB	ASR
385007	441007+442007+444007	EC	SCR	SMB	ASR
385008	441008+442008+444008	EC	SCR	SMB	ASR
385009	441009+442009+444009	EC	SCR	SMB	ASR
385010	441010+442010+444010	EC	SCR	SMB	ASR
385011	441011+442011+444011	EC	SCR	SMB	ASR
385012	441012+442012+444012	EC	SCR	SMB	ASR
385013	441013+442013+444013	EC	SCR	SMB	ASR
385014	441014+442014+444014	EC	SCR	SMB	ASR
385015	441015+442015+444015	EC	SCR	SMB	ASR
385016	441016+442016+444016	EC	SCR	SMB	ASR
385017	441017+442017+444017	EC	SCR	SMB	ASR
385018	441018+442018+444018	EC	SCR	SMB	ASR
385019	441019+442019+444019	EC	SCR	SMB	ASR
385020	441020+442020+444020	EC	SCR	SMB	ASR
385021	441021+442021+444021	EC	SCR	SMB	ASR
385022	441022+442022+444022	EC	SCR	SMB	ASR
385023	441023+442023+444023	EC	SCR	SMB	ASR
385024	441024+442024+444024	EC	SCR	SMB	ASR
385025	441025+442025+444025	EC	SCR	SMB	ASR
385026	441026+442026+444026	EC	SCR	SMB	ASR
385027	441027+442027+444027	EC	SCR	SMB	ASR
385028	441028+442028+444028	EC	SCR	SMB	ASR
385029	441029+442029+444029	EC	SCR	SMB	ASR
385030	441030+442030+444030	EC	SCR	SMB	ASR
385031	441031+442031+444031	EC	SCR	SMB	ASR
385032	441032+442032+444032	EC	SCR	SMB	ASR
385033	441033+442033+444033	EC	SCR	SMB	ASR
385034	441034+442034+444034	EC	SCR	SMB	ASR
385035	441035+442035+444035	EC	SCR	SMB	ASR
385036	441036+442036+444036	EC	SCR	SMB	ASR
385037	441037+442037+444037	EC	SCR	SMB	ASR
385038	441038+442038+444038	EC	SCR	SMB	ASR
385039	441039+442039+444039	EC	SCR	SMB	ASR
385040	441040+442040+444040	EC	SCR	SMB	ASR
385041	441041+442041+444041	EC	SCR	SMB	ASR
385042	441042+442042+444042	EC	SCR	SMB	ASR
385043	441043+442043+444043	EC	SCR	SMB	ASR
385044	441044+442044+444044	EC	SCR	SMB	ASR
385045	441045+442045+444045	EC	SCR	SMB	ASR
385046	441046+442046+444046	EC	SCR	SMB	ASR

Class 385/1
AT200

Vehicle Length: 77ft 3in (23.57m) Horsepower: 1,341hp (1,000kW)
Height: awaited 12ft 2in (3.7m) Seats (total/car): 20F/237S, 20F, 15S/80S/80S/62S
Width: 9ft 2in (2.74m)

Number	Formation DMCO+PTSO+TSO+DMSO	Depot	Livery	Owner	Operator
385101	441101+442101+443101+444101	EC	SCR	SMB	ASR
385102	441102+442102+443102+444102	EC	SCR	SMB	ASR

ScotRail

385103	441103+442103+443103+444103	EC	SCR	SMB	ASR
385104	441104+442104+443104+444104	EC	SCR	SMB	ASR
385105	441105+442105+443105+444105	EC	SCR	SMB	ASR
385106	441106+442106+443106+444106	EC	SCR	SMB	ASR
385107	441107+442107+443107+444107	EC	SCR	SMB	ASR
385108	441108+442108+443108+444108	EC	SCR	SMB	ASR
385109	441109+442109+443109+444109	EC	SCR	SMB	ASR
385110	441110+442110+443110+444110	EC	SCR	SMB	ASR
385111	441111+442111+443111+444111	EC	SCR	SMB	ASR
385112	441112+442112+443112+444112	EC	SCR	SMB	ASR
385113	441113+442113+443113+444113	EC	SCR	SMB	ASR
385114	441114+442114+443114+444114	EC	SCR	SMB	ASR
385115	441115+442115+443115+444115	EC	SCR	SMB	ASR
385116	441116+442116+443116+444116	EC	SCR	SMB	ASR
385117	441117+442117+443117+444117	EC	SCR	SMB	ASR
385118	441118+442118+443118+444118	EC	SCR	SMB	ASR
385119	441119+442119+443119+444119	EC	SCR	SMB	ASR
385120	441120+442120+443120+444120	EC	SCR	SMB	ASR
385121	441121+442121+443121+444121	EC	SCR	SMB	ASR
385122	441122+442122+443121+444122	EC	SCR	SMB	ASR
385123	441123+442123+443123+444123	EC	SCR	SMB	ASR
385124	441124+442124+443124+444124	EC	SCR	SMB	ASR

Left: *Currently ScotRail is taking delivery of a sizeable fleet of Class 385 Hitachi sets, formed as both three and four-car sets. Introduction has been very much delayed and problematic, with major issues surrounding the design of the cab windscreens. Some sets have been constructed at the Hitachi plant in Japan, while the majority have been assembled at the Hitachi plant at Newton Aycliffe in County Durham. Four-car set No. 385122 with its first class end nearest the camera is illustrated at Falkirk High.* **Antony Christie**

Class 68 'UK Light'

Vehicle Length: 67ft 3in (20.5m)		Engine: Caterpillar C175-16
Height: 12ft 6½in (3.82m)		Horsepower: 3,750hp (2,800kW)
Speed: 100mph (161km/h)		Electrical Equipment: ABB

Number	Depot	Pool	Livery	Owner	Operator	Name
68006	CR	XHVE	SCR	BEA	DRS	*Daring*
68007	CR	XHVE	SCR	BEA	DRS	*Valiant*

Left: *Until a full fleet of new electric trains are in service, Abellio ScotRail will continue to use two Class 68 powered loco-hauled sets on a limited number of Fife Circle services. The contract between DRS and Abellio has seen the ScotRail white and blue livery applied to two locos Nos. 68006 and 68007 which the operators try and deploy in Scotland. No. 68007 Valiant is seen at Haymarket with an inbound peak hour service to Edinburgh Waverley.* **Nathan Williamson**

Mk2 Hauled Stock

Vehicle Length: 66ft 0in (20.11m) *Width: 9ft 3in (2.81m)*
Height: 12ft 9½in (3.89m) *Seats (total/car): 60S*

AC2F - TSO *Seating 60S*

Number	Depot	Livery	Op'r
5945	ML	SCR	ASR
5952	ML	SCR	ASR
5955	ML	SCR	ASR
5965	ML	SCR	ASR
5976	ML	SCR	ASR

5987	ML	SCR	ASR
6027	ML	SCR	ASR
6137	ML	SCR	ASR
6176	ML	SCR	ASR
6177	ML	SCR	ASR
6183	ML	SCR	ASR

AE2F - BSO *Seating 32S*

Number	Depot	Livery	Op'r
9521	ML	SCR	ASR
9539	ML	SCR	ASR

Right *To operate with the Class 68s on Abellio ScotRail loco-hauled services, a fleet of Mk2s are hired from DRS and outbased at Millerhill. These 13 vehicles are formed up into two sets and are painted in Scottish Railways blue and white livery. 60 seat TSO No. 5945 is shown at Edinburgh Waverley.*
Antony Christie

Mk3 HST Stock

Vehicle Length: 75ft 0in (22.86m) *Width: 8ft 11in (2.71m)*
Height: 12ft 9in (3.88m) *Bogie Type: BT10*

A total of 121 Mk3 HST trailer vehicles, previously used on Great Western services are transferring to Scotland to operate the Inter7City services. When we closed for press just one fully refurbished set had been released to traffic (HA26), other sets were operating in unrefurbished state, including the use of track deposit toilets and slam doors. All refurbished vehicles have single leaf sliding doors.

Vehicles allocated to ScotRail in January 2019, showing set numbers and formations. These will change.

Unrefurbished with slam doors and track deposit toilets

Set No.	Formation
HA01	42256 42572 41124 44029
HA02	44039 41144 42301 42296
HA03	42208 41104 44066 42206
HA04	42574 42269 42267 42325
HA05	42558 42032 42010 41022
HA06	41158 42200 42129 44086
HA07	44004 42013 42012 41010
HA09	41146 42300 42299 44040
HA10	42255 41135 42279 42280 44035
HA11	44015 42047 42207 40207
HA12	42035 42033 44011 40210

Refurbished with sliding doors and retention toilets

Set No.	Formation
HA25	42045 42292 42562 40602 (41038)
HA26	42046 42561 42004 40601

Right: *A fleet of 121 Mk3 HST vehicles are currently being refurbished and fitted with sliding pocket doors at Wabtec Doncaster for deployment on Abellio ScotRail Inter7City services. Two types of vehicle are under conversion, Trailer Standard Open and Trailer First Micro Buffet. TSO vehicle No. 42561 displays the new grey and blue livery.* **CJM**

Serco Caledonian Sleepers

Address: ✉ 1 Union Street, Inverness, IV1 1PP
          ✆ enquiry@Sleeper.scot ✆ 0330 060 0500
          ⓘ www.sleeper.scot

Managing Director: Ryan Flaherty
Franchise Dates: 1 April 2015 - 1 April 2030
Principal Routes: Inverness, Aberdeen, Fort William, Edinburgh, Glasgow
          to London Euston
Depots: Edinburgh Craigentinny (EC), Inverness (IS), Polmadie (PO)
Parent Company: Serco

Passenger Train Operating Companies - Serco Caledonian

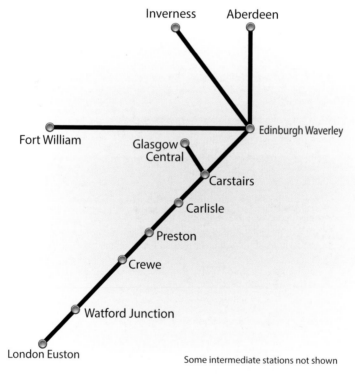

Inverness   Aberdeen

Fort William   Glasgow   Edinburgh Waverley
          Central
               Carstairs

                    Carlisle

                    Preston

                    Crewe

          Watford Junction

London Euston   Some intermediate stations not shown

© TRC.Com Ltd 2015

Serco Caledonian

Class 73/9

Vehicle Length: 53ft 8in (16.35m)
Height: 12ft 5¾in (3.79m)
Width: 8ft 8in (2.64m)
Electrical Equipment: English Electric

Power: MTU 8V4000R43L
Horsepower: diesel - 1,550hp (1,119kW)
ETH index: 96

Number		Depot	Pool	Livery	Owner	Operator
73966	(73005)	EC	GBCS	SCS	GBR	SCS
73967	(73006)	EC	GBCS	SCS	GBR	SCS
73968	(73117)	EC	GBCS	SCS	GBR	SCS
73969	(73105)	EC	GBCS	SCS	GBR	SCS
73970	(73103)	EC	GBCS	SCS	GBR	SCS
73971	(73207/122)	EC	GBCS	SCS	GBR	SCS

Right: *Owned by GB Railfreight and on long lease to Caledonian Sleepers are a fleet of six Class 73/9 locomotives. These original electro-diesel locos, now with electric traction systems isolated and fitted with a 1,550hp MTU 8V4000R43L prime mover operate the sleeper services between Edinburgh and Fort William, Inverness and Aberdeen. Initially working with Mk3 stock, the locos now power the new CAF Mk5 formations, for which the fleet have been fitted with drop-head Dellner couplings. No. 73971 is seen at Edinburgh Waverley.* **Antony Christie**

Class 86

Vehicle Length: 58ft 6in (17.83m)
Height: 13ft 0⅝in (3.97m)
Width: 8ft 8¼in (2.64m)

Power Collection: 25kV ac overhead
Horsepower: 5,900hp (4,400kW)
Electrical Equipment: GEC

Number	Depot	Pool	Livery	Owner	Operator	Name
86101	WN	GBCH	SCS	ETL	GBR	*Sir William Stanier FRS*
86401	WN	GBCH	SCS	ETL	GBR	*Mons Meg*

Class 87

Vehicle Length: 58ft 6in (17.83m)
Height: 13ft 1¼in (3.99m)
Width: 8ft 8¼in (2.64m)

Power Collection: 25kV ac overhead
Horsepower: 7,860hp (5,680kW)
Electrical Equipment: GEC

Number	Depot	Pool	Livery	Owner	Operator	Name
87002	WN	GBCH	SCS	ETL	GBR	*Royal Sovereign*

Right: *To assist with empty stock movements of the Caledonian Sleeper trains, mainly in the London area, Electric Traction Ltd lease one or more of their main line certified Class 86s or 87s to GB Railfreight who hold the Caledonian Sleeper traction contract. The three locos are usually kept at Willesden depot and operate on as required basis. The three sport Caledonian Sleeper teal livery. No. 87002 is seen at London Euston. On the rare occasion one of the ETL locos might be used to power the sleeper service if no other traction is available.* **Antony Christie**

Class 92

Vehicle Length: 70ft 1in (21.34m)			Power Collection: 25kV ac overhead / 750V dc third rail		
Height: 13ft 0in (3.95m)			Horsepower: ac - 6,700hp (5,000kW) / dc - 5,360hp (4,000kW)		
Width: 8ft 8in (2.66m)			Electrical Equipment: Brush		

Number	Depot	Pool	Livery	Owner	Operator	Number	Depot	Pool	Livery	Owner	Operator
92014	WN	GBSL	SCS	GBR	SCS	92028§	WN	GBSL	SCS	GBR	SCS
92018§	WN	GBSL	SCS	GBR	SCS	92033§	WN	GBSL	SCS	GBR	SCS
92023§	WN	GBSL	SCS	GBR	SCS	92038	WN	GBCT	SCS	GBR	SCS

§ Fitted with Dellner coupling

Below: *GB Railfreight has a fleet of six Class 92s dedicated to Caledonian Sleeper haulage, based at Willesden. The locos sport full Caledonian teal livery and are in the process of upgrade with the fitting of Dellner couplings to attach to the new CAF-built Mk5 stock currently entering service. The drop-head Dellners also allow standard hook and shackle coupling if needed. No. 92033 is shown at Edinburgh Waverley, a loco fitted with a Dellner coupling.* **Antony Christie**

Mk2 and Mk3 Hauled Stock

Mk2		Mk3	
Vehicle Length: 66ft 0in (20.11m)	Width: 9ft 3in (2.81m)	Vehicle Length: 75ft 0in (22.86m)	Width: 8ft 11in (2.71m)
Height: 12ft 9½in (3.89m)	Seats (total/car): 60S	Height: 12ft 9in (3.88m)	Bogie Type: BT10

AN1F (Mk2) - RLO *Seating 28-30F*

Number	Depot	Livery	Owner
6700 (3347)	PO	CAS	ERS
6701 (3346)	PO	CAS	EVL
6702 (3421)	PO	SRB	EVL
6703 (3308)	PO	CAS	ERS
6704 (3341)	PO	SRB	EVL
6705 (3310)	PO	SRB	EVL
6706 (3283)	PO	SRB	EVL
6707 (3276)	PO	SRB	EVL
6708 (3370)	PO	SRB	EVL

AN1F (Mk2) - BUO *Seating 31U*

Number	Depot	Livery	Owner
9800 (5751)	PO	CAS	ERS
9801 (5760)	PO	CAS	EVL
9802 (5772)	PO	CAS	EVL
9803 (5799)	PO	SRB	EVL
9804 (5826)	PO	SRB	EVL
9805 (5833)	PO	SRB	EVL
9806 (5840)	PO	SRB	EVL
9807 (5851)	PO	SCR	ERS
9808 (5871)	PO	SCR	EVL
9809 (5890)	PO	SRB	EVL
9810 (5892)	PO	SRB	EVL

AU4G (Mk3) - SLEP *Comps 12*

Number	Depot	Livery	Owner
10501	PO	SRB	PTR

10502	PO	SRB	PTR
10504	PO	SRB	PTR
10513	PO	SRB	PTR
10516(S)	PO	SCR	-
10519	PO	SRB	PTR
10520	PO	SRB	PTR
10522	PO	SRB	PTR
10526	PO	SRB	PTR
10527	PO	SRB	PTR
10529	PO	SRB	PTR
10531	PO	SRB	PTR
10542	PO	SRB	PTR
10543	PO	SRB	PTR
10544	PO	SRB	PTR
10551	PO	SRB	PTR
10553	PO	SRB	PTR
10561	PO	SRB	PTR
10565	PO	SRB	PTR
10580	PO	CAS	PTR
10597	PO	SRB	PTR
10598	PO	SRB	PTR
10600	PO	SRB	PTR
10605	PO	SRB	PTR
10607	PO	SRB	PTR
10610	PO	SRB	PTR
10614	PO	SRB	PTR

AS4G (MK3) - SLE *Comps 13*

Number	Depot	Livery	Owner
10675	PO	SRB	PTR
10683	PO	SRB	PTR
10688	PO	SRB	PTR
10690	PO	SRB	PTR
10693	PO	CAS	PTR
10703	PO	SRB	PTR

AQ4G (Mk3) - SLED *Comps 11*

Number	Depot	Livery	Owner
10648	PO	SRB	PTR
10650	PO	SRB	PTR
10666	PO	SRB	PTR
10680	PO	SRB	PTR
10689	PO	SRB	PTR
10699	PO	SRB	PTR
10706	PO	SRB	PTR
10714	PO	SRB	PTR
10718	PO	SRB	PTR
10719	PO	SRB	PTR
10722	PO	SRB	PTR

§ Stored Long Marston

Right: *Following full introduction of new Mk5 sleeper sets on Caledonian services, the existing Mk2 and Mk3 vehicles will be withdrawn and are likely to be sent for scrap or long term store. Mk2F RLO No. 6701 is shown in Caledonian Sleeper livery.*
Antony Christie

Mk5 Hauled Stock

Mk5 Sleeper Seating Brake
31U, 32.5T

Number	Depot	Livery	Owner
15001	PO	CAS	LOM
15002	PO	CAS	LOM
15003	PO	CAS	LOM
15004	PO	CAS	LOM
15005	PO	CAS	LOM
15006	PO	CAS	LOM
15007	PO	CAS	LOM
15008	PO	CAS	LOM
15009	PO	CAS	LOM
15010	PO	CAS	LOM
15011	PO	CAS	LOM

Mk5 Sleeper Lounge
28U, 35.5T

Number	Depot	Livery	Owner
15101	PO	CAS	LOM
15102	PO	CAS	LOM
15103	PO	CAS	LOM
15104	PO	CAS	LOM
15105	PO	CAS	LOM
15106	PO	CAS	LOM
15107	PO	CAS	LOM
15108	PO	CAS	LOM
15109	PO	CAS	LOM
15110	PO	CAS	LOM

Mk5 Sleeper Accessible
4 Berths, 8 beds, 35.5T

Number	Depot	Livery	Owner
15201	PO	CAS	LOM
15202	PO	CAS	LOM
15203	PO	CAS	LOM
15204	PO	CAS	LOM
15205	PO	CAS	LOM
15206	PO	CAS	LOM
15207	PO	CAS	LOM
15208	PO	CAS	LOM
15209	PO	CAS	LOM
15210	PO	CAS	LOM
15211	PO	CAS	LOM
15212	PO	CAS	LOM
15213	PO	CAS	LOM
15214	PO	CAS	LOM

Mk5 Sleeper
10 berths, 38T

Number	Depot	Livery	Owner
15301	PO	CAS	LOM
15302	PO	CAS	LOM
15303	PO	CAS	LOM
15304	PO	CAS	LOM
15305	PO	CAS	LOM
15306	PO	CAS	LOM
15307	PO	CAS	LOM
15308	PO	CAS	LOM
15309	PO	CAS	LOM
15310	PO	CAS	LOM
15311	PO	CAS	LOM
15312	PO	CAS	LOM
15313	PO	CAS	LOM
15314	PO	CAS	LOM
15315	PO	CAS	LOM
15316	PO	CAS	LOM
15317	PO	CAS	LOM
15318	PO	CAS	LOM
15319	PO	CAS	LOM
15320	PO	CAS	LOM
15321	PO	CAS	LOM
15322	PO	CAS	LOM
15323	PO	CAS	LOM
15324	PO	CAS	LOM
15325	PO	CAS	LOM
15326	PO	CAS	LOM
15327	PO	CAS	LOM
15328	PO	CAS	LOM
15329	PO	CAS	LOM
15330	PO	CAS	LOM
15331	PO	CAS	LOM
15332	PO	CAS	LOM
15333	PO	CAS	LOM
15334	PO	CAS	LOM
15335	PO	CAS	LOM
15336	PO	CAS	LOM
15337	PO	CAS	LOM
15338	PO	CAS	LOM
15339	PO	CAS	LOM
15340	PO	CAS	LOM

Right: *The new CAF-built Mk5 sleeper sets for use on all Caledonian Sleeper services were delivered to Polmadie depot, Scotland from the summer of 2018. The vehicles underwent a major type test programme before entering service in spring 2019 on the 'Lowlander service, Highland services are due to be introduced in mid 2019.*
Antony Christie

South Eastern

Address: ✉ Friars Bridge Court, 41-45 Blackfriars Road, London, SE1 8NZ
📧 info@southeasternrailway.co.uk
📞 08700 000 2222
🌐 www.southeasternrailway.co.uk

Managing Director:	David Stratham
Franchise Dates:	1 April 2006 - running on DfT extension
Principal Routes:	London to Kent and parts of East Sussex, domestic services on HS1
Depots:	Slade Green (SG), Ramsgate (RM), Ashford* (AD) * Operated by Hitachi
Parent Company:	Govia

Class 375/3
Electrostar

Vehicle Length: (Driving) 66ft 9in (20.3m) *Width: 9ft 2in (2.79m)*
(Inter) 65ft 6in (19.96m) *Horsepower: 1,341hp (1,000kW)*
Height: 12ft 4in (3.75m) *Seats (total/car): 16F-170S,60S/16F-50S/60S*

Number	Formation DMSO+MCO+DMSO	Depot	Livery	Owner	Operator	Name
375301	67921+74351+67931	RM	SEB	EVL	SET	
375302	67922+74352+67932	RM	SEB	EVL	SET	
375303	67923+74353+67933	RM	SEB	EVL	SET	
375304	67924+74354+67934	RM	SEB	EVL	SET	
375305	67925+74355+67935	RM	SEB	EVL	SET	
375306	67926+74356+67936	RM	SEB	EVL	SET	
375307	67927+74357+67937	RM	SEB	EVL	SET	
375308	67928+74358+67938	RM	SEB	EVL	SET	
375309	67929+74359+67939	RM	SEB	EVL	SET	
375310	67930+74360+67940	RM	SEB	EVL	SET	

Class 375/6
Electrostar

Vehicle Length: (Driving) 66ft 9in (20.3m) *Width: 9ft 2in (2.79m)*
(Inter) 65ft 6in (19.96m) *Horsepower: 2,012hp (1,500kW)*
Height: 12ft 4in (3.75m) *Seats (total/car): 16F-226S, 60S/16F-50S/56S/60S*

Number	Formation DMSO(A)+MCO+TSO+DMSO(B)	Depot	Livery	Owner	Operator	Name
375601	67801+74251+74201+67851	RM	SEB	EVL	SET	
375602	67802+74252+74202+67852	RM	SEB	EVL	SET	
375603	67803+74253+74203+67853	RM	SEB	EVL	SET	
375604	67804+74254+74204+67854	RM	SEB	EVL	SET	
375605	67805+74255+74205+67855	RM	SEB	EVL	SET	
375606	67806+74256+74206+67856	RM	SEB	EVL	SET	
375607	67807+74257+74207+67857	RM	SEB	EVL	SET	
375608	67808+74258+74208+67858	RM	SEB	EVL	SET	
375609	67809+74259+74209+67859	RM	SEB	EVL	SET	
375610	67810+74260+74210+67860	RM	SEB	EVL	SET	
375611	67811+74261+74211+67861	RM	SEB	EVL	SET	
375612	67812+74262+74212+67862	RM	SEB	EVL	SET	
375613	67813+74263+74213+67863	RM	SEB	EVL	SET	
375614	67814+74264+74214+67864	RM	SEB	EVL	SET	
375615	67815+74265+74215+67865	RM	SEB	EVL	SET	
375616	67816+74266+74216+67866	RM	SEB	EVL	SET	
375617	67817+74267+74217+67867	RM	SEB	EVL	SET	
375618	67818+74268+74218+67868	RM	SEB	EVL	SET	
375619	67819+74269+74219+67869	RM	SEB	EVL	SET	*Driver John Neve*

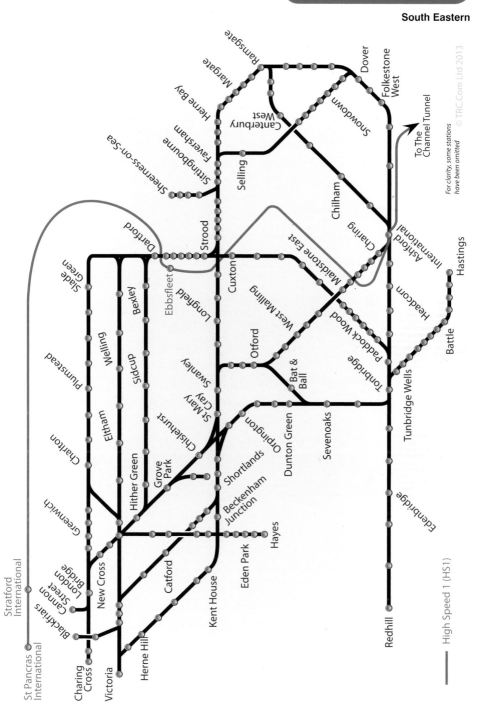

© TRC.Com Ltd 2013

Passenger Train Operating Companies – South Eastern

For clarity, some stations have been omitted

South Eastern

375620	67820+74270+74220+67870	RM	SEB	EVL	SET	
375621	67821+74271+74221+67871	RM	SEB	EVL	SET	
375622	67822+74272+74222+67872	RM	SEB	EVL	SET	
375623	67823+74273+74223+67873	RM	SEB	EVL	SET	*Hospice in the Weald*
375624	67824+74274+74224+67874	RM	SEB	EVL	SET	
375625	67825+74275+74225+67875	RM	SEB	EVL	SET	
375626	67826+74276+74226+67876	RM	SEB	EVL	SET	
375627	67827+74277+74227+67877	RM	SEB	EVL	SET	
375628	67828+74278+74228+67878	RM	SEB	EVL	SET	
375629	67829+74279+74229+67879	RM	SEB	EVL	SET	
375630	67830+74280+74230+67880	RM	SEB	EVL	SET	

Class 375/7
Electrostar

Vehicle Length: (Driving) 66ft 9in (20.3m) *Width: 9ft 2in (2.79m)*
(Inter) 65ft 6in (19.96m) *Horsepower: 2,012hp (1,500kW)*
Height: 12ft 4in (3.75m) *Seats (total/car): 16F-226S, 60S/16F-50S/56S/60S*

Number Formation *Depot Livery Owner Operator Name*
DMSO(A)+MCO+TSO+DMSO(B)

375701	67831+74281+74231+67881	RM	SEB	EVL	SET	*Kent Air Ambulance Explorer*
375702	67832+74282+74232+67882	RM	SEB	EVL	SET	
375703	67833+74283+74233+67883	RM	SEB	EVL	SET	
375704	67834+74284+74234+67884	RM	SEB	EVL	SET	
375705	67835+74285+74235+67885	RM	SEB	EVL	SET	
375706	67836+74286+74236+67886	RM	SEB	EVL	SET	
375707	67837+74287+74237+67887	RM	SEB	EVL	SET	
375708	67838+74288+74238+67888	RM	SEB	EVL	SET	
375709	67839+74289+74239+67889	RM	SEB	EVL	SET	
375710	67840+74290+74240+67890	RM	SEB	EVL	SET	*Rochester Castle*
375711	67841+74291+74241+67891	RM	SEB	EVL	SET	
375712	67842+74292+74242+67892	RM	SEB	EVL	SET	
375713	67843+74293+74243+67893	RM	SEB	EVL	SET	*Rochester Cathedral*
375714	67844+74294+74244+67894	RM	SEB	EVL	SET	
375715	67845+74295+74245+67895	RM	SEB	EVL	SET	

Class 375/8
Electrostar

Vehicle Length: (Driving) 66ft 9in (20.3m) *Width: 9ft 2in (2.79m)*
(Inter) 65ft 6in (19.96m) *Horsepower: 2,012hp (1,500kW)*
Height: 12ft 4in (3.75m) *Seats (total/car): 16F-226S, 60S/16F-50S/56S/60S*

Number Formation *Depot Livery Owner Operator Name*
DMSO(A)+MCO+TSO+DMSO(B)

375801	73301+79001+78201+73701	RM	SEB	EVL	SET	
375802	73302+79002+78202+73702	RM	SEB	EVL	SET	
375803	73303+79003+78203+73703	RM	SEB	EVL	SET	
375804	73304+79004+78204+73704	RM	SEB	EVL	SET	
375805	73305+79005+78205+73705	RM	SEB	EVL	SET	
375806	73306+79006+78206+73706	RM	SEB	EVL	SET	
375807	73307+79007+78207+73707	RM	SEB	EVL	SET	
375808	73308+79008+78208+73708	RM	SEB	EVL	SET	
375809	73309+79009+78209+73709	RM	SEB	EVL	SET	
375810	73310+79010+78210+73710	RM	SEB	EVL	SET	
375811	73311+79011+78211+73711	RM	SEB	EVL	SET	
375812	73312+79012+78212+73712	RM	SEB	EVL	SET	
375813	73313+79013+78213+73713	RM	SEB	EVL	SET	
375814	73314+79014+78214+73714	RM	SEB	EVL	SET	
375815	73315+79015+78215+73715	RM	SEB	EVL	SET	
375816	73316+79016+78216+73716	RM	SEB	EVL	SET	
375817	73317+79017+78217+73717	RM	SEB	EVL	SET	
375818	73318+79018+78218+73718	RM	SEB	EVL	SET	
375819	73319+79019+78219+73719	RM	SEB	EVL	SET	
375820	73320+79020+78220+73720	RM	SEB	EVL	SET	
375821	73321+79021+78221+73721	RM	SEB	EVL	SET	
375822	73322+79022+78222+73722	RM	SEB	EVL	SET	
375823	73323+79023+78223+73723	RM	SEB	EVL	SET	*Ashford Proudly served by rail for 175 years*
375824	73324+79024+78224+73724	RM	SEB	EVL	SET	
375825	73325+79025+78225+73725	RM	SEB	EVL	SET	

375826	73326+79026+78226+73726	RM	SEB	EVL	SET
375827	73327+79027+78227+73727	RM	SEB	EVL	SET
375828	73328+79028+78228+73728	RM	SEB	EVL	SET
375829	73329+79029+78229+73729	RM	SEB	EVL	SET
375830	73330+79030+78230+73730	RM	SEB	EVL	SET

Right: *South Eastern main line domestic services are in the hands of a large fleet of 'Electrostar' Class 375 sets, formed in various sub-classes, allocated to Ramsgate. All have been refurbished and now carry South Eastern dark blue livery. On four-car sets, first class seating has now been repositioned into an intermediate vehicle from its original position in the driving cars. Class 375/8 No. 375819 is shown on the 'Eastern' side at London Victoria.* **Antony Christie**

Class 375/9
Electrostar

Vehicle Length: (Driving) 66ft 9in (20.3m)
(Inter) 65ft 6in (19.96m)
Height: 12ft 4in (3.75m)
Width: 9ft 2in (2.79m)
Horsepower: 2,012hp (1,500kW)
Seats (total/car): 16F-226S, 60S/16F-50S/56S/60S

Number	Formation DMSO(A)+MCO+TSO+DMSO(B)	Depot	Livery	Owner	Operator
375901	73331+79031+79061+73731	RM	SEB	EVL	SET
375902	73332+79032+79062+73732	RM	SEB	EVL	SET
375903	73333+79033+79063+73733	RM	SEB	EVL	SET
375904	73334+79034+79064+73734	RM	SEB	EVL	SET
375905	73335+79035+79065+73735	RM	SEB	EVL	SET
375906	73336+79036+79066+73736	RM	SEB	EVL	SET
375907	73337+79037+79067+73737	RM	SEB	EVL	SET
375908	73338+79038+79068+73738	RM	SEB	EVL	SET
375909	73339+79039+79069+73739	RM	SEB	EVL	SET
375910	73340+79040+79070+73740	RM	SEB	EVL	SET
375911	73341+79041+79071+73741	RM	SEB	EVL	SET
375912	73342+79042+79072+73742	RM	SEB	EVL	SET
375913	73343+79043+79073+73743	RM	SEB	EVL	SET
375914	73344+79044+79074+73744	RM	SEB	EVL	SET
375915	73345+79045+79075+73745	RM	SEB	EVL	SET
375916	73346+79046+79076+73746	RM	SEB	EVL	SET
375917	73347+79047+79077+73747	RM	SEB	EVL	SET
375918	73348+79048+79078+73748	RM	SEB	EVL	SET
375919	73349+79049+79079+73749	RM	SEB	EVL	SET
375920	73350+79050+79080+73750	RM	SEB	EVL	SET
375921	73351+79051+79081+73751	RM	SEB	EVL	SET
375922	73352+79052+79082+73752	RM	SEB	EVL	SET
375923	73353+79053+79083+73753	RM	SEB	EVL	SET
375924	73354+79054+79084+73754	RM	SEB	EVL	SET
375925	73355+79055+79085+73755	RM	SEB	EVL	SET
375926	73356+79056+79086+73756	RM	SEB	EVL	SET
375927	73357+79057+79087+73757	RM	SEB	EVL	SET

Class 376
Electrostar

Vehicle Length: (Driving) 66ft 9in (20.3m)
(Inter) 65ft 6in (19.96m)
Height: 12ft 4in (3.75m)
Width: 9ft 2in (2.79m)
Horsepower: 2,682hp (2,000kW)
Seats (total/car): 216S, 36S/48S/48S/48S/36S + 116 perch

Number	Formation DMSO(A)+MSO+TSO+MSO+DMSO(B)	Depot	Livery	Owner	Operator	Name
376001	61101+63301+64301+63501+61601	SG	SET	EVL	SET	*Alan Doggett*
376002	61102+63302+64302+63502+61602	SG	SET	EVL	SET	
376003	61103+63303+64303+63503+61603	SG	SET	EVL	SET	
376004	61104+63304+64304+63504+61604	SG	SET	EVL	SET	
376005	61105+63305+64305+63505+61605	SG	SET	EVL	SET	

South Eastern

(sidebar, left margin) Passenger Train Operating Companies - South Eastern

376006	61106+63306+64306+63506+61606	SG	SET	EVL	SET
376007	61107+63307+64307+63507+61607	SG	SET	EVL	SET
376008	61108+63308+64308+63508+61608	SG	SET	EVL	SET
376009	61109+63309+64309+63509+61609	SG	SET	EVL	SET
376010	61110+63310+64310+63510+61610	SG	SET	EVL	SET
376011	61111+63311+64311+63511+61611	SG	SET	EVL	SET
376012	61112+63312+64312+63512+61612	SG	SET	EVL	SET
376013	61113+63313+64313+63513+61613	SG	SET	EVL	SET
376014	61114+63314+64314+63514+61614	SG	SET	EVL	SET
376015	61115+63315+64315+63515+61615	SG	SET	EVL	SET
376016	61116+63316+64316+63516+61616	SG	SET	EVL	SET
376017	61117+63317+64317+63517+61617	SG	SET	EVL	SET
376018	61118+63318+64318+63518+61618	SG	SET	EVL	SET
376019	61119+63319+64319+63519+61619	SG	SET	EVL	SET
376020	61120+63320+64320+63520+61620	SG	SET	EVL	SET
376021	61121+63321+64321+63521+61621	SG	SET	EVL	SET
376022	61122+63322+64322+63522+61622	SG	SET	EVL	SET
376023	61123+63323+64323+63523+61623	SG	SET	EVL	SET
376024	61124+63324+64324+63524+61624	SG	SET	EVL	SET
376025	61125+63325+64325+63525+61625	SG	SET	EVL	SET
376026	61126+63326+64326+63526+61626	SG	SET	EVL	SET
376027	61127+63327+64327+63527+61627	SG	SET	EVL	SET
376028	61128+63328+64328+63528+61628	SG	SET	EVL	SET
376029	61129+63329+64329+63529+61629	SG	SET	EVL	SET
376030	61130+63330+64330+63530+61630	SG	SET	EVL	SET
376031	61131+63331+64331+63531+61631	SG	SET	EVL	SET
376032	61132+63332+64332+63532+61632	SG	SET	EVL	SET
376033	61133+63333+64333+63533+61633	SG	SET	EVL	SET
376034	61134+63334+64334+63534+61634	SG	SET	EVL	SET
376035	61135+63335+64335+63535+61635	SG	SET	EVL	SET
376036	61136+63336+64336+63536+61636	SG	SET	EVL	SET

Left: *South Eastern operates a fleet of 36 five-car 'Metro' style Class 376 'Electrostar' sets on the busy inner suburban routes from London to Dartford. The sets have fewer seats and enlarged standing areas to transport the largest number of people. The sets are non gangwayed and carry white livery, off-set by yellow doors and a beige base band. Set No. 376034 is illustrated at Lewisham.* **CJM**

Class 377/5
Electrostar

Vehicle Length: (Driving) 66ft 9in (20.40m)
(Inter) 65ft 6in (19.99m)
Height: 12ft 4in (3.77m)
Width: 9ft 2in (2.79m)
Horsepower: 2,012hp (1,500kW) (ac), dual-voltage sets
Seats (total/car): 20F-221S, 10F-48S/69S/56S/10F-48S

Number	Formation	Depot	Livery	Owner	Operator
	DMCO(A)+MSO+PTSO+DMCO(B)				
377501	73501+75901+74901+73601	RM	SEB	PTR	SET
377502	73502+75902+74902+73602	RM	SEB	PTR	SET
377503	73503+75903+74903+73603	RM	SEB	PTR	SET
377504	73504+75904+74904+73604	RM	SEB	PTR	SET
377505	73505+75905+74905+73605	RM	SEB	PTR	SET
377506	73506+75906+74906+73606	RM	SEB	PTR	SET
377507	73507+75907+74907+73607	RM	SEB	PTR	SET
377508	73508+75908+74908+73608	RM	SEB	PTR	SET
377509	73509+75909+74909+73609	RM	SEB	PTR	SET

377510	73510+75910+74910+73610	RM	SEB	PTR	SET	
377511	73511+75911+74911+73611	RM	SEB	PTR	SET	
377512	73512+75912+74912+73612	RM	SEB	PTR	SET	
377513	73513+75913+74913+73613	RM	SEB	PTR	SET	
377514	73514+75914+74914+73614	RM	SEB	PTR	SET	
377515	73515+75915+74915+73615	RM	SEB	PTR	SET	
377516	73516+75916+74916+73616	RM	SEB	PTR	SET	
377517	73517+75917+74917+73617	RM	SEB	PTR	SET	
377518	73518+75918+74918+73618	RM	SEB	PTR	SET	
377519	73519+75919+74919+73619	RM	SEB	PTR	SET	
377520	73520+75920+74920+73620	RM	SEB	PTR	SET	
377521	73521+75921+74921+73621	RM	SEB	PTR	SET	
377522	73522+75922+74922+73622	RM	SEB	PTR	SET	
377523	73523+75923+74923+73623	RM	SEB	PTR	SET	

Class 395
Javelin

Vehicle Length: (Driving) 67ft 7in (20.6m)
(Inter) 67ft 6in (20.5m)
Height: 12ft 6in (3.81m)
Width: 9ft 2in (2.79m)
Horsepower: 4,504hp (3,360kW)
Seats (total/car): 340S, 28S/66S/66S/66S/66S/48S

Number	Formation	Depot	Livery	Owner	Operator	Name
	DMSO(A)+MSO(A)+MSO(B)+MSO(C)+MSO(D)+DMSO(B)					
395001	39011+39012+39013+39014+39015+39016	AD	HS1	EVL	SET	Dame Kelly Holmes
395002	39021+39022+39023+39024+39025+39026	AD	HS1	EVL	SET	Sebastian Coe
395003	39031+39032+39033+39034+39035+39036	AD	HS1	EVL	SET	Sir Steve Redgrave
395004	39041+39042+39043+39044+39045+39046	AD	HS1	EVL	SET	Sir Chris Hoy
395005	39051+39052+39053+39054+39055+39056	AD	HS1	EVL	SET	Dame Tanni Grey-Thompson
395006	39061+39062+39063+39064+39065+39066	AD	HS1	EVL	SET	Daley Thompson
395007	39071+39072+39073+39074+39075+39076	AD	HS1	EVL	SET	Steve Backley
395008	39081+39082+39083+39084+39085+39086	AD	HS1	EVL	SET	Ben Ainslie
395009	39091+39092+39093+39094+39095+39096	AD	HS1	EVL	SET	Rebecca Adlington
395010	39101+39102+39103+39104+39105+39106	AD	HS1	EVL	SET	Duncan Goodhew
395011	39111+39112+39113+39114+39115+39116	AD	HS1	EVL	SET	Katherine Grainger
395012	39121+39122+39123+39124+39125+39126	AD	HS1	EVL	SET	
395013	39131+39132+39133+39134+39135+39136	AD	HS1	EVL	SET	
395014	39141+39142+39143+39144+39145+39146	AD	HS1	EVL	SET	The Victoria Cross
395015	39151+39152+39153+39154+39155+39156	AD	HS1	EVL	SET	
395016	39161+39162+39163+39164+39165+39166	AD	HS1	EVL	SET	Passchendaele Javelin
395017	39171+39172+39173+39174+39175+39176	AD	HS1	EVL	SET	
395018	39181+39182+39183+39184+39185+39186	AD	HS1	EVL	SET	The Victory Javelin
395019	39191+39192+39193+39194+39195+39196	AD	HS1	EVL	SET	Jessica Ennis
395020	39201+39202+39203+39204+39205+39206	AD	HS1	EVL	SET	Jason Kenny
395021	39211+39212+39213+39214+39215+39216	AD	HS1	EVL	SET	Ed Clancy MBE
395022	39221+39222+39223+39224+39225+39226	AD	HS1	EVL	SET	Alistair Brownlee
395023	39231+39232+39233+39234+39235+39236	AD	HS1	EVL	SET	Ellie Simmonds
395024	39241+39242+39243+39244+39245+39246	AD	HS1	EVL	SET	Jonnie Peacock
395025	39251+39252+39253+39254+39255+39256	AD	HS1	EVL	SET	Victoria Pendleton
395026	39261+39262+39263+39264+39265+39266	AD	HS1	EVL	SET	Marc Woods
395027	39271+39272+39273+39274+39275+39276	AD	HS1	EVL	SET	Hannah Cockcroft
395028	39281+39282+39283+39284+39285+39286	AD	HS1	EVL	SET	Laura Trott
395029	39291+39292+39293+39294+39295+39296	AD	HS1	EVL	SET	David Weir

Right: After opening High Speed 1 (HS1) for International high speed traffic, South Eastern took some paths to operate a high speed domestic service from Kent to London St Pancras. To operate these services a fleet of Hitachi AT300, Class 395 sets were built. These six-vehicle sets based at Ashford hitachi depot are known as 'Javelin' sets and most are named after sportsman associated with speed. Set No. 395012 is seen approaching North Downs Tunnel. **CJM**

Passenger Train Operating Companies - South Eastern

South Eastern

Class 465/0
Networker

Vehicle Length: (Driving) 68ft 6½in (20.89m) Width: 9ft 3in (2.81m)
(Inter) 65ft 9¾in (20.05m) Horsepower: 2,252hp (1,680kW)
Height: 12ft 4½in (3.77m) Seats (total/car): 348S, 86S/90S/86S/86S

Number	Formation DMSO(A)+TSO+TSO+DMSO(B)	Depot	Livery	Owner	Operator
465001	64759+72028+72029+64809	SG	SET	EVL	SET
465002	64760+72030+72031+64810	SG	SET	EVL	SET
465003	64761+72032+72033+64811	SG	SET	EVL	SET
465004	64762+72034+72035+64812	SG	SET	EVL	SET
465005	64763+72036+72037+64813	SG	SET	EVL	SET
465006	64764+72038+72039+64814	SG	SET	EVL	SET
465007	64765+72040+72041+64815	SG	SET	EVL	SET
465008	64766+72042+72043+64816	SG	SET	EVL	SET
465009	64767+72044+72045+64817	SG	SET	EVL	SET
465010	64768+72046+72047+64818	SG	SET	EVL	SET
465011	64769+72048+72049+64819	SG	SET	EVL	SET
465012	64770+72050+72051+64820	SG	SET	EVL	SET
465013	64771+72052+72053+64821	SG	SET	EVL	SET
465014	64772+72054+72055+64822	SG	SET	EVL	SET
465015	64773+72056+72057+64823	SG	SET	EVL	SET
465016	64774+72058+72059+64824	SG	SET	EVL	SET
465017	64775+72060+72061+64825	SG	SET	EVL	SET
465018	64776+72062+72063+64826	SG	SET	EVL	SET
465019	64777+72064+72065+64827	SG	SET	EVL	SET
465020	64778+72066+72067+64828	SG	SET	EVL	SET
465021	64779+72068+72069+64829	SG	SET	EVL	SET
465022	64780+72070+72071+64830	SG	SET	EVL	SET
465023	64781+72072+72073+64831	SG	SET	EVL	SET
465024	64782+72074+72075+64832	SG	SET	EVL	SET
465025	64783+72076+72077+64833	SG	SET	EVL	SET
465026	64784+72078+72079+64834	SG	SET	EVL	SET
465027	64785+72080+72081+64835	SG	SET	EVL	SET
465028	64786+72082+72083+64836	SG	SET	EVL	SET
465029	64787+72084+72085+64837	SG	SET	EVL	SET
465030	64788+72086+72087+64838	SG	SET	EVL	SET
465031	64789+72088+72089+64839	SG	SET	EVL	SET
465032	64790+72090+72091+64840	SG	SET	EVL	SET
465033	64791+72092+72093+64841	SG	SET	EVL	SET
465034	64792+72094+72095+64842	SG	SET	EVL	SET
465035	64793+72096+72097+64843	SG	SET	EVL	SET
465036	64794+72098+72099+64844	SG	SET	EVL	SET
465037	64795+72100+72101+64845	SG	SET	EVL	SET
465038	64796+72102+72103+64846	SG	SET	EVL	SET
465039	64797+72104+72105+64847	SG	SET	EVL	SET

Below: *Suburban services operated by South Eastern are in the hands of Class 465 'Networker' sets, introduced by Network SouthEast to replace EPB slam door stock on local routes. Four sub-classes exist, with the Class 465/0 and 465/1 sets built by BREL/ABB. Class 465/0 No. 465018 is seen heading away from London Bridge. The BREL/ABB sets have now been re-engineered with Hitachi traction equipment.* **CJM**

465040	64798+72106+72107+64848	SG	SET	EVL	SET
465041	64799+72108+72109+64849	SG	SET	EVL	SET
465042	64800+72110+72111+64850	SG	SET	EVL	SET
465043	64801+72112+72113+64851	SG	SET	EVL	SET
465044	64802+72114+72115+64852	SG	SET	EVL	SET
465045	64803+72116+72117+64853	SG	SET	EVL	SET
465046	64804+72118+72119+64854	SG	SET	EVL	SET
465047	64805+72120+72121+64855	SG	SET	EVL	SET
465048	64806+72122+72123+64856	SG	SET	EVL	SET
465049	64807+72124+72125+64857	SG	SET	EVL	SET
465050	64808+72126+72127+64858	SG	SET	EVL	SET

Class 465/1
Networker

Vehicle Length: (Driving) 68ft 6½in (20.89m) (Inter) 65ft 9¾in (20.05m) Height: 12ft 4½in (3.77m) Width: 9ft 3in (2.81m) Horsepower: 2,252hp (1,680kW) Seats (total/car): 348S, 86S/90S/86S/86S

Number	Formation DMSO(A)+TSO+TSO+DMSO(B)	Depot	Livery	Owner	Operator
465151	65800+72900+72901+65847	SG	SET	EVL	SET
465152	65801+72902+72903+65848	SG	SET	EVL	SET
465153	65802+72904+72905+65849	SG	SET	EVL	SET
465154	65803+72906+72907+65850	SG	SET	EVL	SET
465155	65804+72908+72909+65851	SG	SET	EVL	SET
465156	65805+72910+72911+65852	SG	SET	EVL	SET
465157	65806+72912+72913+65853	SG	SET	EVL	SET
465158	65807+72914+72915+65854	SG	SET	EVL	SET
465159	65808+72916+72917+65855	SG	SET	EVL	SET
465160	65809+72918+72919+65856	SG	SET	EVL	SET
465161	65810+72920+72921+65857	SG	SET	EVL	SET
465162	65811+72922+72923+65858	SG	SET	EVL	SET
465163	65812+72924+72925+65859	SG	SET	EVL	SET
465164	65813+72926+72927+65860	SG	SET	EVL	SET
465165	65814+72928+72929+65861	SG	SET	EVL	SET
465166	65815+72930+72931+65862	SG	SET	EVL	SET
465167	65816+72932+72933+65863	SG	SET	EVL	SET
465168	65817+72934+72935+65864	SG	SET	EVL	SET
465169	65818+72936+72937+65865	SG	SET	EVL	SET
465170	65819+72938+72939+65866	SG	SET	EVL	SET
465171	65820+72940+72941+65867	SG	SET	EVL	SET
465172	65821+72942+72943+65868	SG	SET	EVL	SET
465173	65822+72944+72945+65869	SG	SET	EVL	SET
465174	65823+72946+72947+65870	SG	SET	EVL	SET
465175	65824+72948+72949+65871	SG	SET	EVL	SET
465176	65825+72950+72951+65872	SG	SET	EVL	SET
465177	65826+72952+72953+65873	SG	SET	EVL	SET
465178	65827+72954+72955+65874	SG	SET	EVL	SET
465179	65828+72956+72957+65875	SG	SET	EVL	SET
465180	65829+72958+72959+65876	SG	SET	EVL	SET
465181	65830+72960+72961+65877	SG	SET	EVL	SET
465182	65831+72962+72963+65878	SG	SET	EVL	SET
465183	65832+72964+72965+65879	SG	SET	EVL	SET
465184	65833+72966+72967+65880	SG	SET	EVL	SET
465185	65834+72968+72969+65881	SG	SET	EVL	SET
465186	65835+72970+72971+65882	SG	SET	EVL	SET
465187	65836+72972+72973+65883	SG	SET	EVL	SET
465188	65837+72974+72975+65884	SG	SET	EVL	SET
465189	65838+72976+72977+65885	SG	SET	EVL	SET
465190	65839+72978+72979+65886	SG	SET	EVL	SET
465191	65840+72980+72981+65887	SG	SET	EVL	SET
465192	65841+72982+72983+65888	SG	SET	EVL	SET
465193	65842+72984+72985+65889	SG	SET	EVL	SET
465194	65843+72986+72987+65890	SG	SET	EVL	SET
465195	65844+72988+72989+65891	SG	SET	EVL	SET
465196	65845+72990+72991+65892	SG	SET	EVL	SET
465197	65846+72992+72993+65893	SG	SET	EVL	SET

Passenger Train Operating Companies - South Eastern

Class 465/2
Networker

Vehicle Length: (Driving) 68ft 6½in (20.89m)	Width: 9ft 3in (2.81m)
(Inter) 65ft 9¾in (20.05m)	Horsepower: 2,252hp (1,680kW)
Height: 12ft 4½in (3.77m)	Seats (total/car): 348S, 86S/90S/86S/86S

Number	Formation	Depot	Livery	Owner	Operator
	DMSO(A)+TSO+TSO+DMSO(B)				
465235	65734+72787+72788+65784	SG	SET	ANG	SET
465236	65735+72789+72790+65785	SG	SET	ANG	SET
465237	65736+72791+72792+65786	SG	SET	ANG	SET
465238	65737+72793+72794+65787	SG	SET	ANG	SET
465239	65738+72795+72796+65788	SG	SET	ANG	SET
465240	65739+72797+72798+65789	SG	SET	ANG	SET
465241	65740+72799+72800+65790	SG	SET	ANG	SET
465242	65741+72801+72802+65791	SG	SET	ANG	SET
465243	65742+72803+72804+65792	SG	SET	ANG	SET
465244	65743+72805+72806+65793	SG	SET	ANG	SET
465245	65744+72807+72808+65794	SG	SET	ANG	SET
465246	65745+72809+72810+65795	SG	SET	ANG	SET
465247	65746+72811+72812+65796	SG	SET	ANG	SET
465248	65747+72813+72814+65797	SG	SET	ANG	SET
465249	65748+72815+72816+65798	SG	SET	ANG	SET
465250	65749+72817+72818+65799	SG	SET	ANG	SET

Class 465/9
Networker

Vehicle Length: (Driving) 68ft 6½in (20.89m)	Width: 9ft 3in (2.81m)
(Inter) 65ft 9¾in (20.05m)	Horsepower: 2,252hp (1,680kW)
Height: 12ft 4½in (3.77m)	Seats (total/car): 24F-302S, 12F-68S/76S/90S/12F-68S

Number	Formation	Depot	Livery	Owner	Operator
	DMCO(A)+TSO+TSO+DMCO(B)				
465901 (465201)	65700+72719+72720+65750	SG	SET	ANG	SET
465902 (465202)	65701+72721+72722+65751	SG	SET	ANG	SET
465903 (465203)	65702+72723+72724+65752	SG	SET	ANG	SET
465904 (465204)	65703+72725+72726+65753	SG	SET	ANG	SET
465905 (465205)	65704+72727+72728+65754	SG	SET	ANG	SET
465906 (465206)	65705+72729+72730+65755	SG	SET	ANG	SET
465907 (465207)	65706+72731+72732+65756	SG	SET	ANG	SET
465908 (465208)	65707+72733+72734+65757	SG	SET	ANG	SET
465909 (465209)	65708+72735+72736+65758	SG	SET	ANG	SET
465910 (465210)	65709+72737+72738+65759	SG	SET	ANG	SET
465911 (465211)	65710+72739+72740+65760	SG	SET	ANG	SET
465912 (465212)	65711+72741+72742+65761	SG	SET	ANG	SET
465913 (465213)	65712+72743+72744+65762	SG	SET	ANG	SET
465914 (465214)	65713+72745+72746+65763	SG	SET	ANG	SET
465915 (465215)	65714+72747+72748+65764	SG	SET	ANG	SET
465916 (465216)	65715+72749+72750+65765	SG	SET	ANG	SET
465917 (465217)	65716+72751+72752+65766	SG	SET	ANG	SET
465918 (465218)	65717+72753+72754+65767	SG	SET	ANG	SET
465919 (465219)	65718+72755+72756+65768	SG	SET	ANG	SET
465920 (465220)	65719+72757+72758+65769	SG	SET	ANG	SET
465921 (465221)	65720+72759+72760+65770	SG	SET	ANG	SET
465922 (465222)	65721+72761+72762+65771	SG	SET	ANG	SET
465923 (465223)	65722+72763+72764+65772	SG	SET	ANG	SET
465924 (465224)	65723+72765+72766+65773	SG	SET	ANG	SET
465925 (465225)	65724+72767+72768+65774	SG	SET	ANG	SET
465926 (465226)	65725+72769+72770+65775	SG	SET	ANG	SET
465927 (465227)	65726+72771+72772+65776	SG	SET	ANG	SET
465928 (465228)	65727+72773+72774+65777	SG	SET	ANG	SET
465929 (465229)	65728+72775+72776+65778	SG	SET	ANG	SET
465930 (465230)	65729+72777+72778+65779	SG	SET	ANG	SET
465931 (465231)	65730+72779+72780+65780	SG	SET	ANG	SET
465932 (465232)	65731+72781+72782+65781	SG	SET	ANG	SET
465933 (465233)	65732+72783+72784+65782	SG	SET	ANG	SET
465934 (465234)	65733+72785+72786+65783	SG	SET	ANG	SET

Right: *A fleet of 34 of the original Metro-Cammell built Class 465/2 sets have been modified to operate on longer distance outer-suburban services and have been installed with a small first class area in both driving cars, modified sets are reclassified as Class 465/9. All Class 465s are allocated to Slade Green depot. With its first class banding clearly visible behind the driving compartment, set No. 465929 is captured at Victoria (Eastern).*
Antony Christie

Passenger Train Operating Companies - South Eastern

Class 466
Networker

Vehicle Length: (Driving) 68ft 6½in (20.89m)   Horsepower: 1,126hp (840kW)
Height: 12ft 4½in (3.77m)   Seats (total/car): 168S, 86S/82S
Width: 9ft 3in (2.81m)

Number	Formation DMSO+DTSO	Depot	Livery	Owner	Operator
466001	64860+78312	SG	SET	ANG	SET
466002	64861+78313	SG	SET	ANG	SET
466003	64862+78314	SG	SET	ANG	SET
466004	64863+78315	SG	SET	ANG	SET
466005	64864+78316	SG	SET	ANG	SET
466006	64865+78317	SG	SET	ANG	SET
466007	64866+78318	SG	SET	ANG	SET
466008	64867+78319	SG	SET	ANG	SET
466009	64868+78320	SG	SET	ANG	SET
466010	64869+78321	SG	SET	ANG	SET
466011	64870+78322	SG	SET	ANG	SET
466012	64871+78323	SG	SET	ANG	SET
466013	64872+78324	SG	SET	ANG	SET
466014	64873+78325	SG	SET	ANG	SET
466015	64874+78326	SG	SET	ANG	SET
466016	64875+78327	SG	SET	ANG	SET
466017	64876+78328	SG	SET	ANG	SET
466018	64877+78329	SG	SET	ANG	SET
466019	64878+78330	SG	SET	ANG	SET
466020	64879+78331	SG	SET	ANG	SET
466021	64880+78332	SG	SET	ANG	SET
466022	64881+78333	SG	SET	ANG	SET
466023	64882+78334	SG	SET	ANG	SET
466024	64883+78335	SG	SET	ANG	SET
466025	64884+78336	SG	SET	ANG	SET
466026	64885+78337	SG	SET	ANG	SET
466027	64886+78338	SG	SET	ANG	SET
466028	64887+78339	SG	SET	ANG	SET
466029	64888+78340	SG	SET	ANG	SET
466030	64889+78341	SG	SET	ANG	SET
466031	64890+78342	SG	SET	ANG	SET
466032	64891+78343	SG	SET	ANG	SET
466033	64892+78344	SG	SET	ANG	SET
466034	64893+78345	SG	SET	ANG	SET
466035	64894+78346	SG	SET	ANG	SET
466036	64895+78347	SG	SET	ANG	SET
466037	64896+78348	SG	SET	ANG	SET
466038	64897+78349	SG	SET	ANG	SET
466039	64898+78350	SG	SET	ANG	SET
466040	64899+78351	SG	SET	ANG	SET
466041	64900+78352	SG	SET	ANG	SET
466042	64901+78353	SG	SET	ANG	SET
466043	64902+78354	SG	SET	ANG	SET

Right: *To permit the operation of flexible train lengths from anything from two-car to 12, a fleet of 2-car Class 466 'Networker' sets were built by Metro-Cammell. The sets are identical to the four-car Class 465/2 unit. In common with the Class 465 sets, the '466s' are finished in white livery, off-set by sky blue passenger doors and a dark grey base band. Unit No. 466030 is illustrated.*
Antony Christie

South Western Railway

Address: Friars Bridge Court, 41-45 Blackfriars Road, London, SE1 8NZ
✉ customerrelations@swrailway.com
✆ 0345 6000 650   ⓘ www.southwesternrailway.com

Managing Director: Andy Mellors
Franchise Dates: 20 August 2017 - August 2023
Principal Routes: London Waterloo - Weymouth, Exeter, Portsmouth and suburban services in Surrey, Berkshire, Hampshire
Depots: Wimbledon Park (WD), Bournemouth (BM), Clapham Junction (CJ) [Stabling point], Salisbury (SA), Northam (Siemens Transportation) (NT)
Parent Company: First Group (70%) / MTR (30%)

As part of the South Western Railway franchise launched in August 2017, a commitment for new trains was made. This will consist of 30 five-car (Class 701/5) and 60 ten-car (Class 701/0) Bombardier 'Aventra' units to be constructed in the UK at Derby Litchurch lane. These will replace existing Class 455, 456, 458 and 707 stock. The new stock will be funded by RockRail.

In addition, Class 442s will be reinstated for use on the Waterloo to Portsmouth line receiving new electrical equipment at Eastleigh Works.

Class 158

Vehicle Length: 76ft 1¾in (23.21m)   Engine: 1 x Cummins NTA855R of 350hp per vehicle
Height: 12ft 6in (3.81m)   Horsepower: 700hp (522kW)
Width: 9ft 3¼in (2.82m)   Seats (total/car): 13F-114S, 13F-44S/70S

Number	Formation DMCL+DMSL	Depot	Livery	Owner	Operator
158880 (158737)	52737+57737	SA	SWN	PTR	SWR
158881 (158742)	52742+57742	SA	SWN	PTR	SWR
158882 (158743)	52743+57743	SA	SWM	PTR	SWR
158883 (158744)	52744+57744	SA	SWM	PTR	SWR
158884 (158772)	52772+57772	SA	SWM	PTR	SWR
158885 (158775)	52775+57775	SA	SWM	PTR	SWR
158886 (158779)	52779+57779	SA	SWM	PTR	SWR
158887 (158781)	52781+57781	SA	SWR	PTR	SWR
158888 (158802)	52802+57802	SA	SWR	PTR	SWR
158889 (158808)	52808+57808	NM	EMT	PTR	EMT (On loan to East Midlands Trains)
158890 (158814)	52814+57814	SA	SWR	PTR	SWR

Left: *SWR has an allocated of 11 Class 158s, based at Salisbury, with one set (158889) sub-leased to East Midlands Trains. The SWR sets operate alongside the Class 159s from Salisbury as well as operating on the Salisbury-Romsey route. In 2018 a start was made at applying the new South Western Railway livery, with some variations to style being recorded. Set No. 158890 is viewed at Eastleigh showing the new colours.* **CJM**

For clarity, some stations
have been omitted

© TRC.Com Ltd 2013

Passenger Train Operating Companies - South Western Railway

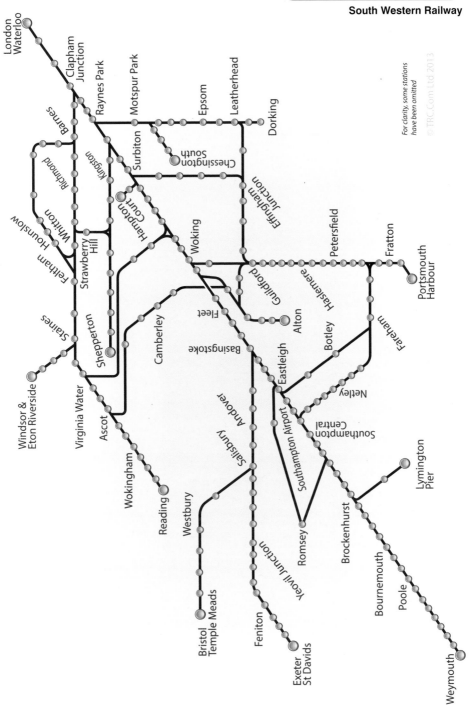

Class 159/0

Vehicle Length: 76ft 1¾in (23.21m) *Engine: 1 x Cummins NTA855R of 400hp per vehicle*
Height: 12ft 6in (3.81m) *Horsepower: 1,200hp (895kW)*
Width: 9ft 3¼in (2.82m) *Seats (total/car): 24F-172S, 24F-28S/72S/72S*

Number	Formation DMCL+MSL+DMS	Depot	Livery	Owner	Operator	Name
159001	52873+58718+57873	SA	SWR	PTR	SWR	
159002	52874+58719+57874	SA	SWM	PTR	SWR	City of Salisbury
159003	52875+58720+57875	SA	SWR	PTR	SWR	
159004	52876+58721+57876	SA	SWM	PTR	SWR	Basingstoke and Deane
159005	52877+58722+57877	SA	SWR	PTR	SWR	
159006	52878+58723+57878	SA	SWR	PTR	SWR	
159007	52879+58724+57879	SA	SWR	PTR	SWR	
159008	52880+58725+57880	SA	SWM	PTR	SWR	
159009	52881+58726+57881	SA	SWR	PTR	SWR	
159010	52882+58727+57882	SA	SWR	PTR	SWR	
159011	52883+58728+57883	SA	SWR	PTR	SWR	
159012	52884+58729+57884	SA	SWR	PTR	SWR	
159013	52885+58730+57885	SA	SWM	PTR	SWR	
159014	52886+58731+57886	SA	SWR	PTR	SWR	
159015	52887+58732+57887	SA	SWM	PTR	SWR	
159016	52888+58733+57888	SA	SWM	PTR	SWR	
159017	52889+58734+57889	SA	SWM	PTR	SWR	
159018	52890+58735+57890	SA	SWM	PTR	SWR	
159019	52891+58736+57891	SA	SWM	PTR	SWR	
159020	52892+58737+57892	SA	SWM	PTR	SWR	
159021	52893+58738+57893	SA	SWM	PTR	SWR	
159022	52894+58739+57894	SA	SWM	PTR	SWR	

Left: *Two batches of Class 159 three-car sets are based at Salisbury and deployed on the busy Waterloo-Salisbury-Exeter/Bristol corridor. Considered by many as the 'Rolls Royce' of the Class 158 design. Members of Class 159/0 were the original 22 sets introduced, with the Class 159/1 sets introduced later due to passenger growth and were modified from existing Class 158 three-car sets. Sets are passing through a refurbishment livery transition period in 2018-2019 with the latest South Western Railways colours now being applied, as shown on set No. 159003.*
Antony Christie

Class 159/1

Vehicle Length: 76ft 1¾in (23.21m) *Engine: 1 x Cummins NTA855R of 350hp per vehicle*
Height: 12ft 6in (3.81m) *Horsepower: 1,050hp (782kW)*
Width: 9ft 3¼in (2.82m) *Seats (total/car): 24F-170S, 24F-28S/70S/72S*

Number	Formation DMCL+MSL+DMSL	Depot	Livery	Owner	Operator
159101 (158800)	52800+58717+57800	SA	SWN	PTR	SWR
159102 (158803)	52803+58703+57803	SA	SWN	PTR	SWR
159103 (158804)	52804+58704+57804	SA	SWN	PTR	SWR
159104 (158805)	52805+58705+57805	SA	SWN	PTR	SWR
159105 (158807)	52807+58707+57807	SA	SWN	PTR	SWR
159106 (158809)	52809+58709+57809	SA	SWN	PTR	SWR
159107 (158811)	52811+58711+57811	SA	SWN	PTR	SWR
159108 (158801)	52801+58701+57801	SA	SWN	PTR	SWR

Class 442

Vehicle Length: (Driving) 75ft 11½in (23.15m) Width: 8ft 11½in (2.73m)
(Inter) 75ft 5½in (22.99m) Horsepower: 1,608hp (1,200kW)
Height: 12ft 4in (3.81m) Seats (total/car): 24F-318S, 74S/76S/24F-28S/66S/74S
To be re-equiped with Kiepe ac traction equipment

Passenger Train Operating Companies - South Western Railway

Number	Formation	Depot	Livery	Owner	Operator
	DTSO(A)+TSO+MBC+TSO+DTSO(B)				
442401	77382+71818+62937+71842+77414	BM	SGX	ANG	SWR (returning to traffic in 2019)
442402	77383+71819+62938+71842+77407	-	-	ANG	- Off lease stored
442403	77384+71820+62941+71843+77408	BM	SWR	ANG	SWR (returning to traffic in 2019)
442404	77385+71821+62939+71844+77409	BM	SWR	ANG	SWR (returning to traffic in 2019)
442405	77386+71822+62944+71845+77410	BM	SGX	ANG	SWR (returning to traffic in 2019)
442406	77389+71823+62942+71846+77411	-	-	ANG	- Off lease stored
442407	77388+71824+62943+71847+77412	BM	SGX	ANG	SWR (returning to traffic in 2019)
442408	77387+71825+62945+71848+77413	BM	SWR	ANG	SWR (returning to traffic in 2019)
442409	77390+71826+62946+71849+77406	BM	SGX	ANG	SWR (returning to traffic in 2019)
442410	77391+71827+62948+71850+77415	-	-	ANG	- Off lease stored
442411	77392+71828+62940+71851+77422	BM	SWR	ANG	SWR (returning to traffic in 2019)
442412	77393+71829+62947+71858+77417	BM	SGX	ANG	SWR (returning to traffic in 2019)
442413	77394+71830+62949+71853+77418	BM	SWR	ANG	SWR (returning to traffic in 2019)
442414	77395+71831+62950+71854+77419	BM	SWR	ANG	SWR (returning to traffic in 2019)
442415	77396+71832+62951+71855+77420	BM	SGX	ANG	SWR (returning to traffic in 2019)
442416	77397+71833+62952+71856+77421	BM	SWR	ANG	SWR (returning to traffic in 2019)
442417	77398+71834+62953+71857+77416	BM	SWR	ANG	SWR (returning to traffic in 2019)
442418	77399+71835+62954+71852+77423	BM	SGX	ANG	SWR (returning to traffic in 2019)
442419	77400+71836+62955+71859+77424	BM	SWR	ANG	SWR (returning to traffic in 2019)
442420	77401+71837+62956+71860+77425	BM	SWR	ANG	SWR (returning to traffic in 2019)
442421	77402+71838+62957+71861+77426	BM	SGX	ANG	SWR (returning to traffic in 2019)
442422	77403+71839+62958+71862+77427	BM	SWR	ANG	SWR (returning to traffic in 2019)
442423	77404+71840+62959+71863+77428	BM	SWR	ANG	SWR (returning to traffic in 2019)
442424	77405+71841+62960+71864+77429	BM	SGX	ANG	SWR (returning to traffic in 2019)

Right: *In November the first of the refreshed Class 442s, No. 442414 emerged from Eastleigh Works, carrying the latest South Western Railway livery. Delays in the supply of revised traction equipment, will see these sets enter traffic with their original traction package, which will be replaced by the planned Kiepe system. Set No. 442414 is seen at Millbrook.*
Mark V. Pike

Class 444
Desiro

Vehicle Length: 77ft 3in (23.57m) Horsepower: 2,682hp (2,000kW)
Height: 12ft 1½in (3.7m) Seats (total/car): 35F-299S, 76S/76S/76S/47/35F-24S
Width: 9ft 2in (2.7m) (refurbished 32F-327S, 76S/76S/76S/59S/32F-40S)

Number	Formation	Depot	Livery	Owner	Operator	Name
	DMSO+TSO+TSO+TSRMB(TSO)+DMCO					
444001	63801+67101+67151+67201+63851	NT	SWM	ANG	SWR	*Naomi House*
444002	63802+67102+67152+67202+63852	NT	SWM	ANG	SWR	
444003	63803+67103+67153+67203+63853	NT	SWM	ANG	SWR	
444004	63804+67104+67154+67204+63854	NT	SWM	ANG	SWR	
444005	63805+67105+67155+67205+63855	NT	SWM	ANG	SWR	
444006	63806+67106+67156+67206+63856	NT	SWM	ANG	SWR	
444007	63807+67107+67157+67207+63857	NT	SWM	ANG	SWR	
444008	63808+67108+67158+67208+63858	NT	SWM	ANG	SWR	
444009	63809+67109+67159+67209+63859	NT	SWM	ANG	SWR	
444010	63810+67110+67160+67210+63860	NT	SWM	ANG	SWR	
444011	63811+67111+67161+67211+63861	NT	SWM	ANG	SWR	
444012	63812+67112+67162+67212+63862	NT	SWR	ANG	SWR	*Destination Weymouth*
444013	63813+67113+67163+67213+63863	NT	SWM	ANG	SWR	
444014	63814+67114+67164+67214+63864	NT	SWM	ANG	SWR	
444015	63815+67115+67165+67215+63865	NT	SWM	ANG	SWR	
444016	63816+67116+67166+67216+63866	NT	SWM	ANG	SWR	
444017	63817+67117+67167+67217+63867	NT	SWM	ANG	SWR	

South Western Railway

444018	63818+67118+67168+67218+63868	NT	SWM	ANG	SWR	*The FAB 444*
444019	63819+67119+67169+67219+63869	NT	SWM	ANG	SWR	
444020	63820+67120+67170+67220+63870	NT	SWM	ANG	SWR	
444021	63821+67121+67171+67221+63871	NT	SWM	ANG	SWR	
444022	63822+67122+67172+67222+63872	NT	SWM	ANG	SWR	
444023	63823+67123+67173+67223+63873	NT	SWM	ANG	SWR	
444024	63824+67124+67174+67224+63874	NT	SWM	ANG	SWR	
444025	63825+67125+67175+67225+63875	NT	SWM	ANG	SWR	
444026	63826+67126+67176+67226+63876	NT	SWM	ANG	SWR	
444027	63827+67127+67177+67227+63877	NT	SWM	ANG	SWR	
444028	63828+67128+67178+67228+63878	NT	SWM	ANG	SWR	
444029	63829+67129+67179+67229+63879	NT	SWM	ANG	SWR	
444030	63830+67130+67180+67230+63880	NT	SWM	ANG	SWR	
444031	63831+67131+67181+67231+63881	NT	SWM	ANG	SWR	
444032	63832+67132+67182+67232+63882	NT	SWM	ANG	SWR	
444033	63833+67133+67183+67233+63883	NT	SWM	ANG	SWR	
444034	63834+67134+67184+67234+63884	NT	SWM	ANG	SWR	
444035	63835+67135+67185+67235+63885	NT	SWM	ANG	SWR	
444036	63836+67136+67186+67236+63886	NT	SWM	ANG	SWR	
444037	63837+67137+67187+67237+63887	NT	SWM	ANG	SWR	
444038	63838+67138+67188+67238+63888	NT	SWM	ANG	SWR	*South Western Railway*
444039	63839+67139+67189+67239+63889	NT	SWM	ANG	SWR	
444040	63840+67140+67190+67240+63890	NT	SWR	ANG	SWR	
444041	63841+67141+67191+67241+63891	NT	SWM	ANG	SWR	
444042	63842+67142+67192+67242+63892	NT	SWM	ANG	SWR	
444043	63843+67143+67193+67243+63893	NT	SWM	ANG	SWR	
444044	63844+67144+67194+67244+63894	NT	SWM	ANG	SWR	

Left: *South Western Railway main line services use five-car Siemens Desiro Class 444s. These are high quality sets, based at Northam depot close to Southampton. Sets are slowly being repainted into the new SWR colours. Set No. 444028 is seen at Eastleigh with a semi-fast Bournemouth to Waterloo service.* **CJM**

Class 450/0
Desiro

Vehicle Length: 66ft 9in (20.4m)	Horsepower: 2,682hp (2,000kW)		
Height: 12ft 1½in (3.7m)	Seats (total/car): 24F-237S, 70S/24F-36S/61S/70S		
Width: 9ft 2in (2.7m)	(refurbished 259S		

Number	Formation	Depot	Livery	Owner	Operator	Name
	DMSO+TCO+TSO+DMSO					
450001	63201+64201+68101+63601	NT	SWO	ANG	SWR	
450002	63202+64202+68102+63602	NT	SWO	ANG	SWR	
450003	63203+64203+68103+63603	NT	SWO	ANG	SWR	
450004	63204+64204+68104+63604	NT	SWO	ANG	SWR	
450005	63205+64205+68105+63605	NT	SWO	ANG	SWR	
450006	63206+64206+68106+63606	NT	SWO	ANG	SWR	
450007	63207+64207+68107+63607	NT	SWO	ANG	SWR	
450008	63208+64208+68108+63608	NT	SWO	ANG	SWR	
450009	63209+64209+68109+63609	NT	SWO	ANG	SWR	
450010	63210+64210+68110+63610	NT	SWO	ANG	SWR	
450011	63211+64211+68111+63611	NT	SWO	ANG	SWR	
450012	63212+64212+68112+63612	NT	SWO	ANG	SWR	
450013	63213+64213+68113+63613	NT	SWO	ANG	SWR	
450014	63214+64214+68114+63614	NT	SWO	ANG	SWR	
450015	63215+64215+68115+63615	NT	SWO	ANG	SWR	*Desiro*
450016	63216+64216+68116+63616	NT	SWR	ANG	SWR	
450017	63217+64217+68117+63617	NT	SWO	ANG	SWR	
450018	63218+64218+68118+63618	NT	SWO	ANG	SWR	
450019	63219+64219+68119+63619	NT	SWO	ANG	SWR	
450020	63220+64220+68120+63620	NT	SWO	ANG	SWR	
450021	63221+64221+68121+63621	NT	SWO	ANG	SWR	

450022	63222+64222+68122+63622	NT	SWO	ANG	SWR
450023	63223+64223+68123+63623	NT	SWO	ANG	SWR
450024	63224+64224+68124+63624	NT	SWO	ANG	SWR
450025	63225+64225+68125+63625	NT	SWO	ANG	SWR
450026	63226+64226+68126+63626	NT	SWO	ANG	SWR
450027	63227+64227+68127+63627	NT	SWO	ANG	SWR
450028	63228+64228+68128+63628	NT	SWO	ANG	SWR
450029	63229+64229+68129+63629	NT	SWO	ANG	SWR
450030	63230+64230+68130+63630	NT	SWO	ANG	SWR
450031	63231+64231+68131+63631	NT	SWO	ANG	SWR
450032	63232+64232+68132+63632	NT	SWO	ANG	SWR
450033	63233+64233+68133+63633	NT	SWO	ANG	SWR	*Treloar College*
450034	63234+64234+68134+63634	NT	SWO	ANG	SWR
450035	63235+64235+68135+63635	NT	SWO	ANG	SWR
450036	63236+64236+68136+63636	NT	SWO	ANG	SWR
450037	63237+64237+68137+63637	NT	SWO	ANG	SWR
450038	63238+64238+68138+63638	NT	SWO	ANG	SWR
450039	63239+64239+68139+63639	NT	SWO	ANG	SWR
450040	63240+64240+68140+63640	NT	SWO	ANG	SWR
450041	63241+64241+68141+63641	NT	SWO	ANG	SWR
450042	63242+64242+68142+63642	NT	SWO	ANG	SWR
450071	63271+64271+68171+63671	NT	SWO	ANG	SWR
450072	63272+64272+68172+63672	NT	SWO	ANG	SWR
450073	63273+64273+68173+63673	NT	SWO	ANG	SWR
450074	63274+64274+68174+63674	NT	SWO	ANG	SWR
450075	63275+64275+68175+63675	NT	SWO	ANG	SWR
450076	63276+64276+68176+63676	NT	SWO	ANG	SWR
450077	63277+64277+68177+63677	NT	SWO	ANG	SWR
450078	63278+64278+68178+63678	NT	SWO	ANG	SWR
450079	63279+64279+68179+63679	NT	SWO	ANG	SWR
450080	63280+64280+68180+63680	NT	SWO	ANG	SWR
450081	63281+64281+68181+63681	NT	SWO	ANG	SWR
450082	63282+64282+68182+63682	NT	SWO	ANG	SWR
450083	63283+64283+68183+63683	NT	SWO	ANG	SWR
450084	63284+64284+68184+63684	NT	SWO	ANG	SWR
450085	63285+64285+68185+63685	NT	SWO	ANG	SWR
450086	63286+64286+68186+63686	NT	SWO	ANG	SWR
450087	63287+64287+68187+63687	NT	SWO	ANG	SWR
450088	63288+64288+68188+63688	NT	SWO	ANG	SWR
450089	63289+64289+68189+63689	NT	SWO	ANG	SWR
450090	63290+64290+68190+63690	NT	SWO	ANG	SWR
450091	63291+64291+68191+63691	NT	SWO	ANG	SWR
450092	63292+64292+68192+63692	NT	SWO	ANG	SWR
450093	63293+64293+68193+63693	NT	SWO	ANG	SWR
450094	63294+64294+68194+63694	NT	SWO	ANG	SWR
450095	63295+64295+68195+63695	NT	SWO	ANG	SWR
450096	63296+64296+68196+63696	NT	SWO	ANG	SWR
450097	63297+64297+68197+63697	NT	SWO	ANG	SWR
450098	63298+64298+68198+63698	NT	SWO	ANG	SWR
450099	63299+64299+68199+63699	NT	SWO	ANG	SWR
450100	63300+64300+68200+63700	NT	SWO	ANG	SWR
450101	63701+66851+66801+63751	NT	SWO	ANG	SWR
450102	63702+66852+66802+63752	NT	SWO	ANG	SWR
450103	63703+66853+66803+63753	NT	SWO	ANG	SWR
450104	63704+66854+66804+63754	NT	SWO	ANG	SWR
450105	63705+66855+66805+63755	NT	SWO	ANG	SWR
450106	63706+66856+66806+63756	NT	SWO	ANG	SWR
450107	63707+66857+66807+63757	NT	SWO	ANG	SWR
450108	63708+66858+66808+63758	NT	SWO	ANG	SWR
450109	63709+66859+66809+63759	NT	SWO	ANG	SWR
450110	63710+66860+66810+63750	NT	SWO	ANG	SWR
450111	63901+66921+66901+63921	NT	SWR	ANG	SWR
450112	63902+66922+66902+63922	NT	ADV	ANG	SWR
450113	63903+66923+66903+63923	NT	SWO	ANG	SWR

South Western Railway

450114	63904+66924+66904+63924	NT	SWO	ANG	SWR	*Fairbridge - investing in the Future*
450115	63905+66925+66905+63925	NT	SWO	ANG	SWR	
450116	63906+66926+66906+63926	NT	SWO	ANG	SWR	
450117	63907+66927+66907+63927	NT	SWO	ANG	SWR	
450118	63908+66928+66908+63928	NT	ADV	ANG	SWR	
450119	63909+66929+66909+63929	NT	SWO	ANG	SWR	
450120	63910+66930+66910+63930	NT	SWO	ANG	SWR	
450121	63911+66931+66911+63931	NT	SWO	ANG	SWR	
450122	63912+66932+66912+63932	NT	SWO	ANG	SWR	
450123	63913+66933+66913+63933	NT	SWO	ANG	SWR	
450124	63914+66934+66914+63934	NT	SWO	ANG	SWR	
450125	63915+66935+66915+63935	NT	SWO	ANG	SWR	
450126	63916+66936+66916+63936	NT	SWO	ANG	SWR	
450127	63917+66937+66917+63937	NT	SWO	ANG	SWR	*Dave Gunson*

Left: When the slam-door stock was replaced on the South Western section, a large fleet of Siemens 'Desiro' units were built, classified 450. These sets mainly sport the previous franchise blue livery with South Western Railway branding. A start has been made on applying the new SWR colours. With SWR branding, set No. 450013 stands at Eastleigh. **CJM**

Class 450/5
Desiro

Vehicle Length: 66ft 9in (20.4m)	*Horsepower: 2,682hp (2,000kW)*	
Height: 12ft 1½in (3.7m)	*Seats (total/car):*	
Width: 9ft 2in (2.7m)	*24F/206S, 64S-24F/32S/56S/54S*	

Number	*Formation* *DMSO+TCO+TSO+DMSO*	*Depot*	*Livery*	*Owner*	*Operator*
450543 (450043)	63243+64243+68143+63643	NT	SWO	ANG	SWR
450544 (450044)	63244+64244+68144+63644	NT	SWO	ANG	SWR
450545 (450045)	63245+64245+68145+63645	NT	SWO	ANG	SWR
450546 (450046)	63246+64246+68146+63646	NT	SWO	ANG	SWR
450547 (450047)	63247+64247+68147+63647	NT	SWO	ANG	SWR
450548 (450048)	63248+64248+68148+63648	NT	SWO	ANG	SWR
450549 (450049)	63249+64249+68149+63649	NT	SWO	ANG	SWR
450550 (450050)	63250+64250+68150+63650	NT	SWO	ANG	SWR
450551 (450051)	63251+64251+68151+63651	NT	SWO	ANG	SWR
450552 (450052)	63252+64252+68152+63652	NT	SWO	ANG	SWR
450553 (450053)	63253+64253+68153+63653	NT	SWO	ANG	SWR
450554 (450054)	63254+64254+68154+63654	NT	SWO	ANG	SWR
450555 (450055)	63255+64255+68155+63655	NT	SWO	ANG	SWR
450556 (450056)	63256+64256+68156+63656	NT	SWO	ANG	SWR
450557 (450057)	63257+64257+68157+63657	NT	SWO	ANG	SWR
450558 (450058)	63258+64258+68158+63658	NT	SWO	ANG	SWR
450559 (450059)	63259+64259+68159+63659	NT	SWO	ANG	SWR
450560 (450060)	63260+64260+68160+63660	NT	SWO	ANG	SWR
450561 (450061)	63261+64261+68161+63661	NT	SWO	ANG	SWR
450562 (450062)	63262+64262+68162+63662	NT	SWO	ANG	SWR
450563 (450063)	63263+64263+68163+63663	NT	SWO	ANG	SWR
450564 (450064)	63264+64264+68164+63664	NT	SWO	ANG	SWR
450565 (450065)	63265+64265+68165+63665	NT	SWO	ANG	SWR
450566 (450066)	63266+64266+68166+63666	NT	SWO	ANG	SWR
450567 (450067)	63267+64267+68167+63667	NT	SWO	ANG	SWR
450568 (450068)	63268+64268+68168+63668	NT	SWO	ANG	SWR
450569 (450069)	63269+64269+68169+63669	NT	SWO	ANG	SWR
450570 (450070)	63270+64270+68170+63670	NT	SWO	ANG	SWR

Right: *A batch of 28 Class 450s were modified soon after introduction to high capacity or HC sets, with some seats removed and extra standing space provided especially in door pocket positions. These sets, reclassified as 450/5 also originally lost their first class seating, but this has subsequently been restored. Class 450/5 set No. 450561 poses at Clapham Junction stabling point.* **CJM**

Class 455/7

Vehicle Length: (Driving) 65ft 0½in (19.83m)	Width: 9ft 3¼in (2.82m)	
(Inter) 65ft 4½in (19.92m)	Horsepower: 1,000hp (746kW)	
Height: 12ft 1½in (3.79m) [TSO- 11ft 6³⁄₂in (3.58m)]	Seats (total/car): 244S, 54S/68S/68S/54S	

Number	Formation DMSO(A)+MSO+TSO+DTSO(B)	Depot	Livery	Owner	Operator	Note
(45)5701	77727+62783+71545+77728	WD	SWS	PTR	SWR	
(45)5702	77729+62784+71547+77730	WD	SWS	PTR	SWR	
(45)5703	77731+62785+71540+77732	WD	SWS	PTR	SWR	
(45)5704	77733+62786+71548+77734	WD	SWS	PTR	SWR	
(45)5705	77735+62787+71565+77736	WD	SWS	PTR	SWR	
(45)5706	77737+62788+71534+77738	WD	SWS	PTR	SWR	
(45)5707	77739+62789+71536+77740	WD	SWS	PTR	SWR	
(45)5708	77741+62790+71560+77742	WD	SWS	PTR	SWR	
(45)5709	77743+62791+71532+77744	WD	SWS	PTR	SWR	
(45)5710	77745+62792+71566+77746	WD	SWS	PTR	SWR	
(45)5711	77747+62793+71542+77748	WD	SWS	PTR	SWR	
(45)5712	77749+62794+71546+77750	WD	SWS	PTR	SWR	
(45)5713	77751+62795+71567+77752	WD	SWS	PTR	SWR	
(45)5714	77753+62796+71539+77754	WD	SWS	PTR	SWR	
(45)5715	77755+62797+71535+77756	WD	SWS	PTR	SWR	
(45)5716	77757+62798+71564+77758	WD	SWS	PTR	SWR	
(45)5717	77759+62799+71528+77760	WD	SWS	PTR	SWR	
(45)5718	77761+62800+71557+77762	WD	SWS	PTR	SWR	
(45)5719	77763+62801+71558+77764	WD	SWS	PTR	SWR	
(45)5720	77765+62802+71568+77766	WD	SWS	PTR	SWR	
(45)5721	77767+62803+71553+77768	WD	SWS	PTR	SWR	
(45)5722	77769+62804+71533+77770	WD	SWS	PTR	SWR	
(45)5723	77771+62805+71526+77772	WD	SWS	PTR	SWR	
(45)5724	77773+62806+71561+77774	WD	SWS	PTR	SWR	
(45)5725	77775+62807+71541+77776	WD	SWS	PTR	SWR	
(45)5726	77777+62608+71556+77778	WD	SWS	PTR	SWR	
(45)5727	77779+62809+71562+77780	WD	SWS	PTR	SWR	
(45)5728	77781+62810+71527+77782	WD	SWS	PTR	SWR	
(45)5729	77783+62811+71550+77784	WD	SWS	PTR	SWR	
(45)5730	77785+62812+71551+77786	WD	SWS	PTR	SWR	
(45)5731	77787+62813+71555+77788	WD	SWS	PTR	SWR	
(45)5732	77789+62814+71552+77790	WD	SWS	PTR	SWR	
(45)5733	77791+62815+71549+77792	WD	SWS	PTR	SWR	
(45)5734	77793+62816+71531+77794	WD	SWS	PTR	SWR	
(45)5735	77795+62817+71563+77796	WD	SWS	PTR	SWR	
(45)5736	77797+62818+71554+77798	WD	SWS	PTR	SWR	
(45)5737	77799+62819+71544+77800	WD	SWS	PTR	SWR	
(45)5738	77801+62820+71529+77802	WD	SWS	PTR	SWR	
(45)5739	77803+62821+71537+77804	WD	SWS	PTR	SWR	
(45)5740	77805+62822+71530+77806	WD	SWS	PTR	SWR	
(45)5741	77807+62823+71559+77808	WD	SWS	PTR	SWR	
(45)5742	77809+62824+71543+77810	WD	SWS	PTR	SWR	
(45)5750§	77811+62825+71538+77812	WD	SWS	PTR	SWR	§ Originally numbered (45)5743

Passenger Train Operating Companies - South Western Railway

Left: *Soon to be replaced by Class 701 stock, the South Western suburban services are currently in the hands of a fleet of Class 455 and 456 sets. All have been refurbished and the 455s have recently received a new ac traction package. Three different sub-classes exist. The Class 455/7s are recognisable in having one vehicle of a different structural design, this came about by inserting an original Class 508 TS vehicle into the Class 455/7s when new. Set No. (45)5705 is shown with the ex '508' coach second from front.* **CJM**

Class 455/8

Vehicle Length: (Driving) 65ft 0½in (19.83m)	Width: 9ft 3¼in (2.82m)
(Inter) 65ft 4½in (19.92m)	Horsepower: 1,000hp (746kW)
Height: 12ft 1½in (3.79m)	Seats (total/car): 268S, 50S/84S/84S/50S

Number	Formation DMSO(A)+MSO+TSO+DTSO(B)	Depot	Livery	Owner	Operator
(45)5847	77671+62755+71683+77672	WD	SWS	PTR	SWR
(45)5848	77673+62756+71684+77674	WD	SWS	PTR	SWR
(45)5849	77675+62757+71685+77676	WD	SWS	PTR	SWR
(45)5850	77677+62758+71686+77678	WD	SWS	PTR	SWR
(45)5851	77679+62759+71687+77680	WD	SWS	PTR	SWR
(45)5852	77681+62760+71688+77682	WD	SWS	PTR	SWR
(45)5853	77683+62761+71689+77684	WD	SWS	PTR	SWR
(45)5854	77685+62762+71690+77686	WD	SWS	PTR	SWR
(45)5855	77687+62763+71691+77688	WD	SWS	PTR	SWR
(45)5856	77689+62764+71692+77690	WD	SWS	PTR	SWR
(45)5857	77691+62765+71693+77692	WD	SWS	PTR	SWR
(45)5858	77693+62766+71694+77694	WD	SWS	PTR	SWR
(45)5859	77695+62767+71695+77696	WD	SWS	PTR	SWR
(45)5860	77697+62768+71696+77698	WD	SWS	PTR	SWR
(45)5861	77699+62769+71697+77700	WD	SWS	PTR	SWR
(45)5862	77701+62770+71698+77702	WD	SWS	PTR	SWR
(45)5863	77703+62771+71699+77704	WD	SWS	PTR	SWR
(45)5864	77705+62772+71700+77706	WD	SWS	PTR	SWR
(45)5865	77707+62773+71701+77708	WD	SWS	PTR	SWR
(45)5866	77709+62774+71702+77710	WD	SWS	PTR	SWR
(45)5867	77711+62775+71703+77712	WD	SWS	PTR	SWR
(45)5868	77713+62776+71704+77714	WD	SWS	PTR	SWR
(45)5869	77715+62777+71705+77716	WD	SWS	PTR	SWR
(45)5870	77717+62778+71706+77718	WD	SWS	PTR	SWR
(45)5871	77719+62779+71707+77720	WD	SWS	PTR	SWR
(45)5872	77721+62780+71708+77722	WD	SWS	PTR	SWR
(45)5873	77723+62781+71709+77724	WD	SWS	PTR	SWR
(45)5874	77725+62782+71710+77726	WD	SWS	PTR	SWR

Above: *The original Class 455 fleet, classified as 455/8 had an earlier front end design, with the warning horns at roof height, with a 'boxey' front roof profile. Class 455/8 No. (45)5863 is seen approaching Raynes Park with a SWR suburban service bound for Waterloo.* **CJM**

Class 455/9

	Vehicle Length: (Driving) 65ft 0½in (19.83m)		Width: 9ft 3¼in (2.82m)		
	(Inter) 65ft 4½in (19.92m)		Horsepower: 1,000hp (746kW)		
	Height: 12ft 1½in (3.79m)		Seats (total/car): 236S, 50S/68S/68S/50S		

Number	Formation DMSO(A)+MSO+TSO+DTSO(B)	Depot	Livery	Owner	Operator
(45)5901	77813+62826+71714+77814	WD	SWS	PTR	SWR
(45)5902	77815+62827+71715+77816	WD	SWS	PTR	SWR
(45)5903	77817+62828+71716+77818	WD	SWS	PTR	SWR
(45)5904	77819+62829+71717+77820	WD	SWS	PTR	SWR
(45)5905	77821+62830+71725+77822	WD	SWS	PTR	SWR
(45)5906	77823+62831+71719+77824	WD	SWS	PTR	SWR
(45)5907	77825+62832+71720+77826	WD	SWS	PTR	SWR
(45)5908	77827+62833+71721+77828	WD	SWS	PTR	SWR
(45)5909	77829+62834+71722+77830	WD	SWS	PTR	SWR
(45)5910	77831+62835+71723+77832	WD	SWS	PTR	SWR
(45)5911	77833+62836+71724+77834	WD	SWS	PTR	SWR
(45)5912	77835+62837+67400+77836	WD	SWS	PTR	SWR
(45)5913	77837+62838+71726+77838	WD	SWS	PTR	SWR
(45)5914	77839+62839+71727+77840	WD	SWS	PTR	SWR
(45)5915	77841+62840+71728+77842	WD	SWS	PTR	SWR
(45)5916	77843+62841+71729+77844	WD	SWS	PTR	SWR
(45)5917	77845+62842+71730+77846	WD	SWS	PTR	SWR
(45)5918	77847+62843+71732+77848	WD	SWS	PTR	SWR
(45)5919	77849+62844+71718+77850	WD	SWS	PTR	SWR
(45)5920	77851+62845+71733+77852	WD	SWS	PTR	SWR

Class 456

	Vehicle Length: (Driving) 65ft 3¼in (19.89m)	Horsepower: 500hp (370kW)
	Height: 12ft 4½in (3.77m)	Seats (total/car): 152S, 79S/73S
	Width: 9ft 3in (2.81m)	

Right: *Previously used on the South Central business, the 24 two-car Class 456 sets were transferred to South Western to allow the operation of a 10-car railway on suburban services. The sets were refurbished in keeping with the Class 455s. The main difference is they are non-gangwayed and retain their dc traction package. Set No. 456006 is shown.* **CJM**

Number	Formation DMSO+DTSO	Depot	Livery	Owner	Operator
456001	64735+78250	WD	SWS	PTR	SWR
456002	64736+78251	WD	SWS	PTR	SWR
456003	64737+78252	WD	SWS	PTR	SWR
456004	64738+78253	WD	SWS	PTR	SWR
456005	64739+78254	WD	SWS	PTR	SWR
456006	64740+78255	WD	SWS	PTR	SWR
456007	64741+78256	WD	SWS	PTR	SWR
456008	64742+78257	WD	SWS	PTR	SWR
456009	64743+78258	WD	SWS	PTR	SWR
456010	64744+78259	WD	SWS	PTR	SWR
456011	64745+78260	WD	SWS	PTR	SWR
456012	64746+78261	WD	SWS	PTR	SWR
456013	64747+78262	WD	SWS	PTR	SWR
456014	64748+78263	WD	SWS	PTR	SWR
456015	64749+78264	WD	SWS	PTR	SWR
456016	64750+78265	WD	SWS	PTR	SWR
456017	64751+78266	WD	SWS	PTR	SWR
456018	64752+78267	WD	SWS	PTR	SWR
456019	64753+78268	WD	SWS	PTR	SWR
456020	64754+78269	WD	SWS	PTR	SWR
456021	64755+78270	WD	SWS	PTR	SWR
456022	64756+78271	WD	SWS	PTR	SWR
456023	64757+78272	WD	SWS	PTR	SWR
456024	64758+78273	WD	SWS	PTR	SWR

Class 458
Juniper

	Vehicle Length: (Driving) 69ft 6in (21.16m)		Width: 9ft 2in (2.79m)		
	(Inter) 65ft 4in (19.91m)		Horsepower: 2,172hp (1,620kW)		
	Height: 12ft 3in (3.73m)		Seats (total/car): 266S, 60S/52S/42S/52S/60S		

Number	Original Number	Formation DMSO(A)+TSO+TSO+MSO+DMSO(B)	Depot	Livery	Owner	Operator
458501	(458001)	67601+74431+74001+74101+67701	WD	SWO	PTR	SWR
458502	(458002)	67602+74421+74002+74102+67702	WD	SWO	PTR	SWR
458503	(458003)	67603+74441+74003+74103+67703	WD	SWO	PTR	SWR
458504	(458004)	67604+74451+74004+74104+67704	WD	SWO	PTR	SWR

South Western Railway

458505	(458005)	67605+74425+74005+74105+67705	WD	SWO	PTR	SWR
458506	(458006)	67606+74436+74006+74106+67706	WD	SWO	PTR	SWR
458507	(458007)	67607+74428+74007+74107+67707	WD	SWO	PTR	SWR
458508	(458008)	67608+74433+74008+74108+67708	WD	SWO	PTR	SWR
458509	(458009)	67609+74452+74009+74109+67709	WD	SWO	PTR	SWR
458510	(458010)	67610+74405+74010+74110+67710	WD	SWO	PTR	SWR
458511	(458011)	67611+74435+74011+74111+67711	WD	SWO	PTR	SWR
458512	(458012)	67612+74427+74012+74112+67712	WD	SWO	PTR	SWR
458513	(458013)	67613+74437+74013+74113+67713	WD	SWO	PTR	SWR
458514	(458014)	67614+74407+74014+74114+67714	WD	SWO	PTR	SWR
458515	(458015)	67615+74404+74015+74115+67715	WD	SWO	PTR	SWR
458516	(458016)	67616+74406+74016+74116+67716	WD	SWO	PTR	SWR
458517	(458017)	67617+74426+74017+74117+67717	WD	SWO	PTR	SWR
458518	(458018)	67618+74432+74018+74118+67718	WD	SWO	PTR	SWR
458519	(458019)	67619+74403+74019+74119+67719	WD	SWO	PTR	SWR
458520	(458020)	67620+74401+74020+74120+67720	WD	SWO	PTR	SWR
458521	(458021)	67621+74438+74021+74121+67721	WD	SWO	PTR	SWR
458522	(458022)	67622+74424+74022+74122+67722	WD	SWO	PTR	SWR
458523	(458023)	67623+74434+74023+74123+67723	WD	SWO	PTR	SWR
458524	(458024)	67624+74402+74024+74124+67724	WD	SWO	PTR	SWR
458525	(458025)	67625+74422+74025+74125+67725	WD	SWO	PTR	SWR
458526	(458026)	67626+74442+74026+74126+67726	WD	SWO	PTR	SWR
458527	(458027)	67627+74412+74027+74127+67727	WD	SWO	PTR	SWR
458528	(458028)	67628+74408+74028+74128+67728	WD	SWO	PTR	SWR
458529	(458029)	67629+74423+74029+74129+67729	WD	SWO	PTR	SWR
458530	(458030)	67630+74411+74030+74130+67730	WD	SWO	PTR	SWR
458531		67913+74418+74446+74458+67912	WD	SWO	PTR	SWR
458532		67904+74417+74447+74457+67905	WD	SWO	PTR	SWR
458533		67917+74413+74443+74453+67906	WD	SWO	PTR	SWR
458534		67914+74414+74444+74454+67918	WD	SWO	PTR	SWR
458535		67915+74415+74445+74455+67911	WD	SWO	PTR	SWR
458536		67906+74416+74448+74456+67902	WD	SWO	PTR	SWR

Left: *A fleet of 36 five-car Class 458s are allocated to Wimbledon for outer suburban use, mainly on the Waterloo Windsor line group of services. The sets are formed of the original four-car '458s' augmented by additional vehicles from Class 460 Gatwick Express stock. Six additional sets were also formed. These units will be phased out following introduction of new Class 701 stock in 2020-2021. Sets Nos. 458511 and 458526 pose at Clapham Junction.* **CJM**

Class 701
Aventra
A fleet of 60 10-car and 30 five-car Bombardier 'Aventra' sets are on order, classified as 701. The are set to replace Class 455, 456, 458 and 707s and should be introduced from 2020.

701001	701014	701027	701040	701053	701505	701518
701002	701015	701028	701041	701054	701506	701519
701003	701016	701029	701042	701055	701507	701520
701004	701017	701030	701043	701056	701508	701521
701005	701018	701031	701044	701057	701509	701522
701006	701019	701032	701045	701058	701510	701523
701007	701020	701033	701046	701059	701511	701524
701008	701021	701034	701047	701060	701512	701525
701009	701022	701035	701048		701513	701526
701010	701023	701036	701049	701501	701514	701527
701011	701024	701037	701050	701502	701515	701528
701012	701025	701038	701051	701503	701516	701529
701013	701026	701039	701052	701504	701517	701530

Class 707
Desiro City

		Vehicle Length: (Driving) 20m	Weight: 160.3 tonnes
		(Inter) 20.16m	Power output: 1,073hp (800kW)
		Height: 3.73m	Seats (total/car): -271S, 46/64/53/62/46S

Number	Formation	Depot	Livery	Owner	Operator
	DMSO(A)+PTSO+TSO+TSO+DMSO(B)				
707001	421001+422001+423001+424001+425001	WD	SWS	ANG	SWR
707002	421002+422002+423002+424002+425002	WD	SWS	ANG	SWR
707003	421003+422003+423003+424003+425003	WD	SWS	ANG	SWR
707004	421004+422004+423004+424004+425004	WD	SWS	ANG	SWR
707005	421005+422005+423005+424005+425005	WD	SWS	ANG	SWR
707006	421006+422006+423006+424006+425006	WD	SWS	ANG	SWR
707007	421007+422007+423007+424007+425007	WD	SWS	ANG	SWR
707008	421008+422008+423008+424008+425008	WD	SWS	ANG	SWR
707009	421009+422009+423009+424009+425009	WD	SWS	ANG	SWR
707010	421010+422010+423010+424010+425010	WD	SWS	ANG	SWR
707011	421011+422011+423011+424011+425011	WD	SWS	ANG	SWR
707012	421012+422012+423012+424012+425012	WD	SWS	ANG	SWR
707013	421013+422013+423013+424013+425013	WD	SWS	ANG	SWR
707014	421014+422014+423014+424014+425014	WD	SWS	ANG	SWR
707015	421015+422015+423015+424015+425015	WD	SWS	ANG	SWR
707016	421016+422016+423016+424016+425016	WD	SWS	ANG	SWR
707017	421017+422017+423017+424017+425017	WD	SWS	ANG	SWR
707018	421018+422018+423018+424018+425018	WD	SWS	ANG	SWR
707019	421019+422019+423019+424019+425019	WD	SWS	ANG	SWR
707020	421020+422020+423020+424020+425020	WD	SWS	ANG	SWR
707021	421021+422021+423021+424021+425021	WD	SWS	ANG	SWR
707022	421022+422022+423022+424022+425022	WD	SWS	ANG	SWR
707023	421023+422023+423023+424023+425023	WD	SWS	ANG	SWR
707024	421024+422024+423024+424024+425024	WD	SWS	ANG	SWR
707025	421025+422025+423025+424025+425025	WD	SWS	ANG	SWR
707026	421026+422026+423026+424026+425026	WD	SWS	ANG	SWR
707027	421027+422027+423027+424027+425027	WD	SWS	ANG	SWR
707028	421028+422028+423028+424028+425028	WD	SWS	ANG	SWR
707029	421029+422029+423029+424029+425029	WD	SWS	ANG	SWR
707030	421030+422030+423030+424030+425030	WD	SWS	ANG	SWR

Above: *A fleet of 30 five-car Class 707 'Desiro City' sets are based at Wimbledon for suburban operations, mainly on the Waterloo-Windsor/Reading routes. These sets have been deemed surplus under the latest franchise and will come off lease when the Class 701s enter traffic. It has been suggested these units might find further work with either TfL or South Eastern.* **CJM**

Class 73/2

		Vehicle Length: 53ft 8in (16.35m)	Power: 750V dc third rail or English Electric 6K
		Height: 12ft 5⅜in (3.79m)	Horsepower: electric - 1,600hp (1,193kW)
		Width: 8ft 8in (2.64m)	Horsepower: diesel - 600hp (447kW)
			Electrical Equipment: English Electric

Number	Depot	Pool	Livery	Owner	Operator
73235 (73125)	BM	HYWD	BLU	SWT	SWT

Transport for Wales
Wales & Borders

Address: ✉ St Mary's House, 47 Penarth Road, Cardiff, CF10 5DJ
⌨ customer.relations@tfwrail.wales
✆ 03333 211202
ⓘ www.tfwrail.wales

Managing Director: Kevin Thomas
Franchise Dates: October 2018 - 14 October 2033
Principal Routes: Cardiff to Swansea and West Wales
Cardiff Valleys
Cardiff - Hereford - Shrewsbury - Crewe - Manchester Piccadilly
Cardiff - Hereford - Shrewsbury - Chester - Bangor - Holyhead
Manchester - Crewe - Bangor - Holyhead
Shrewsbury - Pwllheli / Aberystwyth
Swansea - Shrewsbury
Depots: Cardiff Canton (CV), Chester (CH), Holyhead* (HD)
Machynlleth (MN), Shrewsbury* (SX) * Stabling point
Parent Company: Transport for Wales / Keolis Amey

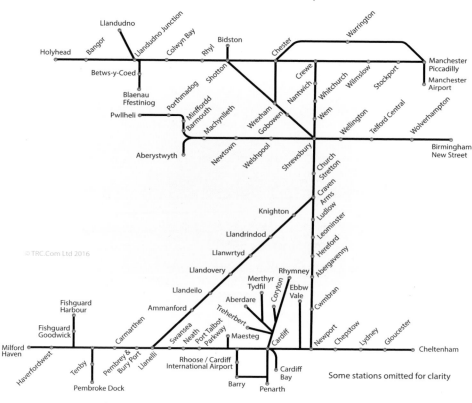

© TRC.Com Ltd 2016

Some stations omitted for clarity

Class 67

		Vehicle Length: 64ft 7in (19.68m)	Engine: EMD 12N-710G3B-EC
		Height: 12ft 9in (3.88m)	Horsepower: 2,980hp (2,223kW)
		Width: 8ft 9in (2.66m)	Electrical Equipment: EMD

Number	Depot	Pool	Livery	Owner	Operator
67001	CE	WAWC	TOQ	DBC	DBC/TFW
67002	CE	WAWC	TOQ	DBC	DBC/TFW
67003	CE	WAAC	TOQ	DBC	DBC/TFW

Right: *Currently the Transport for Wales franchise, operated by Keolis Amey, uses DB Class 67s to power Mk3 rakes on the long distance business trains between Holyhead and Cardiff. Technically three locos Nos. 67001-67003 are the dedicated locos, but in reality any Class 67 is used. The three allocated locos sport turquoise livery of the former Arriva Trains franchise. No. 67002 is illustrated on none-TfW work.* **CJM**

Class 142
Pacer

		Vehicle Length: 51ft 0½in (15.55m)	Engine: 1 x Cummins LTA10-R per vehicle
		Height: 12ft 8in (3.86m)	Horsepower: 460hp (343kW)
		Width: 9ft 2¼in (2.80m)	Seats (total/car): 90S, 46S/44S

Number	Formation DMS+DMSL	Depot	Livery	Owner	Operator
142002	55543+55593	CV	TOQ	ANG	TFW
142006	55547+55597	CV	TOQ	ANG	TFW
142010	55551+55601	CV	TOQ	ANG	TFW
142069	55719+55765	CV	TOQ	ANG	TFW
142072	55722+55768	CV	TOQ	ANG	TFW
142073(S)	55723+55769	CV	TOQ	ANG	-
142074	55724+55770	CV	TOQ	ANG	TFW
142075	55725+55771	CV	TOQ	ANG	TFW
142076	55726+55772	CV	TOQ	ANG	TFW
142077	55727+55773	CV	TOQ	ANG	TFW
142080	55730+55776	CV	TOQ	ANG	TFW
142081	55731+55777	CV	TOQ	ANG	TFW
142082	55732+55778	CV	TOQ	ANG	TFW
142083	55733+55779	CV	TOQ	ANG	TFW
142085	55735+55781	CV	TOQ	ANG	TFW

Name applied
142072 **Myfanwy**

Below: *A fleet of 15 Class 142s are on the books of TfW, but in summer 2018 one set No. 142073 was withdrawn from service due to poor condition. All 'Pacer' sets will be withdrawn by 2020. Sets are painted in the previous Arriva Trains turquoise and grey livery without branding. Set No. 142006 is illustrated from its DMS vehicle at Cardiff.* **CJM**

Passenger Train Operating Companies - Transport for Wales

Class 143
Pacer

Vehicle Length: 51ft 0½in (15.55m)
Height: 12ft 2¼in (3.73m)
Width: 8ft 10½in (2.70m)

Engine: 1 x Cummins LTA10-R per vehicle
Horsepower: 460hp (343kW)
Seats (total/car): 92S, 48S/44S

Number	Formation DMS+DMSL	Depot	Livery	Owner	Operator
143601	55642+55667	CV	ATT	BCC	TFW
143602	55651+55668	CV	ATT	PTR	TFW
143604	55645+55670	CV	ATT	PTR	TFW
143605	55646+55671	CV	ATT	PTR	TFW
143606	55647+55672	CV	ATT	PTR	TFW
143607	55648+55673	CV	ATT	PTR	TFW
143608	55649+55674	CV	ATT	PTR	TFW
143609	55650+55675	CV	TFW	CCC	TFW
143610	55643+55676	CV	TFW	BCC	TFW
143614	55655+55680	CV	TFW	BCC	TFW
143616	55657+55682	CV	ATT	PTR	TFW
143622	55663+55688	CV	ATT	PTR	TFW
143623	55664+55689	CV	ATT	PTR	TFW
143624	55665+55690	CV	ATT	PTR	TFW
143625	55666+55691	CV	TFI	PTR	TFW

Below: *Another TfW fleet which is due for withdrawal by 2020 are the 15 Class 143s, allocated to Cardiff Canton and used with the Class 142s on Valley Line services. The sets display one of two ATW turquoise based liveries, which are now unbranded. Set No. 143607 is illustrated at Radyr.* **CJM**

Class 150/2
Sprinter

Vehicle Length: 64ft 9¾in (19.74m)
Height: 12ft 4½in (3.77m)
Width: 9ft 3⅛in (2.82m)

Engine: 1 x NT855R5 of 285hp per vehicle
Horsepower: 570hp (425kW)
Seats (total/car): 128S, 60S/68S

Number	Formation DMSL+DMS	Depot	Livery	Owner	Operator
150208	52208+57208	CV	ATT	PTR	TFW
150213	52213+57213	CV	ATT	PTR	TFW
150217	52217+57217	CV	ATT	PTR	TFW
150227	52227+57227	CV	ATT	PTR	TFW
150229	52229+57229	CV	ATT	PTR	TFW
150230	52230+57230	CV	ATT	PTR	TFW
150231	52231+57231	CV	ATT	PTR	TFW
150235	52235+57235	CV	ATT	PTR	TFW
150236	52236+57236	CV	ATT	PTR	TFW
150237	52237+57237	CV	ATT	PTR	TFW
150240	52240+57240	CV	ATT	PTR	TFW
150241	52241+57241	CV	ATT	PTR	TFW
150242	52242+57242	CV	ATT	PTR	TFW
150245	52245+57245	CV	ATT	PTR	TFW
150250	52250+57250	CV	ATT	PTR	TFW
150251	52251+57251	CV	ATT	PTR	TFW
150252	52252+57252	CV	ATT	PTR	TFW
150253	52253+57253	CV	ATT	PTR	TFW
150254	52254+57254	CV	ATT	PTR	TFW
150255	52213+57255	CV	ATT	PTR	TFW
150256	52256+57256	CV	ATT	PTR	TFW
150257	52257+57257	CV	ATT	PTR	TFW
150258	52258+57258	CV	ATT	PTR	TFW
150259	52259+57259	CV	ATT	PTR	TFW
150260	52260+57260	CV	ATT	PTR	TFW
150262	52262+57262	CV	ATT	PTR	TFW
150264	52264+57264	CV	ATT	PTR	TFW
150267	52267+57267	CV	ATT	PTR	TFW

150278	52278+57278	CV	ATT	PTR	TFW		150282	52282+57282	CV	ATT	PTR	TFW
150279	52279+57279	CV	ATT	PTR	TFW		150283	52283+57283	CV	ATT	PTR	TFW
150280	52280+57280	CV	ATT	PTR	TFW		150284	52284+57284	CV	ATT	PTR	TFW
150281	52281+57281	CV	ATT	PTR	TFW		150285	52285+57285	CV	ATT	PTR	TFW

Right: *Porterbrook Leasing currently provide a fleet of 36 refurbished Class 150/2 sets to TfW for use on Cardiff Valley Line services, based at Cardiff Canton. The majority of sets sport the later ATW two-tone turquoise colours, now unbranded, as shown on set No. 150229 at Cardiff Central.* **CJM**

Class 153

Vehicle Length: 76ft 5in (23.29m)	Engine: 1 x NT855R5 of 285hp
Height: 12ft 3⅛in (3.75m)	Horsepower: 285hp (213kW)
Width: 8ft 10in (2.70m)	Seats (total/car): 72S

Number	Formation DMSL	Depot	Livery	Owner	Operator						
153303	52303	CV	ATT	ANG	TFW	153323	52323	CV	ATT	PTR	TFW
153312	52312	CV	ATT	ANG	TFW	153327	52327	CV	ATT	ANG	TFW
153320	52320	CV	ATT	PTR	TFW	153353	57353	CV	ATT	ANG	TFW
						153362	57362	CV	ATT	ANG	TFW
						153367	57367	CV	ATT	PTR	TFW

Right: *When the new Transport for Wales franchise was announced in mid 2018, agreement was reached that the franchise would receive five extra Class 153s from GWR in 2019 to assist in the rundown of the 'Pacer' fleets. Painted in the later ATW two-tone turquoise colours, No. 153312 is seen at Cardiff from its small cab end.* **CJM**

Class 158

Vehicle Length: 76ft 1¾in (23.21m)	Engine: 1 x Perkins 2006-TWH of 350hp per vehicle
Height: 12ft 6in (3.81m)	Horsepower: 700hp (522kW)
Width: 9ft 3¼in (2.82m)	Seats (total/car): 134S, 66S/68S

Number	Formation DMSL+DMSL	Depot	Livery	Owner	Operator						
158818	52818+57818	MN	ATT	ANG	TFW	158829	52829+57829	MN	ATT	ANG	TFW
158819	52819+57819	MN	ATT	ANG	TFW	158830	52830+57830	MN	ATT	ANG	TFW
158820	52820+57820	MN	ATT	ANG	TFW	158831	52831+57831	MN	ATT	ANG	TFW
158821	52821+57821	MN	ATT	ANG	TFW	158832	52832+57832	MN	ATT	ANG	TFW
158822	52822+57822	MN	ATT	ANG	TFW	158833	52833+57833	MN	ATT	ANG	TFW
158823	52823+57823	MN	ATT	ANG	TFW	158834	52834+57834	MN	ATT	ANG	TFW
158824	52824+57824	MN	ATT	ANG	TFW	158835	52835+57835	MN	ATT	ANG	TFW
158825	52825+57825	MN	ATT	ANG	TFW	158836	52836+57836	MN	ATT	ANG	TFW
158826	52826+57826	MN	ATT	ANG	TFW	158837	52837+57837	MN	ATT	ANG	TFW
158827	52827+57827	MN	ATT	ANG	TFW	158838	52838+57838	MN	ATT	ANG	TFW
158828	52828+57828	MN	ATT	ANG	TFW	158839	52839+57839	MN	ATT	ANG	TFW
						158840	52840+57840	MN	ATT	ANG	TFW
						158841	52841+57841	MN	ATT	ANG	TFW

Transport for Wales

Left: *The Cambrian depot of Machynlleth is the base for 24 two-car Class 158s, used on longer distance main line services. The sets are all fitted with the European Rail Traffic Management System (ERTMS), which is used on a section of the Cambrian route. Set No. 158839 is illustrated at Cardiff.* **CJM**

Class 175/0
Coradia 1000

Vehicle Length: 75ft 7in (23.06m)
Height: 12ft 4in (3.75m)
Width: 9ft 2in (2.80m)

Engine: 1 x Cummins N14 of 450hp per vehicle
Horsepower: 900hp (671kW)
Seats (total/car): 118S, 54S/64S

Number	Formation DMSL+DMSL	Depot	Livery	Owner	Operator
175001	50701+79701	CH	ATW	ANG	TFW
175002	50702+79702	CH	ATW	ANG	TFW
175003	50703+79703	CH	TFW	ANG	TFW
175004	50704+79704	CH	ATW	ANG	TFW
175005	50705+79705	CH	ATW	ANG	TFW
175006	50706+79706	CH	ATW	ANG	TFW
175007	50707+79707	CH	ATW	ANG	TFW
175008	50708+79708	CH	ATW	ANG	TFW
175009	50709+79709	CH	ATW	ANG	TFW
175010	50710+79710	CH	ATW	ANG	TFW
175011	50711+79711	CH	ATW	ANG	TFW

Left: *Two fleets of Alstom 'Coradia' DMUs are operated by TfW, based at Chester depot, these come in two-and three car form and deployed on longer distance services, mainly on the north-south Wales corridor and services to West Wales from Manchester. From the start of the new franchise in autumn 2018, sets started to appear in the new white and red TfW colours. Three-car set No. 175003 is viewed at Newpor.* **Nathan Williamson**

Class 175/1
Coradia 1000

Vehicle Length: 75ft 7in (23.06m)
Height: 12ft 4in (3.75m)
Width: 9ft 2in (2.80m)

Engine: 1 x Cummins N14 of 450hp per vehicle
Horsepower: 1,350hp (1,007kW)
Seats (total/car): 186S, 54S/68S/64S

Number	Formation DMSL+MSL+DMSL	Depot	Livery	Owner	Op'r
175101	50751+56751+79751	CH	ATW	ANG	TFW
175102	50752+56752+79752	CH	ATW	ANG	TFW
175103	50753+56753+79753	CH	ATW	ANG	TFW
175104	50754+56754+79754	CH	ATW	ANG	TFW
175105	50755+56755+79755	CH	ATW	ANG	TFW
175106	50756+56756+79756	CH	ATW	ANG	TFW
175107	50757+56757+79757	CH	TFW	ANG	TFW
175108	50758+56758+79758	CH	ATW	ANG	TFW
175109	50759+56759+79759	CH	ATW	ANG	TFW
175110	50760+56760+79760	CH	ATW	ANG	TFW
175111	50761+56761+79761	CH	ATW	ANG	TFW
175112	50762+56762+79762	CH	ATW	ANG	TFW
175113	50763+56763+79763	CH	ATW	ANG	TFW
175114	50764+56764+79764	CH	ATW	ANG	TFW
175115	50765+56765+79765	CH	ATW	ANG	TFW
175116	50766+56766+79766	CH	ATW	ANG	TFW

Mk3 Hauled Stock
Class AJ1G / RFM

Vehicle Length: 75ft 0in (22.86m)
Height: 12ft 9in (3.88m)
Width: 8ft 11in (2.71m)

Bogie Type: BT10
Seats: 23F

Number	Type	Depot	Livery	Owner	Operator
10249 (10012)	RFM	CV	ATT	DBR	TFW
10259 (10025)	RFM	CV	ATT	ATW	TFW

Class AD1H / TSO

Vehicle Length: 75ft 0in (22.86m) Width: 8ft 11in (2.71m)
Height: 12ft 9in (3.88m) Bogie Type: BT10

Number	Type	Depot	Livery	Owner	Operator		Number	Type	Depot	Livery	Owner	Operator
12176 (11064)	TSO	CV	ATT	TFW	TFW		12181 (11086)	TSO	CV	ATT	TFW	TFW
12177 (11065)	TSO	CV	ATT	TFW	TFW		12182 (11013)	TSO	CV	ATT	TFW	TFW
12178 (11071)	TSO	CV	ATT	TFW	TFW		12183 (11027)	TSO	CV	ATT	TFW	TFW
12179 (11083)	TSO	CV	ATT	TFW	TFW		12184 (11044)	TSO	CV	ATT	TFW	TFW
12180 (11084)	TSO	CV	ATT	TFW	TFW		12185 (11089)	TSO	CV	ATT	TFW	TFW

Right: *Currently a fleet of 12 Mk3 passenger coaches are based at Cardiff and operate the prime business train each day on the Holyhead to Cardiff corridor as well as a North Wales to Manchester service. The coaches are powered by a hired in DB-C Class 67. In 2019-20 it is expected these will be replaced by Mk4 stock displayed from the LNER route. TSO No. 12180 is shown.* **CJM**

Class NZAG / DVT

Length: 75ft 0in (22.86m) Width: 8ft 11in (2.71m)
Height: 12ft 9in (3.88m) Bogie Type: BT7

NZAG - DVT

Number	Depot	Livery	Owner	Operator		Number	Depot	Livery	Owner	Operator
82306 (82144)	CV	ATT	TFW	TFW		82308 (82108)	CV	ATT	DBR	TFW
82307 (82131)	CV	ATT	TFW	TFW						

Above: *To provide remote driving facilities on the Mk3 push-pull sets powered by Class 67s, three Mk3 DVTs are based at Cardiff. These were cast off vehicles by Virgin Trains West Coast and slightly modified for their Welsh use. No. 82306 is seen at Newport coupled on the west end of a Mk3 set working on the Holyhead to Cardiff corridor.* **CJM**

New Train Orders

As part of the new Wales & Borders and South Wales Metro franchise operated by KeolisAmey and Transport for Wales, a major fleet replacement project has been authorised. This consists of:
51 x two-car and 26 x three-car CAF-built 'Civity' sets,
11 x four-car Stadler 'Flirt' DMU, 7 x three-car and 17 x four-car Stadler 'Flirt' multi-mode (diesel, battery and electric) sets and 36 three-car Stadler 'Citylink' Tram-train sets suitable for main line and street running.

While this stock is under design, construction and delivery, 12 Mk4s displaced by LNER will be deployed on north-south services from 12/19, five Class 153s from Great Western will be used from 05/19. In addition four 2-car and eight 3-car Class 170s displaced from Greater Anglia will be operated.

The franchise will also operate five 3-car Class 230 Vivarail 'D' stock sets and nine Porterbrook Class 769/0 'Flex' conversions able to operate under bi-mode conditions (electric and diesel), to be rebuilt from 319002/003/006-008, to be renumbered as 769002/003/006-008.

Passenger Train Operating Companies - Transport for Wales

Virgin West Coast

Passenger Train Operating Companies - Virgin West Coast

Address: 85 Smallbrook Queensway,
Birmingham, B5 4HA
✉ info@virgintrains.co.uk
✆ 0845 000 8000
ⓘ www.virgintrains.co.uk

Lead Executive: Phil Whittingham

Franchise Dates: 12 December 2006 - March 2020

Principal Routes: London Euston - Birmingham, Holyhead, Manchester Liverpool, Glasgow and Edinburgh

Depots: Edge Hill** (LL), Longsight** (MA), Oxley** (OY), Wembley** (WB), Central Rivers (CZ)
** Operated by Alstom

Parent Company: Virgin Group

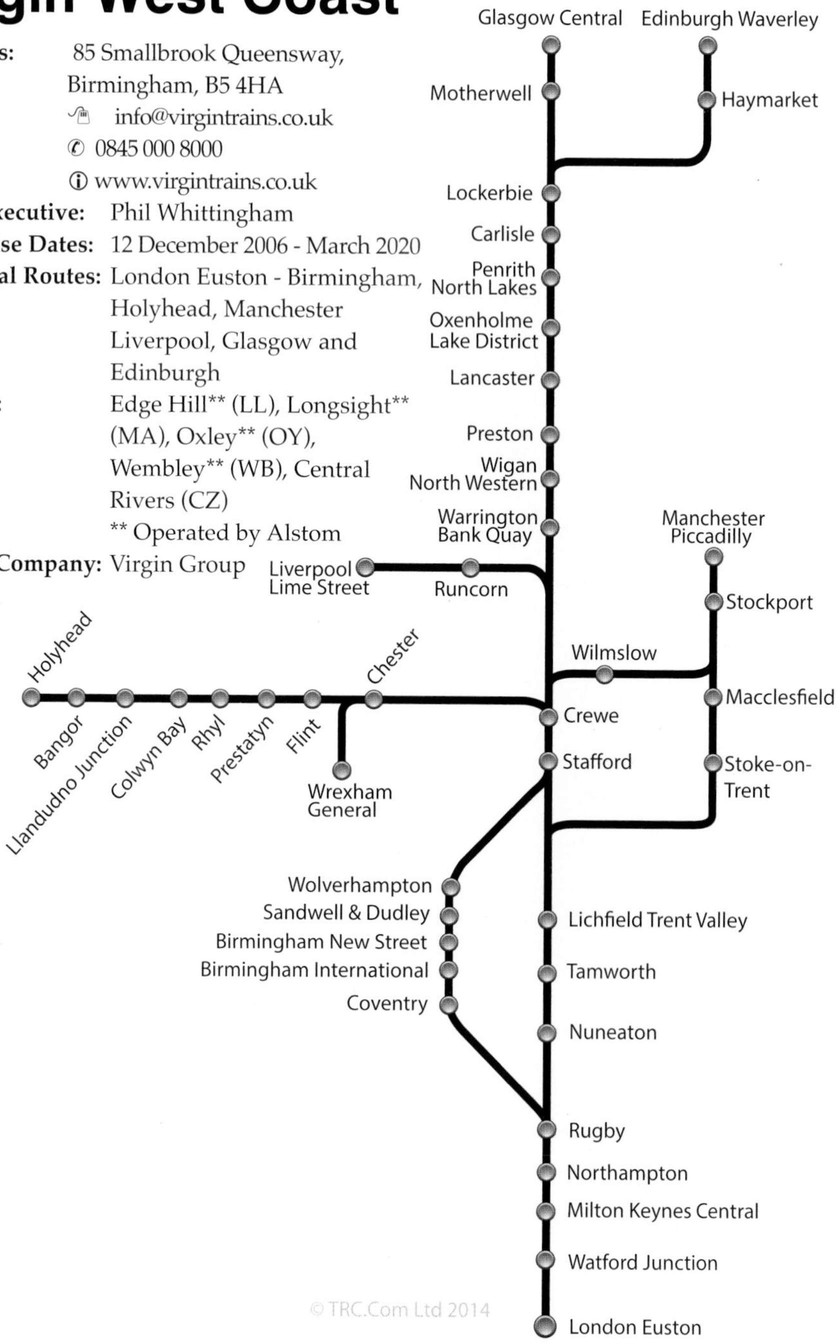

Glasgow Central   Edinburgh Waverley

Motherwell   Haymarket

Lockerbie

Carlisle

Penrith
North Lakes

Oxenholme
Lake District

Lancaster

Preston

Wigan
North Western

Warrington   Manchester
Bank Quay   Piccadilly

Liverpool   Stockport
Lime Street   Runcorn

Holyhead   Wilmslow

Bangor   Llandudno Junction   Colwyn Bay   Rhyl   Prestatyn   Flint   Chester   Macclesfield

Crewe

Wrexham   Stafford   Stoke-on-
General   Trent

Wolverhampton
Sandwell & Dudley
Birmingham New Street   Lichfield Trent Valley
Birmingham International
Coventry   Tamworth

Nuneaton

Rugby

Northampton

Milton Keynes Central

Watford Junction

© TRC.Com Ltd 2014

London Euston

Class 221
Super Voyager

Vehicle Length: 77ft 6in (23.62m)
Height: 12ft 4in (3.75m)
Width: 8ft 11in (2.73m)
Engine: 1 x Cummins 750hp per vehicle
Horsepower: 5-car - 3,750hp (2,796kW). 4-car - 3,000hp (2,237kW)
Seats (total/car): 26F/214S 42S/60S/60S/52S*/26F (*not in 4-car set)

Number	Formation DMS+MS+MS+MSRMB+DMF	Depot	Livery	Owner	Operator	Name
221101	60351+60951+60851+60751+60451	CZ	VWN	BEA	VWC	101 Squadron
221102	60352+60952+60852+60752+60452	CZ	VWC	BEA	VWC	John Cabot
221103	60353+60953+60853+60753+60453	CZ	VWC	BEA	VWC	Christopher Columbus
221104	60354+60954+60854+60754+60454	CZ	VWC	BEA	VWC	Sir John Franklin
221105	60355+60955+60855+60755+60455	CZ	VWC	BEA	VWC	William Baffin
221106	60356+60956+60856+60756+60456	CZ	VWC	BEA	VWC	Willem Barents
221107	60357+60957+60857+60757+60457	CZ	VWC	BEA	VWC	Sir Martin Frobisher
221108	60358+60958+60858+60758+60458	CZ	VWC	BEA	VWC	Sir Ernest Shackleton
221109	60359+60959+60859+60759+60459	CZ	VWC	BEA	VWC	Marco Polo
221110	60360+60960+60860+60760+60460	CZ	VWC	BEA	VWC	James Cook
221111	60361+60961+60861+60761+60461	CZ	VWC	BEA	VWC	Roald Amundsen
221112	60362+60962+60862+60762+60462	CZ	VWC	BEA	VWC	Ferdinand Magellan
221113	60363+60963+60863+60763+60463	CZ	VWC	BEA	VWC	Sir Walter Raleigh
221114	60364+60964+60864+60764+60464	CZ	VWC	BEA	VWC	Royal Air Force Centenary 1918-2018
221115	60365+60965+60865+60765+60465	CZ	VWC¤	BEA	VWC	Polmadie Depot
221116	60366+60966+60866+60766+60466	CZ	VWC	BEA	VWC	
221117	60367+60967+60867+60767+60467	CZ	VWC	BEA	VWC	The Wrekin Giant
221118	60368+60968+60868+60768+60468	CZ	VWC	BEA	VWC	
221142	60392+60992+60986+60792+60492	CZ	VWC	BEA	VWC	Bombardier Voyager
221143	60393+60993+60994+60793+60493	CZ	VWC	BEA	VWC	Auguste Picard

¤ One driving car carries Bombardier branding.

Below: A fleet of 20 five-car 'Super Voyager' Class 221 sets are based at Central Rivers near Burton on Trent and operated by Virgin West Coast. The sets are deployed on non-electrified routes, such as London to Shrewsbury, the North Wales Coast and provide additional resources on the Birmingham and Glasgow corridor, supplementing the Class 390 fleet. Set No. 221101 showing the latest 'Flowing Silk' colours passes South Kenton on 5 November 2018 with a Euston-Shrewsbury service. **CJM**

Class 390
Pendolino

Vehicle Length (Driving): 75ft 6in (23.01m)
Height: 11ft 6in (3.50m)
Width: 8ft 11in (2.71m)

Horsepower: 6,840hp (5,100kW)
Seats (total/car): 147F/300S, 18F/39F/44F/46F/74S/76S/76S/66S/48S/64S/46S
35 sets are now formed of 11 vehicles 147F/450S

Number	*Formation* DMRFO+MFO+PTFO+MFO[MSO]*+(TSO+MSO)+TSO+MSO+PTSRMB+MSO+DMSO	*Depot*	*Livery*	*Owner*	*Operator*	*Name*
390001	69101+69401+69501+69601*+68801+69701+69801+69901+69201	MA	VWN	ANG	VWC	*Bee Together*
390002	69102+69402+69502+69602*+68802+69702+69802+69902+69202	MA	VWN	ANG	VWC	*Stephen Sutton*
390103	69103+69403+69503+69603+65303+68903+68803+69703+69803+69903+69203	MA	VWC	ANG	VWC	*Virgin Hero*
390104	69104+69404+69504+69604+65304+68904+68804+69704+69804+69904+69204	MA	VWN	ANG	VWC	*Alstom Pendolino*
390005	69105+69405+69505+69605*+68805+69705+69805+69905+69205	MA	VWN	ANG	VWC	*City of Wolverhampton*
390006	69106+69406+69606*+68806+69706+69806+69906+69206	MA	VWN	ANG	VWC	*Rethink Mental Illness*
390107	69107+69407+69507+69607+65307+68907+68807+69707+69807+69907+69207	MA	VWN	ANG	VWC	
390008	69108+69408+69508+69608*+68808+69708+69808+69908+69208	MA	VWN	ANG	VWC	*Charles Rennie Mackintosh*
390009	69109+69409+69509+69609*+68809+69709+69809+69909+69209	MA	VWN	ANG	VWC	*Treaty of Union*
390010	69110+69410+69510+69610*+68810+69710+69810+69910+69210	MA	VWN	ANG	VWC	*Cumbrian Spirit*
390011	69111+69411+69511+69611*+68811+69711+69811+69911+69211	MA	VWN	ANG	VWC	*City of Lichfield*
390112	69112+69412+69512+69612+65312+68912+68812+69712+69812+69912+69212	MA	VWN	ANG	VWC	*Virgin Star*
390013	69113+69413+69513+69613*+68813+69713+69813+69913+69213	MA	VWN	ANG	VWC	*Blackpool Belle*
390114	69114+69414+69514+69614+65314+68914+68814+69714+69814+69914+69214	MA	VWN	ANG	VWC	*City of Manchester*
390115	69115+69415+69515+69615+65315+68915+68815+69715+69815+69915+69215	MA	VWN	ANG	VWC	*Virgin Crusader*
390016	69116+69416+69516+69616*+68816+69716+69816+69916+69216	MA	VWN	ANG	VWC	
390117	69117+69417+69517+69617+65317+68917+68817+69717+69817+69917+69217	MA	VWN	ANG	VWC	*Blue Peter*
390118	69118+69418+69518+69618+65318+68918+68818+69718+69818+69918+69218	MA	VWN	ANG	VWC	*Virgin Princess*
390119	69119+69419+69519+69619+65319+68919+68819+69719+69819+69919+69219	MA	VWN	ANG	VWC	*Unkown Soldier*
390020	69120+69420+69520+69620*+68820+69720+69820+69920+69220	MA	VWN	ANG	VWC	*Virgin Cavalier*
390121	69121+69421+69521+69621+65321+68921+68821+69721+69821+69921+69221	MA	VWN	ANG	VWC	*Virgin Dream*
390122	69122+69422+69522+69622+65322+68922+68822+69722+69822+69922+69222	MA	VWN	ANG	VWC	*Penny the Pendolino*
390123	69123+69423+69523+69623+69323+68923+68823+69723+69823+69923+69223	MA	VWN	ANG	VWC	*Virgin Glory*
390124	69124+69424+69524+69624+65324+68924+68824+69724+69824+69924+69224	MA	VWN	ANG	VWC	*Virgin Venturer*
390125	69125+69425+69525+69625+65325+68925+68825+69725+69825+69925+69225	MA	VWC	ANG	VWC	*Virgin Stagecoach*
390126	69126+69426+69526+69626+65326+68926+68826+69726+69826+69926+69226	MA	VWC	ANG	VWC	*Virgin Enterprise*
390127	69127+69427+69527+69627+65327+68927+68827+69727+69827+69927+69227	MA	VWC	ANG	VWC	*Virgin Buccaneer*
390128	69128+69428+69528+69628+65328+68928+68828+69728+69828+69928+69228	MA	VWC	ANG	VWC	*City of Preston*
390129	69129+69429+69529+69629+65329+68929+68829+69729+69829+69929+69229	MA	VWC	ANG	VWC	*City of Stoke-on-Trent*
390130	69130+69430+69530+69630+65330+68930+68830+69730+69830+69930+69230	MA	VWC	ANG	VWC	*City of Edinburgh*
390131	69131+69431+69531+69631+65331+68931+68831+69731+69831+69931+69231	MA	VWC	ANG	VWC	*City of Liverpool*
390132	69132+69432+69532+69632+65332+68932+68832+69732+69832+69932+69232	MA	VWC	ANG	VWC	*City of Birmingham*
390134	69134+69434+69534+69634+65334+68934+68834+69734+69834+69934+69234	MA	VWC	ANG	VWC	*City of Carlisle*
390135	69135+69435+69535+69635+65335+68935+68835+69735+69835+69935+69235	MA	VWC	ANG	VWC	*City of Lancaster*
390136	69136+69436+69536+69636+65336+68936+68836+69736+69836+69936+69236	MA	VWC	ANG	VWC	*City of Coventry*
390137	69137+69437+69537+69637+65337+68937+68837+69737+69837+69937+69237	MA	VWC	ANG	VWC	*Virgin Difference*
390138	69138+69438+69538+69638+65338+68938+68838+69738+69838+69938+69238	MA	VWC	ANG	VWC	*City of London*
390039	69139+69439+69539+69639*+68839+69739+69839+69939+69239	MA	VWN	ANG	VWC	*Virgin Quest*
390040	69140+69440+69540+69640*+68840+69740+69840+69940+69240	MA	VWN	ANG	VWC	*Virgin Radio Star*

Set No	Formation					Name
390141	69141+69441+69541+69641+65341+68941+68841+69741+69841+69941+69241	MA	VWC	ANG	VWC	City of Chester
390042	69142+69442+69542+69642*+68842+69742+69842+69942+69242	MA	VWN	ANG	VWC	
390043	69143+69443+69543+69643*+68843+69743+69843+69943+69243	MA	VWN	ANG	VWC	
390044	69144+69444+69544+69644*+68844+69744+69844+69944+69244	MA	VWN	ANG	VWC	Virgin Lionheart
390045	69145+69445+69545+69645*+68845+69745+69845+69945+69245	MA	VWN	ANG	VWC	Virgin Pride
390046	69146+69446+69546+69646*+68846+69746+69846+69946+69246	MA	VWN	ANG	VWC	Virgin Soldiers
390047	69147+69447+69547+69647*+68847+69747+69847+69947+69247	MA	VWN	ANG	VWC	
390148	69148+69448+69548+69648+65348+68948+68848+69748+69848+69948+69248	MA	VWC	ANG	VWC	Flying Scouseman
390049	69149+69449+69549+69649*+68849+69749+69849+69949+69249	MA	VWN	ANG	VWC	
390050	69150+69450+69550+69650*+68850+69750+69850+69950+69250	MA	VWN	ANG	VWC	
390151	69151+69451+69551+69651+68951+69751+69851+69951+69251	MA	VWC	ANG	VWC	Virgin Ambassador
390152	69152+69452+69552+69652+65352+68952+68852+69752+69852+69952+69252	MA	VWC	ANG	VWC	Alison Waters
390153	69153+69453+69553+69653+65353+68953+68853+69753+69853+69953+69253	MA	VWC	ANG	VWC	Mission Accomplished
390154	69154+69454+69554+69654+65354+68954+68854+69754+69854+69954+69254	MA	VWC	ANG	VWC	Matthew Flinders
390155	69155+69455+69555+69655+68955+69755+69855+69955+69255	MA	VWC	ANG	VWC	X-Men Days of Future Past
390156	69156+69456+69556+69656+68956+69756+69856+69956+69256	MA	VWC	ANG	VWC	Stockport 170
390157	69157+69457+69557+69657+68957+69757+69857+69957+69257	MA	VWC	ANG	VWC	Chad Varah

■ Vehicles 69133 and 69833 have been rebuilt as static training vehicles for use at the Virgin Trains training school in Crewe. Nos. 69933 and 69733 are in use at the fire training school in Moreton-in-Marsh. These coaches came from collision-damaged and withdrawn set No. 390033.

Left: *Virgin Train core West Coast traction are Class 390 'Pendolino sets, formed in either nine or 11 car formations and based at Manchester. During 2017-2019 sets have been refurbished and outshopped by Alstom's Widnes plant in a new 'Floating Silk' white livery with red flashes on the cab sides. The majority of sets now also carry a promotional branding for on board entertainment. Painted in the latest colours, set No. 390039 is seen passing through the Lune Gorge.* **Jamie Squibbs**

Passenger Train Operating Companies - Virgin West Coast

West Midlands

Address: ✉ 34 Edmund Street, Birmingham. B3 2ES
✆ comments@westmidlandsrailway.co.uk
✆ 03333110039 ⓘ www.westmidlandsrailway.co.uk

Managing Director: Jan Chaudhry-van der Velde
Franchise Dates: December 2017 - March 2026
Principal Routes: London Euston - Liverpool Lime Street, West Midlands routes to Stratford-upon-Avon, Worcester, Hereford, Shrewsbury, plus Bedford and St Albans Abbey branches
Depots: Northampton (NN)§, Soho (SI), Tyseley (TS), Stourbridge Junction (SJ) § Operated by Siemens
Parent Company: Abellio, East Japan Railway, Mitsui

36 x 3-car 90mph and 45 5-car EMUs from Bombardier, plus 12 x 2-car and 14 x 4-car DMUs from CAF (funded by Corlink Rail Infrastructure) are on order. The London North Western trading name will be used for main line services.

Class 08

		Vehicle Length: 29ft 3in (8.91m)	Engine: English Electric 6K
		Height: 12ft 8⅝in (3.87m)	Horsepower: 400hp (298kW)
		Width: 8ft 6in (2.59m)	Electrical Equipment: English Electric

Number	Depot	Pool	Livery	Owner	Operator	Name
08616 (3783)	TS	EJLO	LMI	WMT	WMT	*Tyseley 100*
08805	SI	EJLO	GRY	WMT	WMT	

Class 139

	Vehicle Length: 28ft 6in (8.7m)	Engine: 1 x MVH420 2.0ltr LPG, flywheel hybrid
	Width: 7ft 8in (2.4m)	Seats (total/car): 18S

Number	Formation DMS	Depot	Livery	Owner	Operator		Number	Formation	Depot	Livery	Owner	Operator
139001	39001	SJ	LMI	WMT	WMT§		139002	39002	SJ	LMI	WMT	WMT§

Left: *West Midlands Trains in conjunction with Pre-Metro Operations Ltd, operate two Class 139 Parry People Mover vehicles on the Stourbridge Town to Stourbridge Junction 'shuttle' service. The two vehicles are based in a small depot at Stourbridge Junction. Set No. 139002 is seen approaching Stourbridge Town.* **CJM**

§ By Pre-Metro Operations Ltd

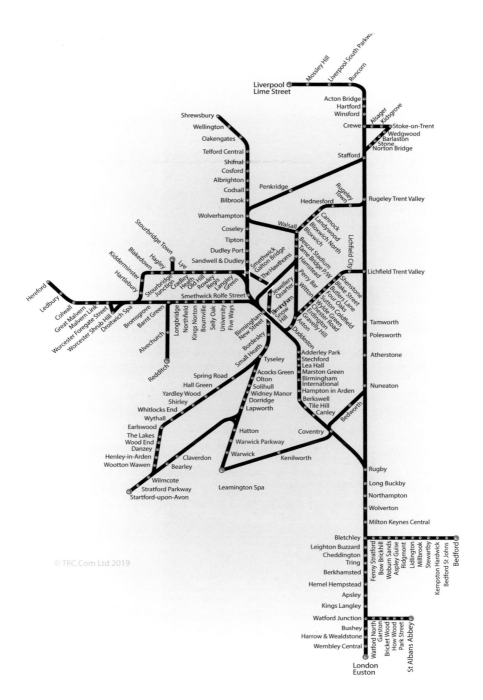

West Midlands

Class 150/1
Sprinter

Vehicle Length: 64ft 9¾in (19.74m)
Height: 12ft 4½in (3.77m)
Width: 9ft 3⅛in (2.82m)

Engine: 1 x NT855R5 of 285hp per vehicle
Horsepower: 570hp (425kW)
Seats (total/car): 148S, 76S/72S

Number	Formation DMSL+DMS	Depot	Livery	Owner	Operator
150105	52105+57105	TS	LMI	ANG	WMT
150107	52107+57107	TS	LMI	ANG	WMT
150109	52109+57109	TS	LMI	ANG	WMT

Left: With West Midlands Trains having a large fleet of new trains on order, the days of Class 150/1s working for the operator are numbered. Currently three Class 150/1s are on the books of Tyseley depot. No. 150105 is shown passing Longbridge. **Nathan Williamson**

Class 153

Vehicle Length: 76ft 5in (23.29m)
Height: 12ft 3⅛in (3.75m)
Width: 8ft 10in (2.70m)

Engine: 1 x NT855R5 of 285hp
Horsepower: 285hp (213kW)
Seats (total/car): 72S

Number	Formation DMSL	Depot	Livery	Owner	Operator						
153334	52334	TS	LMI	PTR	WMT	153364	57364	TS	LMI	PTR	WMT
153354	57354	TS	LMI	PTR	WMT	153365	57365	TS	LMI	PTR	WMT
153356	57356	TS	LMI	PTR	WMT	153366	57366	TS	LMI	PTR	WMT
						153371	57371	TS	LMI	PTR	WMT
						153375	57375	TS	LMI	PTR	WMT

Left: A fleet of eight Class 153 'Bubble' cars are operated by West Midlands Trains, either used on branch line services where patronage is low or to strengthen two-car sets. No. 153356 is shown attached to a Class 170 at Bromsgrove working a Hereford to Birmingham service. **CJM**

Class 170/5
Turbostar

Vehicle Length: 77ft 6in (23.62m)
Height: 12ft 4½in (3.77m)
Width: 8ft 10in (2.69m)

Engine: 1 x MTU 6R 183TD13H of 422hp per vehicle
Horsepower: 844hp (629kW)
Seats (total/car): 122S 55S/67S

Number	Formation DMSL+DMSL	Depot	Livery	Owner	Operator						
						170504	50504+79504	TS	WMT	PTR	WMT
						170505	50505+79505	TS	WMT	PTR	WMT
170501	50501+79501	TS	WMT	PTR	WMT	170506	50506+79506	TS	WMT	PTR	WMT
170502	50502+79502	TS	WMT	PTR	WMT	170507	50507+79507	TS	WMT	PTR	WMT
170503	50503+79503	TS	WMT	PTR	WMT	170508	50508+79508	TS	WMT	PTR	WMT

170509	50509+79509	TS	WMT	PTR	WMT	170514	50514+79514	TS	WMT	PTR	WMT
170510	50510+79510	TS	WMT	PTR	WMT	170515	50515+79515	TS	WMT	PTR	WMT
170511	50511+79511	TS	WMT	PTR	WMT	170516	50516+79516	TS	WMT	PTR	WMT
170512	50512+79512	TS	WMT	PTR	WMT	170517	50517+79517	TS	WMT	PTR	WMT
170513	50513+79513	TS	WMT	PTR	WMT						

Right: *A fleet of both two and three-car Class 170s currently operate West Midlands longer distance services. During 2018-2019 the fleet was in the process of being given the latest gold, white and black livery, as shown on two-car Class 170/5 set No. 170506.* **CJM**

Class 170/6
Turbostar

Vehicle Length: 77ft 6in (23.62m)
Height: 12ft 4½in (3.77m)
Width: 8ft 10in (2.69m)

Engine: 1 x MTU 6R 183TD13H of 422hp per vehicle
Horsepower: 1,266hp (944kW)
Seats (total/car): 196S 55S/74S/67S

Number	Formation	Depot	Livery	Owner	Operator
	DMSL+MS+DMSL				
170630	50630+56630+79630	TS	WMT	PTR	WMT
170631	50631+56631+79631	TS	WMT	PTR	WMT
170632	50632+56632+79632	TS	WMT	PTR	WMT
170633	50633+56633+79633	TS	WMT	PTR	WMT
170634	50634+56634+79634	TS	WMT	PTR	WMT
170635	50635+56635+79635	TS	WMT	PTR	WMT

Class 172/0
Turbostar

Vehicle Length: 73ft 4in (22.37m)
Height: 12ft 4½in (3.77m)
Width: 8ft 8in (2.69m)

Engine: MTU 6H1800R83 of 360kW (483hp) per car
Horsepower: 966hp (720kW)
Seats (total/car): 124S, 60S/64S

Number	Formation	Depot	Livery	Owner	Operator						
	DMS+DMS					172004	59314+59414	TS	LOG	ANG	WMT
						172005	59315+59415	TS	LOG	ANG	WMT
172001	59311+59411	TS	LOG	ANG	WMT	172006	59316+59416	TS	LOG	ANG	WMT
172002	59312+59412	TS	LOG	ANG	WMT	172007	59317+59417	TS	LOG	ANG	WMT
172003	59313+59413	TS	LOG	ANG	WMT	172008	59318+59418	TS	LOG	ANG	WMT

Right: *Following displacement from the London Overground Gospel Oak to Barking route by Class 710s, the eight Willesden-allocated Class 172 have transferred to West Midlands Trains at Tyseley, for suburban diesel services in the West Midlands. Before transfer north and still carrying London Overground livery, set No. 172006 is shown.* **CJM**

Class 172/2
Turbostar

Vehicle Length: 73ft 4in (22.37m)
Height: 12ft 4½in (3.77m)
Width: 8ft 8in (2.69m)

Engine: MTU 6H1800 of of 482hp (360kW) per vehicle
Horsepower: 964hp (720kW)
Seats (total/car): 121S, 53S/68S

Number	Formation	Depot	Livery	Owner	Operator						
	DMS+DMS					172214	50214+79214	TS	LMI	PTR	WMT
						172215	50215+79215	TS	LMI	PTR	WMT
172211	50211+79211	TS	LMI	PTR	WMT	172216	50216+79216	TS	LMI	PTR	WMT
172212	50212+79212	TS	LMI	PTR	WMT	172217	50217+79217	TS	LMI	PTR	WMT
172213	50213+79213	TS	LMI	PTR	WMT	172218	50218+79218	TS	LMI	PTR	WMT

West Midlands

172219	50219+79219	TS	LMI	PTR	WMT	172221	50221+79221	TS	LMI	PTR	WMT
172220	50220+79220	TS	LMI	PTR	WMT	172222	50222+79222	TS	LMI	PTR	WMT

Left: *West Midlands non-electrified services are mainly in the hands of Class 172 'Turbostar' stock which operate in both two and three-car formations. Sets are based at Tyseley and in 2019 a livery change is in progress to apply the latest West Midlands franchise livery. In older green livery but with West Midlands branding, set No. 172215 stands at Birmingham Moor Street.*
Nathan Williamson

Class 172/3
Turbostar

Vehicle Length: (Driving) 73ft 4in (22.37m)
(Inter): 76ft 7in (23.36m)
Height: 12ft 4½in (3.77m)
Width: 8ft 8in (2.69m)
Engine: MTU 6H1800 of 482hp (360kW) per vehicle
Horsepower: 1,446hp (1,080kW)
Seats (total/car): 193S, 53S/72S/68S

Number	Formation	Depot	Livery	Owner	Op'r
	DMSO+MS+DMSO				
172331	50331+56331+79331	TS	WMT	PTR	WMT
172332	50332+56332+79332	TS	WMT	PTR	WMT
172333	50333+56333+79333	TS	WMT	PTR	WMT
172334	50334+56334+79334	TS	WMT	PTR	WMT
172335	50335+56335+79335	TS	WMT	PTR	WMT
172336	50336+56336+79336	TS	WMT	PTR	WMT
172337	50337+56337+79337	TS	WMT	PTR	WMT
172338	50338+56338+79338	TS	WMT	PTR	WMT
172339	50339+56339+79339	TS	WMT	PTR	WMT
172340	50340+56340+79340	TS	WMT	PTR	WMT
172341	50341+56341+79341	TS	WMT	PTR	WMT
172342	50342+56342+79342	TS	WMT	PTR	WMT
172343	50343+56343+79343	TS	WMT	PTR	WMT
172344	50344+56344+79344	TS	WMT	PTR	WMT
172345	50345+56345+79345	TS	WMT	PTR	WMT

Class 230

Vehicle Length: (Driving) 60ft 3in (18.37m)
(Inter) 59ft 5in (18.12m)
Height: 11ft 11in (3.62m)
Width: 9ft 4in (2.85m)
Horsepower: 800hp (597kW)

Number	Formation	Depot	Livery	Owner	Operator
	DMSO+DMSO				
230003	301003+301103	BY	WMT	WMT	WMT
230004	301004+301104	BY	WMT	WMT	WMT
230005	301005+301105	BY	EMT	WMT	WMT

Class 319

Vehicle Length: (Driving) 65ft 0¾in (19.83m)
(Inter) 65ft 4¼in (19.92m)
Height: 11ft 9in (3.58m)
Width: 9ft 3in (2.82m)
Horsepower: 1,326hp (990kW)
Seats (total/car): 12F/277S, 12F-54S/77S/72S/74S

Number	Formation	Depot	Livery	Owner	Operator
	DTSO(A)+MSO+TSO+DTSO(B)				
319005	77299+62895+71776+77298	NN	LMW	PTR	WMT
319008	77305+62898+71779+77304	NN	TLK	PTR	WMT

Above: *A batch of 13 former Thameslink Class 319 sets are allocated to West Midlands Trains and operated by their North Western Railway sector. Based at Northampton, the sets provide extra capacity on the Euston to Northampton corridor during peak periods. An eight-car formation with set No. 319460 nearest the camera is seen passing South Kenton. Examples of sub-classes 319/0, 319/2 and 319/4 can be seen.* **CJM**

319012	77313+62902+71783+77312	NN	LMW	PTR	WMT
319013	77315+62903+71784+77314	NN	LMI	PTR	WMT
319215	77319+62905+71786+77318	NN	LMW	PTR	WMT
319216	77321+62906+71787+77320	NN	LMW	PTR	WMT
319220	77329+62910+71791+77328	NN	TLK	PTR	WMT
319429	77347+62919+71800+77346	NN	LMI	PTR	WMT
319433	77355+62923+71804+77354	NN	LMI	PTR	WMT
319441	77371+62931+71812+77370	NN	LMW	PTR	WMT
319455	77447+62969+71874+77446	NN	LMW	PTR	WMT
319457	77451+62971+71876+77450	NN	LMW	PTR	WMT
319460	77457+62974+71879+77456	NN	LMI	PTR	WMT

Class 323

Vehicle Length: (Driving) 76ft 8¼in (23.37m)
(Inter) 76ft 10¾in (23.44m)
Height: 12ft 4¾in (3.78m)
Width: 9ft 2¼in (2.80m)
Horsepower: 1,565hp (1,168kW)
Seats (total/car): 284S, 98S/88S/98S

Number	Formation DMSO(A)+PTSO+DMSO(B)	Depot	Livery	Owner	Op'r		Number	Formation	Depot	Livery	Owner	Op'r
							323213	64013+72213+65013 SI	WMT	PTR	WMT
323201	64001+72201+65001 SI	WMT	PTR	WMT			323214	64014+72214+65014 SI	WMT	PTR	WMT
323202	64002+72202+65002 SI	WMT	PTR	WMT			323215	64015+72215+65015 SI	WMT	PTR	WMT
323203	64003+72203+65003 SI	WMT	PTR	WMT			323216	64016+72216+65016 SI	WMT	PTR	WMT
323204	64004+72204+65004 SI	WMT	PTR	WMT			323217	64017+72217+65017 SI	WMT	PTR	WMT
323205	64005+72205+65005 SI	WMT	PTR	WMT			323218	64018+72218+65018 SI	WMT	PTR	WMT
323206	64006+72206+65006 SI	WMT	PTR	WMT			323219	64019+72219+65019 SI	WMT	PTR	WMT
323207	64007+72207+65007 SI	WMT	PTR	WMT			323220	64020+72220+65020 SI	WMT	PTR	WMT
323208	64008+72208+65008 SI	WMT	PTR	WMT			323221	64021+72221+65021 SI	WMT	PTR	WMT
323209	64009+72209+65009 SI	WMT	PTR	WMT			323222	64022+72222+65022 SI	WMT	PTR	WMT
323210	64010+72210+65010 SI	WMT	PTR	WMT			323240	64040+72340+65040 SI	WMT	PTR	WMT
323211	64011+72211+65011 SI	WMT	PTR	WMT			323241	64041+72341+65041 SI	WMT	PTR	WMT
323212	64012+72212+65012 SI	WMT	PTR	WMT			323242	64042+72342+65042 SI	WMT	PTR	WMT
							323243	64043+72343+65043 SI	WMT	PTR	WMT

Above: *To be replaced by new stock around 2021, the Hunslet TPL-built Class 323s are currently the mainstay of operations on the Birmingham Cross-City route, from Bromsgrove/Redditch in the south to Lichfield in the north. Currently sets are being re-painted in the latest WMTs gold, while and black livery. Set No. 323202 shows this scheme at Longbridge. After displacement from the Birmingham area, these sets are likely to move to Northern.* **CJM**

Class 350/1
Desiro

Vehicle Length: 66ft 9in (20.4m)
Height: 12ft 1½in (3.78m)
Width: 9ft 2in (2.7m)
Horsepower: 1,341hp (1,000kW)
Seats (total/car): 24F-209S, 60S/24F-32S/57S/60S
110mph max speed

Number	Formation DMSO(A)+TCO+PTSO+DMSO(B)	Depot	Livery	Owner	Operator
350101	63761+66811+66861+63711	NN	LMI	ANG	WMT
350102	63762+66812+66862+63712	NN	LMI	ANG	WMT
350103	63765+66813+66863+63713	NN	LMI	ANG	WMT
350104	63764+66814+66864+63714	NN	LMI	ANG	WMT
350105	63763+66815+66868+63715	NN	LMI	ANG	WMT
350106	63766+66816+66866+63716	NN	LMI	ANG	WMT
350107	63767+66817+66867+63717	NN	LMI	ANG	WMT
350108	63768+66818+66865+63718	NN	LMI	ANG	WMT
350109	63769+66819+66869+63719	NN	LMI	ANG	WMT
350110	63770+66820+66870+63720	NN	LMA	ANG	WMT

West Midlands

350111	63771+66821+66871+63721	NN	LMI	ANG	WMT
350112	63772+66822+66872+63722	NN	LMI	ANG	WMT
350113	63773+66823+66873+63723	NN	LMI	ANG	WMT
350114	63774+66824+66874+63724	NN	LMI	ANG	WMT
350115	63775+66825+66875+63725	NN	LMI	ANG	WMT
350116	63776+66826+66876+63726	NN	LMI	ANG	WMT
350117	63777+66827+66877+63727	NN	LMI	ANG	WMT
350118	63778+66828+66878+63728	NN	LMI	ANG	WMT
350119	63779+66829+66879+63729	NN	LMI	ANG	WMT
350120	63780+66830+66880+63730	NN	LMI	ANG	WMT
350121	63781+66831+66881+63731	NN	LMI	ANG	WMT
350122	63782+66832+66882+63732	NN	LMI	ANG	WMT
350123	63783+66833+66883+63733	NN	LMI	ANG	WMT
350124	63784+66834+66884+63734	NN	LMI	ANG	WMT
350125	63785+66835+66885+63735	NN	LMI	ANG	WMT
350126	63786+66836+66886+63736	NN	LMI	ANG	WMT
350127	63787+66837+66887+63737	NN	LMI	ANG	WMT
350128	63788+66838+66888+63738	NN	LMI	ANG	WMT
350129	63789+66839+66889+63739	NN	LMI	ANG	WMT
350130	63790+66840+66890+63740	NN	LMI	ANG	WMT

Left: West Midlands under its North Western Railway trading name currently operate a fleet of 77 Class 350 'Desiro' sets, based at Northampton. The 30 Class 350/1 sets, owned by Angel Trains are now upgraded for 110mph (177km/h) running to enable operation on longer distance services over the West Coast Main Line where they are sharing paths with Class 390 'Pendolino' stock. Set No. 350117 in West Midlands green livery with NWR branding is seen on the main line at South Kenton. **CJM**

Class 350/2
Desiro

Vehicle Length: 66ft 9in (20.4m)	Horsepower: 1,341hp (1,000kW)
Height: 12ft 1½in (3.78m)	Seats (total/car): 24F-243S, 70S/24F-42S/61S/70S
Width: 9ft 2in (2.7m)	100mph max speed

Left: A fleet of 37 Class 350/2 sets, owned by Porterbrook, but restricted to 100mph (161km/h) top speed are allocated alongside the Class 350/1s. These sets are scheduled to be taken off lease when new WMT stock is commissioned. Set No. 350252 in the latest North Western Railway livery is shown at Crewe. **CJM**

Number	Formation	Depot	Livery	Owner	Operator
	DMSO(A)+TCO+PTSO+DMSO(B)				
350231	61431+65231+67531+61531	NN	LNW	PTR	WMT
350232	61432+65232+67532+61532	NN	LNW	PTR	WMT
350233	61433+65233+67533+61546	NN	LMI	PTR	WMT
350234	61434+65234+67534+61534	NN	LNW	PTR	WMT

350235	61435+65235+67535+61535	NN	LMI	PTR	WMT
350236	61436+65236+67536+61536	NN	LMI	PTR	WMT
350237	61437+65237+67537+61537	NN	LMI	PTR	WMT
350238	61438+65238+67538+61538	NN	LMI	PTR	WMT
350239	61439+65239+67539+61539	NN	LNW	PTR	WMT
350240	61440+65240+67540+61540	NN	LNW	PTR	WMT
350241	61441+65241+67541+61541	NN	LMI	PTR	WMT
350242	61442+65242+67542+61542	NN	LMI	PTR	WMT
350243	61443+65243+67543+61543	NN	LMI	PTR	WMT
350244	61444+65244+67544+61544	NN	LNW	PTR	WMT
350245	61445+65245+67545+61545	NN	LNW	PTR	WMT
350246§	61446+65246+67546+61533	NN	LMI	PTR	WMT
350247	61447+65247+67547+61547	NN	LMI	PTR	WMT
350248	61448+65248+67548+61548	NN	LMI	PTR	WMT
350249	61449+65249+67549+61549	NN	LMI	PTR	WMT
350250	61450+65250+67550+61550	NN	LMI	PTR	WMT
350251	61451+65251+67551+61551	NN	LMI	PTR	WMT
350252	61452+65252+67552+61552	NN	LNW	PTR	WMT
350253	61453+65253+67553+61553	NN	LNW	PTR	WMT
350254	61454+65254+67554+61554	NN	LNW	PTR	WMT
350255	61455+65255+67555+61555	NN	LMI	PTR	WMT
350256	61456+65256+67556+61556	NN	LMI	PTR	WMT
350257	61457+65257+67557+61557	NN	LNW	PTR	WMT
350258	61458+65258+67558+61558	NN	LNW	PTR	WMT
350259	61459+65259+67559+61559	NN	LNW	PTR	WMT
350260	61460+65260+67560+61560	NN	LMI	PTR	WMT
350261	61461+65261+67561+61561	NN	LMI	PTR	WMT
350262	61462+65262+67562+61562	NN	LNW	PTR	WMT
350263	61463+65263+67563+61563	NN	LNW	PTR	WMT
350264§	61464+65264+67564+61564	NN	LMI	PTR	WMT
350265	61465+65265+67565+61565	NN	LMI	PTR	WMT
350266	61466+65266+67566+61566	NN	LMI	PTR	WMT
350267	61467+65267+67567+61567	NN	LNW	PTR	WMT

■ In October 2018, Porterbrook unveiled a project to convert the Class 350/2 sets to battery/electric units after they are returned from WMT use, this would allow greater flexibility for the re-lease of the sets.

Class 350/3
Desiro

Vehicle Length: 66ft 9in (20.4m)
Height: 12ft 1½in (3.78m)
Width: 9ft 2in (2.7m)

Horsepower: 1,341hp (1,000kW)
Seats (total/car): 24F-209S, 60S/24F-32S/57S/60S
110mph max speed

Number	Formation	Depot	Livery	Owner	Operator	Name
	DMSO(A)+TCO+PTSO+DMSO(B)					
350368	60141+60511+60651+60151	NN	LNW	ANG	WMT	
350369	60142+60512+60652+60152	NN	LNW	ANG	WMT	
350370	60143+60513+60653+60153	NN	LNW	ANG	WMT	
350371	60144+60514+60654+60154	NN	LNW	ANG	WMT	
350372	60145+60515+60655+60155	NN	LNW	ANG	WMT	
350373	60146+60516+60656+60156	NN	LNW	ANG	WMT	
350374	60147+60517+60657+60157	NN	LNW	ANG	WMT	
350375	60148+60518+60658+60158	NN	LNW	ANG	WMT	
350376	60149+60519+60659+60159	NN	LNW	ANG	WMT	
350377	60150+60520+60660+60160	NN	LNW	ANG	WMT	*Graham Taylor OBE*

Right: *In 2014 a fleet of 10 Class 350/3 sets were added to stock, owned by Angel Trains. Based at Northampton, these sets now display the latest full London North Western colours. Set No. 350369 is illustrated passing South Kenton.* **CJM**

■ The Class 350/4 s currently working on Trans Pennine are scheduled to transfer to West Midlands.

Colas Rail Freight

Address: ✉ Dacre House, 19 Dacre Street, London, SW1H 0DJ
📧 enquiries@colasrail.co.uk, ☎ 0207 593 5353, ⓘ www.colasrail.co.uk

Managing Director: Debbie Francis

Depots: Washwood Heath (AW), Rugby (RU), Eastleigh Works (ZG), Nottingham Eastcroft (NM), Barrow Hill (BH)

Class 37

Vehicle Length: 61ft 6in (18.74m)
Height: 13ft 0¼in (3.96m)
Width: 8ft 11⅝in (2.73m)
Engine: English Electric 12CSVT
Horsepower: 1,750hp (1,304kW)
Electrical Equipment: English Electric

Number	Depot	Pool	Livery	Owner	Operator	Name/Notes
37025	RU	COTS	BLL	STS	COL	*Inverness TMD*
37057 (D6757)	RU	COTS	GRN	PRI	COL	
37099 (37324)	RU	COTS	COL	COL	COL	*Merl Evans 1947 - 2016*
37116	RU	COTS	COL	COL	COL	
37175	RU	COTS	COL	COL	COL	
37188	-	-	-	-	-	Sold to Europhoenix 01/19
37207(S)	-	-	-	-	-	Sold to Europhoenix 01/19
37219	RU	COTS	COL	COL	COL	
37254	RU	COTS	COL	COL	COL	*Cardiff Canton*
37418 (37271)	BH	COTS	BLL	PRI	COL	
37421 (37267)	RU	COTS	BLL	COL	COL	
37521 (37117)	RU	COTS	COL	COL	COL	
37610 (37687)	BH	COTS	BLL	HNR	COL	

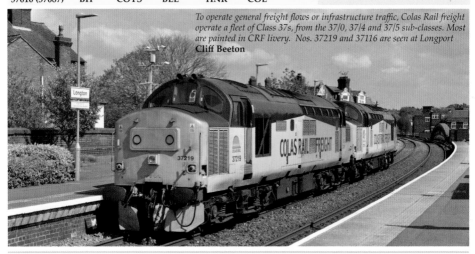

To operate general freight flows or infrastructure traffic, Colas Rail freight operate a fleet of Class 37s, from the 37/0, 37/4 and 37/5 sub-classes. Most are painted in CRF livery. Nos. 37219 and 37116 are seen at Longport **Cliff Beeton**

Class 56

Vehicle Length: 63ft 6in (19.35m)
Height: 13ft 0in (3.96m)
Width: 9ft 2in (2.79m)
Engine: Ruston Paxman 16RK3CT
Horsepower: 3,250hp (2,420kW)
Electrical Equipment: Brush

Number	Depot	Pool	Livery	Owner	Operator	Name
56049	NM	COFS	COL	COL	COL	*Robin of Templecombe 1938-2013*
56051(S)	NM	COLS	?	COL	-	
56078	NM	COFS	COL	COL	COL	
56087	NM	COFS	COL	BEA	COL	
56090(S)	NM	COFS	COL	BEA	-	
56094	NM	COFS	COL	COL	COL	
56096	NM	COFS	COL	BEA	COL	
56105	NM	COFS	COL	BEA	COL	
56113	NM	COFS	COL	BEA	COL	
56302 (56124)	NM	COFS	COL	COL	COL	*Peco The Railway Modeller 2016 70 Years*

Colas Rail Freight

Right: *To power heavier trains, Colas Rail Freight has a fleet of Class 56s, with at the start of 2018, eight being available if needed. All are painted in the yellow and orange CRF house colours. No. 56302 (modified from No. 56124) is seen with its No. 1 end on the right.* **Antony Christie**

Class 66/8

Vehicle Length: 70ft 0½in (21.34m)	Engine: EMD 12N-710G3B-EC
Height: 12ft 10in (3.91m)	Horsepower: 3,300hp (2,462kW)
Width: 8ft 8¼in (2.65m)	Electrical Equipment: EMD

Number		Depot	Pool	Livery	Owner	Operator	Name
66846	(66573)	RU	COLO	COL	BEA	COL	
66847	(66574)	RU	COLO	COL	BEA	COL	
66848	(66575)	RU	COLO	COL	BEA	COL	
66849	(66576)	RU	COLO	COL	BEA	COL	*Wylam Dilly*
66850	(66577)	RU	COLO	COL	BEA	COL	*David Maidment OBE*
							www.railwaychildren.org.uk

Right: *A small fleet of five Class 66s are owned and operated by Colas Rail freight, these are usually deployed on heavy Network Rail engineering trains, especially those operated from Eastleigh, Westbury and Hoo Junction. The locos, officially allocated to Rugby, previously operated for Freightliner. All carry Colas lime and orange livery. No. 66850 is shown passing Totnes with a Network Rail ballast train.* **Nathan Williamson**

Class 67

Vehicle Length: 64ft 7in (19.68m)	Engine: EMD 12N-710G3B-EC
Height: 12ft 9in (3.88m)	Horsepower: 2,980hp (2,223kW)
Width: 8ft 9in (2.66m)	Electrical Equipment: EMD

Number	Depot	Pool	Livery	Owner	Operator	Name
67023	RU	COTS	COL	BEA	COL	*Stella*
67027	RU	COTS	COL	BEA	COL	*Charlotte*

Right: *A pair of former DB Class 67s were purchased by Colas Rail Freight in 2017 to fulfill a contract with Network Rail to provide high speed power for test trains. The two locos were refurbished by Toton depot and repainted in Colas Rail Freight livery. The pair can usually be found operating 'top and tail' with Network Rail yellow-liveried test trains, or standing in for the New Measurement Train (NMT) if the HST set is stood down for maintenance. The two locos with a test formation is seen passing Powderham, Devon.* **CJM**

Freight Operating Companies - Colas Rail Freight

Colas Rail Freight

Class 70 - PH37ACmi

Vehicle Length: 71ft 2½in (21.71m)
Height: 12ft 10in (3.91m)
Width: 8ft 8in (2.64m)

Engine: GE V16-cylinder PowerHaul 616
Horsepower: 3,700hp (2,750kW)
Electrical Equipment: General Electric

Number	Depot	Pool	Livery	Owner	Operator
70801 (70099)	RU	COLO	COL	LOM	COL
70802	RU	COLO	COL	LOM	COL
70803	RU	COLO	COL	LOM	COL
70804	RU	COLO	COL	LOM	COL
70805	RU	COLO	COL	LOM	COL
70806	RU	COLO	COL	LOM	COL
70807	RU	COLO	COL	LOM	COL
70808	RU	COLO	COL	LOM	COL
70809	RU	COLO	COL	LOM	COL
70810	RU	COLO	COL	LOM	COL
70811	RU	COLO	COL	BEA	COL
70812	RU	COLO	COL	BEA	COL
70813	RU	COLO	COL	BEA	COL
70814	RU	COLO	COL	BEA	COL
70815	RU	COLO	COL	BEA	COL
70816	RU	COLO	COL	BEA	COL
70817	RU	COLO	COL	BEA	COL

■ 70099 was built as a demonstrator at the GE plant in Turkey, tested in mainland Europe then transferred to the UK, and sold to Colas Rail Freight.

Left: *The most modern fleet operated by Colas Rail Freight are 17 General Electric Class 70s, introduced new between 2013-2017. The locos operate both freight and infrastructure flows and can be found throughout the country. The most popular locations to find class members is at Westbury and Eastleigh. In immaculate condition following an exam at Tavistock Junction, No. 70816 is recorded at Newton Abbot.* **Antony Christie**

Hauled Stock (NPCCS)

Barrier Vans

Mk1
Vehicle Length: 64ft 6in (19.65m)
Height: 12ft 9½in (3.89m)
Width: 9ft 3in (2.81m)

AW51

Number	Depot	Livery	Owner
6376 (ADB975973, 1021)	Barry	BLU	PTR
6377 (ADB975975, 1042)	Barry	BLU	PTR
6378 (ADB975971, 1054)	Barry	BLU	PTR

6379 (ADB975972, 1039)	Barry	BLU	PTR
6392 (81588/92183)	ZA	COL	COL
6397 (81600/92190)	ZA	COL	COL

Motorail Vans (Operated as brake force runners on Network Rail test trains)

96602 (96150)	RU	COL	NR	96605 (96157)	RU	COL	NR	96608 (96216)	RU	COL	NR
96603 (96155)	RU	COL	NR	96606 (96213)	RU	COL	NR	96609 (96217)	RU	COL	NR
96604 (96156)	RU	COL	NR	96607 (96215)	RU	COL	NR				

Left: *Several of the former Great Western Motorail side loading bogie vehicles are now is use on Network Rail test trains to act as brake force runners. The vehicles are on the books of Colas Rail freight. Painted in NR yellow livery with joint Network Rail and Colas Rail freight branding, No. 96609 is seen formed in a test train at Tonbridge.* **Antony Christie**

DB-Cargo – (EWS)

Address (UK): ✉ Lakeside Business Park, Caroline Way, Doncaster, DN4 5PN
🖳 info@uk.dbcargo.com, ☎ 0870 140 5000
ⓘ https://uk.dbcargo.com

Chief Executive: Hans-Georg Werner
Depots: Crewe Electric (CE), Toton (TO)

Class 58

Vehicle Length: 62ft 9½in (19.13m)		Engine: Ruston Paxman 12RK3ACT	
Height: 12ft 10in (3.91m)		Horsepower: 3,300hp (2,460kW)	
Width: 9ft 1in (2.72m)		Electrical Equipment: Brush	

Number	Hire No.	Depot	Pool	Livery	Owner	Location	Operator	Name
58001	-		WNTS	ETF	DBC	France	ETF	
58004§	-		WNTS	TSO	DBC	France	TSO	
58005§	-		WNTS	ETF	DBC	France	ETF	
58006§	-		WNTS	ETF	DBC	France	ETF	
58007§	-		WNTS	TSO	DBC	France	TSO	
58009§	-		WNTS	TSO	DBC	France	TSO	
58010§	-		WNTS	FER	DBC	France	TSO	
58011§	-		WNTS	TSO	DBC	France	TSO	
58013§	-		WNTS	ETF	DBC	France	ETF	
58015	L54	CON/SS	-	CON	DBC/T	Spain	TRN	
58018	-		WNTS	TSO	DBC	France	TSO	
58020	L43	CON/SS	-	CON	DBC/T	Spain	TRN	
58021§	-		WNTS	TSO	DBC	France	TSO	
58024	L42	CON/SS	-	CON	DBC/T	Spain	TRN	
58025	L41	CON/SS	-	CON	DBC	Spain	CON	
58026§	-		WNTS	TSO	DBC	France	TSO	
58027	L52	CON/SS	-	CON	DBC	Spain	CON	
58029	L44	CON/SS	-	CON	DBC/T	Spain	TRN	
58030	L46	CON/SS	-	CON	DBC/T	Spain	TRN	
58031	L45	CON/SS	-	CON	DBC/T	Spain	TRN	Cabellero Ferroviaro
58032§	-		WNTS	ETF	DBC	France	ETF	
58033§	-		WNTS	TSO	DBC	France	TSO	
58034§	-		WNTS	TSO	DBC	France	TSO	
58035§	-		WNTS	TSO	DBC	France	TSO	
58036§	-		WNTS	ETF	DBC	France	ETF	
58038§	58-038		WNTS	ETF	DBC	France	ETF	
58039§	58-039		WNTS	ETF	DBC	France	ETF	
58040§	-		WNTS	TSO	DBC	France	TSO	
58041	L36	CON/SS	-	CON	DBC/T	Spain	TRN	
58042§	-		WNTS	TSO	DBC	France	TSO	
58043	L37	CON/SS	-	CON	DBC/T	Spain	TRN	
58044±	58-044		WZFF	ETF	DBC	France	ETF	
58046§	-		WNTS	TSO	DBC	France	TSO	
58047	L51	CON/SS	-	CON	DBC/T	Spain	TRN	
58049§	-		WNTS	TSO	DBC	France	ETF	
58050	L53	CON/SS	-	CON	DBC	Spain	CON	

§ Stored at Alizay (Rouen), ± Stored at Metz

Right: *The 50 strong fleet of BREL Class 58s were born into an uncertain world and soon became redundant. Under privatisation and ownership by EWS, many were exported to Mainland Europe for freight and infrastructure work. Today, a large number are stored in France and Spain and unlikely to work again. The SNCF yard at Alizay in Rouen houses a considerable number. No. 58039 is seen in the yard with several others.* **Howard Lewsey**

DB-Cargo

Class 59/2

Vehicle Length: 70ft 0½in (21.34m)
Height: 12ft 10in (3.91m)
Width: 8ft 8¼in (2.65m)

Engine: EMD 16-645 E3C
Horsepower: 3,000hp (2,462kW)
Electrical Equipment: EMD

Number	Depot	Pool	Livery	Owner	Operator	Name
59201	MD	WDAM	DBS	DBC	DBC	
59202	MD	WDAM	DBS	DBC	DBC	Alan Meddows Taylor MD, Mendip Rail Limited
59203	MD	WDAM	DBS	DBC	DBC	
59204	MD	WDAM	DBS	DBC	DBC	
59205	MD	WDAM	DBS	DBC	DBC	
59206	MD	WDAM	DBS	DBC	DBC	John F. Yeoman Rail Pioneer

Above: DB-Cargo currently has a fleet of six Class 59/2s on its books, allocated to Merehead and maintained by Mendip Rail, being used as part of the core Class 59 fleet on Mendip aggregate traffic. The six locos were originally purchased by National Power and used on power station traffic in Yorkshire, later being sold to EWS. No. 59206 is seen at Ealing Broadway. **Antony Christie**

Class 60

Vehicle Length: 70ft 0½in (21.34m)
Height: 12ft 10⅜in (3.92m)
Width: 8ft 8in (2.64m)

Engine: Mirrlees MB275T
Horsepower: 3,100hp (2,240kW)
Electrical Equipment: Brush

Number	Depot	Pool	Livery	Owner	Operator	Name
60001‡	TO	WCAT	DBS	DBC	DBC	
60003	TO	WNWX	EWS	DBC	-	Freight Transport Association
60005	TO	WNTS	EWS	DBC	-	
60007‡	TO	WCBT	DBS	DBC	-	The Spirit of Tom Kendell
60009(S)	TO	WNTS	EWS	DBC	-	
60010‡	TO	WCBT	DBS	DBC	DBC	
60011	TO	WQAA	DBS	DBC	DBC	
60012(S)	TO	WNWX	EWS	DBC	-	
60015‡	TO	WCBT	DBS	DBC	DBC	
60017‡	TO	WCBT	DBS	DBC	DBC	
60019‡	TO	WCAT	DBS	DBC	DBC	Port of Grimsby & Immingham
60020‡	TO	WCBT	DBS	DBC	DBC	The Willows
60022	TO	WNTS	EWS	DBC	-	
60024‡	TO	WCAT	DBS	DBC	DBC	Clitheroe Castle
60025	TO	WNTS	EWS	DBC	-	

60027	TO	WNTS	EWS	DBC	-	
60030	TO	WNTS	EWS	DBC	-	
60032	TO	WNWX	EWS	DBC	-	
60034(S)	TO	WNTS	RFE	DBC	-	Carnedd Llewelyn
60035	TO	WCAT	EWS	DBC	DBC	
60036(S)	TO	WNTS	EWS	DBC	-	GEFCO
60037	TO	WNWX	EWS	DBC	-	
60039‡	TO	WCAT	DBS	DBC	DBC	Dove Holes
60040‡	TO	WCAT	DBS	DBC	DBC	The Territorial Army Centenary
60043(S)	TO	WNWX	EWS	DBC	-	
60044‡	TO	WCAT	DBS	DBC	-	Dowlow
60045(S)	TO	WQBA	EWS	DBC	-	The Permanent Way Institution
60049	TO	WQBA	EWS	DBC	DBC	
60051	TO	WNTS	EWS	DBC	-	
60052	TO	WNTS	EWS	DBC	-	Glofa Twr - The last deep mine in Wales - Tower Colliery
60053(S)	TO	WNTS	EWS	DBC	-	
60054‡	TO	WCBT	DBS	DBC	DBC	
60057(S)	TO	WNWX	RFE	DBC	-	Adam Smith
60059‡	TO	WCBT	DBS	DBC	DBC	Swinden Dalesman
60060(S)	TO	WNWX	RFE	DBC	-	
60062‡	TO	WCAT	DBS	DBC	DBC	Stainless Pioneer
60063‡	TO	WCAT	DBS	DBC	DBC	
60064■	TO	WNWX	RFE	DBC	-	Back Tor
60065	TO	WQAA	EWS	DBC	DBC	Spirit of Jaguar
60066‡	TO	WCAT	ADV	DBC	DRC	
60067(S)	TO	WNWX	RFE	DBC	-	
60069(S)	TO	WNWX	EWS	DBC	-	Slioch
60071(S)	TO	WQBA	DBS	DBC	-	Ribblehead Viaduct
60072(S)	TO	WNWX	RFE	DBC	-	Cairn Toul
60073(S)	TO	WNTS	RFE	DBC	-	Cairn Gorm
60074‡	TO	WCAT	DBS	DBC	DBC	
60077(S)	TO	WNWX	RFE	DBC	-	
60079‡	TO	WQAA	DBS	DBC	DBC	
60083(S)	TO	WNTS	EWS	DBC	-	
60084(S)	TO	WNTS	RFE	DBC	-	Cross Fell
60086(S)	TO	WNWX	RFE	DBC	-	
60088(S)	TO	WNWX	MLG	DBC	-	
60090(S)	TO	WNTS	RFE	DBC	-	Quinag
60091‡	TO	WCBT	DBS	DBC	DBC	Barry Needham
60092‡	TO	WCBT	DBS	DBC	DBC	
60093(S)	TO	WNTS	EWS	DBC	-	
60094(S)	CD	WNTS	EWS	DBC	-	Rugby Flyer
60097(S)	TO	WNTS	EWS	DBC	-	
60099(S)	TO	WQBA	TAT	DBC	-	
60100‡	TO	WCAT	DBS	DBC	DBC	Midland Railway - Butterley
60500(S)*	TO	WNTS	EWS	DBC	-	

* Previously numbered 60016. ‡ Refurbished 'Super 60'. ADV = Drax biomass livery.
■ Offered for sale on December 2018, plus 60028/029/046/055/070/098

Right: *Once numbering a hundred examples, the fleet of DB Class 60s is now down to a handful, kept operational to power DBs heaviest freight trains. All refurbished and mostly sporting DB red livery, the locos are based at Toton but can be found frequently in Humberside and Wales. No. 60059 is shown carrying the now obsolete DB Schenker branding.* **Antony Christie**

DB-Cargo

Class 66

Vehicle Length: 70ft 0½in (21.34m)
Height: 12ft 10in (3.91m)
Width: 8ft 8¼in (2.65m)
Engine: EMD 12N-710G3B-EC
Horsepower: 3,300hp (2,462kW)
Electrical Equipment: EMD

Number	Depot	Pool	Livery	Owner	Operator
66001‡	TO	WBAE	DBS	DBC	DBC
66002‡	TO	WBAT	EWS	DBC	DBC
66003	TO	WBAE	EWS	DBC	DBC
66004	TO	WBAE	EWS	DBC	DBC
66005	TO	WBAT	EWS	DBC	DBC
66006	TO	WBAT	EWS	DBC	DBC
66007	TO	WBAR	EWS	DBC	DBC
66009	TO	WBAE	DBC	DBC	DBC
66010 ●	AZ	WBEN	EWS	DBC	DBC
66011	TO	WBAE	EWS	DBC	DBC
66012	TO	WBAT	EWS	DBC	DBC
66013 ●	TO	WBAE	EWS	DBC	DBC
66014	TO	WBAR	EWS	DBC	DBC
66015	TO	WBAR	EWS	DBC	DBC
66017	TO	WBAR	DBC	DBC	DBC
66018	TO	WBAR	DBC	DBC	DBC
66019	TO	WBAR	DBC	DBC	DBC
66020	TO	WBAE	DBC	DBC	DBC
66021	TO	WBAR	DBC	DBC	DBC
66022 ●	AZ	WBEN	EWS	DBC	DBC
66023	TO	WBAT	EWS	DBC	DBC
66024	TO	WBAE	EWS	DBC	DBC
66025	TO	WBAR	EWS	DBC	DBC
66026 ●	TO	WBEN	EWS	DBC	ECR
66027	TO	WBAT	DBC	DBC	DBC
66028 ●	AZ	WBEN	EWS	DBC	ECR
66029 ●	TO	WGEA	EWS	DBC	DBC
66030	TO	WBAR	EWS	DBC	DBC
66031 ●	TO	WBAT	EWS	DBC	DBC
66032 ●	AZ	WBES	EWS	DBC	ECR
66033 ●	AZ	WBEN	EWS	DBC	DBC
66034	TO	WBAE	DBC	DBC	DBC
66035	TO	WBAE	DBC	DBC	DBC
66036 ●	AZ	WBEN	EWS	DBC	ECR
66037	TO	WBRT	EWS	DBC	DBC
66038 ●	AZ	WBEN	EWS	DBC	ECR
66039	TO	WQAB	EWS	DBC	DBC
66040	TO	WBAR	EWS	DBC	DBC
66041	TO	WBAE	DBC	DBC	DBC
66042 ●	AZ	WFMS	EWS	DBC	ECR
66043	TO	WQAB	EWS	DBC	DBC
66044	TO	WBAE	DBC	DBC	DBC
66045 ●	AZ	WBEN	EWS	DBC	ECR
66047	TO	WBAT	EWS	DBC	DBC
66049 ●	AZ	WBEN	EWS	DBC	ECR
66050	TO	WBAE	EWS	DBC	DBC
66051	TO	WBAR	EWS	DBC	DBC
66052 ●	AZ	WFMS	EWS	DBC	ECR
66053	TO	WBAE	EWS	DBC	DBC
66054	TO	WBAR	EWS	DBC	DBC
66055	TO	WBAR	DBC	DBC	DBC
66056	TO	WBLE	EWS	DBC	DBC
66057	TO	WBAE	EWS	DBC	DBC
66059	TO	WBLE	EWS	DBC	DBC
66060 ‡	TO	WBAE	EWS	DBC	DBC
66061	TO	WBAE	EWS	DBC	DBC
66062 ●	AZ	WBEN	EWS	DBC	DBC
66063	TO	WBAE	EWS	DBC	DBC
66064 ●	AZ	WBEN	EWS	DBC	DBC
66065	TO	WBAR	DBC	DBC	DBC
66066	TO	WBAR	DBC	DBC	DBC
66067	TO	WBRT	EWS	DBC	DBC
66068	TO	WBAR	EWS	DBC	DBC
66069	TO	WBAR	EWS	DBC	DBC
66070	TO	WBAT	EWS	DBC	DBC
66071 ●	AZ	WBEN	EWS	DBC	DBC
66072 ●	AZ	WBEN	EWS	DBC	DBC
66073 ●	AZ	WBEN	EWS	DBC	ECR
66074	TO	WBAE	DBC	DBC	DBC
66075	TO	WBAE	EWS	DBC	DBC
66076	TO	WBAT	EWS	DBC	DBC
66077	TO	WBAR	EWS	DBC	DBC
66078	TO	WBAE	EWS	DBC	DBC
66079	TO	WBAR	EWS	DBC	DBC
66080	TO	WBAE	EWS	DBC	DBC
66082	TO	WBAE	DBC	DBC	DBC
66083	TO	WBAR	EWS	DBC	DBC
66084	TO	WBAR	EWS	DBC	DBC
66085	TO	WBAR	DBC	DBC	DBC
66086	TO	WBAT	EWS	DBC	DBC
66087	TO	WBAT	EWS	DBC	DBC
66088	TO	WBAE	EWS	DBC	DBC
66089	TO	WBAR	EWS	DBC	DBC
66090	TO	WBAE	EWS	DBC	DBC
66091	TO	WBAR	EWS	DBC	DBC
66092	TO	WBAE	EWS	DBC	DBC
66093	TO	WBAE	EWS	DBC	DBC
66094	TO	WBAE	DBC	DBC	DBC
66095	TO	WBAE	EWS	DBC	DBC
66096	TO	WBAR	EWS	DBC	DBC
66097	TO	WBAE	DBS	DBC	DBC
66098	TO	WQAA	EWS	DBC	DBC
66099	TO	WBBE	EWS	DBC	DBC
66100	TO	WBBE	DBC	DBC	DBC
66101	TO	WBBE	DBS	DBC	DBC
66102	TO	WBBE	EWS	DBC	DBC
66103	TO	WBBE	EWS	DBC	DBC
66104	TO	WBRT	DBC	DBC	DBC
66105	TO	WBAR	DBC	DBC	DBC
66106	TO	WBBE	EWS	DBC	DBC
66107	TO	WBAR	DBC	DBC	DBC
66108	TO	WBAE	EWS	DBC	DBC
66109	TO	WBAR	EWS	DBC	DBC
66110	TO	WBBE	EWS	DBC	DBC
66111	TO	WBBT	EWS	DBC	DBC
66112	TO	WBBE	EWS	DBC	DBC
66113	TO	WBBE	EWS	DBC	DBC
66114	TO	WBBE	DBS	DBC	DBC
66115	TO	WBAT	DBC	DBC	DBC
66116	TO	WBAE	EWS	DBC	DBC
66117	TO	WBAT	DBC	DBC	DBC
66118	TO	WQAA	DBC	DBC	DBC
66119	TO	WBAE	EWS	DBC	DBC
66120	TO	WBAE	EWS	DBC	DBC
66121	TO	WBAE	EWS	DBC	DBC
66122	TO	WBAE	EWS	DBC	DBC
66123 ●	AZ	WGEA	EWS	DBC	DBC
66124	TO	WBAR	DBC	DBC	DBC
66125	TO	WBAE	DBC	DBC	DBC
66126	TO	WBAE	EWS	DBC	DBC
66127	TO	WBAT	EWS	DBC	DBC
66128	TO	WBAE	DBC	DBC	DBC
66129	TO	WBAR	EWS	DBC	DBC

66130	TO	WBAR	DBC	DBC	DBC		66180 P	PN	WBEP	EWS	DBC	DBC
66131	TO	WBAE	DBC	DBC	DBC		66181	TO	WBAR	EWS	DBC	DBC
66133	TO	WBAE	EWS	DBC	DBC		66182	TO	WBAE	EWS	DBC	DBC
66134	TO	WBAE	DBC	DBC	DBC		66183	TO	WBAE	EWS	DBC	DBC
66135	TO	WBAE	DBC	DBC	DBC		66185	TO	WBRT	DBS	DBC	DBC
66136	TO	WBAE	DBC	DBC	DBC		66186	TO	WBAT	EWS	DBC	DBC
66137	TO	WBAE	DBC	DBC	DBC		66187	TO	WBAE	EWS	DBC	DBC
66138	TO	WQAB	EWS	DBC	DBC		66188	TO	WBAR	EWS	DBC	DBC
66139	TO	WBAE	EWS	DBC	DBC		66189 P	PN	WBEP	EWS	DBC	DBC
66140	TO	WBAE	EWS	DBC	DBC		66190 ●	AZ	WBEN	EWS	DBC	ECR
66142	TO	WBAR	EWS	DBC	DBC		66191 ●	AZ	WBEN	EWS	DBC	DBC
66143	TO	WBAE	EWS	DBC	DBC		66192	TO	WBAR	DBC	DBC	DBC
66144	TO	WBAR	EWS	DBC	DBC		66193 ●	AZ	WBEN	EWS	DBC	ECR
66145	TO	WQAB	EWS	DBC	DBC		66194	TO	WBAR	EWS	DBC	DBC
66146 P	PN	WBEP	EWS	DBC	DBC		66195 ●	TO	WBEN	EWS	DBC	ECR
66147	TO	WBAT	EWS	DBC	DBC		66196 P	PN	WBEP	EWS	DBC	DBC
66148	TO	WBAE	EWS	DBC	DBC		66197	TO	WBAE	EWS	DBC	DBC
66149	TO	WBAE	DBC	DBC	DBC		66198	TO	WBAR	EWS	DBC	DBC
66150	TO	WBAE	DBC	DBC	DBC		66199	TO	WBAE	EWS	DBC	DBC
66151	TO	WBAE	EWS	DBC	DBC		66200	TO	WBAE	EWS	DBC	DBC
66152	TO	WBRT	DBS	DBC	DBC		66201 ●	AZ	WBEN	EWS	DBC	ECR
66153 P	PN	WBEP	EWS	DBC	DBC		66202 ●	AZ	WBEN	EWS	DBC	ECR
66154	TO	WBAE	EWS	DBC	DBC		66203 ●	AZ	WBEN	EWS	DBC	ECR
66155	TO	WBAE	EWS	DBC	DBC		66204 ●	AZ	WBEN	EWS	DBC	ECR
66156	TO	WBAE	EWS	DBC	DBC		66205 ●	AZ	WBEN	EWS	DBC	ECR
66157 P	PN	WBEP	EWS	DBC	DBC		66206	TO	WBAR	DBC	DBC	DBC
66158	TO	WBAE	EWS	DBC	DBC		66207	TO	WBAE	EWS	DBC	DBC
66159 P	PN	WBEP	EWS	DBC	DBC		66208 ●	AZ	WBEN	EWS	DBC	ECR
66160	TO	WBAE	EWS	DBC	DBC		66209 ●	AZ	WBEN	EWS	DBC	ECR
66161	TO	WBAE	EWS	DBC	DBC		66210 ●	AZ	WBEN	EWS	DBC	ECR
66162	TO	WBAR	EWS	DBC	DBC		66211 ●	TO	WBEN	EWS	DBC	ECR
66163 P	PN	WBEP	DBS	DBC	DBC		66212 ●	AZ	WBEN	EWS	DBC	ECR
66164	TO	WBAE	EWS	DBC	DBC		66213 ●	AZ	WBEN	EWS	DBC	ECR
66165	TO	WBAR	DBC	DBC	DBC		66214 ●	AZ	WBEN	EWS	DBC	ECR
66166 P	PN	WBEP	EWS	DBC	DBC		66215 ●	AZ	WBEN	EWS	DBC	ECR
66167	TO	WBAE	EWS	DBC	DBC		66216 ●	AZ	WBEN	EWS	DBC	ECR
66168	TO	WBAR	EWS	DBC	DBC		66217 ●	AZ	WBEN	EWS	DBC	ECR
66169	TO	WBAR	EWS	DBC	DBC		66218 ●	AZ	WGEA	EWS	DBC	ECR
66170	TO	WBAE	EWS	DBC	DBC		66219 ●	AZ	WGEA	EWS	DBC	ECR
66171	TO	WBAR	EWS	DBC	DBC		66220 P	PN	WBEP	DBC	DBC	DBC
66172	TO	WBAT	EWS	DBC	DBC		66221	TO	WBAT	EWS	DBC	DBC
66173 P	PN	WBEP	EWS	DBC	DBC		66222 ●	AZ	WBEN	EWS	DBC	ECR
66174	TO	WBAE	EWS	DBC	DBC		66223 ●	AZ	WBEN	EWS	DBC	DBC
66175	TO	WBAE	DBC	DBC	DBC		66224 ●	AZ	WBEN	EWS	DBC	ECR
66176	TO	WBRT	EWS	DBC	DBC		66225 ●	AZ	WBEN	EWS	DBC	ECR
66177	TO	WBAT	EWS	DBC	DBC		66226 ●	AZ	WBEN	EWS	DBC	ECR
66178 P	PN	WBEP	EWS	DBC	DBC		66227 P	PN	WBEP	EWS	DBC	DBC
66179 ●	TO	WBAK	EWS	DBC	ECR		66228 ●	AZ	WBEN	EWS	DBC	ECR

Right: *DBs most prolific class of diesel in the UK is the Class 66, however from the original delivered fleet of 250 locos, the UK operational fleet is now down to less than 160, following a large number being modified for use in Europe and a batch sold to GBRf. Painted in DB red, No. 66115 rests between duties at Westbury.* **CJM**

DB-Cargo

66229 ●	AZ	WBEN	EWS	DBC	ECR	66241 ●	AZ	WBEN	EWS	DBC ECR
66230	TO	WQAB	DBC	DBC	DBC	66242 ●	AZ	WGEA	EWS	DBC ECR
66231 ●	AZ	WBEN	EWS	DBC	ECR	66243 ●	TO	WBEN	EWS	DBC ECR
66232 ●	AZ	WBEN	EWS	DBC	ECR	66244 ●	AZ	WBEN	EWS	DBC ECR
66233 ●	AZ	WBEN	EWS	DBC	ECR	66245 ●	AZ	WBEN	EWS	DBC DBC
66234 ●	AZ	WBEN	EWS	DBC	ECR	66246 ●	AZ	WBEN	EWS	DBC ECR
66235 ●	AZ	WBEN	EWS	DBC	ECR	66247 ●	AZ	WBEN	EWS	DBC ECR
66236 ●	AZ	WBEN	EWS	DBC	ECR	66248 P	PN	WBEP	DBS	DBC DBC
66237 P	PN	WBEP	EWS	DBC	DBC	66249 ●	AZ	WBES	EWS	DBC DBC
66239 ●	AZ	WBEN	EWS	DBC	ECR					
66240 ●	AZ	WBEN	EWS	DBC	ECR	‡ Only fitted with standard drawgear				

● Modified to operate with Euro Cargo Rail in mainland Europe.
P Locomotives operated by DB-Schenker in Poland. Only locos from the series 66146-250 can be modified for this contract.

Names applied
66002	*Lafarge Quorn*	66077	*Benjamin Gimbert GC*
66035	*Resourceful*	66079	*James Nightall GC*
66050	*EWS Energy*	66100	*Armistice 100 1918 - 2018*
66055	*Alain Thauvette*	66152	*Derek Holmes Railway Operator*
66066	*Geoff Spencer*	66172	*Paul Melleney*
		66185	*DP World London Gateway*

Above: Although a number of Class 66s from the UK operating pool have been overhauled and repainted into DB red, a significant number still retain their original maroon and gold colours, mostly now devoid of EWS branding and carrying a DB logo on the cab side. No. 66134 shows this livery variation at Acton. This loco now sports DB-C red livery. **CJM**

Class 67

Vehicle Length: 64ft 7in (19.68m)	Engine: EMD 12N-710G3B-EC
Height: 12ft 9in (3.88m)	Horsepower: 2,980hp (2,223kW)
Width: 8ft 9in (2.66m)	Electrical Equipment: EMD

Number	Depot	Pool	Livery	Owner	Operator	Name/Notes
67001	CE	WAWC	ATW	DBC	DBC/ATW	
67002	CE	WAAC	ATW	DBC	DBC/ATW	
67003	CE	WAAC	ATW	DBC	DBC/ATW	
67004	CE	WABC	DBC	DBC	DBC	
67005	CE	WAAC	ROY	DBC	DBC	*Queen's Messenger*
67006	CE	WAAC	ROY	DBC	DBC	*Royal Sovereign*
67007	CE	WABC	EWS	DBC	-	
67008	CE	WAAC	EWS	DBC	DBC	
67009	CE	WABC	EWS	DBC	DBC	
67010	CE	WAAC	DBC	DBC	DBC	
67011	CE	WQBA	EWS	DBC	-	
67012	CE	WAWC	WSR	DBC	DBC	
67013	CE	WAAC	DBS	DBC	DBC	

67014	CE	WAAC	WSR	DBC	DBC	
67015	CE	WAAC	DBS	DBC	DBC	
67016	CE	WAWC	EWS	DBC	DBC	
67017	CE	WQBA	EWS	DBC	-	*Arrow*
67018	CE	WAAC	DBS	DBC	DBC	*Keith Heller*
67019	CE	WQAA	EWS	DBC	-	
67020	CE	WAWC	EWS	DBC	DBC	
67021	CE	WAAC	PUL	DBC	DBC	
67022	CE	WAAC	EWS	DBC	DBC	
67024	CE	WAAC	PUL	DBC	DBC	
67025	CE	WQAA	EWS	DBC	-	*Western Star*
67026	CE	WQBA	ROJ	DBC	-	*Diamond Jubilee*
67028	CE	WAAC	DBC	DBC	DBC	
67029	CE	WACC	EWE	DBC	DBC	*Royal Diamond*
67030	CE	WABC	EWS	DBC	-	

Above: *With DB holding the contract to provide locos for the Belmond GB Pullman, a pair of Class 67s, Nos. 67021 and 67024 have been repainted in Pullman livery to match the train. The impressive looking pair are seen with the Belmond British Pullman at Cockwood in summer 2018.* **CJM**

Right: *A number of operational Class 67s have been repainted into the latest DB red livery with a grey solebar, as demonstrated on No. 67004 stabled at Doncaster and performing 'Thunderbird' duties for LNER. This duty is likely to end once IET stock is introduced.* **CJM**

Class 90

Vehicle Length: 61ft 6in (18.74m)			Power Collection: 25kV ac overhead		
Height: 13ft 0¼in (3.96m)			Horsepower: 7,860hp (5,860kW)		
Width: 9ft 0in (2.74m)			Electrical Equipment: GEC		

Number		Depot	Pool	Livery	Owner	Operator	Name/Notes
90017		CE	WQBA	EWS	DBC	-	
90018		CE	WEAC	DBS	DBC	DBC	*The Pride of Bellshill*
90019		CE	WEDC	DBC	DBC	DBC	*Multimodal*
90020		CE	WEDC	EWS	DBC	DBC	*Collingwood*
90021	(90221)	CE	WEDC	FGS	DBC	DBC	
90022(S)	(90222)	CE	WQBA	RFE	DBC	-	*Freightconnection*
90023(S)	(90223)	CE	WQBA	EWS	DBC	-	
90024	(90224)	CE	WQAA	ADV±	DBC	DBC	
90025	(90225)	CE	WEAC	RFD	DBC	DBC	
90026		CE	WQAA	EWS	DBC	DBC	
90027(S)	(90227)	CE	WQBA	RFD	DBC	-	*Allerton T&RS Depot Quality Approved*

DB-Cargo

90028		CE	WEAC	DBC	DBC	DBC	Sir William McAlpine
90029		CE	WEDC	DBS	DBC	DBC	
90030(S)	(90130)	CE	WQBA	EWS	DBC	-	
90031(S)	(90131)	CE	WQBA	EWS	DBC	-	The Railway Children Partnership - Working for Street Children Worldwide
90032(S)	(90132)	CE	WQBA	EWS	DBC	-	
90033(S)	(90233)	CE	WQBA	RFI	DBC	DBC	
90034	(90134)	CE	WEDC	DRB	DBC	DBC	
90035	(90135)	CE	WEAC	EWS	DBC	DBC	
90036(S)	(90136)	CE	WQBA	DBS	DBC	-	Driver Jack Mills
90037	(90137)	CE	WEAC	EWS	DBC	DBC	Spirit of Dagenham
90038(S)	(90238)	CE	WQBA	RFI	DBC	-	
90039	(90239)	CE	WEDC	EWS	DBC	DBC	
90040	(90140)	CE	WEAC	DBS	DBC	DBC	
90050(S)	(90150)	BA	DHLT	FLG	FLT	-	(Stored at Crewe Basford Hall, for scrap)

± Carries W H Malcolm livery

Above: *Although 24 Class 90s are on the operational books of DB, only around 15 are maintained in a running state, this is dictated by a low level of work for electric locos. Displaying tatty maroon and gold livery and in need of some care and attention, No. 90037 is seen with an automotive train at Willesden Junction low level in summer 2018.* **Nathan Williamson**

Class 92

Vehicle Length: 70ft 1in (21.34m)	Power Collection: 25kV ac overhead / 750V dc third rail
Height: 13ft 0in (3.95m)	Horsepower: ac - 6,700hp (5,000kW) / dc - 5,360hp (4,000kW)
Width: 8ft 8in (2.66m)	Electrical Equipment: Brush

Number	Depot	Pool	Livery	Owner	Operator	Name
92001■	-	WGEE	DBS	HBS	Sold to Locotech, Russia● (91 53 0472 002-1)	Mircea Eliade
92002■	-	WGEE	DBS	DBC	Sold to Locotech, Russia● (91 53 0472 003-9)	
92003±	-	WGEE	RFE	DBC	Exported Bulgaria (91 53 0472 xxx-x)	Beethoven
92004(S)	CE	WQBA	RFE	DBC		Jane Austen
92005±		WGEE	DBS	DBC	Sold to Locotech, Russia● (91 53 0472 005-4)	Emil Cioran
92007(S)	CE	WQAA	RFE	DBC	-	Schubert
92008(S)	CE	WQAB	RFE	DBC	-	Jules Verne
92009§(S)	CE	WQBA	DBS	DBC	-	Marco Polo
92011	CE	WFBC	RFE	DBC	DBC	Handel
92012■	-	WGEE	DBS	HBS	Sold to Locotech, Russia● (91 53 0472 001-3)	Mihai Eminescu

92013(S)	CE	WQBA	RFE	DBC		*Puccini*
92015§	CE	WFBC	DBS	DBC	DBC	
92016§	CE	WQAB	DBS	DBC	DBC	
92017(S)	CE	WQAA	STO	DBC	-	*Bart the Engine*
92019	CE	WFBC	RFE	DBC	DBC	*Wagner*
92022±	-	WGEE	RFE	DBC	*Exported Bulgaria (91 52 1688 022-1)*	*Charles Dickens*
92024■	-	WGEE	DBS	DBC	*Sold to Locotech, Russia● (91 53 0472 004-7)*	*Marin Preda*
92025±	-	WGEE	RFE	HBS	*Exported Bulgaria (91 52 1688 025-1)*	*Oscar Wilde*
92026±	-	WGEE	RFE	DBC	*Exported Romania (91 53 0472 026-x)*	*Britten*
92027±	-	WGEE	RFE	HBS	*Exported Bulgaria (91 70 1688 027-1) OOU*	*George Eliot*
92029±	CE	WQAA	RFE	DBC	-	*Dante*
92030±	-	WGEE	RFE	DBC	*Exported Bulgaria (91 52 1688 030-1)*	
92031§(S)	CE	WQAA	DBS	DBC	-	
92034±	-	WGEE	RFE	HBS	*Exported Bulgaria (91 52 1688 034-3). OOU*	*Kipling*
92035(S)	CE	WQBA	RFE	DBC	-	*Mendelssohn*
92036§	CE	WFBC	RFE	DBC	DBC	*Bertolt Brecht*
92037	CE	WQAA	RFE	DBC	DBC	*Sullivan*
92039■	-	WGEE	DBS	DBC	*Sold to Locotech, Russia● (91 53 0472 006-2)*	*Eugen Ionescu*
92041	CE	WFBC	RFE	DBC	DBC	*Vaughan Williams*
92042§	CE	WFBC	DBS	DBC	DBC	

§ Fitted with equipment to allow operation over HS1, ± Exported to Bulgaria, ■ Exported to Romania
● Sold to Locotech, Russia, leased to Transagent Spediicija, Croatia

Left: *Only a handful of Class 92s remain operational with DB in the UK, the majority having been exported to Eastern Europe. Carrying DB Schenker red livery, No. 92015 is seen working the Tesco train in Southern Scotland.* **Ian Lothian**

Below: *Now exported and working for DB in Bulgaria No. 92034 is seen still with UK markings, BR logo and Channel Tunnel branding and its original name. The loco now carries the number 91 52 1688 034-3.* **Howard Lewsey**

DB-Cargo

Hauled Stock (Passenger)

AD1F - FO

Number	Depot	Livery	Owner
3279	TY	MAR	DBR

AC2B - TSO

Number	Depot	Livery	Owner
5482	TO	BLG	DBR

AE2D - BSO

Number	Depot	Livery	Owner
9494(S)	TY	MAR	DBR/SCR

AE2E - BSO

Number	Depot	Livery	Location
9506	ME	MAR	Brodie Eng

AE2F - BSO

Number	Depot	Livery	Owner
9529(S)	DN	MAR	DBR
9531(S)	DN	MAR	DBR

AJ1G - RFM

Number		Depot	Livery	Owner
10211	(40510)	TO	EWE	DBC
10215	(11032)	LM	BLG	DBR/CRW
10222(S)	(11063)	BU	BLG	DBR
10226(S)	(11015)	LM	VIR	DBR
10233(S)	(10013)	LM	VIR	DBR
10235	(10015)	LM	BLG	DBR/CRW
10237(S)	(10022)	BY	DRU	DBR
10242(S)	(10002)	LM	BLG	DBR
10246	(10114)	CF	BLG	DBR/ATW
10250(S)	(10020)	LM	VIR	DBR
10257(S)	(10007)	BU	BLG	DBR

AU4G - SLEP

Number	Depot	Livery	Owner
10546	TO	EWE	DBC

Number	Depot	Livery	Owner
11033(S)	LM	DRU	DBR
11039	TO	EWE	DBS
11046(S)	ZB	DRU	DBR
11054(S)	ZB	DRU	DBR

Mk2 — Height: 12ft 9½in (3.89m)
Vehicle Length: 66ft 0in (20.11m) — Width: 9ft 3in (2.81m)

Mk 3 — Height: 12ft 9in (3.88m)
Vehicle Length: 75ft 0in (22.86m) — Width: 8ft 11in (2.71m)

GK2G - TRSB

Number		Depot	Livery	Owner
40402(S)	(40002)	LM	VIR	DBR
40403(S)	(40003)	LM	VIR	DBR
40416(S)	(40016)	LM	VIR	DBR
40434(S)	(40234)	LM	VIR	DBR

Saloon

Number	Depot	Livery	Owner
45020(S)	TO	MAR	DBR

AD1G - FO

Number	Depot	Livery	Owner
11019(S)	ZB	DRU	DBR
11028(S)	ZB	VIR	DBR
11030(S)	ZB	DRU	DBR
3A TSO			

Hauled Stock (NPCCS)

Mk 3 (DVT) — Height: 12ft 9in (3.88m)
Vehicle Length: 61ft 9in (18.83m) — Width: 8ft 11in (2.71m)

NZAG - DVT

Number	Depot	Livery	Owner
82116(S)	LM	VIR	DBR
82120(S)	LM	VIR	DBR
82137(S)	LM	VIR	DBR
82138(S)	LM	VIR	DBR
82141(S)	LM	VIR	DBR
82146	TO	DBE	DBC
82148(S)	LM	VIR	DBR
82150(S)	LM	VIR	DBR

NOA1 - H-GUV

Number		Depot	Livery	Owner
95727	(95127)	WE	RES	DBS
95761	(95161)	WE	RES	DBS
95763	(95163)	BS	RES	DBS

Euro Cargo Rail A part of DB-Cargo

Address: ✉ Immeuble la Palacio, 25-29 Place de la Madeleine, Paris, 75008
✒ info@eurocargorail.com, ✆ +33 977 400000, ⓘ www.eurocargorail.com

Class 21
Vehicle Length: (21/5) 48ft 2in (14.70m), (21/6) 46ft 3in (14.13m)   Engine: (21/5) Caterpillar 3512B DITA of 2,011hp
Height: (21/5) 13ft 8in (4.16m), (21/6) 13ft 9in (4.19m)   (21/6) MTU 8V 4000 R41L of 1,475hp
Width: 8ft 8¼in (2.65m)   Hydraulic Equipment: Voith

Number		Depot	Pool	Livery	Owner	Operator							
21544	(FB1544)	DM	WLAN	MAR	ANG	ECR	21547	(FB1547)	DM	WLAN	MAR	ANG ECR
21545	(FB1545)	DM	WLAN	MAR	ANG	ECR	21610	(FB1610)	DM	WLAN	MAR	ANG ECR
21546	(FB1546)	DM	WLAN	MAR	ANG	ECR	21611	(FB1611)	DM	WLAN	MAR	ANG ECR

Class 77
(JT42CWRM)

Vehicle Length: 70ft 0½in (21.34m)
Height: 12ft 10in (3.91m)
Width: 8ft 8¼in (2.65m)

Engine: EMD 12N-710G3B-EC
Horsepower: 3,300hp (2,462kW)
Electrical Equipment: EMD

Number							
	77008	77016	77024	77032	77040	77048	77056
77001	77009	77017	77025	77033	77041	77049	77057
77002	77010	77018	77026	77034	77042	77050	77058
77003	77011	77019	77027	77035	77043	77051	77059
77004	77012	77020	77028	77036	77044	77052	77060
77005	77013	77021	77029	77037	77045	77053	
77006	77014	77022	77030	77038	77046	77054	
77007	77015	77023	77031	77039	77047	77055	

Above: *Ordered by the EWS partner Euro Cargo Rail, a batch of European Class 66, classified as 77 were introduced. Over the years a number have been sold and re-leased. No. 077 012-8 is currently operated by Mitteldeutsche Eisenbahn (MEG), a part of DB Schenker. On 21 September 2018 the loco is seen powering an aggregate train through Berlin Schonefeld.* **CJM**

Right: *Most of the Ex-UK Class 66s exported by EWS to Euro Cargo Rail retain their original maroon and gold livery. These locos are modified for European use but can return to the UK if required. Those exported to Poland can not return to the UK without structural modification. No. 66236 is seen operating in Northern France at Caffiers Quarry near Calais.* **Howard Lewsey**

Royal Mail (operations contracted to DB-Cargo)

Address: ✉ 148 Old Street, London, EC1V 9HQ
✆ press.office@royalmail.com
✆ 0207 250 2468
ⓘ www.royalmailgroup.com

Class 325

Vehicle Length: (Driving) 65ft 0¾in (19.82m) Width: 9ft 2in (2.82m)
(Inter) 65ft 4¼in (19.92m) Horsepower: 1,278hp (990kW)
Height: 12ft 4½in (3.76m) Seats (total/car): None - luggage space

Number	Formation DTPMV+MPMV+TPMV+DTPMV	Depot	Livery	Owner	Operator	Name
325001	68300+68340+68360+68301	CE	RMR	RML	DBC	
325002	68302+68341+68361+68303	CE	RMR	RML	DBC	
325003	68304+68342+68362+68305	CE	RMR	RML	DBC	
325004	68306+68343+68363+68307	CE	RMR	RML	DBC	
325005	68308+68344+68364+68309	CE	RMR	RML	DBC	
325006	68310+68345+68365+68311	CE	RMR	RML	DBC	
325007	68312+68346+68366+68313	CE	RMR	RML	DBC	Peter Howarth C.B.E
325008	68314+68347+68367+68315	CE	RMR	RML	DBC	
325009	68316+68348+68368+68317	CE	RMR	RML	DBC	
325011	68320+68350+68370+68321	CE	RMR	RML	DBC	
325012	68322+68351+68371+68323	CE	RMR	RML	DBC	
325013	68324+68352+68372+68325	CE	RMR	RML	DBC	
325014	68326+68353+68373+68327	CE	RMR	RML	DBC	
325015	68328+68354+68374+68329	CE	RMR	RML	DBC	
325016	68330+68355+68375+68331	CE	RMR	RML	DBC	

Above: *The Class 325 dual voltage EMUs were built as part of the modernisation of the 'Mail by Rail' project as special sets which could transport mail racks between central Royal Mail facilities, of which a number were purpose built at locations including London, Bristol, Doncaster, Warrington, Glasgow and Newcastle. However, soon after introduction Royal Mail decided to opt for other transport methods and the sets became surplus. After a short time some sets were used as hauled stock to transport mail. In more recent times a number of sets have returned to their intended traffic and operate a few longer distance services on the West Coast. One set has been withdrawn and used for spares and most of the operational sets have been overhauled, their dc systems removed and repainted in an all over Royal Mail red. Three sets, led by No. 325005 head south through Stafford bound for the London terminal at Wembley.* **Antony Christie**

Direct Rail Services

Address (UK): ✉ Kingmoor Depot, Etterby Road, Carlisle, Cumbria, CA3 9NZ
📠 info@directrailservices.com © 01228 406600
ⓘ www.directrailservices.com

Managing Director: Debbie Francis
Depots: Carlisle Kingmoor (KM), Crewe Gresty Bridge (CR)

Class 20/3

Vehicle Length: 46ft 9¼in (14.26m)				Engine: English Electric 8SVT Mk2		
Height: 12ft 7⅝in (3.84m)				Horsepower: 1,000hp (745kW)		
Width: 8ft 9in (2.66m)				Electrical Equipment: English Electric		

Number		Depot	Pool	Livery	Owner	Operator	Name / Note
20301(S)	(20047)	BH	XHSS	DRC	DRS	-	
20302(S)	(20084)	KM	XHSS	DRC	DRS	-	
20303(S)	(20127)	KM	XHSS	DRC	DRS	-	*Max Joule 1958 - 1999*
20304(S)	(20120)	KM	XHSS	DRC	DRS	-	
20305(S)	(20095)	KM	XHSS	DRC	DRS	-	
20309(S)	(20075)	BH	XHSS	DRC	DRS	-	
20312(S)	(20042)	KM	XHSS	DRC	DRS	-	Offered for sale 12/16

Right: *Direct Rail Services, with its headquarters in Carlisle and a major depot facility at Crewe, is a major player in the freight sector as well as a provider of traction and train crew for special services. Although currently stored, a fleet of refurbished Class 20s are on the company roster. These carry DRS blue livery. Nos. 20302 and 20303 are seen at York.* **David Farrah**

Class 37/0

Vehicle Length: 61ft 6in (18.74m)				Engine: English Electric 12CSVT	
Height: 13ft 0¼in (3.96m)				Horsepower: 1,750hp (1,304kW)	
Width: 8ft 11⅝in (2.73m)				Electrical Equipment: English Electric	
Class 37/4 - Electric Train Heat fitted					

Number	Depot	Pool	Livery	Owner	Operator
37038	KM	XHNC	DRC	DRS	DRS
37059	KM	XHNC	DRR	DRS	DRS
37069	KM	XHNC	DRR	DRS	DRS
37218	KM	XHNC	DRR	DRS	DBS
37259	KM	XHNC	DRU	DRS	DRS

Class 37/4

Number		Depot	Pool	Livery	Owner	Operator	Name / Note
37401	(37268)	KM	XHAC	BLL	DRS	DRS	*Mary Queen of Scots*
37402	(37274)	KM	XHAC	BLL	DRS	DRS	*Stephen Middlemore 23.12.1954 - 8.6.2013*
37403	(37307)	KM	XHAC	BLL	DRS	DRS	
37405	(37282)	BH	XHAC	DRC	DRS	DRS	
37407(S)	(37305)	KM	XHSS	BLL	DRS	-	*Blackpool Tower*
37409	(37270)	KM	XHAC	BLL	DRS	DRS	*Lord Hinton*
37419	(37291)	KM	XHSS	DRC	DRS	DRS	*Carl Haviland 1954-2012*
37422	(37266)	KM	XHAC	DRB	DRS	DRS	
37423	(37296)	KM	XHAC	BLL	DRS	DRS	*Spirit of the Lakes*
37424	(37279)	KM	XHAC	BLL	DRS	DRS	*Avro Vulcan XH558 (carries No. 37558)*
37425	(37292)	BH	XHAC	DRC	DRS	DRS	*Sir Robert McAlpine / Concrete Bob*

Direct Rail Services

Left: *Now in their more senior years, the English Electric Class 37 fleet still features largely in the DRS roster, with in early 2019 some 14 operational locos in traffic and others stored. Various different liveries are carried, with one of the most popular being the old BR large logo blue. This livery is applied to Class 37/4 No. 37424, which currently carries the number 37558 in recognition of the last operational RAF Vulcan bomber, after which it is named. The loco is seen hauling Network Rail inspection saloon 975025.* **CJM**

Class 37/6

Number		Depot	Pool	Livery	Owner	Operator
37602	(37502)	KM	XHNC	DRC	DRS	DRS
37603(S)	(37504)	KM	XHSS	DRC	DRS	-
37604(S)	(37506)	KM	XHCC	DRC	DRS	-
37605	(37507)	KM	XHNC	DRC	DRS	DRS
37606	(37508)	KM	XHNC	DRS	DRS	DRS
37609(S)	(37514)	KM	XHSS	DRC	DRS	-

Class 37/7

Number		Hire No.	Depot	Pool	Livery	Owner	Operator
37703(S)	(37067)	L25	BH	XHSS	DRR	DRS	-
37716	(37094)	L23	KM	XHNC	DRC	DRS	DRS

Left: *Two heavyweight Class 37/7s are operated by DRS. One No. 37703 is stored and the other No. 37716 is in full front line service. These two locos were part of a batch which were exported by EWS to Spain and operated on infrastructure traffic for high speed line construction operated by GIF. In Spain the loco carried the identity L23. In pristine condition No. 37716 is seen passing Longport.* **Cliff Beeton**

Class 57/0

							Vehicle Length: 63ft 6in (19.38m) Height: 12ft 10½in (3.91m) Width: 9ft 2in (2.79m)	Engine: EMD 645-12E3 Horsepower: 2,500hp (1,864kW) Electrical Equipment: Brush

Number		Depot	Pool	Livery	Owner	Operator	Name
57002	(47322)	KM	XHCK	DRC	DRS	DRS	Rail Express
57003	(47317)	KM	XHSS	DRC	DRS	DRS	
57004(S)	(47347)	KM	XHSS	DRC	DRS	-	
57007	(47332)	KM	XHCK	DRC	DRS	DRS	John Scott 12.5.45 - 22.5.12
57008(S)	(47060)	KM	XHSS	DRC	DRS	-	
57009(S)	(47079)	KM	XHSS	DRC	DRS	-	
57010(S)	(47231)	KM	XHSS	DRC	DRS	-	
57011(S)	(47329)	CR	XHSS	DRC	DRS	-	
57012(S)	(47204)	KM	XHSS	DRC	DRS	-	

Right: *Originally converted for Freightliner before Class 66s were introduced. Nine of the original 12 Class 57/0s are part of the DRS fleet, a number are stored. Painted in immaculate DRS compass livery, No. 57002* Rail Express *is seen stabled at Norwich.* **Antony Christie**

Freight Operating Companies - Direct Rail Services

Class 57/3

Vehicle Length: 63ft 6in (19.38m)
Height: 12ft 10⅛in (3.91m)
Width: 9ft 2in (2.79m)
Engine: EMD 645-12F3B
Horsepower: 2,750hp (2,051kW)
Electrical Equipment: Brush

Number		Depot	Pool	Livery	Owner	Operator	Name
57301	(47845)	KM	XHAC	DRC	DRS	DRS	Goliath
57302(S)	(47827)	KM	XHSS	DRC	PTR	-	Chad Varah
57303	(47705)	KM	XHAC	DRC	DRS	DRS	Pride of Carlisle
57304	(47807)	KM	XHVT	DRC	PTR	DRS	Pride of Cheshire
57305	(47822)	LR	XHAC	NBP	DRS	ROG	Northern Princess
57306	(47814)	KM	XHAC	DRC	DRS	DRS	Her Majesty's Railway Inspectorate 175
57307	(47225)	KM	XHVT	DRA	PTR	DRB	Lady Penelope
57308	(47846)	KM	XHVT	DRC	PTR	DRS	Jamie Ferguson
57309	(47806)	KM	XHVT	DRC	PTR	DRS	Pride of Crewe
57310	(47831)	KM	XHAC	DRS	DRS	DRS	Pride of Cumbria
57311(S)	(47817)	KM	XHSS	DRC	PTR	-	Thunderbird
57312	(47330)	LR	XHAC	NBP	PTR	ROG	Solway Princess

Nos. 57301, 57303 and 57306 fitted with Tightlock couplings, Nos. 57310 and 57312 fitted with modified Dellner couplings.

Right: *A fleet of 12 Class 57/3s are operated by Direct Rail Services, these power mixed traffic operations covering freight and charter passenger. These locos were part of the original Virgin fleet, introduced as Pendolino/Voyager 'Thunderbirds' and have drop head dellner couplings. In recent times some of the Dellners have been exchanged for Tightlock couplings to allow assistance of multiple unit stock. Several of this fleet are always available to hire to Virgin if required. With its coupling covered, No. 57303 pilots a DRS Class 37 on a stock move from Laira to Crewe passing Dawlish.* **CJM**

Class 66/3 & 66/4

Vehicle Length: 70ft 0½in (21.34m)
Height: 12ft 10in (3.91m)
Width: 8ft 8¼in (2.65m)
Engine: EMD 12N-710G3B-EC
Horsepower: 3,300hp (2,462kW)
Electrical Equipment: EMD

Number	Depot	Pool	Livery	Owner	Operator		Number	Depot	Pool	Livery	Owner	Operator
66301	KM	XHIM	DRC	BEA	DRS		66425	KM	XHIM	DRB	HAL	DRS
66302	KM	XHIM	DRB	BEA	DRS		66426	KM	XHIM	DRB	HAL	DRS
66303	KM	XHIM	DRC	BEA	DRS		66427	KM	XHIM	DRC	HAL	DRS
66304	KM	XHIM	DRC	BEA	DRS		66428	KM	XHIM	DRB	HAL	DRS
66305	KM	XHIM	DRB	BEA	DRS		66429	KM	XHIM	DRC	HAL	DRS
66421	KM	XHIM	DRC	HAL	DRS		66430	KM	XHIM	DRS	HAL	DRS
66422	KM	XHIM	DRC	HAL	DRS		66431	KM	XHIM	DRC	HAL	DRS
66423	KM	XHIM	DRC	HAL	DRS		66432	KM	XHIM	DRC	HAL	DRS
66424	KM	XHIM	DRC	HAL	DRS		66433	KM	XHIM	DRC	HAL	DRS
							66434	KM	XHIM	DRC	HAL	DRS

Freight Operating Companies - Direct Rail Services

Direct Rail Services

Names applied
66301   Kingmoor TMD
66421   Gresty Bridge TMD

Left: *A fleet of 19 Class 66s are operated by DRS on freight and infrastructure flows. These display a mix of DRS liveries. Painted in all blue with small DRS branding No. 66432 is shown at Doncaster.*
Antony Christie

Class 68 'UK Light'

Vehicle Length: 67ft 3in (20.5m)
Height: 12ft 6½in (3.82m)
Speed: 100mph (161km/h)

Engine: Caterpillar C175-16
Horsepower: 3,750hp (2,800kW)
Electrical Equipment: ABB

Number	Depot	Pool	Livery	Owner	Operator	Name	
68001	CR	XHVE	DRS	BEA	DRS	Evolution	§ Modified for
68002	CR	XHVE	DRS	BEA	DRS	Intrepid	operation with
68003	CR	XHVE	DRS	BEA	DRS	Astute	push-pull passenger
68004	CR	XHVE	DRS	BEA	DRS	Rapid	stock, fitted with
68005	CR	XHVE	DRS	BEA	DRS	Defiant	AAR controls.
68006	CR	XHVE	SCR	BEA	DRS/SCR	Daring	68019-68032
68007	CR	XHVE	SCR	BEA	DRS/SCR	Valiant	modified to operate
68008§	CR	XHVE	DRS	BEA	DRS	Avenger	with Trans Pennine
68009§	CR	XHVE	DRS	BEA	DRS	Titan	Express Mk5 stock
68010§	CR	XHCE	CRG	BEA	DRS/CRW	Oxford Flyer	
68011§	CR	XHCE	CRG	BEA	DRS/CRW		
68012§	CR	XHCE	CRG	BEA	DRS/CRW		
68013§	CR	XHCE	CRG	BEA	DRS/CRW		
68014§	CR	XHCE	CRG	BEA	DRS/CRW		
68015§	CR	XHCE	CRG	BEA	DRS/CRW		
68016	CR	XHVE	BLU	BEA	DRS	Fearless	
68017	CR	XHVE	BLU	BEA	DRS	Hornet	
68018	CR	XHVE	DRS	BEA	DRS	Vigilant	
68019	CR	XHTP	FTN	BEA	DRS/TPE	Brutus	
68020	CR	XHTP	FTN	BEA	DRS/TPE	Reliance	
68021	CR	XHTP	FTN	BEA	DRS/TPE	Tireless	
68022	CR	XHTP	FTN	BEA	DRS/TPE	Resolution	
68023	CR	XHTP	FTN	BEA	DRS	Achilles	
68024	CR	XHTP	FTN	BEA	DRS	Centaur	
68025	CR	XHTP	FTN	BEA	DRS	Superb	
68026	CR	XHTP	FTN	BEA	DRS	(Nautilus)	
68027	CR	XHTP	FTN	BEA	DRS	(Endeavour)	
68028	CR	XHTP	FTN	BEA	DRS	Lord President	
68029	CR	XHVE	FTN	BEA	DRS	(Destroyer)	
68030	CR	XHTP	FTN	BEA	DRS	Black Douglas	
68031	CR	XHTP	FTN	BEA	DRS	(Excelsior)	
68032	CR	XHVE	FTN	BEA	DRS	(Patriot)	
68033	CR	XHVE	DRB	DRS	DRS	(Courageous)	
68034	CR	XHVE	DRB	DRS	DRS	(Victorious)	

Left: *DRS operate a fleet of 34 Class 68 Vossloh Bo-Bo diesel-electric locos, all but the final two are owned by Beacon Rail, while Nos. 68033 and 68034 are owned by DRS. The locos operate freight and infrastructure flows, as well as some Chiltern Railways and TransPennine Express passenger services, the later with Mk5 passenger stock and driving trailers. Nos. 68025 and 68023 are seen at Bridgwater with a flask train bound for Crewe.* **Antony Christie**

Class 88 'Euro Dual'

Vehicle Length: 67ft 3in (20.5m)
Height: 12ft 6½in (3.82m)
Speed: 100mph (161km/h)
Electric train supply Index: 96

Engine: Caterpillar C27
Horsepower: Diesel - 940hp (700kW)
Electric - 5,360hp (4,000kW)
Electrical Equipment: ABB

Number	Depot	Pool	Livery	Owner	Operator	Name
88001	KM	XHVE	DRS	BEA	DRS	Revolution
88002	KM	XHVE	DRS	BEA	DRS	Prometheus
88003	KM	XHVE	DRS	BEA	DRS	Genesis
88004	KM	XHVE	DRS	BEA	DRS	Pandora
88005	KM	XHVE	DRS	BEA	DRS	Minerva
88006	KM	XHVE	DRS	BEA	DRS	Juno
88007	KM	XHVE	DRS	BEA	DRS	Electra
88008	KM	XHVE	DRS	BEA	DRS	Ariadne
88009	KM	XHVE	DRS	BEA	DRS	Diana
88010	KM	XHVE	DRS	BEA	DRS	Aurora

Currently the most modern fleet of locos operating in the UK
are 10 bi-mode Class 88 electro-diesels built by Stadler for DRS.
No. 88004 Pandora is shown from its pantograph end. **CJM**

Coaching Stock

Mk2
Vehicle Length: 66ft 0in (20.11m)
Height: 12ft 9½in (3.89m)
Width: 9ft 3in (2.81m)

Mk 3
Vehicle Length: 75ft 0in (22.86m)
Height: 12ft 9in (3.88m)
Width: 8ft 11in (2.71m)

Number	Type	Depot	Livery	Operator
5810	AC2E/TSO	KM	DRC	NOR
5919	AC2F/TSO	KM	DBC	NOR
5945	AC2F/TSO	ML	SCR	ASR
5965	AC2F/TSO	ML	SCR	ASR
5971	AC2F/TSO	KM	DRC	NOR
5976	AC2F/TSO	ML	SCR	ASR
5995	AC25/TSO	NR	DRC	NOR
6001	AC2F/TSO	NR	DRC	NOR
6008	AC2F/TSO	ML	DRC	NOR
6046	AC2F/TSO	KM	DRC	DRS
6064	AC2F/TSO	KM	DRC	NOR
6117	AC2F/TSO	KM	DRC	DRS
6122	AC2F/TSO	ML	DRC	NOR
6173	AC2F/TSO	ML	DRS	NOR
6176	AC2F/TSO	ML	SCR	ASR
6177	AC2F/TSO	ML	SCR	ASR
6183	AC2F/TSO	ML	SCR	ASR
9419	AC2E/TSO	KM	DRC	DRS
9428	AE2E/BSO	KM	DRC	DRS
9488	AE2E/BSO	ML	SCR	DRS
9508	AE2E/BSO	ZA	BRC	DRS
9521	AE2E/BSO	KM	DRC	DRS

Number	Type	Depot	Livery	Operator
9525	AE2E/BSO	NR	DRC	DRS
9539	AE2E/BSO	KM	SCR	ASR
9704 (9512)	AF2F/DBSO	KM	DRC	DRS
9705 (9519)	AF2F/DBSO	ZA	DRC	NOR
9707 (9511)	AF2F/DBSO	ZA	DRC	NOR
9709 (9515)	AF2F/DBSO	KM	DRC	DRS
9710 (9518)	AF2F/DBSO	KM	DRC	DRS
11006	AD1G/FO	BU	-	DRS
17159	AB1D/BFK	KM	CCM	GAR
82101(S)	NZAK/DVT	ZA	VIR	DRS
82126	NZAK/DVT	KM	-	DRS

NX5G - NGV (Nightstar Generators)

Number		Depot	Livery	Owner
96372(S)	(10564)	LM	EPS	DRS
96373(S)	(10568)	LM	EPS	DRS
96375(S)	(10587)	LM	EPS	DRS

GB Railfreight (GBRf)

Address: ✉15-25 Artillery Lane, London, E1 7HA

✍ gbrfinfo@gbrailfreight.com ✆ 0207 983 5177 ⓘ www.gbrailfreight.com

Managing Director: John Smith

Depots: Peterborough (PT), Willesden (WN), St Leonards (SE), Coquelles (CQ)

Parent Company: EQT Infrastructure II - Hector Rail

Class 08 & 09

	Vehicle Length: 29ft 3in (8.91m)		Engine: English Electric 6K		
	Height: 12ft 8⅝in (3.87m)		Horsepower: 400hp (298kW)		
	Width: 8ft 6in (2.59m)		Electrical Equipment: English Electric		

Number	Depot	Pool	Livery	Owner	Operator		Number	Depot	Pool	Livery	Owner	Operator
08401	HH	GBWW	GRN	HEC	Hams Hall		09002	BH	GBWM	GRN	GBF	GBR
08925	BH	GBWM	GRN	GBF	March		09009	MR	GBWM	GRN	GBF	Dean Lane
08934	BH	GBWM	GRN	GBF	GBR							

Class 20

	Vehicle Length: 46ft 9¼in (14.26m)		Engine: English Electric 8SVT Mk2
	Height: 12ft 7⅝in (3.84m)		Horsepower: 1,000hp (745kW)
	Width: 8ft 9in (2.66m)		Electrical Equipment: English Electric

Number		Depot	Pool	Livery	Owner	Operator	Name
20142		PG	GBEE	LUL	20189	GBR	Sir John Betjeman
20189		PG	GBEE	BLU	20189	GBR	
20227		SK	MOLO	LUL	c2L	GBR	Sherlock Holmes
20901	(20101)	PG	GBEE	GBN	HNR	GBR	
20905	(20225)	PG	GBEE	GBN	HNR	GBR	

GB Railfreight operates a small fleet of Class 20s for freight and charter use. These are privately owned locos, leased to GBRf. In recent years, the '20s' have been used to haul LUL stock between Bombardier Derby and the LU network as well as being used on charter services. London Transport liveried Nos. 20189 and 20227 are shown.
Mark V. Pike

Class 47/7

	Vehicle Length: 63ft 6in (19.35m)		Engine: Sulzer 12LDA28C
	Height: 12ft 10⅜in (3.91m)		Horsepower: 2,580hp (1,922kW)
	Width: 9ft 2in (2.79m)		Electrical Equipment: Brush
	Electric Train Heat fitted		47739/749 fitted with Dellner couplings

Number		Depot	Pool	Livery	Owner	Operator	Name
47727	(47569)	PG	GBDF	SCS	GBR	GBR	Edinburgh Castle / Caisteal Dhun Eideann
47739	(47594)	PG	GBDF	GBR	GBR	GBR	
47749	(47625)	PG	GBDF	COL	GBR	GBR	

Right: *Three Class 47/7s previously operated by Colas Rail Freight are now on the GBRf roster. The locos operate as required on charter (passenger), freight and Caledonian Sleeper operations as required. To signify the Caledonian Sleeper involvement, No. 47727 carries Caledonian Sleeper branding and was named* Edinburgh Castle / Caisteal Dhun Eideann *in 2018. In the illustration, the loco is seen powering a railtour at Bath.* **Antony Christie**

Class 56

Vehicle Length: 63ft 6in (19.35m)	Engine: Ruston Paxman 16RK3CT
Height: 13ft 0in (3.96m)	Horsepower: 3,250hp (2,420kW)
Width: 9ft 2in (2.79m)	Electrical Equipment: Brush

In 2018, GBRf purchased a fleet of Class 56s for re-engineering, some will be fitted with new power units. The locos are allocated to pool GBGS. It is said that 10 are for re-engineering, three will be operated as standard Class 56s and three will be parts doners. Locos are officially allocated to PG, in Pool GBGS.

56007§	56018§	56032§	56038§	56065*	56077*	56098■	56106*	56311§
56009§	56031§	56037§	56060*	56069§	56081*	56104±	56128§	56312■

No. 56009 owned by EMD

* Stored at Leicester
§ Stored at EMD Longport
± Stored at Castle Donnington
■ In use at Peak Forest

Right: *GBRf for ever looking for additional motive power purchased a batch of Class 56s, many are scheduled to be rebuilt with new prime movers by ElectroMotive, while some will be scrapped and others will retain their original traction equipment. At the start of 2019 the locos were stored awaiting work. No. 56069 carrying Fertis livery is seen being hauled to EMD Longport.* **Cliff Beeton**

Class 59/0

Vehicle Length: 70ft 0½in (21.34m)	Engine: EMD 16-645 E3C
Height: 12ft 10in (3.91m)	Horsepower: 3,000hp (2,462kW)
Width: 8ft 8¼in (2.65m)	Electrical Equipment: EMD

Number	Depot	Pool	Livery	Owner	Operator	Name
59003	PG	GBYH	GBN	GBR	GBR	*Yeoman Highlander*

Right: *A very popular loco in the GBRf portfolio is former Foster Yeoman Class 59/0 No. 59003 Yeoman Highlander, which after several years working in Germany and Eastern Europe was returned to the UK and obtained by GBRf for heavy freight flow duties. At the end of 2018 and the start of 2019, the loco has been operating in the Westbury area powering heavy aggregate trains, the very work the loco was originally ordered to undertake.* **Mark V. Pike**

GBRf

Class 60

	Vehicle Length: 70ft 0½in (21.34m)	Engine: Mirrlees MB275T
	Height: 12ft 10⅝in (3.92m)	Horsepower: 3,100hp (2,240kW)
	Width: 8ft 8in (2.64m)	Electrical Equipment: Brush

Number	Depot	Pool	Livery	Owner	Operator
60002	PG	GBTG	COL	BEA	GBR
60004	-	-	EWS	BEA	BEA
60008	-	-	EWS	BEA	-
60014	-	-	EWS	BEA	-
60018	-	-	EWS	BEA	-
60021	PG	GBTG	COL	BEA	GBR
60026	PG	GBTG	COL	BEA	GBR
60047	PG	GBTG	COL	BEA	GBR
60056	PG	GBTG	COL	BEA	GBR
60076	PG	GBTG	COL	BEA	GBR
60085	PG	GBTG	COL	BEA	GBR
60087	PG	GBTG	COL	BEA	GBR
60095	PG	GBTG	GBN	BEA	GBR
60096	PG	GBTG	COL	BEA	GBR

Right: *In the summer of 2018, GBRf obtained 10 Class 60s, previously operated and owned by Colas Rail Freight. The locos were sold to Beacon Rail Leasing and then hired to GBRf. The locos, with a superior tractive effort to the Class 66 fleet will be used on the operators heaviest trains. In late 2018 a start was made at repainting the locos into standard GBRf colours at Arlington, Eastleigh, the first to be repainted being No. 60095. The loco is seen piloting a GBRf Class 66 at Horbury.* **Peter Marsh**

Class 66/7

	Vehicle Length: 70ft 0½in (21.34m)	Engine: EMD 12N-710G3B-EC
	Height: 12ft 10in (3.91m)	Horsepower: 3,300hp (2,462kW)
	Width: 8ft 8¼in (2.65m)	Electrical Equipment: EMD

Number	Depot	Pool	Livery	Owner	Operator	Name
66701	PG	GBBT	GBR	EVL	GBR	
66702	PG	GBBT	GBN	EVL	GBR	Blue Lightning
66703	PG	GBBT	GBN	EVL	GBR	Doncaster PSB 1981 - 2002
66704	PG	GBBT	GBN	EVL	GBR	Colchester Power Signalbox
66705	PG	GBBT	GBR	EVL	GBR	Golden Jubilee
66706	PG	GBBT	GBN	EVL	GBR	Nene Valley
66707	PG	GBBT	GBN	EVL	GBR	Sir Sam Fay / Great Central Railway
66708	PG	GBBT	GBR	EVL	GBR	Jayne
66709	PG	GBBT	MSC	EVL	GBR	Sorrento
66710	PG	GBBT	GBN	EVL	GBR	Phil Packer
66711	PG	GBBT	AGI	EVL	GBR	Sence
66712	PG	GBBT	GBN	EVL	GBR	Peterborough Power Signalbox
66713	PG	GBBT	GBN	EVL	GBR	Forest City
66714	PG	GBBT	GBN	EVL	GBR	Cromer Lifeboat
66715	PG	GBBT	GBN	EVL	GBR	Valour
66716	PG	GBBT	GBN	EVL	GBR	Locomotive & Carriage Institution Centenary 1911-2011
66717	PG	GBBT	GBN	EVL	GBR	Good Old Boy
66718	PG	GBLT	SPL	EVL	GBR	Sir Peter Hendy CBE
66719	PG	GBLT	GBN	EVL	GBR	Metro-Land
66720	PG	GBLT	SPL	EVL	GBR	
66721	PG	GBLT	SPL	EVL	GBR	Harry Beck
66722	PG	GBLT	GBN	EVL	GBR	Sir Edward Watkin
66723 (ZA723)	PG	GBLT	GBN	EVL	GBR	Chinook
66724	PG	GBLT	GBN	EVL	GBR	Drax Power Station
66725	PG	GBLT	GBN	EVL	GBR	Sunderland
66726	PG	GBLT	GBN	EVL	GBR	Sheffield Wednesday
66727	PG	GBLT	ADV	EVL	GBR	Maritime One
66728	PG	GBLT	GBN	PTR	GBR	Institution of Railway Operators
66729	PG	GBLT	GBN	PTR	GBR	Derby County
66730	PG	GBLT	GBF	PTR	GBR	Whitemoor
66731	PG	GBLT	GBN	PTR	GBR	interhubGB

66732		PG	GBLT	GBN	PTR	GBR	GBRf The First Decade 1999-2009 John Smith - MD
66733	(66401)	PG	GBFM	BLU	PTR	GBR	Cambridge PSB
66735	(66403)	PG	GBBT	GBN	PTR	GBR	
66736	(66404)	PG	GBFM	GBN	PTR	GBR	Wolverhampton Wanderers
66737	(66405)	PG	GBFM	GBN	PTR	GBR	Lesia
66738	(66578)	PG	GBBT	GBN	GBR	GBR	Huddersfield Town
66739	(66579)	PG	GBFM	GBN	GBR	GBR	Bluebell Railway
66740	(66580)	PG	GBFM	GBN	GBR	GBR	Sarah
66741	(66581)	PG	GBBT	GBN	GBR	GBR	Swanage Railway
66742	(66406, 66841)	PG	GBBT	GBN	GBR	GBR	Port of Immingham Centenary 1912 - 2012
66743	(66407, 66842)	PG	GBFM	ROS	GBR	GBR	
66744	(66408, 66843)	PG	GBBT	GBN	GBR	GBR	Crossrail
66745	(66409, 66844)	PG	GBRT	GBN	GBR	GBR	Modern Railways - The first 50 years
66746	(66410, 66845)	PG	GBFM	ROS	GBR	GBR	
66747		PG	GBEB	GBN	GBR	GBR	
66748		PG	GBEB	GBN	GBR	GBR	West Burton 50
66749		PG	GBEB	GBN	GBR	GBR	
66750		PG	GBEB	GBN	GBN	GBR	Bristol Panel Signal Box
66751		PG	GBEB	GBN	BEA	GBR	Inspiration Delivered Hitachi Rail Europe
66752		PG	GBEL	GBN	GBR	GBR	The Hoosier State
66753		PG	GBEL	GBN	GBR	GBR	EMD Roberts Road
66754		PG	GBEL	GBN	GBR	GBR	Northampton Saints
66755		PG	GBEL	GBN	GBR	GBR	Tony Berkley OBE RFG Chairman 1997-2018
66756		PG	GBEL	GBN	GBR	GBR	The Royal Corps Of Signals
66757		PG	GBEL	GBN	GBR	GBR	West Somerset Railway
66758		PG	GBEL	GBN	GBR	GBR	The Pavior
66759		PG	GBEL	GBN	GBR	GBR	Chippy
66760		PG	GBEL	GBN	GBR	GBR	David Gordon Harris
66761		PG	GBEL	GBN	GBR	GBR	Wensleydale Railway Association 25 Years 1990-2015
66762		PG	GBEL	GBN	GBR	GBR	
66763		PG	GBEL	GBN	GBR	GBR	Severn Valley Railway
66764		PG	GBEL	GBN	GBR	GBR	
66765		PG	GBEL	GBN	GBR	GBR	
66766		PG	GBEL	GBN	GBR	GBR	
66767		PG	GBEL	GBN	GBR	GBR	
66768		PG	GBEL	GBN	GBR	GBR	
66769		PG	GBEL	GBN	GBR	GBR	
66770		PG	GBEL	GBN	GBR	GBR	
66771		PG	GBEL	GBN	GBR	GBR	
66772		PG	GBEL	GBN	GBR	GBR	
66773		PG	GBNB	GBN	GBR	GBR	
66774		PG	GBNB	GBN	GBR	GBR	
66775	(F231)	PG	GBNB	GBN	GBR	GBR	HMS Argyll
66776		PG	GBNB	GBN	GBR	GBR	Joanne
66777		PG	GBNB	GBN	GBR	GBR	Annette
66778		PG	GBNB	GBN	GBR	GBR	Darius Cheskin
66779		PG	GBEL	GRN	GBR	GBR	Evening Star
66780	(66008)	PG	GBOG	ADV	GBR	GBR	
66781	(66016)	PG	GBOG	GBN	GBR	GBR	
66782	(66046)	PG	GBOG	SPL	GBR	GBR	
66783	(66058)	PG	GBOG	SPL	GBR	GBR	The Flying Dustman

Right: *The core diesel motive power operated by GBRf is a fleet of 88 Class 66s, this fleet consists of purpose-built Class 66/7s, purchased former European locos and 10 purchased former Class 66/0s from DB. The locos sport a variety of liveries, ranging from standard GBRf blue and orange to heritage colours, including several in customer advertising liveries. Carrying traditional GBRf blue and orange No. 66778* Darius Cheskin *is seen passing Doncaster.* CJM

GBRf

66784	(66081)	PG	GBOG	GBN	GBR	GBR	*Keighley & Worth Valley Railway 50th Anniversary 1968-2018*
66785	(66132)	PG	GBOG	GBN	GBR	GBR	
66786	(66141)	PG	GBOG	GBN	GBR	GBR	
66787	(66184)	PG	GBOG	GBN	GBR	GBR	
66788	(66238)	PG	GBOG	GBN	GBR	GBR	
66789	(66250)	PG	GBOG	SPL	GBR	GBR	*British Rail 1948-1997*
66790	(T66713 From Sweden) *To be modified for UK operation by GBRF in 2019*						
66791	(T66714 From Denmark) *To be modified for UK operation by GBRF in 2019*						
66792	(CD66403 From Norway) *To be modified for UK operation by GBRF in 2019*						
66793	(CD66404 From Norway) *To be modified for UK operation by GBRF in 2019*						

Class 73/1, 73/2

Vehicle Length: 53ft 8in (16.35m)
Height: 12ft 5½in (3.79m)
Width: 8ft 8in (2.64m)

Power: 750V dc third rail or English Electric 6K
Horsepower: electric - 1,600hp (1,193kW)
Horsepower: diesel - 600hp (447kW)
Electrical Equipment: English Electric

Number		Depot	Pool	Livery	Owner	Operator	Name/notes
73101(S)		SE	GBED	PUL	GBR	-	
73107		SE	GBED	GBN	GBR	GBR	*Tracy*
73109		SE	GBED	GBN	GBR	GBR	
73110		SE	GBED	-	GBR	-	
73119		SE	GBED	GBN	GBR	GBR	
73128		SE	GBED	GBN	GBR	GBR	
73136		SE	GBED	GBU	GBR	GBR	*Mhairi*
73139(S)		SE	GBED	NSE	GBR	-	
73141		SE	GBED	GBU	GBR	GBR	*Charlotte*
73201	(73142)	SE	GBED	BLU	GBR	GBR	*Broadlands*
73212	(73102)	SE	GBED	GBU	GBR	GBR	*Fiona*
73213	(73112)	SE	GBED	GBU	GBR	GBR	*Rhodalyn*

Class 73/9

Vehicle Length: 53ft 8in (16.35m)
Height: 12ft 5½in (3.79m)
Width: 8ft 8in (2.64m)
ETH Index 66 or 96 for sleeper locos

Power: 750V dc third rail or MTU 8V 4000 R43L
Horsepower: electric - 1,600hp (1,193kW)
Horsepower: diesel - 1,600hp (1,193kW)
Electrical Equipment: English Electric

73961	(73209/120)	SE/TG	GBNR	GBB	GBR	GBR	*Alison*
73962	(73204/125)	SE/TG	GBNR	GBB	GBR	GBR	*Dick Mabbutt*
73963	(73206/123)	SE/TG	GBNR	GBB	GBR	GBR	*Janice*
73964	(73205/124)	SE/TG	GBNR	GBB	GBR	GBR	*Jeanette*
73965	(73208/121)	SE/TG	GBNR	GBB	GBR	GBR	
73966	(73005)	EC	GBCS	SCS	GBR	SCS	
73967	(73006)	EC	GBCS	SCS	GBR	SCS	
73968	(73117)	EC	GBCS	SCS	GBR	SCS	
73969	(73105)	EC	GBCS	SCS	GBR	SCS	
73970	(73103)	EC	GBCS	SCS	GBR	SCS	
73971	(73207/122)	EC	GBCS	SCS	GBR	SCS	

Left: *Two fleets of Class 73 electro-diesel locos are operated by GBRf. These former BR Southern Region dual power (diesel/electric) locos have found a new lease of life in recent years. GBRf operates a batch of traditional Class 73/1s and 73/2s powered by the original EE6K prime mover. In addition, 11 locos numbered in the 739xx series have been re-engineered by Brush and now house an MTU prime mover. Of this batch the first five retain dual power equipment, while the remaining six have had their electrical traction system isolated and are deployed in Scotland on Caledonian Sleeper services. No. 73961 leading a Network Rail test train is seen passing Honor Oak Park* **CJM**

Class 92

				Vehicle Length: 70ft 1in (21.34m)	Power Collection: 25kV ac overhead / 750V dc third rail

Vehicle Length: 70ft 1in (21.34m) *Power Collection: 25kV ac overhead / 750V dc third rail*
Height: 13ft 0in (3.95m) *Horsepower: ac - 6,700hp (5,000kW) / dc - 5,360hp (4,000kW)*
Width: 8ft 8in (2.66m) *Electrical Equipment: Brush*

Number	Depot	Pool	Livery	Owner	Operator	Name
92006	WN	GBET	SCS	GBR	GBR	
92010	WN	GBST	SCS	GBR	GBR	
92014	WN	GBSL	SCS	GBR	SCS	
92018	WN	GBST	SCS	GBR	SCS	
92020	WN	GBSL	GBN	GBR	GBR	
92021(S)	Brush	GBSD	EU2	GBR	-	Purcell
92023	CQ	GBSL	SCS	GBR	SCS	
92028	WN	GBET	GBN	GBR	SCS	
92032	CQ	GBST	GBN	GBR	GBR	I Mech E Railway Division
92033	WN	GBSL	SCS	GBR	SCS	
92038	WN	GBST	SCS	GBR	SCS	
92040(S)	Brush	GBSD	EU2	GBR	-	Goethe
92043	CQ	GBST	GBN	GBR	GBR	
92044	CQ	GBST	SCS	GBR	GBR	Couperin
92045(S)	Brush	GBSD	EU2	GBR	-	Chaucer
92046(S)	Brush	GBSD	EU2	GBR	-	Sweelinck

Above and Left: *GBRf has a fleet of 18 high-output Class 92s on its books, used for general freight traffic, as well as a dedicated batch deployed on the main line section of the Caledonian Sleeper service. The sleeper locos are in the process of being fitted with drop-head Dellner couplings for attachment to new Mk5 sleeper stock. No. 92014, painted in Caledonian Sleeper livery is seen powering a freight on the West Coast Main Line. The inset image left shows detail of the drop-head coupling.* **Andrew Royle / CJM**

Class Di 8

Vehicle Length: 57ft 1in (17.38m) *Engine: Caterpillar 3516 DITA*
Height: 13ft 3in (4.01m) *Horsepower: 2,100hp (1,566kW)*
Width: 9ft 8in (2.95m) *Electrical Equipment: Siemens*

GBRf purchased 12 former Cargo-Net, Norway, Class Di 8 locos for use within the SSI Lackenby Steelworks in Redcar. The 2,100hp (1,566kW) locos were built in 1996-97 by Mak in Kiel, Germany, as an order for 20 locos. In the UK the fleet is classified by the UIC as 308. With closure of the complex these locos have now been transferred to Scunthorpe to replace Class 20 operations.

8.701	8.704	8.712	8.718
8.702	8.708	8.716	8.719
8.703	8.711	8.717	8.720

Industrial 0-6-0DH

DH50-1 Works No. TH278V - 0-6-0DH 50-ton design, built 1978, fitted with a Cummins engine
DH50-2 Works No. TH246V - 0-6-0DH 50-ton design, built 1973

The above two industrial locos are operated by GBRf at the Celsa steel plant in Cardiff.

Freightliner

Address: ✉ 3rd Floor, 90 Whitfield Street, London. W1T 4EZ
✍ pressoffice@freightliner.co.uk
℘ 0207 200 3900
ⓘ www.freightliner.com

Chief Executive: Gary Long
Managing Director: Adam Cunliffe
Depots: Crewe Basford Hall (CB), Ipswich* (IP),
Leeds Midland Road (LD), Southampton Maritime (SZ)
* Stabling point
Parent Company: Genesee & Wyoming Inc. Managing Director: Gary Long

Class 08/0

Vehicle Length: 29ft 3in (8.91m)
Height: 12ft 8⅝in (3.87m)
Width: 8ft 6in (2.59m)
Engine: English Electric 6K
Horsepower: 400hp (298kW)
Electrical Equipment: English Electric

Number	Depot	Pool	Livery	Owner	Operator	Number	Depot	Pool	Livery	Owner	Operator
08530	SZ	DFLS	FLR	PTR	FLR	08624	FEL	DFLS	FLP	PTR	FLR
08531	FEL	DFLS	FLP	PTR	FLR	08691	bu	DFLS	FLR	FLR	FLR
08575	BU	DHLT	FLR	PTR	-	08785	LH	DFLS	FLR	PTR	FLR
08585	SZ	DFLS	FLP	PTR	FLR	08873	LH	DFLS	FLR	PTR	FLR
						08891	BU	DFLS	FLR	PTR	-

Names applied

08585	*Vicky*	08691	*Terri*	08624	*Rambo Paul Ramsey*

Class 47/4

Vehicle Length: 63ft 6in (19.35m)
Height: 12ft 10⅜in (3.91m)
Width: 9ft 2in (2.79m)
Electric Train Heat fitted
Engine: Sulzer 12LDA28C
Horsepower: 2,580hp (1,922kW)
Electrical Equipment: Brush

Number	Depot	Pool	Livery	Owner	Operator	Name
47830 (47649) D1645	BH	DFLH	GRN	FLR	FLR	*Beeching's Legacy*

Left: *Just one Class 47 is still officially operated by Freightliner, the loco restored to 1960s BR green livery with its original pre-TOPS No. D1645 is frequently used for road learning purposes operating from Crewe Basford Hall. Now named* Beeching's Legacy, *the loco is seen passing Longport.*
Cliff Beeton

Class 66/4

Vehicle Length: 70ft 0½in (21.34m)
Height: 12ft 10in (3.91m)
Width: 8ft 8¼in (2.65m)
Engine: EMD 12N-710G3B-EC
Horsepower: 3,300hp (2,462kW)
Electrical Equipment: EMD

Number	Depot	Pool	Livery	Owner	Operator	Name
66411	*Exported, working in Poland for Freightliner Poland as 66013FPL*					
66412	*Exported, working in Poland for Freightliner Poland as 66015FPL*					
66413	LD	DFIN	GYF	CBR	FLR	*Lest we Forget*
66414	LD	DFIN	FLP	HAL	FLT	

66415	LD	DFIN	DRC	HAL	FLT
66416	LD	DFIN	FLP	HAL	FLT
66417	*Exported, working in Poland for Freightliner Poland as 66014FPL*				
66418	LD	DFIN	FLP	HAL	FLT
66419	LD	DFIN	DRC	HAL	FLT
66420	LD	DFIN	FLP	HAL	FLT

Patriot - In Memory of Fallen Railway Employees (for 66418)

Class 66/5

Vehicle Length: 70ft 0½in (21.34m)
Height: 12ft 10in (3.91m)
Width: 8ft 8¼in (2.65m)

Engine: EMD 12N-710G3B-EC
Horsepower: 3,300hp (2,462kW)
Electrical Equipment: EMD

Number	Depot	Pool	Livery	Owner	Operator	Name
66501	LD	DFIM	FLR	PTR	FLR	*Japan 2001*
66502	LD	DFIM	FLR	PTR	FLR	*Basford Hall Centenary 2001*
66503	LD	DFIM	FLR	PTR	FLR	*The Railway Magazine*
66504	LD	DFIM	FLP	PTR	FLR	
66505	LD	DFIM	FLR	PTR	FLR	
66506	LD	DFIM	FLR	EVL	FLR	*Crewe Regeneration*
66507	LD	DFIM	FLR	EVL	FLR	
66508	LD	DFIM	FLR	EVL	FLR	
66509	LD	DFIM	FLR	EVL	FLR	
66510	LD	DFIM	FLR	EVL	FLR	
66511	LD	DFIM	FLR	EVL	FLR	
66512	LD	DFIM	FLR	EVL	FLR	
66513	LD	DFIM	FLR	EVL	FLR	
66514	LD	DFIM	FLR	EVL	FLR	
66515	LD	DFIM	FLR	EVL	FLR	
66516	LD	DFIM	FLR	EVL	FLR	
66517	LD	DFIM	FLR	EVL	FLR	
66518	LD	DFIM	FLR	EVL	FLR	
66519	LD	DFIM	FLR	EVL	FLR	
66520	LD	DFIM	FLR	EVL	FLR	
66522	LD	DFHG	FLR	EVL	FLR	
66523	LD	DFIM	FLR	EVL	FLR	
66524	LD	DFIM	FLR	EVL	FLR	
66525	LD	DFIM	FLR	EVL	FLR	
66526	LD	DFIM	FLR	PTR	FLR	*Driver Steve Dunn (George)*
66527	*Exported, working in Poland for Freightliner Poland*					
66528	LD	DFIM	FLP	PTR	FLR	*Madge Elliot MBE Borders Railway Opening 2015*
66529	LD	DFIM	FLR	PTR	FLR	
66530	*Exported, working in Poland for Freightliner Poland*					
66531	LD	DFIM	FLR	PTR	FLR	
66532	LD	DFIM	FLR	PTR	FLR	*P&O Nedlloyd Atlas*
66533	LD	DFIM	FLR	PTR	FLR	*Hanjin Express / Senator Express*
66534	LD	DFIM	FLR	PTR	FLR	*OOCL Express*
66535	*Exported, working in Poland for Freightliner Poland*					
66536	LD	DFIM	FLR	PTR	FLR	
66537	LD	DFIM	FLR	PTR	FLR	
66538	LD	DFIM	FLR	EVL	FLR	
66539	LD	DFIM	FLR	EVL	FLR	
66540	LD	DFIM	FLR	EVL	FLR	*Ruby*
66541	LD	DFIM	FLR	EVL	FLR	
66542	LD	DFIM	FLR	EVL	FLR	
66543	LD	DFIM	FLR	EVL	FLR	
66544	LD	DFIM	FLR	PTR	FLR	
66545	LD	DFIM	FLR	PTR	FLR	
66546	LD	DFIM	FLR	PTR	FLR	
66547	LD	DFIM	FLR	PTR	FLR	
66548	LD	DFIM	FLR	PTR	FLR	
66549	LD	DFIM	FLR	PTR	FLR	
66550	LD	DFIM	FLR	PTR	FLR	
66551	LD	DFIM	FLR	PTR	FLR	
66552	LD	DFIM	FLR	PTR	FLR	*Maltby Raider*

Freightliner

66553	LD	DFIM	FLR	PTR	FLR	
66554	LD	DFIM	FLR	EVL	FLR	
66555	LD	DFIM	FLR	EVL	FLR	
66556	LD	DFIM	FLR	EVL	FLR	
66557	LD	DFIM	FLR	EVL	FLR	
66558	LD	DFIM	FLR	EVL	FLR	
66559	LD	DFIM	FLR	EVL	FLR	
66560	LD	DFIM	FLR	EVL	FLR	
66561	LD	DFIM	FLR	EVL	FLR	
66562	LD	DFIM	FLR	EVL	FLR	
66563	LD	DFIM	FLR	EVL	FLR	
66564	LD	DFIM	FLR	EVL	FLR	
66565	LD	DFIM	FLR	EVL	FLR	
66566	LD	DFIM	FLR	EVL	FLR	
66567	LD	DFIM	FLR	EVL	FLR	
66568	LD	DFIM	FLR	EVL	FLR	
66569	LD	DFIM	FLR	EVL	FLR	
66570	LD	DFIM	FLR	EVL	FLR	
66571	LD	DFIM	FLR	EVL	FLR	
66572	LD	DFIM	FLR	EVL	FLR	
66582	*Exported, working in Poland for Freightliner Poland as 66009FPL*					
66583	*Exported, working in Poland for Freightliner Poland as 66010FPL*					
66584	*Exported, working in Poland for Freightliner Poland as 66011FPL*					
66585	LD	DFIN		HAL	FLR	
66586	*Exported, working in Poland for Freightliner Poland as 66008FPL*					
66587	LD	DFIN	FLR	HAL	FLR	
66588	LD	DFIN	FLR	HAL	FLR	
66589	LD	DFIN	FLR	HAL	FLR	
66590	LD	DFIN	FLR	HAL	FLR	
66591	LD	DFIN	FLR	MAG	FLR	
66592	LD	DFIN	FLR	MAG	FLR	*Johnson Stevens Agencies*
66593	LD	DFIN	FLR	MAG	FLR	*3MG Mersey Multimodal Gateway*
66594	LD	DFIN	FLR	MAG	FLR	*NYK Spirit of Kyoto*
66595	*Exported, working in Poland for Freightliner Poland as 66595FPL*					
66596	LD	DFIN	FLR	BEA	FLR	
66597	LD	DFIN	FLR	BEA	FLR	*Viridor*
66598	LD	DFIN	FLR	BEA	FLR	
66599	LD	DFIN	FLR	BEA	FLR	

Below: *The core diesel traction fleet operated by Freightliner, now owned by Genesee & Wyoming Inc, are EMD Class 66s, of which 81 Class 66/4s and 66/5s were in traffic at the start of 2019. Locos mainly carry Freightliner green, but a start has been made at applying the new Genesee & Wyoming colours. No. 66594* NYK Spirit of Kyoto *is illustrated passing Swindon* **CJM**

Class 66/6

Number	Depot	Pool	Livery	Owner	Operator	Name
66601	LD	DFHH	FLR	PTR	FLR	*The Hope Valley*
66602	LD	DFHH	FLR	PTR	FLR	
66603	LD	DFHH	FLR	PTR	FLR	
66604	LD	DFHH	FLR	PTR	FLR	
66605	LD	DFHH	FLR	PTR	FLR	
66606	LD	DFHH	FLR	PTR	FLR	
66607	LD	DFHH	FLR	PTR	FLR	
66608	*Exported, working in Poland for Freightliner Poland as 66603FPL*					
66609	*Exported, working in Poland for Freightliner Poland as 66605FPL*					
66610	LD	DFHH	FLR	PTR	FLR	
66611	*Exported, working in Poland for Freightliner Poland as 66604FPL*					
66612	*Exported, working in Poland for Freightliner Poland as 66606FPL*					
66613	LD	DFHH	FLR	PTR	FLR	
66614	LD	DFHH	FLR	PTR	FLR	*1916 Poppy 2016*
66615	LD	DFHH	FLR	PTR	FLR	
66616	LD	DFHH	FLR	PTR	FLR	
66617	LD	DFHH	FLR	PTR	FLR	
66618	LD	DFHH	FLR	PTR	FLR	*Railways Illustrated Annual Photographic Awards - Alan Barnes*
66619	LD	DFHH	FLR	PTR	FLR	*Derek W. Johnson MBE*
66620	LD	DFHH	FLR	PTR	FLR	
66621	LD	DFHH	FLR	PTR	FLR	
66622	LD	DFHH	FLR	PTR	FLR	
66623	LD	DFHH	AIN	EVL	FLR	*Bill Bolsover*
66624	*Exported, working in Poland for Freightliner Poland as 66602FPL*					
66625	*Exported, working in Poland for Freightliner Poland as 66601FPL*					

Below: *A batch of 25 increased tractive-effort Class 66/6s were built, but today only 19 remain operating in the UK, the balance having been transferred to the Freightliner operation in Poland. These locos tend to be deployed on the heavier Freightliner Heavy Haul freight duties. No. 66605 is shown passing Doncaster at the head of a cement train.* **CJM**

Class 66/9

Number	Depot	Pool	Livery	Owner	Operator	Name
66951	LD	DFIN	FLR	EVL	FLR	
66952	LD	DFIN	FLR	EVL	FLR	
66953	LD	DFIN	FLR	BEA	FLR	
66954	*Exported, working in Poland for Freightliner Poland as 66954FPL*					
66955	LD	DFIN	FLR	BEA	FLR	
66956	LD	DFIN	FLR	BEA	FLR	
66957	LD	DFIN	FLR	BEA	FLR	*Stephenson Locomotive Society 1909-2009*

Freightliner

Class 70 - PH37ACmi

Vehicle Length: 71ft 2½in (21.71m)				Engine: GE V16-cylinder PowerHaul 616			
Height: 12ft 10in (3.91m)				Horsepower: 3,700hp (2,750kW)			
Width: 8ft 8in (2.64m)				Electrical Equipment: General Electric			

Number	Depot	Pool	Livery	Owner	Operator	Name
70001	LD	DHLT	FLP	MAG	FLR	PowerHaul
70002	LD	DFGI	FLP	MAG	FLR	
70003(S)	LD	DFGI	FLP	MAG	-	
70004(S)	LD	DFGI	FLP	MAG	-	The Coal Industry Society
70005(S)	LD	DFGI	FLP	MAG	-	
70006(S)	LD	DFGI	FLP	MAG	-	
70007	LD	DFGI	FLP	MAG	FLR	
70008	LD	DFGI	FLP	MAG	FLR	
70009(S)	LD	DFGI	FLP	MAG	-	
70010	LD	DFGI	FLP	MAG	FLR	
70011	LD	DHLT	FLP	MAG	FLR	
70013(S)	LD	DFGI	FLP	MAG	-	
70014(S)	LD	DFGI	FLP	MAG	-	
70015	LD	DFGI	FLP	MAG	FLR	
70016(S)	LD	DFGI	FLP	MAG	-	
70017(S)	LD	DFGI	FLP	MAG	-	
70018(S)	LD	DFGI	FLP	MAG	-	
70019(S)	LD	DFGI	FLP	MAG	-	
70020	LD	DFGI	FLP	MAG	FLR	

Above: *Freightliner opted to introduce a fleet of General Electric Class 70s in 2009 to improve performance, originally 20 locos were ordered, but one was lost on delivery. The fleet of 19 have had a checkered career and in early 2019 a number were stored with wheelset and bogie issues. No. 70005 is illustrated powering a liner train at Swindon.* **CJM**

Class 86/6

Vehicle Length: 58ft 6in (17.83m)				Power Collection: 25kV ac overhead		
Height: 13ft 0⅝in (3.97m)				Horsepower: 5,900hp (4,400kW)		
Width: 8ft 8¼in (2.64m)				Electrical Equipment: GEC		

Number		Depot	Pool	Livery	Owner	Operator
86604	(86404)	CB	DFNC	FLR	FLR	FLR
86605	(86405)	CB	DFNC	FLR	FLR	FLR
86607	(86407)	CB	DFNC	FLR	FLR	FLR
86608	(86501/86408)	CB	DFNC	FLR	FLR	FLR
86609	(86409)	CB	DFNC	FLR	FLR	FLR

86610	(86410)	CB	DFNC	FLR	FLR	FLR
86612	(86412)	CB	DFNC	FLR	FLR	FLR
86613	(86413)	CB	DFNC	FLR	FLR	FLR
86614	(86414)	CB	DFNC	FLR	FLR	FLR
86622	(86422)	CB	DFNC	FLP	FLR	FLR
86627	(86427)	CB	DFNC	FLR	FLR	FLR
86628	(86428)	CB	DFNC	FLR	FLR	FLR
86632	(86432)	CB	DFNC	FLR	FLR	FLR
86637	(86437)	CB	DFNC	FLP	FLR	FLR
86638	(86438)	CB	DFNC	FLR	FLR	FLR
86639	(86439)	CB	DFNC	FLR	FLR	FLR

Below: *To power Freightliner intermodal services under the wires, mainly from the West Coast route to Ipswich en route to Felixstowe, Freightliner operates a fleet of 16 Class 86/6s based at Crewe. The locos are in a mix of standard Freightliner and 'PowerHaul' livery. Standard liveried Nos. 86604 and 86605 pass Cheddington with a service bound for Crewe.* **Andrew Royle**

Freight Operating Companies - Freightliner

Class 90

Vehicle Length: 61ft 6in (18.74m)   Power Collection: 25kV ac overhead
Height: 13ft 0¼in (3.96m)   Horsepower: 7,860hp (5,860kW)
Width: 9ft 0in (2.74m)   Electrical Equipment: GEC

Number	Depot	Pool	Livery	Owner	Operator
90016	CB	DFLC	FLR	FLR	FLR
90041	CB	DFLC	FLR	FLR	FLR
90042	CB	DFLC	FLP	FLR	FLR
90043	CB	DFLC	FLP	FLR	FLR
90044	CB	DFLC	FLY	FLR	FLR
90045	CB	DFLC	FLP	FLR	FLR
90046	CB	DFLC	FLR	FLR	FLR
90047	CB	DFLC	FLY	FLR	FLR
90048	CB	DFLC	FLY	FLR	FLR
90049	CB	DFLC	FLP	FLR	FLR

Right: *The above illustrated Class 86s share electric work with a fleet of 10 Class 90s, also based at Crewe and display a mix of standard and 'PowerHaul' liveries. It is possible that Freightliner might take on extra Class 90s, when the fleet currently operated by Greater Anglia are replaced by new stock. Class 90 No. 90043 and Class 86 No. 86637 both in 'Power Haul' colours are seen at Crewe.* **Cliff Beeton**

Mendip Rail

Address: ✉ Torr Works, East Cranmore, Shepton Mallet, Somerset, BA4 5SQ
📧 info@mendip-rail.co.uk ☎ 01749 880672 ⓘ www.mendip-rail.co.uk

Managing Director: Alan Taylor
Depots: Merehead (MD), Whatley (WH)
Parent Company: Aggregate Industries and Hanson

Class 08

Vehicle Length: 29ft 3in (8.91m)
Height: 12ft 8⅜in (3.87m)
Width: 8ft 6in (2.59m)
Engine: English Electric 6K
Horsepower: 400hp (298kW)
Electrical Equipment: English Electric

Number	Depot	Pool	Livery	Owner	Operator
08643	MD	MBDL	GRN	FOS	MRL
08650	MD	MBDL	MRL	FOS	MRL
08652	MD	MBDL	HAN	HAN	MRL
08947	WH	MBDL	BLU	FOS	MRL

Class 59/0 & 59/1

Vehicle Length: 70ft 0½in (21.34m)
Height: 12ft 10in (3.91m)
Width: 8ft 8¼in (2.65m)
Engine: EMD 16-645 E3C
Horsepower: 3,000hp (2,462kW)
Electrical Equipment: EMD

Number	Depot	Pool	Livery	Owner	Operator	Name
59001	MD	XYPO	AGI	FLR	MRL	*Yeoman Endeavour*
59002	MD	XYPO	AGI	FLR	MRL	*Alan J Day*
59004	MD	XYPO	AGI	FLR	MRL	*Paul A Hammond*
59005	MD	XYPO	AGI	FLR	MRL	*Kenneth J Painter*
59101	MD	XYPA	HAN	FLR	MRL	*Village of Whatley*
59102	MD	XYPA	HAN	FLR	MRL	*Village of Chantry*
59103	MD	XYPA	HAN	FLR	MRL	*Village of Mells*
59104	MD	XYPA	HAN	FLR	MRL	*Village of Great Elm*

Below: *Mendip Rail, based at Merehead and Whatley Quarries, operate a fleet of eight Class 59/0s and 59/1s originally operated by Foster Yeoman and ARC. The locos operate heavy aggregate trains from the Mendip Quarries to various locations including Acton yard in London. Hanson-liveried No. 59102 is seen passing West Ealing.* **Antony Christie**

■ As part of a new contract, Freightliner will take over the operation of Mendip Rail aggregate duties from November 2019. This will include the transfer of ownership of the eight Class 59s to Freightliner by the end of the 2018-2019 financial year.

SW1001 'Switcher'

Vehicle Length: 40ft 6in (12.34m)
Height: 14ft 3in (4.34m)
Width: 10ft 0in (3.04m)
Engine: GM 8-645E
Horsepower: 1,000hp (746kW)
Electrical Equipment: EMD

Number	Depot	Pool	Livery	Owner	Operator	Name
44	MD	-	FOS	FOS	MRL	*Western Yeoman II*
120	WH	-	HAN	HAN	MRL	*Kenneth John Witcombe*

abc Rail Guide - Main Line Systems 2019

Eurotunnel - Freight / Passenger

Eurotunnel (GetLink)

Address (UK): ✉ The Channel Tunnel Group Ltd, Ashford Road, Folkestone, CT18 8XX
🕯 info@eurotunnel.com ✆ 01303 282222 ⓘ www.eurotunnel.com

Chairman & CEO: Jacques Gounon **Depot:** Coquelles, France (CO)

Shuttle

All locomotives are allocated to the Eurotunnel Maintenance Facility in Coquelles, France, but can be stabled and receive light repair at the Cheriton terminal in the UK.

Class 9/0

Vehicle Length: 72ft 2in (22m) Power Collection: 25kV ac overhead
Height: 13ft 9in (4.20m) Horsepower: 7,720hp (5,760kW)
Width: 9ft 9in (3.01m) Electrical Equipment: Brush

Original loco order, many now rebuilt and upgraded to Class 9/8.

9005	Jessye Norman	9018	Wilhelmena Fernandez	9033	Montserrat Caballé
9007	Dame Joan Sutherland	9022	Dame Janet Baker	9036	Alain Fondary
9011	José Van Dam	9024	Gotthard 1882	9037	Gabriel Bacquier
9013	Maria Callas	9026	Furkatunnel 1982		
9015	Lötschberg 1913	9029	Thomas Allen		

Class 9/7

Vehicle Length: 72ft 2in (22m) Power Collection: 25kV ac overhead
Height: 13ft 9in (4.20m) Horsepower: 9,387hp (7,000kW)
Width: 9ft 9in (3.01m) Electrical Equipment: Brush

9701	9704	9707	9713 (9103)	9716 (9106)	9719 (9109)	9722 (9112)
9702	9705	9711 (9101)	9714 (9104)	9717 (9107)	9720 (9110)	9723 (9113)
9703	9706	9712 (9102)	9715 (9105)	9718 (9108)	9721 (9111)	

Class 9/8

Rebuilt from Class 9/0 locos; 800 added to original running number on conversion.

Vehicle Length: 72ft 2in (22m) Power Collection: 25kV ac overhead
Height: 13ft 9in (4.20m) Horsepower: 9,387hp (7,000kW)
Width: 9ft 9in (3.01m) Electrical Equipment: Brush

9801	Lesley Garrett	9814	Lucia Popp	9827	Barbara Hendricks
9802	Stuart Burrows	9816	Willard White	9828	Dame Kiri Te Kanawa
9803	Benjamin Luxon	9817(S)	José Carreras	9831	
9804		9819	Maria Ewing	9832	Renata Tebaldi
9806	Régine Crespin	9820	Nicolai Ghiaurov	9834	Mirella Freni
9808	Elisabeth Soderstrom	9821	Teresa Berganza	9835	Nicolai Gedda
9809	François Pollet	9823	Dame Elisabeth Legge-	9838	Hildegard Behrens
9810	Jean-Philippe Courtis		Schwarzkopf	9840	
9812	Luciano Pavarotti	9825			

Right: Channel Tunnel passenger and freight 'Shuttle' operations are in the hands of a fleet of GetLink Class 9 tri-bo locos, based at Coquelles (Calais) in France. Trains are operated in the 'top and tail' mode. Of the original Class 9/0 locos built, a number have been upgraded with extra power and modified equipment and reclassified as 9/8. Modified No. 9804 is shown. **Howard Lewsey**

MaK DE1004

Vehicle Length: 54ft 2in (16.50m) Diesel Engine: MTU 12V396tc
Horsepower: 1,260hp (939.5kW) Electrical Equipment: BBC

0001 (21901)	0003 (21903)	0005 (21905)	0007 (21907) [6457]	0009 (21909) [6451]
0002 (21902)	0004 (21904)	0006 (21906) [6456]	0008 (21908) [6450]	0010 (21910) [6457]

Hunslet/Schöma

Diesel Engine: Deutz Mechanical Equipment: Hunslet
Horsepower: 200hp (270kW)

0031	0032	0033	0034	0035	0036	0037	0038	0039	0040	0041	0042

■ In November 2018 Eurotunnel ordered a new fleet of 19 two-axle 40 ton locos from Socofer. They will be battery powered with a diesel engine used to charge the batteries if needed, usually charging will be from an external supply. Delivery is expected in 2021.

Rail Operations Group (ROG)

Address: ✉ ROG, Wyvern House, Railway Terrace, Derby. DE1 2RU
✆ enquiries@railopsgroup.co.uk ⓘ www.railopsgroup.co.uk
Managing Director: K Watts

Rail Operations Group is a Train Operating Company authorised by the ORR. It was formed in 2015 to facilitate the movement of rolling stock between depots and workshops for overhaul, repair and refurbishment. The company also provides drivers and staff on a spot hire basis and is authorised to instruct drivers.

Class 37

Vehicle Length: 61ft 6in (18.74m)
Height: 13ft 0¼in (3.96m)
Width: 8ft 11⅝in (2.73m)
Engine: Ruston
Horsepower: 1,750hp (1,304kW)
Electrical Equipment: English Electric

Number	Depot	Pool	Livery	Owner	Name	Operator/Notes
37608 (37512)	LR	GROG	EPX	EPX	Andromeda	ROG drophead Dellner fitted
37611 (37690)	LR	GROG	EPX	EPX	Pegasus	ROG
37800 (37143)	LR	GROG	EPX	EPX		ROG drophead Dellner fitted
37884 (37183)	LR	GROG	EPX	EPX	Cepheus	ROG drophead Tightlock fitted

Left: *Rail Operations Group, who provide a service of moving rolling stock between depots and works operate a fleet of Europhoenix-owned Class 37s, displaying Europhoenix livery with Rail Operations Group branding. Some locos have drop-head auto couplers to aid attachment to multiple unit stock. Class 37/6 No. 37611 Pegasus is shown. This was an original European Passenger Services loco.* **CJM**

Class 47

Vehicle Length: 63ft 6in (19.35m)
Height: 12ft 10⅜in (3.91m)
Width: 9ft 2in (2.79m)
Electric Train Heat fitted
Engine: Sulzer 12LDA28C
Horsepower: 2,580hp (1,922kW)
Electrical Equipment: Brush

Number	Depot	Pool	Livery	Owner	Operator	
47769 (47491)	CP	RTLO	VIR	ROG	ROG	
47812 D1916 (47657)	LR	SROG	ROG	ROG	ROG	
47813 (47129/658)	LR	GROG	ROZ	ROG	ROG	
47815 D1748 (47660)	LR	GROG	ROG	ROG	ROG	*Lost Boys 68-88*
47843 (47623)	LR	SROG	ROG	ROG	ROG	
47847 (47577)	LR	SROG	ROG	ROG	ROG	
47848 (47632)	LR	GROG	ROG	ROG	ROG	

Left: *Rail Operations Group also operate a fleet of Class 47s, these are allocated to Leicester depot and are in the process of upgrade for main line service. Locos are painted in mid-blue with either a stylised ROG logo or Rail Operations Group branding. No. 47815 Lost Boys 68-88 is seen at Crewe.* **CJM**

▇ ROG also operate under lease two Class 57s from DRS, Nos. 57305 and 57312.

Class 93

Railway Operations Group have a fleet of 10 tri-mode diesel, electric and Lithium Titanate Oxide (LTO) battery, locos, to be classified as 93 from Stadler Rail, funded by Beacon Rail on order. The fleet is a development of the Class 88 and uses a Caterpillar engine. The electric output will be 5438hp, weight will be 97 tonnes, with a top speed of 110mph. No. 93001 Mercury should be delivered in late 2020.

Locomotive Services Ltd, Crewe

Address: Crewe Diesel Depot, Crewe
✉ alex@iconsofsteam.com ⓘ www.iconsofsteam.com
Facilities: Steam and diesel locomotive owner/operator
Managing Director: Jeremy Hosking

Class 08

Vehicle Length: 29ft 3in (8.91m)
Height: 12ft 8⅜in (3.87m)
Width: 8ft 6in (2.59m)

Engine: English Electric 6K
Horsepower: 400hp (298kW)
Electrical Equipment: English Electric

Number	Depot	Pool	Livery	Owner	Operator
08631	CL	LSLO		LSC	LSC
08737	CL	LSLO		LSC	LSC
08780	CL	LSLO		LSC	LSC

Class 37

Vehicle Length: 61ft 6in (18.74m)
Height: 13ft 0¼in (3.96m)
Width: 8ft 11⅝in (2.73m)

Engine: English Electric 12CSVT
Horsepower: 1,750hp (1,304kW)
Electrical Equipment: English Electric

Number	Depot	Pool	Livery	Owner	Operator
37667 (37151)	CL	LSLO	BLU	LSC	LSC

Class 47

Vehicle Length: 63ft 6in (19.35m)
Height: 12ft 10⅜in (3.91m)
Width: 9ft 2in (2.79m)
Electric Train Heat fitted

Engine: Sulzer 12LDA28C
Horsepower: 2,580hp (1,922kW)
Electrical Equipment: Brush

Number			Depot	Pool	Livery	Owner	Operator	Name/Note
47501	D1944		CL	LSLO	GRN	LSC	LSC	*Craftsman*
47712		(47505)	CL	-	SCR	LSC	LSC	(18 month loan from 12/18)
47790(S)		(47272/673)	CL	LSLO	NBP	LSC	-	
47805	D1935	(47257/650)	CL	LSLO	GRN	LSC	LSC	*Roger Hosking MA 1925-2013*
47810		(47247/655)	CL	LSLO	GRN	LSC	LSC	*Crewe Diesel Depot*
47811(S)		(47128/656)	CL	-	GRN	-	-	
47816(S)		(47066/661)	CL	-	GRN	-	-	(For spares)
47841(S)		(47134/622)	CL	LSLS	BLU	LSC	-	
47853	D1733	(47141/614)	CL	LSLO	BLU	LSC	LSC	

Loco Services Ltd also own 'Deltic' Class 55s Nos. 55016 and 55022 and operate Class 40 No. 40013

Right: *Locomotives Services Ltd, based at the former Crewe Diesel Depot is a train operator in its own right and a provider of locos and stock. The business has announced it intends to increase its rolling stock by adding Class 90s and HST stock to its Portfolio. Immaculately restored Class 47 No. D1935 (47805) Roger Hosking MA 1926-2013 is seen carrying 1960s BR green livery with a small yellow warning end.*
Antony Christie

Coaching Stock

Mk1				Height: 12ft 9½in (3.89m)		
Vehicle Length: 64ft 6in (19.65m)				Width: 9ft 3in (2.81m)		

Number	Type	Depot	Livery	Operator
1211 (3305)	AJ1F/RFB	CL	CAR	LSC
1659 (16509)	AJ41/RBR	CL	CAR	LSC
3229	AD1E/FO	CL	CAR	LSC
3231	AD1E/FO	CL	CAR	LSC
3312	AD1E/FO	CL	CAR	LSC
3344	AD1F/FO	CL	CAR	LSC

Mk2				Height: 12ft 9½in (3.89m)		
Vehicle Length: 66ft 0in (20.11m)				Width: 9ft 3in (2.81m)		

Number	Type	Depot	Livery	Operator
3438	AD1F/FO	CL	CAR	LSC
5912	AD2F/TSO	CL	CAR	LSC
5991	AD2F/TSO	CL	CCM	LSC
17080	AO3/BCK	CL	CAR	LSC
35511 (17130)	AB5C	CL	BRN	LSC
99993	Mk1 TSO	CL	CAR	LSC

Network Rail

Address: 1 Melton St, London NW1 2DN

ⓘ www.networkrail.co.uk

✆ Helpline: 08457 114141, Switchboard: 020 7557 8000

Chief Executive: Andrew Haines OBE

Depots: Heaton (HT), Barrow Hill (BH), Derby (DF), Rugby (RU), Eastleigh (ZG)

Class 08

Vehicle Length: 29ft 3in (8.91m)		Engine: English Electric 6K		
Height: 12ft 8⅝in (3.87m)		Horsepower: 400hp (298kW)		
Width: 8ft 6in (2.59m)		Electrical Equipment: English Electric		

Number	Depot	Pool	Livery	Owner	Operator
08417	DF	QADD	NRL	NRL	NRL

08956§ DF QADD GRN NRL NRL
§ At Bombardier, Old Dalby test centre

Class 43

Vehicle Length: 58ft 5in (18.80m)		Engine: MTU 16V4000 R31R		
Height: 12ft 10in (3.90m)		Horsepower: 2,250hp (1,680kW)		
Width: 8ft 11in (2.73m)		Electrical Equipment: Brush		

Number	Depot	Pool	Livery	Owner	Operator	Name
43013	EC	QCAR	NRL	PTR	NRL	*Mark Carne CBE*
43014	EC	QCAR	NRL	PTR	NRL	*The Railway Observer*
43062	EC	QCAR	NRL	PTR	NRL	*John Armitt*

Left: *Network Rail operate a fleet of three Class 43 HST power cars to operate the Mk3 formed New Measurement Train (NMT) which traverses the main lines of the NR system on a timetabled basis. The power cars are finished in NR yellow. The NMT formation is seen led by power car No. 43014.* **Antony Christie**

Class 73/1 & 73/9

Vehicle Length: 53ft 8in (16.35m)		Power: 750V dc third rail or English Electric 6K		
Height: 12ft 5⅞in (3.79m)		Horsepower: electric - 1,600hp (1,193kW)		
Width: 8ft 8in (2.64m)		diesel - 600hp (447kW)		
		Electrical Equipment: English Electric		
Class 73/9 rebuilt with 2 x Cummins CSK19 755hp engines and revised electric equipment				

Number	Depot	Pool	Livery	Owner	Operator	Name
73138(S)	DF	QADD	NRL	NRL	-	
73951 (73104)	DF	QADD	NRL	NRL	NRL	*Malcolm Brinded*
73952 (73211)	DF	QADD	NRL	NRL	NRL	*Janice King*

Left: *Network Rail currently operate a pair of rebuilt Class 73/9 locos, rebuilt by RVEL and installed with two Cummins QSK 19 755hp power units. The loco bodies have been heavily rebuilt with revised cab ends and new bodyside grilles. Nos. 73951/952 are illustrated at East Midlands Parkway.* **Nathan Williamson**

Class 37 & 97/3

Vehicle Length: 61ft 6in (18.74m)
Height: 13ft 0¼in (3.96m)
Width: 8ft 11⅝in (2.73m)

Engine: English Electric 12CSVT
Horsepower: 1,750hp (1,304kW)
Electrical Equipment: English Electric

Number	Depot	Pool	Livery	Owner	Operator	Name
37198(S)	ZA	MBDL	NRL	NRL	-	Chief Engineer (spares doner)
97301 (37100)§	ZA	QETS	NRL	NRL	NRL	
97302 (37170)±	ZA	QETS	NRL	NRL	NRL	
97303 (37178)±	ZA	QETS	NRL	NRL	NRL	
97304 (37217)±	ZA	QETS	NRL	NRL	NRL	John Tiley

§ Fitted with Hitachi ERTMS, ± Fitted with Ansaldo ERTMS

Right: *To power infrastructure trains and perform testing with ERTMS cab-signalling, four Class 37s, modified to Class 97/3s are operated by Network Rail, based at Derby. the four are painted in NR yellow livery. No. 97302 is illustrated.* **Mark V. Pike**

Class 950

Vehicle Length: 64ft 9¾in (19.74m)
Height: 12ft 4½in (3.77m)
Width: 9ft 3⅛in (2.82m)

Engine: 1 x NT855R5 of 285hp per vehicle
Horsepower: 570hp (425kW)
Seats (total/car): 124S, 59S/65S

Number	Formation	Depot	Livery	Owner	Operator	Note
950001	999600+999601	ZA	NRL	NRL	NRL	Track assessment train (Class 150 outline)

Right: *Used for track assessment throughout the Network Rail system, Class 150/1 outline DMU No. 950001 is operated, based at the RTC Derby, but can be seen at virtually any point in the country. The front end sports various infra-red lights and recording systems, which change according to the tests being undertaken. The set sports yellow NR livery, off-set by pictogram bodyside branding. The set is seen on the Great Western route at Dawlish while performing an inspection from Derby to Plymouth.* **CJM**

Class 313/1

Vehicle Length: (Driving) 64ft 11½in (19.80m) Width: 9ft 3in (2.82m)
                (Inter) 65ft 4¼in (19.92m) Horsepower: 880hp (656kW)
Height: 11ft 9in (3.58m)

ERTMS development unit

Number	Formation DMSO+PTSO+BDMSO	Depot	Livery	Owner	Operator
313121(S)	62549+71233+61613	-	YEL	BEA	NRL (stored at Eastleigh)

Infrastructure Companies

Network Rail

Left: *Former Class 313/1 set No. 313121, owned by Beacon Rail, was used for extensive research, testing and development of ERTMS equipment in the North London area, especially over the Hertford Loop line. In 2018 the testing was complete and the set transferred to Eastleigh Works for store. The image shows the set passing Arundel on route from Hornsey to Eastleigh.* **John Vaughan**

Hauled Stock

Mk2	
Vehicle Length: 66ft 0in (20.11m)	Height: 12ft 9½in (3.89m) Width: 9ft 3in (2.81m)

Royal Train

Mk 3	
Vehicle Length: 75ft 0in (22.86m)	Height: 12ft 9in (3.88m) Width: 8ft 11in (2.71m)

Number	Type	Depot	Livery	Operator	Use
2903 (11001)	AT5G	ZN	ROY	NRL/DBC	HM The Queen's Saloon
2904 (12001)	AT5G	ZN	ROY	NRL/DBC	HRH The Duke of Edinburgh's Saloon
2915 (10735)	AT5G	ZN	ROY	NRL/DBC	Royal Household Sleeping Coach
2916 (40512)	AT5G	ZN	ROY	NRL/DBC	HRH The Prince of Wales's Dining Coach
2917 (40514)	AT5G	ZN	ROY	NRL/DBC	Kitchen Car and Royal Household Dining Coach
2918 (40515)	AT5G	ZN	ROY	NRL/DBC	Royal Household Coach
2919 (40518)	AT5G	ZN	ROY	NRL/DBC	Royal Household Coach
2920 (17109)	AT5B	ZN	ROY	NRL/DBC	Generator Coach and Household Sleeping Coach
2921 (17107)	AT5B	ZN	ROY	NRL/DBC	Brake, Coffin Carrier and Household Accommodation
2922	AT5G	ZN	ROY	NRL/DBC	HRH The Prince of Wales's Sleeping Coach
2923	AT5G	ZN	ROY	NRL/DBC	HRH The Prince of Wales's Saloon Coach

Below: *The eleven Mk2 and Mk3 Royal Train vehicles are managed by Network Rail on behalf of the Government and operated by DB. The Royal Claret-liveried coaches are currently kept at Wolverton when not in service. The train is usually powered by the two Royal Train dedicated Class 67s Nos. 67005 and 67006. The pair are seen leading the Royal train through Powderham, Devon in summer 2018.* **CJM**

Hauled Stock

Number	Type	Depot	Livery	Operator	Use
1256 (3296)	AJIF/RFO	ZA	NRL	NRL	Special vehicle - PLPR3
5981	AC2F/TSO	ZA	NRL	NRL	Special vehicle
6260 (92116)	AX51/GEN	ZA	NRL	NRL/LUL	Generator (owned by DBS)
6261 (92988)	AX51/GEN	ZA	NRL	NRL	Generator (owned by DBS)
6262 (92928)	AX51/GEN	ZA	NRL	NRL	Generator (owned by DBS)
6263 (92961)	AX51/GEN	ZA	NRL	NRL	Generator (owned by DBS)
6264 (92923)	AX51/GEN	ZA	NRL	NRL	Generator (owned by DBS)
9481	AE2D/BSO	ZA	NRL	NRL	Radio Survey coach
9516	AE2D/BSO	ZA	NRL	NRL	Ultrasonic test car support
9523	AE2D/BSO	ZA	NRL	NRL	Ultrasonic test car support
9701 (9528)	AF2F/DBSO	ZA	NRL	NRL	Remote driving car (Mentor train)
9702 (9510)	AF2F/DBSO	ZA	NRL	NRL	Remote driving car
9703 (9517)	AF2F/DBSO	ZA	NRL	NRL	Remote driving car
9708 (9530)	AF2F/DBSO	ZA	NRL	NRL	Remote driving car (Structure Gauging)
9713 (9535)	AF2F/DBSO	ZA	NRL	NRL	Remote driving car
9714 (9536)	AF2F/DBSO	ZA	NRL	NRL	Remote driving car
62287	MBS/CIG	ZA	NRL	NRL	Ultrasonic test car
62384	MBS/CIG	ZA	NRL	NRL	Structure Gauging test car (SGT2)
72612 (6156)	Mk2f/TSO	ZA	NRL	NRL	Brake force runner
72616 (6007)	Mk2f/TSO	ZA	NRL	NRL	Brake force runner
72630 (6094)	Mk2f/TSO	ZA	NRL	NRL	Brake force runner
72631 (6096)	Mk2f/TSO	ZA	NRL	NRL	Brake force runner
72639 (6070)	Mk2f/TSO	ZA	NRL	NRL	PLPR Track Inspection
82111	MK3/DVT	CS	NRL	NRL	Driving Van Trailer
82115	MK3/DVT	ZA	VIR	NRL	Driving Van Trailer
82124	MK3/DVT	ZA	NRL	NRL	Driving Van Trailer
82129	MK3/DVT	CS	NRL	NRL	Driving Van Trailer
82145	MK3/DVT	CS	NRL	NRL	Driving Van Trailer
92114 (81443)	Mk1/BG	ZA	NRL	NRL	Special vehicle
92939 (92039)	Mk1/BG	ZA	INT	NRL	Special vehicle
99666 (3250)	Mk2e/FO	ZA	NRL	NRL	Ultrasonic Test Train
971001 (94150)	Mk1/NKA	SP	NRL	NRL	Tool Van
971002 (94190)	Mk1/NKA	SP	NRL	NRL	Tool Van
971003 (94191)	Mk1/NKA	BS	NRL	NRL	Tool Van
971004 (94168)	Mk1/NKA	SP	NRL	NRL	Tool Van
975025 (60755)	6B Buffet	ZA	GRN	NRL	Control Inspection Saloon *Caroline*
975081 (35313)	Mk1/BSK	ZA	NRL	NRL	Structure Gauging Train
975087 (9)	MK1/BSK	SP	NRL	NRL	Recovery train support coach
975091 (34615)	Mk1/BSK	ZA	NRL	NRL	Overhead line test coach *Mentor*
975464 (35171)	Mk1/BSK	SP	NRL	NRL	Snowblower coach *Ptarmigan*
975477 (35108)	MK1/BSK	SP	NRL	NRL	Recovery train support coach
975486 (34100)	Mk1/BSK	SP	NRL	NRL	Snowblower coach *Polar Bear*
975814 (41000)	HST/TF	EC	NRL	NRL	NMT Conference coach
975984 (40000)	HST/TRUB	EC	NRL	NRL	NMT Lecture coach
977868 (5846)	Mk2e/TSO	ZA	NRL	NRL	Radio Survey coach

Right: *Network Rail operate a number of former loco-hauled ex passenger and van stock as part of their test train fleet. Most vehicles are painted in NR yellow and based at Derby. In addition a number of ex coaching stock vehicles are used as recovery train vehicles in case of derailment. Former bogie van No. 92928 is now Network Rail No. 6262 and has been converted as a generator to provide power for test train operations.*
Antony Christie

Network Rail

977869 (5858)	Mk2e/TSO	ZA	NRL	NRL	Radio Survey coach (stored)
977969 (14112)	Mk2/BFK	ZA	NRL	NRL	Staff coach (former Royal Saloon 2906)
977974 (5854)	Mk2e/TSO	ZA	NRL	NRL	Track Inspection coach
977983 (72503)	Mk2f/FO	ZA	NRL	NRL	Overhead Line Inspection EMV (ex FO 3407)
977984 (40501)	HST/TRFK	EC	NRL	NRL	NMT Staff coach
977985 (72715)	Mk2f/TSO	ZA	NRL	NRL	Structure Gauging Train (SGT2) (ex TSO 6019)
977986 (3189)	Mk2d/FO	ZA	NRL	NRL	Track Recording coach
977993 (44053)	HST/TGS	EC	NRL	NRL	NMT Overhead Line Test coach
977994 (44087)	HST/TGS	EC	NRL	NRL	NMT Recording coach
977995 (40719)	HST/TRFM	EC	NRL	NRL	NMT Generator coach
977997 (72613)	Mk2f/TSO	ZA	NRL	NRL	Radio Survey Test Vehicle (originally TSO 6126)
999550	Mk2	ZA	NRL	NRL	Track Recording coach (purpose-built) TRC
999602 (623xx)	Mk1/CIG	ZA	NRL	NRL	Ultrasonic Test coach - UTU3
999605 (62482)	Mk1/REP	ZA	NRL	NRL	Ultrasonic Test coach - UTU2
999606 (62356)	Mk1/CIG	ZA	NRL	NRL	Ultrasonic Test coach - UTU4

Left Upper: *Former Gatwick Express Class 488 vehicle 72639 (the original 6070) is now used by NR as one of several Plain Line Pattern Recognition (PLPR) vehicles, which carry out a detailed inspection of track heads and joints by using an underslung camera. The vehicle is seen at Tonbridge.* **Antony Christie**

Left Middle: *Originally Mk2 TSO No. 6096, this Converted from Mk2e TSO No. 5854, Track Inspection Coach no. 977974 now operates with one of the PLPR sets and is captured in the train formation at Tonbridge.* **Antony Christie**

Below: *Originally a Hastings 6B buffet car and then the Southern Region General managers saloon, 975025 is currently a Network Rail inspection saloon based at Derby. It has a saloon at either end with a central kitchen and toilet, it is blue star fitted and can control blue star fitted locos from its own cab position. The vehicle is seen at Lostwithiel powered by a DRS Class 37.* **Antony Christie**

Snowploughs
Independent Drift Ploughs – ZZA

Number	Allocation				
ADB965203	Motherwell	ADB965219	Carlisle	ADB965235(S)	York Works
ADB965206	York	ADB965223(S)	York Works	ADB965236	Tonbridge
ADB965208	Carlisle	ADB965224	Carlisle KM	ADB965237	March
ADB965209	Taunton	ADB965230	Carlisle KM	ADB965240	Inverness
ADB965210	Tonbridge	ADB965231	Taunton	ADB965241	York
ADB965211	March	ADB965232	Peterborough	ADB965242	Motherwell
ADB965217	Motherwell	ADB965233	Peterborough	ADB965243	Slateford
		ADB965234	Carlisle		

Above: *Network Rail maintains a number of snowploughs located at strategic locations around the country, with usually two ploughs at each location facing different directions. Classified ZZA No. ADB965241, is seen at York. When required locos are hired, usually from DRS.* **Antony Christie**

Beilhack Patrol Ploughs (ex-Class 40 bogies) – ZZA

Number	Allocation				
ADB965576	Doncaster	ADB965578	Carlisle	ADB965581	Wigan
ADB965577	Doncaster	ADB965579	Carlisle	ADB966098	Doncaster
		ADB965580	Wigan	ADB966099	Doncaster

Left: Network Rail also operate four pairs of Beilhack ploughs which are conversions from original Class 40 bogies. Two pairs are based at Doncaster for East Coast Main Line cover with one set each at Wigan and Carlisle for West Coast use. No. ADB965576, one of the Doncaster allocation is shown. **Antony Christie**

Beilhack Snow Blowers – ZWA

Number	Allocation		
ADB968500	Rutherglen	ADB968501	Rutherglen

Track Machines (On-Track Plant)

Plasser & Theurer DTS-62-N – Dynamic Track Stabiliser – ZWA

DR72211	Balfour Beatty	DR72213	Balfour Beatty

Plasser & Theurer 09-16-CSM – Tamper/Liner – ZWA

DR73105(S)	Colas

Plasser & Theurer 09-3X – Tamper/Liner – ZWA

DR73109	SB Rail	DR73110	Peter White	SB Rail

Plasser & Theurer 09-3X-D-RT – Tamper/Liner ZWA

DR73111	Network Rail	DR73116	Network Rail
DR73113 Dai Evans	Network Rail	DR73117	Network Rail
DR73114 Ron Henderson	Network Rail	DR73118	Network Rail
DR73115	Network Rail		

Plasser & Theurer 09-3x – Duomatic Tamper/Liner – ZWA

DR73120 (99 70 9123-120-6)	Network Rail	DR73122 (99 70 9123 122-2)	Network Rail
DR73121 (99 70 9123 121-4)	Network Rail		

Above: *Plasser & Theurer 09-03x Duomatic Tamper and Liner No. DR73120 is seen passing Swindon. Coupled at the far end is Plasser & Theurer USP 5000 Ballast Regulator No. DR77909.* **CJM**

Plasser & Theurer 07-32 – Duomatic Tamper/Liner – ZWA

DR73434(S)	Balfour Beatty

Plasser & Theurer 08-16/90 – Tamper/Liner – ZWA

DR73502	Trackwork

Plasser & Theurer 08-32U RT – Plain Line Tamper – ZWA

DR73803 Alexander Graham Bell	SBRail

Plasser & Theurer 08-16U RT – Plain Line Tamper – ZWA

DR73804 James Watt	SBRail

Plasser & Theurer 08-16(32)U RT – Plain Line Tamper – ZWA

DR73805	Colas	DR73806 Karine	Colas

Plasser & Theurer 08-4x4/4S - RT – Switch/Crossing Tamper – ZWA

DR73904	*Thomas Telford*	SB Rail		DR73908		Colas
DR73905		Colas		DR73909	*Saturn*	Colas
DR73906	*Panther*	Colas		DR73910	*Jupiter*	Colas
DR73907		Colas				

Right: *Displaying Colas livery, Plasser & Theurer 08-4x4/4S-RT Switch and Crossing tamping machineNo. DR73907 is seen passing through Swindon.* **CJM**

Plasser & Theurer 08-16/4x4C - RT – Switch/Crossing Tamper – ZWA

DR73911	*Puma*	Colas		DR73913	Colas
DR73912	*Lynx*	Colas			

Right: *A shorter version of the vehicle shown above is Plasser & Theurer 08-16/4x4C RT Switch and Crossing Tamper. This machine, No. DR73912 is again operated by Colas and carries the name* Lynx. **CJM**

Plasser & Theurer 08-4x4S - RT – Switch/Crossing Tamper – ZWA

DR73914	*Robert McAlpine*	SB Rail

Plasser & Theurer 08-16/4x4C - RT – Switch/Crossing Tamper – ZWA

DR73915	*William Arrol*	SB Rail		DR73916	*First Engineering*	SBRail

Plasser & Theurer 08-4x4S - RT – Switch/Crossing Tamper – ZWA

DR73917		Balfour Beatty	DR73918	Balfour Beatty

Plasser & Theurer 08-16/4x4 C100 - RT – Tamper – ZWA

DR73919	Colas

Plasser & Theurer 08-16/4x4C80 - RT – Tamper – ZWA

DR73920	Colas	DR73921		Colas	DR73922 *John Snowdon*	Colas

Plasser & Theurer 08-4x4S - RT – Switch/Crossing Tamper – ZWA

DR73923	*Mercury*	Colas

Plasser & Theurer 08-16/4x4 C100 - RT – Tamper – ZWA

DR73924		Colas		DR73927	Balfour Beatty
DR73925	*Europa*	Colas		DR73928	Balfour Beatty
DR73926	*Stephen Keith Blanchard*	Balfour Beatty			

Plasser & Theurer 08-4x4S - RT – Switch/Crossing Tamper – ZWA

DR73929	Colas		DR73930	Colas

Network Rail

Plasser & Theurer 08-16/4x4C100 - RT – Tamper – ZWA

DR73931	Colas

Plasser & Theurer 08-4x4/4S - RT – Switch/Crossing Tamper

DR73932	SB Rail

Plasser & Theurer 08-16/4x4C100 - RT – Tamper – ZWA

DR73933	SB Rail	DR73934	SB Rail

Plasser & Theurer 08-4x4/4S - RT – Switch/Crossing Tamper – ZWA

DR73935	Colas	DR73936	Colas

Plasser & Theurer 08-16/4x4 C100 - RT – Tamper – ZWA

DR73937	Balfour Beatty	DR73939 *Pat Best*	Balfour Beatty
DR73938	Balfour Beatty		

Plasser & Theurer 08-4x4/4S - RT – Switch/Crossing Tamper – ZWA

DR73940	SB Rail	DR73941	SB Rail	DR73942	Colas

Plasser & Theurer 08-16/4x4C100 - RT – Tamper – ZWA

DR73943	Balfour Beatty	DR73944	Balfour Beatty	DR73945	Balfour Beatty

Plasser & Theurer Euromat 08-4x4/4S – ZWA

DR73946	VolkerRail

Plasser & Theurer 08-4x4/4S - RT – Switch/Crossing Tamper ZWA

DR73947	Colas	DR73948	Colas

Plasser & Theurer 08-16/90 275 – Switch/Crossing Tamper – ZWA

DR75201 (S)	Balfour Beatty	DR75202 (S)	Balfour Beatty

Plasser & Theurer 08-16/90 SP-T – Switch/Crossing Tamper – ZWA

DR75203	MLP Maintenance

Plasser & Theurer 08-275ZW – Switch/Crossing Tamper – ZWY

DR75204	Trackwork

Matisa B45 Tamper – ZWA

DR75301	VolkerRail	DR75302	VolkerRail	DR75303	VolkerRail
			Gary Wright		

Left: *Painted in Volker Rail white, black and blue livery, Matisa-built B45 Tamping machine No. DR75302 named* Gary Wright *is recorded at Doncaster.* **CJM**

Matisa B41UE Tamper – ZWA

DR75401	VolkerRail	DR75406	Colas	DR75409	Balfour Beatty
DR75402	VolkerRail	*Eric Machell*		DR75410	Balfour Beatty
DR75403(S)	VolkerRail	DR75407	Colas	DR75411	Balfour Beatty
DR75404	VolkerRail	*Gerry Taylor*			
DR75405	VolkerRail	DR75408	Balfour Beatty		

Matisa B66UC Tamper – ZWA

DR75501	Balfour Beatty	DR75502	Balfour Beatty

Plasser & Theurer RM95RT – Ballast Cleaner – ZWA

DR76323(S)	Network Rail	DR76324(S)	Network Rail

Plasser & Theurer RM900RT Ballast Cleaner – ZWA / ZWQ

DR76501	(HOBC-1)	Network Rail	DR76503	(HOBC-3)	Network Rail
DR76502	(HOBC-2)	Network Rail	DR76504	(HOBC-4)	Network Rail

Plasser & Theurer VM80 NR – ZWA

DR76701	(HOBC-3)	Network Rail	DR76710(S)	(HOTRT-2)	Network Rail
DR76702(S)	(HOBC-2)	Network Rail	DR76711(S)	(HOTRT-1)	Network Rail
DR76703(S)	(HOBC-1)	Network Rail			

Matisa D75 Undercutter – ZWA

DR76750	(HRTRT-2)	Network Rail	DR76751	(HRTRT-1)	Network Rail

Plasser & Theurer 09-16 CM NR – ZWA

DR76801	(HOBC-3)	Network Rail	DR76802	(HOBC-4)	Network Rail

Plasser & Theurer AFM 2000 RT – Rail Finishing Machine – ZWA

DR77001	SB Rail	Anthony Lou Phillips	DR77002	SB Rail

Right: *Operated by SB Rail, No. DR77001, named* Anthony Lou Phillips, *is a massive three section Rail Finishing Machine, built by Plasser and Theurer and classified as AFM 2000RT.* **Antony Christie**

Plasser & Theurer USP 6000 – Ballast Regulator – ZWA

DR77010	Network Rail

Plasser & Theurer USP 5000C – Ballast Regulator – ZWA

DR77315(S)	Balfour Beatty	DR77322(S)	Balfour Beatty	DR77336 (S)	Balfour Beatty
DR77316(S)	Balfour Beatty	DR77327	Colas		

Matisa R24S – Ballast Regulator – ZWA

DR77801	VolkerRail	DR77802	VolkerRail

Plasser & Theurer USP 5000RT – Ballast Regulator – ZWA

DR77901	Colas	DR77906	Network Rail
DR77903	Network Rail	DR77907	Network Rail
DR77904	Network Rail	DR77908 (* Previously DR77902)	SB Rail
DR77905	Network Rail	DR77909	Network Rail

Right: *Operated by Network Rail, Plasser & Theurer USP 5000RT Ballast Regulator No. DR77909 is seen passing Swindon.* **CJM**

Network Rail

Plasser & Theurer Self-Propelled Heavy Duty Twin Jib Crane – YJB

DR78213	VolkerRail	DR78218	Balfour Beatty	DR78223	Balfour Beatty
DR78215	SB Rail	DR78219	SB Rail	DR78224	Balfour Beatty
DR78216(S)	Balfour Beatty	DR78221(S)	Balfour Beatty		
DR78217	SB Rail	DR78222(S)	Balfour Beatty		

Cowans Sheldon Self-Propelled Heavy Duty Twin Jib Crane – YJB

DR78226	Colas	DR78231(S)	Network Rail	DR78235	Colas
DR78229(S)	Network Rail	DR78234(S)	Network Rail	DR78237	Network Rail

Donelli PD350 Single Line Track Relayer

DR78416	Balfour Beatty	DR78417	Balfour Beatty	DR78490	VolkerRail

Harsco Track Technologies NTC Power Wagon – YJA

DR78701	Balfour Beatty	DR78702	Balfour Beatty

Matisa P95 Track Renewal Train – YJA

DR78801	Network Rail	DR78811	Network Rail	DR78821	Network Rail	DR78831	Network Rail
DR78802	Network Rail	DR78812	Network Rail	DR78822	Network Rail	DR78832	Network Rail

Schweebau SPML15 – Rail Grinder – ZWA

DR79200 (S)	Loram

Speno RPS 32-2 – Rail Grinder – ZWA

DR79221	Speno	DR79223	Speno	DR79225	Speno
DR79222	Speno	DR79224	Speno	DR79226	Speno

Loram C21 – Rail Grinder – ZWA

Set 2101		Set 2102		Set 2103	
DR79231	Loram	DR79241	Loram	DR79251	Loram
DR79232	Loram	DR79242	Loram	DR79252	Loram
DR79233	Loram	DR79243	Loram	DR79253	Loram
DR79234	Loram	DR79244	Loram	DR79254	Loram
DR79235	Loram	DR79245	Loram	DR79255	Loram
DR79236	Loram	DR79246	Loram	DR79256	Loram
DR79237	Loram	DR79247 *Roger Smith*	Loram	DR79257 *Martin Elwood*	Loram

Left: *Network Rail operate three seven section Loram C21 Rail Grinding machines, which can re-profile and tidy up rail heads in just one pass at walking speed, frequently operating with adjacent lines open to traffic. Usually these machines are only seen working at night. In this view set No. 2103 formed of vehicles DR79251-DR79257 and carrying the name Martin Elwood is seen passing Dawlish during daylight working a transit move from Tavistock Junction to Swindon.*
CJM

Harsco Track Technologies RGH-20C Switch/Crossing Rail Grinder – ZWA

DR79261 + DR79271	Network Rail	DR79263 + DR79273	Network Rail
DR79262 + DR79272	Network Rail	DR79265 + DR79264+DR79274	Network Rail

DR79266 + DR79276   Network Rail   DR79267 + DR79277   Network Rail

Right: *Several Harsco Rail Technology RGH-20C Switch and Crossing Rail Grinding twin sets are in use. Owned by Network Rail, these sets are currently operated under contract by Balfour Beatty until 2022. DR79273 and DR79263 are seen passing Swindon.* **CJM**

Linsinger MG31UK – Rail Miller – ZWA

DR79101 **(99 70 9427 063-1)** For use on Elizabeth Line (CrossRail)

Right: *One of the latest machines to arrive in the UK is this Linsinger MG31 UK Rail Milling machine, which has been purchased to operate on the new Elizabeth line (CrossRail)* **Network Rail**

Pandrol Jackson – Stoneblower – YZA

DR80201	Harsco	DR80206	Network Rail	DR80210	Network Rail
DR80202	Harsco	DR80207	(in Sweden)	DR80211	Network Rail
DR80203	Harsco	DR80208	Network Rail	DR80212	Harsco
DR80205	Network Rail	DR80209	Network Rail		

Harsco Track Technologies – Stoneblower – YZA

| DR80213 | Network Rail | DR80215 | Network Rail | DR80217 | Network Rail |
| DR80214 | Network Rail | DR80216 | Network Rail | | |

Right: *Pandrol Jackson Stoneblower No. DR80302 is seen from its ballast container end at Exeter Riverside in summer 2018. This machine is currently operated by Harsco on behalf of Network Rail.* **Antony Christie**

Network Rail

Harsco Track Technologies – General Purpose Stoneblower – YZA

DR80301	Stephen Cornish	Network Rail	DR80303	Network Rail
DR80302		Network Rail		

Plasser & Theurer Heavy Duty Diesel Hydraulic Crane – YOB

DR81505	Balfour Beatty	DR81513	Balfour Beatty	DR81525	Balfour Beatty
DR81507	Balfour Beatty	DR81517	Balfour Beatty	DR81532	Balfour Beatty
DR81508	Balfour Beatty	DR81519	Balfour Beatty		
DR81511(S)	Balfour Beatty	DR81522(S)	Balfour Beatty		

Cowans Sheldon Heavy Duty Diesel Hydraulic Crane

DR81541	Corus	DR81545	Corus

Kirow KRC810UK 100 tonne Diesel Hydraulic Crane – ZOA

DR81601	Nigel Chester	VolkerRail	DR81602	Balfour Beatty

Kirow KRC1200UK 125 tonne Diesel Hydraulic Crane – ZOA

DR81611	Malcolm L Pearce	Balfour Beatty	DR81613	VolkerRail
DR81612		Colas		

Kirow KRC250UK Heavy Duty Diesel Hydraulic Crane – ZOA
Kirow KRC1200U Heavy Duty Crane - ZOA§

DR81621	VolkerRail		DR81625	SBRail
DR81622	VolkerRail		DR81626	SRRail
DR81623	SBRail		(99 70 9319 012-9)	
DR81624	SBRail		99 70 9319-013-7§	Network Rail

Plasser & Theurer Loading Station

DR88101	Network Rail

Starfer Single Line Spoil Handling System Train

DR92201	Network Rail	DR92204	Network Rail	DR92207	Network Rail	DR92210	Network Rail
DR92202	Network Rail	DR92205	Network Rail	DR92208	Network Rail	DR92211	Network Rail
DR92203	Network Rail	DR92206	Network Rail	DR92209	Network Rail	DR92212	Network Rail

Skako Ballast Distribution Train – YDA 'Octopus'

DR92213	Network Rail	DR92216	Network Rail	DR92219	Network Rail	DR92222	Network Rail
DR92214	Network Rail	DR92217	Network Rail	DR92220	Network Rail		
DR92215	Network Rail	DR92218	Network Rail	DR92221	Network Rail		

Plasser & Theurer NFS-D Ballast Distribution Train Hopper – YDA

DR92223	Network Rail	DR92228	Network Rail	DR92233	Network Rail	DR92238	Network Rail
DR92224	Network Rail	DR92229	Network Rail	DR92234	Network Rail	DR92239	Network Rail
DR92225	Network Rail	DR92230	Network Rail	DR92235	Network Rail	DR92240	Network Rail
DR92226	Network Rail	DR92231	Network Rail	DR92236	Network Rail		
DR92227	Network Rail	DR92232	Network Rail	DR92237	Network Rail		

Plasser & Theurer MFS-D Ballast Distribution Train Hopper – YDA

DR92241	Network Rail	DR92245	Network Rail	DR92249	Network Rail	DR92253	Network Rail
DR92242	Network Rail	DR92246	Network Rail	DR92250	Network Rail	DR92254	Network Rail
DR92243	Network Rail	DR92247	Network Rail	DR92251	Network Rail		
DR92244	Network Rail	DR92248	Network Rail	DR92252	Network Rail		

Plasser & Theurer MFS-SB Swivel Conveyer Wagon – YDA

DR92259	Network Rail	DR92260	Network Rail	DR92261	Network Rail	DR92262	Network Rail

Plasser & Theurer MFS-PW Single Line Handling Train Power Wagon – YOA

DR92263(S)	Network Rail

Plasser & Theurer NB-PW Ballast Distribution Train Power Wagon – YOA

DR92264(S)	Network Rail

Plasser & Theurer MFS-D Ballast Distribution Train Hopper – YDA

DR92265 Network Rail	DR92269 Network Rail	DR92273 Network Rail	DR92277 Network Rail
DR92266 Network Rail	DR92270 Network Rail	DR92274 Network Rail	DR92278 Network Rail
DR92267 Network Rail	DR92271 Network Rail	DR92275 Network Rail	DR92279 Network Rail
DR92268 Network Rail	DR92272 Network Rail	DR92276 Network Rail	

Plasser & Theurer MFS-SB Swivel Conveyer Wagon – YDA

DR92280 Network Rail	DR92281 Network Rail

Plasser & Theurer MFS-A Materials Handling Train Interface Wagon – YDA

DR92282 Network Rail	DR92283 Network Rail

Plasser & Theurer PW-RT Materials Handling Train Power Wagon – YOA

DR92285 Network Rail

Plasser & Theurer NPW-RT Materials Handling Train Power Wagon – YOA

DR92286 Network Rail

Plasser & Theurer MFS-SB Swivel Conveyer Wagon – YDA

DR92287 Network Rail	DR92289 Network Rail	DR92291 Network Rail	DR92293 Network Rail
DR92288 Network Rail	DR92290 Network Rail	DR92292 Network Rail	DR92294 Network Rail

Plasser & Theurer MFS-D Ballast Distribution Train Hopper – YDA

DR92295 Network Rail	DR92304 Network Rail	DR92313 Network Rail	DR92322 Network Rail
DR92296 Network Rail	DR92305 Network Rail	DR92314 Network Rail	DR92323 Network Rail
DR92297 Network Rail	DR92306 Network Rail	DR92315 Network Rail	DR92324 Network Rail
DR92298 Network Rail	DR92307 Network Rail	DR92316 Network Rail	DR92325 Network Rail
DR92299 Network Rail	DR92308 Network Rail	DR92317 Network Rail	DR92326 Network Rail
DR92300 Network Rail	DR92309 Network Rail	DR92318 Network Rail	DR92327 Network Rail
DR92301 Network Rail	DR92310 Network Rail	DR92319 Network Rail	DR92328 Network Rail
DR92302 Network Rail	DR92311 Network Rail	DR92320 Network Rail	DR92329 Network Rail
DR92303 Network Rail	DR92312 Network Rail	DR92321 Network Rail	DR92330 Network Rail

Plasser & Theurer PW-RT Materials Handling Train Power Wagon – YOA

DR92331 Network Rail

Plasser & Theurer NPW-RT Materials Handling Train Power Wagon – YOA

DR92332 Network Rail

Plasser & Theurer MFS-SB Swivel Conveyer Wagon – YDA

DR92333 Network Rail	DR92335 Network Rail	DR92337 Network Rail	DR92339 Network Rail
DR92334 Network Rail	DR92336 Network Rail	DR92338 Network Rail	DR92340 Network Rail

Plasser & Theurer MFS-D Ballast Distribution Train Hopper – YDA

DR92341 Network Rail	DR92352 Network Rail	DR92363 Network Rail	DR92374 Network Rail
DR92342 Network Rail	DR92353 Network Rail	DR92364 Network Rail	DR92375 Network Rail
DR92343 Network Rail	DR92354 Network Rail	DR92365 Network Rail	DR92376 Network Rail
DR92344 Network Rail	DR92355 Network Rail	DR92366 Network Rail	DR92377 Colas
DR92345 Network Rail	DR92356 Network Rail	DR92367 Network Rail	
DR92346 Network Rail	DR92357 Network Rail	DR92368 Network Rail	
DR92347 Network Rail	DR92358 Network Rail	DR92369 Network Rail	
DR92348 Network Rail	DR92359 Network Rail	DR92370 Network Rail	
DR92349 Network Rail	DR92360 Network Rail	DR92371 Network Rail	
DR92350 Network Rail	DR92361 Network Rail	DR92372 Network Rail	
DR92351 Network Rail	DR92362 Network Rail	DR92373 Network Rail	

Plasser & Theurer MFS-A Materials Handling Train Interface Wagon – YDA

DR92400 Colas

Plasser & Theurer PW-RT Materials Handling Train Power Wagon

DR92431 Network Rail

Plasser & Theurer NPW-RT Materials Handling Train Power Wagon

DR92432	Network Rail

Plasser & Theurer MFS-SB Swivel Conveyer Wagon

DR92433	Network Rail	DR92435	Network Rail	DR92437	Network Rail	DR92439	Network Rail
DR92434	Network Rail	DR92436	Network Rail	DR92438	Network Rail	DR92440	Network Rail

Plasser & Theurer MFS-D Ballast Distribution Train Hopper – YDA

DR92441	Network Rail	DR92451	Network Rail	DR92461	Network Rail	DR92471	Network Rail
DR92442	Network Rail	DR92452	Network Rail	DR92462	Network Rail	DR92472	Network Rail
DR92443	Network Rail	DR92453	Network Rail	DR92463	Network Rail	DR92473	Network Rail
DR92444	Network Rail	DR92454	Network Rail	DR92464	Network Rail	DR92474	Network Rail
DR92445	Network Rail	DR92455	Network Rail	DR92465	Network Rail	DR92475	Network Rail
DR92446	Network Rail	DR92456	Network Rail	DR92466	Network Rail	DR92476	Network Rail
DR92447	Network Rail	DR92457	Network Rail	DR92467	Network Rail		
DR92448	Network Rail	DR92458	Network Rail	DR92468	Network Rail		
DR92449	Network Rail	DR92459	Network Rail	DR92469	Network Rail		
DR92450	Network Rail	DR92460	Network Rail	DR92470	Network Rail		

Plasser & Theurer PW/NPW Materials Handling Train Power Wagon

DR92477	(99 70 9310- 477-3)	Network Rail
DR92478	(99 70 9310- 478-1)	Network Rail

Sleeper Delivery Train – Generator Wagon – YFA

DR92501	(Stored)	DR92502	(Stored)	DR92503	(Stored)

Twin Jib Rail Recovery Train 'Slinger' – YFA

DR92504	(Stored)	DR92507	(Stored)	DR92510	(Stored)
DR92505	(Stored)	DR92508	(Stored)	DR92511	(Stored)
DR92506	(Stored)	DR92509	(Stored)	DR92512	(Stored)

Single Jib Rail Recovery Train 'Slinger' – YFA

DR92513	(Stored)	DR92515	(Stored)	DR92517	(Stored)
DR92514	(Stored)	DR92516	(Stored)	DR92518	(Stored)

Sleeper Delivery Train – Twin Crane 'Slinger' – YFA

DR92519	(Stored)

Sleeper Delivery Train – Generator Wagon 'Slinger' – YFA

DR92520	(Stored)	DR92522	(Stored)	DR92524	(Stored)
DR92521	(Stored)	DR92523	(Stored)	DR92525	(Stored)

Sleeper Delivery Train – Twin Crane 'Slinger' – YFA

DR92526	(Stored)	DR92528	(Stored)	DR92530	(Stored)	DR92532	(Stored)
DR92527	(Stored)	DR92529	(Stored)	DR92531	(Stored)		

Sleeper Delivery Train – Generator Wagon 'Slinger' – YFA

DR92533	(Stored)	DR92534	(Stored)

Sleeper Delivery Train – Twin Crane 'Slinger' – YFA

DR92535	(Stored)	DR92538	(Stored)	DR92541	(Stored)	DR92544	(Stored)
DR92536	(Stored)	DR92539	(Stored)	DR92542	(Stored)	DR92545	(Stored)
DR92537	(Stored)	DR92540	(Stored)	DR92543	(Stored)	DR92546	(Stored)

Sleeper Delivery Train – Generator Wagon 'Slinger' – YFA

DR92547	(Stored)	DR92548	(Stored)	DR92549	(Stored)

Sleeper Delivery Train – Twin Crane 'Slinger' – YFA

DR92550	(Stored)	DR92551	(Stored)	DR92552	(Stored)	DR92553	(Stored)

Infrastructure Companies - Network Rail

DR92554	(Stored)	DR92559	(Stored)	DR92564	(Stored)	DR92569	(Stored)
DR92555	(Stored)	DR92560	(Stored)	DR92565	(Stored)	DR92570	(Stored)
DR92556	(Stored)	DR92561	(Stored)	DR92566	(Stored)	DR92571	(Stored)
DR92557	(Stored)	DR92562	(Stored)	DR92567	(Stored)		
DR92558	(Stored)	DR92563	(Stored)	DR92568	(Stored)		

W H Davis Sleeper Wagons – YXA

DR92601	Network Rail	DR92618	Network Rail	DR92635	Network Rail	DR92652	Network Rail
DR92602	Network Rail	DR92619	Network Rail	DR92636	Network Rail	DR92653	Network Rail
DR92603	Network Rail	DR92620	Network Rail	DR92637	Network Rail	DR92654	Network Rail
DR92604	Network Rail	DR92621	Network Rail	DR92638	Network Rail	DR92655	Network Rail
DR92605	Network Rail	DR92622	Network Rail	DR92639	Network Rail	DR92656	Network Rail
DR92606	Network Rail	DR92623	Network Rail	DR92640	Network Rail	DR92657	Network Rail
DR92607	Network Rail	DR92624	Network Rail	DR92641	Network Rail	DR92658	Network Rail
DR92608	Network Rail	DR92625	Network Rail	DR92642	Network Rail	DR92659	Network Rail
DR92609	Network Rail	DR92626	Network Rail	DR92643	Network Rail	DR92660	Network Rail
DR92610	Network Rail	DR92627	Network Rail	DR92644	Network Rail	DR92661	Network Rail
DR92611	Network Rail	DR92628	Network Rail	DR92645	Network Rail	DR92662	Network Rail
DR92612	Network Rail	DR92629	Network Rail	DR92646	Network Rail	DR92663	Network Rail
DR92613	Network Rail	DR92630	Network Rail	DR92647	Network Rail	DR92664	Network Rail
DR92614	Network Rail	DR92631	Network Rail	DR92648	Network Rail	DR92665	Network Rail
DR92615	Network Rail	DR92632	Network Rail	DR92649	Network Rail		
DR92616	Network Rail	DR92633	Network Rail	DR92650	Network Rail		
DR92617	Network Rail	DR92634	Network Rail	DR92651	Network Rail		

International Sleeper Wagons – YXA

3170 4629 001 9	629001	Network Rail	3170 4629 020 9	629020	Network Rail	3170 4629 039 9	629039	Network Rail
3170 4629 002 7	629002	Network Rail	3170 4629 021 7	629021	Network Rail	3170 4629 040 7	629040	Network Rail
3170 4629 003 5	629003	Network Rail	3170 4629 022 5	629022	Network Rail	3170 4629 041 5	629041	Network Rail
3170 4629 004 3	629004	Network Rail	3170 4629 023 3	629023	Network Rail	3170 4629 042 3	629042	Network Rail
3170 4629 005 0	629005	Network Rail	3170 4629 024 1	629024	Network Rail	3170 4629 043 1	629043	Network Rail
3170 4629 006 8	629006	Network Rail	3170 4629 025 8	629025	Network Rail	3170 4629 044 9	629044	Network Rail
3170 4629 007 6	629007	Network Rail	3170 4629 026 6	629026	Network Rail	3170 4629 045 6	629045	Network Rail
3170 4629 008 4	629008	Network Rail	3170 4629 027 4	629027	Network Rail	3170 4629 046 4	629046	Network Rail
3170 4629 009 2	629009	Network Rail	3170 4629 028 2	629028	Network Rail	3170 4629 047 2	629047	Network Rail
3170 4629 010 0	629010	Network Rail	3170 4629 029 0	629029	Network Rail	3170 4629 048 0	629048	Network Rail
3170 4629 011 8	629011	Network Rail	3170 4629 030 8	629030	Network Rail	3170 4629 049 8	629049	Network Rail
3170 4629 012 6	629012	Network Rail	3170 4629 031 6	629031	Network Rail	3170 4629 050 6	629050	Network Rail
3170 4629 013 4	629013	Network Rail	3170 4629 032 4	629032	Network Rail			
3170 4629 014 2	629014	Network Rail	3170 4629 033 2	629033	Network Rail			
3170 4629 015 9	629015	Network Rail	3170 4629 034 0	629034	Network Rail			
3170 4629 016 7	629016	Network Rail	3170 4629 035 7	629035	Network Rail			
3170 4629 017 5	629017	Network Rail	3170 4629 036 5	629036	Network Rail			
3170 4629 018 3	629018	Network Rail	3170 4629 037 3	629037	Network Rail			
3170 4629 019 1	629019	Network Rail	3170 4629 038 1	629038	Network Rail			

Sleeper Delivery Train – Manipulator, Clamp* – JZA

DR93325	Network Rail	DR93346	Network Rail	DR93465	Network Rail	DR93608*	Network Rail
DR93327	Network Rail	DR93383	Network Rail	DR93480	Network Rail	DR93609*	Network Rail
DR93334	Network Rail	DR93418	Network Rail	DR93601*	Network Rail		
DR93339	Network Rail	DR93463	Network Rail	DR93603*	Network Rail		

W H Davis Flat/Workshop/Barrier Wagons – YSA

DR92701	Network Rail	DR92703	Network Rail	DR92705	Network Rail
DR92702	Network Rail	DR92704	Network Rail	DR92706	Network Rail

Cowans Sheldon 75 tonne Diesel Hydraulic Recovery Crane – ZIA* ZIB¤

ARDC96710 (S) ¤	Network Rail (SP)	ARDC96714 (S) *	Network Rail (SP)
ARDC96713 (S) ¤	Network Rail (SP)	ARDC96715 ¤	Network Rail (BS)

Eiv de Brieve DU94BA – TRAMM – ZWA

DR97001	High Speed 1 (HS1)

Infrastructure Companies - Network Rail

Network Rail

Windhoff Overhead Line – MPV – YXA

DR97011	High Speed 1 (HS1)	DR97013	High Speed 1 (HS1)
DR97012	High Speed 1 (HS1)	DR97014	High Speed 1 (HS1)

Robel Self-Propelled 'Mobile Maintenance Train'

DR97501+DR97601+DR97801	Network Rail	DR97505+DR97605+DR97805	Network Rail
DR97502+DR97602+DR97802	Network Rail	DR97506+DR97606+DR97806	Network Rail
DR97503+DR97603+DR97803	Network Rail	DR97507+DR97607+DR97807	Network Rail
DR97504+DR97604+DR97804	Network Rail	DR97508+DR97608+DR97808	Network Rail

Left: *DR97504 is one of the Network Rail fleet of Mobile Maintenance Trains. Supplied by Robel, these allow track maintenance gangs to travel to site by rail and work in a protected environment. The rear vehicle, DR97804, has sides which extend outwards hydraulically, creating a safe covered working area. The intermediate vehicle, DR97604, houses materials and equipment. Kitchen and welfare facilities are in the front vehicle No. DR97504.*
Andrew Royle

Robel/Plasser Self-Propelled 'Mobile Maintenance Train'

DR97599+DR97510+DR97511+DR97512   For use on Elizabeth Line (CrossRail)

Left: *Another of the very new vehicles, introduced for maintenance of the yet to open Elizabeth Line (CrossRail) is Robel/Plasser Self Propelled Mobile Maintenance Train, a four section set with end cars DR97599 and DR97512.*
Network Rail

Windhoff Overhead Line – MPV – YXA

DR98001	Network Rail	DR98005	Network Rail	DR98009	Network Rail	DR98013	Network Rail
DR98002	Network Rail	DR98006	Network Rail	DR98010	Network Rail	DR98014	Network Rail
DR98003	Network Rail	DR98007	Network Rail	DR98011	Network Rail		
DR98004	Network Rail	DR98008	Network Rail	DR98012	Network Rail		

Left: *In conjunction with the electrification of the Great Western main line, Windhoff supplied Network Rail with a number of MPV based works trains. For the duration of GW electrification these vehicles have been housed in purpose built facilities near Swindon. Vehicle DR98007 is seen leading this formation at Swindon.*
Antony Christie

Names applied:
DR98003 *Anthony Wrighton*   DR98006 *Jason McDonnell 1970-2016*   DR98009 *Melvin Smith*
DR98010 *Benjamin Gautrey*   DR98012 *Terence Hand 1962-2016*   DR98013 *David Wood*
DR98014 *Wayne Imlach 1955-2015*

Plasser & Theurer General Purpose Machine (GP-TRAMM) – ZWA

DR98215	Balfour Beatty	DR98217	Balfour Beatty	DR98219	Balfour Beatty
DR98216	Balfour Beatty	DR98218	Balfour Beatty	DR98220	Balfour Beatty

Geismar General Purpose Machine (GP-TRAMM)

DR98303 BAR

Geismar VMT860 PL/UM – ZWA

DR98305 Network Rail	DR98306 Network Rail	DR98307 Colas (PCV)	DR98308(S) Colas

Rail Head Treatment Train (RHTT) FEA-F

642001	Network Rail	642014	Network Rail	642027	Network Rail	642040	Network Rail
642002	Network Rail	642015	Network Rail	642028	Network Rail	642041	Network Rail
642003	Network Rail	642016	Network Rail	642029	Network Rail	642042	Network Rail
642004	Network Rail	642017	Network Rail	642030	Network Rail	642043	Network Rail
642005	Network Rail	642018	Network Rail	642031	Network Rail	642044	Network Rail
642006	Network Rail	642019	Network Rail	642032	Network Rail	642045	Network Rail
642007	Network Rail	642020	Network Rail	642033	Network Rail	642046	Network Rail
642008	Network Rail	642021	Network Rail	642034	Network Rail	642047	Network Rail
642009	Network Rail	642022	Network Rail	642035	Network Rail	642048	Network Rail
642010	Network Rail	642023	Network Rail	642036	Network Rail	642049	Network Rail
642011	Network Rail	642024	Network Rail	642037	Network Rail	642050	Network Rail
642012	Network Rail	642025	Network Rail	642038	Network Rail		
642013	Network Rail	642026	Network Rail	642039	Network Rail		

Loram C44 – Rail Grinder – ZWA

Set C44-01		Set C44-02		Set C44-03	
DR79301	Loram/Network Rail	DR79401	Loram/Network Rail	DR79501	Loram/Network Rail
DR79302	Loram/Network Rail	DR79402	Loram/Network Rail	DR79502	Loram/Network Rail
DR79303	Loram/Network Rail	DR79403	Loram/Network Rail	DR79503	Loram/Network Rail
DR79304	Loram/Network Rail	DR79404	Loram/Network Rail	DR79504	Loram/Network Rail
				DR79505	Loram/Network Rail
				DR79506	Loram/Network Rail
				DR79507	Loram/Network Rail

Windhoff Multi Purpose Vehicle (MPV) – YXA

DR98901 + DR98951	Network Rail	DR98912 + DR98962	Network Rail	DR98923 + DR98973	Network Rail
DR98902 + DR98952	Network Rail	DR98913 + DR98963	Network Rail	DR98924 + DR98974	Network Rail
DR98903 + DR98953	Network Rail	DR98914 + DR98964	Network Rail	DR98925 + DR98975	Network Rail
DR98904 + DR98954	Network Rail	DR98915 + DR98965	Network Rail	DR98926 + DR98976	Network Rail
DR98905 + DR98955	Network Rail	DR98916 + DR98966	Network Rail	DR98927 + DR98977	Network Rail
DR98906 + DR98956	Network Rail	DR98917 + DR98967	Network Rail	DR98928 + DR98978	Network Rail
DR98907 + DR98957	Network Rail	DR98918 + DR98968	Network Rail	DR98929 + DR98979	Network Rail
DR98908 + DR98958	Network Rail	DR98919 + DR98969	Network Rail	DR98930 + DR98980	Network Rail
DR98909 + DR98959	Network Rail	DR98920 + DR98970	Network Rail	DR98931 + DR98981	Network Rail
DR98910 + DR98960	Network Rail	DR98921 + DR98971	Network Rail	DR98932 + DR98982	Network Rail
DR98911 + DR98961	Network Rail	DR98922 + DR98972	Network Rail		

Names applied:
DR98914+DR98964 *Dick Preston*
DR98915+DR98965 *Nigel Cummins*
DR98923+DR98973 *Chris Lemon*
DR98926+DR98976 *John Denyer*

Right: *Windhoff Multi Purpose Vehicles (MPVs) are an important part of todays rail maintenance and upkeep. The flat beds can carry a number of different 'pods' for different types of maintenance work. The MPV illustrated is carrying weed control pods.* **CJM**

Infrastructure Companies - Network Rail

Network Rail

Rail Wagon – YEA 'Perch'

DR979001	N Rail	DR979029	N Rail	DR979057	N Rail	DR979085	N Rail	DR979113	N Rail
DR979002	N Rail	DR979030	N Rail	DR979058	N Rail	DR979086	N Rail	DR979114	N Rail
DR979003	N Rail	DR979031	N Rail	DR979059	N Rail	DR979087	N Rail	DR979115	N Rail
DR979004	N Rail	DR979032	N Rail	DR979060	N Rail	DR979088	N Rail	DR979116	N Rail
DR979005	N Rail	DR979033	N Rail	DR979061	N Rail	DR979089	N Rail	DR979117	N Rail
DR979006	N Rail	DR979034	N Rail	DR979062	N Rail	DR979090	N Rail	DR979118	N Rail
DR979007	N Rail	DR979035	N Rail	DR979063	N Rail	DR979091	N Rail	DR979119	N Rail
DR979008	N Rail	DR979036	N Rail	DR979064	N Rail	DR979092	N Rail	DR979120	N Rail
DR979009	N Rail	DR979037	N Rail	DR979065	N Rail	DR979093	N Rail	DR979121	N Rail
DR979010	N Rail	DR979038	N Rail	DR979066	N Rail	DR979094	N Rail	DR979122	N Rail
DR979011	N Rail	DR979039	N Rail	DR979067	N Rail	DR979095	N Rail	DR979123	N Rail
DR979012	N Rail	DR979040	N Rail	DR979068	N Rail	DR979096	N Rail	DR979124	N Rail
DR979013	N Rail	DR979041	N Rail	DR979069	N Rail	DR979097	N Rail	DR979125	N Rail
DR979014	N Rail	DR979042	N Rail	DR979070	N Rail	DR979098	N Rail	DR979126	N Rail
DR979015	N Rail	DR979043	N Rail	DR979071	N Rail	DR979099	N Rail	DR979127	N Rail
DR979016	N Rail	DR979044	N Rail	DR979072	N Rail	DR979100	N Rail	DR979128	N Rail
DR979017	N Rail	DR979045	N Rail	DR979073	N Rail	DR979101	N Rail	DR979129	N Rail
DR979018	N Rail	DR979046	N Rail	DR979074	N Rail	DR979102	N Rail	DR979130	N Rail
DR979019	N Rail	DR979047	N Rail	DR979075	N Rail	DR979103	N Rail	DR979131	N Rail
DR979020	N Rail	DR979048	N Rail	DR979076	N Rail	DR979104	N Rail	DR979132	N Rail
DR979021	N Rail	DR979049	N Rail	DR979077	N Rail	DR979105	N Rail	DR979133	N Rail
DR979022	N Rail	DR979050	N Rail	DR979078	N Rail	DR979106	N Rail	DR979134	N Rail
DR979023	N Rail	DR979051	N Rail	DR979079	N Rail	DR979107	N Rail		
DR979024	N Rail	DR979052	N Rail	DR979080	N Rail	DR979108	N Rail		
DR979025	N Rail	DR979053	N Rail	DR979081	N Rail	DR979109	N Rail		
DR979026	N Rail	DR979054	N Rail	DR979082	N Rail	DR979110	N Rail		
DR979027	N Rail	DR979055	N Rail	DR979083	N Rail	DR979111	N Rail		
DR979028	N Rail	DR979056	N Rail	DR979084	N Rail	DR979112	N Rail		

Continuous Welded Rail Clamping Wagon – YEA 'Perch'

DR979409	Network Rail	DR979412	Network Rail	DR979415	Network Rail

Continuous Welded Rail End of Train Wagon – YEA 'Porpoise'

DR979505	Network Rail	DR979509	Network Rail	DR979513	Network Rail	DR979515	Network Rail
DR979506	Network Rail	DR979511	Network Rail	DR979514	Network Rail		

Left: *An important function is the safe delivery of continuous long welded rail sections to worksites. These are usually delivered by train, with the rails discharged by way of a Chute wagon onto the track, either between the running rails or into the cess. In this view we see a Welded Rail End of Train Wagon, No. DR979509.* **Antony Christie**

Continuous Welded Rail 'Chute' Wagon – YEA 'Porpoise'

DR979500	Network Rail	DR979502	Network Rail	DR979507	Network Rail	DR979510	Network Rail
DR979501	Network Rail	DR979503	Network Rail	DR979508	Network Rail	DR979512	Network Rail

Continuous Welded Rail Gantry Wagon – YEA 'Perch'

DR979604	Network Rail	DR979611	Network Rail	DR979614	Network Rail
DR979607	Network Rail	DR979612	Network Rail		
DR979609	Network Rail	DR979613	Network Rail		

Plasser & Theurer EM-SAT RT900 Survey Vehicle

DR999800(S) *Richard Spoors*   Network Rail   DR999801(S)   Network Rail

RailVac Machine - Swedish RailVac 18000/500 KFA

99 70 9515 001-4 (99709)	Railcare, Sweden*	* Operated in the UK - based at Totton
99 70 9515 002-2	Railcare, Sweden*	* Operated in the UK - based at Bletchley
99 70 9515 003-0	Railcare, Sweden*	* Operated in the UK - based at Westbury
99 70 9515 004-8	Railcare, Sweden*	* Operated in the UK - based at Westbury
99 70 9515 005-5	Railcare, Sweden*	* Operated in the UK
99 70 9515 006-3	Railcare, Sweden*	* Operated in the UK

Above: *As part of modern rail and trackside maintenance, a fleet of six Railcare 'Railvac' machines operate over the Network Rail area, these are able to suck up by means of vacuum, ballast and other track side debris and place it into an on board vessel for subsequent emptying. Railvac 4 No. 99 70 9515 004-8 is shown from its cab end. These vehicles are usually hauled to and from worksites and are self propelled within work areas.* **CJM**

Windhoff MPV - High Output Plant System (GW electrification train)

DR76901 (99 70 9131 001)	Network Rail	DR76914 (99 70 9131 014)	Network Rail
DR76903 (99 70 9131 003)	Network Rail	DR76915 (99 70 9131 015)	Network Rail
DR76905 (99 70 9131 005)	Network Rail	DR76916 (99 70 9131 016)	Network Rail
DR76906 (99 70 9131 006)	Network Rail	DR76920 (99 70 9131 020)	Network Rail
DR76910 (99 70 9131 010)	Network Rail	DR76921 (99 70 9131 021)	Network Rail
DR76911 (99 70 9131 011)	Network Rail	DR76922 (99 70 9131 022)	Network Rail
DR76913 (99 70 9131 013)	Network Rail	DR76923 (99 70 9131 023)	Network Rail

Names applied
DR76901   *Brunel*
DR76923   *Gavin Roberts*

Winter Snow Patrol Train 'Perch'

99 70 9594 014-1 IS   977986 IS

Electrification Train

SVI RT250 Crane/platform vehicle	DR 99 70 9231 001-7	ABC Electrification
SVI CTF28 Platform	DR 99 70 9231 002-5	ABC Electrification
SVI Crane/drum	DR 99 70 9231 003-3	ABC Electrification
SVI PT500 Wire/platform	DR 99 70 9231 004-1	ABC Electrification
SVI RSM9 Platform	DR 99 70 9231 005-8	ABC Electrification
SVI RSM9 Platform	DR 99 70 9231 006-6	ABC Electrification
SVI APV250 Platform	DR 99 70 9231 007-4	ABC Electrification

Infrastructure Companies - Network Rail

Alstom Transport

Address: ✉ PO Box 70, Newbold Road, Rugby, Warwickshire, CV21 2WR
✎ info@transport.alstom.com ✆ 01788 577111 ⓘ www.transport.alstom.com
Managing Director: Paul Robinson
Facilities: Following the assembly of the Virgin Trains Class 390 'Pendolino' stock, Alstom closed down its UK production facility at Washwood Heath, Birmingham. However, in 2017 a new purpose-built vehicle plant was opened at Widnes, where Class 390 stock is now overhauled. Any future 'new build' contracts would be built at this site.
Depots: Chester (CH), Liverpool - Edge Hill (LL), Wolverhampton - Oxley (OY),
Wembley (WB)

Class 08

Vehicle Length: 29ft 3in (8.91m)			Engine: English Electric 6K		
Height: 12ft 8⅝in (3.87m)			Horsepower: 400hp (298kW)		
Width: 8ft 6in (2.59m)			Electrical Equipment: English Electric		

Number	Depot	Pool	Livery	Owner	Operator
08451	LO	ATLO	BLK	ALS	ALS
08454	WI	ATLO	BLU	ALS	ALS
08611	WB	ATLO	BLU	ALS	ALS
08617	EH	ATLO	BLU	ALS	ALS
08696	WB	ATLO	BLU	ALS	ALS
08721	AT	ATLO	BLU	ALS	ALS
08790	LL	ATLO	BLU	ALS	ALS
08887	PO	ATZZ	BLK	ALS	ALS

Names applied
08451 *Longsight TMD*
08617 *Steve Purser*

Left: *Alstom, with major engineering facilities at Chester, Edge Hill, Manchester, Wolverhampton, Wembley and Widnes, operate a fleet of Class 08 0-6-0 shunting locos for pilotage work. Most have been overhauled and repainted in recent years and sport dark blue livery with wasp warning ends. No. 08696 shows this livery at Wembley.* **Antony Christie**

Bombardier Transportation

Address: ✉ Litchurch Lane, Derby, DE24 8AD
✎ info@bombardier.com ✆ 01332 344666 ⓘ www.bombardier.com
Chief Country Representative: Paul Roberts **Works:** Derby (ZD), Crewe (ZC)
Facilities: Bombardier Transportation is one of the largest transport companies in the world, with offices and facilities in many countries. Its product range extends well beyond rail vehicles and includes aircraft, boats and leisure equipment. In terms of the UK, two main sites are located in Derby (Litchurch Lane) and Crewe. New-build work is undertaken at the Derby site.

Class 08

Vehicle Length: 29ft 3in (8.91m)			Engine: English Electric 6K		
Height: 12ft 8⅝in (3.87m)			Horsepower: 400hp (298kW)		
Width: 8ft 6in (2.59m)			Electrical Equipment: English Electric		

Number	Depot	Pool	Livery	Owner	Operator	Name/Note
08602 (004)	ZD	KDSD	BLU	BOM	BOM	
08682 (D3849)	ZD	KDSD	SPL	BOM	BOM	*Lionheart*

Progress Rail International Inc

Address: ✉ Progress Rail International Inc, 9301 West 55th Street, LaGrange, Illinois, USA, 60525

Progress Rail International Inc, Muncie, Indiana, USA

📠 info@progressrail.com ✆ +1 (800) 255 5355, ⓘ www.progressrail.com

Facilities: Formerly part of General Motors, Progress Rail is one of the two largest loco builders in the world. Its main production facility is in Muncie, Indiana, USA. In terms of the UK, the JT42CWRM or Class 66 locomotives were originally built at the Canadian facility; however, the final order delivered in 2017 for GBRf saw production move to Muncie, Indiana. Progress Rail is part of the Caterpillar Group. In the UK Progress Rail International operates from premises at Longport, near Stoke-on-Trent, where the bodyshell of withdrawn Class 66 No. 66048 is stored.

General Electric (GE)

Address: ✉ GE Transportation Rail, 2901 East Lake Road, Erie, Pennsylvania, USA, 16531

UK office: Inspira House, Martinfield, Welwyn Garden City, Herts, AL7 1GW

📠 info@getransportation.com ✆ 01707 383700 ⓘ www.getransportation.com

Chief Executive Officer: Lorenzo Simonelli

Facilities: General Electric entered the UK loco arena in recent years, and built Class 70s for Freightliner and Colas Rail Freight. GE operates a construction facility in Erie, Pennsylvania, USA.

Hitachi Europe Ltd

Address: ✉ 16 Upper Woburn Place, London, WC1H 0AF

📠 hirofumi.ojima@hitachi-eu.com ✆ 0207 970 2700, ⓘ www.hitachi-rail.com

Facilities: Hitachi's first UK contract was to design, build and introduce the Class 395 EMUs for domestic services on HS1. In 2009 it formed the construction arm of Agility Trains, awarded the IEP project to design, build and introduce new passenger trains in the UK. In 2015 the company opened construction facilities at Newton Aycliffe, County Durham. Soon other contracts were awarded.

At present the company is completing the build of Class 800 and 801 for LNER and Great Western as well as finishing an order for Class 385 stock for ScotRail.

Hitachi also operate a major construction site in Pistoia, Italy, where the Class 802 stock for GWR, Hull Trains and Trans Pennine have been built.

Arlington Fleet Group

Address: ✉ Eastleigh Rail Works, Campbell Road, Eastleigh, Hampshire, SO50 5AD

📠 info@Arlington-fleet.co.uk ✆ 02380 698789 ⓘ www.arlington-fleet.com

Managing Director: Barry Stephens

Facilities: Arlington Fleet Group offers high-quality rail engineering services to all vehicle owners. The company is based in the former loco/carriage works at Eastleigh.

Depots: Eastleigh (ZG), Shoeburyness (SN)

Class 07

Vehicle Length: 26ft 9½in (8.16m)	Engine: Paxman 6RPHL MkIII
Height: 12ft 10in (3.91m)	Horsepower: 275hp (205kW)
Width: 8ft 6in (2.59m)	Electrical Equipment: AEI

Number	Depot	Pool	Livery	Owner	Operator
07007 (D2991)	ZG	MBDL	BLU	AFG	AFG

Class 08

Vehicle Length: 29ft 3in (8.91m)	Engine: English Electric 6K
Height: 12ft 8⅝in (3.87m)	Horsepower: 400hp (298kW)
Width: 8ft 6in (2.59m)	Electrical Equipment: English Electric

Number	Depot	Pool	Livery	Owner	Operator
08567	ZG	MBDL	EWS	AFG	AFG

Class 47

Vehicle Length: 63ft 6in (19.35m)
Height: 12ft 10⅝in (3.91m)
Width: 9ft 2in (2.79m)
Electric Train Heat fitted

Engine: Sulzer 12LDA28C
Horsepower: 2,580hp (1,922kW)
Electrical Equipment: Brush

Number		Depot	Pool	Livery	Owner	Operator
47818(S)	(47240/663)	ZG	MBDL	BLU	AFG	-

Ex-DB (Germany) Class 323

Number	Depot	Pool	Livery	Owner	Operator
323-539-7	ZG	-	GRN	NHR	AFG
323-674-2	ZG	-	GRN	NHR	AFG

Former German shunting locos, built by Gmeinder and now owned by Northumbria Rail and used at Eastleigh Works by Arlington Fleet Group for pilotage.

Ex-Class 508 Barrier Vehicles

Former Class 508 driving cars now used as EMU barrier/translator vehicles, based at Eastleigh.

Number	Depot	Pool	Livery	Owner	Operator	Name
64664	ZG	-	GRN	ANG	AFG	'Livet' Angel of Inventions
64707	ZG	-	GRN	ANG	AFG	'Labezerin' Angel of Success

Left: *Arlington Fleet Group, based at the old Eastleigh Works in Hampshire, are a major provider of engineering facilities in the UK. To transit stock around the rail system, they operate a fleet of barrier vehicles, fitted with standard draw gear at one end and multiple unit compatible couplings at the other, with brake conversion equipment housed inside the vehicles. These two former Class 508 driving cars are frequently used to move EMU stock around the network, The pair are seen at Doncaster West Yard.*
Antony Christie

Barrier Vehicles

Former Class 489 DMBS de-icing vehicles rebuilt as barrier/translator vehicles, based at Eastleigh.

Number	Vehicle	Depot	Livery	Owner	Operator	Notes
489102	68501	LE	GRN	NRL	ROG	Barrier vehicle modified from Class 489 DMBS
489105	68504	LE	GRN	NRL	ROG	Barrier vehicle modified from Class 489 DMBS
489106	68505	ZG	NRL	NRL	ARL	Barrier vehicle modified from Class 489 DMBS

EMU barrier/translator vehicles, based at Eastleigh.

Number	Depot	Pool	Livery	Owner	Operator	Name
975974 (1030)	ZG	-	GRN	ANG	AFG	Paschar
975978 (1025)	ZG	-	GRN	ANG	AFG	Perpetiel

CAF (Construcciones y Auxiliar de Ferrocarriles)

Address: C/ José Miguel Iturrioz, 26 20200 Beasain (Guipúzcoa), Spain

✆ +34 943 88 01 00   ✉ caf@caf.net   ① www.caf.net

Chairman: Andres Arizkorreta Garcia

Facilities: CAF currently operate a major construction plant at Irun, Spain and have recently won a number of orders for the construction of stock for the UK, including orders for Northern, First TransPennine and Caledonian Sleepers, amounting to around 500 vehicles.
CAF are in the process of building a new complex in Llanwern, South Wales, where new vehicle order construction will be undertaken, including an order for Transport for Wales.

Arriva Train Care

Address: ✉ Arriva Train Care, PO Box 111, Crewe, Cheshire, CW1 2FB
✎ allservicedeliverymanagers@lnwr.com ✆ 01270 508000 ⓘ www.lnwr.com
Managing Director: Mark Knowles
Facilities: ATC is a maintenance facility owned by Arriva Trains.
Depots: Crewe (CO), Bristol Barton Hill (BK), Eastleigh (EH), Cambridge (CA), Tyne (TY)

Class 08, 09

Vehicle Length: 29ft 3in (8.91m)			*Engine: English Electric 6K*			
Height: 12ft 8⅝in (3.87m)			*Horsepower: 400hp (298kW)*			
Width: 8ft 6in (2.59m)			*Electrical Equipment: English Electric*			

Number	Depot	Pool	Livery	Owner	Operator	Name
08442	EH	MBDL	BRT	LNW	ATC	*Richard J Wenham Eastleigh Depot December 1989 - July 1999*
08511	EH	MBDL	RSS	RSS	ATC	
08516	BK	MBDL	LNW	LNW	ATC	
08810	EH	MBDL	GRY	LNW	ATC	
08830	CO	MBDL	BLU	LNW	ATC	
09204	CO	MBDL	ATC	LNW	ATC	

Pullman Group (Colas Rail Freight)

Address: ✉ Train Maintenance Depot, Leckwith Road, Cardiff, CF11 8HP
✎ sales@pullmans.net ✆ 029 2036 8850 ⓘ www.pullmans.net
Managing Director: Colin Robinson
Facilities: Maintenance facility based at Canton depot, Cardiff.

Class 08

Vehicle Length: 29ft 3in (8.91m)			*Engine: English Electric 6K*			
Height: 12ft 8⅝in (3.87m)			*Horsepower: 400hp (298kW)*			
Width: 8ft 6in (2.59m)			*Electrical Equipment: English Electric*			

Number	Depot	Pool	Livery	Owner	Operator	Name
08499	CF	WSXX	BLU	DBS	PUL	*Redlight*

Gemini Rail

Address: ✉ Wolverton Works, Stratford Road, Wolverton, Milton Keynes, MK12 5NT
✎ info@railcare.co.uk ✆ 08000 741122 ⓘ www.railcare.co.uk
Managing Director: Colin Love **Depots:** Glasgow (ZH), Wolverton (ZN)
Notes: Previously named Knorr Bremse Rail. Glasgow Works scheduled to close

Class 08

Vehicle Length: 29ft 3in (8.91m)			*Engine: English Electric 6K*			
Height: 12ft 8⅝in (3.87m)			*Horsepower: 400hp (298kW)*			
Width: 8ft 6in (2.59m)			*Electrical Equipment: English Electric*			

Number	Depot	Pool	Livery	Owner	Operator	Name
08568	ZH	RCZH	GEM	GEM	GEM	*St Rollox*
08629	ZN	RCZN	GEM	GEM	GEM	*Wolverton*
08649	ZN	RCZN	GEM	GEM	GEM	*Bradwell*
08730	ZH	RCZH	GEM	GEM	GEM	*The Caley*

Loram UK

Address: ✉ Vehicles Workshop, RTC Business Park, London Road, Derby, DE24 8UP
✎ enquiries@rvel.co.uk ✆ 01332 331210 ⓘ www.rvel.co.uk
Managing Director: Richard Kelly
Depot: Derby (DF)
Parent Company: Loram

Class 31/1 & 31/4

Vehicle Length: 56ft 9in (17.29m)			Engine: English Electric 12SVT		
Height: 12ft 7in (3.91m)			Horsepower: 1,470hp (1,097kW)		
Width: 8ft 9in (2.65m)			Electrical Equipment: Brush		
Class 31/4 - Electric Train Heat fitted					

Number		Depot	Pool	Livery	Owner	Operator
31106(S)		DF	RVLO	BLU	HJA	-
31468(S)	(31568, 31321)	DF	RVLS	BLK	LOR	-

Left: *Currently stored, No. 31106 is seen in blue livery, with a Network Rail test train.* **Mark V. Pike**

Train Engineering Companies – Loram UK, Siemens, Talgo

Siemens Transportation

Address: ✉ Kings Heath Facility, Heathfield Way, Kings Heath, Northampton, NN5 7QP
    ✆ enquiries@siemenstransportation.co.uk ✆ 01604 594500
    ⓘ www.siemenstransportation.co.uk
    ✉ Ashby Park, Ashby de la Zouch, Leicestershire, LE65 1JD
    ✆ uk.mobility@siemens.com ✆ 01530 258000 ⓘ www.siemens.co.uk/mobility

Managing Director UK: Vernon Baker

Depots: Ardwick, Manchester (AK), Kings Heath, Northampton (NN), Three Bridges, Hornsey (HE), Northam (NT), Glasgow Shields (GW)

Facilities: Siemens is a provider of UK EMU and DMU rolling stock with various derivatives of its 'Desiro' and 'Desiro City' product line. With facilities in the UK, and new-build undertakings in mainland Europe at its Krefeld/Uerdingen factory in Germany. Testing of vehicles is also performed in Germany at the world-famous test track at Wildenrath before delivery to customers. It was announced in 2018 that Siemens are to built a new construction facility at Goole, mainly to undertake the deep tube stock build contract.

Siemens operates lifetime maintenance contracts for its Class 185 stock at Ardwick, Manchester, Class 350 stock at Ardwick and Kings Heath, Northampton, Class 380 stock at Shields (Glasgow), Class 444 and 450 stock at Northam near Southampton, Class 700 stock at Three Bridges and Hornsey, Class 717 stock at Hornsey, Wimbledon for Class 707 five-car sets used currently by South West Trains.

Class 01.5

Number	Depot	Pool	Livery	Owner	Operator	Name
01551 (H016)	AK	MBDL	WAB	WAB	SIE	*Lancelot*

Talgo

Spanish train builder Talgo announced in late 2018 that they were to open a new train construction and testing site in the UK, located at the site of the long closed Longannet Power station. A 70,000^{m2} facility will be built from early 2020, with the first trains constructed in 2022. Talgo are hopeful of winning new train orders, including HS2 rolling stock.

Vivarail

Address: ✉ Quinton Rail Technology Centre, Station Road, Long Marston, Stratford-upon-Avon, Warwickshire. CV37 8PL

✐ info@vivarail.co.uk ✆ 07815 010373 ⓘ www.vivarail.co.uk

Chairman: Adrian Shooter

Vivarail, based at Long Marston, has masterminded the re-use of redundant ex-London Transport 'D' stock, rebuilding vehicles to main-line standards as two- or three-car sets, some as DMUs using two 3.2lit Ford underfloor engines and others as battery powered vehicles. Vivarail owns 150 motor cars and 300 trailer vehicles. The West Midlands franchise now operates three 2-car sets.

230001 DM(A) 300001 - ex-LUL 7058, TS 300201 - ex-LUL 17128, DM(B) 300101- ex-LUL 7511
230002 DM(A) 300002, DM(B) 300102 (Battery set)

Above: *Vivarail has masterminded the rebuilding of former LUL 'D' stock into 'new' suburban trains, after building a development three-car set No. 230001, a battery two car set No. 230002 (illustrated) was tested in summer 2018. The first commercial use has been the conversion of three two-car sets for West Midlands Railways.* **CJM**

Wabtec
Brush Traction, Loughborough

Address: ✉ PO Box 17, Loughborough, Leicestershire, LE11 1HS

✐ sales@brushtraction.com ✆ 01509 617000 ⓘ www.brushtraction.com

Managing Director: John Bidewell

Facilities: The world-famous name of Brush Traction, based in Loughborough, is now part of the Wabtec Group. In recent years the site has been responsible for the majority of UK loco building. The company has been synonymous with loco building for the UK and overseas markets for many years. Although recent main-line loco builds have been awarded overseas, the facilities at the Loughborough plant from which the Class 31, 47, 57, 60 and Eurotunnel Shuttle locos emerged are still available for new-build work. Recently the site has concentrated on rebuild operations including the highly successful re-engining of the HST fleet with MTU power units for First Group, East Coast, Grand Central and Network Rail. In 2016 the site was completing work on the re-engining of a Class 73 with an MTU power unit. The site is fully rail-connected. In late 2012, Wabtec purchased L H Group Services.

Doncaster

Address: ✉ PO Box 400, Doncaster Works, Hexthorpe Road, Doncaster, DN1 1SL
📧 wabtecrail@wabtec.com ✆ 01302 340700 ⓘ www.wabtecrail.co.uk

Managing Director: John Meehan   **Depot:**   Doncaster (ZB)

Class 08

Vehicle Length: 29ft 3in (8.91m)				*Engine: English Electric 6K*		
Height: 12ft 8⅝in (3.87m)				*Horsepower: 400hp (298kW)*		
Width: 8ft 6in (2.59m)				*Electrical Equipment: English Electric*		

Number	Depot	Pool	Livery	Owner	Operator	Name
08472	EC	HBSH	BLK	WAB	VEC	
08571	ZB	HBSH	WAB	WAB	VEC	
08596	EC	HBSH	WAB	WAB	VEC	
08615	LH	HBSH	WAB	WAB	-	Uncle Dai
08669	ZB	HBSH	WAB	WAB	WAB	Bob Machin
08724	ZB	HBSH	WAB	WAB	WAB	
08764	PO	MBDL	BLU	WAB	ALS	Old Tom
08853	ZB	HBSH	BLU	WAB	WAB	
08871	IL	MBDL	GRN	WAB	BOM	

Left: *Wabtec is one of the largest railway engineering businesses in the UK with major facilities at Loughborough (locos), Doncaster (locos, units and stock) and Kilmarnock (units and stock). This is an overview of the north end of the Doncaster site.* **CJM**

Kilmarnock (previously Brush Barclay)

Address: ✉ Caledonia Works, West Langlands Street, Kilmarnock, Ayrshire, KA1 2QD
📧 sales@brushtraction.com ✆ 01563 523573 ⓘ www.brushtraction.com

Managing Director: John Bidewell
Facilities: The Wabtec site in Scotland concentrates on vehicle overhaul and refurbishment, including EMU, DMU and loco-hauled vehicles as well as HST stock.

Artemis Engineering

Class 19

Left: *In 2017-2018, Mk3 DVT No. 82113 was obtained by Artemis Intelligent Power, through a deal with Chiltern, and in a joint venture with the RSSB, built a traction development vehicle using two JCB diesel engines powering an E-dyn 96 digital displacement pump, supplying a flow to axle mounted hydraulic displacement motors. A small driving cab was built at the inner end. Based at the SRPS at Bo'ness in Scotland the 'loco' commenced trials in autumn 2018. 19001 is seen at Bo'ness in November 2018.* **Gordon Kirkby**

19001 (82113)   Bo'ness

Europhoenix Ltd

Address: ✉ 58A High Street, Stony Stratford, Milton Keynes, MK11 1AX
✉ info@europhoenix.eu ✆ 01467 624366 ⓘ www.europhoenix.eu

Facilities: Europhoenix has purchased redundant Class 56, 86 and 87 locos; these are offered to Continental European operators fully refurbished and modified to suit customer needs.

Class 37

Vehicle Length: 61ft 6in (18.74m)				Engine: English Electric 12CSVT (37901-Mirrlees)		
Height: 13ft 0¼in (3.96m)				Horsepower: 1,750hp (1,304kW)		
Width: 8ft 11⅝in (2.73m)				Electrical Equipment: English Electric		

Number	Owner	Pool	Depot	Livery	Name	Owner/Operator/Notes
37503 (37021)	EPX	EPUK	LR	EWS		EPX Spares loco
37510 (37112)	EPX	GROG	LR	BLU		EPX ROG deophead coupler
37601 (37501)	EPX	GROG	LR	EPX	*Perseus*	EPX Spot hire
37608 (37512)	EPX	GROG	LR	EPX	*Andromeda*	EPX ROG drophead Dellner fitted
37611 (37690)	EPX	GROG	LR	EPX	*Pegasus*	EPX COL
37800 (37143)	EPX	GROG	LR	EPX		EPX ROG drophead Dellner fitted
37884 (37183)	EPX	GROG	LR	EPX	*Cepheus*	EPX ROG drophead Tightlock fitted
37901 (37150)	EPX	EPUK	LR	EPX	*Mirrlees Pioneer*	EPX

Right: *Europhoenix, based at Leicester depot are the supplier of spot hire locos to main line operators. At the start of 2019, they had a fleet of eight Class 37s, many of which were on long term hire to Rail Operation Group. Some locos are fitted with drop-head auto couplers or either the Dellner or Tightlock type enabling coupling to modern multiple unit stock. No. 37611 Pegasus is seen attached to a Class 345 near Willington on a transit move.*
John Tuffs

Coaching Stock

Mk 3		Height: 12ft 9in (3.88m)	
Vehicle Length: 75ft 0in (22.86m)		Width: 8ft 11in (2.71m)	

NX5G - NGV (Ex 'Nightstar' generator van)

Number	Depot	Livery	Owner	
96371(S) (10545)	LR	EPS	EPX	(for scrap)

Class 56

Vehicle Length: 63ft 6in (19.35m)			Engine: Ruston Paxman 16RK3CT		
Height: 13ft 0in (3.96m)			Horsepower: 3,250hp (2,420kW)		
Width: 9ft 2in (2.79m)			Electrical Equipment: Brush		

Number	Pool	Owner	Location	Livery	Operator
56096	COFS	EPX	WH	COL	COL
56101 (92 55 0659 001-5)		EPX	-	BLK	Hire to Floyd (Hungary)
56115 (92 55 0659 002-3)		EPX	-	BLK	Hire to Floyd (Hungary)
56117 (92 55 0659 003-1)		EPX	-	BLK	Hire to Floyd (Hungary)
56301 (56045)	UKRL	EPX	LR	FLF	-

Right: *Europhoenix was the supplier of three Class 56s to Hungarian operator Floyd, based in Budapest. Modified for European operation the locos power freight traffic and now sport a stunning black and grey livery off-set by a blue and red band, without a yellow warning end. Sadly No. 92 55 0659 002-3 (56115) has been seriously damaged. No. 92 55 0659 001-5 (56101) is illustrated.*
Howard Lewsey

Train Engineering Companies – Europhoenix

Class 86

			Vehicle Length: 58ft 6in (17.83m)	Power Collection: 25kV ac overhead
			Height: 13ft 0⅝in (3.97m)	Horsepower: 5,900hp (4,400kW)
			Width: 8ft 8¼in (2.64m)	Electrical Equipment: GEC

Number	Location	Hire to						
86215	EXP	Floyd (Hungary)	86229	CE	Freightliner *	86250	EXP	Floyd (Hungary)
86217	EXP	Floyd (Hungary)	86233	EXP	Floyd (Hungary)	86251	CE	Freightliner *
86218	EXP	Floyd (Hungary)	86234	LM	-	86424	EXP	Floyd (Hungary)
86228	EXP	Floyd (Hungary)	86242	EXP	Floyd (Hungary)			(for spares)
			86248	EXP	Floyd (Hungary)	* Freightliner for spares		

Class 87

			Vehicle Length: 58ft 6in (17.83m)	Power Collection: 25kV ac overhead
			Height: 13ft 1¼in (3.99m)	Horsepower: 7,860hp (5,680kW)
			Width: 8ft 8¼in (2.64m)	Electrical Equipment: GEC

Number	Owner	Status	Location	Livery	Name
87009	EPX	Operational	EXP	BUL	
87017	EPX	Operational	EXP	EPX	Iron Duke
87023	EPX	Operational	EXP	EPX	Velocity
87025	EPX	Stored	EXP	VIR	

(Hire locomotives in Bulgaria working for short-line operator Bulmarket)

Porterbrook

Address: ✉ Burdett House, Becket Street, Derby, DE1 1JP

✎ enquiries@porterbrook.co.uk ☏ 01332 262405 ⓘ www.porterbrook.co.uk

Chief Executive Officer: Mary Grant

Facilities: Porterbrook Leasing has made available the off-lease Class 87s to mainland European operators, with a significant number being exported to operate in Bulgaria.

Exported

Number	Present operator					
87003	BZK Bulgaria	87010	BZK Bulgaria	87026	BZK Bulgaria
87004	BZK Bulgaria	87012	BZK Bulgaria	87028	BZK Bulgaria
	Britannia	87013	BZK Bulgaria	87029	BZK Bulgaria
87006	BZK Bulgaria	87014	BZK Bulgaria	87033	BZK Bulgaria
87007	BZK Bulgaria	87019	BZK Bulgaria	87034	BZK Bulgaria
87008	BZK Bulgaria	87020	BZK Bulgaria		
		87022	BZK Bulgaria	See Page 277 for numbering

When the Class 87s were displaced on the West Coast Main Line in the UK, the fleet had many more years of life and owner Porterbrook re-leased the locos to BZK in Bulgaria who were at the time looking for extra electric locos. With major modifications 17 locos are currently in Bulgaria carrying a variety of liveries. No. 91 52 0087 012-8 the former 87012 still carries a version of NSE colours. **Howard Lewsey**

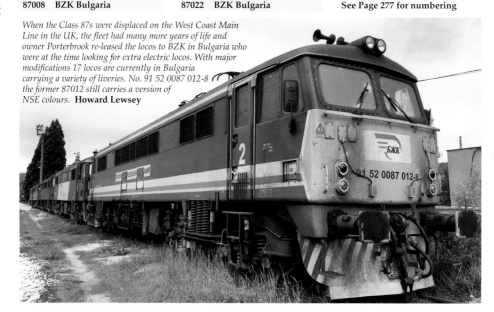

Angel Trains

Address: ✉ Portland House, Bressenden Place, London, SW1E 5BH
🖝 reception@angeltrains.co.uk ✆ 0207 592 0500 ⓘ www.angeltrains.co.uk
Chief Executive: David Jordan **Owned by:** Babcock Brown, AMP Capital and Deutsche Bank

British American Railway Services

Incorporating: RMS Locotec, RT Rail, Dartmoor Railway, Devon & Cornwall Railways, Weardale Railway, Ealing Community Transport and Hanson Rail

Address: ✉ London Riverside, London, SE1 2AQ
President: Ed Ellis **Depots:** RMS Wakefield (ZS), Washwood Heath (WH)
UK operation is part of Iowa Pacific Holdings. BARS is also a Train Operating Company.

Class 08

Vehicle Length: 29ft 3in (8.91m)			Engine: English Electric 6K		
Height: 12ft 8⅝in (3.87m)			Horsepower: 400hp (298kW)		
Width: 8ft 6in (2.59m)			Electrical Equipment: English Electric		

Number	Depot	Pool	Livery	Owner	Operator
08308	W	MRSO	RMS	ECT	Wear
08423	W	INDL	RMS	RMS	IND
08523	IS	MRSO	RMS	RMS	FSR
08573	W	MRSO	BLK	ECT	Wear
08588	WH	MRSO	RMS	ECT	IND
08613	P	MOLO	BLU	RMS	IND
08622	KD	INDL	BLU	RMS	IND
08648	IS	INDL	GTO	BAR	FSR
08754	-	MRSO	BLU	ECT	Wear
08756	MR	MRSO	GRY	ECT	GBR
08762	ZB	MRSO	BLK	ECT	RTC
08870	W	MBDL	BLG	RMS	IND
08873	ZB	MRSO	HUN	ECT	FLR
08874	ZB	MBDL	SIL	RMS	Wear
08885	ZS	INDL	GBR	RMS	GBR
08936	ZS	MBDL	BLU	RMS	IND

§ at Onllwyn, K - Ketton, P - P D Ports, Middlesbrough, W - Weardale

Class 31/1, 31/4

Vehicle Length: 56ft 9in (17.29m)	Engine: English Electric 12SVT
Height: 12ft 7in (3.91m)	Horsepower: 1,470hp (1,097kW)
Width: 8ft 9in (2.65m)	Electrical Equipment: Brush
31/4 Electric Train Heat fitted	

Number		Depot	Pool	Livery	Owner	Location
31190		WH	HTLX	GRN	BAR	Weardale (stored)
31452	(31552, 31279)	-	HTLX	DCG	ECT	Dartmoor Rly (stored)
31454	(31554, 31228)	WH	HTLX	ICS	BAR	Weardale (Stored)

Right: *The BAR owned Class 31s are currently stored and not authorised for main line operations. No. 31452 is shown carrying Devon and Cornwall Railways green livery, attached to a Chiltern Railways Mk3. This was captured in the days when the loco was used for spot hire work over Network Rail tracks.* **Mark V. Pike**

Class 56

Vehicle Length: 63ft 6in (19.35m)		Engine: Ruston Paxman 16RK3CT	
Height: 13ft 0in (3.96m)		Horsepower: 3,250hp (2,420kW)	
Width: 9ft 2in (2.79m)		Electrical Equipment: Brush	

Number		Depot	Pool	Livery	Owner	Operator	Name/Notes
56091		LR	HTLX	GRY	DCR	DCR	
56103		LR	HTLX	DCR	DCR	DCR	
56303(S)	(56125)	LR	HTLX	GRN	BAR	BAR	

UK Rail Leasing

Address: ✉ Leicester Depot, Leicester.

CEO: Mark Winter   **Depot:** Leicester (LR)

Purchaser and restorer of ex-BR locomotives for hire to the UK and overseas rail industries

Class 37/9

	Vehicle Length: 61ft 6in (18.74m)	Engine: Ruston RK270T
	Height: 13ft 0¼in (3.96m)	Horsepower: 1,800hp (1,342kW)
	Width: 8ft 11⅝in (2.73m)	Electrical Equipment: English Electric

Number	Depot	Pool	Livery	Owner	Operator
37905 (D6836, 37136)	LR	UKRS	GRN	URL	URL
37906 (37206)	LR	UKRS	RFD	URL	URL

Left: *UK Rail Leasing, based at Leicester. Two of the prototype re-engined Class 37/9s using Ruston RK270T prime movers are on the roster. No. 37905 (D6936) is seen on the left of this illustration at Leicester depot.* **CJM**

Class 56

	Vehicle Length: 63ft 6in (19.35m)	Engine: Ruston Paxman 16RK3CT
	Height: 13ft 0in (3.96m)	Horsepower: 3,250hp (2,420kW)
	Width: 9ft 2in (2.79m)	Electrical Equipment: Brush

Number	Depot	Pool	Livery	Owner	Operator
56006	LR	UKRS	BLU	URL	ELR

Above: *Until 2018, UK Rail Leasing owned a sizeable fleet of Class 56s, but following a deal, most were sold to GBRf for return to the main line. One loco still remains with UKRL, No. 56006, restored to original BR Rail Blue.* **CJM**

Class 58

	Vehicle Length: 62ft 9½in (19.13m)	Engine: Ruston Paxman 12RK3ACT
	Height: 12ft 10in (3.91m)	Horsepower: 3,300hp (2,460kW)
	Width: 9ft 1in (2.72m)	Electrical Equipment: Brush

Number	Depot	Pool	Livery	Owner	Operator
58016	LR	UKRS	GRY	C58LG	-

Electric Traction Limited

Address: ✉ Woodlands, Manse Road, Inverurie, Aberdeenshire, Scotland, AB51 3UJ

Depot: Long Marston (LM)

Electric Traction Ltd provides spot hire of Class 86 and 87 traction, as well as providing engineering and graphic design services to the rail industry.

Class 86

Vehicle Length: 58ft 6in (17.83m)			Power Collection: 25kV ac overhead		
Height: 13ft 0⅝in (3.97m)			Horsepower: 5,900hp (4,400kW)		
Width: 8ft 8¼in (2.64m)			Electrical Equipment: GEC		

Number	Depot	Pool	Livery	Owner	Operator	Name
86101	WN	GBCH	SCS	ETL	GBR	*Sir William Stanier FRS*
86401	WN	GBCH	SCS	ETL	GBR	*Mons Meg*

Class 87

Vehicle Length: 58ft 6in (17.83m)			Power Collection: 25kV ac overhead		
Height: 13ft 1¼in (3.99m)			Horsepower: 7,860hp (5,680kW)		
Width: 8ft 8¼in (2.64m)			Electrical Equipment: GEC		

Number	Depot	Pool	Livery	Owner	Operator	Name
87002	WN	GBCH	SCS	ETL	GBR	*Royal Sovereign*

Eversholt Rail Group (Previously HSBC Rail)

Address: ✉ PO Box 29499, 1 Eversholt Street, London, NW1 2ZF

🖅 info@eversholtrail.co.uk   ☎ 0207 380 5040   ⓘ www.eversholtrail.co.uk

Chief Operating Officer: Mary Kenny

Owned by C K Investments

One of the three main rolling stock lease companies in the UK, responsible for the ownership and hire of rolling stock of all types to the train operating companies.

Below: *Eversholt Rail Leasing, one of the largest rail vehicle leasing businesses in the UK, was previously HSBC Rail. In recent years the company has made a considerable investment in the procurement of Class 802 IET stock on behalf of Great Western, with 22 five-car and 14 nine-car sets now in traffic. Two five car sets Nos. 802005 and 802006 are seen passing Dawlish.* **CJM**

Harry Needle Railroad Company

Address: ✉ Harry Needle Railway Shed, Barrow Hill Roundhouse, Campbell Drive, Chesterfield, Derbyshire, S43 2PR

Managing Director: Harry Needle

Depot: Barrow Hill (BH), Worksop Wagon Depot

Harry Needle Railroad Company also operates as a scrap dealer in dismantling locomotives and rolling stock.

Class 01.5

Number		Depot	Pool	Livery	Owner	Operator	Note
01552	(TH167V)	BH	HNRL	IND	HNR	IND	
01564	(12088)	-	HNRL	BLK	HNR	IND	Preserved at Aln Valley Railway

Class 08 and 09

Vehicle Length: 29ft 3in (8.91m)
Height: 12ft 8⅝in (3.87m)
Width: 8ft 6in (2.59m)
Engine: English Electric 6K
Horsepower: 400hp (298kW)
Electrical Equipment: English Electric

Number	Depot	Pool	Livery	Owner	Operator	Number	Depot	Pool	Livery	Owner	Operator
08389	BH	HNRL	EWS	HNR	Celsa	08865	BH	HNRL	EWS	HNR	-
08500	BU	HNRL	EWS	HNR	-	08868	CP	HNRL	ATC	HNR	LNW
08527	BH	HNRL	JAR	HNR	Attero	08877	BH	HNRL	BRD	HNR	-
08578	BH	HNRL	EWS	HNR	QRT	08879	BH	HNRL	-	HNR	-
08630	CEL	HNRL	BLK	HNR	Celsa	08892	HE	HNRL	DRS	HNR	HNR
08653	BH	HNRL	EWS	HNR	QRT	08904	BH	HNRL	EWS	HNR	-
08676	-	HNRL	EWS	HNR	EKR	08905	BH	HNRL	EWS	HNR	IND
08685	BH	HNRL	EWS	HNR	EKR	08918	BH	HNRL	EWS	HNR	-
08700	BH	HNRL	BLU	HNR	BOM	08924	BH	HNRL	GBR	HNR	GBR
08701	BH	HNRL	-	HNR	QRT	08929(S)	LM	HNRS	BLK	HNR	-
08714	BH	HNRL	DBS	HNR	Hope	08943	CZ	MBDL	HNR	HNR	NRM
08765	BH	HNRL	ORG	HNR	HNR	08954	LL	HNRS	BLU	HNR	ALS
08786	BH	HNRL	BRD	HNR	HNR	09006§	BH	HNRL	EWS	HNR	-
08802	BH	HNRL	-	HNR	-	09014§	BU	HNRS	ORG	HNR	-
08818	BH	HNRL	GBR	HNR	GBR	09018	BU	HNRS	HNR	HNR	LAF
08824	BH	HNRL	BLK	HNR	-	09106	BH	HNRS	HNR	HNR	HNR
08834	AN	HNRL	HNR	HNR	NOR	09201	BH	HNRL	BRD	HNR	LAF

Name applied
08630 **Celsa Endeavour**

Class 20

Vehicle Length: 46ft 9¼in (14.26m)
Height: 12ft 7⅛in (3.84m)
Width: 8ft 9in (2.66m)
Engine: English Electric 8SVT Mk2
Horsepower: 1,000hp (745kW)
Electrical Equipment: English Electric

Number	Depot	Pool	Livery	Owner	Operator	Number	Depot	Pool	Livery	Owner	Operator
20016(S) §	BH	HNRS	BLU	HNR	-	20118	BH	GBEE	RFG	HNR	HNR
20056	BH	HNRL	COR	HNR	TAT	20121(S)§	WEN	HNRS	ORG	HNR	-
20066	BH	HNRL	TAT	HNR	HCM*	20132‡	BH	GBEE	RFG	HNR	HNR
20081(S) §	LM	HNRS	BLU	HNR	-	20138(S)	LM	HNRS	RFT	HNR	-
20088(S) §	LM	HNRS	RFG	HNR	-	20166	WEN	HNRS	ORG	HNR	HNR
20096	BH	GBEE	BLU	HNR	HNR	20168	BH	HNRL	WHT	HNR	Hope
20107‡	BH	GBEE	ORG	HNR	HNR						
20110§	BH	HNRL	GRN	HNR	-						

‡ Main line certified
* HCM Hope Construction Materials
§ For sale

Number		Depot	Pool	Livery	Owner	Operator	Note
20311	(20102)	BH	GBEE	ORG	HNR	HNR	
20314	(20117)	BH	GBEE	ORG	HNR	HNR	Allocated number 92 70 0020314-5
20903(S)§	(20083)	LM	HNRS	DRS	HNR	-	
20904(S)§	(20041)	LM	HNRS	DRS	HNR	-	
20906	(20219)	LAF	HNRL	WHT	HNR	LAF	

20056 carries Tata Steel No. 81.　　　　20066 carries Tata Steel No. 82.

Names applied

20096	*Ian Goddard 1938-2016*	20132	*Barrow Hill Depot*
20118	*Saltburn-by-the-Sea*	20168	*Sir George Earle*

Class 31

	Vehicle Length: 56ft 9in (17.29m)	Engine: English Electric 12SVT
	Height: 12ft 7in (3.91m)	Horsepower: 1,470hp (1,097kW)
	Width: 8ft 9in (2.65m)	Electrical Equipment: Brush

Number	Depot	Pool	Livery	Owner	Operator
31235	BH	-	-	HNR	-
31285	BH	-	NRL	HNR	-
31459	BH	-	BLU	HNR	-
31465	BH	-	NRL	HNR	At Weardale

Class 37

	Vehicle Length: 61ft 6in (18.74m)	Engine: English Electric 12CSVT
	Height: 13ft 0¼in (3.96m)	Horsepower: 1,750hp (1,304kW)
	Width: 8ft 11⅝in (2.73m)	Electrical Equipment: English Electric

Number	Depot	Pool	Livery	Owner	Operator/Note
37029	BH	HNRS	GRN	HNR	HNR (at Epping & Ongar Railway)
37607 (37511)	BH	COTS	BLU	HNR	COL
37610 (37687)	BH	HNRL	BLU	HNR	HNR
37612 (37691)	BH	COTS	BLU	HNR	COL

Right: *Class 37/6 No. 37607 is one of three former Eurostar UK then DRS Class 37/6s now owned by HNRC. Today, the loco is painted in mid blue and leased to Colas Rail Freight to power Network Rail infrastructure trains. The loco is seen stabled in Doncaster west Yard receiving attention by a HNRC mobile maintenance team.* **CJM**

Class 47

	Vehicle Length: 63ft 6in (19.35m)	Engine: Sulzer 12LDA28C
	Height: 12ft 10⅜in (3.91m)	Horsepower: 2,580hp (1,922kW)
	Width: 9ft 2in (2.79m)	Electrical Equipment: Brush
	Electric Train Heat fitted	

Number	Depot	Pool	Livery	Owner	Operator	Notes/Name
47703 (47514)	Wab	HNRL	-	HNR	heating	
47714 (47511)	OD	HNRL	ANG	HNR	SEC	At RIDC (Old Dalby test track)
47715 (47502)	Lee	HNRL	NSE	HNR	Leemig Bar	Haymarket
47769 (47491)	BH	HNRL	RES	HNR	ROG	

RIDC - Rail Innovation and Development Centre, Old Dalby

Right: *Former ScotRail 'push-pull' Class 47/7 No. 47703, owned by HNRC is currently on hire to Wabtec Doncaster to provide an electric train supply feed to overhauled coaching stock during the test process. It is rumoured that this loco and two others will be overhauled, repainted and returned to front line hire use. In part painted ex FM Rail livery, the loco is seen at Wabtec Doncaster.* **CJM**

Rolling Stock Hire Companies – HNRC

Beacon Rail

Address: ✉ Beacon Rail Leasing, 111 Buckingham Palace Road, London, SW1W 0SR
✐ rail@beaconrail.com.com ✆ 0207 015 00001 ⓘ www.beaconrail.com
UK and international loco, multiple unit and wagon hire company.
Managing Director (UK): Neil Bennett **Parent Company:** J P Morgan

Above: *Beacon Rail is another of the major lease companies, operating within the UK as well as Mainland Europe. In the UK they own a number of multiple unit classes, including the Class 220 and 221 'Voyager' fleets and a number of locomotives and wagons, including most of the Class 68s and all the Class 88s. Beacon Rail-owned, CrossCountry Trains operated 'four-car 'Voyager' No. 220022 is illustrated at Doncaster.* **CJM**

Nemesis Rail

Address: ✉ Nemesis Rail Ltd, Burton Depot, Burton-on-Trent, DE14 1RS
✐ enquiries@ nemesisrail.com ✆ 01246 472331 ⓘ www.nemesisrail.com
Formed from the demise of FM Rail
Depot: Burton (BU)

Class 31/1

	Vehicle Length: 56ft 9in (17.29m)	Engine: English Electric 12SVT
	Height: 12ft 7in (3.91m)	Horsepower: 1,470hp (1,097kW)
	Width: 8ft 9in (2.65m)	Electrical Equipment: Brush

Number	Depot	Pool	Livery	Owner	Operator	Name
31128	BU	NRLO	BLU	NEM	WCR	*Charybdis*

Class 33/1

	Vehicle Length: 50ft 9in (15.47m)	Engine: Sulzer 8LDA28A
	Height: 12ft 8in (3.86m)	Horsepower: 1,550hp (1,156kW)
	Width: 9ft 3in (2.81m)	Electrical Equipment: Crompton Parkinson

Number		Depot	Pool	Livery	Owner	Operator	Name
33103		BU	MBDL	BLU	NEM	-	*Swordfish*

Class 45/1

			Vehicle Length: 67ft 11in (20.70m)			Engine: Sulzer 12LDA28B	
			Height: 12ft 10½in (3.91m)			Horsepower: 2,500hp (1,862kW)	
			Width: 9ft 1½in (2.78m)			Electrical Equipment: Crompton Parkinson	

Number	Depot	Pool	Livery	Owner	Operator	Name
45112	BU	MBDL	BLU	NEM	NEM	*Royal Army Ordnance Corps*

Class 47

			Vehicle Length: 63ft 6in (19.35m)		Engine: Sulzer 12LDA28C	
			Height: 12ft 10⅜in (3.91m)		Horsepower: 2,580hp (1,922kW)	
			Width: 9ft 2in (2.79m)		Electrical Equipment: Brush	
			Class 47/4 and 47/7 - Electric Train Heat fitted			

Number	Depot	Pool	Livery	Owner	Operator	
47488	BU	MBDL	MAR	CRS	NEM	Nos. 47488/701/744 also destined for export to
47701	BU	MBDL	BLK	NEM	NEM	Hungary for Continental Railway Solutions
47744	BU	MBDL	EWS	NEM	NEM	

Porterbrook

Address: ✉ Ivatt House, The Point, Pinnacle Way, Pride Park, Derby, DE24 8ZS

🖰 enquiries@porterbrook.co.uk ✆ 01332 285050 ⓘ www.porterbrook.co.uk

Managing Director: Paul Francis

Owned by: ACP, AIMCo, EDF, Hastings Management

One of the three main UK loco and multiple unit lease companies.

Transmart Trains

Address: ✉ Green Farm House, Falfield, Wootton-under-Edge, Gloucestershire, GL12 8DL

Managing Director: Oliver Buxton

Depots: Cambrian Transport

Class 73/1

			Vehicle Length: 53ft 8in (16.35m)			Power: 750V dc third rail or English Electric 6K	
			Height: 12ft 5⅝in (3.79m)			Horsepower: electric - 1,600hp (1,193kW)	
			Width: 8ft 8in (2.64m)			diesel - 600hp (447kW)	
						Electrical Equipment: English Electric	

‡ At Barry Railway
• Not main-line certified

Number	Depot	Pool	Livery	Owner	Operator	
73118•	‡	-	GRY	TTS	TTS	■ Former 'Gatwick Express' Class 488 vehicles Nos.
73133•	EH	-	GRN	TTS	SWT	72505, 72620, 72621, 72629, 72710 from sets 488206 and 488311 are also owned by Transmart Trains.

Right: *Showing its unique front end design, with body mounted light clusters, fitted after the central headcode box was removed to provide an extra forward facing window, green-liveried Class 73/1 No. 73133 is seen operating on the Swanage Railway during a gala event. The loco is usually kept at Eastleigh Works.* **Antony Christie**

Class 20 Loco Ltd

Class 20

			Vehicle Length: 46ft 9¼in (14.26m)		Engine: English Electric 8SVT Mk2	
			Height: 12ft 7⅜in (3.84m)		Horsepower: 1,000hp (745kW)	
			Width: 8ft 9in (2.66m)		Electrical Equipment: English Electric	

Number	Depot	Pool	Livery	Owner	Operator	
20205	SK	MOLO	BLU	C2L	Spot hire	
20227	SK	MOLO	LUL	C2L	GBR	

L istings provide details of locomotives and stock authorised for operation on the UK National Rail network and that can be seen operating special and charter services.
Preserved locomotives authorised for main-line operation are found in the preserved section.

Bo'ness & Kinneil Railway

Number	Type	Depot	Livery	Operator	Use
464	AO3/BCK	BT	CAL	BOK	Charter train use
1375 (99803)	AO2/TK	BT	CAL	BOK	Charter train use
3096 (99827)	AD11/FO	BT	MAR	BOK	Charter train use
3115	AD11/FO	BT	MAR	BOK	Charter train use
3150	AD11/FO	BT	MAR	BOK	Charter train use
4831 (99824)	AC21/TSO	BT	MAR	BOK	Charter train use
4832 (99823)	AC21/TSO	BT	MAR	BOK	Charter train use
4836 (99831)	AC21/TSO	BT	MAR	BOK	Charter train use
4856 (99829)	AC21/TSO	BT	MAR	BOK	Charter train use
5028 (99830)	AC21/TSO	BT	MAR	BOK	Charter train use
13229 (99826)	AA11/FK	BT	MAR	BOK	Charter train use
13230 (99828)	AA11/FK	BT	MAR	BOK	Charter train use

Flying Scotsman Railway Ltd

Number	Type	Depot	Livery	Operator	Notes/Name
316 (S) (975608)	AO11/PFK	CS	PUL	FSL	Pullman *Magpie*
321 (S)	AO11/PFK	CS	PUL	FSL	Pullman *Swift*
337 (S)	AO11/PSK	CS	PUL	FSL	Pullman Car No. 337

Great Scottish & Western Railway Co

Number	Type	Depot	Livery	Operator	Notes
313 (S) (99964)	AO11/PFK	CS	MAR	WCR	Royal Scotsman
317 (99967)	AO11/PFK	CS	MAR	WCR	Royal Scotsman
319 (99965)	AO11/PFK	CS	MAR	WCR	Royal Scotsman
324 (99961)	AO11/PFP	CS	MAR	WCR	Royal Scotsman
329 (99962)	AO11/PFP	CS	MAR	WCR	Royal Scotsman - *StateCar No. 1*
331 (99963)	AO11/PFP	CS	MAR	WCR	Royal Scotsman
1999 (99131)	AO10/SAL	CS	MAR	WCR	Royal Scotsman

Hastings Diesels Limited

The following vehicles are owned by Hastings Diesels Ltd and kept at St Leonards. Usually a six-car train is formed, which is fitted with central door locking and is main-line certified (original class numbers shown in brackets).
60000 (201), 60019 (202), 60116 (202), 60118 (202), 60501 (201), 60528 (202), 60529 (202), 69337 (422 EMU), 70262 (411 EMU).
Set **1001** is formed of **60116+60529+70262+69337+60501+60118**

Left: The superbly restored Hastings DEMU set, now supplemented by an ex CEP TS and a BIG buffet car is a frequent operator on the main line, powering enthusiasts specials. The set is based at St Leonards. The set does not always operate in the given formation. The set is illustrated forming the '60 Marches' private charter near Hawkeridge Junction.
Mark V. Pike

Mid-Hants Railway

Number	Type	Depot	Livery	Operator
1105	AJ41/RG	RL	GRN	MHR

21252	AB31/BCK	RL	GRN	MHR

North Yorkshire Moors Railway

Class 08

Vehicle Length: 29ft 3in (8.91m)
Height: 12ft 8⅜in (3.87m)
Width: 8ft 6in (2.59m)

Engine: English Electric 6K
Horsepower: 400hp (298kW)
Electrical Equipment: English Electric

Number	Depot	Pool	Livery	Owner	Operator	Note
08850	NY	MBDL	BLU	NYM	NYM	Restricted main-line use

Class 25

Vehicle Length: 50ft 6in (15.39m)
Height: 12ft 8in (3.86m)
Width: 9ft 1in (2.76m)

Engine: Sulzer 6LDA28B
Horsepower: 1,250hp (932kW)
Electrical Equipment: Brush

Number	Depot	Pool	Livery	Owner	Operator	Name	Note
25278	NY	MBDL	GRN	NYM	NYM	Sybilia	Restricted main-line use

Coaching Stock

Number	Type	Depot	Livery	Operator
1823	AN21/RMB	NY	MAR	NYM
3860	AC21/TSO	NY	MAR	NYM
3872	AC21/TSO	NY	MAR	NYM
3948	AC2I/TSO	NY	CAR	NYM
4198	AC21/TSO	NY	CAR	NYM
4252	AC21/TSO	NY	CAR	NYM
4290	AC21/TSO	NY	MAR	NYM
4455	AC21/TSO	NY	CAR	NYM
4786	AC21/TSO	NY	MAR	NYM
4817	AC21/TSO	NY	CHC	NYM
5000	AC21/TSO	NY	MAR	NYM
5029	AC21/TSO	NY	MAR	NYM
9267	AE21/BSO	NY	CHC	NYM
9274	AE21/BSO	NY	CHC	NYM
16156 (7156)	AA31/CK	NY	MAR	NYM
21100	AB31/BCK	NY	CHC	NYM
35089	AB2I/BSK	NY	MAR	NYM

Railfilms Limited/Statesman Rail

Number	Type	Depot	Livery	Operator	Name
84 (99884)	Mk1 Pantry	CS	PUL	RAF	
310 (99107)	AO11/PFL	BO	PUL	RAF	Pegasus / Trianon Bar
1659 (16509)	AJ41/RBR	CL	PUL	RAF	
3188	AD1D/FO	CL	PUL	RAF	
3231	AD1E/FO	CL	PUL	RAF	
3312	AD1E/FO	CL	PUL	RAF	
3438	AD1F/FO	CL	PUL	RAF	
4362	AC21/SO	BU	-	RAF	
5912	AD2F/TSO	CL	PUL	RAF	
5991	AD2F/TSO	CL	PUL	RAF	
9005	GWR	SDR	GWR	RAF	
13508	AA1B/FK	BU	MAR	RAF	
17080	AO3/BCK	CS	PUL	RAF	
35511 (17130)	AB5C	CS	PUL	RAF	

Ridings Railtours

Number	Type	Depot	Livery	Operator
5520 (S)	AC2C/TSO	SV	PUL	RRS

13581 (S)	AA1D/FK	SV	ICS	RRS
13583 (S)	AA1D/FK	SV	ICS	RRS

Riviera Trains

Class 08

Vehicle Length: 29ft 3in (8.91m)
Height: 12ft 8⅜in (3.87m)
Width: 8ft 6in (2.59m)

Engine: English Electric 6K
Horsepower: 400hp (298kW)
Electrical Equipment: English Electric

Number	Depot	Pool	Livery	Owner	Operator	Name
08507	BU	RTLO	RIV	RIV	RIV	Hannah

Coaching Stock

Number	Type	Depot	Livery	Operator	Name
1200 (6459)	AJ1F/RFO	EH	BLG	RIV	
1203 (3291)	AJ1F/RFO	PO	CCM	RIV	
1212 (6453)	AJ1F/RFO	PO	BLG	RIV	
1651	AJ41/RBR	EH	RIV	RIV	
1657	AJ41/RBR	BU	BLG	RIV	
1671	AJ41/RBR	EH	CHC	RIV	
1683	AJ41/RBR	BO	BLU	RIV	Carol
1691	AJ41/RBR	BU	BLG	RIV	
1813	AN21/RMB	CP	CHC	RIV	
1832	AN21/RMB	EH	CCM	RIV	
1863	AN21/RMB	CL	CHC	RIV	
3066 (99566)	AD11/FO	EH	CCM	RIV	
3068 (99568)	AD11/FO	EH	CCM	RIV	
3069 (99540)	AD11/FO	EH	CCM	RIV	
3097	AD11/FO	EH	CCM	RIV	
3098	AD11/FO	EH	CHC	RIV	
3100	AD11/FO	CL	CHC	RIV	
3110 (99124)	AD11/FO	EH	CHC	RIV	
3112 (99357)	AD11/FO	CL	CHC	RIV	
3119	AD11/FO	EH	CCM	RIV	
3120	AD11/FO	EH	CHC	RIV	
3121	AD11/FO	EH	CHC	RIV	
3122	AD11/FO	CL	CHC	RIV	
3123	AD11/FO	EH	CHC	RIV	
3125	AD11/FO	CL	CCM	RIV	
3141 (3608)	AD11/FO	ZG	CHC	RIV	
3144 (3602)	AD11/FO	BQ	MRN	RIV	
3146	AD11/FO	ZG	CHC	RIV	
3147 (3604)	AD11/FO	EH	LNE	RIV	
3148	AD11/FO	CL	CHC	RIV	
3149	AD11/FO	EH	CHC	RIV	
3181 (S)	AD1D/FO	EH	RIV	RIV	Topaz
3223 (S)	AD1E/FO	CL	RIV	RIV	Diamond
3227	AD1E/FO	EH	RIV	RIV	
3240	AD1E/FO	CL	RIV	RIV	Sapphire
3278	AD1F/FO	EH	BLG	RIV	
3304	AD1F/FO	EH	BLG	RIV	
3314	AD1F/FO	BO	BLG	RIV	
3325	AD1F/FO	EH	VIR	RIV	
3330	AD1F/FO	CL	CCM	RIV	
3333	AD1F/FO	EH	BLG	RIV	
3334	AD1F/FO	§	ANG	RIV	
3336	AD1F/FO	§	RIV	RIV	
3340	AD1F/FO	EH	BLG	RIV	
3345	ADIF/FO	EH	BLG	RIV	
3356	AD1F/FO	EH	BLG	RIV	
3364	AD1F/FO	EH	BLG	RIV	
3379	AD1F/FO	§	ANG	RIV	
3384	AD1F/FO	CL	PUL	RIV	Pen-y-Ghent
3386	AD1F/FO	EH	BLG	RIV	
3390	AD1F/FO	EH	BLG	RIV	
3397	AD1F/FO	EH	BLG	RIV	
3417	AD1F/FO	§	ANG	RIV	
3426	AD1F/FO	CL	CCM	RIV	
4927	AC21/TSO	EH	CHC	RIV	
4946	AC21/TSO	EH	CHC	RIV	
4949	AC21/TSO	EH	CHC	RIV	
4959	AC21/TSO	ZA	CHC	RIV	
4991	AC21/TSO	EH	CHC	RIV	
4998	AC21/TSO	EH	CHC	RIV	
5007	AC21/TSO	WH	CHC	RIV	
5009	AC21/TSO	EH	CHC	RIV	
5027 (S)	AC21/TSO	BU	GRN	RIV	

5292	AC2A/TSO	EH	CHC	RIV
5309 (S)	AC2A/TSO	EH	CHC	RIV
5366	AC2A/TSO	EH	CHC	RIV
5494 (S)	AC2B/TSO	SV	NSE	RIV
5647 (S)	AC2D/TSO	EH	RIV	RIV
5910	AC2F/TSO	BU	BLG	RIV
5921	AC2F/TSO	EH	ANG	RIV
5929	AC2F/TSO	EH	BLG	RIV
5937	AC2F/TSO	KM	DRS	RIV
5950	AC2F/TSO	EH	RIV	RIV
5961	AC2F/TSO	BU	BLG	RIV
5964	AC2F/TSO	EH	ANG	RIV
5985	AC2F/TSO	EH	ANG	RIV
5998	AC2F/TSO	EH	BLG	RIV
6006	AC2F/TSO	BU	ANG	RIV
6024	AC2F/TSO	BU	BLG	RIV
6042	AC2F/TSO	EH	ANG	RIV
6051	AC2F/TSO	EH	BLG	RIV
6054	AC2F/TSO	EH	BLG	RIV
6059	AC2F/TSO	EH	BLG	RIV
6067	AC2F/TSO	EH	BLG	RIV
6141	AC2F/TSO	BU	RIV	RIV
6158	AC2F/TSO	EH	BLG	RIV
6310 (81448)	AX51/GEN	EH	CHC	RIV
6320	AZ5Z/SAL	SK	MRN	RIV
6722 (6611)	AN1D/RMBF	LM	FSW	RIV
9504	AC2E/BSO	BU	BLG	RIV
9507	AC2E/BSO	BU	BLG	NOR
9509	AE2E/BSO	BO	ATW	RIV
9520	AE2F/BSO	EH	RIV	RIV
9526	AC2F/BSO	PO	RIV	RIV
9527	AC2F/BSO	ML	SCR	SCR
9537	AE2F/BSO	BU	ADV	RIV
17056 (14056)	AB1A/BFK	CP	CCM	RIV
17105 (2905)	AX5B/BFK	EH	RIV	RIV
21224	AB31/BCK	EH	MAR	RIV
21245 (99356)	AB31/BCK	ZG	MAR	RIV
21269	AB31/BCK	EH	CCM	RIV
21272 (99129)	AB31/BCK	EH	CHC	RIV
35469 (99763)	AB21/BSK	EH	CCM	RIV
80041 (1690)	AK51/RK	EH	MAR	RIV
80042 (1646)	AJ41/RK	ZG	CHC	RIV

§ Stored East Dereham

Directors Saloon

Right: *Mk2F TSO No. 6051, restored to 1960s BR blue and grey, but without a double-arrow logo, is part of a full train sporting this colour scheme, which is frequently used for modern traction railtours and charters.*
Antony Christie

Private Train Operators – Riviera

Above: *Catering on charter trains these days is a very important feature and Riviera, like most operators have a number of certified catering vehicles on their roster. Painted in pleasing BR chocolate and cream livery we see No. W1813, a Mk2 RMB, these vehicles have a central catering area with seating at either end.*
Antony Christie

Left: *More up market catering, including full at seat silver service, can be provided by full length catering RK coach No. 80042, rebuilt from buffet No. 1646. The coach is seen sporting chocolate and cream livery.*
Antony Christie

Scottish Railway Preservation Society

Number	Type	Depot	Livery	Operator
1859 (99822)	AN21/RMB	BT	MAR	SRP
21241	AB31/BCK	BT	MAR	SRP
35185	AB21/BSK	BT	MAR	SRP

Stratford Class 47 Group

Vehicle Length: 63ft 6in (19.35m)
Height: 12ft 10⅝in (3.91m)
Width: 9ft 2in (2.79m)
Electric Train Heat fitted

Engine: Sulzer 12LDA28C
Horsepower: 2,580hp (1,922kW)
Electrical Equipment: Brush

Number		Depot	Pool	Livery	Owner	Operator	Name
47580 (S)	(47167/732)	MNR	MBDL	LLB	S4G	S4G	*County of Essex*

Right: *The Stratford Class 47 Group own an excellently restored Class 47 No. 47580* County of Essex, *which carries BR Rail Blue and a full body height Union Jack flag on the bodyside. The loco usually operates with West Coast Railway. The loco is shown from its No. 2 end at Kensington Olympia. At the start of 2019 the loco was out of use.* **Antony Christie**

Venice Simplon Orient Express (VSOE)
Belmond British Pullman

Number	Name	Type	Depot	Livery	Operator
213 (99535)	Minerva	AO40/PFP	SL	PUL	VSO
239 (S)	Agatha	AO40/PFP	SL	PUL	VSO
243 (99541)	Lucille	AO40/PFP	SL	PUL	VSO
245 (99534)	Ibis	AO40/PFK	SL	PUL	VSO
254 (99536)	Zena	AO40/PFP	SL	PUL	VSO
255 (99539)	Ione	AO40/PFK	SL	PUL	VSO
261 (S)	Car No. 83	AO40/PTP	SL	PUL	VSO
264 (S)	Ruth	AO40/PCK	SL	PUL	VSO
280 (99537)	Audrey	AO40/PFK	SL	PUL	VSO
281 (99546)	Gwen	AO40/PFK	SL	PUL	VSO
283 (S)	Mona	AO40/PFK	SL	PUL	VSO
284 (99543)	Vera	AO40/PFK	SL	PUL	VSO
285 (S)	Car No. 85	AO40/PTP	SL	PUL	VSO
286 (S)	Car No. 86	AO40/PTP	SL	PUL	VSO
288 (S)	Car No. 88	AO40/PTB	SL	PUL	VSO
292 (S)	Car No. 92	AO40/PTB	SL	PUL	VSO
293 (S)	Car No. 93	AO40/PTB	SL	PUL	VSO
301 (99530)	Perseus	AO41/PFP	SL	PUL	VSO
302 (99531)	Phoenix	AO41/PFP	SL	PUL	VSO
307 (S)	Carina	AO41/PFK	SL	PUL	VSO
308 (99532)	Cygnus	AO41/PFP	SL	PUL	VSO
6313 (92167)		AX51/GEN	SL	PUL	VSO
9502		AE2E/BSO	SL	PUL	VSO
35466 (99545)		AB21/BSK	SL	PUL	VSO

Right: *Without doubt the most prestigious train to operate in the UK is the Stewarts Lane-based Belmond British Pullman, formed of the immaculate VSOE Pullman stock. The fleet, usually powered by like-liveried Class 67s provided by DB operate around 200 trips every year. Vehicle No. 254 Zena (99536) is illustrated. This coach was ordered by the GWR in 1928 operating in the Ocean sets before taking up duty in the long gone Torquay Pullmam train.* **Antony Christie**

Vintage Trains

Class 47

	Vehicle Length: 63ft 6in (19.35m)	Engine: Sulzer 12LDA28C
	Height: 12ft 10⅜in (3.91m)	Horsepower: 2,580hp (1,922kW)
	Width: 9ft 2in (2.79m)	Electrical Equipment: Brush
	Electric Train Heat fitted	

Number	Depot	Pool	Livery	Owner	Operator
47773 (47541)	TM	MBDL	GRN	VTN	VTN

Coaching Stock

Number	Type	Depot	Livery	Owner	Operator
335 (99361)	AO11/PSK	TM	PUL	VTN	VTN
349 (99349)	AO11/PSP	TM	PUL	VTN	VTN
353 (99353)	AO11/PSP	TM	PUL	VTN	VTN
1201 (6445)	AJ1F/RFO	TM	CHC	VTN	VTN
3351	AD1F/FO	TM	CHC	VTN	VTN
5157	AC2Z/TSO	TM	CHC	VTN	VTN
5177	AC2Z/TSO	TM	CHC	VTN	VTN
5191	AC2Z/TSO	TM	CHC	VTN	VTN
5198	AC2Z/TSO	TM	CHC	VTN	VTN
5212	AC2Z/TSO	TM	CHC	VTN	VTN
5928	AC2F/TSO	TM	CHC	VTN	VTN
9101 (9398)	AH2Z/BSOT	TM	CHC	VTN	VTN
9496	AE2E/BSO	TM	MAR	VTN	VTN
17018 (99108)	AB11/BFK	TM	CHC	VTN	VTN
17090	AB1A/BFK	TM	CHC	VTN	VTN
96100 (86374)	GUV	TM	BRN	VTN	VTN

Boden Rail Engineering Ltd

Class 50

	Vehicle Length: 68ft 6in (20.88m)	Engine: English Electric 16CSVT
	Height: 12ft 10¼ (3.92m)	Horsepower: 2700hp (2013kW)
	Width: 9ft 1¼in (2.77m)	Electrical Equipment: English Electric

Number	Depot	Pool	Livery	Owner	Operator	Name
50008 (D408)	NM	HTLX	BLU	BRE	BRE	Thunderer
50017 (D417)	NM	MBDL	NSE	BRE	BRE	Royal Oak
50050 (D400)	NM	MBDL	BLU	BRE	BRE	Fearless

West Coast Railway Company

Class 03

	Vehicle Length: 26ft 3in (7.92m)	Engine: Gardner 8L3
	Height: 12ft 7⅞in (3.72m)	Horsepower: 204hp (149kW)
	Width: 8ft 6in (2.59m)	Mechanical Equipment: Wilson-Drewry

Number	Depot	Pool	Livery	Owner	Operator	Name
03196(S)	CS	MBDL	GRN	WCR	WCR	Joyce
D2381(S)	CS	MBDL	BLK	WCR	WCR	

Class 08

	Vehicle Length: 29ft 3in (8.91m)	Engine: English Electric 6K
	Height: 12ft 8⅜in (3.87m)	Horsepower: 400hp (298kW)
	Width: 8ft 6in (2.59m)	Electrical Equipment: English Electric

Number	Depot	Pool	Livery	Owner	Operator
08418	CS	MBDL	EWS	WCR	WCR
08485	CS	MBDL	BLU	WCR	WCR
08678	CS	AWCX	WCR	WCR	WCR

Class 33

	Vehicle Length: 50ft 9in (15.47m)	Engine: Sulzer 8LDA28A
	Height: 12ft 8in (3.86m)	Horsepower: 1,550hp (1,156kW)
	Width: 33/0, 9ft 3in (2.81m),	Electrical Equipment: Crompton
	33/2, 8ft 8in (2.64m)	Parkinson

Number	Depot	Pool	Livery	Owner	Operator	Name
33025	CS	AWCA	WCR	WCR	WCR	
33029	CS	AWCA	WCR	WCR	WCR	
33207	CS	AWCA	WCR	WCR	WCR	Jim Martin

Right: *West Coast Railway operates a sizeable fleet of locomotives mainly used for charter or special traffic operations. One of their front line locomotives is Class 33/0 No. 33025, which now carries WCRC maroon livery with small yellow ends. The loco is seen from its No. 2 end on the Swanage Railway coupled to London Underground operated 4TC stock.*
CJM

Class 37

Vehicle Length: 61ft 6in (18.74m)			Engine: English Electric 12CSVT			
Height: 13ft 0¼in (3.96m)			Horsepower: 1,750hp (1,304kW)			
Width: 8ft 11⅝in (2.73m)			Electrical Equipment: English Electric			

Number	Depot	Pool	Livery	Owner	Operator	Name
37516 (37086)	CS	AWCA	WCR	WCR	WCR	Loch Laidon
37517 (S) (37018)	CS	MBDL	LHL	WCR	-	
37518 (37076)	CS	AWCA	WCR	WCR	WCR	
37668 (37257)	CS	AWCA	WCR	WCR	WCR	
37669 (37129)	CS	AWCA	WCR	WCR	WCR	
37676 (37126)	CS	AWCA	WCR	WCR	WCR	Loch Rannoch
37685 (37234)	CS	AWCA	WCR	WCR	WCR	Loch Arkaig
37706 (37016)	CS	AWCA	WCR	WCR	WCR	
37710 (S) (37044)	CS	MBDL	LHL	WCR	-	
37712 (37102)	CS	AWCX	WCR	WCR	WCR	

Nos. 37668 and 37669 fitted with Hitachi ETRMS for Cambrian Line duties

Right: *West Coast operates a sizeable fleet of Class 37s, again these are mainly deployed on charter train operations. Operational locos display WCRC maroon livery, with small yellow warning ends. No. 37516* Loch Laidon *is illustrated at York.*
Antony Christie

Class 47

Vehicle Length: 63ft 6in (19.35m)			Engine: Sulzer 12LDA28C			
Height: 12ft 10⅜in (3.91m)			Horsepower: 2,580hp (1,922kW)			
Width: 9ft 2in (2.79m)			Electrical Equipment: Brush			
Class 47/4, 47/7 and 47/8 Electric Train Heat fitted						

Number	Depot	Pool	Livery	Owner	Operator	Name
47194 (S)	CS	AWCX	TLF	WCR	-	
47237	CS	AWCA	WCR	WCR	WCR	
47245	CS	AWCA	WCR	WCR	WCR	
47270	CS	AWCA	BLU	WCR	WCR	Swift
47355 (S)	CS	AWCX	BLK	WCR	-	
47492	CS	AWCX	RES	WCR	WCR	
47500 (S) (47770)	CS	AWCX	WCR	WCR	-	
47746 (47605)	CS	AWCA	WCR	WCR	WCR	Chris Fudge 29.7.70-22.6.10
47760 (47562)	CS	AWCA	WCR	WCR	WCR	
47768 (47490)	CS	AWCX	EWS	WCR	WCR	
47772 (47537)	CS	AWAC	WCR	WCR	WCR	Carnforth TMD

Private Train Operators – WCRC

WCRC

47776 (S) (47578)	CS	AWCX	RES	WCR	-	
47786 (47821)	CS	AWCA	WCR	WCR	WCR	*Roy Castle OBE*
47787 (47823)	CS	AWCX	WCR	WCR	WCR	
47802 (47552)	CS	AWCA	WCR	WCR	WCR	
47804 (47792)	CS	AWCA	WCR	WCR	WCR	
47826 (47637)	CS	AWCA	WCR	WCR	WCR	
47832 (47560)	CS	AWCA	WCR	WCR	WCR	
47851/D1648 (47639)	CS	AWCA	WCR	WCR	WCR	
47854 (47674)	CS	AWCA	WCR	WCR	WCR	*Diamond Jubilee*

Left: *A sizeable fleet of Class 47s are on the roster of West Coast Railway, allocated to their Carnforth base. Most of the operational and certified locos carry standard WCRC maroon livery. The majority are of the electric train supply type, suitable for powering passenger services. No. 47760 is seen at London Euston.* **Antony Christie**

Class 57

Vehicle Length: 63ft 6in (19.38m)	Engine: EMD 645-12E3
Height: 12ft 10½in (3.91m)	Horsepower: 2,500hp (1,860kW)
Width: 9ft 2in (2.79m)	Electrical Equipment: Brush

Number	Depot	Pool	Livery	Owner	Operator	Name
57001 (47356)	CS	AWCX	WCR	WCR	WCR	
57005 (47350)(S)	CS	AWCX	WCR	WCR	-	
57006 (47187)(S)	CS	AWCX	WCR	WCR	-	
57313 (47371)	CS	AWCA	WCR	WCR	WCR	
57314 (47372)	CS	AWCA	WCR	WCR	WCR	
57315 (47234)	CS	AWCA	WCR	WCR	WCR	
57316 (47290)	CS	AWCA	WCR	WCR	WCR	
57601 (47165/590/825)	CS	AWCA	PUL	WCR	WCR	*Windsor Castle*

Left: *Eight General Motors powered Class 57s are owned by West Coast, three of the original 57/0s with no provision for train heat, four former Virgin Trains Class 57/3s fitted with electric train supply and previously fitted with drop-head Dellner couplings (now removed) and one Class 57/6. Showing the space where the original Dellner coupling was once housed, Class 57/3 No. 57313 is seen under the great trainshed roof at York.* **Antony Christie**

Coaching Stock

Number	Name	Type	Depot	Livery	Operator	Notes	
159 (99980)		AO10/SAL		CS	MAR	WCR*	LNWR saloon (ex-'Q of Scots')
325 (99025)	*Amber*	AO11/PFP		CS	PUL	WCR	
326 (S) (99402)	*Emerald*	AO11/PFP		CS	PUL	WCR	

347 (99347)	Car No. 347	AO11/PSO	CS	WCR	WCR	
348 (99348)	Topaz	AO11/PSP	CS	WCR	WCR	
350 (99350)	Car No. 350	AO11/PSP	CS	WCR	WCR	
351 (99351)	Sapphire	AO11/PSP	CS	WCR	WCR	
352 (99352)	Amethyst	AO11/PSP	CS	PUL	WCR	
354 (99354)	The Hadrian Bar	AO11/PSP	CS	PUL	WCR	
504 (99678)	Ullswater	AP1Z/PFK	CS	PUL	WCR	
506 (99679)	Windermere	AP1Z/PFK	CS	PUL	WCR	
546 (S) (99670)	City of Manchester	AQ1Z/PFP	CS	PUL	WCR	
548 (99671)	Grasmere	AQ1Z/PFP	CS	PUL	WCR	
549 (99672)	Bassenthwaite	AQ1Z/PFP	CS	PUL	WCR	
550 (99673)	Rydal Water	AQ1Z/PFP	CS	PUL	WCR	
551 (99674)	Buttermere	AQ1Z/PFP	CS	PUL	WCR	
552 (99675)	Ennerdale Water	AQ1Z/PFP	CS	PUL	WCR	
553 (99676)	Crummock Water	AQ1Z/PFP	CS	PUL	WCR	
586 (99677)	Derwent Water	AR1Z/PFB	CS	PUL	WCR	
807 (99881)		AO10/SAL	CS	SPL	WCR*	GNR Saloon (ex-Q of Scots)
1207		AJ1F/RFO	CS	VIR	WCR	
1221		AJ1F/RFO	CS	ICS	WCR	
1644 (S)		AJ41/RBR	CS	ICS	WCR	
1650 (S)		AJ41/RBR	CS	ICS	WCR	
1652 (S)		AJ41/RBR	CS	ICS	WCR	
1655 (S)		AJ41/RBR	CS	ICS	WCR	
1663 (S)		AJ41/RBR	CS	ICS	WCR	
1666		AJ41/RBR	CS	WCR	WCR	
1670 (S)		AJ41/RBR	CS	ICS	WCR	
1730		AJ41/RBR	CS	WCR	WCR	
1840		AN21/RMB	CS	WCR	WCR	
1860		AN21/RMB	CS	WCR	WCR	
1861 (99132)		AN21/RMB	CS	WCR	WCR	
1882 (99311)		AN21/RMB	CS	WCR	WCR	
1961		AJ41/RBR	CS	WCR	WCR	
2127 (S)		AO11/SLF	CS	MAR	WCR	
3058	Florence	AD11/FO	CS	WCR	WCR	
3093 (977594)	Florence	AD11/FO	CS	WCR	WCR	
3105 (99121)	Julia	AD11/FO	CS	WCR	WCR	
3106 (99122)	Alexandra	AD11/FO	CS	WCR	WCR	
3113 (99125)	Jessica	AD11/FO	CS	WCR	WCR	
3117 (99127)	Christina	AD11/FO	CS	WCR	WCR	
3128 (99371)	Victoria	AD11/FO	CS	WCR	WCR	
3130 (99128)	Pamela	AD11/FO	CS	WCR	WCR	
3136 (3605)	Diana	AD11/FO	CS	WCR	WCR	
3143 (3609)	Patricia	AD11/FO	CS	WCR	WCR	
3313		AD1F/FO	CS	WCR	WCR	
3326		AD1F/FO	CS	WCR	WCR	
3348		AD1F/FO	CS	PUL	WCR	
3350		AD1F/FO	CS	WCR	WCR	
3352		AD1F/FO	CS	WCR	WCR	
3359		AD1F/FO	CS	WCR	WCR	
3360		AD1F/FO	CS	ICS	WCR	
3362		AD1F/FO	CS	WCR	WCR	
3395		AD1F/FO	CS	WCR	WCR	
3431		AD1F/FO	CS	WCR	WCR	
4854		AD1F/FO	CS	WCR	WCR	
4860 (S) (99193)		AC21/TSO	CS	MAR	WCR	
4905		AC21/TSO	CS	WCR	WCR	
4912 (99318)		AC21/TSO	CS	WCR	WCR	
4931 (99329)		AC21/TSO	CS	WCR	WCR	
4932 (S)		AC21/TSO	CS	BLG	WCR	
4940		AC21/TSO	CS	WCR	WCR	
4951		AC21/TSO	CS	WCR	WCR	
4954 (99326)		AC21/TSO	CS	WCR	WCR	
4958		AC21/TSO	CS	WCR	WCR	
4960		AC21/TSO	CS	WCR	WCR	
4973		AC21/TSO	CS	WCR	WCR	
4984		AC21/TSO	CS	WCR	WCR	
4994		AC21/TSO	CS	WCR	WCR	
4997 (S)		AC21/TSO	CS	BLG	WCR	
5032 (99194)		AC21/TSO	CS	WCR	WCR	

WCRC

5033 (99328)		AC21/TSO	CS	WCR	WCR	
5035 (99195)		AC21/TSO	CS	WCR	WCR	
5044 (99327)		AC21/TSO	CS	WCR	WCR	
5125 (S)		AC2Z/TSO	BH	GRN	WCR	
5171		AC2Z/TSO	CS	MAR	WCR	
5200		AC2Z/TSO	CS	GRN	WCR	
5216		AC2Z/TSO	CS	MAR	WCR	
5222		AC2Z/TSO	CS	MAR	WCR	
5229	The Green Knight	AC2Z/SO	CS	MAR	WTN	
5236		AC2Z/SO	CS	MAR	WCR	
5237		AD2Z/SO	CS	MAR	WCR	
5239	The Red Knight	AD2Z/SO	CS	MAR	WTN	
5249		AD2Z/SO	CS	MAR	WCR	
5278	Melisande	AC2A/TSO	CS	CHC	WTN	
5419		AC2A/TSO	CS	WCR	WTN	
5487		AC2C/TSO	CS	WCR	WCR	
5756 (S)		AC2E/TSO	CS	WCR	WCR	
6000		AC2F/TSO	CS	WCR	WCR	
6012		AC2F/TSO	CS	WCR	WCR	
6014 (S)		AC2F/TSO	CS	ICS	WCR	
6021		AC3F/TSO	CS	WCR	WCR	
6022		AC2F/TSO	CS	WCR	WCR	
6103		AC2F/TSO	CS	WCR	WCR	
6115		AC2F/TSO	CS	WCR	WCR	
6135 (S)		AC2F/TSO	CS	ICS	WCR	
6312 (92925)		AX51/GEN	CS	WCR	WCR	
6528 (5592)		AG2C/TSOT	CS	WCR	WCR	
6723		AN1D/RMBF	CS	WCR	WCR	
6724		AN1D/RMBF	CS	WCR	WCR	
9104 (S) (9401)		AH2Z/BSOT	CS	WCR	WCR	
9391	Pendragon	AE2Z/BSO	CS	PUL	WTN	
9392		AE2Z/BSO	CS	WCR	WCR	
9448 (S)		AE2C/BSO	CS	WCR	WCR	
9493		AE2D/BSO	CS	WCR	CWR	
13227		AA11/FK	CD	WCR	WCR	
13306 (S)		AA11/FK	CS	WCR	WCR	
13320	Anna	AA11/FO	CS	WCR	WCR	
13321 (99316)		AA11/FK/RBR	CS	WCR	WCR	
13440 (S)		AA1A/FK	CS	GRN	WCR	
17102 (99680)		AB1A/BFK	CS	MAB	WCR	
17168 (S) (99319)		AB1D/BFK	CS	WCR	WCR	
18756 (25756)		AA21/SK	SH	MAR	WCR	
18806 (99722)		AA21/SK	CS	WCR	WCR	
18893 (99712)		Kitchen	CS	WCR	WCR	
19208 (99884)	Car No. 84	AA21/SK	CS	WCR	WCR	
21256 (99304)		AB31/BCK	CS	WCR	WCR	
21266		AB31/BCK	CS	WCR	WCR	
34525 (S) (99966)		AR51/GEN	CS	WCR	WCR	
35407 (99886)		AB21/BSK	CS	MAR	WCR	LNWR livery ('Q of Scots')
45018 (99052)		AO10/SAL	CS	QOS	WCR	
45026 (S)		SAL	CS	MAR	WCR	LMS Inspection Saloon
80043 (1680)		AJ41/RBR	CS	PUL	WCR	
96175		GUV	CS	MAR	WCR	Water carrier
99723 (35459)		AB21/BSK	CS	WCR	WCR	

WCR* - Owned by Scottish Highland Railway Co

Left: *Although sometimes looking a little drab in their overall dark maroon livery, the West Coast passenger fleet always looks neat and impressive. Mk2f TSO No. 6115 is seen at York.*
Antony Christie

Above: *Previously operated as part of the Queen of Scots train, service Car No. 1 (99886) was previously Mk1 BSK No. 35407. rebuilt with a generator in the former luggage compartment, the vehicle is seen at York in charter train use.* **Antony Christie**

Northern Belle

Number	Name	Type	Depot	Livery	Operator	Notes
325 (2907)	Durat	AJ11/RFO	CS	PUL	WCR	
1207 (6422)		AJ11/RFO	CS	-	WCR	
1211 (3305)	Snaefell	AJ11/RFO	CS	PUL	WCR	
1221 (3371)		AJ11/RFO	CS	PUL	WCR	
1566	Caerdydd	AK51/RKB	CS	PUL	WCR	
1953		AJ41/RBR	CS	PUL	WCR	
3174	Glamis	AD1D/FO	CS	PUL	WCR	
3182	Warwick	AD1D/FO	CS	PUL	WCR	
3232		AD1E/FO	CS	PUL	WCR	
3247	Chatsworth	AD1E/FO	CS	PUL	WCR	
3267	Belvoir	AD1E/FO	CS	PUL	WCR	
3273	Alnwick	AD1E/FO	CS	PUL	WCR	
3275	Harlech	AD1E/FO	CS	PUL	WCR	
10541 (99968)		AO4G/SSV	CS	MRN	WCR	Royal Scotsman - State Car 5
10556 (99969)		AO4G/SSV	CS	MRN	WCR	Royal Scotsman - Service Car
10569 (S)	Leviathan	AU4G/SLEP	CS	PUL	WCR	
10729	Crewe	AS4G/SLE	CS	PUL	VSO	
10734 (2914)	Balmoral	AS4G/SLE	CS	PUL	WCR	
17167 (14167)	Mow Cop	AB1D/BFK	CS	PUL	WCR	
92904		NBA	CS	PUL	VSO	

Right: *West Coast Railway are the present operators of the Northern Belle luxury land cruise train, mainly formed of Mk2 vehicles, painted in Pullman Car Co livery. RFO No. 1211, rebuilt from FO No. 3305 is shown from its seating end.* **Antony Christie**

Most preserved locomotives authorised for main-line operation, either steam or diesel, operate with a support coach conveying owners' representatives, engineering staff and light maintenance equipment. Support coaches can be allocated to a specific locomotive or operate with a pool of locos.

Number	Type	Depot	Livery	Support Coach for
14007 (99782) *Mercator*	AB11/BSK	NY	MAR	61264 or 60163
14060 (17060)	AB11/BSK	TM	MAR	45596
17019 (14019)	AB11/BFK	CS	MAR	61994
17025 (14025)	AB11/BFK	CS	MAR	45690
17096	AB1B/BFK	SL	CHC	35028 named *Mercator*
21096 (99080)	AB31/BCK	NY	MAR	60007
21232 (99040)	AB31/BCK	SK	MAR	46201
21236 (99120)	AB31/BCK	ZG	GRN	30828
21249	AB21/BCK	SL	CCM	60163
35317	AD21/BSK	BQ	GRN	46100/70000
35322 (99035)	AB21/BSK	CS	MAR	70000 and WCRC traction
35329	AB21/BSK	RL	GRN	Mid-Hants fleet
35449 (99241)	AB21/BSK	CS	MAR	45231
35451	AB21/BSK	MI	GRN	34046
35461 (99720)	AB21/BSK	CL	CHC	5029
35463 (99312)	AB21/BSK	CS	WCR	WCR fleet
35464	AB21/BSK	PR	MAR	Swanage Railway
35465 (99991)	AB21/BSK	CL	CCM	Jeremy Hosking / 70000
35468 (99953)	AB21/BSK	YK	MAR	National Railway Museum, 60103
35470	AB21/BSK	TM	CHC	Vintage Trains fleet
35476 (99041)	AB21/BSK	SK	MAR	46233
35479	AB21/BSK	SH	MAR	61306
35486 (99405)	AB21/BSK	--	MAR	60009 or 61994
35508	AB1C/BSK	BQ	MAR	45212, 44871, 45407
35517 (17088)	AB1K/BSK	BQ	MAR	45212, 44871, 45407
35518 (17097)	AB11/BFK	SH	GRN	34067
80204 (35297)	NNX	TN	MAR	61994
80217 (35299)	NNX	CS	MAR	WCRC fleet
80220 (35276)	NNX	NY	MAR	62005

Below: *When preserved traction, steam or modern traction operates over the National network, a support coach is usually attached for the support staff to use and provide space for a limited amount of spare parts and tools in case anything goes wrong. The Merchant Navy Loco preservation Society operate Mk2 BFK No. 17096* Mercator *as their support coach for loco No. 35028 Clan Line. The coach is usually based with the loco at Stewarts Lane.* **Antony Christie**

Electric Multiple Units

Class 319/0

Vehicle Length: (Driving) 65ft 0¾in (19.83m) Width: 9ft 3in (2.82m)
(Inter) 65ft 4¼in (19.92m) Horsepower: 1,326hp (990kW)
Height: 11ft 9in (3.58m) Seats (total/car): 319S, 82S/82S/77S/78S

Number	Formation	Depot	Livery	Owner	Operator	Note
	DTSO(A)+MSO+TSO+DTSO(B)					
319001	77291+62891+71772+77290	-	TLK	PTR	-	For 'HydroFlex' Project at Chrysalis Rail
319003	77295+62893+71774+77294	-	TLK	PTR	-	
319006	77301+62896+71777+77300	-	TLK	PTR	-	
319007	77303+62897+71778+77302	-	TLK	PTR	-	
319009	77307+62899+71780+77306	-	TLK	PTR	-	
319010	77309+62900+71781+77308	-	TLK	PTR	-	
319011	77311+62901+71782+77310	-	TLK	PTR	-	

Class 319/2

Vehicle Length: (Driving) 65ft 0¾in (19.83m) Width: 9ft 3in (2.82m)
(Inter) 65ft 4¼in (19.92m) Horsepower: 1,326hp (990kW)
Height: 11ft 9in (3.58m) Seats (total/car): 18F/212S, 64S/60S/52S/18F-36S

Number	Formation	Depot	Livery	Owner	Operator	Note
	DTSO+MSO+TSO+DTCO					
319214	77317+62904+71785+77316	-	TLK	PTR	-	At Crewe
319217	77323+62907+71788+77322	-	TLK	PTR	-	

Class 319/3

Vehicle Length: (Driving) 65ft 0¾in (19.83m) Width: 9ft 3in (2.82m)
(Inter) 65ft 4¼in (19.92m) Horsepower: 1,326hp (990kW)
Height: 11ft 9in (3.58m) Seats (total/car): 300S, 70S/78S/74S/78S

Number	Formation	Depot	Livery	Owner	Operator
	DTSO(A)+MSO+TSO+DTSO(B)				
319384	77979+63096+71982+77980	-	FCC	PTR	-

Class 319/4

Vehicle Length: (Driving) 65ft 0¾in (19.83m) Width: 9ft 3in (2.82m)
(Inter) 65ft 4¼in (19.92m) Horsepower: 1,326hp (990kW)
Height: 11ft 9in (3.58m) Seats (total/car): 12F/277S, 12F-54S/77S/72S/74S

Number	Formation	Depot	Livery	Owner	Operator	Note
	DTCO+MSO+TSO+DTSO					
319421	77331+62911+71792+77330	-	TLK	PTR	-	
319422	77333+62912+71793+77332	-	TLK	PTR	-	
319423	77335+62913+71794+77334	-	TLK	PTR	-	
319425	77339+62915+71796+77338	-	TLK	PTR	-	
319426	77431+62916+71797+77430	-	NOR	PTR	-	
319427	77343+62917+71798+77342	-	TLK	PTR	-	
319428	77345+62918+71799+77344	-	TLK	PTR	-	
319430	77349+62920+71801+77348	-	TLK	PTR	-	
319432	77353+62922+71803+77352	-	TLK	PTR	-	
319435	77359+62925+71806+77358	-	TLK	PTR	-	
319436	77361+62926+71807+77360	-	TLK	PTR	-	
319437	77363+62927+71808+77362	-	TLK	PTR	-	
319438	77365+62928+71809+77364	-	TLK	PTR	-	
319439	77367+62929+71810+77366	-	TLK	PTR	-	
319440	77369+62930+71811+77368	-	TLK	PTR	-	
319443	77375+62933+71814+77374	-	TLK	PTR	-	
319444	77377+62934+71815+77376	-	TLK	PTR	-	
319445	77379+62935+71816+77378	-	TLK	PTR	-	
319447	77431+62961+71866+77430	-	TLK	PTR	-	
319449	77435+62963+71868+77434	-	TLK	PTR	-	
319451	77439+62965+71870+77438	-	FCC	PTR	-	
319452	77441+62966+71871+77440	-	FCC	PTR	-	
319453	77443+62967+71872+77442	-	FCC	PTR	-	
319454	77445+62968+71873+77444	-	FCC	PTR	-	
319459	77455+62973+71878+77454	-	TLK	PTR	-	

Class 365
Networker Express

Vehicle Length: (Driving) 68ft 6½in (20.89m) Width: 9ft 2½in (2.81m)
(Inter) 65ft 9¼in (20.89m) Horsepower: 1,684hp (1,256kW)
Height: 12ft 4½in (3.77m) Seats (total/car): 24F/239S, 12F-56S/59S/68S/12F-56S

Number	Formation	Depot	Livery	Owner	Operator
	DMCO(A)+TSO+PTSO+DMCO(B)				
365501	65894+72241+72240+65935	-	TLK	EVL	-

365503	65896+72245+72244+65937	-	TLK	EVL	-	
365505	65898+72249+72248+65939	IL	TLK	EVL	-	
365507	65900+72253+72252+65941	-	TLK	EVL	-	
365515	65908+72269+72268+65949	-	TLK	EVL	-	
365527	65920+72293+72292+65961	-	TLK	EVL	-	
365535	65928+72309+72308+65969	-	TLK	EVL	-	

Coaching Stock - Passenger

Number	Type	Owner	Location
1209 (6457)	RFO	EVL	ZH
1219 (3418)	RFO	EVL	KT
5636	TSO	EVL	PM
5888	TSO	EVL	CS
6121	TSO	EVL	KT
6160	TSO	EVL	LM
6164	TSO	EVL	KT

10204 (40502)	RFM	PTR	3M
10231 (10016)	RFM	PTR	§
10232	RFM	PTR	LM
10241 (10009)	RFM	PTR	IL
10256 (10028)	RFM	PTR	YO¶
10260 (10001)	RFM	PTR	YO¶

¶ Instruction vehicle - Yoker
§ Fire Training School

10547	SLE	PTR	IS
10661 Concept vehicle at Wolverton			
10667	SLE	-	LM
10698	SLE	-	LM
10733	SLE	-	MM

Coaching Stock - NPCCS

Number	Type	Owner	Location
82109	DVT	PTR	ZB
82149	DVT	PTR	FC

92159 (81534)	BG	EVL	KT
92901 (92001)	BG	EVL	WB
92931 (92031)	BG	EVL	PY

96139 (93751)	GUV	EVL	WB
96181 (93875)	GUV	EVL	LM

Coaching Stock - HST

Number	Type	Owner	Location
40105 (42084)	TSRB	PTR	LM
40106 (42162)	TRSB	PTR	LM
40108 (42314)	TSRB	PTR	LM
40110 (421870	TRSB	PTR	LM
40210	TRS	ANG	EL
40402 (40002)	TRSB	DBR	ZR
40417 (40017)	TRSB	DBR	ZK
40424 (40024)	TRSB	ANG	DY
40425 (40025)	TRSB	DBR	ZK
40426 (40026)	TRSB	ANG	EL
40433 (40033)	TRSB	ANG	EL
40802	TRFB	PTR	LM
40804	TRFB	PTR	LM
40806	TRFB	PTR	LM
41006	TF	ANG	RTC
41006	TF	ANG	EL
41010	TF	ANG	EL
41012	TF	ANG	EL
41016	TF	ANG	EL
41020	TF	ANG	EL
41052	TF	ANG	EL
41103	TF	ANG	EL
41104	TF	ANG	EL
41108	TF	PTR	LM
41116	TF	ANG	EL
42118	TF	ANG	EL
41126	TF	ANG	EL
41128	TF	ANG	EL
41130	TF	ANG	EL
41135	TF	ANG	EL
41136	TF	ANG	EL
41137	TF	ANG	EL
41140	TF	ANG	EL
41142	TF	ANG	EL
41169	TF	PTR	LM
41176	TF	PTR	LM
41180	TF	ANG	EL
41192	TF	PTR	LM
42006	TS	ANG	EL
42009	TS	ANG	EL
42012	TS	ANG	EL
42013	TS	ANG	EL
42014	TS	ANG	EL
42028	TS	ANG	EL

42029	TS	ANG	EL
42030	TS	ANG	EL
42031	TS	ANG	EL
42043	TS	ANG	EL
42054	TS	ANG	EL
42056	TS	ANG	EL
42060	TS	ANG	EL
42061	TS	ANG	EL
42069	TS	ANG	EL
42070	TS	ANG	EL
42072	TS	ANG	EL
42075	TS	ANG	EL
42077	TS	ANG	EL
42078	TS	ANG	EL
42096	TS	ANG	EL
42099	TS	ANG	EL
42107	TS	ANG	EL
42115	TS	PTR	LM
42144	TS	ANG	EL
42185	TS	ANG	EL
42197	TS	ANG	EL
42206	TS	ANG	EL
42216	TS	ANG	EL
42232	TS	PTR	LM
42245	TS	ANG	EL
42250	TS	ANG	EL
42252	TS	ANG	EL
42253	TS	ANG	EL
42255	TS	ANG	EL
42257	TS	ANG	EL
42259	TS	ANG	EL
42261	TS	ANG	EL
42263	TS	ANG	EL
42265	TS	ANG	EL
42268	TS	ANG	EL
42272	TS	ANG	EL
42277	TS	ANG	EL
42279	TS	ANG	EL
42280	TS	ANG	EL
42281	TS	ANG	EL
42287	TS	ANG	EL
42289	TS	ANG	EL
42291	TS	ANG	EL
42293	TS	ANG	EL
42297	TS	ANG	EL
42308	TS	PTR	LM
42319	TS	PTR	LM

42333	TS	ANG	EL
42344	TS	ANG	EL
42350	TS	ANG	EL
42351	TS	ANG	EL
42360	TS	ANG	EL
42382 (121280	TS	PTR	LM
42502 (40731)	TS	ANG	EL
42507 (40209)	TS	ANG	EL
42508 (40725)	TS	ANG	EL
42511 (40709)	TS	ANG	EL
42513 (40738)	TS	ANG	EL
42551 (41013)	TS	ANG	EL
42553 (41009)	TS	ANG	EL
42555 (41015)	TS	ANG	EL
42557 (41019)	TS	ANG	EL
42564 (41051)	TS	ANG	EL
42572 (41123)	TS	ANG	EL
42573 (41127)	TS	ANG	EL
42577 (41141)	TS	ANG	EL
44000	TGS	PTR	LM
44001	TGS	ANG	EL
44004	TGS	ANG	EL
44007	TGS	ANG	EL
44009	TGS	ANG	EL
44010	TGS	ANG	EL
44018	TGS	ANG	EL
44020	TGS	ANG	EL
44023	TGS	ANG	EL
44024	TGS	ANG	EL
44025	TGS	ANG	EL
44028	TGS	ANG	EL
44030	TGS	ANG	EL
44032	TGS	ANG	EL
44035	TGS	ANG	EL
44037	TGS	ANG	EL
44038	TGS	ANG	EL
44049	TGS	ANG	EL
44089	TGS	AUT	LM
46001 (41005)	TC	ANG	EL
46008 (41109)	TC	PTR	LM
46010 (41125)	TC	ANG	EL
46011 (41147)	TC	ANG	EL
46012 (41147)	TC	PTR	LM
46014 (41168)	TC	PTR	LM
46016 (41181)	TC	PTR	LM
46018 (411910	TC	PTR	LM

O ver the years a number of former BR locomotives have, after withdrawal from normal duties, been taken up for use by industrial operators. The list below represents those that are understood to be still in existence in late 2018. Some locos operated at preservation sites are deemed to be 'industrial' but these are grouped in the preserved section.

Class 08/09

08220	Traditional Traction, working at EMD Longport
08375	Hanson Cement, Ketton
08411	RSS Rye Farm, Wishaw
08441	LNER, Bounds Green
08445	Daventry International Railfreight Terminal (DIRFT) – at LH Group, Burton
08447	John G. Russell Transit, Hillington, Glasgow
08460	RSS, at Marcroft
08480	RSS Norwich Crown Point
08484	Hitachi, Newton Aycliffe
08502	Garston Car Terminal, Liverpool
08503	Barry Island Railway
08535	Corus, Shotton Works
08536	RSS, Wishaw, Sutton Coldfield
08580	LNER Bounds Green
08593	RSS Rye Farm, Wishaw
08598	A V Dawson, Middlesbrough
08600	LH Group Services, Barton-under-Needwood
08623	Hope Cement Works
08632	RSS at Leeds Neville Hill
08670	Virgin East Coast, Bounds Green
08683	RSS Norwich Crown Point
08794	Ecclesbourne Valley Railway
08709	Traditional Traction, Colne Valley Railway
08728	St Modwen Storage, Long Marston
08731	Aggregate Industries, Merehead
08738	Colne Valley Railway
08743 *Bryan Turner*	LH Group Services, Barton-under-Needwood
08774 *Arthur Vernon Dawson*	AV Dawson, Middlesbrough
08782	HNRC, Barrow Hill
08787	Hanson Aggregates, Machen
08788	Tata Steel, Shotton
08807	AV Dawson, Middlesbrough
08809	Tata Steel, Rotherham
08823 (D3991) *Kelva*	Tata Steel, Shotton
08846	RSS, Wishaw, Sutton Coldfield
08847	Rail America / RMS
08872	HNRC, European Metal Reprocessing, Attercliffe
08903 *John W. Antill*	SembCorp Utilities Teesside, Wilton
08912	AV Dawson, Middlesbrough
08915	Stephenson Railway Museum
08921	RSS Rye Farm, Wishaw
08927	Axiom Rail, Stoke-on-Trent
08933	Aggregate Industries, Merehead
08939	Colne Valley Railway
09022	Boston Docks Co
09023	European Metal Reprocessing, Attercliffe

Class 11

12088	Butterwell

Class 14

D9529 (14029)	Aggregate Industries, Bardon Quarry

Industrial

These lists give details of former UK diesel and electric locos exported for further use overseas and understood to be still operational.

Class 03/04
D2013 Italy
D2032 Italy
D2033 Italy
D2036 Italy

D2216 Italy
D2232 Italy
D2295 Italy

Class 08
D3047 Lamco Liberia as 101
D3092 Lamco Liberia as 102
D3094 Lamco Liberia as 103
D3098 Lamco Liberia as 104
D3100 Lamco Liberia as 105

Class 10
D3639 Conakry (Guinea) - cut up
D3649 Conakry (Guinea) - cut up

Class 14
D9534 Bruges

Class 47
47375 CRS, Hungary
      92 70 0047-375-5

Class 56
56101 Floyd, Hungary
      92 55 0659-001-5
56115 Floyd, Hungary
      92 55 0659-002-3
56117 Floyd, Hungary
      92 55 0659-003-1

Class 58
58001 ETF France
58004 TSO France
58005 ETF France
58006 ETF France
58007 TSO France
58009 TSO France
58010 TSO France
58011 TSO France
58013 ETF France
58015 Transfesa, Spain
58018 TSO France
58020 Transfesa, Spain
58021 TSO France
58024 Transfesa, Spain
58025 Cont'l Rail, Spain
58026 TSO France
58027 Con'l Rail, Spain
58029 Transfesa, Spain
58030 Transfesa, Spain

58031 Transfesa, Spain
58032 ETF France
58033 TSO France
58034 TSO France
58035 TSO France
58036 ETF France
58038 ETF France
58039 ETF France
58040 TSO France
58041 Transfesa, Spain
58042 TSO France
58043 Transfesa, Spain
58044 ETF France
58046 TSO France
58047 Transfesa, Spain
58049 ETF France
58050 Cont'l Rail, Spain

Class 66
66010 ECR, France
66022 ECR, France
66026 ECR, France
66032 ECR, France
66036 ECR, France
66038 ECR, France
66042 ECR, France
66045 ECR, France
66049 ECR, France
66052 ECR, France
66064 ECR, France
66072 ECR, France
66073 ECR, France
66123 ECR, France
66146 ECR, Poland
66153 ECR, Poland
66157 ECR, Poland
66159 ECR, Poland
66163 ECR, Poland
66166 ECR, Poland
66173 ECR, Poland
66178 ECR, Poland
66179 ECR, France
66180 ECR, Poland
66189 ECR, Poland
66190 ECR, France
66195 ECR, France
66196 ECR, Poland
66202 ECR, France
66203 ECR, France
66205 ECR, France
66208 ECR, France
66209 ECR, France
66210 ECR, France
66211 ECR, France
66212 ECR, France
66214 ECR, France

66215 ECR, France
66216 ECR, France
66217 ECR, France
66218 ECR, France
66219 ECR, France
66220 ECR, Poland
66222 ECR, France
66223 ECR, France
66224 ECR, France
66225 ECR, France
66226 ECR, France
66228 ECR, France
66229 ECR, France
66231 ECR, France
66233 ECR, France
66234 ECR, France
66235 ECR, France
66236 ECR, France
66237 ECR, Poland
66240 ECR, France
66241 ECR, France
66242 ECR, France
66244 ECR, France
66246 ECR, France
66247 ECR, France
66248 ECR, Poland
66411 Freightliner PL,
      As 66013FPL
66412 Freightliner PL,
      As 66015FPL
66417 Freightliner PL,
      As 66014FPL
66527 Freightliner PL
      As No. 66016FPL
66530 Freightliner PL,
      As No. 66017FPL
66582 Freightliner PL,
      As 66009FPL
66583 Freightliner PL,
      As 66010FPL
66584 Freightliner PL,
      As 66011FPL
66586 Freightliner PL,
      As 66008FPL
66595 Freightliner PL,
      As 66595FPL
66608 Freightliner PL,
      As 66603FPL
66609 Freightliner PL,
      As 66605FPL
66611 Freightliner PL,
      As 66604FPL
66612 Freightliner PL,
      As 66606FPL
66624 Freightliner PL,
      As 66602FPL

66625 Freightliner PL,
   As 66601FPL
66954 Freightliner PL
   As 66954FPL

Class 86
86213 Bul', Bulgaria
   91 52 00 85003-9
86215 Floyd, Hungary
   91 55 0450-005-8
86217 Floyd, Hungary
   91 55 0450-006-?
86218 Floyd, Hungary
   91 55 0450-004-1
86228 Floyd, Hungary
   91 55 0450-007-
86231 Bul', Bulgaria
   91 52 00 85005-4
86232 Floyd, Hungary
   91 55 0450-003-3
86233 Bulgaria (spares)
86234 Bul', Bulgaria
   91 52 00 85006-2
86235 Bul', Bulgaria
   91 52 00 85004-7
86242 Floyd, Hungary
   91 55 0450-008-
86248 Floyd, Hungary
   91 55 0450-001-7
86250 Floyd, Hungary
   91 55 0450-002-5
86424 Floyd, Hungary
   91 55 0450-009
86701 Bul', Bulgaria
   91 52 00 85001-3
86702 Bul', Bulgaria
   91 52 00 85002-1

Class 87
87003 BZK Bulgaria
   91 52 00 87003-7
87004 BZK Bulgaria
   91 52 00 87004-5
87006 BZK Bulgaria
   91 52 00 87006-0
87007 BZK Bulgaria
   91 52 00 87007-8
87008 BZK Bulgaria
   91 52 00 87008-9
87009 BUL Bulgaria
   91 52 00 87009-4
87010 BZK Bulgaria
   91 52 00 87010-2
87012 BZK Bulgaria
   91 52 00 87012-8
87013 BZK Bulgaria
   91 52 00 87013-6
87014 BZK Bulgaria
   91 52 00 87014-7
87017 BUL Bulgaria
   91 52 00 87017-7
87019 BZK Bulgaria
   91 52 00 87019-3
87020 BZK Bulgaria
   91 52 00 87020-1
87022 BZK Bulgaria
   91 52 00 87022-7
87023 BUL Bulgaria
   91 52 00 87023-5
87025 BUL Bulgaria
   91 52 00 87025-0
87026 BZK Bulgaria
   91 52 00 87026-8
87028 BZK Bulgaria
   91 52 00 87028-4
87029 BZK Bulgaria
   91 52 00 87029-2
87033 BZK Bulgaria
   91 52 00 87033-4

87034 BZK Bulgaria
   91 52 00 87034-2

Class 92
92001 LocoTech, Russia,
   Lease to Transagent,
   Rijeka, Croatia
   91 53 0472-002-1
92002 LocoTech, Russia,
   Lease to Transagent,
   Rijeka, Croatia
   91 53 0472-003-9
92003 DBS Romania
   91 53 0472 xxx-x
92005 LocoTech, Russia,
   Lease to Transagent,
   Rijeka, Croatia
   91 53 0472-005-4
92012 LocoTech, Russia,
   Lease to Transagent,
   Rijeka, Croatia
   91 53 0472-001-3
92022 DBS Bulgaria
   91 52 1688 022-1
92024 LocoTech, Russia,
   Lease to Transagent,
   Rijeka, Croatia
   91 53 0472-004-7
92025 DBS Bulgaria
   91 52 1688 025-1
92026 DBS Romania
   91 53 0472-026-x
92027 DBS Bulgaria
   91 70 1688 027-1
92030 DBS Bulgaria
   91 52 1688 030-1
92034 DBS Bulgaria
   91 52 1688 034-3
92039 DBS Romania
   91 53 0472-006-2

Right: *A number of ex UK-based locomotives have been exported to various countries of World for further use, as well as locos, some multiple units and coaches have been exported. After withdrawal a significant number of Class 87s were exported by Porterbrook to Bulgaria. In this image we see No. 87003, now running as No. 91 52 00 87003-7 BG-BZK.*
Howard Lewsey

Northern Ireland Railways (NIR)

Class 3000

Three-car suburban sets for use in the Belfast area. Built by CAF, with seating for 200 standard class passengers. Each vehicle powered by one MAN D2876 LUH03 of 453hp (338kW). Max speed 90mph (145km/h). Introduced in 2004-05.

3001	3005	3009	3013	3017	3021
3002	3006	3010	3014	3018	3022
3003	3007	3011	3015	3019	3023
3004	3008	3012	3016	3020	

Sets 3001-3006 are fitted with CAWS and Irish Rail safety equipment to allow cross-border operation if needed.

These sets can not operate in multiple with 40xx sets in passenger traffic.

Left: *Northern Ireland Railway (NIR) passenger services based around Belfast are operated by two fleets of CAF three-car DMUs. The 3000 series were introduced in 2004-2005. Set No. 3023 is seen at Bangor.* **CJM**

Class 4000

Three-car suburban sets for use in the Belfast area. Built by CAF, with seating for 212 standard class passengers. Each vehicle powered by one MTU 6H1800 R84 of 520hp (390kW). Max speed 90mph (145km/h). Introduced in 2010-12.

4001	4005	4009	4013	4017	These sets can not
4002	4006	4010	4014	4018	operate in multiple
4003	4007	4011	4015	4019	with 30xx sets in
4004	4008	4012	4016	4020	passenger traffic.

In December 2018, 21 extra intermediate vehicles were ordered for delivery in 2021-2022, to form 7, six-car sets.

Above: *In 2010-2012 a second batch of CAF units were introduced numbered in the 4000 series, these have slightly different front end design. Set No. 4007 is viewed at Moira.* **CJM**

Class 111

These three locomotives are the same as the Irish Rail Class 071s and were built by General Motors in the late 1970s. The 57ft (17.37m)-long double-cab design is mounted on a Co-Co wheel configuration and carries an EMD 12-645-E3C prime mover. They have a top speed of 90mph (145km/h). Today the NIR fleet operates in departmental service.

8111	*Great Northern*	8112	*Northern Counties*	8113	*Belfast & County Down*

Right: *Three Class 111 locomotives are on the roster of Northern Ireland Railways and based at Belfast York Road depot. The locos see occasional engineering train use. Painted in NIR blue livery, No. 112 (8112)* Northern Counties *is seen running light power at Porterdown.* **CJM**

Class 201

Two locomotives of the 34-strong Class 201 fleet are owned by NIR for use on the Belfast-Dublin 'Enterprise' services. Built by General Motors EMD in Canada in 1994-95, these 3200hp (2400kW) locos are classified as JT42HCW, and have a top speed of 102mph (164km/h). They are fitted with retractable buffers, auto couplers, event recorders and NIR cab controls.

8208	*River Lagan*	8209	*(River Foyle)*

Service Stock

Five former Class 80 DMU vehicles and one Class 450 DMU set are retained by NIR for autumn sandite and rail cleaning, and are usually to be found at Yorkgate depot, Belfast. These vehicles are likely to be replaced by on-track plant in the near future.

Class 80

8069 (DMBSO)	8097 (DMBSO)	8752 (DTSO)
8094 (DMBSO)	8749 (DTSO)	

Class 450

Set 5 8455+8795+8785 *Galgorm Castle*
Stored at Ballymena

Irish Railways (IR)

Class 071

A fleet of 18 Irish Rail Class 071s was built by General Motors, Canada, in the late 1970s. The 57ft (17.37m)-long double-cab design is mounted on a Co-Co wheel configuration and have a EMD 12-645-E3C prime mover. They have a top speed of 90mph (145km/h). These locos are currently going through an overhaul project.

071		078		083
072		079		084
073		080		085
074		081		086
075		082	*Cumann Na nInnealtoiri /*	087
076			*The Institution Of*	088
077			*Engineers Of Ireland*	

Right: *The Irish Railways Class -071 fleet are the same as the Northern Ireland Railways Class 111, being built by General Motors in the 1970s. The locos can be found powering a handful of freight services operating each day, consisting mainly of container and log traffic. No. 079 is recorded passing through Kildare with a Ballina to Dublin Harbour container train.* **CJM**

Class 201

IR has a fleet of 32 Class 201 main-line diesel-electric locos. Built by General Motors EMD in Canada in 1994-95, these 3200hp (2400kW) locos are classified as JT42HCW and have a top speed of 102mph (164km/h). Several different variants exist within the current fleet. Locos Nos. 201-207/210-214 have fixed buffers and use shackle couplings. Nos. 215-226/229/232/234 have push-pull control, retractable buffers, electronic fuel systems and both knuckle and shackle couplings. Nos. 206-207/228/230/231/233 are similar to the 215 batch but have event recorders and cab equipment to allow operation on the NIR network.
Loco No. 216 dedicated to Belmond Pullman Train and painted in Belmond blue livery.

201(S)	Abhainn na Sionnainne	River Shannon		219	(Abhainn na Tulchann)	River Tolka
202(S)	Abhainn na Laoi	River Lee		220	An Abhainn Dhubh	River Blackwater
203(S)	Abhainn na Coiribe	River Corrib		221	Abhainn na Feilge	River Fealge
204(S)	Abhainn na Bearu	River Barrow		222	(Abhainn na Dargaile)	River Dargle
205(S)	Abhainn na Feoire	River Nore		223	Abhainn na hAinnire	River Anner
206	(Abhainn na Life)	River Liffey		224	Abhainn na Féile	(River Feale)
207	Abhainn na Bóinne	River Boyne		225(S)	Abhainn na Daoile	River Deel
210(S)	Abhainn na hEirne	River Erne		226	Abhainn na Siuire	(River Suir)
211(S)	Abhainn na Suca	River Suck		227	(Abhainn na Leamhna)	River Laune
212(S)	Abhainn na Slaine	River Slaney		228	An Abhainn Bhui	(River Owenboy)
213(S)	Abhainn na Muaidhe	River Moy		229	Abhainn na Mainge	River Maine
214(S)	Abhainn na Broshai	River Brosna		230	Abhainn na Bandan	(River Bandon)
215	An Abhainn Mhor	River Avonmore		231	Abhainn na Maighe	(River Maigue)
216*	Abhainn na Dothra	River Dodder		232	(Abhainn na Chaomaraigh)	River Cummeragh
217	Abhainn na Fleisce	River Flesk		233	Abhainn na Chlair	River Clare
218	Abhainn na Garbhoige	River Garavogue		234	(Abhainn na hEatharlai)	River Aherlow

Left: *The largest fleet of diesel locos working in Ireland are the Class 201, which now consists of 32 locos. Painted in InterCity passenger livery, No. 223 operates in push-pull mode on a Cork to Dublin service at Kildare.* **CJM**

Below: *Class 201 No. 216 is painted in Belmond Pullman 'Grand Hibernian' dark blue livery and is usually dedicated to powering the luxury land cruise train. No. 216 named River Dodder is seen at Portarlington. Note the Grand Hibernian logo on the lower cab side.* **CJM**

Class 2600

A fleet of 17 Class 2601 vehicles was introduced in 1993-94, built by Tokyu Car in Japan. Each two-car set seats 130 standard class passengers. The top speed is 70mph (110km/h). Today the remaining 16 vehicles operate in eight pairs allocated to Cork, usually working on the Mallow, Midleton and Cobh routes, occasionally being seen in the Limerick area.

2601 + 2602	2605 + 2616	2607 + 2608	2611 + 2612
2603 + 2604	2606 + 2615	2610 + 2613	2614 + 2617

Right: *A fleet of 16 Class 2600 cars are based at Cork for local branch line services. The vehicles usually operate in numeric pairs. Built by Tokyu Car, these cars retain their original end gangways. Nos. 2601 and 2602 are seen at Cork with a Cobh service.* **CJM**

Class 2800

A fleet of 10 Class 2801 vehicles was introduced in 2000, built by Tokyu Car in Japan. Each two-car set seats 85 standard class passengers. The top speed is 75mph (120km/h). Today the sets are allocated to Limerick, working local services.

2801 + 2802	2805 + 2806	2809 + 2810	2813 + 2814	2817 + 2818
2803 + 2804	2807 + 2808	2811 + 2812	2815 + 2816	2819 + 2820

Right: *Introduced in 2000 are a fleet of 20 Class 2800 DMU vehicles, again these operate in numeric pairs. The class is allocated to Limerick Town and usually operate branch services in the area. This class have lost their front gangways. Nos 2815 and 2816 are seen arriving at Limerick Town.* **CJM**

Irish Railways

Class 22000

As part of the modernisation of the IR passenger system a total of 234 22000 class vehicles are now in service operating commuter and Intercity services. The sets are presently formed into three-, four- and five-car sets. The stock was built by the partnership of Mitsui of Japan and Rotem of South Korea. Sets have a top speed of 100mph (160km/h) and each vehicle is powered by an underfloor MTU 6H 1800 R83 engine of 483hp (327kW).

Three-car Intercity/commuter sets able to operate into Northern Ireland

22001	22002	22003	22004	22005	22006

Three-car Intercity/commuter sets

22007	22008	22009	22010

Four-car Intercity/commuter sets

22011	22014	22017	22020	22023	22026	22029
22012	22015	22018	22021	22024	22027	22030
22013	22016	22019	22022	22025	22028	

Left: *The largest fleet of Irish DMUs is the Class 22000 series, which are formed and operate in a number of different configurations. Four-car Intercity formed set 023 with driving cars 22323/023 is seen calling at Bray with a Dublin to Rosslare duty.* **CJM**

Five-car Intercity sets with premier seating (first class)

22031	22033	22035	22037	22039
22032	22034	22036	22038	22040

Left: *Ten sets 031-040 are formed of five coaches and set out for Intercity operation with premier seating for first class, including a quality catering vehicle, identifiable by the plated windows in the first class driving car. A five car set with driving cars 22140/040 departs from Kildare bound for Dublin.* **CJM**

Four-car Intercity/commuter high-capacity sets

22041	22042	22043	22044	22045

Three-car Intercity/commuter sets

22046	22048	22050	22052	22054	22056	22058	22060	22062
22047	22049	22051	22053	22055	22057	22059	22061	22063

Left: *Formed as a three car Intercity/ Commuter set, driving cars 22351/051 await departure from Portarlington with a service bound for Dublin.* **CJM**

Class 29000

Introduced between 2002 and 2005, a fleet of 29 four-car CAF-built sets is allocated to the Dublin area for commuter work. Each set seats 185 standard class passengers and each vehicle is powered by an underfloor MAN D2876 LUH01 engine developing 400hp (298kW).

29001	29005	29009	29013	29017	29021	29025	29029
29002	29006	29010	29014	29018	29022	29026	
29003	29007	29011	29015	29019	29023	29027	
29004	29008	29012	29016	29020	29024	29028	

Right: *A fleet of 29 four-car CAF-built sets operate in the Dublin area. The sets sport either the green, blue and grey livery shown or all-over green. With driving car 29113 nearest the camera, set 13 is seen at Dublin Connolly.* **CJM**

Hauled Stock

'Enterprise' stock used on Belfast-Dublin route, built 1997 by De Dietrich Ferroviaire

Driving Trailer Brake First (DTBF)

9001	9002	9003	9004

Trailer First (TF)

9101	9102	9103	9104

Trailer Standard (TS)

9201	9205	9209	9213
9202	9206	9210	9214
9203	9207	9211	9215
9204	9208	9212	9216

Trailer Cafe (TC)

9401	9402	9403	9404

Right: *The 'Enterprise service between Belfast and Dublin is operated by a fleet of 1997-built De Dietrich and have a number of resemblances to UK e300 Class 383 Eurostar stock. Trailer Cafe car No. 9403 is illustrated.* **CJM**

Generator Car (GEN)

9602	9604	9605	9608	9613

Right: *To provide hotel power for the Enterprise operation, each train has a Generator Coach, coupled between the loco and train. These are of the Mk 2 design. No. 9604 is shown.* **CJM**

Odd-numbered sets are owned by Irish Rail, even-numbered sets are owned by Northern Ireland Railways.

Irish Railways

Mk4 Inter-City stock built by CAF in 2006. Operated on Dublic to Cork route

Driving Van Trailer (DVT)

4001	4002	4003	4004	4005	4006	4007	4008

Left: *To operate InterCity services, a fleet of CAF-built loco-hauled stock was introduced in 2006 to provide remote driving controls (usually at the Dublin end of formations), a fleet of Driving Van Trailers were introduced, with a rather unusual front end style. These vehicles also house a generator. No. 4005 is seen passing Kildare with a service from Cork to Dublin.* **CJM**

Trailer Standard (*End) (TSO)

4101	4107	4113	4119	4125*	4131	4137	4143
4102	4108	4114	4120*	4126	4132	4138	
4103	4109	4115*	4121	4127	4133	4139	
4104	4110*	4116	4122	4128	4134	4140*	
4105*	4111	4117	4123	4129	4135*	4141	
4106	4112	4118	4124	4130*	4136	4142	

Left: *Standard class seating in the 2+2 style is provided by a fleet of Trailer Standard and Trailer Standard End coaches, numbered in the 41xx series. All vehicles have sliding plug doors and carry Irish Rail two-tone green and grey livery. Vehicle No. 4111 is shown.* **CJM**

Trailer First (TFO)

4201	4202	4203	4204	4205	4206	4207	4208

Trailer Buffet (RBR)

4401	4402	4403	4404	4405	4406	4407	4408

Belmond Pullman 'Grand Hibernian'

In 2016 luxury train operator Belmond launched an Irish high-quality land cruise train. Formed of 10 former CIE Mk3s first introduced in 1980-85 and withdrawn in 2009, the coaches have been totally rebuilt by Brodie Engineering in Kilmarnock, Scotland, and fitted out at Mivan Engineering in Ireland. The train is usually powered by IR Class 201 No. 216 which carries the Belmond blue livery.

Sleeping Cabin Cars

7116 (55 60 76 87001-8)	Fermanagh	
7129 (55 60 76 87003-4)	Waterford	
7137 (55 60 76 87005-0)	Kerry	
7149 (55 60 76 87004-2)	Down	

7158 (55 60 76 87002-6)   Leitrim

Dining Cars

7169 (55 60 88 87102-0)   Wexford
7171 (55 60 88 87101-2)   Sligo

Observation/Bar Car
7104 (55 60 89 **87103**-7)   **Kildare**

Crew Car
7130 (55 60 89 **87110**-2)   **Donegal**

Generator Car
7601 (55 60 99 **87104**-3)   **Carlow**

Vehicle No. 7122 is also owned by Belmond and stored unrefurbished in Dublin.

Right: *The impressive Belmond Pullman 'Grand Hibernian' luxury land cruise train is formed of a rake of 10 redundant CIE BREL-built Mk3 coaches, hugely rebuilt. The stock is now finished in a dark blue livery with cast nameplates on the bodyside of each vehicle and a cast 'Grand Hibernian' logo. Sleeping/Cabin Car 7149 Down is shown.* **CJM**

Left: *Dining car No. 7169 Wexford.* **CJM**

Below: *Rebuilding included for formation of two high quality Observation/Bar cars. No. 7104 Kildare is illustrated from its observation end.* **CJM**

Irish Railways

Dublin DART

The Dublin Area Rapid Transit (DART) is a local network around Dublin, opened in 1983. It is electrified at 1500V dc overhead. The original stock supplied by GEC / Linke Hofmall Busch has been supplemented by stock from Tokyu Car. All sets are maintained at Fairview, Dublin. Trains are formed as four-car sets with driving trailers at the outer end and driving motor cars in the middle.

Class 8100

Original two-car sets built by GEC / LHB - 8100 series

8101+8301	8108+8308	8115+8315	8122+8322	8129+8329	8137+8337
8102+8302	8109+8309	8116+8316	8123+8323	8130+8330	8138+8338
8103+8303	8110+8310	8117+8317	8124+8324	8131+8331	8139+8339
8104+8304	8111+8311	8118+8318	8125+8325	8132+8332	8140+8340
8105+8305	8112+8312	8119+8319	8126+8326	8133+8333	
8106+8306	8113+8313	8120+8320	8127+8327	8134+8334	
8107+8307	8114+8314	8121+8321	8128+8328	8135+8335	

Left: *GEC/LHB-built DART set No. 8333, one of the original two-car sets, which usually operate in eight-car formations is seen on an inbound service to Dublin at Howth Junction.* **CJM**

Class 8500

2000-built four-car sets by Tokyu Car - 8500 series

8601+8501+8502+8602	8603+8503+8504+8604	8605+8505+8506+8606	8607+8507+8508+8608

Class 8510

2001-built four-car sets by Tokyu Car - 8510 series

8611+8511+8512+8612	8613+8513+8514+8614	8615+8515+8516+8616

Class 8520

2003-04-built four-car sets by Tokyu Car - 8520 series

8621+8521+8522+8622	8627+8527+8528+8628	8633+8533+8534+8634	8639+8539+8540+8640
8623+8523+8524+8624	8629+8529+8530+8630	8635+8535+8536+8636	
8625+8525+8526+8626	8631+8531+8532+8632	8637+8537+8538+8638	

Left: *The 8500, 8510 and 8520 class sets are four-car units built by Tokyu Car and have a two window front end arrangement. Four-car set No. 8627 forms the rear set of a train from Howth to Dublin seen departing from Howth Junction.* **CJM**

With the introduction of modern traction from the 1950s a number of different methods of multiple operation were introduced, covering the different control principles of locomotives, for example those using electro-pneumatic or electro-magnetic systems.

Six main systems are in operation today:

Blue Star ★ using the electro-pneumatic system and fitted to Classes 20, 25, 31, 33, 37, 40 and 73.

Green Spot ● a unique system installed on some Class 47s operated by the freight sector.

Orange Square ■ an English Electric system used only on the Class 50s.

Red Diamond ♦ a 1970s system developed for the modern freight locos of Classes 56 and 58.

In addition to the above coded systems, the American-developed main-line locos of Classes 59, 66, 67 and 70 use the US standard AAR (Association of American Railroads) system. Direct Rail Services (DRS) has also developed a unique system, which is installed on some of the company's Class 20, 37, 47 and 57 locos.

A number of locomotives have either been built with or modified to incorporate Time Division Multiplex (TDM) remote operation equipment, which uses coach lighting-type Railway Clearing House (RCH) nose-end jumper cables.

Some of the surviving first generation DMMU sets carry a **Blue Square** ■ multiple operation system.

Details of the main coupling systems in operation in the UK are included in the accompanying illustrations.

Standard Coupling

Above: *Class 59 and 66 front-end layout (non-DB-S operated). 1-Coupling hook, 2-Coupling shackle, 3-Air brake pipe (red), 4-Main reservoir pipe (yellow), 5-Buffer, 6-Association of American Railroads (AAR) jumper socket. No. 66726 is illustrated.* **CJM**

Standard Coupling

Above: *Standard coupling arrangement to be found on many classes of UK loco. 1-Electric Train Supply (ETS) jumper socket, 2-Main reservoir air pipe (yellow), 3-Vacuum brake pipe, 4-Coupling hook and shackle, 5-Air brake pipe (red), 6-Electric Train Supply (ETS) jumper cable. No. 47580 is illustrated.* **CJM**

Drophead Buckeye with TDM Coupling

Above: *The unique front-end layout of the Royal Mail Class 325. 1-Brake pipe (red), 2-Main reservoir pipe (yellow), 3-Electric Train Supply (ETS) socket, 4-Time Division Multiplex (TDM) jumper socket, 5-Drophead buckeye coupling, 6-Electric Train Supply (ETS) cable.* **CJM**

Couplings

Drophead Dellner Coupling

Above: *Following the introduction of Virgin Trains 'Voyager' and 'Pendolino' stock, a fleet of 16 Class 57/3s was introduced with drophead Dellner couplers and cabling to provide 'hotel power'. The coupling is seen in this illustration in the raised position. 1-Electric Train Supply (ETS) jumper socket, 2-Main reservoir pipe (yellow), 3-Air brake pipe (red), 4-Coupling hook, 5-Dellner coupling face, 6-Electric Train Supply (ETS) jumper cable.* **CJM**

BSI Coupling

Above: *With the birth of modern multiple unit trains came the Bergische Stahl Industrie (BSI) automatic coupling, first seen in the UK on the Tyne & Wear Metro vehicles in 1978. The modern generation of UK DMUs now concentrates on the Compact BSI coupler with a CK2 coupling interface. The couplers are engaged by the compression of the two coupling faces, which completes a physical connection and also opens a watertight cover to an electrical connection box. The full train air connection is made during the coupling compression process. The coupling is completed by the driver pressing a 'couple' button in the driving cab. 1-Emergency air connection, 2-Coupling face, 3-Electric connection (behind plate), 4-Air connection. The coupling shown is on a Class 166.* **CJM**

Tightlock with Drum Connection

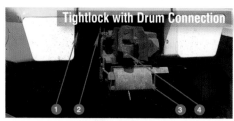

Above: *The Tightlock coupler is a derivative of the Association of American Railroads (AAR) Type H coupler, later under the control of the American Public Transportation Association (APTA). A modified Type H coupler was introduced in the UK from the early 1970s and has become a standard fitting on many of the later BR and several post-privatisation EMUs. The UK Tightlock design can be supplied with or without an electrical connection box and with or without a pneumatic connection. This view shows a fully automated version as fitted to the 'Networker' fleet. Attachment is achieved by driving the two vehicles together, which physically connects them, while a 'roll-cover' box opens to connect electric and pneumatic services. 1-Emergency air connector, 2-Manual release handle, 3-Semi-rotary electric/pneumatic cover, 4-Physical coupler.* **CJM**

Tightlock with Nose End Connections

Above: *The BR Southern Region-designed Class 455 and 456 units have a semi-automatic Tightlock used for physical connections, while air and electrical connections are made by waist-height flexible pipes. 1-Main reservoir pipe (yellow), 2-Control jumper, 3-Tightlock coupler, 4-Couple/Uncouple drum switch, 5-Manual release handle, 6-Control jumper receptacle.* **CJM**

Dellner Coupling with Drum Connector

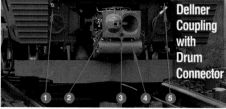

Above: *Dellner couplers have become the standard in the UK and much of Europe; these are fully automatic and come in various forms. 1-Emergency air supply, 2-Dellner coupling plate, 3-Pneumatic connection, 4-Roll-cover to electrical connections, 5-Air supply. Coupling of a Class 360 is illustrated.* **CJM**

Dellner Coupling

Above: *A large number of different designs of Dellner couplers exist on UK rolling stock. Some feature full automatic operation including pneumatic and electrical connections, while others only provide physical coupling. This view shows a pair of 'Voyager' units coupled together with Dellner couplers. The electrical connection box is above the physical coupler. After trains are 'pushed' together the driver operates a 'couple' button in the cab to complete the attachment. Uncoupling is achieved by the driver pressing an 'uncouple' button and driving the trains apart.* **CJM**

Dellner Coupling

Right: *The Virgin Trains 'Pendolino' stock uses Dellner couplers with a rotary covered electrical connector plate above. These couplers are supplemented by electric train supply connections on either side to provide 'hotel power' to Class 390 sets from attached Class 57 locos. 1-Electric Train Supply (ETS) socket, 2-Emergency air connector, 3-Electrical connector plate under semi-rotary cover, 4-Dellner physical coupler, 5-Pneumatic connections. In normal use the Dellner coupler on 'Pendolino' stock is covered by a front fairing.* **CJM**

Dellner Coupling Without Electric Connector

Above: *Under the front-end fairing of the Eurostar Class 373 stock a standard Scharfenberg coupler is located for assistance purposes and shunting. No electrical provision is made and the couplers are seldom used. 1-Scharfenberg coupling face, 2-Pneumatic connections, 3-Manual uncoupling handle.* **CJM**

Dellner Coupling With Electric Connector

Above: *In as-installed condition and having never been coupled to another set, a Class 380 Scharfenberg coupler is viewed, showing the auto opening electrical connection box above. 1-Electrical connection box, 2-Coupling face plate, 3-Pneumatic connection.* **CJM**

Couplings

Emergency HST Bar Coupling

Left: *If High Speed Trains are required to be coupled to conventional hook couplings an adaptor coupling is carried on the HST for this purpose. It has to be first attached to the front of the HST by opening the front panel and attaching the aluminium bar to a coupling lug. The other end is then at the right level and length to attach to a standard loco hook coupling without the loco's buffers touching the HST's bodywork. Standard air connection is provided. Locos fitted with swing-head or combination couplers cannot be used to assist HST stock. A Class 59/1 is seen attached to HST power car No. 43150 in this view at Westbury.* **Greg Welsh**

Emergency HST Bar / Combination Coupling

Left: *With the introduction of combination couplings on Class 66s and 67s and the deployment of Class 67s as East Coast 'Thunderbirds' came the need to develop a revised HST bar coupling, which could attach to the extended jaw of the auto coupler. To use this coupling method, a pair of short extension air hoses are required to bridge the increased space between the HST and Class 67 hoses. The Class 67 to HST coupling using the auto coupler and extension hoses is shown with the attachment of No. 67030 and East Coast power car No. 43315.* **Antony Christie**

DBS Combination Coupler

Left Below: *All DBS Class 66s (except Nos. 66001/002) and all Class 67s are fitted with swing-head combination couplers allowing attachment to other like-fitted locos or rolling stock using a knuckle coupling. Two Class 66s are seen here attached using the swing-head coupler. Note that the buffers do not touch and that all traction and braking forces are transmitted through the coupler. Standard buffer-beam air connections are provided on one main reservoir and one brake pipe. The auto coupler can be disconnected by using the white uncoupling handle seen on the left.* **Antony Christie**

Right: *Front end equipment positions for the latest 'state-of-the-art Class 88 electro-diesel locomotives now in service with DRS. 1: Air warning horns located behind grill panel, 2: High level marker light, 3: Multiple control jumper connections (cable for use is carried in engine compartment). 4: Light cluster (headlight, marker and tail light), 5: Lamp bracket, 6: Electric Train Supply (ETS) jumper cable, 7: Main reservoir pipe (yellow), 8: Air brake pipe (red), 9: Coupling shackle and hook, 10: Electric Train Supply jumper socket, 11: Adjustable height obstacle deflector plate.* **CJM**

Right: *Class 800, 801 and 802 Dellner coupling, showing bi-parting doors in open position. Above the physical 'cup and cone' coupling is the electrical connection box, at the base of the coupling plate is a main reservoir pipe connection. A shore electrical connection socket (orange) is on the far side.* **CJM**

Couplings

Rail Data Tables

Livery Codes

Code	Description
AGI	Aggregate Industries - green, silver and green
AIN	Aggregate Industries - blue
ALS	Alstom Transportation
ANG	Anglia - mid blue
ANN	Anglia - turquoise/white with Greater Anglia branding
ATE	Arriva Trains Executive - turquoise/cream with branding
ATT	Arriva Trains Wales - Welsh Government
ATW	Arriva Trains Wales - turquoise/cream
AWT	Abellio - white Greater Anglia
AXC	Arriva Cross Country - brown, silver, pink
AZU	LNER 'Azuma' red and white
BBR	Balfour Beatty Rail - blue/white
BLG	Blue and grey
BLK	Black
BLL	BR Rail Blue with large logo
BLU	Blue
BLW	Carillion Rail - blue/white
BOM	Bombardier Transportation
BPM	Blue Pullman - Nankin blue and white
BRD	BR Departmental mid-grey
BRT	BR Trainload two-tone grey
C2C	c2c - blue/pink
CAL	Caledonian Railway
CAS	Caledonian Sleepers
CAR	Carmine and cream
CEN	Central Trains - blue and two-tone green
CHC	Chocolate and cream
CIV	BR Civil Engineers - grey and yellow
COL	Colas - orange, lime green and black
CON	Continental Rail - light/mid-blue
COR	Corus Steel - light blue or yellow
COX	Connex - white and yellow
CRG	Chiltern Railways - grey
CRO	CrossRail
CRR	Chitern Railways local revised
CRW	Chiltern Railways - white/blue
CTL	Central Trains - blue, green with yellow doors
CWR	Cotswold Rail - silver with branding
DBB	DB-Schenker - light blue
DBM	DB-Schenker - maroon
DBS	DB-Schenker - red
DCG	Devon & Cornwall Railways - green
DCN	Devon & Cornwall Railways - grey
DRB	Direct Rail Services - blue
DRC	Direct Rail Services - blue 'Compass' branding
DRO	Direct Rail Services - Ocean Liner blue
DRS	Direct Rail Services - blue
DRU	Direct Rail Services - unbranded blue
ECG	East Coast - grey
ECR	European Cargo Rail - grey
ECS	East Coast - silver
ECW	East Coast - white
ECT	East Coast - branded National Express livery
EMT	East Midlands Trains - white, blue, swirl cab ends
EPR	Europhoenix - red/silver with ROG brand
EPS	European Passenger Services
EPX	Europhoenix - red/silver
ETF	ETF Rail - yellow with green band
EUB	Eurostar new style - blue/grey
EUS	Eurostar - white, yellow and blue
EWE	DBS Executive
EWS	English Welsh & Scottish - red with gold band
FER	Fertis - grey with branding
FGB	First Great Western - blue
FGF	First Group - GBRf (Barbie)
FGL	First Great Western - local lines
FGS	First Group ScotRail with EWS branding
FGW	First Great Western - as FST with FGW branding
FHT	First Hull Trains - as FST with Hull Trains branding
FLG	Freightliner - green unbranded
FLP	Freightliner - green/yellow - PowerHaul
FLR	Freightliner - green/yellow - original
FLU	Freightliner - green/yellow - unbranded
FLY	Freightliner - grey
FNA	First livery with National Express East Anglia branding
FSN	Northern branded First Group
FST	First Group - dark blue, pink and white swirl
FSW	First Group - green and white with gold branding
FTN	First TransPennine - silver, blue and mauve
FTP	First TransPennine - as FST with FTP branding
GAR	Greater Anglia Railways
GAZ	Greater Anglia Railways - Renatus
GBE	GB Railfreight - Europorte branding
GBF	GB Railfreight - swirl
GBN	GB Railfreight/Eurotunnel new livery
GBR	GB Railfreight - blue
GBU	GB Railfreight - swirl (no First branding)
GEM	Gemini Rail Services
GLX	Glaxochem - grey, blue and black
GRN	Green
GRY	Grey
GSW	Great Scottish & Western Railway - maroon
GTO	Grand Central Railway - black with orange
GWG	Great Western - green
GWR	Great Western Railway - green
GYF	Genesee & Wyoming / Freightliner - orange
HAN	Hanson
HEC	Heathrow Connect - grey, orange
HEL	Heathrow Connect - Terminal 4 'Link'
HEX	Heathrow Express - silver, grey
HNR	Harry Needle Railroad - yellow/grey
HS1	High Speed 1 - blue with powder blue doors
HUN	Hunslet
ICS	InterCity Swallow
IND	Industrial colours of operator
INT	InterCity - two-tone grey offset with red and white body band

JAR	Jarvis - maroon	SCF	Stagecoach - white with East Midlands branding modified
KBR	Knorr Bremse Rail - blue, white, green	SCI	ScotRail Intercity
LAF	Lafarge Aggregates - green/white	SCR	Scottish Railways - blue with Saltire
LHL	Loadhaul Freight - black and orange	SCS	Serco Caledonian Sleepers
LLB	Large Logo Blue	SCT	ScotRail Caledonian Sleepers - mauve/white
LMI	London Midland - grey, green and black	SCQ	Scottish Railways - White
LNE	LNER white/red	SEB	South Eastern Trains - blue
LNR	LNER Red (ex Virgin)	SEC	Serco
LNW	West Midlands Trains LNW branding	SET	South Eastern Trains - white with branding
LOG	London Overground - white and blue/orange	SGK	Southern Gatwick Express - blue, white and red with swirl ends
LON	London Overground - New style	SIL	Silver
LUL	London Underground - red	SKL	Silverlink London Overground, SLK with London Overground branding
MAI	MainTrain - blue with branding	SLF	Silverlink, with First Great Western branding
MAL	Malcolm Rail	SLK	Silverlink - mauve, green and white
MAR	Maroon	SNF	Railfreight grey with SNCF branding
MER	Merseyrail - silver and yellow	SNT	SNCF domestic on Eurostar - silver, white and yellow
MLF	Mainline Freight - aircraft blue	SOU	Southern - white, black and green
MLG	Mainline Freight - branded double grey	SPL	Special livery
MML	Midland Main Line - turquoise/white	SRB	Scotrail blue
MRS	Mutares Rail Services	STN	Stansted Express
MSC	Mediterranean Shipping Company	SWM	South West Trains - main-line white and blue
NBP	Northern Belle Pullman - cream/umber	SWN	South West Trains - main-line white (modified)
NE2	National Express with c2c branding	SWO	South West Trains - outer-suburban blue
NGE	First Great Eastern - grey/blue with cab end swirl, branded National Express	SWR	South Western Railway
NRE	Northern Rail - Electric	SWS	South West Trains - suburban red
NNR	New Northern Rail - blue/white	SWT	South West Trains - blue, red, grey
NOM	Northern Rail - blue Metro branded	TAT	Tata Steel - blue
NOR	Northern Rail - blue, purple, grey	TES	Tesco
NOU	Northern Rail - unbranded	TEX	TransPennine Express - as FST with TPE brand
NRL	Network Rail - yellow with branding	TFI	Transport for Wales - ATW with TfW branding
NSE	Network SouthEast - red, white and blue	TFW	Transport for Wales white/red
NUB	Northern Rail blue - unbranded ScotRail	TGG	Transrail - grey with 'T' branding
NWT	North West Trains - dark blue	THM	Thameslink - blue, white, yellow
GAR	National Express East Anglia (now Abellio)	TLF	Trainload Freight - grey
NXU	National Express unbranded white/grey	TLK	Thameslink new
ONE	One Anglia - mid-blue (now Abellio)	TLL	Trainload - grey with Loadhaul branding
ORA	One Railway with Greater Anglia branding	TOQ	Turquoise, former Arriva Trains Wales
ORG	HNRC - orange	TSO	Travaux du Sud Ouest - yellow
PTR	Porterbrook	TTG	Two-tone grey
PUL	Pullman - umber/cream	VIR	Virgin - red/grey
QOS	Queen of Scots Pullman	VSN	VSOE Northern
RFD	Railfreight Distribution	VWC	Virgin West Coast - silver, red, white and black
RFE	Railfreight - grey with EWS branding	VWN	Virgin West Coast - revised
RFG	Railfreight - grey	WAB	Wabtec Rail - black
RFI	Railfreight International	WAG	West Anglia Great Northern - purple
RFP	Railfreight with Petroleum branding	WCR	West Coast Railway - maroon
RFT	BR Railfreight - grey, red and yellow, with large logo and numbers	WES	Wessex Trains - maroon
RIV	Riviera Trains - maroon	WET	Wessex Trains - silver, maroon/pink doors
RML	Royal Mail Limited - red	WEX	Wessex Rail Engineering
ROG	Rail Operations Group - branding	WHT	White
ROZ	Rail Operations Group - blue with flash	WMT	West Midlands Trains - mauve
ROY	Royal Train - claret	YEL	Yellow
RTB	Railtrack - blue		
RTK	Railtrack - grey/brown		
SCC	Strathclyde - carmine and cream (some with turquoise band)		
SCE	Stagecoach - white with East Midlands branding original		

Data Tables

Rail Data Tables

Operational Pool Codes

ATLO	West Coast Traincare - Locomotives	MBDL	Private operators - Diesel traction
AWCX	West Coast Railway - Stored locos	PTXX	Eurotunnel - Europorte2 Class 92
COFS	Colas Rail - Class 56	QCAR	Network Rail - HST power cars
COLO	Colas Rail - Operational locomotives	QETS	Network Rail - Class 97/3
COLS	Colas Rail - Stored locomotives	RCZH	Railcare Springburn - Class 08
COTS	Colas Rail - For refurbishment	RCZN	Railcare Wolverton - Class 08
DFFT	Freightliner - Restricted duties	RFSH	Wabtec Rail Doncaster - Class 08
DFGC	Freightliner - Class 86/5 trials locomotive	RVLO	Rail Vehicle Engineering Derby - Locos
DFGH	Freightliner - Heavy Haul Class 70	RVLS	Rail Vehicle Engineering Derby - Stored locos
DFGI	Freightliner - Class 70	SROG	Rail Operations Group - stored locos
DFHH	Freightliner - Heavy Haul Class 66/6	TTLS	Traditional Traction - Locomotives
DFIM	Freightliner - Class 66/5	WAAC	DB-Cargo - Class 67
DFIN	Freightliner - Class 66/5 low emission	WABC	DB-Cargo - Class 67 RETB fitted
DFLC	Freightliner - Class 90	WACC	DB-Cargo - Class 67 hire to Chiltern
DFLH	Freightliner - Class 47	WAWC	DB-Cargo - Class 67 hire to Arriva T W
DFLS	Freightliner - Class 08	WBAE	DB-Cargo - Class 66 stop/start fitted
DFNC	Freightliner - Class 86/6	WBAR	DB-Cargo - Class 66 RHTT
DFRT	Freightliner - Class 66 Infrastructure contracts	WBAT	DB-Cargo - Class 66 general
DFTZ	Freightliner - Stored Class 66	WBBE	DB-Cargo - Class 66 stop/start fitted, RETB
DHLT	Freightliner - Awaiting repairs	WBBT	DB-Cargo - Class 66 RETB fitted
EFOO	First Great Western - Class 57	WBLE	DB-Cargo - Class 66 Lickey banker stop/start
EFPC	First Great Western - HST power cars	WBLT	DB-Cargo - Class 66 Lickey banker
EFSH	First Great Western - Class 08	WBRT	DB-Cargo - Class 66 RHTT general
EHPC	CrossCountry Trains - HST power cars	WBSN	DB-Cargo - Class 66 RHTT general
EJLO	London Midland - Class 08	WCAT	DB-Cargo - Class 60 standard fuel capacity
EMPC	East Midlands Trains - HST power cars	WCBT	DB-Cargo - Class 60 extended fuel capacity
EMSL	East Midlands Trains - Class 08	WDAM	DB-Cargo - Class 59/2
EPXX	Europhoenix - Class 86	WEAC	DB-Cargo - Class 90 general
GBBR	GBRf - Class 73/9	WEDC	DB-Cargo - Class 90 hire Virgin
GBBT	GBRf - Class 66 large fuel tanks	WFMS	DB-Cargo - Class 60 Fleet Management
GBCD	GBRf - Class 92 Channel Tunnel	WGEA	DB-Cargo - Class 66 for Export
GBCM	GBRf - Class 66 commercial contracts	WLAN	DB-Cargo - Euro Cargo Rail Class 21
GBDR	GBRf - Class 66 new ex-DB	WNTS	DB-Cargo - Stored locos, serviceable
GBEB	GBRf - Class 66 Euro large tanks	WNXX	DB-Cargo - Stored locos, unserviceable
GBED	GBRf - Class 73/1, 73/2	WNYX	DB-Cargo - Stored locos, parts recovery
GBEL	GBRf - Class 66 Euro small tanks	WNZX	DB-Cargo - Awaiting disposal
GBET	GBRf - Class 92	WFAC	DB-Cargo - Class 92 general
GBFM	GBRf - Class 66 modified with RETB	WFBC	DB-Cargo - Class 92 HS1 equipped
GBHN	GBRf - HNRC locos on loan	WFCC	DB-Cargo - Class 92 HS1 equipped DRS
GBLT	GBRf - Class 66 small fuel tanks	WFDC	DB-Cargo - Class 92 Hire DRS
GBMU	GBRf - Class 66 modified for MU	XHAC	Direct Rail Services - Class 47
GBNL	GBRf - Class 66 new ex-NL	XHCE	Direct Rail Services - Class 68 Chiltern
GBOB	GBRf - Class 66 ex DB-Cargo	XHCK	Direct Rail Services - Class 57
GBRT	GBRf - Class 66 Infrastructure	XHNB	Direct Rail Services - Northern Belle
GBSL	GBRf - Class 92 Caledonian Sleepers	XHND	Direct Rail Services - Class 37 Network Rail
GBST	GBRf - Class 92 Sleeper & C Tunn	XHHP	Direct Rail Services - Holding Pool
GBTG	GBRf - Class 60	XHIM	Direct Rail Services - Class 66, Intermodal
GBWM	GBRf - Class 08	XHNC	Direct Rail Services - Nuclear Traffic
GBZZ	GBRf - Stored locomotives	XHSS	Direct Rail Services - Stored
GCHP	Grand Central - HST power cars	XHTP	Direct Rail Services - Class 68 Trans Pennine
GPSS	Eurostar UK - Class 08	XHVE	Direct Rail Services - Class 68
GROG	Rail Operations Group - operational locos	XHVT	Direct Rail Services - Class 57 Thunderbird
HNRL	Harry Needle Railroad - Class 08, 20 hire locos	XYPA	Mendip Rail - Hanson Group
HNRS	Harry Needle Railroad - Stored locomotives	XYPO	Mendip Rail - Foster Yeoman (Aggregate Inds)
HTCX	Hanson Traction - Class 56		
IANA	Abellio East Anglia - Class 90		
IECA	LNER - Class 91		
IECP	LNER - HST power cars		
LSLO	Loco Services - operational		
LSLS	Loco Services - stored		

■ Pools are given only for locomotive groups which are included in this book. Pool codes for multiple units are not included.

Data Tables

Operator Codes

AFG	Arlington Fleet Group
ALL	Allelys Heavy Haul
ALS	Alstom
AMS	Amec Spie Rail
ASR	Abellio Scottish Railways
ATW	Arriva Trains Wales
AXC	Arriva Cross Country
AXI	Axiom Rail
BAR	British American Railway Services
BBR	Balfour Beatty
BHE	Barrow Hill Roundhouse
BOK	Bo'ness & Kinneil
BOM	Bombardier
BRM	Birmingham Railway Museum
BTL	Brush Traction Limited
C2C	c2c Rail
CAR	Carillion
CHS	Crewe Heritage Centre
COL	Colas Rail
CON	Continental Rail (Spain)
COR	Corus Steel
CRW	Chiltern Railways
DBA	DB Arriva
DBR	DB Regio
DBS	DB-Schenker West
DRS	Direct Rail Services
ECR	Euro Cargo Rail (DBS)
ELR	East Lancashire Railway
EMT	East Midlands Trains
ERS	Eastern Rail Services
ETF	ETF Freight (France)
ETL	Electric Traction Ltd
EUR	Eurotunnel
EUS	Eurostar
FDH	Felixstowe Dock & Harbour
FHT	First Hull Trains
FIL	First Island Line
FLR	Freightliner
FSL	Flying Scotsman Railway Ltd
FTP	First TransPennine
GBR	GB Railfreight
GEM	Gemini Rail Services
GRP	Grant Rail Plant
GTL	Grand Central Railway
GTR	Govia Thameslink Railway
GWR	Great Western Railway
GWS	Great Western Society
HEC	Heathrow Connect
HEX	Heathrow Express
HIT	Hitachi
HNR	Harry Needle Railroad
IND	Industrial operator
IRY	Ian Riley
JHS	Jeremy Hosking
KBR	Knorr Bremse Rail
KRS	Knights Rail Services
LAF	Lafarge Aggregates
LNW	L&NWR Railway Co
LOG	London Overground
LOR	Loram UK
LUL	London Underground Ltd
MER	Merseyrail
MHR	Mid-Hants Railway
MoD	Ministry of Defence
MRC	Midland Railway Centre
MRL	Mendip Rail Ltd
NDZ	NedTrains
NOR	Northern Rail
NOT	Northumbria Rail
NRL	Network Rail
NRM	National Railway Museum
NVR	Nene Valley Railway
NYM	North Yorkshire Moors Railway
OLD	Old Dalby Test Track
POB	Port of Boston
PUL	Pullman Group
RAF	Railfilms Ltd
RCL	Railcare Ltd
RIV	Riviera Trains
RRS	Ridings Railtours
S4G	Stratford 47 Group
SCR	Scottish Railways
SET	SouthEastern Trains
SIE	Siemens
SLR	St Leonards Rail Engineering
SNB	Société Nationale des Chemins de fer Belges
SNF	Société Nationale des Chemins de fer Français
SOU	Southern
SRP	Scottish Railway Preservation Society
SVR	Severn Valley Railway
SWR	South West Railway
TfL	Transport for London
TfW	Transport for Wales
TRN	Transfesa
TSO	Travaux du Sud Ouest (France)
TTS	Transmart Trains
VSO	Venice Simplon Orient Express
VTN	Vintage Trains
VEC	Virgin East Coast
VWC	Virgin West Coast
WAB	Wabtec
WCR	West Coast Railway Co
WMR	West Midlands Trains

Above: *Displaying the latest 'flowing silk' colours, Class 390 No. 390117 passes South Kenton with a Euston bound service on 5 November 2018.* **CJM**

Data Tables

Depot Codes

Code	Facility	Name	Operator
AB	SD	Aberdeen Guild Street	DBS
AC	CSD	Aberdeen Clayhills	ICE
AD	EMUD	Ashford Hitachi	HIT/SET
AF	T&RSMD	Ashford Chart Leacon	BOM
AH	MoD	Ashchurch	MoD
AK	DMUD	Ardwick	SIE/FTP
AL	DMUD	Aylesbury	CRW
AN	TMD/WRD	Allerton, Liverpool	DBS/NOR
AP	TMD	Ashford Rail Plant	BBR
AS	Store	Allelys	ALL
AT	TMD	Various sites	ALS
AW	SD	Washwood Heath	Hanson
AZ	TMD	Ashford	BBR
AZ	TMD	Alizay (France)	ECR (DBS)
BA	TMD	Crewe Basford Hall	FLR
BC	MoD	Bicester	MoD
BD	T&RSMD	Birkenhead North	MER
BF	EMUD	Bedford Cauldwell Walk	GTR
BG	SD	Hull Botanic Gardens	NOR
BH	Eng	Barrow Hill Roundhouse	BHE
BI	EMUD	Brighton	GTR
BK	T&RSMD	Barton Hill	LNWR
BL	T&RSMD	Crewe Basford Hall	FLR
BM	T&RSMD	Bournemouth	SWR
BN	T&RSMD	Bounds Green	VEC
BO	T&RSMD	Burton	Nemesis
BP	SD	Blackpool CS	NOR
BQ	TMD	Bury	ELR
BR	SD	Bristol Kingsland Road	NRL, FLR
BS	TMD	Bescot	DBS
BT	TMD	Bo'ness	BOK
BW	SD	Barrow-in-Furness	NOR
BZ	T&RSMD	St Blazey	DBS
CA	SD	Cambridge Coldhams Ln	AXI
CB	STORE	Crewe Brook Sidings	DBS
CC	T&RSMD	Clacton	GAR
CD	SD	Crewe Diesel	LSL
CE	IEMD	Crewe Electric	DBS
CF	DMUD	Cardiff Canton	PUL
CG	TMD	Crewe Gresty Bridge	DRS
CH	DMUD	Chester	ALS, ATW
CJ	SD	Clapham Junction	SWR
CK	DMUD	Corkerhill	SCR
CL	TMD	Crewe Loco Services	LSC
CO	IEMD	Coquelles (France)	EUR
CP	CARMD	Crewe Carriage Shed	LNW
CQ	T&RSMD	Crewe Railway Age	CHC
CR	SD	Colchester	GAR
CS	T&RSMD	Carnforth	WCR
CT	SD	Cleethorpes	FTP
CV	TMD	Cardiff Canton	ATW
CW	MoD	Caerwent	MoD
CX	Store	Cardiff Tidal	DBS
CY	Store	Crewe Coal/South Yards	DRS/RIV
CZ	TMD	Central Rivers	BOM
DD	SD	Doncaster Wood Yard	DBS
DF	T&RSMD	Rail Vehicle Engineering	RVE
DI	Pres	Didcot Railway Centre	GWS
DM	TMD	Dollands Moor	DBS
DO	Store	Donnington Railfreight	-
DT	SD	Didcot Triangle	DBS
DV	SD	Dover	SET
DW	SD	Doncaster West Yard	NRL, WAB
DY	T&RSMD	Derby Etches Park	EMT
EA	SD	Earles Sidings	DBS
EC	T&RSMD	Craigentinny (Edinburgh)	VEC
ED	DMUD	Eastfield	SCR
EF	MPVD	Effingham Junction	AMS
EH	SD	Eastleigh	DBS
EM	EMUD	East Ham	c2c
EN	CARMD	Euston Downside	NRL
EU	SD	Euston Station Sidings	VWC
EZ	DMUD	Exeter	FGW
FB	Store	Ferrybridge	DBS
FC*		Fire College (Moreton-in-Marsh)	
FD	Mobile	Diesel loco	FLR
FE	Mobile	Electric loco	FLR
FF	TRSMD	Forest, Brussels	SNCB, NMBS, EUS
FH	TRACK	Frodingham	GRP
FN	Hire	France	ECR
FP	CSD	Ferme Park	VEC
FR	EMUD	Fratton	SWR
FS	Mobile	Diesel Shunter	FLR
FW	SD	Fort William	DBS
FX	TMD	Felixstowe	FDH
GI	EMUD	Gillingham	SET
GP	SD	Grove Park	SET
GW	EMUD	Glasgow Shields	SCR
HA	TMD	Haymarket	SCR
HD	SD	Holyhead	ATW
HE	EMUD	Hornsey	GTR
HF	SD	Hereford	DBS
HG	Store	Hither Green	DBS
HI	TM	Hitchin	BBR
HJ	SD	Hoo Junction	DBS
HM	SD/WRD	Healey Mills	DBS
HT	T&RSMD	Heaton	NOR, GTL
HY	SD	Oxford Hinksey Yard	NRL
IL	T&RSMD	Ilford	GAR
IM	SD	Immingham	DBS
IP	SD	Ipswich	FLR
IS	TMD	Inverness	SCR
KC	Store	Carlisle Currock WRD	DBS
KD	SD	Kingmoor Yard	DRS
KK	EMUD	Kirkdale	MER
KM	TMD	Carlisle Kingmoor	DRS
KR	T&RSMD	Kidderminster	SVR
KT	MoD	Kineton	MoD
KY	SD/WRD	Knottingley	DBS
LA	T&RSMD	Laira	FGW
LB	Eng	Loughborough	BTL
LD	TMD	Leeds Midland Road	FLR
LE	T&RSMD	Landore	FGW
LG	T&RSMD	Longsight Electric	ALT
LH	Eng	LH Group	LHG
LL	CSD	Liverpool Edge Hill	ALS
LM	Store	Long Marston	MLS
LO	T&RSMD	Longsight Diesel	NOR
LP*	Eng	EMD Longport	EMD
LR	Eng	Leicester	UKR

Rail Data Tables

Code	Type	Name	Operator
LU	MoD	Ludgershall	MoD
LW	MoD	Longtown	MoD
LY	T&RSMD	Le Landy (Paris)	SNCF, EUS
MA	CARMD	Manchester International	ALS
MD	TMD	Merehead	MRL
MG	TMD	Margam	DBS
MH	SD	Millerhill	DBS
ML	SD	Motherwell	DRS
MM	Store	Moreton-in-Marsh	-
MN	DMUD	Machynlleth	ATW
MQ	Store	Meldon Quarry	BAR
MR	SD	March	GBR
MW	MoD	Marchwood Military Port	MoD
MY	SD/Store	Mossend Yard	DBS, FLR
NA	Eng	Newton Aycliffe	Hitachi
NB	SD	New Brighton	MER
NC	T&RSMD	Norwich Crown Point	GAR
ND	Works	NedTrans, Tilburg	NDZ
NG	T&RSMD	New Cross Gate	LOL
NH	DMUD	Newton Heath	NOR
NL	T&RSMD	Neville Hill (Leeds)	EMT, VEC
NM	SD	Nottingham Eastcroft	EMT
NN	EMUD	Northampton, Kings Heath	SIE, WMT
NT	EMUD	Northam	SIE, SWR
NY	T&RSMD	Grosmont	NYM
OC	T&RSMD	Old Oak Common	CRO
OD	Eng	Old Dalby	ALS
OH	EMUD	Old Oak Common Electric	SIE
ON	SD	Orpington	SET
OX	CSD	Oxford Carriage Sidings	FGW
OY	CARMD	Oxley	ALS
PB	SD	Peterborough	DBS
PC	TRSMD	Polmadie	ALS
PE	SD	Peterborough Nene	GTR
PF	SD	Peak Forest	DBS
PH	SD	Perth	SCR
PM	TRSMD	St Philip's Marsh (Bristol)	FGW
PN	SD	Preston Station	NOR
PN	TMD	Poznan (Poland)	ECR (DBS)
PQ	SD	Harwich Parkeston Quay	DBS
PT	SD	Peterborough	GBR
PY	MoD	Shoeburyness (Pigs Bay)	MoD, KRS
PZ	TRSMD	Penzance (Long Rock)	FGW
RE	EMUD	Ramsgate	SET
RG	DMUD	Reading	FGW
RH	SD	Redhill	DBS
RL	TRSMD	Ropley	MHR
RO	SD	Rotherham Steel	DBS
RU	TMD	Rugby Rail Plant	GRP
RY	EMUD	Ryde	SWR
SA	DMUD	Salisbury	SWR
SB	TMD	Shrewsbury	NOR
SE	TRSMD	St Leonards	SLR
SG	EMUD	Slade Green	SET
SH	CARMD	Southall Railway Centre	WCR
SI	EMUD	Soho	WMT
SJ	TRSMD	Stourbridge Junction	WMT
SK	TRSMD	Swanwick	MRC
SL	TRSMD	Stewarts Lane	DBS, VSO, GTR
SM	SP	Sheringham	NOR
SN	SD	Shoeburyness	c2c
SO*		Southend	-
SP	CRDC	Springs Branch	DBS
SQ	SD	Stockport	NOR
ST	SD	Southport	MER
SU	TRSMD	Selhurst	GTR
SX	SD	Shrewsbury	ATW
SZ	TMD	Southampton Maritime	FLR
TB	TMD	Three Bridges	GTR
TE	TMD	Thornaby/Tees Yard	TLK
TF	SD	Orient Way	GAR
TG	SD	Tonbridge	GBR
TI	TRSMD	Temple Mills	EUS
TJ	TMD	Tavistock Junction	COL
TM	SD	Tyseley Loco Works	BRM
TN	SD	Taunton Fairwater	NRL, FLR
TO	TMD	Toton	DBS
TS	DMUD	Tyseley	WMT
TT	Store	Toton Training Compound	DBS
TY	Store	Tyne Yard	DBS
VI	SD	Victoria	SET
VR	SD	Aberystwyth	ATW
VZ	EMUD	Strawberry Hill	SIE, SWR
WA	SD	Warrington Arpley	DBS
WB	TRSMD	Wembley	ALS
WD	EMUD	East Wimbledon	SWR
WE	SD	Willesden Brent	DBS
WF	SD	Wansford	NVR
WH	Eng	Whatley	MRL
WK	SD	West Kirby	MER
WN	EMUD	Willesden	BOM
WO	TMD	Wolsingham	WER
WP	SD	Worksop	DBS
WS	SD	Worcester	WMT
WW	SD	West Worthing	GTR
WY	SD/CSD	Westbury Yard	DBS
WZ*	TRSMD	Washwood Heath	HAN
XW	TMD	Crofton	BOM
XX	-	Exported	-
YK	DMUD	Siemens York	SIE, FTP
YL	TMD	York Leeman Road	JAR, FLF
YM	Store	National Railway Museum	NRM
YN	SD	York North Yard	DBS
YO	SD	Yoker	SCR
ZA	Eng	RTC Derby	SER, NRL, AEA
ZB	Eng	Doncaster	WAB
ZC	Eng	Crewe	BOM
ZD	Eng	Derby Litchurch Lane	BOM
ZE	Eng	Washwood Heath	COL
ZG	Eng	Eastleigh Works	KRS
ZH	Eng	Glasgow	RCL
ZI	Eng	Ilford	BOM
ZK	Eng	Kilmarnock	BTL
ZL	SD	Cardiff Canton	PUL
ZN	Eng	Wolverton	RCL
ZE	Eng	York	N Rail
ZS	Eng	Locotech Wakefield	BAR
ZW	Eng	Stoke-on-Trent (Marcroft)	AXI
WZ		Warsaw (Poland)	DBS
3M*		3M Industries, Bracknell	

* Unofficial code

Data Tables

Rail Data Tables

Owner Codes

201	20189 Ltd (Michael Owen)
AEA	AEA Rail Technology
ALS	Alstom
ANG	Angel Trains
ATW	Arriva Trains Wales
AUT	Arriva UK Trains
BAA	British Airports Authority
BCC	Bridgend County Council
BEA	Beacon Rail
BOM	Bombardier
BOT	Bank of Tokyo (Mitsubishi)
BRO	Brodie Engineering
BTM	BTMU Capital Corporation
C20	Class 20 Locomotive Ltd
CBR	CB Rail
CCC	Cardiff County Council
COL	Colas Rail
CRW	Chiltern Railways
CWR	Cotswold Rail
DBR	DB Regio
DBS	DB-Schenker West
DBS/T	DB-Schenker/Transfesa
DRS	Direct Rail Services
ECR	Euro Cargo Rail (DBS)
ECT	ECT Main Line Rail
EMT	East Midlands Trains
ETL	Electric Traction Ltd
EU2	Eurotunnel Europorte2
EUR	Eurotunnel
EUS	Eurostar
EVL	Eversholt Leasing
FGP	First Group
FLF	Fastline Freight
FLR	Freightliner
FOS	Foster Yeoman
GBR	GB Railfreight
GEM	Gemini Rail Services
GTL	Grand Central Railway Ltd
HAN	Hanson Traction
HEC	Hunslet Engine Co
HBS	Halifax-Bank of Scotland
HJA	Howard Johnson Associates
HNR	Harry Needle Railroad
IRY	Ian Riley
JAR	Jarvis
KBR	Knorr Bremse Rail
KRS	Knights Rail Services
LOM	Lombard Finance
LOR	Loram UK
MAG	Macquarie Euro Rail
NRL	Network Rail
NYM	North Yorkshire Moors Railway
PTR	Porterbrook
QWR	QW Rail Leasing
RCL	Railcare Limited
RIV	Riviera Trains
RML	Royal Mail
RMS	RMS Locotech
RTR	RT Rail
S4G	Stratford Class 47 Group
SCS	Serco Caledonian Sleepers
SEC	Serco
SIE	Siemens
SNB	Société Nationale des Chemins de fer Belges
SNF	Société Nationale des Chemins de fer Français
SOU	Southern (Govia)
SWT	South Western Railway
TTS	Transmart Trains
UKG	UK Government
URL	UK Rail Leasing
VTN	Vintage Trains
WAB	Wabtec
WCR	West Coast Railway Co
WMT	West Midlands Trains
WYP	West Yorkshire PTE

DMU and EMU Vehicle Codes

BDMSO	Battery Driving Motor Standard Open		MFL	Motor First Lavatory
DM	Driving Motor		MPMV	Motor Parcels Mail Van
DMBO	Driving Motor Brake Open		MS	Motor Standard
DMBS	Driving Motor Brake Standard		MSL	Motor Standard Lavatory
DMCL	Driving Motor Composite Lavatory		MSLRB	Motor Standard Lavatory Restaurant Buffet
DMCO	Driving Motor Composite Open		MSO	Motor Standard Open
DMF	Driving Motor First		MSRMB	Motor Standard Restaurant Micro Buffet
DMFLO	Driving Motor First Luggage Open		PTSO	Pantograph Trailer Standard Open
DMRFO	Driving Motor Restaurant First Open		RB	Restaurant Buffet
DMS	Driving Motor Standard		TBFO	Trailer Brake First Open
DMSL	Driving Motor Standard Lavatory		TCO	Trailer Composite Open
DMSO	Driving Motor Standard Open		TFO	Trailer First Open
DTCO	Driving Trailer Composite Open		TPMV	Trailer Parcels Mail Van
DTPMV	Driving Trailer Parcels Mail Van		TSO	Trailer Standard Open
DTSO	Driving Trailer Standard Open		TSRMB	Trailer Standard Restaurant Micro Buffet
MBC	Motor Brake Composite			
MBSO	Motor Brake Standard Open		(A) - A Car	
MC	Motor Composite		(B) - B Car	

This cross number checklist indicates in which section of the *abc Rail Guide - Main Line Systems 2019* full details of rolling stock can be found.

Number Cross-Link Codes

3MP	3M Productions
AFG	Arlington Fleet Group
ALS	Alstom
ASR	Abellio ScotRail
ATC	Arriva Train Care
ATW	Arriva Trains Wales
AXC	Arriva CrossCountry
BAR	British American Railway
BOK	Bo'ness & Kinneil Railway
BOM	Bombardier Transportation
C2C	c2c Railway
COL	Colas
CRW	Chiltern Railways
DBC	DB Cargo
DBR	DB Regio
DRS	Direct Rail Services
ECR	Euro Cargo Rail
EMT	East Midlands Trains
EPX	Europhoenix Ltd
ETL	Electric Traction Ltd
EUR	Eurotunnel / Europorte 2
EUS	Eurostar UK
EXP	Exported
FHT	First Hull Trains
FLR	Freightliner
FSL	Flying Scotsman Railway Ltd
FTP	First TransPennine
GAR	Abellio Greater Anglia
GBR	GB Railfreight
GSW	Great Scottish & Western Rly
GTL	Grand Central Railway
GWR	Great Western Railway
HAN	Hanson Traction
HEC	Heathrow Connect
HEX	Heathrow Express
HNR	Harry Needle Railroad Co
IND	Industrial
JHS	Jeremy Hosking
LOG	London Overground
MER	Merseyrail
MHR	Mid-Hants Railway
MRL	Mendip Rail Ltd
NEM	Nemesis Rail
NOR	Northern Railways
NRL	Network Rail Limited
NYM	North Yorkshire Moors Railway
OLS	Off Lease
PUL	Pullman Rail
RAF	Railfilms
RCL	Railcare
RIV	Riviera Trains
RRS	Ridings Railtours
RVE	Rail Vehicle Engineering
S4L	Stratford Class 47 Group
SEC	Serco Railtest
SET	South Eastern Trains
SCS	Serco Caledonian Sleepers
SIE	Siemens
SIL	Stagecoach Island Line
SNF	SNCF (French Railways)
SRP	Scottish Railway Preservation Soc
SUP	Support Coaches
SWT	South West Trains
TSG	Thameslink, Southern and Great Northern
TTS	Transmart Trains
URL	UK Rail Leasing
VEC	Virgin East Coast
VSO	Venice Simplon Orient Express
VTN	Vintage Trains
VWC	Virgin West Coast
WAB	Wabtec
WCR	West Coast Railway
WMT	West Midlands Trains

Locomotives – Diesel & Electric

No.	Code	No.	Code	No.	Code	No.	Code	No.	Code
		9714	EUR	9831	EUR	08445	IND	08580	IND
		9715	EUR	9832	EUR	08447	IND	08585	FLR
		9716	EUR	9834	EUR	08451	ALS	08588	BAR
44	MRL	9717	EUR	9835	EUR	08454	ALS	08593	IND
120	MRL	9718	EUR	9838	EUR	08460	IND	08596	WAB
		9719	EUR	9840	EUR	08472	WAB	08598	IND
9005	EUR	9720	EUR			08480	IND	08600	IND
9007	EUR	9721	EUR	01509	CRW	08483	GWR	08602	BOM
9011	EUR	9722	EUR	01551	SIE	08484	IND	08611	ALS
9013	EUR	9723	EUR	01552	HNR	08485	WCR	08613	BAR
9015	EUR			01564	HNR	08499	PUL	08615	WAB
9018	EUR	9801	EUR			08500	HNR	08616	WMT
9022	EUR	9802	EUR	03196	WCR	08502	IND	08617	ALS
9024	EUR	9803	EUR	03381	WCR	08503	IND	08622	BAR
9026	EUR	9804	EUR			08507	RIV	08623	IND
9029	EUR	9806	EUR	07007	AFG	08511	ATC	08624	FLR
9033	EUR	9808	EUR			08516	ATC	08629	MRS
9036	EUR	9809	EUR	08220	IND	08523	BAR	08630	HNR
9037	EUR	9810	EUR	08308	BAR	08525	EMT	08631	LSC
		9812	EUR	08375	IND	08527	HNR	08632	IND
9701	EUR	9814	EUR	08389	HNR	08530	FLR	08641	GWR
9702	EUR	9816	EUR	08401	GBR	08531	FLR	08643	MRL
9703	EUR	9817	EUR	08405	EMT	08535	IND	08644	GWR
9704	EUR	9819	EUR	08410	GWR	08536	IND	08645	GWR
9705	EUR	9820	EUR	08411	IND	08567	AFG	08648	BAR
9706	EUR	9821	EUR	08417	NRL	08568	MRS	08649	MRS
9707	EUR	9823	EUR	08418	WCR	08571	WAB	08650	MRL
9711	EUR	9825	EUR	08423	BAR	08573	BAR	08652	MRL
9712	EUR	9827	EUR	08441	IND	08575	FLR	08653	HNR
9713	EUR	9828	EUR	08442	ATC	08578	HNR	08663	GWR

Data Tables

No.	Code	No.	Code	No.	Code	No.	Code	No.	Code
08669	WAB	08891	FLR	20309	DRS	37422	DRS	43032	ASR
08670	IND	08892	HNR	20311	HNR	37423	DRS	43033	ASR
08676	HNR	08899	EMT	20312	DRS	37424	DRS	43034	ASR
08678	WCR	08903	IND	20314	HNR	37425	DRS	43035	ASR
08682	BOM	08904	HNR	20901	GBR	37503	EPX	43036	ASR
08683	IND	08905	HNR	20903	HNR	37510	EPX	43037	ASR
08685	HNR	08908	EMT	20904	HNR	37516	WCR	43040	GWR
08690	EMT	08912	IND	20905	GBR	37517	WCR	43041	GWR
08691	FLR	08915	IND	20906	HNR	37518	WCR	43042	GWR
08696	ALS	08918	HNR			37521	COL	43043	EMT
08700	HNR	08924	HNR			37601	EPX	43044	EMT
08701	HNR	08925	GBR	21544	ECR	37602	DRS	43045	EMT
08704	IND	08929	HNR	21545	ECR	37603	DRS	43046	EMT
08709	IND	08933	IND	21546	ECR	37604	DRS	43047	EMT
08714	HNR	08934	GBR	21547	ECR	37605	DRS	43048	EMT
08721	ALS	08936	BAR			37606	DRS	43049	EMT
08724	WAB	08939	IND	21610	ECR	37607	HNR	43050	EMT
08728	IND	08943	HNR	21611	ECR	37608	ROG	43052	EMT
08730	MRS	08947	MRL			37609	DRS	43053	GWR
08731	MRL	08948	EUS	25278	NYM	37610	COL	43054	EMT
08737	LSC	08950	EMT			37611	ROG	43055	EMT
08738	IND	08954	HNR	31105	NRL	37612	HNR	43056	GWR
08743	IND	08956	NRL	31106	LOR	37667	LSC	43058	EMT
08754	BAR			31128	NEM	37668	WCR	43059	EMT
08756	BAR	09002	GBR	31190	BAR	37669	WCR	43060	EMT
08762	BAR	09006	HNR	31233	NRL	37676	WCR	43061	EMT
08764	WAB	09007	LOG	31235	HNR	37685	WCR	43062	NRL
08765	HNR	09009	GBR	31285	HNR	37703	DRS	43063	GWR
08774	IND	09014	HNR	31452	BAR	37706	WCR	43064	EMT
08782	IND	09018	HNR	31454	BAR	37710	WCR	43066	EMT
08785	FLR	09022	IND	31459	HNR	37712	WCR	43069	GWR
08786	HNR	09023	IND	31465	HNR	37716	DRS	43070	GWR
08787	IND	09106	HNR	31468	LOR	37800	ROG	43071	GWR
08788	IND	09201	HNR			37884	ROG	43073	EMT
08790	ALS	09204	ATC	33025	WCR	37901	EPX	43075	EMT
08795	GWR			33029	WCR	37905	URL	43076	EMT
08802	HNR	12088	IND	33103	NEM	37906	URL	43078	GWR
08805	WMT			33207	WCR			43079	GWR
08807	IND	19001	ATE			43002	GWR	43081	EMT
08809	IND			37025	COL	43003	ASR	43082	EMT
08810	ATC	20016	HNR	37029	HNR	43004	GWR	43083	EMT
08818	HNR	20056	HNR	37038	DRS	43005	GWR	43086	GWR
08822	GWR	20066	HNR	37057	COL	43009	GWR	43087	GWR
08823	IND	20081	HNR	37059	DRS	43010	GWR	43088	GWR
08824	HNR	20088	HNR	37069	DRS	43012	ASR	43089	EMT
08830	ATC	20096	HNR	37099	COL	43013	NRL	43091	GWR
08834	HNR	20107	HNR	37116	COL	43014	NRL	43092	GWR
08836	GWR	20110	HNR	37146	COL	43015	ASR	43093	GWR
08846	IND	20118	HNR	37715	COL	43016	GWR	43094	GWR
08847	IND	20121	HNR	37188	COL	43017	GWR	43097	GWR
08850	NYM	20132	HNR	37198	NRL	43018	GWR	43098	GWR
08853	WAB	20138	HNR	37207	COL	43020	GWR	43122	GWR
08865	HNR	20142	GBR	37218	DRS	43021	ASR	43124	ASR
08868	HNR	20166	HNR	37219	COL	43022	GWR	43125	ASR
08870	BAR	20168	HNR	37254	COL	43023	GWR	43126	ASR
08871	WAB	20189	GBR	37259	DRS	43024	GWR	43127	ASR
08872	IND	20205	C2L	37401	DRS	43025	GWR	43128	ASR
08873	FLR	20227	GBR	37402	DRS	43026	ASR	43129	ASR
08874	BAR	20301	DRS	37403	DRS	43027	GWR	43130	ASR
08877	HNR	20302	DRS	37405	DRS	43028	ASR	43131	ASR
08879	HNR	20303	DRS	37407	DRS	43029	GWR	43132	ASR
08885	BAR	20304	DRS	37409	DRS	43030	ASR	43133	ASR
08887	ALS	20305	DRS	37419	DRS	43031	ASR	43134	ASR
				37421	COL				

Data Tables

No.	Code	No.	Code	No.	Code	No.	Code	No.	Code
43135	ASR	43251	LNE	47744	NEM	56105	COL	58026	DBC
43136	ASR	43257	LNE	47746	WCR	56106	GBR	58027	DBC
43137	ASR	43272	LNE	47749	GBR	56113	COL	58029	DBC
43138	ASR	43274	LNE	47760	WCR	56115	EXP	58030	DBC
43139	ASR	43277	LNE	47768	WCR	56117	EXP	58031	DBC
43140	ASR	43285	AXC	47769	ROG	56128	GBR	58032	DBC
43141	ASR	43290	LNE	47772	WCR	56301	EPX	58033	DBC
43142	ASR	43295	LNE	47773	VTN	56302	COL	58034	DBC
43143	ASR	43296	LNE	47776	WCR	56303	BAR	58035	DBC
43144	ASR	43299	LNE	47786	WCR	56311	GBR	58036	DBC
43145	ASR	43300	LNE	47787	WCR	56312	GBR	58038	DBC
43146	ASR	43301	AXC	47790	LSC			58039	DBC
43147	ASR	43302	LNE	47802	WCR	57001	WCR	58040	DBC
43148	ASR	43303	AXC	47804	WCR	57002	DRS	58041	DBC
43149	ASR	43304	AXC	47805	LSC	57003	DRS	58042	DBC
43150	ASR	43305	LNE	47810	LSC	57004	DRS	58043	DBC
43151	ASR	43306	LNE	47811	LSC	57005	WCR	58044	DBC
43152	ASR	43307	LNE	47812	ROG	57006	WCR	58046	DBC
43153	GWR	43308	LNE	47813	ROG	57007	DRS	58047	DBC
43154	GWR	43309	LNE	47815	ROG	57008	DRS	58048	URL
43155	GWR	43310	LNE	47816	LSC	57009	DRS	58049	DBC
43156	GWR	43311	LNE	47818	AFG	57010	DRS	58050	DBC
43158	GWR	43312	LNE	47826	WCR	57011	DRS		
43159	GWR	43313	LNE	47830	FLR	57012	DRS	59001	MRL
43160	GWR	43314	LNE	47832	WCR	57301	DRS	59002	MRL
43161	GWR	43315	LNE	47841	LSC	57302	DRS	59003	GBR
43162	GWR	43316	LNE	47843	ROG	57303	DRS	59004	MRL
43163	ASR	43317	LNE	47847	ROG	57304	DRS	59005	MRL
43164	ASR	43318	LNE	47848	ROG	57305	DRS		
43165	GWR	43319	LNE	47851	WCR	57306	DRS	59101	MRL
43168	ASR	43320	LNE	47853	LSC	57307	DRS	59102	MRL
43169	ASR	43321	AXC	47854	WCR	57308	DRS	59103	MRL
43170	GWR	43357	AXC			57309	DRS	59104	MRL
43171	GWR	43366	AXC	50007	C5A	57310	DRS		
43172	GWR	43367	LNE	50008	BRE	57311	DRS	59201	DBC
43174	GWR	43378	AXC	50017	BRE	57312	DRS	59202	DBC
43175	ASR	43384	AXC	50050	BRE	57313	WCR	59203	DBC
43176	ASR	43423	EMT			57314	WCR	59204	DBC
43177	ASR	43465	EMT	56006	URL	57315	WCR	59205	DBC
43179	ASR	43467	EMT	56007	GBR	57316	WCR	59206	DBC
43180	GWR	43468	EMT	56009	GBR	57601	WCR		
43181	ASR	43480	EMT	56018	GBR	57602	GWR	60001	DBC
43182	ASR	43484	EMT	56031	GBR	57603	GWR	60002	GBR
43183	ASR			56032	GBR	57604	GWR	60003	GBR
43185	GWR	45112	NEM	56037	GBR	57605	GWR	60004	GBR
43186	GWR			56038	GBR			60005	DBC
43187	GWR	47194	WCR	56049	COL	58001	DBC	60007	DBC
43188	GWR	47237	WCR	56051	COL	58004	DBC	60008	GBR
43189	GWR	47245	WCR	56060	GBR	58005	DBC	60009	DBC
43190	GWR	47270	WCR	56065	GBR	58006	DBC	60010	DBC
43191	GWR	47355	WCR	56069	GBR	58007	DBC	60011	DBC
43192	GWR	47375	EXP	56077	GBR	58009	DBC	60012	DBC
43193	GWR	47488	NEM	56078	COL	58010	DBC	60015	DBC
43194	GWR	47492	WCR	56081	GBR	58011	DBC	60017	DBC
43195	GWR	47500	WCR	56087	COL	58013	DBC	60018	GBR
43196	GWR	47501	LSC	56091	BAR	58015	DBC	60019	DBC
43197	GWR	47580	S4G	56090	COL	58016	URL	60020	DBC
43198	GWR	47701	NEM	56094	COL	58017	DBC	60021	GBR
43206	LNE	47703	HNR	56096	COL	58018	DBC	60022	DBC
43207	AXC	47714	HNR	56098	GBR	58020	DBC	60024	DBC
43208	LNE	47715	HNR	56101	EXP	58021	DBC	60025	DBC
43238	LNE	47727	GBR	56103	BAR	58024	DBC	60026	GBR
43239	LNE	47739	GBR	56104	GBR	58025	DBC	60027	DBC

Data Tables

Number	Code	Number	Code	Number	Code	Number	Code	Number	Code
60030	DBC	66012	DBC	66079	DBC	66145	DBC	66209	EXP
60032	DBC	66013	EXP	66080	DBC	66146	EXP	66210	EXP
60034	DBC	66014	DBC	66082	DBC	66147	DBC	66211	EXP
60035	DBC	66015	DBC	66083	DBC	66148	DBC	66212	EXP
60036	DBC	66017	DBC	66084	DBC	66149	DBC	66213	EXP
60037	DBC	66018	DBC	66085	DBC	66150	DBC	66214	EXP
60039	DBC	66019	DBC	66086	DBC	66151	DBC	66215	EXP
60040	DBC	66020	DBC	66087	DBC	66152	DBC	66216	EXP
60043	DBC	66021	DBC	66088	DBC	66153	EXP	66217	EXP
60044	DBC	66022	EXP	66089	DBC	66154	DBC	66218	EXP
60045	DBC	66023	DBC	66090	DBC	66155	DBC	66219	EXP
60047	GBR	66024	DBC	66091	DBC	66156	DBC	66220	DBC
60049	DBC	66025	DBC	66092	DBC	66157	EXP	66221	DBC
60051	DBC	66026	EXP	66093	DBC	66158	DBC	66222	EXP
60052	DBC	66027	DBC	66094	DBC	66159	EXP	66223	EXP
60053	DBC	66028	EXP	66095	DBC	66160	DBC	66224	EXP
60054	DBC	66029	EXP	66096	DBC	66161	DBC	66225	EXP
60056	GBR	66030	DBC	66097	DBC	66162	DBC	66226	EXP
60057	DBC	66031	DBC	66098	DBC	66163	EXP	66227	EXP
60059	DBC	66032	EXP	66099	DBC	66164	DBC	66228	EXP
60060	DBC	66033	EXP	66100	DBC	66165	DBC	66229	EXP
60062	DBC	66034	DBC	66101	DBC	66166	EXP	66230	DBC
60063	DBC	66035	DBC	66102	DBC	66167	DBC	66231	EXP
60064	DBC	66036	EXP	66103	DBC	66168	DBC	66232	EXP
60065	DBC	66037	DBC	66104	DBC	66169	DBC	66233	EXP
60066	DBC	66038	EXP	66105	DBC	66170	DBC	66234	EXP
60067	DBC	66039	DBC	66106	DBC	66171	DBC	66235	EXP
60069	DBC	66040	DBC	66107	DBC	66172	DBC	66236	EXP
60071	DBC	66041	DBC	66108	DBC	66173	EXP	66237	EXP
60072	DBC	66042	EXP	66109	DBC	66174	DBC	66239	EXP
60073	DBC	66043	DBC	66110	DBC	66175	DBC	66240	EXP
60074	DBC	66044	DBC	66111	DBC	66176	DBC	66241	EXP
60076	GBR	66045	EXP	66112	DBC	66177	DBC	66242	EXP
60077	DBC	66047	DBC	66113	DBC	66178	EXP	66243	EXP
60079	DBC	66049	EXP	66114	DBC	66179	EXP	66244	EXP
60083	DBC	66050	DBC	66115	DBC	66180	EXP	66245	EXP
60084	DBC	66051	DBC	66116	DBC	66181	DBC	66246	EXP
60085	GBR	66052	EXP	66117	DBC	66182	DBC	66247	EXP
60086	DBC	66053	DBC	66118	DBC	66183	DBC	66248	EXP
60087	GBR	66054	DBC	66119	DBC	66184	DBC	66249	EXP
60088	DBC	66055	DBC	66120	DBC	66186	DBC		
60090	DBC	66056	DBC	66121	DBC	66187	DBC	66301	DRS
60091	DBC	66057	DBC	66122	DBC	66188	DBC	66302	DRS
60092	DBC	66059	DBC	66123	EXP	66189	EXP	66303	DRS
60093	DBC	66060	DBC	66124	DBC	66190	EXP	66304	DRS
60094	DBC	66061	DBC	66125	DBC	66191	EXP	66305	DRS
60095	GBR	66062	EXP	66126	DBC	66192	DBC		
60096	GBR	66063	DBC	66127	DBC	66193	EXP	66411	EXP
60097	DBC	66064	EXP	66128	DBC	66194	DBC	66412	EXP
60099	DBC	66065	DBC	66129	DBC	66195	EXP	66413	FLR
60100	DBC	66066	DBC	66130	DBC	66196	EXP	66414	FLR
60500	DBC	66067	DBC	66131	DBC	66197	DBC	66415	FLR
		66068	DBC	66133	DBC	66198	DBC	66416	EXP
66001	DBC	66069	DBC	66134	DBC	66199	DBC	66417	EXP
66002	DBC	66070	DBC	66135	DBC	66200	DBC	66418	FLR
66003	DBC	66071	EXP	66136	DBC	66201	EXP	66419	FLR
66004	DBC	66072	EXP	66137	DBC	66202	EXP	66420	FLR
66005	DBC	66073	EXP	66138	DBC	66203	EXP	66421	DRS
66006	DBC	66074	DBC	66139	DBC	66204	EXP	66422	DRS
66007	DBC	66075	DBC	66140	DBC	66205	EXP	66423	DRS
66009	DBC	66076	DBC	66142	DBC	66206	EXP	66424	DRS
66010	EXP	66077	DBC	66143	DBC	66207	EXP	66425	DRS
66011	DBC	66078	DBC	66144	DBC	66208	EXP	66426	DRS

No.		No.		No.		No.		No.	
66427	DRS	66556	FLR	66702	GBR	66766	GBR	67025	DBC
66428	DRS	66557	FLR	66703	GBR	66767	GBR	67026	DBC
66429	DRS	66558	FLR	66704	GBR	66768	GBR	67027	COL
66430	DRS	66559	FLR	66705	GBR	66769	GBR	67028	DBC
66431	DRS	66560	FLR	66706	GBR	66770	GBR	67029	DBC
66432	DRS	66561	FLR	66707	GBR	66771	GBR	67030	DBC
66433	DRS	66562	FLR	66708	GBR	66772	GBR		
66434	DRS	66563	FLR	66709	GBR	66773	GBR	68001	DRS
		66564	FLR	66710	GBR	66774	GBR	68002	DRS
66501	FLR	66565	FLR	66711	GBR	66775	GBR	68003	DRS
66502	FLR	66566	FLR	66712	GBR	66776	GBR	68004	DRS
66503	FLR	66567	FLR	66713	GBR	66777	GBR	68005	DRS
66504	FLR	66568	FLR	66714	GBR	66778	GBR	68006	ASR
66505	FLR	66569	FLR	66715	GBR	66779	GBR	68007	ASR
66506	FLR	66570	FLR	66716	GBR	66780	GBR	68008	DRS
66507	FLR	66571	FLR	66717	GBR	66781	GBR	68009	DRS
66508	FLR	66572	FLR	66718	GBR	66782	GBR	68010	CRW
66509	FLR	66582	EXP	66719	GBR	66783	GBR	68011	CRW
66510	FLR	66583	EXP	66720	GBR	66784	GBR	68012	CRW
66511	FLR	66584	EXP	66721	GBR	66785	GBR	68013	CRW
66512	FLR	66585	FLR	66722	GBR	66786	GBR	68014	CRW
66513	FLR	66586	EXP	66723	GBR	66787	GBR	68015	CRW
66514	FLR	66587	FLR	66724	GBR	66788	GBR	68016	DRS
66515	FLR	66588	FLR	66725	GBR	66789	GBR	68017	DRS
66516	FLR	66589	FLR	66726	GBR			68018	DRS
66517	FLR	66590	FLR	66727	GBR	66846	COL	68019	TPE
66518	FLR	66591	FLR	66728	GBR	66847	COL	68020	TPE
66519	FLR	66592	FLR	66729	GBR	66848	COL	68021	TPE
66520	FLR	66593	FLR	66730	GBR	66849	COL	68022	TPE
66522	FLR	66594	FLR	66731	GBR	66850	COL	68023	TPE
66523	FLR	66595	EXP	66732	GBR			68024	TPE
66524	FLR	66596	FLR	66733	GBR	66951	FLR	68025	TPE
66525	FLR	66597	FLR	66735	GBR	66952	FLR	68026	TPE
66526	FLR	66598	FLR	66736	GBR	66953	FLR	68027	TPE
66527	EXP	66599	FLR	66737	GBR	66954	EXP	68028	TPE
66528	FLR			66738	GBR	66955	FLR	68029	TPE
66529	FLR	66601	FLR	66739	GBR	66956	FLR	68030	TPE
66530	EXP	66602	FLR	66740	GBR	66957	FLR	68031	TPE
66531	FLR	66603	FLR	66741	GBR			68032	TPE
66532	FLR	66604	FLR	66742	GBR	67001	TFW	68033	DRS
66533	FLR	66605	FLR	66743	GBR	67002	TFW	68034	DRS
66534	FLR	66606	FLR	66744	GBR	67003	TFW		
66535	EXP	66607	FLR	66745	GBR	67004	DBC	70001	FLR
66536	FLR	66608	EXP	66746	GBR	67005	DBC	70002	FLR
66537	FLR	66609	EXP	66747	GBR	67006	DBC	70003	FLR
66538	FLR	66610	FLR	66748	GBR	67007	DBC	70004	FLR
66539	FLR	66611	EXP	66749	GBR	67008	DBC	70005	FLR
66540	FLR	66612	EXP	66750	GBR	67009	DBC	70006	FLR
66541	FLR	66613	FLR	66751	GBR	67010	DBC	70007	FLR
66542	FLR	66614	FLR	66752	GBR	67011	DBC	70008	FLR
66543	FLR	66615	FLR	66753	GBR	67012	DBC	70009	FLR
66544	FLR	66616	FLR	66754	GBR	67013	DBC	70010	FLR
66545	FLR	66617	FLR	66755	GBR	67014	DBC	70011	FLR
66546	FLR	66618	FLR	66756	GBR	67015	DBC	70013	FLR
66547	FLR	66619	FLR	66757	GBR	67016	DBC	70014	FLR
66548	FLR	66620	FLR	66758	GBR	67017	DBC	70015	FLR
66549	FLR	66621	FLR	66759	GBR	67018	DBC	70016	FLR
66550	FLR	66622	FLR	66760	GBR	67019	DBC	70017	FLR
66551	FLR	66623	FLR	66761	GBR	67020	DBC	70018	FLR
66552	FLR	66624	EXP	66762	GBR	67021	DBC	70019	FLR
66553	FLR	66625	EXP	66763	GBR	67022	DBC	70020	FLR
66554	FLR			66764	GBR	67023	COL		
66555	FLR	66701	GBR	66765	GBR	67024	DBC	70801	COL

Data Tables

❏ 70802	COL	❏ 77014	ECR	❏ 86604	FLR	❏ 90011	GAR	❏ 91124	LNE
❏ 70803	COL	❏ 77015	ECR	❏ 86605	FLR	❏ 90012	GAR	❏ 91125	LNE
❏ 70804	COL	❏ 77016	ECR	❏ 86607	FLR	❏ 90013	GAR	❏ 91126	LNE
❏ 70805	COL	❏ 77017	ECR	❏ 86608	FLR	❏ 90014	GAR	❏ 91127	LNE
❏ 70806	COL	❏ 77018	ECR	❏ 86609	FLR	❏ 90015	GAR	❏ 91128	LNE
❏ 70807	COL	❏ 77019	ECR	❏ 86610	FLR	❏ 90016	FLR	❏ 91129	LNE
❏ 70808	COL	❏ 77020	ECR	❏ 86612	FLR	❏ 90017	DBC	❏ 91130	LNE
❏ 70809	COL	❏ 77021	ECR	❏ 86613	FLR	❏ 90018	DBC	❏ 91131	LNE
❏ 70810	COL	❏ 77022	ECR	❏ 86614	FLR	❏ 90019	DBC	❏ 91132	LNE
❏ 70811	COL	❏ 77023	ECR	❏ 86622	FLR	❏ 90020	DBC		
❏ 70812	COL	❏ 77024	ECR	❏ 86627	FLR	❏ 90021	DBC	❏ 92001	EXP
❏ 70813	COL	❏ 77025	ECR	❏ 86628	FLR	❏ 90022	DBC	❏ 92002	EXP
❏ 70814	COL	❏ 77026	ECR	❏ 86632	FLR	❏ 90023	DBC	❏ 92003	EXP
❏ 70815	COL	❏ 77027	ECR	❏ 86637	FLR	❏ 90024	DBC	❏ 92004	DBC
❏ 70816	COL	❏ 77028	ECR	❏ 86638	FLR	❏ 90025	DBC	❏ 92005	EXP
❏ 70817	COL	❏ 77029	ECR	❏ 86639	FLR	❏ 90026	DBC	❏ 92006	GBR
		❏ 77030	ECR	❏ 86701	EXP	❏ 90027	DBC	❏ 92007	DBC
❏ 73101	GBR	❏ 77031	ECR	❏ 86702	EXP	❏ 90028	DBC	❏ 92008	DBC
❏ 73107	GBR	❏ 77032	ECR			❏ 90029	DBC	❏ 92009	DBC
❏ 73109	GBR	❏ 77033	ECR	❏ 87002	GBR	❏ 90030	DBC	❏ 92010	GBR
❏ 73110	GBR	❏ 77034	ECR	❏ 87003	EXP	❏ 90031	DBC	❏ 92011	DBC
❏ 73118	TTS	❏ 77035	ECR	❏ 87004	EXP	❏ 90032	DBC	❏ 92012	EXP
❏ 73119	GBR	❏ 77036	ECR	❏ 87006	EXP	❏ 90033	DBC	❏ 92013	DBC
❏ 73128	GBR	❏ 77037	ECR	❏ 87007	EXP	❏ 90034	DBC	❏ 92014	SCS
❏ 73133	TTS	❏ 77038	ECR	❏ 87008	EXP	❏ 90035	DBC	❏ 92015	DBC
❏ 73136	GBR	❏ 77039	ECR	❏ 87009	EXP	❏ 90036	DBC	❏ 92016	DBC
❏ 73138	NRL	❏ 77040	ECR	❏ 87010	EXP	❏ 90037	DBC	❏ 92017	DBC
❏ 73139	GBR	❏ 77041	ECR	❏ 87012	EXP	❏ 90038	DBC	❏ 92018	SCS
❏ 73141	GBR	❏ 77042	ECR	❏ 87013	EXP	❏ 90039	DBC	❏ 92019	DBC
❏ 73201	GBR	❏ 77043	ECR	❏ 87014	EXP	❏ 90040	DBC	❏ 92020	GBR
❏ 73202	GTR	❏ 77044	ECR	❏ 87017	EXP	❏ 90041	FLR	❏ 92021	GBR
❏ 73212	GBR	❏ 77045	ECR	❏ 87019	EXP	❏ 90042	FLR	❏ 92022	EXP
❏ 73213	GBR	❏ 77046	ECR	❏ 87020	EXP	❏ 90043	FLR	❏ 92023	SCS
❏ 73235	SWR	❏ 77047	ECR	❏ 87022	EXP	❏ 90044	FLR	❏ 92024	EXP
		❏ 77048	ECR	❏ 87023	EXP	❏ 90045	FLR	❏ 92025	EXP
❏ 73951	NRL	❏ 77049	ECR	❏ 87025	EXP	❏ 90046	FLR	❏ 92026	EXP
❏ 73952	NRL	❏ 77050	ECR	❏ 87026	EXP	❏ 90047	FLR	❏ 92027	EXP
		❏ 77051	ECR	❏ 87028	EXP	❏ 90048	FLR	❏ 92028	SCS
❏ 73961	GBR	❏ 77052	ECR	❏ 87029	EXP	❏ 90049	FLR	❏ 92029	DBC
❏ 73962	GBR	❏ 77053	ECR	❏ 87033	EXP	❏ 90050	FLR	❏ 92030	EXP
❏ 73963	GBR	❏ 77054	ECR	❏ 87034	EXP			❏ 92031	DBC
❏ 73964	GBR	❏ 77055	ECR			❏ 91101	LNE	❏ 92032	GBR
❏ 73965	GBR	❏ 77056	ECR	❏ 88001	DRS	❏ 91102	LNE	❏ 92033	SCS
❏ 73966	SCS	❏ 77057	ECR	❏ 88002	DRS	❏ 91103	LNE	❏ 92034	EXP
❏ 73967	SCS	❏ 77058	ECR	❏ 88003	DRS	❏ 91104	LNE	❏ 92035	DBC
❏ 73968	SCS	❏ 77059	ECR	❏ 88004	DRS	❏ 91105	LNE	❏ 92036	DBC
❏ 73969	SCS	❏ 77060	ECR	❏ 88005	DRS	❏ 91106	LNE	❏ 92037	DBC
❏ 73970	SCS			❏ 88006	DRS	❏ 91107	LNE	❏ 92038	SCS
❏ 73971	SCS	❏ 86101	GBR	❏ 88007	DRS	❏ 91108	LNE	❏ 92039	DBC
		❏ 86213	EXP	❏ 88008	DRS	❏ 91109	LNE	❏ 92040	GBR
		❏ 86215	EXP	❏ 88009	DRS	❏ 91110	LNE	❏ 92041	DBC
❏ 77001	ECR	❏ 86217	EXP	❏ 88010	DRS	❏ 91111	LNE	❏ 92042	DBC
❏ 77002	ECR	❏ 86218	EXP			❏ 91112	LNE	❏ 92043	GBR
❏ 77003	ECR	❏ 86228	EXP	❏ 90001	GAR	❏ 91113	LNE	❏ 92044	GBR
❏ 77004	ECR	❏ 86229	EPX	❏ 90002	GAR	❏ 91114	LNE	❏ 92045	GBR
❏ 77005	ECR	❏ 86233	EXP	❏ 90003	GAR	❏ 91115	LNE	❏ 92046	GBR
❏ 77006	ECR	❏ 86234	EPX	❏ 90004	GAR	❏ 91116	LNE		
❏ 77007	ECR	❏ 86242	EXP	❏ 90005	GAR	❏ 91117	LNE	❏ 97301	NRL
❏ 77008	ECR	❏ 86248	EXP	❏ 90006	GAR	❏ 91118	LNE	❏ 97302	NRL
❏ 77009	ECR	❏ 86250	EXP	❏ 90007	GAR	❏ 91119	LNE	❏ 97303	NRL
❏ 77010	ECR	❏ 86251	EPX	❏ 90008	GAR	❏ 91120	LNE	❏ 97304	NRL
❏ 77011	ECR	❏ 86401	GBR	❏ 90009	GAR	❏ 91121	LNE		
❏ 77012	ECR	❏ 86424	EXP	❏ 90010	GAR	❏ 91122	LNE	❏ 323 539-7	AFG
❏ 77013	ECR								

Data Tables

323 674-2	AFG	142030	NOR	142094	NOR	150109	WMT	150222	NOR
		142031	NOR	142095	NOR	150110	NOR	150223	NOR
DH50-1	GBR	142032	NOR	142096	NOR	150111	NOR	150224	NOR
DH50-2	GBR	142033	NOR			150112	NOR	150225	NOR
8.701	GBR	142034	NOR	143601	TFW	150113	NOR	150226	NOR
8.702	GBR	142035	NOR	143602	TFW	150114	NOR	150227	TFW
8.703	GBR	142036	NOR	143603	GWR	150115	NOR	150228	NOR
8.704	GBR	142037	NOR	143604	TFW	150116	NOR	150229	TFW
8.708	GBR	142038	NOR	143605	TFW	150117	NOR	150230	TFW
8.711	GBR	142039	NOR	143606	TFW	150118	NOR	150231	TFW
8.712	GBR	142040	NOR	143607	TFW	150119	NOR	150232	GWR
8.716	GBR	142041	NOR	143608	TFW	150120	NOR	150233	GWR
8.717	GBR	142042	NOR	143609	TFW	150121	NOR	150234	GWR
8.718	GBR	142043	NOR	143610	TFW	150122	NOR	150235	TFW
8.719	GBR	142044	NOR	143611	GWR	150123	NOR	150236	TFW
8.720	GBR	142045	NOR	143612	GWR	150124	NOR	150237	TFW
		142046	NOR	143614	TFW	150125	NOR	150238	GWR

Diesel Multiple Units

		142047	NOR	143616	TFW	150126	NOR	150239	GWR
		142048	NOR	143617	GWR	150127	NOR	150240	TFW
60000	HDL	142049	NOR	143618	GWR	150128	NOR	150241	TFW
60019	HDL	142050	NOR	143619	GWR	150129	NOR	150242	TFW
60116	HDL	142051	NOR	143620	GWR	150130	NOR	150243	GWR
60118	HDL	142052	NOR	143621	GWR	150131	NOR	150244	GWR
60501	HDL	142053	NOR	143622	TFW	150132	NOR	150245	TFW
60528	HDL	142054	NOR	143623	TFW	150133	NOR	150246	GWR
60529	HDL	142055	NOR	143624	TFW	150134	NOR	150247	GWR
		142056	NOR	143625	TFW	150135	NOR	150248	GWR
69337	HDL	142057	NOR			150136	NOR	150249	GWR
		142058	NOR	144001	NOR	150137	NOR	150250	TFW
70262	HDL	142060	NOR	144002	NOR	150138	NOR	150251	TFW
		142061	NOR	144003	NOR	150139	NOR	150252	TFW
139001	WMT	142062	NOR	144004	NOR	150140	NOR	150253	TFW
139002	WMT	142063	NOR	144005	NOR	150141	NOR	150254	TFW
		142064	NOR	144006	NOR	150142	NOR	150255	TFW
142001	NOR	142065	NOR	144007	NOR	150143	NOR	150256	TFW
142002	TFW	142066	NOR	144008	NOR	150144	NOR	150257	TFW
142003	NOR	142067	NOR	144009	NOR	150145	NOR	150258	TFW
142004	NOR	142068	NOR	144010	NOR	150146	NOR	150259	TFW
142005	NOR	142069	TFW	144011	NOR	150147	NOR	150260	TFW
142006	TFW	142070	NOR	144012	NOR	150148	NOR	150261	GWR
142007	NOR	142071	NOR	144013	NOR	150149	NOR	150262	TFW
142009	NOR	142072	TFW	144014	NOR	150150	NOR	150263	GWR
142010	TFW	142073	TFW	144015	NOR			150264	TFW
142011	NOR	142074	TFW	144016	NOR	150201	NOR	150265	GWR
142012	NOR	142075	TFW	144017	NOR	150202	GWR	150266	GWR
142013	NOR	142076	TFW	144018	NOR	150203	NOR	150267	TFW
142014	NOR	142077	TFW	144019	NOR	150204	NOR	150268	NOR
142015	NOR	142078	NOR	144020	NOR	150205	NOR	150269	NOR
142016	NOR	142079	NOR	144021	NOR	150206	NOR	150270	NOR
142017	NOR	142080	TFW	144022	NOR	150207	GWR	150271	NOR
142018	NOR	142081	TFW	144023	NOR	150208	TFW	150272	NOR
142019	NOR	142082	TFW			150209	GWR	150273	NOR
142020	NOR	142083	TFW	150001	GWR	150210	NOR	150274	NOR
142021	NOR	142084	NOR	150002	GWR	150211	NOR	150275	NOR
142022	NOR	142085	TFW			150213	TFW	150276	NOR
142023	NOR	142086	NOR	150101	NOR	150214	NOR	150277	NOR
142024	NOR	142087	NOR	150102	NOR	150215	NOR	150278	TFW
142025	NOR	142088	NOR	150103	NOR	150216	GWR	150279	TFW
142026	NOR	142089	NOR	150104	NOR	150217	TFW	150280	TFW
142027	NOR	142090	NOR	150105	WMT	150218	NOR	150281	TFW
142028	NOR	142091	NOR	150106	NOR	150219	GWR	150282	TFW
142029	NOR	142092	NOR	150107	WMT	150220	NOR	150283	TFW
		142093	NOR	150108	NOR	150221	GWR	150284	TFW

Data Tables

Number	Code	Number	Code	Number	Code	Number	Code	Number	Code
150285	TFW	153376	EMT	156445	ASR	156508	ASR	158780	EMT
		153377	ASR	156446	ASR	156509	ASR	158782	NOR
153301	NOR	153378	NOR	156447	NOR	156510	ASR	158783	EMT
153302	EMT	153379	EMT	156448	NOR	156511	ASR	158784	NOR
153303	TFW	153380	NOR	156449	NOR	156512	ASR	158785	EMT
153304	NOR	153381	EMT	156450	ASR	156513	ASR	158786	NOR
153305	NOR	153382	EMT	156451	NOR	156514	ASR	158787	NOR
153306	GAR	153383	EMT	156452	NOR			158788	EMT
153307	NOR	153384	EMT	156453	ASR	158701	ASR	158789	NOR
153308	EMT	153385	EMT	156454	NOR	158702	ASR	158790	NOR
153309	GAR			156455	NOR	158703	ASR	158791	NOR
153310	EMT	155341	NOR	156456	ASR	158704	ASR	158792	NOR
153311	EMT	155342	NOR	156457	ASR	158705	ASR	158793	NOR
153312	TFW	155343	NOR	156458	ASR	158706	ASR	158794	NOR
153313	EMT	155344	NOR	156459	NOR	158707	ASR	158795	NOR
153314	GAR	155345	NOR	156460	NOR	158708	ASR	158796	NOR
153315	NOR	155346	NOR	156461	NOR	158709	ASR	158797	NOR
153316	NOR	155347	NOR	156462	ASR	158710	ASR	158798	GWR
153317	NOR			156463	NOR	158711	ASR	158799	EMT
153318	EMT	156401	EMT	156464	NOR	158712	ASR		
153319	EMT	156402	GAR	156465	NOR	158713	ASR	158806	EMT
153320	TFW	156403	EMT	156466	NOR	158714	ASR	158810	EMT
153321	EMT	156404	EMT	156467	ASR	158715	ASR	158812	EMT
153322	GAR	156405	EMT	156468	NOR	158716	ASR	158813	EMT
153323	TFW	156406	EMT	156469	NOR	158717	ASR	158815	NOR
153324	NOR	156407	GAR	156470	EMT	158718	ASR	158816	NOR
153325	GWR	156408	EMT	156471	NOR	158719	ASR	158817	NOR
153326	EMT	156409	GAR	156472	NOR	158720	ASR	158818	TFW
153327	TFW	156410	EMT	156473	EMT	158721	ASR	158819	TFW
153328	NOR	156411	EMT	156474	ASR	158722	ASR	158820	TFW
153329	GWR	156412	GAR	156475	NOR	158723	ASR	158821	TFW
153330	NOR	156413	EMT	156476	ASR	158724	ASR	158822	TFW
153331	NOR	156414	EMT	156477	ASR	158725	ASR	158823	TFW
153332	NOR	156415	EMT	156478	ASR	158726	ASR	158824	TFW
153333	GWR	156416	GAR	156479	NOR	158727	ASR	158825	TFW
153334	WMT	156417	GAR	156480	NOR	158728	ASR	158826	TFW
153335	GAR	156418	GAR	156481	NOR	158729	ASR	158827	TFW
		156419	GAR	156482	NOR	158730	ASR	158828	TFW
153351	NOR	156420	NOR	156483	NOR	158731	ASR	158829	TFW
153352	NOR	156421	NOR	156484	NOR	158732	ASR	158830	TFW
153353	TFW	156422	GAR	156485	NOR	158733	ASR	158831	TFW
153354	WMT	156423	NOR	156486	NOR	158734	ASR	158832	TFW
153355	EMT	156424	NOR	156487	NOR	158735	ASR	158833	TFW
153356	WMT	156425	NOR	156488	NOR	158736	ASR	158834	TFW
153357	EMT	156426	NOR	156489	NOR	158737	ASR	158835	TFW
153358	NOR	156427	NOR	156490	NOR	158738	ASR	158836	TFW
153359	NOR	156428	NOR	156491	NOR	158739	ASR	158837	TFW
153360	NOR	156429	NOR	156492	ASR	158740	ASR	158838	TFW
153361	GWR	156430	ASR	156493	ASR	158741	ASR	158839	TFW
153362	TFW	156431	ASR	156494	ASR	158752	NOR	158840	TFW
153363	NOR	156432	ASR	156495	ASR	158753	NOR	158841	TFW
153364	WMT	156433	ASR	156496	NOR	158754	NOR	158842	NOR
153365	WMT	156434	ASR	156497	EMT	158755	NOR	158843	NOR
153366	WMT	156435	ASR	156498	EMT	158756	NOR	158844	NOR
153367	TFW	156436	ASR	156499	ASR	158757	NOR	158845	NOR
153368	EMT	156437	ASR	156500	ASR	158758	NOR	158846	EMT
153369	GWR	156438	NOR	156501	ASR	158759	NOR	158847	EMT
153370	WMT	156439	ASR	156502	ASR	158763	GWR	158848	NOR
153371	WMT	156440	NOR	156503	ASR	158766	GWR	158849	NOR
153372	EMT	156441	NOR	156504	ASR	158770	EMT	158850	NOR
153373	NOR	156442	ASR	156505	ASR	158773	EMT	158851	NOR
153374	EMT	156443	NOR	156506	ASR	158774	EMT	158852	EMT
153375	WMT	156444	NOR	156507	ASR	158777	EMT	158853	NOR

Data Tables

Number	Code
158854	EMT
158855	NOR
158856	EMT
158857	EMT
158858	EMT
158859	NOR
158860	NOR
158861	NOR
158862	EMT
158863	EMT
158864	EMT
158865	EMT
158866	EMT
158867	NOR
158868	NOR
158869	NOR
158870	NOR
158871	NOR
158872	NOR
158880	SWR
158881	SWR
158882	SWR
158883	SWR
158884	SWR
158885	SWR
158886	SWR
158887	SWR
158888	SWR
158889	EMT
158890	SWR
158901	NOR
158902	NOR
158903	NOR
158904	NOR
158905	NOR
158906	NOR
158907	NOR
158908	NOR
158909	NOR
158910	NOR
158950	GWR
158951	GWR
158952	GWR
158953	GWR
158954	GWR
158955	GWR
158956	GWR
158957	GWR
158958	GWR
158959	GWR
158960	GWR
158961	GWR
159001	SWR
159002	SWR
159003	SWR
159004	SWR
159005	SWR
159006	SWR
159007	SWR

Number	Code
159008	SWR
159009	SWR
159010	SWR
159011	SWR
159012	SWR
159013	SWR
159014	SWR
159015	SWR
159016	SWR
159017	SWR
159018	SWR
159019	SWR
159020	SWR
159021	SWR
159022	SWR
159101	SWR
159102	SWR
159103	SWR
159104	SWR
159105	SWR
159106	SWR
159107	SWR
159108	SWR
165001	CRW
165002	CRW
165003	CRW
165004	CRW
165005	CRW
165006	CRW
165007	CRW
165008	CRW
165009	CRW
165010	CRW
165011	CRW
165012	CRW
165013	CRW
165014	CRW
165015	CRW
165016	CRW
165017	CRW
165018	CRW
165019	CRW
165020	CRW
165021	CRW
165022	CRW
165023	CRW
165024	CRW
165025	CRW
165026	CRW
165027	CRW
165028	CRW
165029	CRW
165030	CRW
165031	CRW
165032	CRW
165033	CRW
165034	CRW
165035	CRW
165036	CRW
165037	CRW
165038	CRW

Number	Code
165039	CRW
165101	GWR
165102	GWR
165103	GWR
165104	GWR
165105	GWR
165106	GWR
165107	GWR
165108	GWR
165109	GWR
165110	GWR
165111	GWR
165112	GWR
165113	GWR
165114	GWR
165116	GWR
165117	GWR
165118	GWR
165119	GWR
165120	GWR
165121	GWR
165122	GWR
165123	GWR
165124	GWR
165125	GWR
165126	GWR
165127	GWR
165128	GWR
165129	GWR
165130	GWR
165131	GWR
165132	GWR
165133	GWR
165134	GWR
165135	GWR
165136	GWR
165137	GWR
166201	GWR
166202	GWR
166203	GWR
166204	GWR
166205	GWR
166206	GWR
166207	GWR
166208	GWR
166209	GWR
166210	GWR
166211	GWR
166212	GWR
166213	GWR
166214	GWR
166215	GWR
166216	GWR
166217	GWR
166218	GWR
166219	GWR
166220	GWR
166221	GWR

Number	Code
168001	CRW
168002	CRW
168003	CRW
168004	CRW
168005	CRW
168106	CRW
168107	CRW
168108	CRW
168109	CRW
168110	CRW
168111	CRW
168112	CRW
168113	CRW
168214	CRW
168215	CRW
168216	CRW
168217	CRW
168218	CRW
168219	CRW
168321	CRW
168322	CRW
168323	CRW
168324	CRW
168325	CRW
168326	CRW
168327	CRW
168328	CRW
168329	CRW
170101	AXC
170102	AXC
170103	AXC
170104	AXC
170105	AXC
170106	AXC
170107	AXC
170108	AXC
170109	AXC
170110	AXC
170111	AXC
170112	AXC
170113	AXC
170114	AXC
170115	AXC
170116	AXC
170117	AXC
170201	GAR
170202	GAR
170203	GAR
170204	GAR
170205	GAR
170206	GAR
170207	GAR
170208	GAR
170270	GAR
170271	GAR
170272	GAR
170273	GAR
170393	ASR
170394	ASR

Number	Code
170395	ASR
170396	ASR
170397	AXC
170398	AXC
170401	ASR
170402	ASR
170403	ASR
170404	ASR
170405	ASR
170406	ASR
170407	ASR
170408	ASR
170409	ASR
170410	ASR
170411	ASR
170412	ASR
170413	ASR
170414	ASR
170415	ASR
170416	ASR
170417	ASR
170418	ASR
170419	ASR
170420	ASR
170425	ASR
170426	ASR
170427	ASR
170428	ASR
170429	ASR
170430	ASR
170431	ASR
170432	ASR
170433	ASR
170434	ASR
170450	ASR
170451	ASR
170452	ASR
170453	NOR
170454	NOR
170455	NOR
170456	NOR
170457	NOR
170458	NOR
170459	NOR
170460	NOR
170461	NOR
170470	NOR
170471	NOR
170472	NOR
170473	NOR
170474	NOR
170475	NOR
170476	NOR
170477	NOR
170478	NOR
170501	WMT
170502	WMT
170503	WMT
170504	WMT
170505	WMT
170506	WMT

Data Tables

Number Cross-Link

170507	WMT	172102	CRW	180102	GTL	185150	FTP	220017	AXC
170508	WMT	172103	CRW	180103	GTL	185151	FTP	220018	AXC
170509	WMT	172104	CRW	180104	GTL			220019	AXC
170510	WMT			180105	GTL	195001	NOR	220020	AXC
170511	WMT	172211	WMT	180106	GTL	195002	NOR	220021	AXC
170512	WMT	172212	WMT	180107	GTL	195003	NOR	220022	AXC
170513	WMT	172213	WMT	180108	GTL	195004	NOR	220023	AXC
170514	WMT	172214	WMT	180109	FHT	195005	NOR	220024	AXC
170515	WMT	172215	WMT	180110	FHT	195006	NOR	220025	AXC
170516	WMT	172216	WMT	180111	FHT	195007	NOR	220026	AXC
170517	WMT	172217	WMT	180112	GTL	195008	NOR	220027	AXC
170518	AXC	172218	WMT	180113	FHT	195009	NOR	220028	AXC
170519	AXC	172219	WMT	180114	GTL	195010	NOR	220029	AXC
170520	AXC	172220	WMT			195011	NOR	220030	AXC
170521	AXC	172221	WMT	185101	FTP	195012	NOR	220031	AXC
170522	AXC	172222	WMT	185102	FTP			220032	AXC
170523	AXC			185103	FTP	195101	NOR	220033	AXC
		172331	WMT	185104	FTP	195102	NOR	220034	AXC
170630	WMT	172332	WMT	185105	FTP	195103	NOR		
170631	WMT	172333	WMT	185106	FTP	195104	NOR	221101	VWC
170632	WMT	172334	WMT	185107	FTP	195105	NOR	221102	VWC
170633	WMT	172335	WMT	185108	FTP	195106	NOR	221103	VWC
170634	WMT	172336	WMT	185109	FTP	195107	NOR	221104	VWC
170635	WMT	172337	WMT	185110	FTP	195108	NOR	221105	VWC
170636	AXC	172338	WMT	185111	FTP	195109	NOR	221106	VWC
170637	AXC	172339	WMT	185112	FTP	195110	NOR	221107	VWC
170638	AXC	172340	WMT	185113	FTP	195111	NOR	221108	VWC
170639	AXC	172341	WMT	185114	FTP	195112	NOR	221109	VWC
		172342	WMT	185115	FTP	195113	NOR	221110	VWC
171201	GTR	172343	WMT	185116	FTP	195114	NOR	221111	VWC
171202	GTR	172344	WMT	185117	FTP	195115	NOR	221112	VWC
		172345	WMT	185118	FTP	195116	NOR	221113	VWC
171401	GTR			185119	FTP	195117	NOR	221114	VWC
171402	GTR	175001	TFW	185120	FTP	195118	NOR	221115	VWC
		175002	TFW	185121	FTP	195119	NOR	221116	VWC
171721	GTR	175003	TFW	185122	FTP	195120	NOR	221117	VWC
171722	GTR	175004	TFW	185123	FTP	195121	NOR	221118	VWC
171723	GTR	175005	TFW	185124	FTP	195122	NOR	221119	AXC
171724	GTR	175006	TFW	185125	FTP	195123	NOR	221120	AXC
171725	GTR	175007	TFW	185126	FTP	195124	NOR	221121	AXC
171726	GTR	175008	TFW	185127	FTP	195125	NOR	221122	AXC
171727	GTR	175009	TFW	185128	FTP	195126	NOR	221123	AXC
171728	GTR	175010	TFW	185129	FTP	195127	NOR	221124	AXC
171729	GTR	175011	TFW	185130	FTP	195128	NOR	221125	AXC
171730	GTR			185131	FTP	195129	NOR	221126	AXC
		175101	TFW	185132	FTP	195130	NOR	221127	AXC
171801	GTR	175102	TFW	185133	FTP			221128	AXC
171802	GTR	175103	TFW	185134	FTP	220001	AXC	221129	AXC
171803	GTR	175104	TFW	185135	FTP	220002	AXC	221130	AXC
171804	GTR	175105	TFW	185136	FTP	220003	AXC	221131	AXC
171805	GTR	175106	TFW	185137	FTP	220004	AXC	221132	AXC
171806	GTR	175107	TFW	185138	FTP	220005	AXC	221133	AXC
		175108	TFW	185139	FTP	220006	AXC	221134	AXC
172001	WMT	175109	TFW	185140	FTP	220007	AXC	221135	AXC
172002	WMT	175110	TFW	185141	FTP	220008	AXC	221136	AXC
172003	WMT	175111	TFW	185142	FTP	220009	AXC	221137	AXC
172004	WMT	175112	TFW	185143	FTP	220010	AXC	221138	AXC
172005	WMT	175113	TFW	185144	FTP	220011	AXC	221139	AXC
172006	WMT	175114	TFW	185145	FTP	220012	AXC	221140	AXC
172007	WMT	175115	TFW	185146	FTP	220013	AXC	221141	AXC
172008	WMT	175116	TFW	185147	FTP	220014	AXC	221142	VWC
				185148	FTP	220015	AXC	221143	VWC
172101	CRW	180101	GTL	185149	FTP	220016	AXC	221144	AXC

Data Tables

Number	Code
222001	EMT
222002	EMT
222003	EMT
222004	EMT
222005	EMT
222006	EMT
222007	EMT
222008	EMT
222009	EMT
222010	EMT
222011	EMT
222012	EMT
222013	EMT
222014	EMT
222015	EMT
222016	EMT
222017	EMT
222018	EMT
222019	EMT
222020	EMT
222021	EMT
222022	EMT
222023	EMT
222101	EMT
222102	EMT
222103	EMT
222104	EMT
230001	VIV
230002	VIV
230003	WMT
230004	WMT
230005	WMT

Electric Multiple Units

Number	Code
62384	NRL
313018	GTR
313024	GTR
313025	GTR
313026	GTR
313027	GTR
313028	GTR
313029	GTR
313030	GTR
313031	GTR
313032	GTR
313033	GTR
313035	GTR
313036	GTR
313037	GTR
313038	GTR
313039	GTR
313040	GTR
313041	GTR
313042	GTR
313043	GTR
313044	GTR
313045	GTR
313046	GTR
313047	GTR
313048	GTR
313049	GTR
313050	GTR
313051	GTR
313052	GTR
313053	GTR
313054	GTR
313055	GTR
313056	GTR
313057	GTR
313058	GTR
313059	GTR
313060	GTR
313061	GTR
313062	GTR
313063	GTR
313064	GTR
313121	NRL
313122	GTR
313123	GTR
313134	GTR
313201	GTR
313202	GTR
313203	GTR
313204	GTR
313205	GTR
313206	GTR
313207	GTR
313208	GTR
313209	GTR
313210	GTR
313211	GTR
313212	GTR
313213	GTR
313214	GTR
313215	GTR
313216	GTR
313217	GTR
313219	GTR
313220	GTR
314201	ASR
314202	ASR
314203	ASR
314204	ASR
314205	ASR
314206	ASR
314207	ASR
314208	ASR
314209	ASR
314210	ASR
314211	ASR
314212	ASR
314213	ASR
314214	ASR
314215	ASR
314216	ASR
315801	LOG
315802	LOG
315803	LOG
315804	LOG
315805	LOG
315806	LOG
315807	LOG
315808	LOG
315809	LOG
315810	LOG
315811	LOG
315812	LOG
315813	LOG
315814	LOG
315815	LOG
315816	LOG
315817	LOG
315818	CRO
315819	CRO
315820	CRO
315821	CRO
315822	CRO
315823	CRO
315824	CRO
315825	CRO
315826	CRO
315827	CRO
315829	CRO
315830	CRO
315831	CRO
315833	CRO
315834	CRO
315836	CRO
315837	CRO
315838	CRO
315839	CRO
315840	OLS
315842	CRO
315843	CRO
315844	CRO
315845	CRO
315847	CRO
315848	CRO
315849	CRO
315851	CRO
315852	CRO
315853	CRO
315854	CRO
315855	CRO
315856	CRO
315857	CRO
315858	CRO
315859	CRO
315860	OLS
315861	OLS
317337	GAR
317338	GAR
317339	GAR
317340	GAR
317341	GAR
317342	GAR
317343	GAR
317344	GAR
317345	GAR
317346	GAR
317347	GAR
317348	GAR
317501	GAR
317502	GAR
317503	GAR
317504	GAR
317505	GAR
317506	GAR
317507	GAR
317508	GAR
317509	GAR
317510	GAR
317511	GAR
317512	GAR
317513	GAR
317514	GAR
317515	GAR
317649	GAR
317650	GAR
317651	GAR
317652	GAR
317653	GAR
317654	GAR
317655	GAR
317656	GAR
317657	GAR
317658	GAR
317659	GAR
317660	GAR
317661	GAR
317662	GAR
317663	GAR
317664	GAR
317665	GAR
317666	GAR
317667	GAR
317668	GAR
317669	GAR
317670	GAR
317671	GAR
317672	GAR
317708	LOG
317709	LOG
317710	LOG
317714	LOG
317719	LOG
317723	LOG
317729	LOG
317732	LOG
317881	GAR
317882	GAR
317883	GAR
317884	GAR
317885	GAR
317886	GAR
317887	LOG
317888	LOG
317889	LOG
317890	LOG
317891	LOG
317892	LOG
318250	ASR
318251	ASR
318252	ASR
318253	ASR
318254	ASR
318255	ASR
318256	ASR
318257	ASR
318258	ASR
318259	ASR
318260	ASR
318261	ASR
318262	ASR
318263	ASR
318264	ASR
318265	ASR
318266	ASR
318267	ASR
318268	ASR
318269	ASR
318270	ASR
319001	OLS
319002	OLS
319003	OLS
319004	NOR
319005	WMT
319006	OLS
319007	OLS
319008	WMT
319009	OLS
319010	OLS
319011	OLS
319012	WMT
319013	WMT
319214	OLS
319215	OLS
319216	WMT
319217	OLS
319218	NOR
319219	NOR
319220	WMT
319361	NOR
319362	NOR
319363	NOR
319364	NOR
319365	NOR
319366	NOR
319367	NOR
319368	NOR
319369	NOR
319370	NOR
319371	NOR
319372	NOR
319373	NOR
319374	NOR

Data Tables

Number	Code	Number	Code	Number	Code	Number	Code	Number	Code
319375	NOR	320318	ASR	321345	GAR	322481	NOR	325015	DBC
319376	NOR	320319	ASR	321346	GAR	322482	NOR	325016	DBC
319377	NOR	320320	ASR	321347	GAR	322483	NOR		
319378	NOR	320321	ASR	321348	GAR	322484	NOR	331001	NOR
319379	NOR	320322	ASR	321349	GAR	322485	NOR	331002	NOR
319380	NOR			321350	GAR			331003	NOR
319381	NOR	320401	ASR	321351	GAR	323201	WMT	331004	NOR
319382	NOR	320402	ASR	321352	GAR	323202	WMT	331005	NOR
319383	NOR	320404	ASR	321353	GAR	323203	WMT	331006	NOR
319384	OLS	320411	ASR	321354	GAR	323204	WMT	331007	NOR
319385	NOR	320412	ASR	321355	GAR	323205	WMT	331008	NOR
319386	NOR	320413	ASR	321356	GAR	323206	WMT	331009	NOR
		320414	ASR	321357	GAR	323207	WMT	331010	NOR
319421	OLS	320415	ASR	321358	GAR	323208	WMT	331011	NOR
319422	OLS	320416	ASR	321359	GAR	323209	WMT	331012	NOR
319423	OLS	320417	ASR	321360	GAR	323210	WMT	331013	NOR
319425	OLS	320418	ASR	321361	GAR	323211	WMT	331014	NOR
319426	OLS	320420	ASR	321362	GAR	323212	WMT	331015	NOR
319427	OLS			321363	GAR	323213	WMT	331016	NOR
319428	OLS	321301	GAR	321364	GAR	323214	WMT	331017	NOR
319429	WMT	321302	GAR	321365	GAR	323215	WMT	331018	NOR
319430	OLS	321303	GAR	321366	GAR	323216	WMT	331019	NOR
319432	OLS	321304	GAR			323217	WMT	331020	NOR
319433	WMT	321305	GAR	321403	GAR	323218	WMT	331021	NOR
319435	OLS	321306	GAR	321405	GAR	323219	WMT	331022	NOR
319436	OLS	321307	GAR	321406	GAR	323220	WMT	331023	NOR
319437	OLS	321308	GAR	321407	GAR	323221	WMT	331024	NOR
319438	OLS	321309	GAR	321408	GAR	323222	WMT	331025	NOR
319439	OLS	321310	GAR	321409	GAR	323223	NOR	331026	NOR
319440	OLS	321311	GAR	321410	GAR	323224	NOR	331027	NOR
319441	WMT	321312	GAR	321419	GAR	323225	NOR	331028	NOR
319443	OLS	321313	GAR	321421	GAR	323226	NOR	331029	NOR
319444	OLS	321314	GAR	321422	GAR	323227	NOR	331030	NOR
319445	OLS	321315	GAR	321423	GAR	323228	NOR	331031	NOR
319446	NOR	321316	GAR	321424	GAR	323229	NOR	331101	NOR
319447	OLS	321317	GAR	321425	GAR	323230	NOR	331102	NOR
319449	OLS	321318	GAR	321426	GAR	323231	NOR	331103	NOR
319451	OLS	321319	GAR	321427	GAR	323232	NOR	331104	NOR
319452	OLS	321320	GAR	321428	GAR	323233	NOR	331105	NOR
319453	OLS	321321	GAR	321429	GAR	323234	NOR	331106	NOR
319454	OLS	321322	GAR	321430	GAR	323235	NOR	331107	NOR
319455	WMT	321323	GAR	321431	GAR	323236	NOR	331108	NOR
319457	WMT	321324	GAR	321432	GAR	323237	NOR	331109	NOR
319459	OLS	321325	GAR	321433	GAR	323238	NOR	331110	NOR
319460	WMT	321326	GAR	321434	GAR	323239	NOR	331111	NOR
		321327	GAR	321435	GAR	323240	WMT	331112	NOR
320301	ASR	321328	GAR	321436	GAR	323241	WMT		
320302	ASR	321329	GAR	321437	GAR	323242	WMT	332001	HEX
320303	ASR	321330	GAR	321438	GAR	323243	WMT	332002	HEX
320304	ASR	321331	GAR	321439	GAR			332003	HEX
320305	ASR	321332	GAR	321440	GAR	325001	DBC	332004	HEX
320306	ASR	321333	GAR	321441	GAR	325002	DBC	332005	HEX
320307	ASR	321334	GAR	321442	GAR	325003	DBC	332006	HEX
320308	ASR	321335	GAR	321443	GAR	325004	DBC	332007	HEX
320309	ASR	321336	GAR	321444	GAR	325005	DBC	332008	HEX
320310	ASR	321337	GAR	321445	GAR	325006	DBC	332009	HEX
320311	ASR	321338	GAR	321446	GAR	325007	DBC	332010	HEX
320312	ASR	321339	GAR	321447	GAR	325008	DBC	332011	HEX
320313	ASR	321340	GAR	321448	GAR	325009	DBC	332012	HEX
320314	ASR	321341	GAR			325011	DBC	332013	HEX
320315	ASR	321342	GAR	321901	NOR	325012	DBC	332014	HEX
320316	ASR	321343	GAR	321902	NOR	325013	DBC		
320317	ASR	321344	GAR	321903	NOR	325014	DBC	333001	NOR

Data Tables

No.		No.		No.		No.		No.	
333002	NOR	345007	CRO	345070	CRO	350261	WMT	357034	C2C
333003	NOR	345008	CRO			350262	WMT	357035	C2C
333004	NOR	345009	CRO	350101	WMT	350263	WMT	357036	C2C
333005	NOR	345010	CRO	350102	WMT	350264	WMT	357037	C2C
333006	NOR	345011	CRO	350103	WMT	350265	WMT	357038	C2C
333007	NOR	345012	CRO	350104	WMT	350266	WMT	357039	C2C
333008	NOR	345013	CRO	350105	WMT	350267	WMT	357040	C2C
333009	NOR	345014	CRO	350106	WMT			357041	C2C
333010	NOR	345015	CRO	350107	WMT	350368	WMT	357042	C2C
333011	NOR	345016	CRO	350108	WMT	350369	WMT	357043	C2C
333012	NOR	345017	CRO	350109	WMT	350370	WMT	357044	C2C
333013	NOR	345018	CRO	350110	WMT	350371	WMT	357045	C2C
333014	NOR	345019	CRO	350111	WMT	350372	WMT	357046	C2C
333015	NOR	345020	CRO	350112	WMT	350373	WMT		
333016	NOR	345021	CRO	350113	WMT	350374	WMT	357201	C2C
		345022	CRO	350114	WMT	350375	WMT	357202	C2C
334001	ASR	345023	CRO	350115	WMT	350376	WMT	357203	C2C
334002	ASR	345024	CRO	350116	WMT	350377	WMT	357204	C2C
334003	ASR	345025	CRO	350117	WMT			357205	C2C
334004	ASR	345026	CRO	350118	WMT	350401	FTP	357206	C2C
334005	ASR	345027	CRO	350119	WMT	350402	FTP	357207	C2C
334006	ASR	345028	CRO	350120	WMT	350403	FTP	357208	C2C
334007	ASR	345029	CRO	350121	WMT	350404	FTP	357209	C2C
334008	ASR	345030	CRO	350122	WMT	350405	FTP	357210	C2C
334009	ASR	345031	CRO	350123	WMT	350406	FTP	357211	C2C
334010	ASR	345032	CRO	350124	WMT	350407	FTP		
334011	ASR	345033	CRO	350125	WMT	350408	FTP	357312	C2C
334012	ASR	345034	CRO	350126	WMT	350409	FTP	357313	C2C
334013	ASR	345035	CRO	350127	WMT	350410	FTP	357314	C2C
334014	ASR	345036	CRO	350128	WMT			357315	C2C
334015	ASR	345037	CRO	350129	WMT	357001	C2C	357316	C2C
334016	ASR	345038	CRO	350130	WMT	357002	C2C	357317	C2C
334017	ASR	345039	CRO			357003	C2C	357318	C2C
334018	ASR	345040	CRO	350231	WMT	357004	C2C	357319	C2C
334019	ASR	345041	CRO	350232	WMT	357005	C2C	357320	C2C
334020	ASR	345042	CRO	350233	WMT	357006	C2C	357321	C2C
334021	ASR	345043	CRO	350234	WMT	357007	C2C	357322	C2C
334022	ASR	345044	CRO	350235	WMT	357008	C2C	357323	C2C
334023	ASR	345045	CRO	350236	WMT	357009	C2C	357324	C2C
334024	ASR	345046	CRO	350237	WMT	357010	C2C	357325	C2C
334025	ASR	345047	CRO	350238	WMT	357011	C2C	357326	C2C
334026	ASR	345048	CRO	350239	WMT	357012	C2C	357327	C2C
334027	ASR	345049	CRO	350240	WMT	357013	C2C	357328	C2C
334028	ASR	345050	CRO	350241	WMT	357014	C2C		
334029	ASR	345051	CRO	350242	WMT	357015	C2C	360101	GAR
334030	ASR	345052	CRO	350243	WMT	357016	C2C	360102	GAR
334031	ASR	345053	CRO	350244	WMT	357017	C2C	360103	GAR
334032	ASR	345054	CRO	350245	WMT	357018	C2C	360104	GAR
334033	ASR	345055	CRO	350246	WMT	357019	C2C	360105	GAR
334034	ASR	345056	CRO	350247	WMT	357020	C2C	360106	GAR
334035	ASR	345057	CRO	350248	WMT	357021	C2C	360107	GAR
334036	ASR	345058	CRO	350249	WMT	357022	C2C	360108	GAR
334037	ASR	345059	CRO	350250	WMT	357023	C2C	360109	GAR
334038	ASR	345060	CRO	350251	WMT	357024	C2C	360110	GAR
334039	ASR	345061	CRO	350252	WMT	357025	C2C	360111	GAR
334040	ASR	345062	CRO	350253	WMT	357026	C2C	360112	GAR
		345063	CRO	350254	WMT	357027	C2C	360113	GAR
345001	CRO	345064	CRO	350255	WMT	357028	C2C	360114	GAR
345002	CRO	345065	CRO	350256	WMT	357029	C2C	360115	GAR
345003	CRO	345066	CRO	350257	WMT	357030	C2C	360116	GAR
345004	CRO	345067	CRO	350258	WMT	357031	C2C	360117	GAR
345005	CRO	345068	CRO	350259	WMT	357032	C2C	360118	GAR
345006	CRO	345069	CRO	350260	WMT	357033	C2C	360119	GAR

Data Tables

Number Cross-Link

Number	Code	Number	Code	Number	Code	Number	Code	Number	Code
360120	GAR	373208	EUS	375307	SET	375812	SET	376016	SET
360121	GAR	373209	EUS	375308	SET	375813	SET	376017	SET
		373210	EUS	375309	SET	375814	SET	376018	SET
360201	HEC	373211	EUS	375310	SET	375815	SET	376019	SET
360202	HEC	373212	EUS			375816	SET	376020	SET
360203	HEC	373213	EUS	375601	SET	375817	SET	376021	SET
360204	HEC	373214	EUS	375602	SET	375818	SET	376022	SET
360205	HEC	373215	EUS	375603	SET	375819	SET	376023	SET
		373216	EUS	375604	SET	375820	SET	376024	SET
365501	OLS	373217	EUS	375605	SET	375821	SET	376025	SET
365502	GTR	373218	EUS	375606	SET	375822	SET	376026	SET
365503	OLS	373219	EUS	375607	SET	375823	SET	376027	SET
365504	GTR	373220	EUS	375608	SET	375824	SET	376028	SET
365505	OLS	373221	EUS	375609	SET	375825	SET	376029	SET
365506	GTR	373222	EUS	375610	SET	375826	SET	376030	SET
365507	OLS	373223	EUS	375611	SET	375827	SET	376031	SET
365508	GTR	373224	EUS	375612	SET	375828	SET	376032	SET
365509	ASR	373229	EUS	375613	SET	375829	SET	376033	SET
365510	GTR	373230	EUS	375614	SET	375830	SET	376034	SET
365511	GTR			375615	SET			376035	SET
365512	GTR	373399	EUS	375616	SET	375901	SET	376036	SET
365513	ASR			375617	SET	375902	SET		
365514	GTR	374001	EUS	375618	SET	375903	SET	377101	GTR
365515	OLS	374002	EUS	375619	SET	375904	SET	377102	GTR
365516	GTR	374003	EUS	375620	SET	375905	SET	377103	GTR
365517	ASR	374004	EUS	375621	SET	375906	SET	377104	GTR
365518	GTR	374005	EUS	375622	SET	375907	SET	377105	GTR
365519	ASR	374006	EUS	375623	SET	375908	SET	377106	GTR
365520	GTR	374007	EUS	375624	SET	375909	SET	377107	GTR
365521	ASR	374008	EUS	375625	SET	375910	SET	377108	GTR
365522	GTR	374009	EUS	375626	SET	375911	SET	377109	GTR
365523	ASR	374010	EUS	375627	SET	375912	SET	377110	GTR
365524	GTR	374011	EUS	375628	SET	375913	SET	377111	GTR
365525	ASR	374012	EUS	375629	SET	375914	SET	377112	GTR
365527	OLS	374013	EUS	375630	SET	375915	SET	377113	GTR
365528	GTR	374014	EUS			375916	SET	377114	GTR
365529	ASR	374015	EUS	375701	SET	375917	SET	377115	GTR
365530	GTR	374016	EUS	375702	SET	375918	SET	377116	GTR
365531	GTR	374017	EUS	375703	SET	375919	SET	377117	GTR
365532	GTR	374018	EUS	375704	SET	375920	SET	377118	GTR
365533	ASR	374019	EUS	375705	SET	375921	SET	377119	GTR
365534	GTR	374020	EUS	375706	SET	375922	SET	377120	GTR
365535	OLS	374021	EUS	375707	SET	375923	SET	377121	GTR
365536	GTR	374022	EUS	375708	SET	375924	SET	377122	GTR
365537	ASR	374023	EUS	375709	SET	375925	SET	377123	GTR
365538	GTR	374024	EUS	375710	SET	375926	SET	377124	GTR
365539	GTR	374025	EUS	375711	SET	375927	SET	377125	GTR
365540	GTR	374026	EUS	375712	SET			377126	GTR
365541	GTR	374027	EUS	375713	SET	376001	SET	377127	GTR
		374028	EUS	375714	SET	376002	SET	377128	GTR
373007	EUS	374029	EUS	375715	SET	376003	SET	377129	GTR
373008	EUS	374030	EUS			376004	SET	377130	GTR
373015	EUS	374031	EUS	375801	SET	376005	SET	377131	GTR
373016	EUS	374032	EUS	375802	SET	376006	SET	377132	GTR
373021	EUS	374033	EUS	375803	SET	376007	SET	377133	GTR
373022	EUS	374034	EUS	375804	SET	376008	SET	377134	GTR
				375805	SET	376009	SET	377135	GTR
373105	EUS	375301	SET	375806	SET	376010	SET	377136	GTR
373106	EUS	375302	SET	375807	SET	376011	SET	377137	GTR
		375303	SET	375808	SET	376012	SET	377138	GTR
373205	EUS	375304	SET	375809	SET	376013	SET	377139	GTR
373206	EUS	375305	SET	375810	SET	376014	SET	377140	GTR
373207	EUS	375306	SET	375811	SET	376015	SET	377141	GTR

377142	GTR	377324	GTR	377458	GTR	377621	GTR	378227	LOG
377143	GTR	377325	GTR	377459	GTR	377622	GTR	378228	LOG
377144	GTR	377326	GTR	377460	GTR	377623	GTR	378229	LOG
377145	GTR	377327	GTR	377461	GTR	377624	GTR	378230	LOG
377146	GTR	377328	GTR	377462	GTR	377625	GTR	378231	LOG
377147	GTR			377463	GTR	377626	GTR	378232	LOG
377148	GTR	377401	GTR	377464	GTR			378233	LOG
377149	GTR	377402	GTR	377465	GTR	377701	GTR	378234	LOG
377150	GTR	377403	GTR	377466	GTR	377702	GTR	378255	LOG
377151	GTR	377404	GTR	377467	GTR	377703	GTR	378256	LOG
377152	GTR	377405	GTR	377468	GTR	377704	GTR	378257	LOG
377153	GTR	377406	GTR	377469	GTR	377705	GTR		
377154	GTR	377407	GTR	377470	GTR	377706	GTR	379001	GAR
377155	GTR	377408	GTR	377471	GTR	377707	GTR	379002	GAR
377156	GTR	377409	GTR	377472	GTR	377708	GTR	379003	GAR
377157	GTR	377410	GTR	377473	GTR			379004	GAR
377158	GTR	377411	GTR	377474	GTR	378135	LOG	379005	GAR
377159	GTR	377412	GTR	377475	GTR	378136	LOG	379006	GAR
377160	GTR	377413	GTR			378137	LOG	379007	GAR
377161	GTR	377414	GTR	377501	SET	378138	LOG	379008	GAR
377162	GTR	377415	GTR	377502	SET	378139	LOG	379009	GAR
377163	GTR	377416	GTR	377503	SET	378140	LOG	379010	GAR
377164	GTR	377417	GTR	377504	SET	378141	LOG	379011	GAR
		377418	GTR	377505	SET	378142	LOG	379012	GAR
377201	GTR	377419	GTR	377506	SET	378143	LOG	379013	GAR
377202	GTR	377420	GTR	377507	SET	378144	LOG	379014	GAR
377203	GTR	377421	GTR	377508	SET	378145	LOG	379015	GAR
377204	GTR	377422	GTR	377509	SET	378146	LOG	379016	GAR
377205	GTR	377423	GTR	377510	SET	378147	LOG	379017	GAR
377206	GTR	377424	GTR	377511	SET	378148	LOG	379018	GAR
377207	GTR	377425	GTR	377512	SET	378149	LOG	379019	GAR
377208	GTR	377426	GTR	377513	SET	378150	LOG	379020	GAR
377209	GTR	377427	GTR	377514	SET	378151	LOG	379021	GAR
377210	GTR	377428	GTR	377515	SET	378152	LOG	379022	GAR
377211	GTR	377429	GTR	377516	SET	378153	LOG	379023	GAR
377212	GTR	377430	GTR	377517	SET	378154	LOG	379024	GAR
377213	GTR	377431	GTR	377518	SET			379025	GAR
377214	GTR	377432	GTR	377519	SET	378201	LOG	379026	GAR
377215	GTR	377433	GTR	377520	SET	378202	LOG	379027	GAR
		377434	GTR	377521	SET	378203	LOG	379028	GAR
377301	GTR	377435	GTR	377522	SET	378204	LOG	379029	GAR
377302	GTR	377436	GTR	377523	SET	378205	LOG	379030	GAR
377303	GTR	377437	GTR			378206	LOG		
377304	GTR	377438	GTR	377601	GTR	378207	LOG	380001	ASR
377305	GTR	377439	GTR	377602	GTR	378208	LOG	380002	ASR
377306	GTR	377440	GTR	377603	GTR	378209	LOG	380003	ASR
377307	GTR	377441	GTR	377604	GTR	378210	LOG	380004	ASR
377308	GTR	377442	GTR	377605	GTR	378211	LOG	380005	ASR
377309	GTR	377443	GTR	377606	GTR	378212	LOG	380006	ASR
377310	GTR	377444	GTR	377607	GTR	378213	LOG	380007	ASR
377311	GTR	377445	GTR	377608	GTR	378214	LOG	380008	ASR
377312	GTR	377446	GTR	377609	GTR	378215	LOG	380009	ASR
377313	GTR	377447	GTR	377610	GTR	378216	LOG	380010	ASR
377314	GTR	377448	GTR	377611	GTR	378217	LOG	380011	ASR
377315	GTR	377449	GTR	377612	GTR	378218	LOG	380012	ASR
377316	GTR	377450	GTR	377613	GTR	378219	LOG	380013	ASR
377317	GTR	377451	GTR	377614	GTR	378220	LOG	380014	ASR
377318	GTR	377452	GTR	377615	GTR	378221	LOG	380015	ASR
377319	GTR	377453	GTR	377616	GTR	378222	LOG	380016	ASR
377320	GTR	377454	GTR	377617	GTR	378223	LOG	380017	ASR
377321	GTR	377455	GTR	377618	GTR	378224	LOG	380018	ASR
377322	GTR	377456	GTR	377619	GTR	378225	LOG	380019	ASR
377323	GTR	377457	GTR	377620	GTR	378226	LOG	380020	ASR

Data Tables

No.		No.		No.		No.		No.	
380021	ASR	385044	ASR	387135	GWR	387223	GTR	390152	VWC
380022	ASR	385045	ASR	387136	GWR	387224	GTR	390153	VWC
		385046	ASR	387137	GWR	387225	GTR	390154	VWC
380101	ASR			387138	GWR	387226	GTR	390155	VWC
380102	ASR	385101	ASR	387139	GWR	387227	GTR	390156	VWC
380103	ASR	385102	ASR	387140	GWR			390157	VWC
380104	ASR	385103	ASR	387141	GWR	387301	C2C		
380105	ASR	385104	ASR	387142	GWR	387302	C2C	395001	SET
380106	ASR	385105	ASR	387143	GWR	387303	C2C	395002	SET
380107	ASR	385106	ASR	387144	GWR	387304	C2C	395003	SET
380108	ASR	385107	ASR	387145	GWR	387305	C2C	395004	SET
380109	ASR	385108	ASR	387146	GWR	387306	C2C	395005	SET
380110	ASR	385109	ASR	387147	GWR			395006	SET
380111	ASR	385110	ASR	387148	GWR	390001	VWC	395007	SET
380112	ASR	385111	ASR	387149	GWR	390002	VWC	395008	SET
380113	ASR	385112	ASR	387150	GWR	390103	VWC	395009	SET
380114	ASR	385113	ASR	387151	GWR	390104	VWC	395010	SET
380115	ASR	385114	ASR	387152	GWR	390005	VWC	395011	SET
380116	ASR	385115	ASR	387153	GWR	390006	VWC	395012	SET
		385116	ASR	387154	GWR	390107	VWC	395013	SET
385001	ASR	385117	ASR	387155	GWR	390008	VWC	395014	SET
385002	ASR	385118	ASR	387156	GWR	390009	VWC	395015	SET
385003	ASR	385119	ASR	387157	GWR	390010	VWC	395016	SET
385004	ASR	385120	ASR	387158	GWR	390011	VWC	395017	SET
385005	ASR	385121	ASR	387159	GWR	390112	VWC	395018	SET
385006	ASR	385122	ASR	387160	GWR	390013	VWC	395019	SET
385007	ASR	385123	ASR	387161	GWR	390114	VWC	395020	SET
385008	ASR	385124	ASR	387162	GWR	390115	VWC	395021	SET
385009	ASR			387163	GWR	390016	VWC	395022	SET
385010	ASR	387101	GTR	387164	GWR	390117	VWC	395023	SET
385011	ASR	387102	GTR	387165	GWR	390118	VWC	395024	SET
385012	ASR	387103	GTR	387166	GWR	390119	VWC	395025	SET
385013	ASR	387104	GTR	387167	GWR	390020	VWC	395026	SET
385014	ASR	387105	GTR	387168	GWR	390121	VWC	395027	SET
385015	ASR	387106	GTR	387169	GWR	390122	VWC	395028	SET
385016	ASR	387107	GTR	387170	GWR	390123	VWC	395029	SET
385017	ASR	387108	GTR	387171	GWR	390124	VWC		
385018	ASR	387109	GTR	387172	GWR	390125	VWC	399201	NOR
385019	ASR	387110	GTR	387173	GWR	390126	VWC	399202	NOR
385020	ASR	387111	GTR	387174	GWR	390127	VWC	399203	NOR
385021	ASR	387112	GTR			390128	VWC	399204	NOR
385022	ASR	387113	GTR	387201	GTR	390129	VWC	399205	NOR
385023	ASR	387114	GTR	387202	GTR	390130	VWC	399206	NOR
385024	ASR	387115	GTR	387203	GTR	390131	VWC	399207	NOR
385025	ASR	387116	GTR	387204	GTR	390132	VWC		
385026	ASR	387117	GTR	387205	GTR	390134	VWC	442401	SWR
385027	ASR	387118	GTR	387206	GTR	390135	VWC	442402	OLS
385028	ASR	387119	GTR	387207	GTR	390136	VWC	442403	SWR
385029	ASR	387120	GTR	387208	GTR	390137	VWC	442404	SWR
385030	ASR	387121	GTR	387209	GTR	390138	VWC	442405	SWR
385031	ASR	387122	GTR	387210	GTR	390039	VWC	442406	OLS
385032	ASR	387123	GTR	387211	GTR	390040	VWC	442407	SWR
385033	ASR	387124	GTR	387212	GTR	390141	VWC	442408	SWR
385034	ASR	387125	GTR	387213	GTR	390042	VWC	442409	SWR
385035	ASR	387126	GTR	387214	GTR	390043	VWC	442410	OLS
385036	ASR	387127	GTR	387215	GTR	390044	VWC	442411	SWR
385037	ASR	387128	GTR	387216	GTR	390045	VWC	442412	SWR
385038	ASR	387129	GTR	387217	GTR	390046	VWC	442413	SWR
385039	ASR	387130	GWR	387218	GTR	390047	VWC	442414	SWR
385040	ASR	387131	GWR	387219	GTR	390148	VWC	442415	SWR
385041	ASR	387132	GWR	387220	GTR	390049	VWC	442416	SWR
385042	ASR	387133	GWR	387221	GTR	390050	VWC	442417	SWR
385043	ASR	387134	GWR	387222	GTR	390151	VWC	442418	SWR

Number	Code	Number	Code	Number	Code	Number	Code	Number	Code
442419	OLS	450011	SWR	450102	SWR	455708	SWR	455827	GTR
442420	SWR	450012	SWR	450103	SWR	455709	SWR	455828	GTR
442421	SWR	450013	SWR	450104	SWR	455710	SWR	455829	GTR
442422	SWR	450014	SWR	450105	SWR	455711	SWR	455830	GTR
442423	SWR	450015	SWR	450106	SWR	455712	SWR	455831	GTR
442424	SWR	450016	SWR	450107	SWR	455713	SWR	455832	GTR
		450017	SWR	450108	SWR	455714	SWR	455833	GTR
444001	SWR	450018	SWR	450109	SWR	455715	SWR	455834	GTR
444002	SWR	450019	SWR	450110	SWR	455716	SWR	455835	GTR
444003	SWR	450020	SWR	450111	SWR	455717	SWR	455836	GTR
444004	SWR	450021	SWR	450112	SWR	455718	SWR	455837	GTR
444005	SWR	450022	SWR	450113	SWR	455719	SWR	455838	GTR
444006	SWR	450023	SWR	450114	SWR	455720	SWR	455839	GTR
444007	SWR	450024	SWR	450115	SWR	455721	SWR	455840	GTR
444008	SWR	450025	SWR	450116	SWR	455722	SWR	455841	GTR
444009	SWR	450026	SWR	450117	SWR	455723	SWR	455842	GTR
444010	SWR	450027	SWR	450118	SWR	455724	SWR	455843	GTR
444011	SWR	450028	SWR	450119	SWR	455725	SWR	455844	GTR
444012	SWR	450029	SWR	450120	SWR	455726	SWR	455845	GTR
444013	SWR	450030	SWR	450121	SWR	455727	SWR	455846	GTR
444014	SWR	450031	SWR	450122	SWR	455728	SWR	455847	SWR
444015	SWR	450032	SWR	450123	SWR	455729	SWR	455848	SWR
444016	SWR	450033	SWR	450124	SWR	455730	SWR	455849	SWR
444017	SWR	450034	SWR	450125	SWR	455731	SWR	455850	SWR
444018	SWR	450035	SWR	450126	SWR	455732	SWR	455851	SWR
444019	SWR	450036	SWR	450127	SWR	455733	SWR	455852	SWR
444020	SWR	450037	SWR			455734	SWR	455853	SWR
444021	SWR	450038	SWR	450543	SWR	455735	SWR	455854	SWR
444022	SWR	450039	SWR	450544	SWR	455736	SWR	455855	SWR
444023	SWR	450040	SWR	450545	SWR	455737	SWR	455856	SWR
444024	SWR	450041	SWR	450546	SWR	455738	SWR	455857	SWR
444025	SWR	450042	SWR	450547	SWR	455739	SWR	455858	SWR
444026	SWR	450071	SWR	450548	SWR	455740	SWR	455859	SWR
444027	SWR	450072	SWR	450549	SWR	455741	SWR	455860	SWR
444028	SWR	450073	SWR	450550	SWR	455742	SWR	455861	SWR
444029	SWR	450074	SWR	450551	SWR	455750	SWR	455862	SWR
444030	SWR	450075	SWR	450552	SWR			455863	SWR
444031	SWR	450076	SWR	450553	SWR	455801	GTR	455864	SWR
444032	SWR	450077	SWR	450554	SWR	455802	GTR	455865	SWR
444033	SWR	450078	SWR	450555	SWR	455803	GTR	455866	SWR
444034	SWR	450079	SWR	450556	SWR	455804	GTR	455867	SWR
444035	SWR	450080	SWR	450557	SWR	455805	GTR	455868	SWR
444036	SWR	450081	SWR	450558	SWR	455806	GTR	455869	SWR
444037	SWR	450082	SWR	450559	SWR	455807	GTR	455870	SWR
444038	SWR	450083	SWR	450560	SWR	455808	GTR	455871	SWR
444039	SWR	450084	SWR	450561	SWR	455809	GTR	455872	SWR
444040	SWR	450085	SWR	450562	SWR	455810	GTR	455873	SWR
444041	SWR	450086	SWR	450563	SWR	455811	GTR	455874	SWR
444042	SWR	450087	SWR	450564	SWR	455812	GTR		
444043	SWR	450088	SWR	450565	SWR	455813	GTR	455901	SWR
444044	SWR	450089	SWR	450566	SWR	455814	GTR	455902	SWR
444045	SWR	450090	SWR	450567	SWR	455815	GTR	455903	SWR
		450091	SWR	450568	SWR	455816	GTR	455904	SWR
450001	SWR	450092	SWR	450569	SWR	455817	GTR	455905	SWR
450002	SWR	450093	SWR	450570	SWR	455818	GTR	455906	SWR
450003	SWR	450094	SWR			455819	GTR	455907	SWR
450004	SWR	450095	SWR	455701	SWR	455820	GTR	455908	SWR
450005	SWR	450096	SWR	455702	SWR	455821	GTR	455909	SWR
450006	SWR	450097	SWR	455703	SWR	455822	GTR	455910	SWR
450007	SWR	450098	SWR	455704	SWR	455823	GTR	455911	SWR
450008	SWR	450099	SWR	455705	SWR	455824	GTR	455912	SWR
450009	SWR	450100	SWR	455706	SWR	455825	GTR	455913	SWR
450010	SWR	450101	SWR	455707	SWR	455826	GTR	455914	SWR

Data Tables

Number	Code	Number	Code	Number	Code	Number	Code	Number	Code
455915	SWR	458532	SWR	465157	SET	465905	SET	466033	SET
455916	SWR	458533	SWR	465158	SET	465906	SET	466034	SET
455917	SWR	458534	SWR	465159	SET	465907	SET	466035	SET
455918	SWR	458535	SWR	465160	SET	465908	SET	466036	SET
455919	SWR	458536	SWR	465161	SET	465909	SET	466037	SET
455920	SWR			465162	SET	465910	SET	466038	SET
		465001	SET	465163	SET	465911	SET	466039	SET
456001	SWR	465002	SET	465164	SET	465912	SET	466040	SET
456002	SWR	465003	SET	465165	SET	465913	SET	466041	SET
456003	SWR	465004	SET	465166	SET	465914	SET	466042	SET
456004	SWR	465005	SET	465167	SET	465915	SET	466043	SET
456005	SWR	465006	SET	465168	SET	465916	SET		
456006	SWR	465007	SET	465169	SET	465917	SET	483002	SWR
456007	SWR	465008	SET	465170	SET	465918	SET	483004	SWR
456008	SWR	465009	SET	465171	SET	465919	SET	483006	SWR
456009	SWR	465010	SET	465172	SET	465920	SET	483007	SWR
456010	SWR	465011	SET	465173	SET	465921	SET	483008	SWR
456011	SWR	465012	SET	465174	SET	465922	SET	483009	SWR
456012	SWR	465013	SET	465175	SET	465923	SET		
456013	SWR	465014	SET	465176	SET	465924	SET	489102	AFG
456014	SWR	465015	SET	465177	SET	465925	SET	489105	AFG
456015	SWR	465016	SET	465178	SET	465926	SET	489106	AFG
456016	SWR	465017	SET	465179	SET	465927	SET		
456017	SWR	465018	SET	465180	SET	465928	SET	507001	MER
456018	SWR	465019	SET	465181	SET	465929	SET	507002	MER
456019	SWR	465020	SET	465182	SET	465930	SET	507003	MER
456020	SWR	465021	SET	465183	SET	465931	SET	507004	MER
456021	SWR	465022	SET	465184	SET	465932	SET	507005	MER
456022	SWR	465023	SET	465185	SET	465933	SET	507006	MER
456023	SWR	465024	SET	465186	SET	465934	SET	507007	MER
456024	SWR	465025	SET	465187	SET			507008	MER
		465026	SET	465188	SET	466001	SET	507009	MER
458501	SWR	465027	SET	465189	SET	466002	SET	507010	MER
458502	SWR	465028	SET	465190	SET	466003	SET	507011	MER
458503	SWR	465029	SET	465191	SET	466004	SET	507012	MER
458504	SWR	465030	SET	465192	SET	466005	SET	507013	MER
458505	SWR	465031	SET	465193	SET	466006	SET	507014	MER
458506	SWR	465032	SET	465194	SET	466007	SET	507015	MER
458507	SWR	465033	SET	465195	SET	466008	SET	507016	MER
458508	SWR	465034	SET	465196	SET	466009	SET	507017	MER
458509	SWR	465035	SET	465197	SET	466010	SET	507018	MER
458510	SWR	465036	SET			466011	SET	507019	MER
458511	SWR	465037	SET	465235	SET	466012	SET	507020	MER
458512	SWR	465038	SET	465236	SET	466013	SET	507021	MER
458513	SWR	465039	SET	465237	SET	466014	SET	507023	MER
458514	SWR	465040	SET	465238	SET	466015	SET	507024	MER
458515	SWR	465041	SET	465239	SET	466016	SET	507025	MER
458516	SWR	465042	SET	465240	SET	466017	SET	507026	MER
458517	SWR	465043	SET	465241	SET	466018	SET	507027	MER
458518	SWR	465044	SET	465242	SET	466019	SET	507028	MER
458519	SWR	465045	SET	465243	SET	466020	SET	507029	MER
458520	SWR	465046	SET	465244	SET	466021	SET	507030	MER
458521	SWR	465047	SET	465245	SET	466022	SET	507031	MER
458522	SWR	465048	SET	465246	SET	466023	SET	507032	MER
458523	SWR	465049	SET	465247	SET	466024	SET	507033	MER
458524	SWR	465050	SET	465248	SET	466025	SET		
458525	SWR			465249	SET	466026	SET	508103	MER
458526	SWR	465151	SET	465250	SET	466027	SET	508104	MER
458527	SWR	465152	SET			466028	SET	508108	MER
458528	SWR	465153	SET	465901	SET	466029	SET	508110	MER
458529	SWR	465154	SET	465902	SET	466030	SET	508111	MER
458530	SWR	465155	SET	465903	SET	466031	SET	508112	MER
458531	SWR	465156	SET	465904	SET	466032	SET	508114	MER

508115	MER	700043	GTR	700145	GTR	701052	SWR	707023	SWR
508117	MER	700044	GTR	700146	GTR	701053	SWR	707024	SWR
508120	MER	700045	GTR	700147	GTR	701054	SWR	707025	SWR
508122	MER	700046	GTR	700148	GTR	701055	SWR	707026	SWR
508123	MER	700047	GTR	700149	GTR	701056	SWR	707027	SWR
508124	MER	700048	GTR	700150	GTR	701057	SWR	707028	SWR
508125	MER	700049	GTR	700151	GTR	701058	SWR	707029	SWR
508126	MER	700050	GTR	700152	GTR	701059	SWR	707030	SWR
508127	MER	700051	GTR	700153	GTR	701060	SWR		
508128	MER	700052	GTR	700154	GTR			710101	LOG
508130	MER	700053	GTR	700155	GTR	701501	SWR	710102	LOG
508131	MER	700054	GTR			701502	SWR	710103	LOG
508134	MER	700055	GTR	701001	SWR	701503	SWR	710104	LOG
508136	MER	700056	GTR	701002	SWR	701504	SWR	710105	LOG
508137	MER	700057	GTR	701003	SWR	701505	SWR	710106	LOG
508138	MER	700058	GTR	701004	SWR	701506	SWR	710107	LOG
508139	MER	700059	GTR	701005	SWR	701507	SWR	710108	LOG
508140	MER	700060	GTR	701006	SWR	701508	SWR	710109	LOG
508141	MER			701007	SWR	701509	SWR	710110	LOG
508143	MER	700101	GTR	701008	SWR	701510	SWR	710111	LOG
		700102	GTR	701009	SWR	701511	SWR	710112	LOG
700001	GTR	700103	GTR	701010	SWR	701512	SWR	710113	LOG
700002	GTR	700104	GTR	701011	SWR	701513	SWR	710114	LOG
700003	GTR	700105	GTR	701012	SWR	701514	SWR	710115	LOG
700004	GTR	700106	GTR	701013	SWR	701515	SWR	710116	LOG
700005	GTR	700107	GTR	701014	SWR	701516	SWR	710117	LOG
700006	GTR	700108	GTR	701015	SWR	701517	SWR	710118	LOG
700007	GTR	700109	GTR	701016	SWR	701518	SWR	710119	LOG
700008	GTR	700110	GTR	701017	SWR	701519	SWR	710120	LOG
700009	GTR	700111	GTR	701018	SWR	701520	SWR	710121	LOG
700010	GTR	700112	GTR	701019	SWR	701521	SWR	710122	LOG
700011	GTR	700113	GTR	701020	SWR	701522	SWR	710123	LOG
700012	GTR	700114	GTR	701021	SWR	701523	SWR	710124	LOG
700013	GTR	700115	GTR	701022	SWR	701524	SWR	710125	LOG
700014	GTR	700116	GTR	701023	SWR	701525	SWR	710126	LOG
700015	GTR	700117	GTR	701024	SWR	701526	SWR	710127	LOG
700016	GTR	700118	GTR	701025	SWR	701527	SWR	710128	LOG
700017	GTR	700119	GTR	701026	SWR	701528	SWR	710129	LOG
700018	GTR	700120	GTR	701027	SWR	701529	SWR	710130	LOG
700019	GTR	700121	GTR	701028	SWR	701530	SWR	710131	LOG
700020	GTR	700122	GTR	701029	SWR				
700021	GTR	700123	GTR	701030	SWR	707001	SWR	710256	LOG
700022	GTR	700124	GTR	701031	SWR	707002	SWR	710257	LOG
700023	GTR	700125	GTR	701032	SWR	707003	SWR	710258	LOG
700024	GTR	700126	GTR	701033	SWR	707004	SWR	710259	LOG
700025	GTR	700127	GTR	701034	SWR	707005	SWR	710260	LOG
700026	GTR	700128	GTR	701035	SWR	707006	SWR	710261	LOG
700027	GTR	700129	GTR	701036	SWR	707007	SWR	710262	LOG
700028	GTR	700130	GTR	701037	SWR	707008	SWR	710263	LOG
700029	GTR	700131	GTR	701038	SWR	707009	SWR	710264	LOG
700030	GTR	700132	GTR	701039	SWR	707010	SWR	710265	LOG
700031	GTR	700133	GTR	701040	SWR	707011	SWR	710266	LOG
700032	GTR	700134	GTR	701041	SWR	707012	SWR	710267	LOG
700033	GTR	700135	GTR	701042	SWR	707013	SWR	710268	LOG
700034	GTR	700136	GTR	701043	SWR	707014	SWR	710269	LOG
700035	GTR	700137	GTR	701044	SWR	707015	SWR		
700036	GTR	700138	GTR	701045	SWR	707016	SWR	717001	GTR
700037	GTR	700139	GTR	701046	SWR	707017	SWR	717002	GTR
700038	GTR	700140	GTR	701047	SWR	707018	SWR	717003	GTR
700039	GTR	700141	GTR	701048	SWR	707019	SWR	717004	GTR
700040	GTR	700142	GTR	701049	SWR	707020	SWR	717005	GTR
700041	GTR	700143	GTR	701050	SWR	707021	SWR	717006	GTR
700042	GTR	700144	GTR	701051	SWR	707022	SWR	717007	GTR

Data Tables

717008	GTR	720522	GAR	720585	GAR	755421	GAR	800113	LNE
717009	GTR	720523	GAR	720586	GAR	755422	GAR		
717010	GTR	720524	GAR	720587	GAR	755423	GAR	800201	LNE
717011	GTR	720525	GAR	720588	GAR	755424	GAR	800202	LNE
717012	GTR	720526	GAR	720589	GAR			800203	LNE
717013	GTR	720527	GAR					800204	LNE
717014	GTR	720528	GAR	745001	GAR	769424	NOR	800205	LNE
717015	GTR	720529	GAR	745002	GAR	769431	NOR	800206	LNE
717016	GTR	720530	GAR	745003	GAR	769434	NOR	800207	LNE
717017	GTR	720531	GAR	745004	GAR	769442	NOR	800208	LNE
717018	GTR	720532	GAR	745005	GAR	769448	NOR	800209	LNE
717019	GTR	720533	GAR	745006	GAR	769450	NOR	800210	LNE
717020	GTR	720534	GAR	745007	GAR	769456	NOR		
717021	GTR	720535	GAR	745008	GAR	769458	NOR	800301	GWR
717022	GTR	720536	GAR	745009	GAR			800302	GWR
717023	GTR	720537	GAR	745010	GAR	800001	GWR	800303	GWR
717024	GTR	720538	GAR			800002	GWR	800304	GWR
717025	GTR	720539	GAR	745101	GAR	800003	GWR	800305	GWR
		720540	GAR	745102	GAR	800004	GWR	800306	GWR
720101	GAR	720541	GAR	745103	GAR	800005	GWR	800307	GWR
720102	GAR	720542	GAR	745104	GAR	800006	GWR	800308	GWR
720103	GAR	720543	GAR	745105	GAR	800007	GWR	800309	GWR
720104	GAR	720544	GAR	745106	GAR	800008	GWR	800310	GWR
720105	GAR	720545	GAR	745107	GAR	800009	GWR	800311	GWR
720106	GAR	720546	GAR	745108	GAR	800010	GWR	800312	GWR
720107	GAR	720547	GAR	745109	GAR	800011	GWR	800313	GWR
720108	GAR	720548	GAR	745110	GAR	800012	GWR	800314	GWR
720109	GAR	720549	GAR			800013	GWR	800315	GWR
720110	GAR	720550	GAR	755325	GAR	800014	GWR	800316	GWR
720111	GAR	720551	GAR	755326	GAR	800015	GWR	800317	GWR
720112	GAR	720552	GAR	755327	GAR	800016	GWR	800318	GWR
720113	GAR	720553	GAR	755328	GAR	800017	GWR	800319	GWR
720114	GAR	720554	GAR	755329	GAR	800018	GWR	800320	GWR
720115	GAR	720555	GAR	755330	GAR	800019	GWR	800321	GWR
720116	GAR	720556	GAR	755331	GAR	800020	GWR		
720117	GAR	720557	GAR	755332	GAR	800021	GWR	801101	LNE
720118	GAR	720558	GAR	755333	GAR	800022	GWR	801102	LNE
720119	GAR	720559	GAR	755334	GAR	800023	GWR	801103	LNE
720120	GAR	720560	GAR	755335	GAR	800024	GWR	801104	LNE
720121	GAR	720561	GAR	755336	GAR	800025	GWR	801105	LNE
720122	GAR	720562	GAR	755337	GAR	800026	GWR	801106	LNE
		720563	GAR	755338	GAR	800027	GWR	801107	LNE
720501	GAR	720564	GAR			800028	GWR	801108	LNE
720502	GAR	720565	GAR	755401	GAR	800029	GWR	801109	LNE
720503	GAR	720566	GAR	755402	GAR	800030	GWR	801110	LNE
720504	GAR	720567	GAR	755403	GAR	800031	GWR	801111	LNE
720505	GAR	720568	GAR	755404	GAR	800032	GWR	801112	LNE
720506	GAR	720569	GAR	755405	GAR	800033	GWR		
720507	GAR	720570	GAR	755406	GAR	800034	GWR	801201	LNE
720508	GAR	720571	GAR	755407	GAR	800035	GWR	801202	LNE
720509	GAR	720572	GAR	755408	GAR	800036	GWR	801203	LNE
720510	GAR	720573	GAR	755409	GAR			801204	LNE
720511	GAR	720574	GAR	755410	GAR	800101	LNE	801205	LNE
720512	GAR	720575	GAR	755411	GAR	800102	LNE	801206	LNE
720513	GAR	720576	GAR	755412	GAR	800103	LNE	801207	LNE
720514	GAR	720577	GAR	755413	GAR	800104	LNE	801208	LNE
720515	GAR	720578	GAR	755414	GAR	800105	LNE	801209	LNE
720516	GAR	720579	GAR	755415	GAR	800106	LNE	801210	LNE
720517	GAR	720580	GAR	755416	GAR	800107	LNE	801211	LNE
720518	GAR	720581	GAR	755417	GAR	800108	LNE	801212	LNE
720519	GAR	720582	GAR	755418	GAR	800109	LNE	801213	LNE
720520	GAR	720583	GAR	755419	GAR	800110	LNE	801214	LNE
720521	GAR	720584	GAR	755420	GAR	800111	LNE	801215	LNE
						800112	LNE		

801216	LNE	802210	FTP	504	WCR	2922	NRL	3344	LSC
801217	LNE	802211	FTP	506	WCR	2923	NRL	3345	RIV
801218	LNE	802212	FTP	546	WCR			3348	WCR
801219	LNE	802213	FTP	548	WCR	3058	WCR	3350	WCR
801220	LNE	802214	FTP	549	WCR	3066	RIV	3351	VTN
801221	LNE	802215	FTP	550	WCR	3068	RIV	3352	WCR
801222	LNE	802216	FTP	551	WCR	3069	RIV	3356	RIV
801223	LNE	802217	FTP	552	WCR	3093	WCR	3359	WCR
801224	LNE	802218	FTP	553	WCR	3096	BOK	3360	WCR
801225	LNE	802219	FTP	586	WCR	3097	RIV	3362	WCR
801226	LNE			807	WCR	3098	RIV	3364	RIV
801227	LNE	802301	FHT			3100	RIV	3379	RIV
801228	LNE	802302	FHT	1105	MHR	3105	WCR	3384	RIV
801229	LNE	802303	FHT	1200	RIV	3106	WCR	3386	RIV
801230	LNE	802304	FHT	1201	VTN	3110	RIV	3390	RIV
		802305	FHT	1203	RIV	3112	RIV	3395	WCR
802001	GWR			1207	WCR	3113	WCR	3397	RIV
802002	GWR	**Coaching Stock**		1209	OLS	3115	BOK	3417	RIV
802003	GWR	84	RAF	1211	LSC	3117	WCR	3426	RIV
802004	GWR	159	WCR	1212	RIV	3119	RIV	3431	WCR
802005	GWR	213	VSO	1219	OLS	3120	RIV	3438	LSC
802006	GWR	239	VSO	1221	WCR	3121	RIV	3860	NYM
802007	GWR	243	VSO	1256	NRL	3122	RIV	3872	NYM
802008	GWR	245	VSO	1375	BOK	3123	RIV	3948	NYM
802009	GWR	254	VSO	1566	WCR	3125	RIV		
802010	GWR	255	VSO	1644	WCR	3128	WCR	4198	NYM
802011	GWR	261	VSO	1650	WCR	3130	WCR	4252	NYM
802012	GWR	264	VSO	1651	RIV	3136	WCR	4290	NYM
802013	GWR	280	VSO	1652	WCR	3141	RIV	4362	RAF
802014	GWR	281	VSO	1655	WCR	3143	WCR	4455	NYM
802015	GWR	283	VSO	1657	RIV	3144	RIV	4786	NYM
802016	GWR	284	VSO	1659	LSC	3146	RIV	4817	NYM
802017	GWR	285	VSO	1663	WCR	3147	RIV	4831	BOK
802018	GWR	286	VSO	1666	WCR	3148	RIV	4832	BOK
802019	GWR	288	VSO	1670	WCR	3149	RIV	4836	BOK
802020	GWR	292	VSO	1671	RIV	3150	BOK	4854	WCR
802021	GWR	293	VSO	1683	RIV	3174	WCR	4856	BOK
802022	GWR	301	VSO	1691	RIV	3181	RIV	4860	WCR
		302	VSO	1730	WCR	3182	WCR	4905	WCR
802101	GWR	307	VSO	1813	RIV	3188	RAF	4912	WCR
802102	GWR	308	VSO	1823	NYM	3223	RIV	4927	RIV
802103	GWR	310	RAF	1832	RIV	3227	RIV	4931	WCR
802104	GWR	313	WCR	1840	WCR	3229	LSC	4932	WCR
802105	GWR	316	FSL	1859	SRP	3231	LSC	4940	WCR
802106	GWR	317	WCR	1860	WCR	3232	WCR	4946	RIV
802107	GWR	319	WCR	1861	WCR	3240	RIV	4949	RIV
802108	GWR	321	FSL	1863	RIV	3247	WCR	4951	WCR
802109	GWR	324	WCR	1882	WCR	3267	WCR	4954	WCR
802110	GWR	325	WCR	1953	WCR	3273	WCR	4958	RIV
802111	GWR	326	WCR	1961	WCR	3275	WCR	4959	RIV
802112	GWR	329	WCR	1999	WCR	3278	RIV	4960	WCR
802113	GWR	331	WCR			3279	DBR	4973	WCR
802114	GWR	335	VTN	2127	WCR	3304	RIV	4984	WCR
		337	FSL			3312	LSC	4991	RIV
802201	FTP	347	WCR	2903	NRL	3313	WCR	4994	WCR
802202	FTP	348	WCR	2904	NRL	3314	RIV	4997	WCR
802203	FTP	349	VTN	2915	NRL	3325	RIV	4998	RIV
802204	FTP	350	WCR	2916	NRL	3326	WCR		
802205	FTP	351	WCR	2917	NRL	3330	RIV	5000	NYM
802206	FTP	352	WCR	2918	NRL	3333	RIV	5007	RIV
802207	FTP	353	VTN	2919	NRL	3334	RIV	5009	RIV
802208	FTP	354	WCR	2920	NRL	3336	RIV	5027	RIV
802209	FTP	464	BOK	2921	NRL	3340	RIV	5028	BOK

Data Tables

5029	NYM	6021	WCR	9508	DRS	10304	LNE	10553	SCS
5032	WCR	6022	WCR	9509	RIV	10305	LNE	10556	WCR
5033	WCR	6024	RIV	9516	NRL	10306	LNE	10561	SCS
5035	WCR	6027	ASR	9520	RIV	10307	LNE	10563	GWR
5044	WCR	6042	RIV	9521	ASR	10308	LNE	10565	SCS
5125	WCR	6046	DRS	9522	DBR	10309	LNE	10569	WCR
5157	VTN	6051	RIV	9523	NRL	10310	LNE	10580	SCS
5171	WCR	6054	RIV	9525	DRS	10311	LNE	10584	GWR
5177	VTN	6059	RIV	9526	RIV	10312	LNE	10589	GWR
5191	VTN	6064	DRS	9527	RIV	10313	LNE	10590	GWR
5198	VTN	6067	RIV	9529	DBR	10315	LNE	10594	GWR
5200	WCR	6103	WCR	9531	DBR	10317	LNE	10596	GWR
5212	VTN	6115	WCR	9537	RIV	10318	LNE	10597	SCS
5216	WCR	6117	DRS	9539	ASR	10319	LNE	10598	SCS
5222	WCR	6121	OLS	9704	DRS	10320	LNE		
5229	WCR	6122	DRS	9705	DRS	10321	LNE	10600	SCS
5236	WCR	6135	WCR	9707	DRS	10323	LNE	10601	GWR
5237	WCR	6137	ASR	9709	DRS	10324	LNE	10605	SCS
5239	WCR	6141	RIV	9710	DRS	10325	LNE	10607	SCS
5249	WCR	6158	RIV	9800	SCS	10326	LNE	10610	SCS
5278	WCR	6160	OLS	9801	SCS	10328	LNE	10612	GWR
5292	RIV	6164	OLS	9802	SCS	10329	LNE	10614	SCS
5309	RIV	6173	DRS	9803	SCS	10330	LNE	10616	GWR
5341	RIV	6176	ASR	9804	SCS	10331	LNE	10648	SCS
5366	RIV	6177	ASR	9805	SCS	10332	LNE	10650	SCS
5419	WCR	6183	ASR	9806	SCS	10333	LNE	10661	OLS
5482	DBR	6310	RIV	9807	SCS			10666	SCS
5487	WCR	6312	WCR	9808	SCS	10401	GAR	10667	OLS
5494	RIV	6313	VSO	9809	SCS	10402	GAR	10675	SCS
5636	OLS	6320	RIV	9810	SCS	10403	GAR	10680	SCS
5647	RIV	6528	WCR			10404	GAR	10683	SCS
5756	WCR	6700	SCS	10204	3MP	10405	GAR	10688	SCS
5810	DRS	6701	SCS	10211	DBC	10406	GAR	10689	SCS
5888	OLS	6702	SCS	10212	FTP	10411	GAR	10690	SCS
5910	RIV	6703	SCS	10215	DBR	10412	GAR	10693	SCS
5912	LSC	6704	SCS	10217	GWR	10413	GAR	10698	OLS
5919	DRS	6705	SCS	10219	GWR	10414	GAR	10699	SCS
5921	RIV	6706	SCS	10222	DBR	10415	GAR	10703	SCS
5928	VTN	6707	SCS	10225	GWR	10416	GAR	10706	SCS
5929	RIV	6708	SCS	10226	DBR	10417	GAR	10714	SCS
5937	RIV	6722	RIV	10229	GWR			10718	SCS
5945	ASR	6723	WCR	10231	OLS	10501	SCS	10719	SCS
5950	RIV	6724	WCR	10232	OLS	10502	SCS	10722	SCS
5952	ASR			10233	DBR	10504	SCS	10729	WCR
5955	ASR	9005	RAF	10235	DBR	10506	SCS	10733	OLS
5961	RIV	9101	VTN	10237	DBR	10513	SCS	10734	WCR
5964	RIV	9104	WCR	10241	OLS	10516	SCS		
5965	ASR	9267	NYM	10242	DBR	10519	SCS	11006	DRS
5971	DRS	9274	NYM	10246	DBR	10520	SCS	11007	FTP
5976	ASR	9391	WCR	10249	TFW	10522	SCS	11018	FTP
5981	NRL	9392	WCR	10250	DBR	10526	SCS	11019	DBR
5985	RIV	9419	DRS	10256	OLS	10527	SCS	11028	DBR
5987	ASR	9428	DRS	10257	DBR	10529	SCS	11029	CRW
5991	LSC	9448	WCR	10259	TFW	10531	SCS	11030	DBR
5995	DRS	9481	NRL	10260	OLS	10532	GWR	11031	CRW
5998	RIV	9488	DRS	10271	CRW	10534	GWR	11033	DBR
		9493	WCR	10272	CRW	10541	WCR	11039	DBC
6000	WCR	9494	DBR	10273	CRW	10542	SCS	11046	DBR
6001	DRS	9496	VTN	10274	CRW	10543	SCS	11048	FTP
6006	RIV	9502	VSO	10300	LNE	10544	SCS	11054	DBR
6008	DRS	9504	RIV	10301	LNE	10546	DBC	11066	GAR
6012	WCR	9506	DBR	10302	LNE	10547	OLS	11067	GAR
6014	WCR	9507	RIV	10303	LNE	10551	SCS	11068	GAR

Data Tables

Number	Code	Number	Code	Number	Code	Number	Code	Number	Code
❏ 11069	GAR	❏ 11311	LNE	❏ 11513	FTP	❏ 12037	GAR	❏ 12154	GAR
❏ 11070	GAR	❏ 11312	LNE			❏ 12040	GAR	❏ 12159	GAR
❏ 11072	GAR	❏ 11313	LNE	❏ 11701	FTP	❏ 12041	GAR	❏ 12161	GWR
❏ 11073	GAR	❏ 11314	LNE	❏ 11702	FTP	❏ 12042	GAR	❏ 12164	GAR
❏ 11075	GAR	❏ 11315	LNE	❏ 11703	FTP	❏ 12043	CRW	❏ 12166	GAR
❏ 11076	GAR	❏ 11316	LNE	❏ 11704	FTP	❏ 12046	GAR	❏ 12167	GAR
❏ 11077	GAR	❏ 11317	LNE	❏ 11705	FTP	❏ 12049	GAR	❏ 12170	GAR
❏ 11078	GAR	❏ 11318	LNE	❏ 11706	FTP	❏ 12051	GAR	❏ 12171	GAR
❏ 11080	GAR	❏ 11319	LNE	❏ 11707	FTP	❏ 12056	GAR	❏ 12176	TFW
❏ 11081	GAR	❏ 11320	LNE	❏ 11708	FTP	❏ 12057	GAR	❏ 12177	TFW
❏ 11082	GAR	❏ 11321	LNE	❏ 11709	FTP	❏ 12060	GAR	❏ 12178	TFW
❏ 11085	GAR	❏ 11322	LNE	❏ 11710	FTP	❏ 12061	GAR	❏ 12179	TFW
❏ 11087	GAR	❏ 11323	LNE	❏ 11711	FTP	❏ 12062	GAR	❏ 12180	TFW
❏ 11088	GAR	❏ 11324	LNE	❏ 11712	FTP	❏ 12064	GAR	❏ 12181	TFW
❏ 11090	GAR	❏ 11325	LNE	❏ 11713	FTP	❏ 12066	GAR	❏ 12182	TFW
❏ 11091	GAR	❏ 11326	LNE	❏ 11714	FTP	❏ 12067	GAR	❏ 12183	TFW
❏ 11092	GAR	❏ 11327	LNE	❏ 11715	FTP	❏ 12073	GAR	❏ 12184	TFW
❏ 11093	GAR	❏ 11328	LNE	❏ 11716	FTP	❏ 12078	FTP	❏ 12185	TFW
❏ 11094	GAR	❏ 11329	LNE	❏ 11717	FTP	❏ 12079	GAR		
❏ 11095	GAR	❏ 11330	LNE	❏ 11718	FTP	❏ 12081	GAR	❏ 12200	LNE
❏ 11096	GAR	❏ 11401	LNE	❏ 11719	FTP	❏ 12082	GAR	❏ 12201	LNE
❏ 11098	GAR	❏ 11402	LNE	❏ 11720	FTP	❏ 12084	GAR	❏ 12202	LNE
❏ 11099	GAR	❏ 11403	LNE	❏ 11721	FTP	❏ 12089	GAR	❏ 12203	LNE
❏ 11100	GAR	❏ 11404	LNE	❏ 11722	FTP	❏ 12090	GAR	❏ 12204	LNE
❏ 11101	GAR	❏ 11405	LNE	❏ 11723	FTP	❏ 12091	GAR	❏ 12205	LNE
❏ 11201	LNE	❏ 11406	LNE	❏ 11724	FTP	❏ 12093	GAR	❏ 12207	LNE
❏ 11219	LNE	❏ 11407	LNE	❏ 11725	FTP	❏ 12094	CRW	❏ 12208	LNE
❏ 11229	LNE	❏ 11408	LNE	❏ 11726	FTP	❏ 12097	GAR	❏ 12209	LNE
❏ 11237	LNE	❏ 11409	LNE	❏ 11727	FTP	❏ 12098	GAR	❏ 12210	LNE
❏ 11241	LNE	❏ 11410	LNE	❏ 11728	FTP	❏ 12099	GAR	❏ 12211	LNE
❏ 11244	LNE	❏ 11411	LNE	❏ 11729	FTP	❏ 12100	GWR	❏ 12212	LNE
❏ 11273	LNE	❏ 11412	LNE	❏ 11730	FTP	❏ 12103	GAR	❏ 12213	LNE
❏ 11277	LNE	❏ 11413	LNE	❏ 11731	FTP	❏ 12105	GAR	❏ 12214	LNE
❏ 11278	LNE	❏ 11414	LNE	❏ 11732	FTP	❏ 12107	GAR	❏ 12215	LNE
❏ 11279	LNE	❏ 11415	LNE	❏ 11733	FTP	❏ 12108	GAR	❏ 12216	LNE
❏ 11280	LNE	❏ 11416	LNE	❏ 11734	FTP	❏ 12109	GAR	❏ 12217	LNE
❏ 11281	LNE	❏ 11417	LNE	❏ 11735	FTP	❏ 12110	GAR	❏ 12218	LNE
❏ 11282	LNE	❏ 11418	LNE	❏ 11736	FTP	❏ 12111	GAR	❏ 12219	LNE
❏ 11283	LNE	❏ 11419	LNE	❏ 11737	FTP	❏ 12114	GAR	❏ 12220	LNE
❏ 11284	LNE	❏ 11420	LNE	❏ 11738	FTP	❏ 12115	GAR	❏ 12222	LNE
❏ 11285	LNE	❏ 11421	LNE	❏ 11739	FTP	❏ 12116	GAR	❏ 12223	LNE
❏ 11286	LNE	❏ 11422	LNE			❏ 12118	GAR	❏ 12224	LNE
❏ 11287	LNE	❏ 11423	LNE	❏ 11998	LNE	❏ 12119	CRW	❏ 12225	LNE
❏ 11288	LNE	❏ 11424	LNE	❏ 11999	LNE	❏ 12120	GAR	❏ 12226	LNE
❏ 11289	LNE	❏ 11425	LNE	❏ 12005	GAR	❏ 12122	FTP	❏ 12227	LNE
❏ 11290	LNE	❏ 11426	LNE	❏ 12009	GAR	❏ 12125	GAR	❏ 12228	LNE
❏ 11291	LNE	❏ 11427	LNE	❏ 12011	FTP	❏ 12126	GAR	❏ 12229	LNE
❏ 11292	LNE	❏ 11428	LNE	❏ 12012	GAR	❏ 12129	GAR	❏ 12230	LNE
❏ 11293	LNE	❏ 11429	LNE	❏ 12013	GAR	❏ 12130	GAR	❏ 12231	LNE
❏ 11294	LNE	❏ 11430	LNE	❏ 12015	GAR	❏ 12132	GAR	❏ 12232	LNE
❏ 11295	LNE			❏ 12016	GAR	❏ 12133	FTP		
❏ 11298	LNE	❏ 11501	FTP	❏ 12017	CRW	❏ 12137	GAR	❏ 12300	LNE
❏ 11299	LNE	❏ 11502	FTP	❏ 12019	GAR	❏ 12138	FTP	❏ 12301	LNE
❏ 11301	LNE	❏ 11503	FTP	❏ 12021	GAR	❏ 12139	GAR	❏ 12302	LNE
❏ 11302	LNE	❏ 11504	FTP	❏ 12024	GAR	❏ 12141	GAR	❏ 12303	LNE
❏ 11303	LNE	❏ 11505	FTP	❏ 12026	GAR	❏ 12142	GWR	❏ 12304	LNE
❏ 11304	LNE	❏ 11506	FTP	❏ 12027	GAR	❏ 12143	GAR	❏ 12305	LNE
❏ 11305	LNE	❏ 11507	FTP	❏ 12030	GAR	❏ 12146	GAR	❏ 12307	LNE
❏ 11306	LNE	❏ 11508	FTP	❏ 12031	GAR	❏ 12147	GAR	❏ 12308	LNE
❏ 11307	LNE	❏ 11509	FTP	❏ 12032	GAR	❏ 12148	GAR	❏ 12309	LNE
❏ 11308	LNE	❏ 11510	FTP	❏ 12034	GAR	❏ 12150	GAR	❏ 12310	LNE
❏ 11309	LNE	❏ 11511	FTP	❏ 12035	GAR	❏ 12151	GAR	❏ 12311	LNE
❏ 11310	LNE	❏ 11512	FTP	❏ 12036	CRW	❏ 12153	GAR	❏ 12312	LNE

Data Tables

Number	Code	Number	Code	Number	Code	Number	Code	Number	Code
12313	LNE	12450	LNE	12620	CRW	15208	SCS	17174	GWR
12315	LNE	12452	LNE	12621	CRW	15209	SCS	17175	GWR
12316	LNE	12453	LNE	12623	CRW	15210	SCS	18756	WCR
12317	LNE	12454	LNE	12625	CRW	15211	SCS	18806	WCR
12318	LNE	12455	LNE	12627	CRW	15212	SCS	18893	WCR
12319	LNE	12456	LNE			15213	SCS	19208	WCR
12320	LNE	12457	LNE	12801	FTP	15214	SCS		
12321	LNE	12458	LNE	12802	FTP			21096	SUP
12322	LNE	12459	LNE	12803	FTP	15301	SCS	21100	NYM
12323	LNE	12460	LNE	12804	FTP	15302	SCS	21224	RIV
12324	LNE	12461	LNE	12805	FTP	15303	SCS	21232	SUP
12325	LNE	12462	LNE	12806	FTP	15304	SCS	21236	SUP
12326	LNE	12463	LNE	12807	FTP	15305	SCS	21241	SRP
12327	LNE	12464	LNE	12808	FTP	15306	SCS	21245	RIV
12328	LNE	12465	LNE	12809	FTP	15307	SCS	21249	SUP
12329	LNE	12466	LNE	12810	FTP	15308	SCS	21252	MHR
12330	LNE	12467	LNE	12811	FTP	15309	SCS	21256	WCR
12331	LNE	12468	LNE	12812	FTP	15310	SCS	21266	WCR
		12469	LNE	12813	FTP	15311	SCS	21269	RIV
12400	LNE	12470	LNE	12814	FTP	15312	SCS	21272	RIV
12401	LNE	12471	LNE			15313	SCS		
12402	LNE	12472	LNE	13227	WCR	15314	SCS	34525	WCR
12403	LNE	12473	LNE	13229	BOK	15315	SCS		
12404	LNE	12474	LNE	13230	BOK	15316	SCS	35089	NYM
12405	LNE	12476	LNE	13306	WCR	15317	SCS	35185	SRP
12406	LNE	12477	LNE	13320	WCR	15318	SCS	35317	SUP
12407	LNE	12478	LNE	13321	WCR	15319	SCS	35322	SUP
12409	LNE	12480	LNE	13440	WCR	15320	SCS	35329	SUP
12410	LNE	12481	LNE	13508	RAF	15321	SCS	35407	WCR
12411	LNE	12483	LNE			15322	SCS	35449	SUP
12414	LNE	12484	LNE	14007	SUP	15323	SCS	35451	SUP
12415	LNE	12485	LNE	14060	SUP	15324	SCS	35461	SUP
12417	LNE	12486	LNE			15325	SCS	35463	SUP
12419	LNE	12488	LNE	15001	SCS	15326	SCS	35464	SUP
12420	LNE	12489	LNE	15002	SCS	15327	SCS	35465	SUP
12421	LNE	12513	LNE	15003	SCS	15328	SCS	35466	VSO
12422	LNE	12514	LNE	15004	SCS	15329	SCS	35468	SUP
12423	LNE	12515	LNE	15005	SCS	15330	SCS	35469	RIV
12424	LNE	12518	LNE	15006	SCS	15331	SCS	35470	SUP
12425	LNE	12519	LNE	15007	SCS	15332	SCS	35476	SUP
12426	LNE	12520	LNE	15008	SCS	15333	SCS	35479	SUP
12427	LNE	12522	LNE	15009	SCS	15334	SCS	35486	SUP
12428	LNE	12526	LNE	15010	SCS	15335	SCS	35508	SUP
12429	LNE	12533	LNE	15011	SCS	15336	SCS	35511	LSC
12430	LNE	12534	LNE			15337	SCS	35517	SUP
12431	LNE	12538	LNE	15101	SCS	15338	SCS	35518	SUP
12432	LNE			15102	SCS	15339	SCS		
12433	LNE	12602	CRW	15103	SCS	15340	SCS	40101	GWR
12434	LNE	12603	CRW	15104	SCS	16156	NYM	40102	GWR
12436	LNE	12604	CRW	15105	SCS			40103	GWR
12437	LNE	12605	CRW	15106	SCS	17018	VTN	40104	GWR
12438	LNE	12606	CRW	15107	SCS	17019	SUP	40106	GWR
12439	LNE	12607	CRW	15108	SCS	17025	SUP	40107	GWR
12440	LNE	12608	CRW	15109	SCS	17056	RIV	40108	OLS
12441	LNE	12609	CRW	15110	SCS	17080	LSC	40109	GWR
12442	LNE	12610	CRW			17090	VTN	40110	GWR
12443	LNE	12613	CRW	15201	SCS	17096	SUP	40111	OLS
12444	LNE	12614	CRW	15202	SCS	17102	WCR	40112	GWR
12445	LNE	12615	CRW	15203	SCS	17105	RIV	40113	GWR
12446	LNE	12616	CRW	15204	SCS	17159	DRS	40114	GWR
12447	LNE	12617	CRW	15205	SCS	17167	WCR	40115	GWR
12448	LNE	12618	CRW	15206	SCS	17168	WCR	40116	GWR
12449	LNE	12619	CRW	15207	SCS	17173	GWR	40117	GWR

Data Tables

No.	Code	No.	Code	No.	Code	No.	Code	No.	Code
40118	GWR	40801	GWR	41088	LNE	41187	GWR	42057	LNE
40119	GWR	40802	OLS	41089	GWR	41189	GWR	42058	LNE
		40803	GWR	41090	LNE	41190	LNE	42059	LNE
40204	EMT	40804	GWR	41091	LNE	41192	OLS	42060	GWR
40205	EMT	40805	EMT	41092	LNE	41193	AXC	42061	GWR
40207	GWR	40806	GWR	41094	ASR	41194	AXC	42062	GWR
40210	OLS	40807	GWR	41095	LNE	41195	AXC	42063	LNE
40221	EMT	40808	GWR	41097	LNE	41204	EMT	42064	LNE
40231	GWR	40809	GWR	41098	LNE	41205	EMT	42065	LNE
		40810	GWR	41099	LNE	41206	EMT	42066	GWR
40402	DBR	40811	GWR	41100	LNE	41207	EMT	42067	GWR
40403	DBR			41102	GWR	41208	EMT	42068	GWR
40416	DBR	40900	GWR	41103	GWR	41209	EMT	42069	GWR
40417	OLS	40901	GWR	41104	ASR			42070	GWR
40424	OLS	40902	GWR	41106	GWR	42003	GWR	42071	GWR
40425	OLS	40903	GWR	41108	GWR	42004	ASR	42072	OLS
40426	OLS	40904	GWR	41110	GWR	42005	GWR	42073	GWR
40433	OLS			41111	EMT	42006	OLS	42074	GWR
40434	DBR	41004	GWR	41112	LNE	42007	GWR	42075	GWR
		41006	OLS	41113	EMT	42008	GWR	42076	GWR
40602	ASR	41008	GWR	41115	LNE	42009	GWR	42077	GWR
40700	EMT	41010	GWR	41116	OLS	42010	GWR	42078	GWR
40701	LNE	41012	GWR	41117	EMT	42012	GWR	42079	GWR
40702	LNE	41016	OLS	41118	LNE	42013	GWR	42080	GWR
40703	GWR	41018	GWR	41120	LNE	42014	GWR	42081	GWR
40704	LNE	41020	GWR	41122	GWR	42015	GWR	42083	GWR
40705	LNE	41022	OLS	41124	OLS	42016	GWR	42085	GWR
40706	LNE	41024	GWR	41126	GWR	42019	GWR	42087	GWR
40707	GWR	41026	AXC	41128	GWR	42021	GWR	42089	GWR
40708	LNE	41028	GWR	41130	OLS	42023	GWR	42091	LNE
40710	GWR	41030	GWR	41132	GWR	42024	GWR	42092	GWR
40711	LNE	41032	ASR	41134	OLS	42025	GWR	42094	GWR
40713	GWR	41034	GWR	41135	OLS	42026	GWR	42095	GWR
40715	GWR	41035	AXC	41136	ASR	42027	GWR	42096	OLS
40716	GWR	41039	LNE	41137	OLS	42028	GWR	42097	AXC
40718	GWR	41040	LNE	41138	GWR	42029	GWR	42098	GWR
40720	LNE	41041	EMT	41140	GWR	42030	GWR	42099	GWR
40721	GWR	41043	LNE	41142	GWR	42031	GWR	42100	EMT
40722	GWR	41044	LNE	41144	GWR	42032	GWR	42101	GWR
40727	GWR	41046	EMT	41146	OLS	42033	GWR	42102	GWR
40728	EMT	41052	GWR	41149	GWR	42034	GWR	42103	GWR
40730	EMT	41056	GWR	41150	LNE	42035	GWR	42105	GWR
40732	LNE	41057	EMT	41151	LNE	42036	AXC	42106	LNE
40733	GWR	41058	LNE	41152	LNE	42037	AXC	42107	ASR
40734	GWR	41059	GWR	41154	LNE	42038	AXC	42108	ASR
40735	LNE	41061	EMT	41156	EMT	42039	GWR	42109	LNE
40737	LNE	41062	LNE	41158	OLS	42040	GWR	42110	LNE
40739	GWR	41063	EMT	41159	LNE	42041	GWR	42111	EMT
40740	LNE	41064	EMT	41160	GWR	42042	GWR	42113	EMT
40741	EMT	41066	LNE	41161	GWR	42043	GWR	42115	OLS
40742	LNE	41067	EMT	41162	GWR	42044	GWR	42116	LNE
40743	GWR	41068	LNE	41164	LNE	42045	ASR	42117	LNE
40746	EMT	41069	EMT	41165	LNE	42046	ASR	42118	GWR
40748	LNE	41070	EMT	41166	GWR	42047	ASR	42119	EMT
40749	EMT	41071	EMT	41167	GWR	42048	GWR	42120	EMT
40750	LNE	41072	EMT	41169	OLS	42049	GWR	42121	EMT
40751	LNE	41075	EMT	41170	LNE	42050	GWR	42122	LNE
40752	GWR	41076	EMT	41176	GWR	42051	AXC	42123	LNE
40753	EMT	41077	EMT	41180	OLS	42052	AXC	42124	EMT
40754	EMT	41079	EMT	41182	GWR	42053	AXC	42125	LNE
40755	GWR	41083	LNE	41183	GWR	42054	ASR	42126	GWR
40756	EMT	41084	EMT	41185	LNE	42055	ASR	42127	LNE
40757	GWR	41087	LNE	41186	GWR	42056	GWR	42128	LNE

Data Tables

Number	Code
42129	OLS
42130	LNE
42131	EMT
42132	EMT
42133	EMT
42134	LNE
42135	EMT
42136	EMT
42137	EMT
42138	GWR
42139	EMT
42140	EMT
42141	EMT
42143	ASR
42144	ASR
42145	ASR
42146	LNE
42147	LNE
42148	EMT
42149	EMT
42150	LNE
42151	EMT
42152	EMT
42153	EMT
42154	LNE
42155	EMT
42156	EMT
42157	EMT
42158	LNE
42159	LNE
42160	LNE
42161	LNE
42163	LNE
42164	EMT
42165	EMT
42166	GWR
42167	GWR
42169	GWR
42171	LNE
42172	LNE
42173	GWR
42174	GWR
42175	GWR
42176	GWR
42178	GWR
42179	LNE
42180	LNE
42181	LNE
42182	LNE
42183	ASR
42184	ASR
42185	ASR
42186	LNE
42188	LNE
42189	LNE
42190	LNE
42191	LNE
42192	LNE
42193	LNE
42194	LNE
42195	GWR
42196	GWR
42197	GWR

Number	Code
42198	LNE
42199	LNE
42200	OLS
42201	GWR
42202	GWR
42203	GWR
42204	GWR
42205	LNE
42206	ASR
42207	ASR
42208	ASR
42209	ASR
42210	LNE
42211	GWR
42212	GWR
42213	GWR
42214	GWR
42215	LNE
42216	GWR
42217	GWR
42218	GWR
42219	LNE
42220	EMT
42221	GWR
42222	GWR
42224	GWR
42225	LNE
42226	LNE
42227	LNE
42228	LNE
42229	LNE
42230	EMT
42231	GWR
42232	OLS
42233	GWR
42234	AXC
42235	LNE
42236	GWR
42237	LNE
42238	LNE
42239	LNE
42240	LNE
42241	LNE
42242	LNE
42243	LNE
42244	LNE
42245	OLS
42247	GWR
42250	GWR
42251	GWR
42252	GWR
42253	GWR
42255	GWR
42256	GWR
42257	GWR
42258	GWR
42259	GWR
42260	GWR
42261	GWR
42263	GWR
42264	GWR
42265	GWR
42266	GWR

Number	Code
42267	ASR
42268	GWR
42269	GWR
42271	GWR
42272	GWR
42273	GWR
42275	GWR
42276	GWR
42277	GWR
42279	GWR
42280	GWR
42281	GWR
42283	GWR
42284	GWR
42285	GWR
42286	LNE
42287	GWR
42288	GWR
42289	GWR
42290	AXC
42291	GWR
42292	ASR
42293	GWR
42294	GWR
42295	GWR
42296	GWR
42297	GWR
42299	OLS
42300	OLS
42301	OLS
42302	GWR
42303	GWR
42304	GWR
42305	GWR
42306	LNE
42307	LNE
42308	GWR
42310	GWR
42315	GWR
42317	GWR
42319	OLS
42321	OLS
42322	LNE
42323	LNE
42324	OLS
42325	GWR
42326	LNE
42327	EMT
42328	EMT
42329	EMT
42330	LNE
42331	EMT
42332	GWR
42333	GWR
42335	LNE
42337	EMT
42339	EMT
42340	LNE
42341	EMT
42342	AXC
42343	ASR
42344	GWR
42345	GWR

Number	Code
42346	GWR
42347	GWR
42348	GWR
42349	GWR
42350	GWR
42351	OLS
42352	LNE
42353	GWR
42354	LNE
42355	LNE
42356	GWR
42357	LNE
42360	GWR
42361	GWR
42362	GWR
42363	LNE
42364	GWR
42365	GWR
42366	AXC
42367	AXC
42368	AXC
42369	AXC
42370	AXC
42371	AXC
42372	AXC
42373	AXC
42374	AXC
42375	AXC
42376	AXC
42377	AXC
42378	AXC
42379	AXC
42380	AXC
42381	GWR
42382	OLS
42383	GWR
42384	EMT
42401	EMT
42402	EMT
42404	EMT
42405	EMT
42407	EMT
42408	EMT
42501	GWR
42502	GWR
42503	GWR
42504	GWR
42505	GWR
42506	GWR
42507	GWR
42508	GWR
42509	GWR
42510	GWR
42511	ASR
42512	GWR
42513	GWR
42514	GWR
42515	GWR
42516	GWR
42517	GWR
42518	GWR
42519	GWR

Number	Code
42520	GWR
42551	ASR
42552	GWR
42553	GWR
42554	GWR
42555	OLS
42556	GWR
42557	GWR
42558	GWR
42559	GWR
42560	GWR
42561	ASR
42562	ASR
42563	GWR
42564	GWR
42565	GWR
42566	GWR
42567	ASR
42568	GWR
42569	GWR
42570	GWR
42571	GWR
42572	OLS
42573	GWR
42574	GWR
42575	GWR
42576	GWR
42577	GWR
42578	GWR
42579	OLS
42580	GWR
42581	GWR
42582	GWR
42583	GWR
42584	EMT
42585	EMT
42586	EMT
44000	OLS
44001	OLS
44002	GWR
44003	GWR
44004	GWR
44005	GWR
44007	OLS
44008	GWR
44009	GWR
44010	OLS
44011	OLS
44012	AXC
44013	GWR
44014	GWR
44015	GWR
44016	GWR
44017	AXC
44018	GWR
44019	LNE
44020	GWR
44021	AXC
44022	GWR
44023	GWR
44024	OLS
44025	OLS

Data Tables

44026	GWR	44101	GWR	48133	GWR	99537	VSO	9393	LNE
44027	LNE			48134	GWR	99539	VSO	9394	LNE
44028	OLS	45001	AXC	48135	GWR	99541	VSO		
44029	OLS	45002	AXC			99543	VSO	9701	NRL
44030	GWR	45003	AXC	49101	GWR	99545	VSO	9702	NRL
44031	LNE	45004	AXC	49102	GWR	99546	VSO	9703	NRL
44032	OLS	45005	AXC	49103	GWR	99678	WCR	9708	NRL
44033	GWR			49104	GWR	99679	WCR	9713	NRL
44034	GWR	45018	WCR	49105	GWR	99670	WCR	9714	NRL
44035	GWR	45020	DBR	49106	GWR	99671	WCR		
44036	GWR	45026	WCR	49107	GWR	99672	WCR	62287	NRL
44037	GWR			49108	GWR	99673	WCR	62384	NRL
44038	OLS	46001	GWR	49109	GWR	99674	WCR		
44039	GWR	46002	GWR	49110	GWR	99675	WCR	64664	AFG
44040	OLS	46003	GWR	49111	GWR	99676	WCR	64707	AFG
44041	EMT	46004	GWR	49112	GWR	99677	WCR		
44042	GWR	46005	GWR	49113	GWR	99680	WCR	72612	NRL
44043	GWR	46006	GWR			99706	WCR	72616	NRL
44044	EMT	46007	GWR	80041	RIV	99710	WCR	72630	NRL
44045	LNE	46008	OLS	80042	RIV	99712	WCR	72631	NRL
44046	EMT	46009	GWR	80043	WCR	99713	WCR	72639	NRL
44047	EMT	46010	GWR			99717	WCR		
44048	EMT	46011	GWR	99025	WCR	99718	WCR	80204	SUP
44049	OLS	46012	OLS	99035	SUP	99720	SUP	80217	SUP
44050	LNE	46013	GWR	99040	SUP	99721	WCR	80220	SUP
44051	EMT	46014	GWR	99041	SUP	99722	WCR		
44052	AXC	46015	GWR	99080	SUP	99723	WCR	82101	DRS
44054	EMT	46016	OLS			99782	SUP	82102	GAR
44056	LNE	46017	GWR	99108	VTN	99792	SUP	82103	GAR
44057	LNE	46018	OLS	99120	SUP	99884	WCR	82105	GAR
44058	LNE			99121	WCR			82107	GAR
44059	GWR	48101	GWR	99125	WCR	99953	SUP	82109	OLS
44060	GWR	48102	GWR	99127	WCR	99966	WCR	82111	NRL
44061	LNE	48103	GWR	99128	WCR	99968	VSO	82112	GAR
44063	LNE	48104	GWR	99132	WCR	99969	VSO	82113	ATE
44064	GWR	48105	GWR	99193	WCR			82114	GAR
44066	OLS	48106	GWR	99194	WCR	99991	SUP	82115	NRL
44067	GWR	48107	GWR	99195	WCR	99993	LSC	82116	DBR
44068	GWR	48108	GWR	99241	SUP	99995	SUP	82118	GAR
44069	GWR	48109	GWR	99304	WCR			82120	DBR
44070	EMT	48110	GWR	99311	WCR	**NPCCS Stock**		82121	GAR
44071	EMT	48111	GWR	99312	SUP	6260	NRL	82124	NRL
44072	AXC	48112	GWR	99316	WCR	6261	NRL	82126	DRS
44073	LNE	48113	GWR	99318	WCR	6262	NRL	82127	GAR
44074	GWR	48114	GWR	99319	WCR	6263	NRL	82129	NRL
44075	LNE	48115	GWR	99326	WCR	6264	NRL	82132	GAR
44076	GWR	48116	GWR	99327	WCR	6330	GWR	82133	GAR
44077	LNE	48117	GWR	99328	WCR	6336	GWR	82136	GAR
44078	GWR	48118	GWR	99329	WCR	6338	GWR	82137	DBR
44079	OLS	48119	GWR	99348	WCR	6340	LNE	82138	DBR
44080	LNE	48120	GWR	99349	VTN	6344	LNE	82139	GAR
44081	GWR	48121	GWR	99350	WCR	6346	LNE	82141	DBR
44083	GWR	48122	GWR	99353	VTN	6348	GWR	82143	GAR
44085	EMT	48123	GWR	99354	WCR	6352	LNE	82145	NRL
44086	OLS	48124	GWR	99361	VTN	6353	LNE	82146	DBC
44089	OLS	48125	GWR	99402	WCR	6376	COL	82148	DBR
44090	GWR	48126	GWR	99405	SUP	6377	COL	82149	OLS
44091	GWR	48127	GWR	99530	VSO	6378	COL	82150	DBR
44093	GWR	48128	GWR	99531	VSO	6379	COL	82152	GAR
44094	LNE	48129	GWR	99532	VSO	6392	COL		
44097	GWR	48130	GWR	99534	VSO	6397	COL	82200	LNE
44098	LNE	48131	GWR	99535	VSO	6398	EMT	82201	LNE
44100	GWR	48132	GWR	99536	VSO	6399	EMT	82202	LNE

Data Tables

❏ 82203	LNE	❏ 82226	LNE	❏ 92939	NRL	❏ 96609	COL	❏ 975978	AFG
❏ 82204	LNE	❏ 82227	LNE	❏ 95727	DBC	❏ 99666	NRL	❏ 975984	NRL
❏ 82205	LNE	❏ 82228	LNE	❏ 95761	DBC			❏ 977337	NRL
❏ 82206	LNE	❏ 82229	LNE	❏ 95763	DBC	**Service Stock**		❏ 977868	NRL
❏ 82207	LNE	❏ 82230	LNE			❏ 950001	NRL	❏ 977869	NRL
❏ 82208	LNE	❏ 82231	LNE	❏ 96100	VTN	❏ 960014	CRW	❏ 977969	NRL
❏ 82209	LNE	❏ 82301	CRW	❏ 96139	OLS			❏ 977974	NRL
❏ 82210	LNE	❏ 82302	CRW	❏ 96175	WCR	❏ 971001	NRL	❏ 977983	NRL
❏ 82211	LNE	❏ 82303	CRW	❏ 96181	OLS	❏ 971002	NRL	❏ 977984	NRL
❏ 82212	LNE	❏ 82304	CRW			❏ 971003	NRL	❏ 977985	NRL
❏ 82213	LNE	❏ 82305	CRW	❏ 96371	EPX	❏ 971004	NRL	❏ 977986	NRL
❏ 82214	LNE	❏ 82306	TFW	❏ 96372	DRS			❏ 977993	NRL
❏ 82215	LNE	❏ 82307	TFW	❏ 96373	DRS	❏ 975025	NRL	❏ 977994	NRL
❏ 82216	LNE	❏ 82308	TFW	❏ 96374	WAB	❏ 975081	NRL	❏ 977995	NRL
❏ 82217	LNE	❏ 82309	CRW	❏ 96375	DRS	❏ 975087	NRL	❏ 977997	NRL
❏ 82218	LNE			❏ 96602	COL	❏ 975091	NRL		
❏ 82219	LNE	❏ 92114	NRL	❏ 96603	COL	❏ 975464	NRL	❏ 999550	NRL
❏ 82220	LNE	❏ 92159	OLS	❏ 96604	COL	❏ 975477	NRL	❏ 999602	NRL
❏ 82222	LNE			❏ 96605	COL	❏ 975486	NRL	❏ 999605	NRL
❏ 82223	LNE	❏ 92901	OLS	❏ 96606	COL	❏ 975814	NRL	❏ 999606	NRL
❏ 82224	LNE	❏ 92904	WCR	❏ 96607	COL	❏ 975974	AFG		
❏ 82225	LNE	❏ 92931	OLS	❏ 96608	COL				

Also by Colin J Marsden

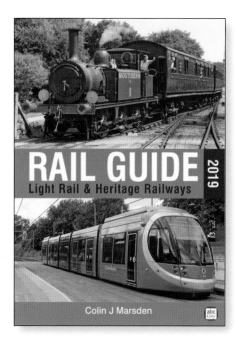

abc Rail Guide 2019
Light Rail & Heritage Railways

As a result of the ever growing network of light rail tramways and heritage lines Colin Marsden has expanded part of his highly successful *abc Rail Guide* to form the *abc Rail Guide Light Rail & Heritage Railways.*

   This new separate book incorporates additional details and illustrations of the UK's Light Rail systems including numbers and data for all London Underground lines and stock, both tube and surface lines.

   Details of all preserved railways and museum sites, including names, addresses and satnav codes together with tables listing the numbers and names of all preserved steam and modern traction locomotives and multiple units are provided as well as their locations and details of preserved traction authorised to operate on the national network.

   This welcome addition to Crecy's *abc* range of reference books is an accurate, portable and heavily illustrated guide to these fascinating areas of our transport infrastructure and heritage. A fascinating source of detailed information for all railway, light rail and tramway enthusiasts.

Hardback
210mm x 148mm
112 pages
ISBN: 9781910809563
£12.95

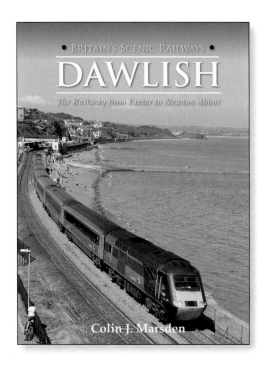

Britain's Scenic Railways: Dawlish

In this book author Colin Marsden who has an unrivalled archive of historical information on the railways of this area, presents a detailed history of the line from Exeter to Newton Abbot, concentrating on the scenic section between Starcross and Bishopsteighton, with previously unpublished photographs and accompanying text.

The Dawlish Sea Wall has been a popular site for railway enthusiasts and photographers for many generations and the final section of the book is devoted to the closure, rebuilding and triumphant reopening of the Sea Wall after the devastating storms of 2014.

A fresh new look to this scenic part of Britain's railway network.

Hardback
210mm x 280mm
128 pages
ISBN 978 07110 38387
£22.50

Available from all good bookshops

Crécy Publishing Ltd
www.crecy.co.uk